RENFER

1493

D1613541

Law of the
real estate business

Law of the real estate business

HAROLD F. LUSK
Professor Emeritus
Indiana University

and

WILLIAM B. FRENCH
Vice President and Trust Officer
Director of the Trust Division
National Bank and Trust Company
of South Bend, Indiana

 Third Edition 1975

RICHARD D. IRWIN, INC. *Homewood, Illinois 60430*

Irwin-Dorsey Limited Georgetown, Ontario L7G 4B3

Third Edition

First Printing, February 1975
Second Printing, October 1975
Third Printing, January 1976
Fourth Printing, April 1976
Fifth Printing, August 1976
Sixth Printing, November 1976
Seventh Printing, January 1977
Eighth Printing, June 1977

ISBN 0-256-01576-7
Library of Congress Catalog Card No. 74–25807

Printed in the United States of America

Preface

THE OBJECTIVE of this book, as of its previous edition, is to serve as a guide not only for real estate dealers but also for those who are less directly involved in the real estate business. It is hoped that this third edition will also prove valuable to lenders, property managers, investors, and individual property owners.

While the technical rules of law that establish and govern basic rights of ownership and use of real estate have been historically slow to change, the needs of the modern and constantly changing world of business have forced us to find new ways of structuring a real estate transaction. The closely related areas of taxation, finance, and general business law do change quite frequently, and they have an impact on real estate law that is very real even though it is often indirect and subtle.

New material has been added to this 3rd edition in the areas of taxation, governmental regulation, and methods of investment in real estate. In these areas I am indebted to the many resourceful and inventive attorneys with whom I have been privileged to be associated over the years in both the commercial banking and trust banking areas as well as various projects for the Indiana State Bar Association. Special gratitude is owed to my associate in the trust banking business, C. LaMar Gemberling, whose assistance in the area of taxation has been invaluable.

In addition to the new sections that have been added, another major reason for this revision has been a complete reorganization of the existing materials. The new order of presentation is the result of my experience in using this book for some ten years as an instructor of real estate business law at Indiana University and in the Real Estate Certification Program conducted by the university for the Real Estate Commission of the State of Indiana. To all of my associates in these programs I am indebted for helpful suggestions but most especially to George F. Bloom of Indiana University and Stephen J. Martin, Coordinator of the Real Estate Certification Program.

Endless hours of work and a great deal of understanding as well as practical advice have been contributed to this revision by a practicing real estate broker, my wife, Bernadine.

I am deeply grateful to Harold F. Lusk of Indiana University for the privilege of working on this revision of his original book. It has been a most challenging task to attempt to improve upon his earlier work. His vast experience as an educator and his astute guidance have made this revision possible. Nevertheless, the responsibility for any errors or omissions remains mine.

January 1975   WILLIAM B. FRENCH

Contents

vii

ers *of security interest in attached personalty versus owner. Vendee versus holder of security interest. Landlord and tenant. Trade fixtures. Rights under renewal lease. Agricultural fixtures.* Crops, trees, and shrubs: *Rights in crops, trees, and shrubs. Standing timber. Nursery stock.* Mechanics' liens: *Nature of statutory liens. Nature of mechanic's lien statutes. Necessity for compliance with statute. Necessity of contract for improvements. Co-owned property. Improvements by lessee. Property sold on land contract. Infant's 'contract. Persons entitled to a mechanic's lien. Nature of improvements. Labor for which lien may be claimed. Materials for which liens may be claimed. Rights of lien claimant. Waiver of lien rights. Perfecting the lien. Time for filing. Estate subject to lien. Sale of real estate subject to lien. Assignment of mechanic's liens. Priorities of mechanics' liens. Duration of mechanics' liens. Discharge of mechanics' liens. Foreclosure of mechanics' liens. Public improvements.*

1

Introduction

THE STUDY of the legal framework of the real estate business is an ambitious undertaking for it necessarily leads the serious student into a vast array of subjects, each of which is by itself complex. It is true that there is a recognizable body of law related to rights in real estate and this book could have been restricted to that field, however, it would not then live up to its title. It is the intent of this book to cover all of those phases of law which are essential to the conduct of a business in which real estate or the right to its use is the basic commodity.

The study of the law relating to any business today is a complex matter. The laws relating to ownership, contracts, principal and agent, finance and security, taxation, and governmental regulations are all significant areas of investigation for any business study. Against this general complexity of the modern business world we must view the real estate business. What makes it different from other businesses? How does it differ from the automobile business for example? What makes a separate study of the law of the real estate business necessary or worthwhile?

The answer to these questions lies in the character of real estate itself. The law has traditionally considered real estate legally indestructible. Buildings can be destroyed; the ground upon which they are built cannot. This fact results in a body of law which is quite distinctive. The subject matter of this law cannot be destroyed. As a result the law relating to it must be, as near as we may make it, unchangeable. We must be able to be certain about the rights of ownership of real estate not just today, but for countless tomorrows. Fundamental real estate law assumes that absolute ownership carries with it rights that will last forever, in spite of the fact that the owner of those rights today cannot expect to enjoy them forever. The law cannot comprehend the notion that real estate and the rights to its ownership will ever terminate. It is not simply a matter of saying that real estate may exist indefinitely. It is a matter of being compelled to accept the idea that real estate *cannot* be legally destroyed. The laws which shape and govern the rights of ownership of real estate are all based upon the premise that the real estate will always exist and that the law must recognize this fact. From a legal standpoint we are therefore dealing with a very unusual commodity.

The indestructibility of real estate is enough to make the study of the law of the real estate business a specialized one, but there is more. Basic fundamental real estate law in the United States has always been based upon the concept that each parcel of ground is unique. Under our law there is no such thing as two identical pieces of real estate. No matter that there are two lots in a subdivision with exactly equal road frontage, identical dimensions, the same terrain and slope, facing the same direction; no matter that they are obviously identical; the law says that they are *not* identical. Each is unique unto itself. When a bargain is struck for one of them the purchaser cannot be compelled to accept the other in its place. He is entitled to that precise piece of real estate for which he has contracted. He may compel his seller to deliver that piece of real estate. Our law says that he cannot be made whole by being paid money damages for the difference in value because each piece of real estate is unique and there is no way to assess his damages in terms of mere money.

Both of the above concepts which permeate all of the law of real estate have had a significant effect on the development of the laws which govern the conduct of the real estate business. Other concepts of real estate law have also had a significant impact. Consider, for example, the possession of real estate. How does one demonstrate that he is in actual, physical possession of real estate? He cannot put it in his pocket, as he can with cash, and thus clearly control it as well as obviously claim its ownership. He can of course erect boundary markers such as fences, but these are symbolic only of his claim to ownership. He needs some way of establishing his claim to ownership that must be recognized by his neighbors and the rest of society. This difficulty in establishing the fact of ownership has had a dramatic effect on real estate law and, therefore, upon the real estate business. It has resulted in the creation of a mammoth system of records by which the legality of one's claim to ownership is proven and preserved. All documents which relate to the ownership of real estate are meticulously preserved and cataloged from the time that an organized government appears. With it we have occasionally confusion, contradiction, and ambiguity; without it we would have absolute chaos.

Ingredients like those above give the real estate business a flavor all its own. It is exceedingly complex in terms of the legal framework upon which it rests. It is demanding in terms of its emphasis upon attention to minute details. It is frustrating in terms of the lack of knowledge and appreciation of its intricacies on the part of buyers and sellers, landlords and tenants, builders and lenders, and brokers and salesmen. Yet, it is a vibrant business, an area of tremendous opportunity for one who is knowledgeable and capable and in which significant personal achievement is possible. The real estate business is fundamental to other businesses and to each of us personally.

In embarking upon the study of the law of the real estate business one must of necessity chart a course through a wide range of apparently unrelated topics. Necessarily the law relating to finance and the creation of the security interests which have developed must be given careful consideration. The unique economic and legal characteristics of real estate have dictated the creation of specialized security interests which require precise care in their creation and application in order to be valid. Certain lending institutions have been designed for the primary, if not the sole purpose of providing real estate financing. By the same token special contract rules have developed because of the unusual treatment accorded to real estate under the law. Certain forms of agreements have developed which have become standard and custom has become law regarding their use in some situations. The ownership and use of real estate are subject to many limitations which result from such diverse areas as individual property rights of others, private restrictions imposed by contract, regulation by governmental units under the police power of federal, state, and local governments and even the taking away of the right of private ownership for the public good by eminent domain proceedings. The impact on the rights to own and use real estate from each of these sources must be explored. Sales of real estate are affected, shaped and governed by many forms of governmental regulations ranging from licensing provisions for real estate brokers and salesmen to control of advertising the terms of a proposed sale under disclosure regulations. These and other areas must be explored in varying degrees of depth in order to cover the full range of the law of the real estate business. None of them can be treated exhaustively in a single book of reasonable length. Therefore, the materials presented herein represent a survey of them with what is hoped will be direction to the sources of more detailed investigation.

It is worth noting at this point that certain basic terminology should be understood in connection with this book and this introduction. The term "real estate business" has a wide variety of meanings. It may be simply the sale of one's own residence; it may mean speculation in raw ground for an anticipated profit; it may mean the development and management of a shopping center, apartment complex, or office building; it may mean investment in debt instruments such as mortgages or land contracts; it may even mean the securities business in the form of selling shares in a real estate investment trust. It is apparent that the variety of forms which the real estate business may take will result in the application of a wide variety of laws. The term "the law" also has a wide range of meanings. It may mean the rule established by an appellate court considering for the first time some unique question of property rights; it may mean a statute which defines the rights or obligations which flow from the creation of some interest in land; it may mean a federal regulation of an industry which has the effect of limiting or expanding rights to real estate. In short, terms used in connection with the law of the real estate business are not necessarily fixed or unchanging. A pet theory of lawyers, law students and law instructors has been that real estate law is notoriously slow to change. Were this true there would be no need for continuous revision of books on the subject. In fact, this theory is true only with respect to certain basic concepts in the law directly related to rights to ownership of real estate. Such ancient terms as "fee simple absolute" still define the same basic rights they did over a hundred years ago. On the other hand, however, there has been and continues to be volatile change in the controls or limitations upon the exercise of the traditional rights of ownership. Who can deny the impact which the exercise of traditional rights of ownership have had upon our environment or the impact of the movement to protect and clean up that environment which is taking place today? We may someday look back upon the 1970s as the decade of our history marked by a dramatic change in the fundamental law of real property rights. The erosion of the concept of absolute rights to the ownership and use of real estate has been apparent for many years, but it has never been so pronounced as it has been in the 1970s. Far from being a subject that is a sure cure for insomnia the law of the real estate business is dynamic, vital, constantly changing and, most significantly, *fundamental* to most business and personal decisions. Throughout the chapters which follow there has been a concerted effort to point out the possibilities of change and emphasis has been placed on the need to either keep current with the developments or consult with those whose business it is to keep current. In the face of the almost bewildering variety of laws which affect the real estate business, their volatility and the goal of this work of brevity, the organization and method of presentation of the material which follows has been a task of major proportions. There is no pretense that the order of presentation is the only good one that exists. Quite the contrary, the use of earlier editions by instructors has shown that the order of presentation is unique to each instructor's plan, the makeup of his class, and the educational and business background of his students. The order of presentation which has been selected is based, to some extent at least, on the notion that this book might be appropriately subtitled "The Language of the Real Estate Business." As with other major industries the real estate business has developed its own lexicon in which terms have a precise and peculiar meaning which is quite different from that normally meant. For instance, the term "fee" does not always mean "compensation," it frequently means a form of ownership of real estate which is more or less absolute. Definition of the terms used in the material which follow should be ascertained and kept in mind throughout the book.

The initial chapters deal with the basic rights in real estate which are recognized today and which distinguish them from rights recognized in personal property. The historical background and evolution of the basic rights in real estate are explored at the outset. Understanding the forces which shaped the early beginnings of real estate law is helpful in understanding the terminology which has resulted and which has been in use, in some cases, for several hundred years. The rights to own and use real estate today range from "absolute" ownership which will last indefinitely, at least in theory, all the way down to the simple right to go upon the land belonging to another for a specific purpose. While there may still exist some of the ancient interests in land which were once recognized only those commonly recognized today are considered.

Because of the fact that the character of property may change under certan circumstances it is important to recognize that, at a given time, a transaction may be governed by either real estate law or personal property law depending upon the form which the property takes. This confusing phenomenon is the law of "fixtures." When personal property such as lumber, brick and mortar are brought onto real estate and used to construct a house upon that real estate they cease to be personal property and become "fixtures" and are treated as though they were in fact real property. (The reverse can also occur of course; that is, real property may be converted into personal property as in the mining of minerals and their removal from the premises.) At first blush this transformation may appear to be a legal curiosity of only passing interest. Be assured that the difference is critically important in determining the rights of sellers, buyers, and creditors. Consider the supplier of lumber to a builder who finds that the material sold has been used to build a house which becomes real estate and simply adds to the security of the holder of the mortgage on the real estate and is lost to the supplier. There is great practical significance in the difference. How does the supplier protect himself? One obvious way is for him to insist on payment in cash at the time he supplies materials and labor, but this approach would tend to impede the normal course of construction and interrupt schedules since the supplier of money cannot be assured that the labor and materials will in fact be put into the building to enhance his security and to justify the advance of funds. The solution to this dilemma which has been devised by our legal system is the "mechanic's lien" or "materialman's lien." As the names suggest, the law permits the supplier of labor or material to protect himself by perfecting a lien or claim against the property itself in order to provide some measure of security and the assurance that he will be paid. The statutes which create this right are highly technical and the procedure which must be followed is very detailed. The basic rules are emphasized in Chapter 3 while specific applications are reserved for later consideration in the book when dealing with construction.

A wide variety of forms of co-ownership of real estate are recognized today. Many of these have been designed for the primary purpose of permitting investment in real estate by a number of persons at the same time. In Chapter 4, however, are considered the basic forms of co-ownership which have been traditionally recognized at common law and whose purposes have typically been for other than investment such as convenience of transfer or to recognize interests in several parties at the same time which often result quite by accident. Herein are discussed the joint tenancy with right of survivorship under which the survivor takes the deceased owner's share automatically. Also discussed is the tenancy in common under which each owner has a recognizable individual interest in real estate which does not go to the surviving owners at his death, but goes instead to his legal heirs or designated beneficiaries of his will thereby resulting in a substitution of owners. The unusual forms of co-ownership between spouses, the tenancy by the entirety and the community under community property systems are also covered. The relatively recent developments of cooperative ownership of apartments and the condominium are discussed as well. Some form of co-ownership is particularly common for residential property and a clear understanding of its results is essential in the real estate business.

Chapters 5, 6, and 7 take up the overall subject of the acquisition of "title" or ownership of real estate. There are several ways in which title may be acquired, each of them operating in a different fashion and under different legal principles. By far the most common method of acquiring title is through a sale from one owner to another. It is at this point that the full significance of the complexity of the real estate business is brought home with emphasis. The transfer of title from one owner to another is accomplished through a "conveyance" or a "deed." The mystique which surrounds the preparation of a legally effective conveyance borders upon the ridiculous. Tradition and hundreds of years of development have made the preparation of a deed the work of the expert, the attorney. The business of preparation of deeds is not for the unskilled and untrained layman. Attorneys speak of it as the "art" of conveyancing and the term is accurate for it requires careful attention to many minute details in order to make the deed legally effective to transfer title. These details run from establishing the competency of the seller, the precise and correct description of the property being conveyed, the magic words of conveyance which transfer title and which specify the "estate" or interest being transferred, all the way to delivery and acceptance of the deed by the purchaser. The deed is the most important document used in the real estate sale. Its preparation appears deceptively simple, but its preparation requires legal skill and knowledge. It is not the statements which are made in a deed which can create subsequent difficulty. Rather, it is those provisions which are implied or "read into" the simple deed by statute which are troublesome. An awareness of the legal consequences of a simple deed is important to an understanding of the real estate business itself. The second most common way by which title to real estate is transferred is the death of its owner. Aside from the transfer which may result from some form of co-ownership which includes the element of survivorship, discussed in detail in Chapter 4, title is frequently obtained by inheritance. While the laws of inheritance vary widely from state to state to such a point that it is dangerous to generalize, two conclusions will be apparent: the transfer is cumbersome and it is usually very time consuming. Formal probate proceedings are almost universally required which generally require publication of notice of the owner's death and a "reasonable" time for creditors to appear and file their claims. This reasonable time will frequently be six months or more. While it is not uncommon for state law to provide that title to the real estate "vests" in the heirs immediately, it is also not uncommon for their interests to be of questionable quality until the estate is settled. Sales of real estate during the administration of the deceased owner's estate generally require formal court proceedings and substantial delays. Last, but by no means least, the death taxes must be paid to clear the title from that obligation since state and federal governments are preferred creditors of the estate. Acquisition of title by inheritance is too common not to be studied so that the basic workings of the probate system will be understood in terms of their impact on the real estate business.

In spite of the many safeguards with which our law surrounds the ownership of real estate, our real estate law has always recognized some form of acquisition of title to real estate by simply taking it and holding it for some prescribed period of time. In the early days of development of our country when there were frequently large open tracts of ground it was not uncommon for one to simply take possession of another's real estate, claim it as his own and maintain this position for a period of years, apparently on the theory that if the true owner did not object for a period of many years (formerly 21, and now down to 10 in many states) to the fact that a stranger was in possession of his property the law would no longer help him to protect that ownership. Today we seldom encounter the classic case of adverse possession in which a stranger legally "steals" another's real estate and ultimately becomes its lawful owner. The doctrine is quite viable, however, and is very useful in settling disputes which arise from time to time between adjoining property owners. It is not uncommon today to find that, as a result of modern surveying techniques which are more accurate than those used in the past, a building constructed many years ago was in fact built in such a way that it encroaches upon the adjoining real estate. By applying the doctrine of adverse possession it is frequently possible to establish the building owner's right to the land actually occupied and thereby make his title to it marketable.

In Chapter 8, the legal system by which the right to ownership of real estate is established is considered in detail. As noted earlier it is difficult to demonstrate exclusive possession and control of real estate, particularly of a large tract of ground. In addition, the indestructibility of real estate and the permanent nature of ownership of it require some clear-cut evidence of the rights claimed by an owner, tenant, or user of real estate. The method devised by our real estate law is the recording system, a vast collection of legal documents which affect the title to all real estate. Such systems, which provide for the filing of documents with a public official whose duty it is to protect and preserve them and make them available for public reference, have been in existence in most states from the time of their organization. In major metropolitan areas which have been organized for 100 years or more the sheer number of documents is overwhelming. Cataloging and indexing of these records is a truly formidable problem. Unfortunately we have yet to establish a generally accepted solution to the problem of proving the history of the title to a piece of real estate so that we can clearly establish ownership of it today. Greatly oversimplified, the system works like this: a specialist, called an abstractor, searches the records and digests those which affect a particular parcel of land which he delivers to the selling property owner who in turn furnishes it to his buyer; the buyer will deliver the abstract to an attorney who studies it and determines who, in his opinion, is the legal owner of that property. This is called the abstract and opinion method of title assurance. Myriad problems have developed over the accuracy of the recording system, the abstractor's digest and the attorney's opinion and consequent losses which may result from inaccuracy. Due to the difficulty in establishing a claim for damages the owner or buyer will frequently resort to insurance of his title by an established title insurance company. The title insurance industry is the bastard child of the recording system. As with other insurance the risk of loss is spread over many policyholders and losses are paid from the reserves created by the insurance premiums paid. The basic steps of the abstract and opinion method are preserved but the feature of a guarantee of accuracy backed by money is added. The limitations of both systems on the protection afforded to the purchaser of real estate are basic to the real estate business.

As with other types of commodities real estate has developed its own system of financing. In Chapter 9, the basic financing vehicle, the real estate mortgage, is considered in detail. Financing of real estate purchases or development is made possible by the relatively long useful life of the commodity with which we are dealing. This long life permits the creation of a long-term security interest which provides some assurance to the lender or investor that the loan will be repaid or that, if it is not, there is something of value which the lender may seize and sell to recoup his loss. Consider for a moment the typical loan which is used in the standard residential real estate transaction: there is an individual's promissory note, a fixed rate of interest, a long-term repayment schedule. Such a long-term commitment of funds by a lender or investor is relatively unattractive when compared to similar investments which are available such as U.S. government notes or bonds, municipal bonds offering tax-exempt interest and high-grade corporate debt issues. The individual financing the purchase of a home must, in a very real way, compete for available funds. The two most obvious ways in which he can do this are to pay a higher rate of interest or to provide security, or both. The security which he provides is the creation of a lien against his real estate in favor of the lender; that is, he mortgages the real estate. In the event of default on the part of the borrower in repayment of the loan' the lender, as a last resort, forecloses on the mortgage, compels a sale of the property and the proceeds of that sale are applied to the repayment of the loan. Because the mortgage creates an important potential interest in land our legal system requires that it be created with all of the formalities which are required in the preparation and execution of a deed. The legal rules relating to the creation of the mortgage lien and the foreclosure of the mortgage are perhaps the most complicated and cumbersome rules encountered in the real estate business. This is unfortunate since the ready availability of long-term financing is the lifeblood of the real estate business. Curiously, to a very great extent, the technicalities introduced into the law of mortgages have been aimed at helping the borrower to secure financing. In fact, they frequently work to his disadvantage. An additional factor which must be considered is the regulatory system which governs the financial institutions which are active in real estate financing. All of these matters are considered in Chapter 9.

The fact that mortgage financing is not always available has led to the development of alternative methods of financing which are essentially private between the buyer and seller. This aspect of real estate financing is considered in Chapter 10 in which the deed of trust and land contract are discussed in some detail. In some states the deed of trust, under which a third party holds legal title to the property until the indebtedness is paid, is quite common. In this arrangement the third party, the "trustee," is actually the legal owner of the real estate during the time that the indebtedness exists. He is obligated, however, to deal with the property for the benefit of the buyer (the borrower) and the lender (who may also be the seller) in accordance with the terms of the agreement between the parties. If the debt is paid the trustee must convey the property to the buyer. If it is not he must convey it to the lender. This arrangement has the advantage (to the lender) of speed in acquiring title to the security, the real estate. Mortgage foreclosure proceedings, on the other hand, might take months. In some states the advantages of the deed of trust are lost because, as a matter of public policy, those states have declared that the deed of trust is in fact a mortgage and mortgage foreclosure rules apply. The "land contract," on the other hand, is a device under which the seller of real estate retains legal title until the entire purchase price is paid at which time he is obligated to convey the legal title to the buyer. It is essentially the same as a conditional sales contract of personal property except, however, that the subject matter of the contract is real estate and some special rules apply. The land contract has been under heavy fire in recent years as a tool of oppression by which unscrupulous sellers have taken advantage of those who do not have the resources to obtain commercial financing. There is no doubt that the criticism is justified in some cases. On the other hand, the land contract is not used solely for the sale of low-grade residential housing. Quite the contrary, many very sophisticated, high dollar real estate sales utilize the land contract because of some very important income tax advantages which may be obtained. These are discussed in detail in the later chapter on taxation, but it is worth noting here that the income tax advantages of installment sales of real estate which permit the seller to spread his capital gain over several tax years can be extremely important. The device is quite frequently used in the sale of development ground for this reason. At this point it is also worth pointing out that many very old, seemingly archaic devices which have developed over the years in real estate law are not obsolete. It takes imagination and ingenuity to adapt them to the modern real estate transaction, but it can be and has been done by capable real estate people and their counselors. This cannot be successfully accomplished, however, without a good working knowledge of the fundamentals of real estate law.

After establishing the basic interests in real estate recognized by our present-day legal system, the various forms of co-ownership, and methods of acquisition and financing we will have established a sufficient basis upon which to consider the real estate business itself. In Chapter 11 the real estate brokerage business is considered in detail. A substantial body of law bears directly upon this subject. At the outset it is necessary to establish the legal basis of real estate brokerage itself. Initially the relationship between the real estate broker and his client must be examined. This requires an analysis of the law of principal and agent since this is the relationship which almost universally exists between the two. A careful analysis of this "fiduciary relationship," the close personal and confidential relationship which exists between principal and agent, is most important in understanding the rights and duties of the parties. Due to the confidential nature of this relationship it will become apparent why our legal system imposes a positive duty of good faith between the parties and imposes harsh penalties when this obligation is breached. In addition to the obligation imposed by the general law of principal and agent state regulation of the real estate brokerage business is rapidly becoming universal. In many cases the licensing requirements and the regulations imposed upon brokers and salesmen simply codify duties that would exist under common-law rules even without legislative control. In others they go far beyond the normal rules of principal and agent. Not to be outdone by the states the federal government has moved into the brokerage area and has regulated many aspects of the brokerage business, indirectly perhaps but effectively nonetheless. The brokerage industry itself has established certain self-imposed regulations in the form of canons of ethics which further delineate the duties of those brokers who choose to be governed by them. No matter how knowledgeable or well qualified a broker may be he must bear in mind that he may not perform some functions which are critically important to his business: he may not engage in the practice of law. This problem is not unique to the real estate brokerage business but it is nevertheless an important limitation on the scope of the broker's activities. Certain formalities exist in the creation of the broker's relationship with his client which have resulted from custom, business practice, or regulation as well as the law of principal and agent. Several types of agency relationships are recognized and certain forms of agreement have been developed which are in widespread use. This chapter examines the "listing contract" and the varying degrees of authority the broker may be given by his principal. It also considers in detail the rights of both parties under these various agency relationships ranging from the "open listing," under which many brokers may represent the same principal to the "exclusive right to sell listing," under which not even the owner may sell his own property without becoming obligated to pay the broker's commission. This area of the law of real estate business is of obvious practical importance.

The purchase agreement or contract of sale between the seller and buyer of real estate is without doubt the most important single document in the real estate business. For reasons considered in Chapter 12 it must be in writing and with very few exceptions it represents the final agreement between the parties to such an extent that they are normally precluded from proving that there was any other agreement beforehand. That is, once the parties reduce their agreement to writing it is presumed to reflect all of the terms of their agreement and all previous agreements are "merged" into it. From the time the written agreement is signed it is almost impossible for either party to successfully maintain that there was an earlier verbal agreement which contradicts the terms of the written agreement. For this reason the purchase agreement must be drafted with great care, making sure that it does indeed reflect the entire agreement between the buyer and seller. Due to its importance this chapter includes a review of basic contract principles which would apply generally to any contract with special emphasis on the unusual contract law rules which become applicable when real estate is the subject matter. There is, however, another reason why the purchase agreement is so important in a study of the law of the real estate business and that is that this contract will dictate the terms of performance for both parties. The purchase agreement defines the subject matter of the sale by describing both the real estate and the interest in it which is being sold. It will also determine the quality of the title which the buyer is to receive by specifying the guarantees or "warranties" that the seller will make in his deed. The typical purchase agreement for real estate is a lengthy and very technical instrument. At the same time the performance of the agreement by the parties is also relatively complex. Once the parties have reached final agreement on the terms of the contract it is usually a matter of several weeks before the sale is "closed" or completed. The reasons for this are related primarily to financing arrangements and the work required to search the history of the title and to obtain assurance of its quality. Typically the purchase agreement is based upon assumptions as to both of these subjects which are reflected in the agreement as conditions which must be met before performance is required. From a practical standpoint it is difficult to find any other area of real estate law in which the practicing broker must be more knowledgeable. The pressures of the business do not permit the luxury of lengthy consultation with an attorney in preparing this agreement. It must be prepared *now* while the parties are in agreement on the wide range of details which must be included in this contract. The use of standard forms which have been prepared by an attorney is of great assistance, but it is still necessary that the broker have an in-depth understanding of all of the essential terms of the purchase agreement. Perhaps nowhere else in the brokerage business is the difference in qualifications from one broker to another more meaningful in terms of his ability to properly and profitably represent his client.

The real estate brokerage business depends of course upon the availability of products to be offered for sale. Raw land, once in abundance, no longer represents the most common commodity in the real estate market. Buildings, whether commercial, industrial, or residential now represent a most important part of the brokerage business. Obviously the creation of these buildings is still another major part of the overall real estate business. Chapter 13 discusses the important elements of the real estate development, building, management, and appraisal areas of the business. The development of raw ground into a residential subdivision is a very important segment of the real estate industry. It is the catalyst that transforms vacant ground which is worth $750 an acre into a planned community in which, by the additions of streets, sewers, lighting, power and orderly division into attractive homesites, the value of even the vacant lots may be increased tenfold. Such an achievement appears to be a simple matter until the complexities of zoning, restrictive covenants, finance, dedications to public use, and compliance with local regulations are carefully considered. The financial risk involved is a matter of significance to the developer; mistakes and delays are costly; knowledge and skill are essential ingredients of success. Even after the basic development is completed the construction of improvements to obtain maximum utilization of the real estate is still another complex area of activity with a different set of problems and different contractual arrangements not to mention a highly specialized type of financing. In the area of real estate management as it has developed for apartment complexes, shopping centers, and even entire planned communities a new real estate business has developed in which skilled specialists command a handsome price for their services. The pronounced trend today toward widely held ownership of such investments has placed a premium upon managerial competence. The professional manager must have a solid working knowledge of real estate law, an awareness of its impact on profitability, both short term and long term, and must have this knowledge at his fingertips in order to be an effective negotiator. A highly professional individual in the real estate business is the appraiser who must be able to establish values for raw land, buildings, long-term leases, and construction costs with a high degree of accuracy. The appraisal of real estate is a demanding business which requires a solid background in real estate law in order to arrive at meaningful estimates of value. There is a significant difference, for example, between absolute ownership of a piece of real estate and the exclusive right to use it for 30 years. It is still the same piece of ground but the difference in value between the legal rights is quite significant. The determination of the dollar value of this difference is a difficult job. All of these aspects are at least introduced in Chapter 13 so that they will be in mind in considering the matters covered by later chapters.

Due to the complexity of the terms of the typical contract used in the real estate business and the length of time generally required for performance it is inevitable that some detailed steps cannot be completed within a reasonable time thereby delaying complete performance. Quite often the detail may be relatively minor and will constitute more a cause for aggravation than real damage to the parties. Rather than postpone performance of the basic contract and suffer the loss of expenses incurred in preparing for performance, the parties will frequently elect to enter into an ancillary arrangement which will permit basic performance to be completed. The device used to accomplish this is the escrow agreement discussed in detail in Chapter 14. In its simplest form the escrow agreement brings into the transaction an independent third party who acts in the capacity of stakeholder. While he is frequently referred to as an escrow "agent" this is a misnomer for in order to act as, more correctly, the "escrow holder" he cannot be the agent of either of the parties. The selection of the escrow holder is done with great care by the two parties to assure his independence. The key to the preparation of a good escrow is the careful establishment of a condition that can be easily verified by the escrow holder without the necessity of making a judgment. The escrow holder who agrees to serve under an agreement which does not contain this key element runs a substantial risk because the crucial rule of law from his standpoint is that an escrow holder is absolutely liable for misdelivery. In a typical escrow arrangement the escrow holder may hold both the purchase price and the deed until a mortgage on the property is released so that clear title will exist at the time the deed is delivered and becomes legally effective. Should he make delivery without proof that the mortgage has in fact been released he exposes himself to liability to the purchaser for whatever damage results up to and including the full amount of the purchase price. Knowledge of the law of escrows is important so as to be able to make use of the device in practice. It is even more helpful in understanding why escrow work should be left to those who are experienced in this field; that is, title insurance companies and banks.

One very important, if not the most important contractual relationship, which exists in the real estate industry is that of landlord and tenant.

In Chapter 15 the subjects of the creation of that relationship and the rights and duties of the parties which flow from it are discussed in detail. Through the lease it is possible to have the use of real estate, even for a very extended length of time, on an exclusive basis without actually owning it. The common law on the subject, and even most of the statutory law as well, is both unique and archaic and frequently leads to results which are neither intended nor desired by the parties. This stems from some unusual common-law rules which are still in effect today which treat the tenant as the *owner* of the property for many purposes during the term of the lease. The results which flow from this concept, which is based on the theory that the landlord has granted an "estate in land" to the tenant, are quite unexplainable in terms of modern contract law. The reason for this is that the court decisions which have created these rules do not proceed on contract principles at all; they proceed on real property principles under which the granting of the exclusive right to use real estate creates an "estate," a form of ownership. Some of the results are distressing: if the buildings on leased real estate burn to the ground halfway through the term of the lease the tenant may be required to continue paying rent while the landlord may have no duty to rebuild the buildings. It is precisely this kind of result which has led to the modern form lease by which the landlord and tenant by contract create a relationship which makes more business sense. Then why study the old property law concepts of landlord and tenant? The best reason is that it gives one an awareness of the significance of the terms which are used in a well-drafted lease and why they must be used. The reason, for example, that most modern apartment leases include a clause which permits the landlord to enter at reasonable times for the purpose of inspection does not appear obvious at first. Business practice would seem to require that he have this right whether stated in the lease or not. The reason it must be stated is that under the common law of leases he very well may not have this right. It will be readily apparent from the study of landlord and tenant law that it is essential to understand it in order to know how to avoid it by the careful drafting of a good lease contract. One more very important reason for understanding leases is that, no matter how modified, they still create an interest in land which can be used to provide security for financing. The tenant's right under his lease can create an interest which is the equivalent of ownership, at least for security purposes, without the necessity of expending the capital necessary to purchase it. This procedure, using the ancient leasehold estate as the vehicle for sophisticated modern financing, represents still another example of the value of a clear understanding of basic real estate law.

Just as our legal system clearly recognizes the concept of absolute ownership which permits the individual to freely contract for its sale or to create lesser interests in it, such as leaseholds, that same system permits him to impose some limited restrictions upon its use even after he sells it. Since he owns the property theoretically forever he may sell all or as much of that ownership as he sees fit, within reason. The result is that he may sell the "fee simple absolute," the equivalent of absolute ownership, while imposing certain limitations on its use by the new owner. The most frequent vehicle is the "covenant" which "runs with the land." In more modern terms there is simply a promise by the buyer (implied from his acceptance of the deed which contains the covenant or restriction) that he will refrain from exercising all of the rights of absolute ownership and will restrict himself in his use of the property. Since he has agreed to some limitation upon the rights of ownership he has something less than absolute ownership and when he sells the property he cannot sell more than he owns. Hence the expression "runs with the land," which simply means that the burden of the restriction is on the land itself and subsequent owners must also comply with it. Only such restrictions as are "reasonable" are permitted and their effective life may be cut off when they have outlived their usefulness and therefore become "unreasonable." The right to impose reasonable restrictions on the use of real estate is crucial to the real estate development business. It permits the developer to impose restrictions upon the type and minimum cost of buildings in a subdivision, the location of such buildings with respect to the boundaries of the lot, the control of density of population, and the amount of free and open space available for each dwelling. The impact of such restrictions which are privately imposed by the developer is readily apparent when we drive through a modern residential subdivision. Certain characteristics of each property which are common to all of them will be apparent and, unfortunately, sometimes monotonous and depressing.

In addition to the restrictions which may be placed upon the use of real property by private owners there is an extremely important system of restrictions placed upon the use of real estate by local governments under "zoning ordinances." The purpose of these local laws is to control the overall development and use of privately owned real estate. The patterns thus established tend to group single-family residential areas in such a way that they are segregated from multifamily residential areas, commercial, and industrial areas. That is, each broad category of use is gathered into its own area or areas in such a way that it does not interfere with other uses. Zoning ordinances are usually general in application although there are some well-recognized exceptions. They have a drastic impact on the value of individual parcels of real estate since they effectively limit the market for those parcels. For example, in most major metropolitan areas a ten acre tract of ground will have limited value for single-family residential development because of its small size, may have a greater value for an apartment building and an astronomical value for industrial purposes. The key will be the zoning which applies and which effectively dictates the limitations of the owner's market. In connection with the publicly imposed zoning regulations and the privately imposed restrictions used by developers it must be kept in mind that these are two separate and distinct systems which are independent of each other and will *both* apply to a given piece of real estate at the same time. The owner or user in such a case must comply with the more restrictive provisions of each of them. Both restrictive covenants and zoning are considered in Chapter 16.

In addition to the regulatory powers of government to restrict the use of private property there also exists the inherent power of government to absolutely *take* private property when it is necessary for the welfare of the general public. This right of "eminent domain" is discussed in some detail in Chapter 17 because of its importance in the real estate business. The immediately preceding subject of zoning regulations should be kept in mind when studying the power of eminent domain because there is a gray area between the two powers. Zoning regulations can, in some cases, become so restrictive that they look suspiciously like a "taking" of property rights and therefore constitute an exercise of the power of eminent domain. What is the practical difference? Compensation. The property owner is not compensated for restrictions upon the use of his property but he must be paid when his property is taken from him. That is, eminent domain is not the equivalent of confiscation. Two aspects of eminent domain are considered in this chapter: when is a taking legal and what is the extent of compensation. Related problems include: what is a "taking," who may take private property, and when is a taking reasonable? The development of the law in this area is hardly reassuring to the property owner. We will see that all governmental units have the power of eminent domain; it can be and is freely delegated to utilities and others; the limits of reasonableness are elastic enough to include such things as recreational use rather than clear necessity; a taking does not include the abandonment of adjoining property, such as the highway in front of the motel or gas station; the damages actually suffered by a taking are difficult and expensive to establish and collect. On the other hand, the eminent domain process frequently has the unintended effect of causing a substantial enhancement in the value of adjoining property which creates very important opportunities. Clearly, a good working knowledge of the subject is an important tool in the conduct of a successful real estate business.

While we will determine in Chapter 17 what is a "taking" with a great degree of care we find out rather quickly in Chapter 18 that it is also a "sale" when viewed by the income taxing authorities and that since it is a sale which may generate a profit that profit will be taxable. This paradox is as good as any to introduce the subject of taxation of real estate. It is characteristic of the contrast between legal definitions which apply in the field of taxation as opposed to the field of real estate law. Recognition must initially be given to the fact that the law of taxation is not based upon logic; it is based upon the need to generate the massive amounts of money that are required in order to pay for the care and feeding of government and to provide the wide range of services we need and have come to expect. Brought down to practical realities the impact of taxation is so significant in the real estate business that we cannot effectively operate without a knowledge of the basic fundamentals of tax law nor without continuous access to expert advice and counseling. The profitability of the real estate business is seriously affected by the laws of taxation, particularly the federal income tax. Even the casual sale of one's own residence has important income tax consequences. Since the income tax laws and their application are in an almost constant state of change it is impossible in a book of this type to provide information that will remain up to date for any great length of time. On the other hand, the subject is far too important to be ignored. Therefore, the general rules which apply to sales and leases of real estate are included with the caution that competent tax counsel should be sought for all real estate transactions. Nowhere in the real estate business is the need for qualified expert advice more pronounced. The dollar value of the average real estate transaction and its consequent importance to the parties involved makes this conclusion even more compelling than in other businesses. A sale or lease of real estate may result in a handsome pre-tax profit with an after-tax loss. Since, in the final analysis, it is only the net after taxes which is available to be spent the significance of taxes on the real estate transaction is of the utmost importance. There are other forms of taxation in addition to federal income taxes and these are also considered, however, the wide variety of forms which these taxes may take makes it almost impossible to do more than introduce them and to provide some guidance toward further study of the subject.

Even under the income tax laws the unique treatment accorded to real estate is reflected. That is, real estate provides an investment that offers a certain amount of "shelter" from current income taxes. As a result of this fact and the notoriety that has been given to the fortunes which have been ammassed by real estate investors there has resulted a phenomenal demand by investors for an opportunity to participate. One major problem until recent years has been the fact that real estate investment or speculation required a substantial amount of capital or credit. Inventive and imaginative real estate people, their lawyers, accountants, and investment counselors have found a wide variety of solutions to this problem by adapting existing forms of co-ownership, including the trust and partnership, to the needs of the investing public. A bonus which has resulted from the use of forms of co-ownership other than widely held corporations is the income tax treatment accorded to them which permits the profit to be taxed once instead of twice. The simple syndicate, which in its purest form is simply a "tenancy in common," discussed in Chapter 2, has been found to be quite useful; the ancient "trust" has evolved into the modern real estate investment trust and has had immense appeal and success because it permits great numbers of small investors to participate in mortgages and ownership of high dollar value projects; the limited partnership has been used for the more sophisticated investor to invest primarily for income tax advantages that are not really beneficial for the low-income investor. The interesting legal aspect of all of these vehicles is that the basic vehicles have been available for many, many years but have not been utilized for investment by large numbers of participants. More impressive, it has opened up a whole new industry, the sale of securities in real estate. It has also brought to the real estate business a whole new set of regulations, those which have been traditionally applied to the stock broker. These developments are considered in Chapter 19 in an introductory fashion.

Finally, in Chapter 20, an effort is made to bring some semblance of order out of the chaotic hodgepodge of governmental regulations of the real estate business. It has been stated that no other industry is as heavily regulated with the possible exception of the narcotics business. After reviewing the wide array of regulatory systems to which the real estate business is subject one doubts that there is any exception. Real estate licensing laws are quite common today and will undoubtedly become universal in the United States before too long. The civil rights acts in force today single out the real estate business for special controls, undoubtedly because of the basic reliance we all have upon real estate in our daily lives. Truth in lending regulations exert an influence not only in the area of real estate finance but also by controlling advertising content and practices. Interstate land sales disclosure acts have an impact on many sales which were previously thought to be immune from classification as interstate commerce: the impact of television and radio which beam advertising over a very broad range have been instrumental in the resulting regulation by the federal government. The movement to protect our environment is beginning to shape and add a new dimension of control to the real estate business. Add to these the regulations of other related industries such as the banking, securities, and insurance industries which have an indirect but significant impact on the real estate business and it becomes apparent that any operation in the real estate industry requires almost constant vigilance to avoid violation of some regulation with its consequent sanctions.

It should be apparent at this point that the study of the law of the real estate business is a demanding one. It requires that one see not only the forest but also the trees, each and every one of them. Problems lurk behind each one, but so does opportunity. Perhaps the gravest danger to one who is active in the real estate business is the tendency to become complacent about his knowledge and command of the wide variety of laws which govern the modern real estate business. The material presented herein does not purport to be exhaustive. What we hope to accomplish is the creation of an awareness of the complexity of the business without discouraging pursuit of additional knowledge and competency which includes the key element of humility which permits consultation with experts: the attorney, the accountant, the banker, the title insurer, and so on *ad infinitum*.

2

Rights in real estate

Historical background

ORIGIN OF REAL ESTATE LAW

LAND AND RIGHTS in land play an important part in the social, economic, and political development of all peoples. The earth's surface was here when we arrived; and no matter how we may alter its exterior, it will be here to be used by generations which follow us. This self-evident fact has been and is basic in the development of laws relating to rights in land. Another fundamental fact is that laws do not exist except as a part of some social organization; that is, some form of government, no matter how primitive. Since land has always been of prime importance in the lives of the people, it was only natural that as soon as men began to band together in some form of social organization, they developed laws defining rights in land.

REAL ESTATE LAW AND SOCIAL DEVELOPMENT

The development of land law tended to parallel general social evolution. When a people changed from a social structure of nomadic tribes into an agricultural society with established farms and accompanying villages and cities, land law was developed which served to define the

22

rights of the people in the land which they were cultivating and the houses in which they lived. Many of our present-day concepts in regard to rights in land were known to and practiced by the Egyptians long before the birth of Christ. The Egyptians had laws regulating the conveyance of land, the recording of titles to land, rights to dispose of land by will, and other land laws which were similar in many respects to our present ones.

FEUDAL SYSTEM

Although the land law of any country might be traced back to primitive times, there is, as a general rule, some particular event of outstanding importance which scholars select as the beginning point in discussing the historical development in a particular area. The Norman conquest in 1066 is universally accepted as marking the beginning of our land law. After the conquest the Normans established in England the feudal system of land tenure, the underlying theory of which was that title to all land was vested in the king, and that all land was held either directly or indirectly from the king. The feudal system involved more than mere rights in land. In its entirety, it incorporated a system of government, a military organization, and the economic structure of the people. We are primarily interested in the rights in land under feudalism.

The king was the source of all rights in land; in theory, he was title owner of all land. The king, as lord, granted land in large tracts to the great lords, who held as tenants of the king. The great lords, in turn, granted their land in smaller tracts to lesser nobles, who held as tenants of the great lords. These lesser lords might, in turn, grant to still lesser noblemen and on down to the villeins, who lived on and cultivated the land. Under this system, with the exception of the highest lord and the lowest villein, each person occupied a double relation: He was tenant as to his overlord and lord as to his tenant. Under the feudal system as originally established, the highest estate which anyone, other than the king, could hold in land was a life estate. The tenant owed duties of fealty, faith, and feudal service to his lord; in return, he was entitled to receive protection from his lord.

DEVELOPMENT OF REAL ESTATE LAW IN ENGLAND

Although land law is—and, under the English law, has been—conservative, it has nevertheless been in a state of growth from its beginning.

The feudal system of land tenure was establihsed at a time when mutual protection was of paramount importance and when the feudal obligations which were imposed on the tenancies were not unduly oppressive. The more onerous duties were connected, either directly or indirectly, with military service; at this early period the performance of these services was necessary for the defense of the realm. As the country developed, the need for protection diminished, and the old feudal services became burdensome. The tenants attempted to devise ways to avoid these duties and were successful to a degree. As early as 1290, legislation was adopted which protected the rights of the lord to feudal services.

Another important feature of the feudal land law was the tenant's right to convey his interest in the land. One of the rights acquired by the lords from the king through the Magna Carta was the right to pass their interest in the land they held to their heirs. Little reliable information is available regarding the right of alienation of land during the first 200 years of the existence of the feudal system in England. It is known that in the latter part of the 13th century, tenants did alienate their interest in the lands they held. The Statute Quia Emptores (1290) recognized the tenant's right to convey his interest in the land and also protected the lord's rights by providing, in effect, that he would have the same rights against the transferee, that he had against the original tenant.

In the year 1660, substantially all the old feudal services were abolished by Statute of Charles II C 24; but this legislation did not do away with the idea that land was "held" from an overlord, either the king or someone lower down in the hierarchy of noblemen.

Feudal rights versus individual rights

Under the feudal system of land tenure the government, which at that time was synonymous with the king, held the majority of the rights in the land; the individual had relatively few rights. The individual was, in most respects, a tenant having only the right of occupation and use. Under the real estate law as it exists in the United States today, the individual has the maximum of rights in the land he owns. The powers of the government—federal, state, and local—are limited to the right to tax; the right, under its police power, to control the use made of the land in order to protect the health, safety, and general welfare of the people; and the right, under the power of eminent domain, to take the land for a public use.

All land privately owned in the United States is alodial land—that is, land held in absolute independence, without being subject to any rent, service, or acknowledgment to a superior. Such an estate in land is the opposite of a feudal estate.

REAL ESTATE LAW IN THE UNITED STATES

This brings us down to the time of the colonization of America. Land in America which was discovered and settled by English subjects or which was acquired by military conquest was claimed in the name of the king and was granted by the crown to the colonies. These grants were made under terms which recognized many of the features of the feudal system. However, the recipient of such a grant paid only a nominal rental; he was not subject to the payment of feudal dues and the performance of feudal services; and his relation to the king was no different than that of any other subject—that is, he did not have to swear fealty or do homage.

After the Revolution the states succeeded to the rights of the crown. All unoccupied land was recognized as the property of the federal government. Since that time, the states have passed statutes which have abolished substantially all of the burdens incident to feudal tenure. In general, the individual does not hold his land from the state as overlord. The state does have jurisdiction over the land within its borders; it has the right to tax; it has the right of eminent domain; and if an owner of land dies intestate and without heirs, his land escheats to the state.

Ownership

NATURE OF OWNERSHIP

When we say that Arthur owns an 80-acre farm, a house and lot in the city, or a country estate, what do we mean? We mean that Arthur has certain rights in the farm, the house and lot, or the country estate. Ownership in real estate consists of a bundle of rights in described land and those things attached to the land; these rights will be recognized by the courts, and protected and enforced by the state. Rights in land may range from the right of absolute ownership to the right of temporary possession.

ESTATES IN LAND

Ownership in land is referred to in legal terminology as an *estate in land*. Estates in land are divided into two major classifications: (1)

freehold estates and (2) leaseholds (less than freehold estates). This classification is historical rather than logical, and all rights in land are not included in these two classes.

At common law, only freehold estates were recognized as estates in land and classified as real estate. Leaseholds were considered as contracts for the possession and use of real estate, and were held to be personal property. In the United States today a leasehold is held, in most of the states, to be personal property.

The classification of an estate as a freehold estate is based on its quantity or duration. A freehold estate continues for an indefinite period. It may be an estate in inheritance or a life estate.

The freehold estates are (1) fee simple, (2) fee tail, (3) determinable fee (also called *qualified* or *base fee*), and (4) life estate. A fee simple, a fee tail, and a determinable fee are estates of inheritance—that is, they do not terminate on the death of the owner but pass to his heirs or devisees. A life estate terminates on the death of the person or persons on whose life or lives it is based.

Leasehold estates are divided into four classes: (1) estates for years, (2) estates from year to year (also termed *estates from period to period*), (3) estates at will, and (4) estates at sufferance.[1]

FEE SIMPLE

An estate in fee simple is the highest type of ownership in real estate known to the law. A fee simple estate is one in which the owner is entitled to all the rights incident to the property. He has the unconditional power to dispose of the property during his lifetime; and on his death, if he dies intestate (without leaving a will), the property descends to his heirs. The terms *fee, fee simple,* and *fee simple absolute* are equivalent. At one time the term *fee simple* was used to distinguish the estate from a fee tail or conditional estate.[2]

Even though the fee simple owner has a maximum of rights in the property, he does not have the unrestricted right to do whatever he wishes with it. Individual rights flowing from ownership are always subject to the superior rights of society, which are based on the furtherance of the general public welfare. A fee simple owner may use his property for any lawful purpose. He has the right to sell it, dispose of it on his death by will (with limitations), encumber it, or lease it. He has

---

[1] Leasehold estates are discussed in Chapter 15, "Landlord and Tenant."

[2] *Hay's Estate et al.* v. *Commissioner of Internal Revenue,* 181 F.2d 169.

the right to open mines, drill for gas and oil, remove sand or gravel or other aggregate which may be on the land, cut the timber, burn the buildings if he does not endanger the property of his neighbors in the process, flood the land, and so forth, so long as his acts do not jeopardize the health, safety, or welfare of others.

A fee simple owner will not be permitted to maintain a nuisance on his property. For example, such an owner of a lot in a high-class residential district, even though there were no zoning ordinances or restrictions on the use of the lot, would have no right to use it as a public dump, since such use would create a nuisance. The property of any owner, including the fee simple owner, may be taken for the benefit of the public under the right of eminent domain, and the use of all property may be restricted under the police power of the state.

The fee simple estate is the source of all lesser estates and rights in real property; when these lesser estates terminate, they merge into the fee simple estate. In other words, the entire bundle of rights making up ownership in land is vested in and controlled by the owner in fee; he may grant these rights to others on whatever terms he wishes; and when the granted right terminates, the fee owner may enjoy it himself or regrant it.

For example, Allen, who owns real estate in fee simple, may give Beech a mortgage on land, may grant Call an easement of right of way over the land, may lease the land to Faris for a period of years, and may grant Gale a license to hunt on the land. Although he has granted rights to Beech, Call, Faris, and Gale, Allen still owns the land in fee simple. On the termination of the rights of Beech, Call, Faris, and Gale, such rights merge into Allen's fee and may be regranted by him. Different persons may own different segments of a tract of land in fee. For example, Allen may own the surface of a tract of land in fee simple, and Beech may own the minerals in the same land in fee simple.

Etheridge conveyed to the United States ten acres of seashore property under a statute authorizing the Treasury of the United States to acquire ". . . the right to use and occupy sites for life saving or life boat stations." The consideration was $100, and the deed included the following: ". . . the said Secretary . . . deems it advisable to acquire . . . the right to use and occupy the hereinafter described land as a site for a Life Savings Station." The land was used as a life saving station from 1912 until July 16, 1956, when the United States began to use it for other purposes. Etheridge claimed the right to the land and demanded rent for the period from July 16, 1956, to the time the United States surrendered possession of the land to him. The United States claimed that it owned the land in fee simple. The court held that the deed conveyed limited rights in the land and did not convey a fee simple.

District Judge Larkins said: "A good title in fee simple is indefeasible, marketable and unencumbered. By definition a fee simple title cannot be qualified or limited, but carries with it full legal rights with respect to the property." *Etheridge* v. *United States,* 218 F. Supp. 809 (1963).

DETERMINABLE FEE

A determinable, qualified, or base fee is an estate of inheritance, and the holder of the fee has all the rights that the holder of a fee simple has. However, the estate of the holder of the determinable fee will be extinguished on the occurrence of a designated event, the time of the happening of which must be uncertain.[3] The event on the happening of which the determinable fee is to be extinguished may be an event which is certain to happen, although the time of its happening is uncertain, or it may be an event which may never happen.

Whether a conveyance creates a determinable fee, places a limitation on the use of the real property conveyed, or creates a fee simple conditional will depend on the wording of the conveyance. There is a lack of harmony in the decisions of the courts as to the interpretation of language used. In addition, this branch of real estate law (future interests in real estate) is exceedingly technical. If a person engaged in the real estate business should encounter a transaction involving the rights of parties to such a conveyance, the wise course of action would be to refer the entire matter to a competent attorney and follow his advice in the matter.

In the above case of *Etheridge* v. *United States,* the court held that the deed conveyed a fee simple determinable. Judge Larkins, quoting from Tiffany, *Law of Real Property,* 3rd Ed., Section 220, said, " '. . . So, when land is granted for certain purposes, as for a schoolhouse, a church, a public building, or the like, and it is evidently the grantor's intention that it shall be used for such purpose only, and on the cessation of such use, the estate shall end, without any re-entry by the grantor, an estate of the kind now under consideration is created. It is necessary, it has been said, that the event named as terminating the estate be such that it may by possibility never happen at all, since it is an essential characteristic of a fee that it may possibly endure forever.

The court said: "The conveyance in question falls squarely within the preceding definition. The language employed by the grantors in the deed clearly manifests their intention that the land be used and occupied as a site for

[3] *Coquillard* v. *Coquillard et al.,* 62 Ind. App. 489, 113 N.E. 481.

a lifesaving station and for that purpose only. It is sufficiently evident that the grantors intended that, on the cessation of such use, the estate would terminate without a re-entry by them. When the defendant ceased using the land for a lifesaving station the land automatically reverted to the plaintiffs by operation of law."

FEE TAIL

An estate tail or fee tail is an estate given to a person and the heirs of his body. At common law, such property was, in effect, owned by the bloodline and could not be alienated. If the bloodline terminated, as it would in the event there were no heirs of the body of the grantee, the title to the land would revert to the original grantor. At an early date, methods were devised whereby the inalienability of an estate tail could be defeated. In the United States today the estate tail has been abolished by statute in all but a few states.[4] In those states which recognize it, the duration of an estate tail is usually limited to life or lives in being.

The deeds in litigation conveyed certain farm land to Carl M. Thompson and wife and to Raymond T. Thompson and wife. The granting clause in each of the deeds conveyed the land to the above-named grantees and "the heirs of their bodies." In other portions of the deeds the grant was to "their heirs and assigns." The question presented to the court was whether a fee simple or a fee tail was conveyed. The court held that a fee tail was granted.

Judge Fisher said: "It is universally conceded in English and American Jurisprudence that an absolute fee simple estate is the entire interest in the land, with infinite duration, and inheritable by the collateral as well as the lineal heirs of the person having such estate; whereas an estate in fee tail is one restricted in its course of descent at law to certain heirs, namely, those of the body. The first matter for consideration is, therefore, whether the 1949 deed conveyed a fee simple or a fee tail estate.

"The word 'heirs' was necessary to create a fee simple estate by deed at common law, but in 1925 a statute was enacted in Ohio, declaring that words of inheritance or succession are not necessary to create an estate in fee simple and that every grant or conveyance shall be construed to pass the whole estate or interest unless it clearly appears by the deed that the grantor intended to convey a lesser estate. The usual form of conveyance in fee simple is a grant 'to A and his heirs and assigns forever,' and one of the incidents of such an estate is the power of unlimited alienation. However, in a fee tail estate

---

[4] *Restatement of the Law—Property,* Vol. 1, chap. v. pp. 202–3, Special Notes 1 and 2.

the course of descent is usually restricted to the heirs of the donee's body. The form most generally used is 'to A and the heirs of his body.' These latter estates are of common law origin, having derived their existence from the statute de donis which had the effect of making them inalienable where the limitation was to some particular heir or class of issue of the grantee instead of the general heirs. If there were no heirs of the class to whom the estate was limited, the property reverted to the donor. If the donee in tail died leaving heirs of the class to whom the estate was limited by the grant, as heirs of the body, it passed to them in fee simple by operation of law. Thus, where lands were conveyed by deed 'to A, the heirs of his body and assigns, forever,' A took an estate tail." *Guida* v. *Thompson,* 80 Ohio Abs. 148, 160 N.E.2d 153 (1957).

Life estates

NATURE AND CREATION OF LIFE ESTATE

A life estate is a freehold estate in land and is limited in duration to the life of the owner, or to the life or lives of some other person or persons. It is not an estate of inheritance.[5] A life estate may be terminated on the happening of a future, uncertain event. For example, a devise to "my wife Ann for her natural life or so long as she shall remain my widow" creates a life estate in Ann which would terminate on her remarriage.[6]

There are two classes of life estates: (1) conventional and (2) legal. The conventional life estate is created by the acts of the parties; a legal life estate is created by operation of the law. The life estate created by the acts of the parties may be for the life of the life tenant, or for the life of some other person or persons. The latter is known technically as an estate *pur autre vie.* Legal life estates are dower, curtesy, and, in some states, homesteads.

NATURE OF LIFE TENANT'S OWNERSHIP

The life tenant possesses legal title to the real estate, since the life estate is a freehold; but his rights in the property are limited both as

---

[5] *Weekley* v. *Weekley et al.,* 126 W. Va. 90, 27 S.E.2d 591.

[6] *Greenleaf et al.* v. *Greenleaf et al.,* 332 Mo. 277, 58 S.W.2d 448.

to their scope and as to their duration. Since a life estate is real estate, it must be created by a grant, that is, by a deed or will. No formal wording need be used to create such an estate. If the grantor or testator uses in the deed or will language which indicates, with reasonable certainty, his intention to grant a life estate, such phraseology will be sufficient.

Under the statute of frauds, any contract for the sale of land or any interest in or concerning land must, if it is to be enforceable, be evidenced by a note or memorandum in writing signed by the party to be bound or his duly authorized agent. A life estate is an interest in land; consequently, any contract affecting a life estate, if it is to be enforceable, would have to comply with the statute of frauds.

Since the life tenant's estate in real property terminates on his death, or on the death of the person or persons upon whose life the duration of the estate is limited, the life tenant does not own the entire property in the real estate. That portion of the entire property not owned by the life tenant is owned either by the original grantor of the life estate, by his heirs or assigns, or by the remainderman. When the life estate terminates, the rights of the life tenant merge into the fee. If the grantor has retained the fee, the interest of the life tenant will revert to him, in which case his interest in the property during the existence of the life estate is known as a *reversion.*

If the grantor has granted a life estate to one person and the fee to another person, the interest of the fee owner is known as a *remainder.* For example, if Ames, who owns real estate in fee simple, grants it to Bell for life, Bell's interests, on the termination of the life estate, merge into the fee retained by Ames. During the period of the life estate, Ames has a reversionary interest in the real estates. If Ames grants the real estate to Bell for life and the remainder to Call in fee simple, Call will have the fee in the land subject to Bell's outstanding life estate. Bell is life tenant, and Call is remainderman.

William D. Robinson left a will in which he devised all of his real estate as follows: "Third: I give all my Real Estate to my wife, Lelia S. Robinson, and at her death it goes to F. M. Robinson (Frank M. Robinson), and at his death to his two boys, David Robinson and Richard Robinson." Caldwell and other heirs of Lelia S. Robinson claimed that a fee simple title vested in Lelia and that Frank M. Robinson and his two sons would take nothing. The trial court decided in favor of Caldwell *et al., and Robinson appealed.* The judgment was reversed.

Justice Miller said: "The devises in the wills to the first takers are general devises and use no words indicative of intent to give more than a life estate.

At common law such a general devise to the first taker created only a life estate.

"But unless the intent appears upon the face of the devise to give more than a life estate, the common law rule applies to devises as to conveyances, and nothing but an estate for life passes. . . .

"Section 55–11, Code 1950, has, however, changed this common law rule, and such a general devise now conveys the fee simple unless a contrary intention shall appear by the will, conveyance or grant.

"Though neither will devises an express life estate, yet the respective wills clearly disclose that the testator and testatrix intended to and did, by the limiting phrases that they employed, create mere life estates in the first takers with vested remainders in David and Richard Robinson." *Robinson* v. *Caldwell,* 200 Va. 353, 105 S.E.2d 852 (1958).

EXTENT OF LIFE TENANT'S RIGHTS

The life tenant's interest in the real property is an ownership interest; he is not answerable to a superior owner. However, since he is not absolute owner, his rights are limited; and in the enjoyment of his rights, he must not encroach upon those of the remainderman or the reversioner, as the case may be.

The life tenant is entitled to all the income and profits arising from the property during the term of his tenancy.[7] He may sell his interest, or he may lease or mortgage the property. If he leases the property, the lease will end on the termination of the life estate. If he mortgages the property, the mortgagee acquires a lien only on the life tenant's interest; consequently, on the termination of the life estate the mortgagee would have no lien on the real property. The life tenant cannot create a lien on the interest of the remainderman or reversioner.

If mines, quarries, or oil or gas wells are open at the time of or before the creation of the life estate, the life tenant, unless expressly precluded, has a right to work such mines, quarries, or wells to exhaustion. He may sell the production thereof without having to account to the remainderman or reversioner for depletion.[8] If there are no mines, quarries, or wells open at the time of the creation of the life estate, the life tenant has no right, unless such right is provided for, to open new mines, quarries, or wells. However, if the owner, prior to the creation of the life estate, has granted the right to mine or to drill for gas and oil, the life tenant will be entitled to the royalties from the mines opened

---

[7] *Croasdale* v. *Butell,* 177 Kan. 487, 280 P.2d 593.

[8] *In re Crozer's Estate,* 336 Pa. 266, 9 A.2d 535.

or to the income and profits from the gas and oil wells drilled under the grant or lease for the duration of the life estate.[9]

DUTIES AND LIABILITIES OF LIFE TENANT

The life tenant owes a duty to refrain from conduct which does permanent injury to the remainder or reversion. An act which does permanent injury to the real estate subject to the life estate is known as *waste*. No exact statement can be made as to what acts on the part of the life tenant will be held to be waste. For example, the cutting, selling, and removal of timber would, as a general rule, be considered waste; but if the cutting of the timber enhances the value of the property (clearing land for cultivation or other beneficial purposes), the cutting and removal of the timber would not be considered waste.[10]

As a general rule, the removal or destruction of buildings which are a permanent part of the real estate is waste, even though the life tenant is tearing down a building to make room for a better one. If a life tenant tears down a structure and sells the material to a third person, the third person is liable to the remainderman or reversioner for the value of the material.[11]

Failure on the part of the life tenant to make ordinary repairs is waste, but he owes no duty to make permanent improvements. There is no clearcut line of distinction between ordinary repairs and permanent improvements. In borderline situations, each case must be decided on the basis of its particular facts.

If the life tenant fails to make ordinary repairs and, after due notice and request, refuses or fails to make them within a reasonable time, the remainderman or reversioner may bring an appropriate action to require him to make such repairs or may have them made and recover the cost from the life tenant.[12]

If the life tenant makes permanent improvements for his own benefit and convenience, he must pay the entire cost of the improvement. If the life tenant completes improvements begun by the donor, makes permanent improvements required by municipal authority, or makes permanent improvements necessary to assure a reasonable return on the property, the courts have generally held that the entire cost of the improvement

---

[9] *Benson* v. *Nyman*, 136 Kan. 455, 16 P.2d 963.

[10] *Sallee et al.* v. *Daneri et al.*, 49 Cal. App.2d 324, 121 P.2d 781.

[11] *Hayden* v. *Boetler*, 263 Ky. 722, 93 S.W.2d 831.

[12] *In re Stout's Estate*, 151 Ore. 411, 50 P.2d 768.

need not be borne by him. No basic standard for the distribution of the cost of permanent improvements between the life tenant and the remainderman or reversioner has been developed by the courts. They have attempted to make an equitable adjustment based on the facts of each individual case.

If the life tenant and remainderman or reversioner enter into an agreement for the making of the improvement and the apportionment of the cost, the courts will, in the absence of fraud, duress, or undue influence, enforce the agreement. A contract in writing, setting out the agreement for apportionment of the cost of the improvement, will, as a general rule, prevent expensive litigation.

The life tenant in possession sold the standing timber on the land. The remainderman brought suit against the purchaser of the timber, who had cut and removed it, to recover a judgment for the value of such timber. The court granted a judgment to the remainderman.

Judge Franklin said: "Under the theory on which the case was tried, the only question on which the defendant's liability depended was whether the tenant had authority in the exercise of her rights under her life estate tenancy to sell the timber in question. She could rightfully cut only such timber as she needed for firewood or for making repairs to the premises or such as was necessary to clear up the land for cultivation, or such as was necessary to be cut in the exercise of good husbandry or forestry. In this case there was not one shred of evidence that the cutting of timber here involved was for the purpose of providing the life tenant with firewood or for the purpose of clearing up and for cultivation or the exercise of good husbandry or forestry. *Ola B. Campion* v. *McLeod,* 108 Ga. App. 261, 132 S.E.2d 848 (1963).

Property was conveyed by will to Toler. The will provided: "I give, devise and bequeath to my brother, Benjamin Edward Toler, for and during his natural life, with the right to full use and benefit of all the rents, issues and profits therefrom with the remainder over in fee to the following persons. . . ."

Ponder, the remainderman, contended that the court improperly determined income allocable to the life tenant, and that it should have charged operational expenses to income. The court held that the life tenant was liable for operational expenses.

Justice Shepard said: "Ordinarily where the will is silent on the subject of expenses, the owner of the life estate will be held responsible for the upkeep of the improvements, against waste and for taxes, and a just proportion of extraordinary assessments benefiting the whole inheritance. . . . The charging of taxes to corpus in any year in which a loss occurred is amply supported by precedent." *In re Toler's Estate,* 18 Cal. Rptr. 684, 345 P.2d 152 (1959).

INSURING THE PROPERTY

Both the life tenant and the remainderman or reversioner have an insurable interest in the property. Neither owes to the other a duty to insure the property. If either insures it for his individual benefit, the other party does not share in the insurance. The life tenant and the remainderman or reversioner may join in insuring the property.

Under some circumstances, the life tenant may owe a duty to keep the property insured. For example, when there is a mortgage on the property executed by the donor, which mortgage requires the mortgagor to keep the premises insured, there have been instances in which the life tenant has been required to insure the premises.[13]

A life estate in a 400-acre farm was devised to Bertha Adams subject to a power in William Adams to operate the farm during Bertha's tenancy. William was directed to pay Bertha the reasonable rental value of the farm. A controversy arose as to the life tenant's obligation to pay taxes, insurance, repairs, and improvements. The court held that these items were chargeable to the life tenant, not to the remainderman.

Judge Montgomery said: "In such cases the rules are plain and of long standing. It is the duty of the life tenant to keep up the property and preserve the estate for the remainderman. To that end the life tenant is bound to pay taxes, insurance, repairs and improvements and cannot charge them against the remainderman. Under this rule it is obligatory that appellant [Bertha Adams] pay the items mentioned. *Adams* v. *Adams,* Ky. App., 371 S.W.2d 637 (1963).

PAYMENT OF TAXES AND ASSESSMENTS

The life tenant in possession owes a duty to pay all ordinary taxes. Failure on his part to do so is the commission of waste. However, the courts have generally held that the duty to pay taxes is limited to the amount of the income of the property and that if the taxes exceed the income, the life tenant is not obligated to pay the excess out of his own funds.[14]

In the majority of the states, taxes assessed against real estate are a lien on the property; if they are not paid, the property may be sold at tax sale. If the life tenant fails to pay the taxes, the remainderman or reversioner may pay them and recover from the life tenant the amount disbursed.

In the event of the death of the person on whose life the tenancy is based, thus terminating the tenancy, the courts have in most instances

---

[13] *Livesay* v. *Boyd et al.,* 164 Va. 528, 180 S.E. 158.

[14] *Schofield et al.* v. *Green,* 115 Ind. App. 160, 56 N.E.2d 506.

apportioned the taxes, charging the life tenant for the portion of the tax year during which he was in possession and charging the remainder-man or reversioner for the remaining portion of the year. If taxes have not been paid, they are a charge against the life tenant's estate.

MORTGAGES, LIENS, AND OTHER CHARGES

If, at the time of the creation of a life estate, the property is encumbered by a mortgage, lien, or other charge, the life tenant owes a duty to pay the interest on the encumbrance, but not the principal.[15] Some authorities have held that the life tenant's duty to pay interest on an encumbrance is limited to the amount of income received from the property or to the rental value thereof. If the life tenant mortgages the property or permits a lien to be obtained on the property for his debt, he must pay both interest and principal. Only the interest of the life tenant, on default, is subject to foreclosure or sale. If the remainderman or the reversioner mortgages the property or permits a lien to be obtained on the property for his debt, the life tenant is not obligated to pay either the interest or the principal; and any foreclosure or sale, on default, must be made subject to the outstanding life estate.

If the life tenant and the remainderman or reversioner join in mortgaging the property, and enter into an agreement defining the obligation of each to the other, each is obligated to pay his agreed share of both interest and principal. In the absence of an agreement, expressed or implied, both the interest and the principal will be apportioned between them. In the event of default, the entire property is subject to foreclosure and sale.

The life tenant may, in order to preserve the estate, pay off an encumbrance. If the life tenant pays off an encumbrance which the remainderman or reversioner is obligated to pay, he acquires a lien on the share of the property belonging to the remainderman or reversioner; he is, prima facie, a creditor. The remainderman or reversioner may, if he acts within a reasonable time, reimburse the life tenant for the amount paid and thus discharge the lien of the life tenant.

The rule frequently applied in determining the amount due the life tenant in the event he has redeemed from a mortgage or other lien or charge is to subtract from the amount paid by the life tenant the amount of an annuity equal to the annual interest for the life expectancy of the life tenant. In the event the remainderman or reversioner redeems

---

[15] *Oldham et al.* v. *Noble et al.*, 117 Ind. App. 68, 66 N.E.2d 614.

the property, the life tenant may protect his interest by contributing his share of the indebtedness. The life tenant's contribution is the equivalent of the interest on the encumbrance during the continuance of the life estate.

Neither the life tenant nor the remainderman or reversioner can cut off the rights of the other by permitting a default, foreclosure, or sale and then purchasing the property at the sale, either in his own name or through a third person. If either party buys the property, he will be deemed to have purchased it for the benefit of all interested parties; the purchaser will, by operation of law, be converted into an involuntary trustee holding for the benefit of all; and he will be required to convey to the other interested party or parties on terms which are equitable. Other interested parties may lose their right to claim an interest in the property by delaying an unreasonable length of time before offering to make contribution.

In June, 1919, a life estate in 120 acres of land was granted to Bethea, Sr., and the remainder to his issue. In 1925, Bethea, Sr., gave Bank of Lotta a mortgage on the land to secure a $5,543.38 loan. The loan was not paid. Bank of Lotta assigned the claim and mortgage to Bass, who foreclosed the mortgage and purchased the property at foreclosure sale. The master's deed purported to convey a fee in the property. Bass took possession on March, 1931, and remained in possession until his death in May, 1954, when his interest in the property passed to his wife and children, who continued in possession. Bethea, Sr., died on November 29, 1959, leaving Bethea, Jr., his sole surviving issue. Bethea, Jr., brought this action to recover possession of the property. The court held that the mortgage encumbered only the interest of the life tenant and that Bethea, Jr., was entitled to possession of the property.

Acting Justice Legge said: "The grant in the case at bar not being within the rule in Shelly's case, Thomas M. Bethea, Sr., took a life estate only, and the respondent, Thomas M. Bethea, Jr., a contingent remainder, which became vested upon his father's death in 1959. The mortgage from Thomas M. Bethea, Sr., in 1925, though purporting to include the fee, covered only his life estate, for that was all he had; and the Master's deed in the foreclosure could convey no more. Nor did the length of possession under the deed bar respondent's claim, for his cause of action did not accrue until his father's death. *Bethea v. Bass*, 240 S.C. 398, 126 S.E.2d 354 (1962).

TERMINATION AND RIGHTS ON TERMINATION

A life estate terminates on the death of the person on whose life it is limited. If it is based on the life of two or more persons, it terminates on the death of the last survivor. The instrument creating the life estate may provide that it shall terminate on the happening of some stipulated, future, uncertain event, as, for instance, where a conveyance is so worded that it would create a life estate in the widow which would terminate on her remarriage.

Whenever a greater and a lesser estate in real property vest in the same person, the lesser estate is merged into the greater and is terminated. If the interest of a life tenant is conveyed to the remainderman or reversioner or the fee of the remainderman or reversioner is conveyed to the life tenant, the life estate is terminated by merger, since the interest of both the life tenant and the remainderman or reversioner vests in the same person. If the remainder or reversion is vested in two or more persons, a conveyance of the life estate to one of the remaindermen or reversioner will not terminate the life estate, since both the greater and the lesser estates, in such situation, are not vested in one and the same person.

A life estate may be terminated by forfeiture. Under the statutes of some states a life tenant forfeits his estate by the willful commission of waste.[16] Also, under the statutes of some states the life tenant forfeits his estate if he fails to pay taxes and permits the property to be sold on tax sale, and then fails to redeem the property within the permitted period.

On the termination of the life estate, all the rights of the life tenant and those claiming under him are cut off. One exception to this general rule is the right of the life tenant or a lessee of the life tenant to harvest annual crops planted before the termination of the tenancy.[17]

Legal life estates

NATURE OF LEGAL LIFE ESTATES

Legal life estates are curtesy, dower, and, in some states, homesteads. Curtesy, at common law, was the husband's life estate in the real property of the wife. At common law, two kinds of curtesy were recognized: curtesy initiate and curtesy consummate. There were three requisites for curtesy initiate: (1) a valid marriage, (2) title or seizin of real estate in the wife, and (3) a child born alive who could inherit. A fourth requisite—

[16] *McCartney et al.* v. *Titsworth et al.,* 104 N.Y.S. 45, 119 App. Div. 547.
[17] *In re Mischke's Estate,* 136 Neb. 875, 287 N.W. 760.

the death of the wife, the husband surviving—was necessary for curtesy consummate. On the fulfillment of the three requisites for curtesy, a life estate vested in the husband, and he had a freehold estate in the real estate of the wife.

Modern married women's statutes enacted by the states have abolished curtesy initiate, or have at least materially altered the rights of the husband. Likewise, the married women's acts have not necessarily abolished curtesy consummate, but they have substantially changed the rights of the husband in most states. To determine the rights of a husband in his wife's real estate, the statutes of the state in which the real estate is located must be consulted.

DOWER

Dower is the provision which the law makes for the widow out of the husband's property at his death. The purpose of dower is to provide the widow with means of support for herself and her children. It is of ancient origin and is generally recognized throughout the United States.

A widow's dower rights are determined by the laws of the state in which the real property is located.[18] At common law the widow's dower was a life estate in one third of all the real estate to which the husband had held title during his lifetime, provided she had not joined the husband in a conveyance or encumbrance of the property. The common-law rule has been altered by statute in substantially all states. In some states the widow takes a fee in a designated portion of the husband's real estate, title to which was held during his lifetime, provided she had not joined him in the conveyance or encumbrance of the property. In a few states the widow has dower rights only in the real estate to which the husband held title at the time of his death.

EXTENT OF DOWER

The extent of the widow's dower may depend on other relationships. For example, the widow of a second childless marriage, children of a former marriage by the husband surviving, may take only a life estate; whereas a widow of a first marriage or of any subsequent marriage, if children were born to such union, would take a fee interest in the husband's real estate.

On the basis of the general rule that one cannot convey greater rights

---

[18] *In re Clemmon's Estate*, 242 Iowa 1248, 49 N.W.2d 883.

in property than he has, the courts have held that a widow's dower rights are subject to outstanding rights in and encumbrances on the real estate, title to which was in the husband at the time of the marriage, and that her dower rights are subject to a purchase-money mortgage given by the husband at the time he acquired the property, even though she did not join him in the execution of the mortgage.

In some states the widow is entitled to dower in the husband's equitable interests in real estate. For example, if the husband has contracted to purchase real estate, and has paid part or all of the purchase price, but has not yet been given a deed to the property, the wife is entitled to dower in the equitable interest acquired by the husband. The wife has no dower right in property held by the husband as a joint tenant with others, since the interest of the husband passes to the surviving joint tenants by right of survivorship. However, the widow is entitled to dower in the husband's interest in real estate held with others as tenant in common.

The wife may not convey her inchoate dower to others, but she may cut off her right to dower by joining the husband in a conveyance or mortgage of the property. In the event of a forced sale of the husband's real estate, such as an execution sale on a judgment against the husband, or bankruptcy of the husband, or the taking of the husband's property by eminent domain, the value of the inchoate dower of the wife will be determined and provision made to protect it.

NATURE OF DOWER

The widow's dower may be (1) inchoate, (2) consummate, or (3) assigned or vested. Inchoate dower is a potential interest in the real estate of the husband which arises as soon as a valid marriage is consummated. Inchoate dower is not an estate in real estate but is recognized as a valuable interest, and it will be protected by the courts.

Consummate dower arises on the death of the husband, the wife surviving; that is, the widow acquires an estate in the real estate of the deceased husband, but this estate is incomplete until its extent is determined. It becomes assigned or vested when the court determines the extent of the widow's dower and the required orders fixing her rights are entered by the judge.

In a case involving a question of a widow's right to a marital deduction, the federal district court, in computing the federal estate tax assessed against the deceased husband's estate, was required to determine the nature and scope of the widow's dower rights in a farm, the title to which was held by the husband at the time of his death.

District Judge Lewis said: "It is well settled in Virginia that until a widow's dower has been assigned to her, her dower right is merely a right to sue for and compel the setting aside of her dower interest. It is not an estate in itself.

"When the widow's dower is laid off and assigned to her it becomes a life estate (terminable) in the land assigned." (NOTE: Under the statutes of some states the estate acquired by the widow would be a fee held as tenant in common with the other heirs of the deceased husband.) *National Bank of Orange* v. *United States,* 218 F. Supp. 907 (1963).

HOMESTEAD

In its popular sense the term *homestead* signifies the dwelling house in which the family resides. Homestead laws provide that the homestead shall be immune from seizure to satisfy creditors. Homestead rights were unknown at common law. They are peculiar to the United States and are created either by the constitutions or by the statutes of the several states. The objective of homestead laws is the protection of the family against eviction from its home by creditors. The homestead laws, in general, protect the wife and family from the improvidence of the husband and, in some states, give the widow protection against the creditors of the husband in addition to the protection afforded her by her dower rights.

The homestead laws of the states having such laws are not uniform in their wording or in their scope; consequently, our discussion of homestead rights must be very general.

In order to create a homestead, (1) there must be a family, (2) the family must occupy the premises as a home, and (3) the head of the family or householder must have an ownership interest in the property. In some states the homestead interest attaches by operation of law; in others the homestead interest must be perfected by a filing, as required by the state statutes.

Although there is considerable diversity in the wording of the homestead statutes as to what constitutes a family, there must be, as a general rule, two or more persons living together as a unit under one head, who owns a property interest in the premises, and who owes some duty of support to the other members of the unit. Usually, the husband is the head of the family; but if the husband is dead or has abandoned the family, or if the husband and wife are divorced and the wife has custody of the children, the widow or wife could qualify as the head of the family. In fact, anyone supporting the other members of the unit, if he is under a legal or moral obligation to do so, could qualify, under the homestead laws of most states, as the head of a family.

To constitute a homestead, the premises must be occupied by the family as a home. The householder, in order to claim homestead rights in the premises, need not own the property in fee but must have some property rights in it. He may, for instance, have a determinable fee or life estate; he may be purchasing the property on contract, thereby acquiring an equitable interest; he may have a lease on the premises; or he may own as joint tenant or as a tenant in common with others. His homestead rights cannot exceed his property interest in the premises.

The courts of some states have held that the homestead laws of the state create an estate in the homestead property, whereas the courts of other states have held that their homestead laws do not create an estate in the property but exempt it from sale for the obligations of the householder.

There are some differences as to the protection provided by the homestead laws of the several states. Under the laws of some states the homestead is not protected against debts in existence at the time of the declaration of the homestead; whereas under the homestead laws of other states the homestead is protected against all debts, regardless of when created. The homestead laws do not protect against liens and encumbrances on the property at the time the homestead claimant acquired it nor against mechanics' liens acquired for reason of improvement of the homestead property, nor against taxes and assessments.

The homestead may be mortgaged or conveyed; but as a general rule, if the householder is married, his or her spouse must join in the execution of the mortgage or deed. Under the laws of some states the mortgage or deed must contain a clause expressly waiving homestead rights.

EXTENT OF HOMESTEAD

The extent of the property which may be claimed as a homestead varies widely. It will depend somewhat on whether the property in which the homestead is claimed is an urban home or a farm home. In the case of an urban home the property may be limited, for instance, to a single-family dwelling and the lot on which it stands, whereas in the case of a farm home the property may be limited to the home and the outbuildings and not to exceed 40 acres of land on which they stand. In some instances a dollar value may be placed on the homestead, such as, for instance, "not exceeding $8.000 in value."

Under the laws of some of the states the homestead, on the death of the householder, passes to the surviving spouse and minor children, and is not subject to the debts of the deceased householder. As a general rule, under such statutes the widow has no homestead right in property which was not occupied as a homestead at her husband's death. However, under the laws of some states the widow and minor children are entitled to homestead rights in the property of the deceased husband, even though he had made no declaration of homestead during his lifetime. Such homesteads are known as *probate homesteads.*

TERMINATION OF HOMESTEAD

The homestead rights in property may be lost by abandonment. Whether or not a householder has abandoned the homestead is primarily a question of intention to be determined from all the surrounding circumstances. A temporary cessation of occupancy is not an abandonment. The declaration of a homestead in other property or the use of the property for purposes not permitted for a homestead is an abandonment.

Easement

NATURE OF EASEMENT

An easement is a nonpossessory interest in the real estate of another. It is an interest in land and is classed as real estate but is not an estate in land. It is intangible and does not carry with it any rights or interest in the corpus of the land. An easement may be appurtenant or in gross, and may be affirmative or negative.

To have an easement appurtenant, there must be two tracts of land owned by different parties. The one tract having the benefit of the easement is known as the *dominant tenement,* and the tract subject to the easement is known as the *servient tenement.* The dominant and servient tenements do not have to be adjoining tracts of land, but one of the termini of the easement must be on the dominant tenement. For example, dominant tenement lot A, which is at the north end of a block of lots, could have an easement of right of way over servient tenement lot E, which is at the south end of the block and lots, even though lot A is separated from lot E by lots B, C, and D, and each is owned by a different owner, provided one of the termini of the easement is located on lot A. If it were necessary for the right of way to begin on lot B, C, or D, then lot A could not have an easement of right of way over lot E.

An easement appurtenant is considered as part of the dominant tenement, and on the conveyance of the dominant tenement the easement passes with the title. In assessing the dominant tenement for taxation, the value of the easement is included. The easement is an encumbrance on the servient tenement, and any conveyance of the servient tenement is subject to the encumbrance of the easement.

AFFIRMATIVE AND NEGATIVE EASEMENTS

An easement may be affirmative or negative. An affirmative easement is the right to make some use of the property of another, such as an easement of right of way over the land of another. A negative easement is the right to have another refrain from making certain lawful use of his land. For example, an easement of light and air is the right to have an adjoining landowner refrain from erecting on his land a structure which will cut off light and air from the property of the owner of the easement.

EASEMENTS IN GROSS

An easement in gross is a mere personal interest in, or right to use, the land of another. It is not appurtenant to any estate in land. At common law an easement in gross was purely a personal right; it could not be assigned, conveyed, or inherited. This is still true if the easement in gross is held by an individual and the benefits to be derived from the easement are personal in their nature. However, it is not true if the easement is one that is sometimes referred to as a *commercial easement in gross,* such as a railroad right of way, or the right of way for a pipeline or high-tension lines, for examples. Such an easement in gross may be assigned or conveyed and, if owned by an individual, may be inherited.

Smith owned lot M and granted to Didion Brothers, Inc., an easement of right of way over lot M "for use as a walkway by pedestrians from the Hultz Manor Plan of Lots to and from the Pittsburgh Railways Company car stop." Didion Brothers, Inc., had divided a tract of land adjoining lot M and sold the lots to various persons. Smith interfered with the use of the right of way by the residents of Hultz Manor Plan of Lots, and an action was brought to enjoin Smith from further interference. Smith contended that the easement granted to Didion Brothers, Inc., was an easement in gross and could not be assigned. The court held that the easement was an easement appurtenant and enjoined further interference with its use.

Judge Montgomery said: "An easement will never be presumed to be a mere personal right when it can fairly be construed to be appurtenant to some other estate. Whether an easement is in gross or appurtenant must be determined by the fair interpretation of the grant or reservation creating the easement, aided if necessary by the situation of the parties and the surrounding circumstances.

"We have no trouble in finding that the easement in this case was appurtenant to the land owned by Didion Brothers, Inc., in the Hultz Manor Plan. Clearly, it was intended to benefit the Didions in the use of their land, and not personally." *Rusciolelli* v. *Smith,* 195 Pa. Super. 562, 171 A.2d 802 (1961).

Acquisition of easement

An easement may be acquired by express grant, by a reservation in a grant, by implication, by estoppel, by necessity, or by prescription. Under the statutes of most states a grant of an easement must be executed with the same formality as is the grant of a fee in real estate. There is some controversy as to the creation of an easement by an exception or a reservation in a deed. For example, suppose that Anthony is the owner in fee of 80 acres of land. Anthony deeds 40 acres of the land to Bates and includes in the deed a clause excepting and reserving, for the benefit of the 40 acres retained, an easement of right of way over the 40 acres sold. Some courts have held that since no easement could exist at the time of the conveyance (a person cannot have an easement in his own property), an easement cannot be created by exception. An easement could probably be reserved in such a case.

Under the modern rule followed in most states, the courts would hold that an easement can be created by either an exception or a reservation. Some conveyancers recommend that instead of attempting to create an easement by exception or reservation in a deed, the grantee named in the deed execute a separate grant giving to the grantor of the property the desired easement right. If this practice is followed, the uncertainty surrounding the effectiveness of an exception or reservation in a deed is avoided.

An easement by implication may be created when the circumstances surrounding the transfer indicate with reasonable certainty that the parties had intended to create the easement. An easement by implication is an exception to the rule that an easement can be created only by a grant in writing. In order to have an easement created by implication, there must be in existence a quasi easement which must be apparent, reasonably permanent, and reasonably necessary to the enjoyment of the dominant tenement. For example, if the grantor,[19] at the time the grantee acquired title, was using one portion of his land for the benefit of the portion sold, it would indicate that the parties intended the benefits to continue.

An easement by estoppel arises when the grantor conveys a part of his land knowing that the grantee intends to make a certain use of the part granted which will interfere with the enjoyment of the part retained. The grantee will have an easement which will enable him to make the intended specific use of his land.

An easement by necessity arises when it is necessary for the enjoyment of the part of the land granted. For example, if Adams grants land to Bates, and this land is so located that Bates cannot reach it unless he travels over the land retained by Adams or over the land of others, Bates would have an easement of right of way by necessity over the land of Adams.

An easement is acquired by prescription when the claimant has made use of the land, for the prescriptive period, openly, notoriously, continuously, and exclusively, with claim of right and adversely to the owner. It is analogous to the acquisition of possessory rights in land by adverse possession.[20]

Richardson owned adjoining lots 5 and 6. A building had been constructed on lot 6, the eaves of which overhung lot 5 by about sixteen inches. In 1949, Richardson constructed a building on lot 5, and the rainwater from the roof of the building on lot 6 was discharged on the roof of the building of lot 5. Lot 5 and the building thereon were sold by Richardson, Brannin's predecessor in title, in the year 1954. Lot 6 and the building thereon were conveyed by Richardson to Tangner in the year 1954. The deeds to the lots conveyed to each grantee rights in a party wall. Brannin sued Tangner to recover a judgment for damage to his building caused by water dripping from the eaves of Tangner's building onto his building. Tangner claimed that he had an easement right to discharge the water onto Brannin's building. The court held that Tangner had an implied easement as claimed.

Justice Welch said: "A deed may, of course, grant or reserve an easement and the instrument should be construed to carry out the intention of the parties. But an easement may be implied also and the intention of the parties is determined by all the facts and circumstances in order that effect may be given

[19] *Lane* v. *Flautt*, 176 Md. 620, 6 A.2d 228.

[20] Acquisition of title to real estate by adverse possession is discussed in a subsequent chapter.

to the apparent intent. An implied easement is based upon the theory that whenever one conveys property he includes in the conveyance whatever is necessary for the use and enjoyment of the land retained. . . .

"There is ample evidence in the case at bar indicative of knowledge by the plaintiffs of the servitude of the property they purchased. The existence of the party-wall clause in the deed by which plaintiffs acquired title to Lot 5 directed attention to the probability of the overhanging of the roof-eave. Ordinary observation would have confirmed it as a fact." *Tangner* v. *Brannin,* Okla., 381 p.2d 321 (1963).

Rights and duties of parties to easements

The scope and extent of an easement depend on the wording of the grant or, if acquired by prescription, on the use made by the dominant tenement at the time of acquisition. The owner of the servient tenement may use the entire premises for any purpose he desires so long as such use does not interfere with the enjoyment of the easement.

The owner of the servient tenement may erect gates or put up bars across a right of way if they do not unreasonably interfere with its use. An easement which gives the owner exclusive possession of a portion of the premises, such as a railroad right of way, does not give the owner of the easement the right to drill oil or gas wells thereon. Such use would be in excess of the scope of the easement.

The owner of the easement must keep the affected part of the servient tenement in repair and has the right to enter upon the servient tenement for the purpose of making repairs or improvements reasonably necessary to the enjoyment of the easement. If the easement is acquired for the general benefit of the dominant tenement, a change in the use of the dominant tenement will not affect the easement. However, if the easement is limited in its scope, its use will be confined to the designated scope.

Also, if the owner of the dominant tenement acquires additional property adjoining the dominant tenement, the easement cannot be enlarged to include use for the benefit of the additional property. For example, suppose that Albert owns a factory and the land upon which it stands, and has an easement of right of way over the land of Bates. Albert purchases an additional tract of land adjacent to his factory and enlarges his factory so that it is partly on the additional tract of land. Albert cannot use the right of way over the land of Bates for the benefit of the enlarged factory.[21] The scope of an easement may be enlarged by prescription.

---

[21] *D. M. Goodwillie Co.* v. *Commonwealth Electric Co.,* 241 Ill. 42, 89 N.E. 272.

DESCRIPTION OF EASEMENT

If an easement is imperfectly described in a grant, or in an exclusion or reservation clause in a grant, a court will interpret the instrument and resolve the uncertainties and, if necessary, establish the location of the easement.

EXTINGUISHMENT OF EASEMENT

An easement is extinguished if the ownership of the fee of both the dominant and the servient tenement is in the same person, but this rule does not apply if one of the tenements is held in a representative capacity. For example, Albert may own the dominant tenement in his own right and have title to the servient tenement as trustee for Bates.

An easement granted for a specific purpose or for a limited time, or an easement by necessity, is extinguished by the fulfillment of the purpose, the expiration of the time, or the ceasing of the necessity. Also, an easement is extinguished by abandonment. A mere nonuse of an easement without an accompanying intent to relinquish the right to it is not an abandonment of the easement.

An easement may be extinguished by prescription. If the owner of the servient tenement uses his land in a manner inconsistent with the rights of the owner of the easement and continues such use for the statutory period, the easement will be extinguished. The sale of the servient tenement for nonpayment of taxes does not extinguish the easement.

UNRECORDED EASEMENT

An unrecorded easement created by a grant will be extinguished by a conveyance of the servient tenement to a bona fide purchaser for value who has no notice or knowledge of the existence of the easement.[22]

Profits

NATURE OF PROFITS

A profit in land, technically known as a *profit a pendre,* is the right to take part of the soil or produce of land owned by someone else. The

---

[22] Recording of instruments and the effects of recording on the rights of parties will be discussed in a subsequent chapter.

term includes the right to take soil, gravel, minerals, oil, gas, and the like from the land of another. A profit is like an easement in almost all respects. It may be appurtenant—that is, the profits may be taken only for the benefit of the dominant tenement—or it may be in gross.

Frequently, it is difficult to determine whether a grant conveys a fee in the minerals underlying the surface or conveys a profit in the land. The wording of the grant, interpreted in the light of the surrounding circumstances, will determine the nature of the interest conveyed.

License

NATURE OF LICENSE

A license is a privilege to go upon the land of another. It is not an estate in land and is personal to the one to whom it is given; and it has been held, with some exceptions, that a license cannot be assigned or inherited. Since a license is not an interest in land, it can be created orally.

Permission to hunt or fish on the land of another is an example of a typical license, as is also the right of a person to attend a theatrical performance or ball game after purchasing a ticket.

As a general rule, a license is revocable at the will of the licensor. If the license is created by contract, written or oral, and is to continue for a specified time, the licensor, under the general rule, may revoke the license at any time. However, if his revocation would be a breach of the contract granting the license, he would be liable to the licensee for damages for breach of the contract.

Under some circumstances, a license has been held to be irrevocable. For example, if a license which contemplates expenditures on the part of the licensee in the improvement of the premises is granted, it has been held by some courts that after substantial expenditures have been made, the power of revocation is suspended until the term of the license expires or the purpose of the license is accomplished.[23] The effect of such a holding is to convert a license into an easement. Some courts have refused to hold such cases to be exceptions to the general rule.

An oral grant of an easement which is unenforceable under the statute of frauds creates a license which is revocable before it is acted upon. Some courts have held that when the oral grant has been acted upon

---

[23] *Binder* v. *Weinberg,* 94 Miss. 817, 48 So. 1013.

and the grantee has expended substantial sums in the improvement of the premises, he has an easement; but other courts do not so hold.[24]

Du Bose contracted to sell to Bishop timber to be cut by Bishop from a tract of land owned by Du Bose. The contract was in writing and, in addition to stating the price per thousand feet to be paid for logs cut, provided that the seller had the right to direct the portions of the tract from which the trees were to be cut. It did not state the quantity of timber to be cut, nor did it state that all merchantable timber on the tract should be cut.

After Bishop had cut between 30,000 and 40,000 feet of timber, Du Bose ordered him to cease cutting timber and denied him the right to come onto the land. Bishop sued Du Bose to recover damages for breach of contract. Bishop claimed that he had acquired title to the timber on the tract. Du Bose claimed that the contract was unenforceable for uncertainty of terms and that Bishop had only a license to cut timber. The court gave judgment to Bishop, and Du Bose appealed. The judgment was reversed.

Justice Moore said: "The contract in the case at bar is not a conveyance of standing timber. Defendant 'agrees to sell' and plaintiff 'agrees to pay for . . . logs on the stump' from defendant's Avery Creek farm at a specified price per thousand feet to be paid before removal of the logs from the land. This is an executory contract for sale of 'logs,' title to pass after logs are severed, measured, and paid for, with license to enter the land, sever and remove the logs.

"A contract to remove timber, providing for measurement of logs before removal from the premises and for payment at the time the logs are measured and containing no direct promise on the part of the buyer to sever or pay for the timber in any event, lacks mutuality to pass present title and is a mere license revocable at any time by the landowner without liability. 'A license to enter on land and cut timber, while it remains executory, is revocable at any time. It is revocable at the will of the licensor, and terminates when he gives notice not to cut the timber further or refuses permission of the licensee to perform.' However, there are exceptions to this rule: (1) a license coupled with an interest may not be revoked; (2) 'a license cannot be revoked as to acts done under it; the revocation is prospective not retrospective'; (3) . . . Where the licensee has made expenditures upon the faith of the license, . . . it cannot be revoked at the will of the licensor unless the license is placed in statu quo.

"Plaintiff's evidence fails to bring him within either of the enumerated exceptions." *Bishop* v. *Du Bose,* 252 N.C. 158, 113 S.E.2d 309 (1960).

---

[24] *Baird* v. *Westberg,* 341 Ill. 616, 173 N.E. 820.

3

Personal property, fixtures, and mechanics' liens

Personal property

DISTINCTION BETWEEN PERSONAL PROPERTY AND REAL ESTATE

THE DISTINCTION between personal property and real estate is both practical and logical. It was recognized at an early period in the social development of people and is now a part of the law of all civilized nations. Simply stated, the earth's crust and all things attached thereto are real estate; all other property is personal property. However, this elementary rule is inadequate as the basis for the solution of problems arising in our complex society. We change the character of property from real estate to personal property by severance, and we change personal property to real estate by attachment. Stone, in its natural condition in the earth's crust, is real estate; but when it is severed from the earth's crust—quarried—it becomes personal property, and is bought and sold as such. When the quarried stone is fashioned into a building, it becomes real estate, and is bought and sold as such along with the land on which the structure has been erected.

In dealing with real estate, many situations arise in which it is necessary to determine whether or not a particular item of property passes as real estate to the purchaser of land or remains the personal property of the seller. This area of the law is known as the *law of fixtures*.

Fixtures

NATURE OF FIXTURES

From a technical legal standpoint a fixture is personal property which is so attached to or used with the real estate that it is considered to be a part of the real estate. The term *fixture* is also used to designate personal property which appears to be a part of the real estate but is not permanently attached thereto and is removable, such as, for instance, store fixtures. In its broadest sense the term is applied to any personal property attached to or used with real estate, whether irremovable or movable, and imparts nothing which would designate the category into which of the preceding categories the property would fall but leaves that to be determined by consideration of the circumstances and the relation of the parties.[1]

BASIC PRINCIPLES

Certain basic principles have particular significance in real estate law and are frequently applied in the solution of problems involving the determination of whether an item of property is personal property or is a fixture and passes with the land. The following brief statements of these basic principles will help clarify some of the points raised by the courts in their determination of controversies involving fixtures:

1. Within certain not too well-defined limits the parties involved may determine their rights in property by mutual agreement.
2. An agreement cannot affect the property rights of persons who are not parties to the agreement.
3. As a general rule, a party is bound by his knowledge or notice of the rights of others.
4. As a general rule, a person takes property with notice of the rights of the party in possession of it.
5. A person takes property with notice of rights of others which are matters of public record.
6. A person cannot convey greater rights in property than he has.
7. When one of two innocent parties must suffer a loss, the party whose fault has contributed most to the loss must bear it.

---

[1] *New Castle Theater Company* v. *Ward,* 57 Ind. App. 473, 104 N.E. 526.

Standard tests

INTENTION OF PARTIES

The courts, in determining whether or not an item of property is a fixture, attempt to ascertain the intention of the parties. It is obvious that in many cases the parties did not consider the question and could not have entertained an intention regarding it. Consequently, the courts have set up the following standard which they apply: What would a man of ordinary prudence, familiar with the business at hand, with the customs of the community, and with all the facts and circumstances of the transaction, be justified in believing the parties intended? In applying this standard, certain factual elements are important, but none are conclusive.

The lessee drilled a well on the leased premises and installed pumping equipment costing between $20,000 and $25,000. The well was a failure, and at the time of the expiration of the lease the pumping equipment was standing on wooden blocks, unattached to the land. The lessee claimed the pumping equipment as his personal property, and the lessor claimed it was a fixture. The court held that it was personal property.

Presiding Justice Conley said: "The authorities apply a threefold test in determining whether or not an article is a a fixture: '(1) the manner of its annexation; (2) its adaptability to the use and purpose for which the realty is used; and (3) the intention of the parties making the annexation.' . . . It was reasonable for the trial court to consider that there was no intention to make a gift of equipment costing $20,000 or $25,000 to the owner of the premises. *Banks* v. *Clintworth*, 20 Cal. Rptr. 431 (1963).

EXPRESS AGREEMENT

If parties agree that personal property attached to or used with real estate shall remain personal property and may be detached and removed, the courts will enforce the agreement. However, if personal property is built into a structure and the severance of such property would destroy or seriously injure the structure, the courts will refuse to enforce the agreement. An agreement was enforced whereby a landlord permitted a tenant to install an oil burner in the furnace on the leased premises with the right to remove it on the termination of the lease, provided the tenant restored the furnace to its original condition.[2]

If the owner of real estate purchases under a conditional sales contract

---

[2] *Brandt* v. *Koppelman et al.,* 169 Pa. Super. 236, 82 A.2d 666.

supporting I-beams which are to be used in the construction of a building on the premises, and the contract expressly provides that the I-beams shall remain personal property and may be repossessed if not paid for, the courts, in case there is a default, will not permit the removal of the I-beams, since such removal would destroy or seriously damage the structure. The courts have held that a person purchasing real estate from an owner not in possession takes it subject to the right of the person in possession to remove attached personal property.[3]

Haverfield Company leased from Siegel certain designated space in a building which, at the time the lease was executed, was under construction. Eight wall cases were specially constructed for the building. The cases served as a partition wall between the sales area and the fitting rooms. The lease provided that the lessee would pay for the cases and their installation; that they would be depreciated at the rate of 10 per cent per year; and that if the lease were terminated, the lessor would pay the lessee the cost of the cases less the depreciated value. The lease further provided that "the fixtures, except trade fixtures, shall become the property of the lessor." The lessee had possession of the premises for twelve years; consequently, under the terms of the lease the price of the cases was completely depreciated. Haverfield Company claimed the cases as trade fixtures. The court held that by the terms of the lease the cases were fixtures and the property of the lessor, Siegel.

Justice Pope said: "The intention of the parties is expressed and governed by the lease agreement. . . . The parties contemplated that those items which were part of the permanent construction, . . . were the items termed (fixtures) in the lease." *Haverfield Company* v. *Siegel,* Tex. Civ. App., 366 S.W.2d 790 (1963).

MODE OF ATTACHMENT.   At one period in the development of the law of fixtures, the only test applied by the courts was that of attachment. Today, attachment or—more specifically—the mode of attachment is of outstanding importance but is not controlling. If personal property has been firmly attached to the real estate, it is strong evidence that the party so attaching the property intended it to become a part of the real estate; but if the property is so affixed that it can be easily removed without injury to it or to the real estate to which it is attached, then there is strong evidence that the parties intended it to retain its character as personal property.

At one time, lighting fixtures were owned by the tenant and were generally held to be the personal property of the tenant. Today, lighting

---

[3] *Sarafin* v. *Wolff et ux.,* 5 N.J. Super. 386, 69 A.2d 347.

fixtures, furnaces, and similar equipment installed in a building are generally held to be fixtures, even though they are so attached that they can be removed without injury to either the equipment or the real estate to which they are attached. Such items are usually considered as part of the completed structure.[4]

Whether appliances such as gas and electric stoves, refrigerators, freezers, washers, and dryers are held to be fixtures or personal property will depend more on the surrounding circumstances than on the mode of attachment. The courts may come to opposite conclusions in cases in which the mode of attachment is substantially the same. A careful analysis of the facts of the cases, however, will usually reveal differences in the surrounding circumstances which justify the variance in the decisions of the courts.[5] In the absence of an agreement to the contrary, the courts have been consistent in holding that "built-in" appliances are fixtures.

At one stage in the development of the law of fixtures, the courts held that if a structure was set up on blocks or stones which were not embedded in the earth, there was no attachment, and the structure was personal property. However, under present-day law a building, in the absence of an express agreement to the contrary, will be held to be a fixture, even though its foundation is not embedded in the earth.[6] In one case the court held that a statue and sun dial set on a cement foundation, not fastened by bolts or clamps but held in place by gravity, was a fixture.[7]

If a building is set on a foundation, or is joined with the land by being set over a basement and is connected with the sewer and water mains, it will be held to be real estate, unless there is an agreement to the contrary.[8]

ADAPTATION TO USE WITH REAL ESTATE. Another important consideration is the adaptation or appropriation of the personal property to the use or purpose of the real estate to which it is attached. If personal property has been attached to the real estate to promote the purpose for which the realty is held, the courts will presume that the party affixing

---

[4] *Batcheler* v. *Lally*, Pa. Com. Pl., 40 Luz. L. Reg. Rep. 166.

[5] *Leisle* v. *Welfare Building and Loan Association*, 232 Wis. 440, 287 N.W. 739.

[6] *Cornell College* v. *Crain et al.*, 211 Iowa 1343, 235 N.W. 731.

[7] *Snedeker* v. *Warring*, 12 N.Y. 170.

[8] *Standard Oil Company* v. *Braun*, 53 N.D. 104, 204 N.W. 972; *Crawford-Fayram Lumber Co.* v. *Mann*, 203 Iowa 748, 211 N.W. 225.

it to the realty intended it to become a part of the real estate, regardless of the mode of attachment.[9] In the more recent cases the courts have, as a general rule, given more weight to the adaptation of the article to the use of the real estate than they have to the method of attachment. If the personal property is attached to the real estate for the purpose of improving it and making it more valuable, it will generally be held to be a fixture; but if it is brought onto the realty for temporary use which does not enhance the value of the realty and may be removed at the pleasure of the person making the attachment without injury to the realty, it will usually be held to retain its character as personal property, even though it is attached to the realty.

UNATTACHED PROPERTY. The courts have held, with a few exceptions, that an article of personal property particularly adapted for use with certain real estate, but useful elsewhere and not attached to the real estate, is not a fixture.[10] However, in a few cases the courts have held that such articles are fixtures if it was reasonably clear that the owner intended them to be used permanently with the real estate. In one case the court held that rollaway beds were fixtures, since closets had been constructed for the sole purpose of receiving the beds when not in use.[11] The courts have held machinery and other articles brought into and fastened to a building to be fixtures if they were essential to the carrying-on of the business to which the building was devoted.[12] And in some instances the courts have held such machinery to be a fixture even though it was not physically attached to the building.[13]

Relation of parties

OWNER

Since the owner of property is free, within limits, to use his property as he wishes, he is at liberty to attach personal property to his real estate and detach it at will, and no question arises as to whether the property

---

[9] *Citizens Bank of Greenfield* v. *Mergenthaler Linotype Co.,* 216 Ind. 573, 25 N.E.2d 444.

[10] *Fry et al.* v. *Lost Key Mine, Inc., et al.,* 108 Col. App. 568, 239 P.2d 69.

[11] *Leisle* v. *Welfare Building and Loan Association,* 232 Wis. 440, 287 N.W. 739.

[12] *Atlantic Die Casting Co.* v. *Whiting Tubular Products, Inc.,* 337 Mich. 414, 60 N.W.2d 174.

[13] *Pennsylvania Chocolate Co.* v. *Hershey Bros.,* 316 Pa. 292, 175 A. 694.

attached remains personal property or becomes a fixture. The ownership of both the attached property and the real estate is vested in the same person, and the character of such attached property is immaterial. It is only when the real estate is sold, mortgaged, or leased that a question may arise as to the character of personal property which is attached to or used with the real estate.

VENDEE

When the owner of real estate attaches to it personal property which is appropriate for the purpose for which the real estate is used, there is a strong presumption that he intended the article to be a fixture. If the property is sold and there is no reservation in the contract of sale or deed, the courts will resolve all doubt in favor of the purchaser.

Frequently, articles have been held to be fixtures as between vendor and vendee which would not have been held to be fixtures if the relation of the parties had been different—landlord and tenant, for example.[14]

The same rules apply to a mortgage transaction. The mortgagee of real estate acquires all the rights of a vendee; that is, the mortgage is a lien on all fixtures which were a part of the realty at the time the mortgage was executed, unless they are excluded by an agreement in writing or by a provision in the mortgage.[15]

Peed owned a duplex, which he sold to Bennett. At the time of the sale, Peed was living in the lower apartment, and the upper apartment was rented. Peed had installed in the upper apartment a refrigerator and stove for the use of tenants occupying the apartment. At the time of the sale, Peed told Bennett that the apartment rented for $60 per month by reason of the fact that the refrigerator and stove were furnished to the apartment. There was no reference to the refrigerator and stove in the purchase agreement or deed. Peed claimed the refrigerator and stove as personal property, and Bennett claimed them as fixtures. The court held that the refrigerator and stove were fixtures.

Judge Dowell said: "The instant case is one between vendor and purchaser of real estate and of this much there can be little doubt, that as between such parties the modern doctrine is that the rule for determining what is a fixture is strongly construed against the vendor and in favor of the purchaser. . . .

"Many chattels have been held to be fixtures as between vendor and purchaser

---

[14] *Peed* v. *Bennett,* 114 Ind. App. 412, 52 N.E.2d 629.

[15] *Fusor* v. *Whittaker et al.,* 28 Tenn. App. 338, 190 S.W.2d 305.

of lands or as between mortgagor and mortgagee thereof which do not lose their character of personal chattels when the question is between landlord and tenant or others." *Peed* v. *Bennett,* 114 Ind. App. 412, 52 N.E.2d 629 (1944).

EXCEPTIONS AND RESERVATIONS. In handling a transaction, if there is any question as to the character of items, one should clearly state in the contract of sale the items which are to become the property of the vendee, and those which are excepted from the sale and reserved by the vendor. As a general rule, an oral exception or reservation is ineffective, although under some circumstances, such an exception or reservation might be enforced.

Under the statute of frauds, any contract affecting an interest in real estate is unenforceable unless it is evidenced by a note or memorandum in writing. Since a fixture is real estate, a reservation, in order to be enforceable, must be in writing.[16] In addition, under the parol evidence rule, oral evidence is inadmissible to add to, alter, or vary the terms of a written instrument; consequently, if there is no exception or reservation in the contract or deed, oral evidence offered to prove an oral exception or reservation would be inadmissible.[17]

HOLDERS OF SECURITY INTEREST IN ATTACHED PERSONALTY VERSUS OWNER

If the owner of real estate purchases personal property and gives a security interest in it under the provisions of the Uniform Commercial Code; or if the owner gives a chattel mortgage or buys on a conditional sales contract in a non-Code state; or if a security interest either under the Code or under a chattel mortgage, in a non-Code state, is given on attached personal property to secure an obligation, the court will hold that the security transaction is, in effect, an agreement that the attached property shall be personal property, and the secured party, in the event there is a default, will have the right to detach the property from the real estate and proceed to foreclose his lien.[18]

As a general rule, if the owner of real estate permits another, as a licensee, to affix to the real estate personal property owned by the licensee, the attached article remains personal property and may be removed by the licensee.[19]

---

[16] *Bricker* v. *Whisler,* 65 Ind. App. 492, 117 N.E. 550.

[17] *Wellman* v. *Tomblin,* W. Va., 84 S.E.2d 617.

[18] *Swift Lumber and Fuel Company* v. *Elwanger et al.,* 127 Neb. 740, 256 N.W. 875.

[19] *Wilson* v. *Modica,* Tex. Civ. App., 80 S.W.2d 411.

VENDEE VERSUS HOLDER OF SECURITY INTEREST

If, at the time a person purchases real estate, there is attached to it personal property on which there is a perfected security interest under the Uniform Commercial Code, or under a chattel mortgage or conditional sales contract if the property is in a non-Code state, the rights of the vendee will depend on whether or not he had notice or knowledge of the outstanding interest in such attached personal property. The vendee will have notice if the purchase agreement or deed contains provisions excepting or reserving the personal property or if the purchase agreement states that the real estate is sold subject to the outstanding security interest in the specific attached personal property.

Under the Uniform Commercial Code, provision is made for perfecting a security interest in fixtures; and if the secured party complies with the requirements of the Code, his security interest in the fixture will have priority over all persons subsequently acquiring an interest in the real estate, subject to certain stated exceptions.[20]

The Uniform Conditional Sales Act, Section 7, provides for the recording in the real estate records of conditional sales contracts of personal property which is to be attached to real estate; and if a conditional sales contract is properly recorded under the provisions of the act, a subsequent purchaser or mortgagee of the real estate takes subject to the rights of the conditional vendor. An improperly recorded or an unrecorded chattel mortgage or conditional sales contract is void against a bona fide purchaser or an innocent mortgagee of the real estate to which the article is attached.[21]

LANDLORD AND TENANT

DOMESTIC FIXTURES. Domestic or ornamental fixtures are fixtures which are attached to a dwelling for the purpose of making it a more comfortable and attractive place in which to live. The early English courts held that any personal property attached to leased real estate by the tenant became the property of the landlord; but the modern courts favor the tenant and have held that he may remove such fixtures, provided they can be detached without material injury to the real estate. If the article attached is a substitute for one which was there at the time of the lease,

---

[20] *Uniform Commercial Code,* Sec. 9–313.

[21] The rights of a real estate mortgagee against the holder of a security interest in fixtures is discussed in Chapter 9.

it may not be removed unless the old fixture has been preserved and can be reinstalled without material injury to the real estate.

In those cases in which the landlord and tenant have entered into an agreement which gives the tenant the right to remove personal property which the tenant has attached to the leased premises, the court will enforce such agreement. In the event the agreement does not state a time within which such property shall be removed, the courts have generally held that the tenant will have a reasonable time after the termination of the lease in which to remove attached property.[22] Some courts have held, however, that if the lease is a term lease, the tenant must remove the property before the expiration of the lease.

TRADE FIXTURES

A trade fixture is an article attached to the leased real estate by the tenant to aid him in carrying on the business or profession he is operating on the leased premises. In determining whether or not an article is a trade fixture, the mode of annexation and the size of the article are of secondary importance. However, if a tenant incorporates an article into the building in such a manner that its removal would weaken the structure, the courts have held that the article is not a trade fixture, even though it was attached to the building by the tenant for the purpose of making the structure more suitable for carrying on the business conducted on the premises.[23] A provision in a lease stating that certain items attached to the real estate shall or shall not become a part of the realty will be enforced.

Under the common-law rule, if the tenant did not remove trade fixtures before the expiration of a term lease, the fixtures became the property of the landlord. Some courts based the rule on the ground that if the fixtures were not removed before the end of the term, the tenant must have intended them to be permanent additions to the realty. Other courts held that if the tenant entered the premises after the expiration of the term, he would be a trespasser and that therefore he forfeited his right to remove the fixtures if he did not remove them during the term. A majority of the courts have held that if the tenant is left in possession of the premises, with the consent of the landlord, after the expiration of the lease, the tenant has the right to remove trade fixtures during

---

[22] *Hubert* v. *Collard,* Tex. Civ. App., 141 S.W.2d 677.

[23] *Stockton* v. *Tester,* Mo. App., 273 S.W.2d 783.

the period of possession.[24] If the lease is for an indefinite period, such as a life lease, the tenant has a reasonable time after the termination of the lease within which to remove his trade fixtures.

Kelm owned a building which he leased as a tavern to Timper. Without the consent of Kelm, Timper removed a bar which was built against one of the walls and replaced it with a circular bar built in the center of the room. In installing this bar, approximately twelve holes differing in diameter from one to six inches were drilled in the floor. These holes were made so that the bar could have the necessary electrical and water connections, and so that beer could be piped from the basement of the building. A bottle chute was also installed. The cost of restoring the floor to its original condition would be about $350. In order to make the change in the bar, Timper borrowed money and gave Loan Corporation a chattel mortgage on the bar as security. Timper abandoned the lease, and Loan Corporation claimed the bar. Kelm claimed that the bar was a fixture, not a trade fixture, and that it was his property. The court held that the bar was a fixture and was the property of Kelm.

Justice Wilkie said: "The most important single fact in this case is that when defendant [Kelm] leased the premises to the tenant as a 'tavern' it contained a 'bar.' From this it is easy to conclude that there was an intention on the part of the tenant and landloard to make the new bar part of the premises. ' When the tenant, who had been utilizing the premises for four years, substituted a new fixture and discarded the old fixture, which he did not initially own, it is reasonable to conclude that he intended that the new fixture was to be substituted for the old fixture and to become the property of the owner of the old fixture." *Auto Acceptance and Loan Corporation* v. *Kelm,* Wis.2d 178, 118 N.W.2d 175 (1962).

RIGHTS UNDER RENEWAL LEASE

The courts are in conflict as to whether or not a tenant's right to remove trade fixtures is lost if he takes a renewal lease or a new lease which does not, by its terms, specifically reserve his right to remove the trade fixtures attached to the premises during the prior terms. The early view, which is still adhered to by some courts, is that if, on the expiration of the first term, the tenant did not remove the fixtures and, on renewal or on the making of a new lease, he did not reserve his right to the fixtures, he thereby abandoned such right.[25]

Some courts have repudiated the rule; some have held that it does

---

[24] *Anderson-Tully Company* v. *United States,* 189 F.2d 192.

[25] *Niestadt* v. *Joseph,* 81 Ind. App. 355, 139 N.E. 336.

not apply to trade fixtures; and some have inferred an understanding, from the circumstances of the case, that the fixtures are removable.

In some states the tenants' rights are protected by statute.[26] If the right to remove fixtures is expressly reserved in the renewal lease or new lease, the courts will enforce the provision.

AGREEMENT THAT TENANT SHALL NOT REMOVE PROPERTY. As a general rule, the courts have held that a provision in a lease to the effect that all "alterations, additions, or improvements" to the premises shall, on the expiration of the lease, become the property of the landlord does not include trade fixtures. What would be included as alterations, additions, and improvements is a question of fact to be determined according to all the surrounding circumstances.

AGRICULTURAL FIXTURES

Today, we consider the operation of a farm as a business and apply to agriculture fixtures the rules of law relating to trade fixtures.[27]

Crops, trees, and shrubs

RIGHTS IN CROPS, TREES, AND SHRUBS

Technically, crops, trees, and shrubs are not fixtures; but in real estate transactions the problems relating to crops, trees, and shrubs are, from a practical standpoint, similar in many respects to the problems relating to fixtures. Vegetation growing on land is divided into two categories: (1) vegetation which is produced annually by the labor of man and (2) vegetation which is the natural product of the soil and which is perennial in nature. The former is classed as personal property and the latter as real estate.

As in all classifications, there is no natural, clear line of demarcation between the classes, and disputes often arise as to the classification in which a particular article belongs.

In general, crops which are planted and cultivated annually and fruits, berries, and so forth, which are harvested annually are personal property, and may be bought and sold as such. However, if the land on which

---

[26] *Handler* v. *Horns*, 2 N.J. 18, 65 A.2d 523; Maryland, *Flock Annotated Code, 1951*, Art. 53, Sec. 38.

[27] *Old Line Life Insurance Company of America* v. *Hawn et al.*, 225 Wis. 627, 275 N.W. 542.

such crops are growing is transferred and there is no reservation or exception of the growing crops, the crops pass with the land and become the property of the transferee.

Some courts have enforced oral reservations of crops; at the same time, other courts have held that evidence of an oral reservation of crops is inadmissible under the parol evidence rule or that the reservation must be in writing to satisfy the statute of frauds.[28]

The courts have distinguished between growing crops, matured crops, and severed crops. Growing crops, if not excepted or reserved, pass with the land; severed crops do not. Matured crops—that is, crops that are ripe and ready for harvest but have not been severed from the land—do not, as a general rule, pass with the land.

In all real estate transactions, controversies regarding the rights to crops, trees, and shrubs may be avoided, or at least minimized, by including in the purchase agreement or deed a provision defining the rights of the parties.

The courts are in substantial accord in holding that trees and shrubs are a part of the land and that any exception or reservation relating to them must be in writing.

Standing timber

The sale of standing timber, to be left on the land for an appreciable period of time, is the sale of real estate and must be treated as such. A sale of trees to be cut, either by the seller or by the buyer, within a short period of time has been held to be a sale of personal property. The courts so holding have based their decisions on a theory of constructive severance. They hold that the sale is a sale of the severed logs, not of the standing trees.[29]

Nursery stock

Nursery stock is personal property. The operation of a nursery is considered to be the operation of a business, and the nursery stock is considered to be the stock in trade of the business. Plants, trees, and shrubs in the nursery are all held to be personal property.[30]

The city of Los Angeles condemned a tract of land owned by Pedersen

---

[28] *Dick* v. *Horn*, 97 Okla. 258, 223 P. 393.

[29] *Edwards* v. *Glaske*, 165 Pa. Super. 108, 67 A.2d 798.

[30] *Story* v. *Christin et al.*, 14 Cal.2d 592, 95 P.2d 925.

and leased to Hoover Nursery Company. The lease gave Hoover Nursery Company the right to remove the nursery stock. A controversy arose as to the right of Hoover Nursery Company to compensation for condemned nursery stock. The court held that the nursery stock was part of the real estate and that under the terms of the lease, Hoover Nursery Company had an interest in the real estate and was entitled to compensation for it.

The court said: "Respondent [City of Los Angeles] contends, however, that, because the lease between the parties provided that nursery stock might be planted and grown by the nursery company for resale by it, such trees and plants acquired the character of personal property exclusively. . . . Growing trees, shrubs and other plants were generally considered a part of the realty to which they are attached by their roots, and continued to be such until they were severed, when they became personal property. The occasion to declare trees, plants, crops, etc., to be personal property while they were attached to the land by their roots, was merely to apply a fiction in law in order to arrive at a just determination in particular cases." *City of Los Angeles* v. *Hughes,* 202 Col. 731, 262 P. 737 (1927).

Mechanics' liens

NATURE OF STATUTORY LIENS

At common law a person who made improvements to the real estate of another by his labor or by the addition of his materials could acquire no lien on such real estate for the value of his improvements. Neither could a person acquire a lien on real estate by operation of law, and the early chancery courts did not grant equitable liens on real estate. Under present-day law, liens on real estate are granted by statutory enactment.

All states have enacted statutes providing for mechanics' liens on real estate, judgment liens, attachment liens, execution liens, and tax liens. The scope of such liens and the rights and liabilities of the parties involved will depend on the provisions of the lien statute of the state in which the real estate is located and the interpretation of the statute by the courts of that state. Under the federal law the federal government is entitled to a tax lien on a delinquent taxpayer's property, including his real estate, for any unpaid income, estate, or gift tax.

NATURE OF MECHANIC'S LIEN STATUTES

The mechanic's lien on real estate is based on the principles of the common-law artisan's lien. The objective of each is the same: the protection of anyone who by his labor or by the addition of his material improves the property of another. The artisan's lien is a possessory lien on personal property, and the artisan must have the possession of the property improved before such a lien can be granted him; whereas the mechanic's lien on real estate is not a possessory lien, since the property improved remains in the possession of the owner. Under the mechanic's lien statutes the owner must have contracted, either expressly or impliedly, for the improvement of his real estate, and the lien claimant must have improved the real estate by his labor or by the addition of his materials. A lien can then be granted for the reasonable value of the labor or materials furnished, which normally is the contract price.

Although the mechanic's lien statutes are based on the same fundamental principle, they vary widely in their provisions as to who is entitled to a lien; the property subject to the lien; the procedure followed in perfecting the lien; the rights of materialmen, laborers, and subcontractors; priorities; waivers; assignment of lien rights; and similar details. In addition, the statutes are, in many respects, general in their terminology; and the right to a lien depends, in particular situations, on the court's interpretation of the statute. The mechanic's lien statutes of the various states differ in so many particulars that it is impossible to discuss them in detail in a work of this nature.

NECESSITY FOR COMPLIANCE WITH STATUTE

Since the mechanic's lien on real estate is created by constitutional provision or statutory enactment, the lien claimant, in order to obtain a lien, must comply strictly with the provisions of the law. A person engaging in any phase of the real estate business should familiarize himself with the general provisions of the mechanic's lien law. However, if he should have occasion to avail himself of the benefits of the law, he would be wise to consult a competent local attorney at the inception of his transaction. Failure to comply with some detail of the lien law could result in the loss of lien rights.

On August 23, 1956, J. T. Evans Co. filed a mechanic's lien notice against property owned by the Reidingers, and the lien was perfected on April 12, 1957. On November 25, 1957, J. T. Evans Co. obtained a judgment against the Reidingers for the unpaid balance owed for labor and materials furnished, for which the mechanic's lien had been perfected. J. T. Evans Co. did not levy an execution on the Reidinger's property.

On March 11, 1958, Fanelli recovered a judgment against the Reidingers and levied an execution on the property on which J. T. Evans Co. had a mechanic's lien. Fanelli claimed that since J. T. Evans Co. did not levy an execution on the Reidingers' property, the Fanelli execution had priority, and that the bringing of suit and recovering of a judgment by the J. T. Evans Co. on its claim resulted in a waiver of its rights under its mechanic's lien. The court held that J. T. Evans Co.'s mechanic's lien had priority over Fanelli's judgment.

Judge Dzick said: "There are generally three kinds of liens recognized in our judicial system: (1) common law, (2) equitable, and (3) statutory. There is, of course, no common-law lien under which the plaintiff could claim any right of priority for the payment of materials furnished by it in the construction of the homes on the lands in question, nor is the plaintiff entitled to an equitable lien by reason of supplying the materials to the builder contractor. It becomes apparent, therefore, that the lien, if any, to which plaintiff was entitled must be a statutory lien and must arise as a result of N.J.S. 2A:44–64 et seq., N.J.S.A., commonly referred to as the Mechanic's Lien Act. The plaintiff, if it is entitled to any priority, is so entitled by virtue of said act, and is entitled also only to a statutory lien.

"Generally, common-law liens pertained exclusively to personal property, and normally required for their continued efficacy a continuance of possession in the lienor. Over the years, however, the word has acquired much more extended significance and is now generally recognized as a charge upon a particular piece of property including realty, for the payment or discharge of a particular debt or duty in priority to the general debts or duty of the owner.

"The purpose of the Mechanic's Lien Act is very aptly expressed in Friedman v. Stein:

> 'The mechanic's and materialman's liens had their genesis in the civil law. They are unknown to the common law; and they had no recognition in equity except as prescribed by statute. Thus it is that these liens are exclusively statutory in origin; and, being in derogation of the common law, the provisions of the statute giving rise to the lien are to be strictly construed, while the provisions for the enforcement of the lien thereby created are to be liberally construed to effectuate the remedial statutory policy of providing priority of payment of the price or value of work performed and materials furnished in the erection or reparation of a building or other structure and . . . the security of the land and buildings for the payment of that which has made for an assumed enhancement of the value of the property.'

"The claim by a supplier for materials furnished is an inchoate lien until all statutory requisites are met, at which time the statutory lien arises.

> 'The statutory lien is separate and distinct from the underlying debt; the lien affords a cumulative remedy for the enforcement of the debt. The

claimant's status is that of general creditor until those things are done which give him the security of the statutory lien. Until then, the lien is inchoate merely.'

"The Legislature must therefore have intended that although by the judgment the original cause of action is extinguished and a new cause of action is created, advantages to which the plaintiff was entitled with respect to the original cause of action may not be destroyed by the judgment. Thus, if a creditor has a lien upon the property of the debtor and obtains a judgment against him, he does not thereby lose the benefit of the lien. The court determines that an execution on plaintiff's judgment after defendant's sale relates back over defendant's rights, subject to any payments herein above mentioned to which the defendant is entitled to be subrogated." *J. T. Evans Co. v. Fanelli,* 59 N.J. Super. 19, 157 A.2d 36 (1959).

NECESSITY OF CONTRACT FOR IMPROVEMENTS

Under a basic principal of law, universally followed, an obligation cannot be imposed on a person without his knowledge or consent, either expressed or implied, or unless the person has so acted that he is estopped from denying liability. Under this principle, if a person who has no right or interest in a piece of real estate contracts for the erection of a building on the real estate, and the building is erected without the knowledge or consent of the owner of the real estate and without the owner's being negligent in failing to discover that a building is being erected on his real estate, the persons furnishing labor and material for the erection of the building are not entitled to a lien on the real estate. Whether or not a person, in order to be entitled to a mechanic's lien on real estate, must have a contract with the owner of the real estate depends on the wording of the mechanic's lien statute of the state in which the real estate is located.

Under the mechanic's lien laws of all states, if the owner has contracted for the improvement, the contractor who has furnished labor and materials is entitled to a lien. Under the provisions of some mechanic's lien statutes, if the labor or material is furnished "under a contract with the owner or with the consent of the owner," the person furnishing the labor or material is entitled to a lien on the real estate. Several of the statutes pertaining to mechanics' liens on real estate make no mention of the necessity of the contract with or without the consent of the owner.

As a general rule, mere knowledge by the owner that improvements are being made on the real estate in which he has an ownership interest is not sufficient to subject his interest to a mechanic's lien.[31] However, if the owner has ratified the contract, or, under some mechanic's lien laws, if the owner has authorized, requested, or consented to the making of the improvement, his interest in the real estate is subject to the lien. Whether or not an owner has ratified, authorized, requested, or consented to an improvement to his real estate is a question of fact to be decided by the court trying the case.

Anna Simon owned a three-story building which was leased to Beider and was being used as a girls' club. Beider contracted with Fetters, Love and Sieben, Inc. (hereinafter referred to as Fetters), a plumbing firm, to have nine bathrooms added to the building. During the time the work was in progress, Joseph Simon, Anna's husband, went to the building to collect on a rent check which had been returned for nonsufficient funds. At this time, Beider pointed out to Joseph the work in progress.

Beider did not pay Fetters for the work, and Fetters filed a mechanic's lien on the building. On the foreclosure of the lien, Anna Simon defended on the ground that she had not contracted for, nor consented to, the performance of the work. The only evidence offered to establish Anna's knowledge or consent was that Beider had pointed out the work in progress to Joseph, Anna's husband. The trial court rendered a judgment for Fetters. The judgment was reversed on appeal.

Presiding Justice Burke said: "Proof of the existence of the marital relation does not establish the husband's agency for his wife. The agency of the husband is a question of fact to be proved by direct or circumstantial evidence. There is no presumption that the husband has the authority to act for the wife. In an action against the wife to hold her responsible for the act or contract of her husband, plaintiff has the burden of showing the agency and authority of the husband or a ratification by the wife.

"The foundation of a mechanic's lien is the contract with the owner of the land for the improvement thereof and the furnishing of material and labor according to the contract, in connection with the Statute giving the lien. The contract for the improvements must either have been made with the owner or with one whom the owner has authorized or knowingly permitted to have done the work for him.

"The defendant in the present case did not enter into any contract, either express or implied, with the plaintiffs nor did she perform any acts which would indicate that she gave her husband authority to act for her as her agent. She cannot be said to have knowingly permitted the alterations to be made on the premises since there was no evidence that she knew the work was being undertaken nor did she acquiesce in accepting the alleged benefits. On the record presented plaintiff cannot enforce its claim under the Mechanic's

---

[31] *Brown et al.* v. *Ward et al.,* 221 N.C. 344, 20 S.E.2d 324; *Weinstein* v. *V. & J. Realty & Investment Co.,* 127 N.J.L. 198, 21 A.2d 862.

Lien Act against her property." *Fetters, Love and Sieben, Inc.* v. *Simon,* 46 Ill. App.2d 232, 196 N.E.2d 700 (1964).

CO-OWNED PROPERTY

Several different persons may have ownership interests in the same piece of real estate. If one of the owners contracts, authorizes, or consents to an improvement, the right of the person making the improvement to a mechanic's lien affecting the ownership interests of the other owners who are not parties to the contract or have not authorized or consented to the improvement will depend on the relationship of the several owners and the circumstances of the particular case. As a general rule, a person furnishing labor or materials for the improvement of real estate must ascertain the ownership interest in the real estate of the person engaging him.

If the owners of the real estate are tenants in common or joint tenants, one or more of the tenants cannot, by contracting for or consenting to the improvement of the co-owned property, subject the interest of a co-owner or of co-owners of the property to a mechanic's lien, unless it can be established that such co-owner or co-owners have expressly or impliedly authorized the party or parties contracting for the improvement to act as their agent, or have consented to the improvement or have so acted that he or they are estopped from setting up the defense of lack of consent. The interest of the contracting or consenting co-owner or co-owners will be subject to a mechanic's lien.

If the property is owned by husband and wife as joint tenants, the rules relative to the subjecting of co-owned property to a mechanic's lien apply; but if the property is owned by husband and wife as tenants by the entirety, both must join in the contract for the improvement, since neither can by his or her individual act encumber the entirety of the property.[32]

However, the New York statute pertaining to mechanics' liens on real estate provides that if the real estate is the property of the husband or wife, or both, each will be presumed to be agent for the other; and if a contract is negotiated by one, the other will be bound, unless such other, having knowledge of the improvement, shall, within ten days after learning of the contract, give the contractor written notice of his or her refusal to consent to the improvement.

---

[32] *Badger Lumber & Coal Co.* v. *Pugsley et al.,* 227 Mo. App. 1203, 61 S.W. 2d 425.

Generally, the husband has the right to manage community property; consequently, a contract with the husband for the improvement of community real estate would entitle the contractor to a lien on the real estate. Whether or not a person furnishing labor or materials for the improvement of a homestead is entitled to a mechanic's lien on the homestead will depend on the provisions of the mechanic's lien laws and the homestead laws of the state in which the real estate is located. As a general rule, dower and curtesy are cut off by a mechanic's lien.

IMPROVEMENTS BY LESSEE

The mere existence of the landlord-tenant relationship does not empower the tenant to subject the leased premises to a mechanic's lien. He may subject his interest, however, since he does have a property interest in such premises. Whether or not he may subject the landlord's title to a mechanic's lien will depend on the provisions of the mechanic's lien statutes of the state, on the terms of the lease, on the knowledge and the conduct of the landlord relative to the making of the improvements, and on all circumstances of the case. In many cases the court must determine whether or not the landlord has consented to the improvement. In general, if the lease expressly provides that the lessee shall make improvements to the leased real estate, or if he has made any improvements under a contract with the lessor, the lessor's title to the real estate will be subject to a mechanic's lien.[33]

In those states in which consent is sufficient ground for allowing a mechanic's lien, the lessor, if he has knowledge of the making of the improvement and does not give the contractor notice of his nonresponsibility, will be held to have consented to the improvement, and his interest in the property will be subject to a mechanic's lien. However, mere knowledge of the making of the improvement, in the absence of some affirmative act, is generally not sufficient to subject the lessor's interest to a mechanic's lien.[34]

If a lease contains a provision that the lessor's interest shall not be subject to a mechanic's lien for improvements contracted for by the lessee, the lessor will be protected under some circumstances, especially if the contractor has notice of the provision against liens.

The owner of multiple-unit rental property should post notices of non-

---

[33] *Denniston & Partridge Company* v. *Romp et al.,* 244 Iowa 204, 56 N.W.2d 601.

[34] *P. Delany & Co.* v. *Duvoli et al.,* 278 N. Y. 328, 16 N.E.2d 354.

responsibility; and if a tenant of such property has contracted for substantial improvements to the leased property, the lessor or his manager should give the contractor written notice of nonresponsibility as soon as he learns that the improvement is being made. Under the terms of some statutes the lessor can protect his interest in the leased property by filing or recording a notice of nonresponsibility.

Katzentine was the owner and lessor of a business building which he had leased to Grady on a 99-year lease. The lease contained the following provision: "The lessee covenants with the lessor to keep the leased premises in good repair and in a clean and wholesome and tenantable condition and further the lessee agrees to make improvements [the lease set out in detail improvements to be made] to and upon the leased premises." The improvements provided for in the lease called for a permanent building. In addition, the lease provided that no lien should arise or be created for labor or materials or otherwise against the land superior to the rights of the lessors, and further provided that the lessee would not make any written contract in connection with repairs or improvements on or about the demised premises without first providing in such contract that no such lien would arise.

Grady entered into a contract with Ideal Roofing and Sheet Metal Works, Inc. (hereinafter referred to as Roofing Co.), for the roofing of the building provided for in the lease. There was no provision in this contract whereby Roofing Co. waived its right to a lien.

The lien statute of the state provides: "When an improvement is made by a lessee, in accordance with a contract between such lessee and his lessor, liens shall extend also to the interest of the lessor." Roofing Co. was not paid for its work, and it filed a lien claim against the building and land. Katzentine claimed that Roofing Co. was not entitled to a lien on the land (the lessor's interest), since the 99-year lease included a no-lien clause. The trial court held that Roofing Co. was not entitled to a mechanic's lien on the land, and it appealed. The holding was reversed.

Chief Judge Horton said: "The mechanic's lien law provides: 'When an improvement is made by a lessee, in accordance with a contract between such lessee and his lessor, liens shall extend also to the interest of such lessor.' Where as here, it affirmatively appears from the amended complaint that the labor and materials were furnished to the lessee, as contemplated by the parties to the lease, upon proof thereof, the lessor's estate may be burdened with a mechanic's lien.

"The courts have further held that a provision in a lease to the effect that the lessee is without power to subject the lessor's interest in the leased premises to a mechanic's lien does not prevent the acquisition of such a lien by a laborer or materialman dealing with the lessee if the lease requires the lessee to make the improvement.

"In the Anderson case, Justice Terrell, in discussing a similar attempt by a lessor to evade (Chapter 84, Fla. Stat., F.S.A.) said 'One cannot by contract read the clear intent of the legislature out of the books, neither can he, in the manner shown, contract the coat off the back of him who furnishes labor or materials to improve his premises. In historical setting, the very purpose of equity and the statutory mechanic's lien was to prevent hardship like that pointed out in this case.' " *Ideal Roofing and Sheet Metal Works, Inc.* v. *Katzentine,* Fla., 127 So.2d 116 (1961).

PROPERTY SOLD ON LAND CONTRACT

As a general rule, when real estate has been sold on a land contract, the buyer of the real estate cannot subject the seller's interest to a mechanic's lien, and the seller cannot subject the buyer's interest to such a lien. Each can subject his own interest to a mechanic's lien. In most respects, the situation of the buyer and seller is like that of lessee and lessor. Under the mechanic's lien laws of some states, if a lessee or buyer under a land contract has improved the property, the contractor is entitled to a mechanic's lien on the improvement.[35]

INFANT'S CONTRACT

As a general rule, an infant cannot subject his real estate to a mechanic's lien, since he is under a disability and his contracts are voidable.

PERSONS ENTITLED TO A MECHANIC'S LIEN

There is no uniformity in the provisions of the mechanic's lien statutes as to the persons who are entitled to a mechanic's lien on real estate. Some statutes state in general terms who will be entitled to such a lien—for instance, contractors, subcontractors, and materialmen—and leave it to the courts to interpret the statute. The statute of the state of Washington specifies "any person who, at the request of the owner, his agent, contractor or subcontractor. . . ."[36] Other statutes, in addition to a general statement, list specifically the persons who are entitled to a lien. For example, the statute of the state of New York provides: ". . . contractor, subcontractor, laborer, materialman, landscape gardner, nurseryman, person or corporation selling fruit or ornamental trees, roses, shrub-

---

[35] *Strand Lumber Company* v. *Dostie et al.,* 260 Mich. 422, 245 N.W. 777.

[36] Revised Code of Washington (May 1, 1952), Title 60, "Liens," p. 60-04-040.

bery, vines and small fruit, persons who perform labor or furnish materials for the improvement of real property. . . .[37] In general, the courts have held that lien rights extend to a person who performs work for or furnishes materials to a general contractor who has a contract with the owner, provided such work or materials enhance the value of the owner's real estate.[38]

The courts are not in accord in their interpretation of the term *subcontractor.* The owner may let the contract to a general contractor, who will in turn contract with others to perform defined units of the work. Such persons clearly come within the definition of a subcontractor. The owner may contract directly with persons to have units of the work performed. Such persons are prime contractors; but if they, in turn, engage others to perform parts of the work, there is a question as to whether these others would qualify as subcontractors. The subcontractor under a general contractor may contract with others to do portions of the work, in which case there is diversity in the holdings as to whether such persons qualify as subcontractors. Some courts have held that the relation of a subcontractor of a subcontractor is too remote to entitle him to a lien. However, the courts have generally held that an employee of a contractor or subcontractor, if such employee works on the improvement, is entitled to a lien.

A person furnishing materials to a contractor or subcontractor is generally entitled to a mechanic's lien, but a person who furnishes materials to a materialman is not entitled to a lien. For example, it was held that a person who sold water softeners to a plumber (materialman), who in turn installed them in houses, was not entitled to a lien on the houses.[39]

NATURE OF IMPROVEMENTS

If a laborer or materialman is to be entitled to a lien on real estate, the labor expended or materials furnished must become a part of the real estate.[40] The nature and scope of the building or improvement for which a lien may be claimed will be set out in the statute of the state in which the real estate is located. Some states have statutes which are

---

[37] *McKinney's Consolidated Laws of New York Annotated,* Book 32, "Lien Law" (1940), Art. 2, § 3.

[38] *Morin Lumber Company* v. *Person et al.,* 110 Mont. 114, 99 P.2d 206.

[39] *Harris & Stunston, Inc., Limited* v. *Yorba Linda Citrus Association,* 135 Cal. App. 154, 26 P.2d 654.

[40] *Stone* v. *Rosenfield et al.,* 141 Conn. 188, 104 A.2d 545.

very general in their terms, whereas other states have statutes which set out in detail the nature and scope of the improvement for which a lien may be claimed.

As a general rule, the improvement must be permanent in nature.[41] Under the statutes of some states a person furnishing fixtures, such as lighting fixtures, heating equipment, and other types of "built-in" fixtures, is entitled to a mechanic's lien on the real estate if such fixtures are intended as permanent additions to the building; but if the fixtures are such as would be classed as trade fixtures, the person furnishing them is not entitled to a lien.[42]

Under special provisions of some state statutes, improvements such as repairs, alterations, additions, excavations, the moving or wrecking of a building, the laying of foundations, the addition of machinery that is firmly attached to the building, landscaping, the drilling of wells, the building of roads or sidewalks, and so forth, are specifically included in the improvements which will entitle the person making the improvement to a lien on the real estate.

Liberto owned a building which was leased to Landers for the operation of a grocery. Landers, with the knowledge and consent of Liberto, contracted for the installation of shelving in the store. The shelving was constructed at Landers' home in eight-foot sections and then brought to the store and placed against the wall. The sections were screwed together and attached to the wall by first nailing a 1 × 8-inch plywood strip along the wall at the height of the cabinets and attaching the cabinets to this strip. The only purpose of attaching the cabinets to the strip was to keep the shelves from toppling over when filled with groceries. The parties admitted that the shelves could be removed without material injury to the shelves or to the building. Broadmoor Lumber Co., Inc., sold the plywood and lumber for the shelves to Landers, who did not pay for it. Broadmoor Lumber Co., Inc., filed a lien on the building, and Liberto contended that the shelves were not an improvement to the building and that Broadmoor Lumber Co., Inc., was not entitled to a lien. The trial court held for Broadmoor Lumber Co., Inc., and Liberto appealed. The judgment was reversed.

Judge Hall said: "It is immaterial where the shelves were constructed. The fact that they were prefabricated and brought to the building does not of itself prevent application of the lien law. What is material is whether they were attached to the building in such manner that they became immovables

---

[41] *Alexander Lumber Co.* v. *Swindlehurst et al.,* 309 Ill. App. 433, 32 N.E.2d 637.

[42] *Silverman* v. *Mazer Lumber & Supply Co.,* 252 Ala. 627, 42 So.2d 542.

by destination. We conclude that the cabinets are movables and have not become immovables by destination.

"Since the lien statute is restricted to immovables and since plaintiff has no recourse against the owner except by virtue of the lien statute, we conclude that plaintiff cannot recover for the materials amounting to $303.68 which were used in the construction of the cabinets." *Broadmoor Lumber Co., Inc., v. Liberto,* La. App., 162 So.2d 800 (1964).

LABOR FOR WHICH LIEN MAY BE CLAIMED

Labor, manual or physical, expended in the making of an improvement for which a daily wage is paid is clearly the basis for a lien under the mechanic's lien statutes. The statute may, in addition, extend the scope of the lien right to include personnel in a supervisory capacity or those performing professional services directly connected with the improvement. Generally, an architect would not, under such a statutory provision, be entitled to a lien for his charges for preparing preliminary sketches or plans and specifications, if he performed no further services; but if, in addition, he supervised the work, he would be entitled to a lien.

The courts of some states have held that the work need not, in all instances, be done on the premises. A person preparing, in the shop of the contractor, materials for inclusion in a building may, under the terms of some mechanic's lien statutes, have a lien on the real estate for the value of such services.[43]

MATERIALS FOR WHICH LIENS MAY BE CLAIMED

As a general rule, the laws pertaining to mechanics' liens do not define specifically the nature of the materials for which a lien may be claimed. If the materials used are such as are usual and reasonably necessary for the job which is the subject matter of the contract, the person or persons who furnish the materials will be entitled to a mechanic's lien on the real estate. The materials must be actually furnished for the particular job. Under the statutes of some states the materials must be furnished for a particular building and on the credit of the building, not on the general credit of the purchaser of the materials.[44]

Under the mechanic's lien laws of some states, if the contractor has contracted to build several buildings on a tract, a materialman furnishing

[43] *Wells* v. *Christian et al.,* 165 Ind. 622, 76 N.E. 518.
[44] *Rosebud Lumber & Coal Co.* v. *Homes et al.,* 155 Neb. 459, 52 N.W.2d 313; *Schuman* v. *Teague et al.,* 195 Okla. 328, 156 P.2d 1010.

materials for the erection of the buildings is entitled to a lien. He does not have to prove that the materials were used in a particular building. Proof that the materials were used in the performance of the contract is sufficient.[45]

In some states, if materials have been ordered for the improvement of particular real estate, and the materials are specially fabricated and not suitable for use in the performance of any other contract, the material-man will be entitled to a lien on the real estate, even though the general contract is canceled and the materials are not used.[46]

Under the mechanic's lien laws of some states the materialman, in order to be entitled to a lien, must prove that the materials were used in the building. Generally, if the materialman proves that the materials were delivered to the site of the building for inclusion in the building, he has established his case; the owner, if he is to defeat the materialman's right to a lien, would have to prove that the materials were not used in the building. The owner cannot defeat the materialman's right to a lien by diverting to some other use, without the materialman's knowledge or consent, materials delivered for incorporation into a building.[47]

In most states, proof that the materials were purchased for use in a proposed building and that they were delivered to or near the site of the building is sufficient to entitle the materialman to a lien. He does not have to prove that the materials were actually incorporated into the building.[48]

As a general rule, the materials the materialman has furnished must be incorporated in and become a part of the building, or the materialman will not be entitled to a mechanic's lien on the property. Under this rule a person supplying tools, machinery, equipment, or appliances used in the erection of the building is not entitled to a lien on the real estate.[49]

Under the laws of some states a person furnishing materials which are destroyed in use but are not actually incorporated into the building— for example, lumber, wire, and nails used in making concrete forms,

---

[45] *Caird Engineering Works* v. *Seven-Up Gold Mining Company, Inc.*, 111 Mont. 471, 111 P.2d 267.

[46] *Surf Properties, Inc.* v. *Markowitz Bros., Inc.* Fla., 75 So.2d 298.

[47] *Ohio Oil Company* v. *Fidelity & Deposit Company of Maryland*, 112 Ind. App. 452, 42 N.E.2d 406.

[48] *Idaho Lumber & Hardware Company* v. *Digiacomo et ux.*, 61 Idaho 383, 102 P.2d 637.

[49] *Consolidated Cut Stone Company et al.* v. *Seidenbach et al.*, 118 Okla. 578, 75 P.2d 442; *Mann et al.* v. *Schnarr*, 228 Ind. 654, 95 N.E.2d 138.

and so forth, necessary in building—is entitled to a lien on the real estate.[50]

Whether or not a person furnishing shoring, scaffolding, fuel for heating the building while under construction or for operating machinery used in the construction of the building, oil, or other similar materials is entitled to a lien on the real estate will depend on the wording of the mechanic's lien statute of the state in which the real estate is located.

Lembke Construction Co., Inc., contracted to construct a shopping center. The excavation work was subcontracted to Harris, who leased from J. D. Coggins Company earth-moving equipment for use in the project. Harris did not pay the rent for the leased equipment, and J. D. Coggins Company filed a mechanic's lien claim against the real estate of the shopping center. Lembke Construction Co., Inc., contested the claim on the ground that rent for the equipment did not come within the scope of the mechanic's lien statute. The trial court denied the claim; and on appeal, the judgment was affirmed.

District Judge Garnett R. Burks said: "The general rule with reference to machinery or equipment used in performing the work is stated in 57 C.J.S. Mechanics' Liens, p. 44, as follows: 'Ordinarily, unless expressly so provided by statute, no lien may be acquired for the value or use of tools, machinery, equipment, or appliances furnished or lent for the purposes of facilitating the work, where they remain the property of the contractor and are not consumed in their use, but remain capable of use in other construction or improvement work. . . .'

"Generally a lien may be acquired for materials which, although not incorporated in the building or improvement, are used in the construction and, by their use, are actually or practically consumed, wasted, destroyed, or rendered worthless or unfit for further use.

"We feel that a proper construction of a statute similar to our own was expressed in Hall v. Cowen, . . . where it was said: 'It seems to us too plain to admit of extended argument or discussion that a claim for the rental of scrapers is neither for labor performed or materials furnished within the purview of this section.'

"The appellant urges that if the rental for the equipment is not a lienable item as labor it is such as material furnished and used up in the construction of the project. With this we cannot agree. Here the same reasoning applies to both theories, as the court found it did in Hall v. Cowen, supra.

"While we may feel that in view of our changed methods and conditions in construction work generally, and the increased and ever-increasing use of machinery to replace manual labor, the rental of such machinery might well be the basis of a claim of lien, we do not find such to be the law as it

---

[50] *Tway et al.* v. *Thompson et al.,* 160 Okla. 279, 16 P.2d 76.

exists in New Mexico today; nor do we believe we should enlarge the scope of our present lien law by judicial construction, but that the wisdom and necessity of so doing should be determined by and left to the legislature." *Lembke Construction Co., Inc.* v. *J. D. Coggins Company,* 72 N.M. 259, 382 P.2d 983 (1963).

RIGHTS OF LIEN CLAIMANT

There are two distinct and essentially different systems of mechanics' liens in force in the United States. Under one system—generally referred to as the *Pennsylvania system*—the laborers, subcontractors, and materialmen who furnish labor or material for the improvement of real estate are given a direct lien on the building and the land on which it stands; the general contractor's lien is subordinate to the liens of the laborers, subcontractors, and materialmen.[51]

Under such a system the total amount of the liens of laborers, subcontractors, and materialmen could exceed the total contract price of the improvement. Also, the mere fact that the owner has paid the contractor in full will not bar the right of laborers, subcontractors, or materialmen to a lien if their claims have not been paid.

Under the other system—commonly referred to as the *New York system*—the original contractor is the only person who has a direct lien on the improvement. Laborers, subcontractors, and materialmen may, if they give proper notice, be subrogated to the rights of the original contractor; but the total of the liens of laborers, subcontractors, and materialmen cannot exceed the total contract price.[52] Furthermore, if the owner has paid to the contractor a part of the contract price before he (the owner) is given notice of lien claims of laborers, subcontractors, or materialmen, the owner's liability will be limited to the unpaid balance of the contract price.

Some states have borrowed from both the Pennsylvania and the New York systems and consequently do not fall in either category.

---

[51] The following states have adopted the Pennsylvania system: Arizona, Arkansas, California, Colorado, Georgia, Idaho, Indiana, Kansas, Massachusetts, Michigan, Montana, Nebraska, New Mexico, North Dakota, Oregon, Pennsylvania, South Dakota, Washington, West Virginia, and Wisconsin.

[52] The following states have adopted the New York system: Alabama, Connecticut, Florida, Illinois, Kentucky, Louisiana, Mississippi, New Jersey, New York, Nevada, North Carolina, and Texas.

WAIVER OF LIEN RIGHTS

Whether or not an express provision in a contract to improve real estate waiving all rights of the contractor, subcontractors, laborers, and materialmen to claim a lien on the real estate under the mechanic's lien laws of the state will be effective will depend on the wording of the waiver provision, the provisions of the mechanic's lien statutes of the state in which the property is located, and the court decisions of the state. A clearly worded waiver provision in the contract may, in some states, preclude the contractor from claiming a lien, but not preclude subcontractors, laborers, and materialmen from so doing.[53] In other states the courts have held that such a waver provision will preclude subcontractors, laborers, and materialmen from claiming a lien.[54] A few states have held that such a waiver-of-lien provision in the contract will not preclude the principal contractor from claiming a lien,[55] whereas a few other states have held that it will.[56]

PERFECTING THE LIEN

Since the right to a mechanic's lien on real estate is created by statute, which is in derogation of the common law, the lien claimant must comply with all the material provisions of the lien statute to obtain a lien. There

---

[53] Apparently, a waiver in the principal contract does not affect the rights of subcontractors, laborers, and materialmen to a lien, especially if they do not have notice of the waiver provision, in the following states: Alabama, Arizona, Arkansas, Colorado, Indiana, Maine, Massachusetts, Michigan, Montana, Nebraska, New York, Ohio, Oregon, Washington, and Wisconsin.

[54] Apparently, the following states have adhered to this rule: California, Illinois, Missouri, and New Jersey. In Indiana the mechanic's lien statute provides that the contract containing the waiver provision must be in writing, must be acknowledged before a notary public, and must be filed in the recorder's office in the county wherein the real estate is situated within five days after execution; the owner must post, and keep posted, on the premises a sign, no smaller than three feet by three feet, giving notice that the work is being done under a no-lien contract.

[55] Arkansas, Idaho, Massachusetts, Texas, and Washington.

[56] Arizona, Connecticut, Indiana (if statute is complied with), Iowa, Maryland, Minnesota, Missouri, Nebraska, Oregon, Pennsylvania, and Wisconsin. Illinois and New York have cases holding that under some circumstances, the contractor is not precluded from claiming a lien; whereas under other circumstances, he is precluded from doing so.

is an almost complete lack of uniformity in the requirements which the lien claimant must satisfy in order to perfect his lien. In all of the states, some type of notice of the claim of a lien must be given to the owner of the property interest to which the lien is to attach.

Generally, the lien claimant or his authorized agent must file, in the office of a designated county officer, a verified statement of claim.[57] Everything required by the statute should be stated in reasonably clear and concise language. The statement should be compared with the statute to make certain that all the information required by the statute is included, since all such information is material and its omission would defeat the right to the lien.

The statement must describe the property. The property need not be described with the same technical accuracy as that required in a deed, but information must be given which is sufficient to enable one familiar with the locality to identify the property with reasonable accuracy. The statement of claim must show a prima facie right to a lien. It must show that the improvement was made under a contract with the owner or with his consent, express or implied, and that the work was completed or that the materials were furnished. Usually, a statement of account is required. Under the provisions of some statutes, all that need be stated is the amount for which the lien is claimed, whereas under the provisions of other statutes the statement must show charges and credits in some detail.

The owner or reputed owner must be named. If the property is owned by husband and wife as tenants by the entirety, both should be named. In some states, however, the courts have held that the name of the husband is sufficient. In community property states, both husband and wife must be named if the lien is against community property.

Under the statutes of some states a subcontractor must give the owner notice of his intention to claim a lien. The purpose of this requirement is to enable the owner to withold money sufficient to pay the subcontractor's claim. Failure to give notice defeats the subcontractor's right to a lien or reduces his rights to a recovery out of the unpaid balance of the contract price of the improvement.

---

[57] Alabama, judge of probate; Arizona, county recorder; California, county recorder of county or city and county in which such property or some part thereof is situated; Connecticut, town clerk of town in which building is located; Delaware, office of prothonotary; District of Columbia, clerk of Supreme Court.

TIME FOR FILING

The lien claim and notice of the lien must be filed or served within the time designated in the statute. Failure to do so is fatal to the claim, since the courts cannot excuse a late filing or extend, by judicial order, the time for service of notice or filing. Usually, the time for filing the lien claim or serving the notice is computed from the time the last labor was performed or the last materials were furnished, the determination of which is primarily a question of fact to be determined by the court. In general, the test applied is whether all the labor has been performed or all the materials necessary to the fulfillment of the contract have been furnished. The courts have not permitted a contractor, subcontractor, laborer, or materialman to extend the time for filing by returning to the job to correct trivial imperfections in the work.

In some states, all claimants must file within the specified time; in others the statutes make a distinction between classes of lien claimants. For example, in Pennsylvania, claims against leasehold estates and for repair work must be filed within three months after the contract is completed. In New York the claim must be filed within six months after the contract is completed. In Alabama the original contractor must file within six months, journeymen and day laborers within 30 days, and every other person within four months after the indebtedness accrues.

The filing of a claim for a mechanic's lien or notice of a mechanic's lien should be handled by a competent attorney familiar with the law pertaining to mechanics' liens on real estate in the state in which the real estate is located. Failure to comply with the mandatory provisions of the statute will result in loss of the lien.

Djureen and Carpenter entered into a contract for the construction of a house. Carpenter ordered the lumber and other building materials to be used in the construction of the house from Joyce Lumber Company. Materials were delivered on the job by Joyce Lumber Company between September 22, 1961, and November 13, 1961. Additional materials were delivered to the premises on February 7, 1962, which Joyce Lumber Company claimed were used in the Djureen house. Joyce Lumber Company filed its claim for a mechanic's lien on March 12, 1962. This claim included all materials delivered on the Djureen job from September 22, 1961, to and including February 7, 1962. The mechanic's lien statute provides that the claim for a lien must be filed within three months "from the performing of such labor or furnishing of such material." Djureen defended on the ground that the lien for materials delivered between September 22, 1961, and November 13, 1961, was void since it was not filed within the three-month period. Joyce Lumber Company contended that its lien was valid, since the claim was filed within three months of the delivery of the last materials on February 7, 1962. The trial court held that the lien was not valid as to the September 22, 1961, to November 13, 1961, deliveries. This holding was affirmed on appeal.

Justice Messmore said: "The trial court was correct in holding that the order dated February 7, 1962, could not be tacked onto the previous orders for the purpose of extending the plaintiff's lien-filing time.

"We conclude that the mechanic's lien of the plaintiff was not filed within time as provided for by section 52–102, R.R.S. 1943." *Joyce Lumber Company* v. *Djureen,* 176 Neb. 86, 125 N.W.2d 109 (1963).

ESTATE SUBJECT TO LIEN

Under a basic principle of property law a person cannot convey a greater interest in property than he has. This principle applies in determining the scope of a lien claimant's rights in the property he has improved. Only the property interest of the person who has contracted for or consented to the improvement is subject to a lien. The nature and scope of this interest was discussed under the heading "Necessity of Contract for Improvements" above.

In some of the states the extent of the property which may be subjected to the lien is set out in the statute. For example, in California the statute provides that the lien shall be on the improvement and so much of the ground around the same as is required for its use and occupation; in Delaware, the building and the land on which it is situated; and in Minnesota, not exceeding 40 acres, if the improvement is outside the limits of an incorporated city or village, and 1 acre, if it is within such limits. Provisions such as those in the California and Delaware statutes predominate.

SALE OF REAL ESTATE SUBJECT TO LIEN

Real estate which is subject to a mechanic's lien may be sold, but the purchaser takes subject to existing lien rights. Since, in most states, notice of a lien does not have to be filed or recorded, or does not have to be given until some designated period of time after the last labor is performed or the last materials furnished, a purchaser cannot rely entirely on the records to determine whether or not there are outstanding mechanic's lien rights. The purchaser should inspect the property to determine whether or not work is being done on the property or has been done recently. For additional protection, he may retain a percentage of the agreed price until the time for filing liens expires. In some instances, it may be good business to obtain from the seller an affidavit stating that no work has been performed on the premises and that the premises are not subject to mechanics' liens.

ASSSIGNMENT OF MECHANICS' LIENS

The courts have distinguished between an assignment of a debt due a contractor, subcontractor, laborer, or materialman for which he is entitled to a lien; an assignment of such a debt as security; an assignment of a contract for improvements; and an assignment of a perfected mechanic's lien. In all the states a debt due, in the absence of a provision in the contract to the contrary, is assignable; but there is a diversity of opinion as to the right of the assignee of the debt to perfect the mechanic's lien. In some states the courts have held that the right to the mechanic's lien is personal and cannot be assigned;[58] in other states the courts have held that a debt and the right to a mechanic's lien are assignable.[59]

The assignment of a debt arising under a contract to improve real estate does not defeat the right to a mechanic's lien. Under such an assignment the contractor, subcontractor, laborer, or materialman making the assignment remains the owner of the debt, subject to the security rights of the assignee.

If the contract for improvement is assigned with the consent of the owner, such an assignment has been considered a novation, and the assignee who completes the work is entitled to a mechanic's lien.[60]

The courts are in accord in holding that a perfected mechanic's lien is assignable. In all material respects, a perfected mechanic's lien is like a real estate mortgage, and the rules relating to the assignment of real estate mortgages apply to the assignment of mechanics' liens on real estate.

The general rules of law applicable to assignments apply in all assignment situations. The assignee acquires no greater rights than the assignor had at the time of the assignment.

---

[58] *Williams Lumber & Manufacturing Co.* v. *Ginsburg et al.*, 347 Mo. 119, 146 S.W.2d 604.

[59] *Brown* v. *Home Development Company*, 129 N.J. Eq. 172, 18 A.2d 742.

[60] *Smith* v. *Gunniss et ux.*, 115 Mont. 362, 144 P.2d 186.

PRIORITIES OF MECHANICS' LIENS

The mechanic's lien statutes of the several states define the priority rights of the various classes of persons who may claim security rights in the real estate; however, they are not uniform in their priority provisions. In some states the priority provisions of the statutes are elaborate and set up several classes of security claimants, whereas in other states the priority provisions of the statutes are relatively simple.

The general rule of "first in time is first in right" governs mechanics' liens. The concept of first in time, however, when determining the priority rights of mechanics' liens, is not based on recording, as is generally the case with mortgages and similar liens. The time for computing priority rights of mechanics' liens is, in most states, from the time the first labor is performed or the first materials are furnished, although filing of the lien is postponed by statute, and subsequent purchasers or lienees take subject to the mechanics' liens. In a few states the mechanic's lien dates from the execution of the contract for the improvement, thus in effect creating a potential secret lien for one who acquires rights in the property between the time of the execution of the contract and the commencement of the work.

There is no priority between mechanics' liens claimants. Since all laborers and materialmen have contributed to the improvement of the property, it is only fair that all should share ratably in the finished result; and those who, by the nature of their contribution, performed their labor or furnished their materials first should not be given priority over later contributors.

In some states, lien claimants have priority in the order in which the lien claims are filed, the first in time having superior rights; whereas in other states, lien claimants are given priority according to a classification set up in the statute. For example, the Oregon mechanic's lien statute provides:

In case the proceeds of any sale [under O.R.S. 87.005 to 87.075 foreclosure of lien] are insufficient to pay all lienholders claiming under such statute, the liens of all persons other than the original contractor and subcontractors shall be paid in full, or pro rata, if the proceeds are insufficient to pay them in full; and out of the remainder, if any, the subcontractors shall be paid in full, or pro rata, if the proceeds are insufficient to pay them in full; and the remainder, if any, shall be paid to the original contractor.[61]

---

[61] Oregon Revised Statutes (1953–55), 87.060 (2).

Also, under the provisions of some statutes, liens for labor are given priority over those of contractors, subcontractors, and materialmen.

In a majority of situations, mechanics' liens have priority over mortgages which have not been recorded until after the performance of the work on the improvement has commenced, even though the money was loaned and the mortgage executed before the beginning of the work. A mortgage must be recorded before the work is started on the improvement if such mortgage is to have priority over mechanics' liens. In a few states, mechanics' liens are given priority, at least in part, over their liens. This rule is justified on the ground that the property has been enhanced in value by the expenditure of labor by the lien claimants and by the addition of their materials, and they should therefore share in the total property in proportion to their contribution to its value.

A mortgage given to secure future advances, if made in good faith, and if recorded before the commencement of work on the improvement, is entitled, as a general rule, to priority over liens for labor or materials, although the advancements are not made until after the commencement of the work. If the mortgagee is not obligated to make the advancements, he is not entitled to priority.

Under the statutes of some states, mechanics' liens on a building constructed on certain land have priority over a mortgage on the land given and recorded prior to the commencement of the work on the building.

Crochet and Martin entered into a written agreement in which Martin agreed to construct a building for Crochet. Martin purchased lumber for the job from Lumber Products, Inc., and did not pay for it. Lumber Products, Inc., filed a mechanic's lien on the property and brought an action to foreclose its lien.

Justice Summers said: "We are concerned with the privilege against the property or the in rem action, the personal action having been abandoned. Such a privilege is granted, as the term implies, in derogation of common rights, for there is no preference granted to these creditors by the owner. The privilege is granted by law without the consent of the owners. For this reason, statutes creating privileges having the character of that under review, being in derogation of common rights, must be considered as stricti juris and rigidly construed. Such a privilege is superior to all other claims against the land and improvements, except taxes and local assessments for public improvements or a bona fide vendor's privilege or mortgage recorded before the work or labor is begun or any material furnished. Such a privilege supersedes the homestead exemption which may be due on the affected property. It is a right which the nature of a debt gives to a creditor and which entitles him to be preferred before other creditors. Privileges can be claimed only for those debts to which they are expressly granted by law." *Lumber Products, Inc.* v. *Crochet,* 244 La. 1060, 156 So.2d 438 (1963).

DURATION OF MECHANICS' LIENS

The mechanic's lien statutes of all states provide that unless action is brought to foreclose the mechanic's lien within a stated time after the perfecting of the lien, the lien will be lost. The time for starting foreclosure proceedings varies from six months to six years, with the periods of six months and one year predominating.

In some states, if the owner gives the lien claimant notice, as required by the provisions of the statute, the lienholder's right to foreclose his lien will be barred, unless he brings his action within the time stated in the statute—usually 30 or 60 days.

DISCHARGE OF MECHANICS' LIENS

Under the mechanic's lien statutes of some states a mechanic's lien may be discharged by the owner's posting a bond or depositing in court a sum sufficient to pay the claim. A mechanic's lien is discharged by merger—that is, the lienholder acquires the owner's interest in the real estate which is subject to the lien. A mechanic's lien is also discharged by a release given for a sufficient consideration.

If a mechanic's lien is discharged but the lienholder refuses to release the lien of record and thereby remove the lien as an encumbrance on the owner's title to the property, the court, in a proper action, will force the lienholder to discharge the lien of record.[62]

FORECLOSURE OF MECHANICS' LIENS

A perfected mechanic's lien on real estate is comparable in most respects to a real estate mortgage, and the procedure followed in the foreclosure of the lien is similar to that followed in the foreclosure of a real estate mortgage by action and sale. The action will be brought in the court having jurisdiction over the real estate involved, and the laws of the state in which the land is located will apply. All parties having an interest in the real estate which will be affected by the foreclosure of the lien,

---

[62] *Gibson et al.* v. *Koutsky-Brennan-Vana Company,* 143 Neb. 326, 9 N.W.2d 298.

including all mechanics' lienholders, are made parties to the suit. Any party in interest may appear and defend. The court will determine the validity of the claimant's lien and will find the amount due the lienholder if the claim is held to be valid.

This foreclosure of a mechanic's lien has some of the characteristics of a receivership. Consequently, if there is more than one mechanic's lien on the property, the court will, as a general rule, determine the validity and the amount of the claims of all other such holders. In addition, the court may, if the circumstances require, determine the priority right of lien claimants other than mechanic's lien claimants. The court will then order the real estate sold and the proceeds distributed according to the priority rights of the various lien claimants as set out in the mechanic's lien statutes of the state in which the real estate is located.

PUBLIC IMPROVEMENTS

Public improvements and, as a general rule, improvements to public utilities are not subject to mechanics' liens. Each state has regulated, by special statutes, the rights of laborers and materialmen furnishing labor and materials for public improvements; but a discussion of these statutes is outside the scope of this work.

4

Co-ownership

NATURE OF CO-OWNERSHIP

IF TITLE to real estate is vested in one person or organization, that person or organization is said to own the property in severalty. When the title to real estate is vested in two or more persons or organizations, such persons or organizations are said to be co-owners of the property. Co-owners may hold as joint tenants, as tenants by the entirety, or as tenants in common. In addition to these types of common-law ownership, we· recognize tenancy in partnership and, in some states, community property as types of co-ownership.

Modern living has given rise to two kinds of community ownership of real property: the cooperative apartment and the condominium. The real estate trust and real estate syndicate have afforded those persons who are not financially able to purchase real estate outright or who do not wish to be burdened with the management of real estate an opportunity to share the profits and risks of real estate investment. None of these arrangements is recognized as co-ownership under common-law legal rules, yet they are new types of ownership wherein two or more persons acquire interests in real property.

Joint tenancy

CHARACTERISTICS OF JOINT TENANCY

A joint tenancy is a single estate in land owned by two or more persons. The basic idea of the joint tenancy is that of unity of ownership; that is, there is only one title, and it is vested in the unit, which is made up of two or more persons. The death of one of the joint tenants does not destroy the unit; it only reduces by one the number of persons who make it up. The remaining joint tenants take the rights of the deceased joint tenant by right of survivorship. The last survivor takes title in severalty, and on his death the property goes to his heirs or devisees. This right of survivorship is the distinguishing characteristic of a joint tenancy.[1]

Although joint tenancies were favored at common law, many states have enacted statutes which either abolish joint tenancies or abolish the right of survivorship. A reason given for the abolition of joint tenancies or the right of survivorship is that a husband may, by holding his property in joint tenancy with others, defeat the statutory rights of his wife and family to share in his property on his death. Under the law of survivorship the surviving joint tenant or tenants take the jointly owned property by right of survivorship, and there is no title or right which could descend to the estate of the deceased joint tenant; consequently, there is no estate in which the wife or family can share.

CREATION OF JOINT TENANCY

A joint tenancy cannot be created by operation of law but must be created by grant, purchase, or devise.[2] Four unities are required to create a joint tenancy: unity of title, unity of time, unity of interest, and unity of possession. Unless all four of the unities are present, a joint tenancy is not created. Consequently, the joint tenancy must be created by one and the same instrument, executed and delivered at one and the same time, and convey equal interests to the grantees, who must hold undivided possession.

Today, joint tenancies are not favored; and in order to create a joint tenancy, the instrument must show clearly that such was the intention of the parties. A grant to "Amos and Bert" or to "Amos and Bert jointly" will not create a joint tenancy. A grant to "Amos and Bert as joint tenants" will be sufficient to create a joint tenancy in some states but not in others.[3] A careful conveyancer prefers using "to Amos and Bert as joint tenants, with right of survivorship and not as tenants in common." When such language is used, there is no room for doubt as to the grantor's intention to create a joint tenancy.

---

[1] *In re King's Estate,* 261 Wis. 266, 52 N.W.2d 885.

[2] *Porter et al.* v. *Porter et al.,* 381 Ill. 322, 45 N.E.2d 635.

[3] *Howell* v. *Kline et al.,* 156 Pa. Super. 628, 41 A.2d 580.

At common law, if the owner in severalty of real estate wished to create a joint tenancy between himself and another or others, he would have to convey the property to an intermediary and have the intermediary convey it back to the parties as joint tenants. The reason for this holding was that if the owner in severalty attempted to convey directly to another a joint interest in the property, a joint tenancy could not result, since the four unities essential to its creation would not be present. The title would not be created by one and the same instrument at one and the same time. Moreover, under the early common law the courts held that a person could not make a grant of his own property to himself.

In some states the necessity of using an intermediary has been abolished by statutory enactment; in other states the courts, holding that the clear intention of a party should not be defeated by a technicality, have refused to follow the common-law rule.[4] However, in case of doubt, the use of an intermediary is recommended.

RIGHTS OF JOINT TENANTS

One of the unities of a joint tenancy is the right of possession. Each tenant has equal right to the enjoyment of the joint property, and the possession of one is considered the possession of all. If the joint tenants occupy the premises as a house, or if the joint property is a farm and the joint tenants work the farm as a cooperative venture, each is, in contemplation of law, exercising his right of possession of the entire property. The idea of unity of possession would be carried out even though each tenant, by mutual agreement, occupied a portion of the house or worked certain fields.

If the joint property is rental property and is not occupied by any of the tenants, no problem is presented. In such a case the rent received, after deductions for taxes, insurance, and necessary repairs, is distributed equally.

If one or more, but not all, of the joint tenants occupy the joint property, the tenant who does not occupy the property is not entitled to rent from the occupying tenants, unless there has been an agreement to the contrary, ·or unless the occupying tenants have excluded him from living on the premises.

If one of two or more joint tenants is in sole possession of the joint property, he is considered as possessing not only for himself, but also

---

[4] *Lipps* v. *Crowe*, 28 N.J. Super. 131, 100 A.2d 361.

for his cotenants; and he is not liable to his cotenants for rent, unless there has been an agreement to the contrary, or unless he has excluded his cotenants.[5]

John Black, who was contemplating a second marriage, conveyed, through a dummy, an orange grove to himself and his three sons as joint tenants. John Black remarried, and he and his wife operated the orange grove, retaining for themselves all of the income therefrom. On the death of John Black the sons brought an action against the widow, asking an accounting for the profits realized from the operation of the orange grove. The request was denied.

Presiding Justice Moore said: "A joint tenant in the sole and exclusive occupancy of the land is not required to account to his cotenant for any portion of the revenues derived therefrom so long as they are the fruitage of his own capital, labor and skill. The risks incurred by the occupier of the land (held jointly) in the cultivation of crops are his as are also the profits he may enjoy or the losses he may sustain in producing crops by his industry. In taking all the fruits grown upon the land, decedent herein received no more than his just share inasmuch as it is no more than the reward for his own labor and capital to no part of which is his cotenant entitled. It is thus seen that there is no equity in the claim that the mere fact of being named as joint tenant entitled one to share in the revenue produced on the land as the result of the labor, management and money of him who is in sole possession when the claiming cotenant has neither demanded possession, contributed to the expense of production nor previously made himself liable for possible losses." *Black* v. *Black,* 91 Cal. App.2d 328, 204 P.2d 950 (1949).

TERMINATION OF JOINT TENANCY

A joint tenancy is destroyed when any of the essential unities is destroyed. A joint tenant has the right to convey his interest in the joint property, but such a conveyance destroys the unity of interest and consequently destroys the jointure insofar as the interest conveyed is concerned. If the unity holding title is composed of three or more persons and one of the joint tenants conveys his interest, the grantee would hold his interest as a tenant in common with the remaining joint tenants, but the remaining joint tenants would hold in jointure as to each other. For example, suppose that Amos, Bert, Charles, and David own real property as joint tenants and Amos deeds his interest to Earl. Earl will hold his interest with Bert, Charles, and David as tenant in common; but Bert, Charles, and David will continue to hold as joint tenants as to each other. Since the

---

[5] *Swartzbaugh* v. *Sampson et al.,* 11 Cal. App.2d 451, 54 P.2d 73.

interest of a joint tenant goes, on his death, to the surviving tenant or tenants, an attempt by a joint tenant to devise his interest in the joint property is inoperative; consequently, a joint tenancy cannot be destroyed by a devise.

If a joint tenant or all the joint tenants enter into a conditional land contract whereby the joint tenant or tenants contract to sell his or their interest in the joint property to another and give the vendee possession, and contract to execute a deed to the property on the payment of the purchase price, the joint tenancy is destroyed. The conditional vendee becomes the equitable owner of the property, and the conditional vendor or vendors hold the legal title as security for the payment of the purchase price. The unity of possession is destroyed.[6]

MORTGAGING JOINT ESTATE.   A joint tenant or all the joint tenants may mortgage his or their interest in the joint property without destroying the joint tenancy. However, if there is default, foreclosure, and sale of the property, and one of the joint tenants does not redeem the property from the foreclosure sale, the joint tenancy is destroyed. If a joint tenant redeems from the foreclosure sale, he will be deemed to have done so for the benefit of the defaulting tenant or tenants. However, if the defaulting tenant or tenants do not reimburse the redeeming tenant within a reasonable time, the court will, after appropriate action is brought, enter a decree cutting off the right of the defaulting tenant or tenants and vesting title in the redeeming tenant.

When the joint property is sold at an execution sale, if the interest of the debtor tenant's creditor is purchased by a person other than one of the joint tenants, the joint tenancy is destroyed in the same manner and to the same extent as though the debtor tenant had deeded his interest in the property to the purchaser at the execution sale. If one of the joint tenants purchases at the execution sale, the situation is the same as that arising when one of the joint tenants purchases on a mortgage foreclosure sale.

A judgment creditor of one of the joint tenants may levy an execution on the judgment debtor's interest in the joint property. Such a levy does not destroy the jointure; and if the judgment debtor tenant dies before the execution sale, the judgment debtor tenant's interest in the joint property passes to his cotenant or cotenants by right of survivorship, and the judgment creditor takes nothing.

SALE OF JOINT ESTATE FOR TAXES.   If the joint property is sold for

[6] *Buford* v. *Dahlke et al.,* 158 Neb. 39, 62 N.W.2d 252.

taxes and one of the joint tenants purchases the property at the tax sale, the joint tenancy is not destroyed, since the purchasing tenant will be deemed to have acted for the benefit of his cotenants. The situation is the same as when one of the joint tenants buys the joint property on a mortgage foreclosure sale or on an execution sale.

If one of the joint tenants arranges to have a third person purchase the property at the tax sale and the property is then deeded to the joint tenant, the rights of his cotenants will not be cutoff. However, if the third-party buyer is a bona fide purchaser and the later sale to one of the joint tenants is a bona fide sale, the joint tenancy will have been destroyed, and the purchasing joint tenant will hold the property free from any rights of his former joint tenants.

On November 1, 1944, Juanita I. Ellis and W. O. Ellis purchased a two-story duplex and took title as joint tenants with right of survivorship and not as tenants in common. In 1951, Juanita I. Ellis was granted a divorce from W. O. Ellis, and the decree of divorce provided that the property be sold and the proceeds be divided equally, W. O. Ellis to pay certain expenses and costs out of his one half of the proceeds. Juanita I. Ellis was given a 60-day option to purchase W. O. Ellis' one-half interest at its appraised value. On the expiration of the 60 days the parties, by written contract, agreed to sell the property for $20,000, each to live in and maintain one of the apartments until the property was sold. Before the sale of the property, W. O. Ellis died, leaving a will whereby he devised his one half of the premises to his daughter, Mrs. Carson. Juanita I. Ellis claimed the entire property by right of survivorship. The court held that Mrs. Carson took a one-half interest in the property, and Juanita I. Ellis appealed. The judgment was affirmed.

Justice Wertz said: "The four essential elements of a joint tenancy are unity of interest, title, time and possession. To meet these equirements, the several tenants must have one and the same conveyance commencing at the same time and held by one and the same undivided possession. A joint tenancy will be severed by the destruction of any one or more of its necessary units.

"It has also been held that a joint tenancy may be terminated by a mutual agreement between the parties, or by any conduct or course of dealing sufficient to indicate that all parties have mutually treated their interests as belonging to them in common.

"An analysis of the two contracts entered into between the parties clearly reveals it was their intent to sever the joint tenancy. The contracts and the actions of the parties obviously destroyed the unity of possession. These contracts and the acts and conduct of the parties were clearly inconsistent with the existence of a joint tenancy and indicated an intention and agreement that such relationship should no longer exist." *Carson* v. *Ellis,* 186 Kan. 112, 348 P.2d 807 (1960).

Tenancy in common

CHARACTERISTICS OF TENANCY IN COMMON

A tenancy in common is a holding by two or more persons of separate titles in the same real estate. The estate of each tenant in common is an estate of inheritance. Since each tenant holds separate title, his interest in the common property descends on his death to his heirs or goes to his devisees. If a contenant of a tenancy in common leaves a wife surviving, she takes the same widow's rights in his interest in the common property as she takes in his property which he held in severalty. A tenant in common acquires no rights in the common property by right of survivorship.

The only unity in a tenancy in common is the unity of possession. The interests of the tenants in common need not be acquired at the same time; they may be acquired by separate deed, and the interests need not be equal, but they do have equal rights of possession. These rights of possession held by a tenant in common are substantially the same as the rights of possession of a joint tenant in the joint property.

CREATION OF TENANCY IN COMMON

A tenancy in common can be created by grant, by purchase, by devise, or by operation of law. If a person dies intestate and leaves real estate, his heirs will take the real estate as tenants in common. Also, if two or more persons take real estate by operation of law, they generally take as tenants in common. A grant of real estate to two or more persons, not husband and wife, will create a tenancy in common, unless appropriate language clearly indicating a contrary intent is used in the grant. For example, a grant to "Amos and Bert" or to "Amos and Bert jointly" will create a tenancy in common.

The owner of real estate in severalty can create a tenancy in common between himself and another or others by a direct grant. For example, if Amos owns real estate, he can create a tenancy in common in the real estate between himself and Bert by granting to Bert a designated interest in the real estate, such as, for instance, a one-fourth interest.

TERMINATION OF TENANCY IN COMMON

A tenancy in common may be destroyed by partition of the real estate held by the tenants in common. The tenants may enter into an agreement for the partition of the property, in which event each tenant would grant to his cotenant his interest in the portion of the real estate set aside to him. For example, suppose that Amos and Bert own 80 acres of land as tenants in common, each owning an undivided one-half interest, and they agree to partition the land—Amos to take the north 40 acres and Bert the south 40 acres. Amos would grant Bert his (Amos') one-half interest in the south 40 acres, and Bert would grant to Amos his (Bert's) one-half interest in the north 40 acres. As a result, Amos would own the north 40 acres in severalty, and Bert would own the south 40 acres in severalty. If the property is such that it cannot be partitioned, it may be sold, each tenant in common executing the deed of conveyance, and each tenant taking his share of the proceeds of the sale in proportion to his interest in the property.

If the parties cannot agree as to the division of the property, any of the tenants may bring court action asking for partition of the real estate held by them as tenants in common. The court may decree a partition in kind if the nature of the property is such that an equitable division can be made. If an equitable division cannot be made, the court will order the property sold and the proceeds of the sale distributed among the tenants in proportion to their interest in the property.

A tenancy in common is also destroyed by merger—that is, by vesting in one person the interests of all the tenants in common.

A tenant in common may sell, mortgage, devise, or dispose in any way of his interest in the property held with his cotenants without destroying the tenancy in common.

If real property held by tenants in common is sold for taxes and one of the tenants in common bids the property in at the tax sale, the purchasing tenant will be deemed to have acted for the benefit of all the tenants in common, and the tenancy will not be destroyed. However, the tenant paying the taxes is entitled to contribution from his cotenants; if they refuse to contribute, he will have a lien on their interest for their share of the tax paid.

Pennie Shull and Morris Shepherd, while living together as husband and wife although they were not married, purchased in July, 1949, the real property in issue. They lived together in the house until 1953, when they separated; and Shepherd then continued to live there alone. Both subsequently married other persons. Following their separation, Shepherd offered Shull $800 for her interest in the property, but she refused to sell. On March 31, 1961, Shull brought this action to recover her interest in the property. Shepherd claimed that he had acquired her interest in the property by adverse possession.

The court held that Shepherd had not acquired Shull's interest and that Shull owned a 45.2 per cent interest in the property and Shepherd owned a 54.8 per cent interest.

Judge Hamilton said: "In the absence of additional facts or circumstances sufficient to show an ouster, exclusive possession by one tenant is not adverse as against his cotenant, but is ordinarily the possession of both. Mere possession by one cotenant alone will not ripen into title by adverse possession, even though it be continued without interruption for the period of the statute of limitations. There must be an ouster followed by adverse possession for the statutory period to determine the estate of the tenant not in possession.

"Property acquired with contributions from both parties is held as tenants in common, and the courts will presume they intended to share the property, in proportion to the amount contributed, where it can be traced, otherwise they share it equally." *Shull* v. *Shepherd,* Wash.2d, 387 P.2d 767 (1963).

Tenancy by the entirety

CHARACTERISTICS OF TENANCY BY THE ENTIRETY

A tenancy by the entirety is a joint tenancy between husband and wife. At early common law a husband and wife were held to be one legal person. The woman, on marriage, lost her identity as a legal person; her legal personality merged with that of her husband, and the husband was the sole legal representative of the unity. This legal concept is the basis for the law relating to tenancies by the entirety. Property so owned is considered as being held by one indivisible legal unity.[7]

There are two distinguishing characteristics of a tenancy by the entirety: (1) The tenants must be husband and wife, and (2) there must be right of survivorship. The four unities of a joint tenancy are essential to the existence of a tenancy by the entirety. However, the tenants by the entirety, since husband and wife are considered as a legal unit, do not own equal shares in the property.

At common law the husband, during the continuance of the marriage, had the exclusive right of control over the property, and was entitled to all the rents and profits from the property. This rule is still in effect in some of the states which recognize tenancy by the entirety.[8]

Some states have held that under their statutes relating to the separate

---

[7] *Wilson et al.* v. *Florida National Bank & Trust Co. at Miami et al.,* Fla., 64 So.2d 309.

[8] *Hale* v. *Hale,* 332 Mass. 329, 125 N.E.2d 142.

property of married women, the husband and wife each have an interest in the rents and profits derived from the real estate held by them as tenants by the entirety; and a few states have held that during the continuance of the marriage, each spouse holds one half of the estate in common with the other.[9]

CREATION OF TENANCY BY THE ENTIRETY

A tenancy by the entirety, like a joint tenancy, cannot be created by operation of law, but must be created by grant, purchase, or devise. It is not an estate of inheritance. Tenancies by the entirety are recognized in less than one half of the states. In those states which recognize tenancy by the entirety, the holdings of the courts are not in harmony as to the language which will be interpreted as creating such a tenancy.

In most of the states, if land is granted to persons who, at the time of the grant, are husband and wife, and the grant contains no language indicating a contrary intent, the court will interpret the grant as creating a tenancy by the entirety. For example, a deed naming John Jones and Mary Jones as grantees would create a tenancy by the entirety; likewise, a grant to John Jones and Mary Jones, husband and wife, would create a tenancy by the entirety in most of the states recognizing such tenancy. However, in some states the grant would have to state clearly the intent to create a tenancy by the entirety. A grant to "John Jones and Mary Jones, husband and wife, as tenants by the entirety with right of survivorship," would be sufficient under the laws of any state recognizing tenancies by the entirety.

The states are not in accord as to whether or not a tenancy by the entirety can be created by a direct grant. The same rules are applied to the creation of a tenancy by the entirety as are applied to the creation of a joint tenancy in this same situation, with like results.[10]

TERMINATION OF TENANCY BY THE ENTIRETY

Neither the husband nor the wife, without the consent of the other, can dispose of or encumber any part of the real estate held by them as tenants by the entirety. As a general rule, any real estate which is held by a husband and wife as tenants by the entirety is not subject to levy of execution and sale for the individual obligations of either

---

[9] *Ross* v. *Ross,* 35 N.J. Super. 242, 113 A.2d 700.

[10] See p. 90.

spouse, but is subject to levy and sale in satisfaction of a judgment against both.[11] In those states which hold that the husband has the exclusive right to control the real estate owned with his wife as tenants by the entirety and the exclusive right to the rents and profits from such real estate, the courts have held that the husband can convey or encumber the rents and profits; but such conveyance or encumbrances will not be valid after the death of the husband, the wife surviving.

If a mortgage, contract to sell, or deed to real estate which is held by a husband and wife as tenants by the entirety is signed by the husband alone, such signing will not defeat the right of the wife, on the death of the husband, to take the property free of any claim of the mortgagee, contractee, or grantee. If the husband lists such property for sale with a broker and the broker finds a customer ready, able, and willing to buy, the wife is under no obligation to convey the property. However, the husband will be individually liable to the broker for his commission. Neither the husband nor the wife has any power to convey, by will, any interest in property which is held by husband and wife as tenants by the entirety.

In the event of divorce, the rights of the husband and wife in property held as tenants by the entirety will be determined by the courts according to the statutes of the state. As a general rule, after an absolute divorce, property formerly held by the husband and wife as tenants by the entirety will be held as tenants in common.[12]

If either spouse redeems property held as tenants by the entirety from foreclosure, judgment, or tax sale, or purchases the property at such sale, he will be deemed to have redeemed or to have bought the property for the benefit of both, and the property will be held by them as tenants by the entirety.

On February 15, 1954, Andrew Bradish contracted to purchase a tract of land. On July 14, 1956, Bradish applied to Western Pennsylvania National Bank for a loan of $3,500, the money to be used to pay the unpaid balance of the contract price of the tract of land. The Bank made the loan to Bradish, and he executed his promissory note, signed only by Bradish, to the Bank for the amount of the loan. The money was used as agreed to pay the balance of the purchase price of the land. The title to the land was taken in the name of Andrew Bradish and Virginia Bradish, husband and wife, as tenants by the entirety.

Andrew Bradish was killed in an automobile accident on July 17, 1956.

---

[11] *Lake* v. *Callis et al.*, 202 Md. 581, 97 A.2d 316.

[12] *In re Cochran's Real Estate*, 31 Del Ch. 545, 66 A.2d 497.

There were insufficient assets in his estate to pay his debts in full. Western Pennsylvania National Bank claimed that since the $3,500 loaned to Andrew Bradish was loaned for the purpose of paying the unpaid balance of the purchase price of the land deeded to Andrew and Virginia and was used for that purpose, the Bank should be granted a lien on the land for the unpaid balance of the $3,500 loan. Virginia Bradish claimed that she took the land by right of survivorship free from the claims of the individual creditors of Andrew Bradish and that since the Bank was an individual creditor of Andrew Bradish, it had no right to a lien on the land. The court held that the Bank was not entitled to a lien on the land.

Judge Gunther said: "In order to seek the enforcement of an equitable lien under the circumstances here present, the evidence must be clear, precise and indubitable as to the intention of the parties. We agree with the court below that the evidence offered lacks the clearness and sincereity upon which the equitable doctrine of a lien may be applied. These proceedings were commenced only after a claim for the sum in question had been made upon the estate and when it was discovered that payment in full might not be realized on the note. In connection with this claim against the estate, the evidence discloses that the estate, without the claim, is not insolvent but becomes so if the full amount of the note be paid off.

"Appellant [bank] knew how to obtain a valid lien against the real estate here involved. It has done so in the past and its negligent practice cannot be made the basis of an equitable lien." *Western Pennsylvania National Bank* v. *Bradish,* 194 Pa. Supp. 126, 166 A.2d 104 (1960).

Community property

CHARACTERISTICS OF COMMUNITY PROPERTY

Community property is property which is owned in common by a husband and wife as a kind of marital partnership. It had its origin in the Spanish law and was adopted by Mexico, and has been adopted by eight of the western and southwestern states.[13] Under the early Spanish law the husband was the owner of the community property and could dispose of it during his lifetime without the wife joining in the conveyance. The interest of the wife in the community property was an expectancy; that is, the wife took a one-half interest in it on the death of the husband, and this right could not be defeated by a testamentary disposition by the husband.

---

[13] Arizona, California, Idaho, Louisiana, Nevada, New Mexico, Texas, and Washington.

In the United States the community property laws of the states are statutory, and they are not uniform in their provisions as to the nature of ownership of community property. They are alike, however, in their basic provisions.

ACQUISITION OF COMMUNITY PROPERTY

Regarding the acquisition of community property, the statutes make no distinction between real and personal property. The statutes likewise make no distinction in the character of community property based upon its sources as between the spouses. Each has an equal, present, and existing interest therein, whether it originates entirely from the earnings of the husband, entirely from the earnings of the wife, or partly from each.

The statutes do, however, define separate property; and the courts have held that all property which does not come within the definition of separate property is community property. For example, the California Code (Civil Code, §162) defines the separate property of the wife as follows: "All property of the wife owned by her before marriage, and that acquired afterwards by gift, bequest, devise, or descent with the rents, issues, and profits thereof, is her separate property. The wife may, without the consent of her husband, convey her separate property." The definition of the separate property of the husband is stated in almost identical language (Civil Code, §163).

MANAGEMENT OF COMMUNITY PROPERTY

In general, the husband has the right to manage the community property. Under the early community property statutes the husband's power of disposal of community property was absolute and unrestricted; whereas under the existing community property statutes the husband is given the right to manage the community property, but his right of disposal of it is restricted. Generally, the wife must join the husband in any conveyance or mortgage of community real estate. The statutes of the community property states and the holdings of their courts are not in accord as to the rights of creditors to have their claims satisfied out of community real estate. No general statement can be made in this regard, since a creditor's rights depend primarily on whether the claim is for a prenuptial debt of the wife or husband, a postnuptial separate debt of the husband or wife, or a community debt. As to the husband's right to dispose of community property, the California Code (Civil Code, §172) provides that the husband may not dispose of community property by gift; or he may not sell or encumber furniture, furnishings, or fittings of the home, or clothing or wearing apparel of the wife or minor children, without the written consent of the wife.

EFFECT OF MUTUAL AGREEMENT

In community property states a husband and wife may hold real estate as joint tenants or as tenants in common. They may also, by mutual agreement, declare property which would otherwise be community property to be the separate property of either the husband or the wife. Under the statutes of some of the states, such an agreement, if it is to be enforceable, would have to be entered into before the marriage.

The statutes of some states permit married persons moving into the state to enter into such an agreement, provided the agreement is made within a designated period of time after they move into the state.

RIGHTS ON DIVORCE OR DEATH

In the event of divorce between a man and wife who are holding property as community property, each spouse is generally granted a one-half interest. However, the statutes of some states provide that if the grounds for the divorce are adultery, extreme cruelty, or other such reasons, the judge may, in his discretion, grant a greater portion of the community property to the innocent spouse.

There is a lack of uniformity as to the disposition of the community property in the event of the death of the husband or wife. As a general rule, on the death of the husband the wife is entitled to one half of the community property. The husband may make a testamentary disposal of one half of the community property; but under the statutes of some of the states, if he dies intestate, the wife takes all of the community property. Under the laws of some states the wife may make a testamentary disposal of one half of the community property; whereas under the statues of other states the husband, on the death of the wife, takes all the community property.

Earl Wiggins sold to Fairchild the timber on a tract of land which was community property. Alice M. Wiggins, Earl's wife, did not join him in the execution of the bill of sale of the timber. Fairchild brought an action asking that he be adjudged the owner of the timber. The court held that the timber was community real estate and that since Alice M. Wiggins did not join her husband in the execution of the bill of sale, it was void, and Fairchild acquired no title to the timber.

Justice McFadden said: 'I.C. § 32-912 provides: 'The husband has the management and control of the community property, except the earnings of the wife for her personal services and the rents and profits of her separate estate. But he cannot sell, convey or encumber the community real estate unless the wife joins him in executing and acknowledging the deed or other instrument of conveyance, by which the real estate is sold, conveyed or encumbered. . . . '

"That the bill of sale to the timber created an encumbrance upon community real estate is not disputed, and hence the attempted conveyance of such an interest in the community real estate, without the wife's signature and acknowledgement, is void." *Fairchild* v. *Wiggins*, 85 Idaho 402, 380 P.2d 6 (1963).

Partnership property

NATURE OF PARTNERSHIP PROPERTY

At common law the ownership of real estate by a partnership was not recognized. A partnership is not a legal entity; and from a technical, common-law standpoint, a partnership cannot own real property. The title must vest in the partners, not in the firm.

At common law, if a partnership was named in a deed as grantee and the partnership name did not include the name of any of the partners, no title to the real estate would pass by the deed. The Uniform Partnership Act provides that any real estate may be acquired in the partnership name and that title so acquired can be conveyed only in the partnership name. In those states which have adopted the Uniform Partnership Act or have enacted statues of similar import, the common-law rule is not followed.

Partnership ownership of real estate is a type of quasi-entity ownership. No partner has a particular interest in partnership property; he holds as a tenant in partnership with his partners. The incidents of a tenancy in partnership are set out in Section 25 of the Uniform Partnership Act.

Only real estate intended by the partners to be partnership property is partnership property. Although the form of a conveyance is not conclusive of the nature of the rights conveyed, it is of great weight in determining whether or not property is partnership property. The grantee, if a partnership, should be named in the deed in such a way that the intent of the parties is clearly indicated. For example, if John Jones and Henry Smith, who are partners doing business as "The Big Busy Bee," purchase real estate as partnership property, the deed should clearly indicate this intent. If the grantee is named as "John Jones and Henry Smith, partners, doing business as The Big Busy Bee," the deed will clearly indicate that the real estate is acquired as partnership property. If the grantee is named as "John Jones and Henry Smith," title technically vests in John Jones and Henry Smith as tenants in common. However, in an equitable proceeding for an accounting or for a dissolution and winding-up of the partnership business, parol (oral) evidence would be admitted to prove that the property was partnership property. Under the Uniform Partnership Act a deed naming "The Big Busy Bee" as grantee would vest title to the property in the partnership.

Conveyance of Partnership Real Estate

Under the general law of partnership, every partner is a general agent of the firm, with authority to execute in the name of the partnership any instrument for apparently carrying on in the usual way the business of the partnership. Under this rule, any partner has the power to execute a deed in the name of the partnership conveying partnership real estate, provided such conveyance is for the apparent purpose of carrying on in the usual way the business of the partnership.

If a partnership is organized for the purpose of buying and selling real estate, any partner (unless his authority is limited by the agreement of the partners and such limitation is known to the purchaser) may execute in the partnership name a deed conveying partnership real estate sold in the regular course of the partnership business.[14]

If a partnership is dissolved by the bankruptcy or death of a partner, the partners not bankrupt, or the surviving partner or partners, have the right to wind up the partnership business. In the event the partnership is dissolved by the death of a partner, the title to real estate held by the partnership in the partnership name vests in the surviving partner or partners—subject, however, to a duty to wind up the partnership business and pay over to the estate of the deceased the deceased partner's interest in the partnership. The surviving partner or partners have the power to transfer to a bona fide purchaser for value good title to partnership real estate. If there are no partnership creditors, the estate of the deceased partner and the surviving partner or partners may, by mutual agreement, distribute partnership real estate in kind or hold it as tenants in common.

---

[14] *Robinson* v. *Daughtry*, 171 N.C. 200, 88 S.E. 252.

O. L. Littleton loaned $10,000 to L. T. Littleton; and as security, L. T. Littleton deeded a dairy farm to O. D. Littleton. During the years 1953 and 1954 the Littletons operated the dairy farm as partners. O. L. Littleton claimed the farm. L. T. Littleton claimed that the farm became partnership property and that he (L. T. Littleton) owned a one-half interest in it. The court held that the farm was not partnership property and that even if it were, L. T. Littleton, as a partner, would not have a one-half interest in it.

Chief Justice Bell said: "If the partnership continued to exist, appellant [L. T. Littleon] would not own title to any specific property belonging to the partnership. If the property under the evidence was shown to be partnership property, the court could not legally award a judgment decreeing title to one half of specific property. The court could merely declare ownership in the partnership with a particular interest in such partnership being owned by apellant." *Littleton* v. *Littleton*, Tex. Civ. App., 341 S.M.2d 484 (1960).

Modern types of common ownership

SOCIAL AND ECONOMIC NEEDS

As society developed and the population began to concentrate in urban areas, there arose a need for some type of multiunit housing, and the apartment building seemed to fulfill this need. The apartment dweller was, however, a tenant and as such was not free, as a general rule, to make any changes and improvements he might desire to make to the apartment which he was occupying. Those who wished to own their own apartments and thereby acquire some, if not all, of the freedom of individual ownership found it difficult to work out such an arrangement under the types of coownership recognized by the common law. In order to overcome this difficulty, two different plans were devised which gave the multiunit housing resident ownership rights in the apartment which he occupied. Under these plans, he obtained some, but not all, of those freedoms enjoyed by an owner of a single-family residence.

In the United States the first plan used for this type of living was the cooperative. Recent legislation, usually termed the Horizontal Property Act, lays the foundation for a second type of ownership of apartments— the condominium. This is a plan whereby a party is the owner of his own apartment and, in addition, is co-owner of the common elements of the apartment building and grounds.

The desire of persons who do not wish to own and manage real property or who do not have funds sufficient to purchase income real property, yet would like to invest in real estate, has given rise to the real estate investment trust and the real estate syndicate.

THE COOPERATIVE

The cooperative plan of ownership of real estate was, in its origin, applied almost exclusively to apartment buildings. In recent years, it has been expanded to include developments involving ownership of city lots and the single-family homes erected thereon. From the standpoint of types of ownership of land the cooperative property is owned in severalty.

Ordinarily, the title to the cooperative property is vested in either a stock or a membership corporation. If a stock corporation is used as the vehicle, stock of a total par value equal to the purchase price of the cooperative property will be authorized. If a membership corporation is used, the total value of the memberships issued will be equal to the purchase price of the cooperative property. If a stock corporation is used, the authorized stock will be allocated between the individual units according to their estimated relative value. The value of a membership in a membership corporation is determined on the same basis.

A party wishing to "buy" an apartment or house and lot pays the agreed price (subscription) equal to the money value of the unit involved. The "buyer" is then issued stock or a membership of a value equal to the price of the unit "purchased" and is granted a proprietary lease to a particular unit for the life of the corporation. The operating expenses of the cooperative are divided among the individual units in the form of monthly assessments. This, with the payment on the subscription, comprises the monthly outlay of the owner.

In this manner the residents of the cooperative property control the corporation that owns and manages the entire property. Each cooperative member has one vote, regardless of the number of shares or the value of his membership, and the majority can determine the proper management and expenditure policies in the light of their own best interests as they see them. It is the right of the "unit owners" to have a voice in choosing those who will be their neighbors. Most cooperatives provide that the lease and stock or membership cannot be transferred without the approval of the buyer by the elected representatives of the members.

RESTRAINT ON ALIENATION

Our courts have been consistent in holding that a direct restraint on the alienation of property is against public policy and is void. Yet, if a cooperative is to function successfully, it is necessary that extensive restraints be placed on the alienation of the cooperative units. This restraint has been accomplished by several devices which accomplish the desired objective without placing a direct restraint on the alienation of the cooperative unit. A common plan used is one which provides that the proprietary lease cannot be assigned or the unit sublet without the written consent of a committee of unit owners or of a stated portion of the unit owners, or without the consent of the board of directors. Another plan provides that the corporation would have the first right to purchase the stock or membership and lease of the unit owner. The courts have recognized the desirability of permitting extensive restraints in cooperative cases.[15]

RESTRICTIONS ON USE

A cooperative has been called a municipality within a municipality. Our courts have recognized the right of corporations, fraternal organizations, churches, and similar associations to adopt rules and regulations for the guidance and control of their members, and have enforced such rules and regulations provided they were reasonable and not against public policy or illegal. The broad rule has been applied to the rules and regulations adopted by cooperatives. The community type of living, which is part of the cooperative plan, necessitates the adoption of extensive rules setting out the rights of the unit owners to use and alter their units and their rights in the common property, such as halls, elevators, grounds, and so on, and also the duties they owe to other unit owners. The penalty for violation of such rules and regulations is, as a general rule, cancellation of the unit owner's lease. However, other penalties may be available, depending on the circumstances of the individual case.

Carolyn Green, a member of Greenbelt Homes, Inc., a cooperative, was found to be guilty of violation of the rules and regulations of the corporation. The procedure set out in the contract of membership and in the bylaws of the corporation was followed, and the required number of members voted to terminate Mrs. Green's membership. Mrs. Green contended that she owned the house she occupied and that she could not be deprived of her ownership by the action of the corporation. The court upheld the termination of Mrs.

[15] *Penthouse Properties, Inc.* v. *1158 Fifth Avenue, Inc.,* 256 N.Y. App. 685, 11 N.Y.S.2d 417; *Gale* v. *York Center Community Center, Inc.,* 21 Ill.2d 86, 171 N.E.2d 30.

Green's membership in the corporation and held that she had forfeited her right to the continued possession and occupation of the unit she had acquired.

Judge Horney said: "We think it is clear from the mutual ownership contract that the restrictions on the use of the cooperative dwelling unit were covenants between the member and the corporation, the breach of which gave the corporation the right to terminate the contract. We see no practical difference between this contract and a lease which provides that it can be terminated by the lessor when its provisions as to the use to be made of the premises by the lessee are breached. . . . It is apparent, we think, that the objectionable conduct of the member was a sufficient breach of covenant to warrant the corporation exercising its right to terminate the interest of the members in the dwelling unit." *Green* v. *Greenbelt Homes, Inc.,* 232 Md. 666, 194 A.2d 273 (1963).

CONDOMINIUM

The condominium has many of the features of a cooperative, but it has one major distinguishing characteristic: The units of the condominium are owned in fee by the members. The common areas, that is, the walls, roof, footings, halls, elevators, heating system, plumbing, and so forth, and the land on which the building stands are held by the owners as tenants in common. Under the usual arrangement the transfer of a unit in the condominium includes a transfer of the unit owner's interest in the common areas. Several states have enacted enabling statutes, generally titled Horizontal Property Acts, which set out the procedure to be followed in the organization of a condominium. At the same time the National Housing Act has been amended,[16] authorizing the Federal Housing Administration to insure a first mortgage given to secure the unpaid purchase price of a fee interest in a one-family unit or in an apartment in a multi-family structure together with the purchaser's undivided interest in the common area and facilities that serve the structure.

CONDOMINIUM STATUTES

Condominium statutes usually provide that each apartment, together with its undivided interest in common areas and facilities, shall for all purposes constitute real property. The rights in the common areas are defined in detail, and the statutes provide that the common areas are not subject to partition. Provision is made for the filing in the office in which records of the title to real estate are filed or recorded of a declaration which includes a description of the land on which the building

---

[16] National Housing Act, Sec. 234.

and improvements are to be located, a description of the building to be erected, a description of the common areas, a statement of the value of the property and of each apartment, a statement of the purpose for which the building and each apartment are to be used, the voting rights, the restrictions on use of the apartment and common areas, and other details necessary for the effective organization of the condominium. The floor plan of the building must be recorded and each unit described. The requirements for the conveyance of the individual units and for the recording of the title to the units must be set out.

The owner of a unit may mortgage his unit or subject it to a lien; but he cannot, by his individual act, impose a lien on the property as a whole. By authorized acts of the managers the property as a whole may be subjected to a lien for repairs or improvements of the common area. The owner of a unit may discharge his unit and his interest in the common area by paying his proportionate share of the indebtedness secured by the lien.

Under the statutes of some states, taxes and assessments are assessed against and collected on each individual apartment. Each unit owner may insure his holding, and the manager may insure the whole property; and the rights of the unit owners in the event of damage to or destruction of the building are set out.

MANAGEMENT

The Horizontal Property Acts usually set out general guidelines for the management of the condominium, but the details of the management plan are left for the unit owners to work out. A person may be appointed as manager; a board of trustees elected by the unit owners may be authorized to manage the property; a nonprofit corporation may be organized, and its board of directors act as managers, or some other plan may be adopted. In general, the management of a condominium follows the general pattern of the management of a corporation. For instance, monthly assessments are made to cover the costs of maintaining the common areas and facilities, rules are adopted for the conduct of the occupants of the units, and provision is made for the enforcement of these rules; and such other matters as are necessary for the efficient operation of the whole property are delegated to the management.

Although there is some diversity of opinion as to the procedure to be followed in the enforcement of the rules and regulations, the general expectation is that the courts will hold that the rules and regulations are covenants between the unit owners and are enforceable as such by the managers. The remedies which are available to a landlord against a defaulting tenant in the operation of a cooperative will not be available to the managers of the condominium.

CONCLUSIONS

The condominium provides for individual ownership of the units involved in communal property. This individual ownership permits the owner to finance his unit as he wishes within the scope of the general plan, and it gives him some tax advantages. To some extent, it relieves him from the burden imposed on a unit owner in a cooperative in the event a co-owner defaults, since liens on the condominium are on the individual units, whereas liens on a cooperative are on the whole property. Which form of community ownership will be the better will depend on the objectives of the parties, the laws of the state, and many intangible elements.

5

Acquisition of title by conveyance

Introduction

✔ ORIGINAL TITLE TO LAND

TITLE TO LAND is based on a conveyance from a government which has acquired sovereignty over it. When the original 13 states gained their independence, much of the land within their boundaries had been granted to individuals who held either directly or indirectly from crown grants made by the country which had acquired sovereignty over the land through discovery and settlement, or by conquest or treaty. Each state had sovereignty over the vacant and unappropriated land within its borders. The Northwest Territory was granted to the United States by the states having claims thereto, and the vacant and unappropriated lands in this area came under federal jurisdiction.

Most of the land within the borders of the United States other than that of the 13 original states and the Northwest Territory was acquired by purchase or treaty from France, Spain, and Mexico. The land obtained from Spain and Mexico was partially settled. The owners of such land traced their titles to grants from the crown of the government which had colonized and settled the areas and the rights of these owners were preserved under the terms of the treaties whereby these lands were acquired. There were no established settlements in the area acquired from France—the Louisiana Purchase. At the present time most of the unowned land acquired by the United States has been granted to individuals under laws enacted by Congress. The basis for private ownership of this land is a patent from the U.S. government.

CONVEYANCE OF REAL ESTATE

The right of alienation, that is, the right to convey ownership of real estate to another, is of outstanding importance. At one time in the long period of the evolution of real estate law an individual could not freely convey his rights in real estate; his only right was to possess and use. In the United States the free alienation of real estate is held to be in the interest of the public. If the right of alienation could be denied to an owner of real estate, large holdings in real estate could become frozen; and as a result, social and economic development would be retarded. However, we do recognize the fact that reasonable restraints on the free alienation of real estate are necessary, but a total restraint is against public policy and is void.

Deeds

DEFINITION AND CLASSSIFICATION

In the broadest sense, a deed is any instrument in writing which is signed, sealed, and delivered. However, technically, a deed is an instrument in writing whereby the owner of land (the grantor) conveys to the grantee some right, title, or interest in or to real estate. In this chapter, we shall use the word *deed* in the latter sense.

CLASSIFICATION OF DEEDS

Deeds in common use in the United States today are classed as quitclaim deeds, warranty deeds (general and special), and deeds of bargain and sale.

QUITCLAIM DEED. A quitclaim deed does not purport to convey the property; it conveys only the grantor's right, title, and interest therein.[1] The quitclaim deed conveys all the interest of the grantor in the property at the time of the execution and delivery of the deed. If, at that time, the grantor owns the property in fee simple, the grantee in the quitclaim

---

[1] *Frandson* v. *Casey*, N.D. 73 N.W.2d 436.

deed will acquire a fee simple interest. However, if the grantor has no right, title, or interest in the property, the grantee will acquire nothing by virtue of the quitclaim deed.

A quitclaim deed is frequently used in a situation in which a deed is necessary to cure a technical defect in the chain of title to property. In such a case the grantor may claim no right, title, or interest in the property. A quitclaim deed is also used when the grantor, although he has a merchantable title to the property, does not wish, for some reason, to warrant his title.

WARRANTY DEED.   A general warranty deed purports to convey the property and, in addition, contains covenants of warranty whereby the grantor warrants that he has title to the property conveyed; that he transfers to the grantee title which is good against third persons; that the property is free from liens and encumbrances; and that, upon failure of title, either in whole or in part, he will make compensation in money for the loss sustained.

A special warranty deed purports to convey the property; in addition, the grantor covenants against any defects in title or encumbrances which arose after he acquired the property. In the general warranty deed the grantor warrants against all defects in title and all encumbrances, whereas in the special warranty deed the grantor warrants against only those defects in title or encumbrances which arose after he acquired title. There are no covenants of warranty in a quitclaim deed.

DEED OF BARGAIN AND SALE.   A deed that recites a consideration and conveys real estate to the grantee is a deed of bargain and sale. The language of conveyance commonly used in a deed of bargain and sale is "bargain and sell," although wording of similar import may be used. Many quitclaim deeds and warranty deeds are deeds of bargain and sale. In many states, deeds executed by corporations in which the words of conveyance are "grant, bargain, sell, and convey" are held to be deeds of bargain and sale.

George W. Hudson owned 160 acres of land. After his death, this land was sold for delinquent taxes. Under the laws of descent and distribution, his widow, Myrtle Hudson, took a one-third interest in the land in fee, and each of his four children took one quarter of the remaining two thirds in fee. Jackson, the husband of a daughter, redeemed the land from the tax sale; and a deed naming George W. Hudson as grantee was executed by the county and delivered to Myrtle Hudson. She executed and delivered a deed which read as follows: "Said party of the first part [Myrtle Hudson] do hereby convey and quit to the said party of the second part, [Hans Frandson] his heirs and assigns forever, all right, title and interest in and to a certain tract of land in the county of Mountrail, State of North Dakota, described as follows" [there followed a description of the 160 acres of land].

Frandson died, and his heirs claimed the land. The four children of George W. Hudson claimed a two-thirds interest in the land. The court held that the deed executed by Myrtle Hudson conveyed only her one-third interest in the land and that the heirs of Frandson acquired only such one-third interest.

Judge Johnson said: "We must next determine whether the quitclaim deed issued by Myrtle Hudson purporting to convey all of the property to Hans Frandson did in fact convey anything more than a one-third interest in the property. . . . The deed is labeled as a quitclaim deed and is on a printed form. It did not operate to convey the entire fee in the land, although it was color of title. Nowhere does the word 'grant' appear in the instrument. Where such word is used in a conveyance by which an estate of inheritance or fee is to be passed, certain covenants are implied. The quitclaim deed contains no covenants of warranty. A quitclaim deed is one which purports to convey, and is understood to convey, nothing more than the interest or estate in the property described of which the grantor is seised or possessed, if any, at the time, rather than the property itself. A quitclaim deed does not purport to convey the property, but only the grantor's right, title and interest therein." *Frandson* v. *Casey*, N.D., 73 N.W.2d 436 (1955).

EQUITABLE RIGHTS AND LEGAL TITLE

An instrument which does not fulfill the legal requirements for a valid deed may convey to the grantee an equitable interest in the property. That is, although the instrument is not sufficient to convey to the grantee the legal title to the property, it will transfer to him the equitable owner- ship of the property. Such ownership is valid as between the parties, but it is not good against a bona fide purchaser for value.[2]

For example, suppose Arnett, as grantor, deeds real estate to Bennett, but the deed does not comply with statutory requirements, although it does state clearly that Arnett thereby conveys the real estate to Bennett. As between Arnett and Bennett, Bennett becomes the owner of the real estate. However, if Arnett thereafter deeds the real estate by a valid deed to Clark, who has no knowledge or notice of the prior conveyance to Bennett, and who purchases the property in good faith, paying value therefor, Clark will acquire good title to the real estate. If Arnett refuses to give a deed which cures the defects, a court of equity, on proper action brought by Bennett, will quiet title to the land in Bennett.

[2] *Mertzger* v. *Miller*, 291 F. 780.

In our discussion of the requirements of a valid deed, we shall set out those elements which must be contained in a deed if it is to convey legal title to the real estate and if it is to be eligible for record under the laws of the state in which the real estate is located.

Formal requirements

✓ IMPORTANCE OF FORM

The drafting of deeds demands the highest skill and the greatest care. There are many reported cases that have arisen due to the fact that the deeds involved were improperly drafted or handled. Carelessness, sloppiness, or ignorance in handling a real estate transaction may result in an expensive lawsuit or costly action to quiet title, or, at best, in inconvenience and some expense to clear the record of technical defects.

✓ BASIC REQUIREMENTS

Although the formal requirements for a valid deed are not uniform throughout the United States, there are certain requirements which are the basis for all deeds:

1. A grantor having capacity to execute a deed.
2. A grantee named with reasonable certainty, so that he can be identified.
3. A recital of consideration.
4. Words of conveyance.
5. A description of the land conveyed.
6. A signing by the grantor.
7. Delivery of the deed.
8. Acceptance of the deed.

In addition to these, there will be, in substantially all deeds, exceptions and reservations, and an acknowledgement. In some states, there must be witnesses to the grantor's signature, and the instrument must be sealed.

Nations conveyed to Lundy all the merchantable timber on the 13.74-acre tract of land described in the deed and granted him the right to cut and remove it at any time within six months. Lundy sold the timber to New Home Building Supply Company and attempted to transfer these rights to that Company by executing the following endorsement on the reverse side of the deed:

"March 27, 1962, 'I, A. S. Lundy, do hereby transfer this deed in its entirety to New Home Building Supply Company, Inc., with the exception of pulp wood.' Seal A. S. Lundy, Witness Alma W. Crumley."

The check given by Lundy to Nations in payment for the timber was dishonored, and Nations refused to permit New Home Building Supply Company to cut and remove the timber, claiming that the endorsement on the back of the deed was not a valid conveyance. The court held that the endorsement was sufficient to convey the timber.

Justice Sharp said: "Standing timber is a part of the realty and can be conveyed only by an instrument which is sufficient to convey any other realty. . . .

"Today in North Carolina, the word *deed* ordinarily denotes an instrument in writing, sealed and delivered by the grantor whereby an interest in realty is transferred from the grantor to the grantee. A grantor, a grantee, and a thing granted are necessary requisites. The description of the thing granted must identify the land or furnish the means of identifying it with certainty by reference to something extrinsic. However, it is the seal which distinguishes a deed from a simple contract.

"An effective deed must, of course, contain operative words of conveyance which indicate the grantor's intention to convey his property. The absence of such words cannot be supplied, but the failure to use *technically* operative words will not usually defeat an intention which is plainly though not technically expressed. Ordinary words in common parlance may be effectively used, informality alone will not defeat an instrument which is intended as a deed." *New Home Building Supply Company* v. *Nations,* 259 N.C. 681, 131 S.E.2d 425 (1963).

Grantor

✓ GENERAL REQUIREMENTS

To have a valid conveyance of real estate, the grantor must have legal existence and legal capacity to contract. In general, an unincorporated association, club, or society, except a partnership, does not have legal existence and cannot own or convey real estate in its name.[3] Under the statutes of some states, certain special types of unincorporated associations have been granted legal capacity to own and convey real estate conferred on them.

---

[3] *Popovich et al.* v. *Yugoslav National Home Society, Inc. et al.,* 106 Ind. App. 195, 18 N.E.2d 948.

✓ NATURAL PERSON AS GRANTOR

A deed is in many respects a contract, and the rules relative to a natural person's capacity to contract apply in determining his capacity to convey his real estate. To make a valid conveyance, he must be of lawful age and of sound mind. At common law a person reached his majority at the age of 21 years. The age of infancy has been modified in most states today for many purposes. Unfortunately, there is no uniform rule which has been established and the statutes of each state must be consulted. Even in those states which have reduced the age of majority to 18 this has frequently been done on a selective basis so that age 18 is not the age of majority for all purposes.

A deed executed by an infant is voidable, not void. The rule generally followed is that an infant cannot disaffirm a conveyance of real estate until he reaches his majority. After reaching his majority, he has a reasonable time in which to disaffirm. What constitutes a reasonable time is a question to be determined by the court. Each case must be decided according to its particular facts and circumstances.

A grantor is generally held to have sufficient mental capacity to execute a deed if he is capable of understanding the nature and effect of his act. A deed executed by a person of unsound mind is voidable, not void, and may be set aside by proper court action, usually an action in equity to set aside the deed, brought by the grantor on regaining his sanity, or by a guardian or conservator of his estate. If such action is brought, the person of unsound mind must restore the grantee to his original position. Under the statutes of many states a deed is void if it is executed by a person who has been officially adjudged insane and is under guardianship at the time he executes the deed.

At common law a married woman had no capacity to contract, and any deed executed by a married woman was a nullity. In the United States today the married women's property acts enacted by many of the states permit a married woman to convey her separate estate as though she were a *femme sole* (unmarried woman). However, the married women's property acts are not uniform in their provisions; and in several states, unless the husband of a married woman joins in the execution of a deed, it is a nullity.

✓ ARTIFICIAL PERSON AS GRANTOR

A duly incorporated corporation may hold real estate in the corporate name and has the power to convey its real estate in the corporate name.

However, if a corporation is the grantor in a deed, the corporate name must be signed by some duly authorized officer or officers of the corporation. Generally, the officers who sign the deed in the name of the corporation must be authorized to execute the deed by a resolution, duly adopted, at a legally called meeting of the directors or trustees.

If the sale involves a substantial portion of the corporate assets, a favorable vote of a designated portion, frequently two thirds, of the outstanding stock having voting rights is required. Often, a favorable vote of a majority of the members of a nonprofit corporation is required to authorize the sale of real estate.

A New York statute provides that: "A religious corporation shall not sell, mortgage or lease for a term exceeding five years any of its real estate without applying for and obtaining leave of the court therefor pursuant to the provisions of Article five of the general corporation law. . . ."[4]

The requirements for the execution of deeds by municipal corporations and by other governmental agencies and units are set out in the statutes of the state in which the real estate is located. These statutes vary in their provisions; therefore, no general statements regarding the required procedure can be made.

A government official has only those powers which are conferred on him by the statutes of the state. Consequently, in conveying public property, government officials must comply strictly with all the material provisions of the enabling statute. Likewise, the requirements for the execution of deeds by sheriffs, trustees in bankruptcy, receivers, guardians, and so forth, are set out by statute.

The powers of trustees of trust estates and executors of the estates of deceased persons to convey real estate will be set out in the trust instrument or will. These instruments must be examined to determine the extent of the power of the trustee or executor.

GRANTOR'S SPOUSE

Whether or not both the husband and the wife must join as grantors in the execution of a deed depends on the laws of the state in which the property is located. The right of a married woman to convey her separate estate without the husband joining is discussed above.

If the real property is held by the husband and wife as co-owners, the rules discussed in Chapter 4 "Co-ownership," apply. Briefly, if they

---

[4] *McKinney's Consolidated Laws of New York*, "Religious Corporations," Book 50, Sec. 12, as amended.

own as joint tenants or tenants in common, either may convey his or her interest in the property subject to the limitations placed by local law on the right of a husband or wife to convey his or her separate real estate. If they hold as tenants by the entirety, both must execute the deed as grantors.

If the wife, under the statutes of the state in which the property is located, is entitled to dower, or some substitute for dower, in all real estate which her husband has owned during the marriage, she must join in the execution of the deed, or the grantee will take subject to the inchoate dower of the wife. This outstanding interest is a defect in the title to the land until the wife dies, the husband surviving. In some states the deed, in order to convey the inchoate dower interest of the wife, must include appropriate language of conveyance; and under the statutes of some states a separate acknowledgment by the wife is required. In at least one state the wife has a dower interest only in the real estate owned by the husband at the time of his death. Under such a statute the wife would not have to join the husband as grantor.

In states having homestead laws, if the real property is occupied by the husband and wife as a homestead, both, as a general rule, must join as grantors in the execution of the deed. In most of the states with community property laws the husband and wife must join as grantors of community real property.

For practical as well as legal reasons the grantor or grantors should be described in a deed as husband, wife, unmarried, widow, widower, or divorced and not remarried, as the case may be. If the marital status of the grantor or grantors is properly stated in the deed, the deed will show on its face whether or not it has been properly executed. Failure to indicate the marital status of the grantor or grantors creates a technical defect in the record, which may have to be corrected later at no little inconvenience and expense.

THE GRANTOR'S NAME

The greatest care should be exercised to be certain that the grantor's name is spelled correctly and that there is no variation in the name or in the spelling of the name wherever it appears in the deed. Moreover, the name should be spelled the same as it was spelled in the deed or will whereby the grantor acquired the property. For example, if the grantor, in the instrument conveying the property to him, was designated as John Edward Doe, and in the deed whereby he conveys the property is designated as J. E. Doe, John E. Doe, or J. Edward Doe, such a change in the name would create a technical defect in the record, since there would be nothing on the record to show that John Edward Doe was the same person as J. E. Doe, John E. Doe, or J. Edward Doe. Some attorneys would insist that this technical defect be corrected before they would approve the title to the real estate.

From a legal standpoint, a mistake in the spelling of the grantor's name, or a variance in the spelling of the name in the body of the deed and the signature, does not affect the validity of the deed.[5]

In all deeds, there must be a grantor named. In a properly drafted deed, the grantor will be named in the body of the deed; but if the deed reads, "I hereby sell and convey," or if similar language is used and it is signed by the grantor, this is sufficient to satisfy the legal requirement that the grantor be named in the deed.

Grantee

GRANTEE MUST BE NAMED

From the earliest times the courts have held that the title to real estate must vest in someone; consequently, every valid deed must have a grantee. The grantee must be named or indicated in the deed in such a way that it will be possible to identify him. The early courts were strict in their interpretation of the language in deeds, whereas the modern trend is to read the deed in its entirety and attempt to determine the intent of the parties. For example, a deed naming the heirs of Amos, a living person, would, under strict rules of interpretation, be held to be void for the lack of a grantee, since a living person cannot have heirs.[6] Under the more liberal approach, however, if the deed in its entirety would so indicate, the court would interpret "heirs" as "children" and hold the deed to be valid. A deed naming the grantees as "Amos and wife" indicates the grantees with reasonable certainty and is valid; nevertheless, a carefully drafted deed would name the grantees as "John Amos and Mary Amos, husband and wife."

A deed naming a fictitious grantee is a nullity.[7] Likewise, a deed naming an unincorporated association, society, or club as grantee is a nullity,

---

[5] *Lyon* v. *Kain,* 36 Ill. 362.

[6] *Hickel* v. *Starcher,* 90 W. Va. 369, 110 S.E. 695.

[7] *Cox* v. *Pearson,* 212 Ga. 294, 92 S.E.2d 25.

since such an organization cannot sue or be sued and has no capacity to own or convey real estate.[8] However, the natural persons who are members of an unincorporated association may take title to the real estate and hold it in trust for the association.

√ GRANTEE'S NAME LEFT BLANK

A closely related question concerns the validity of a deed in which no grantee is named at the time the grantor executes the deed. The courts have litigated such a question in four different situations, as follows:

1. If the omission of the name of the grantee is a clerical error and the name of the grantee is filled in when the error is discovered, the courts have generally held that the deed is valid.
2. If the name of the grantee is left blank and a grantee's name is filled in without authority, the deed is void.[9] However, if the grantor has been guilty of negligence in the execution of the deed, he may be estopped from setting up the invalidity of the deed against an innocent purchaser or mortgagee for value.
3. If the name of the grantee is left blank and the deed, after execution is given to the grantor's agent, who is authorized in writing to fill in the grantee's name, and does so before delivery of the deed, the deed is valid.[10]
4. If the grantee's name is left blank at the time the deed is executed and the agent of the grantor is given oral or implied authority to fill in the name of a grantee, the courts are not in accord as to the validity of such a deed. A majority of the courts have held that oral authority to fill blanks is sufficient,[11] but there are holdings to the contrary.

Mrs. Green acquired title to several parcels of real estate which she wished to sell. At the direction of her attorney, MacAdam, she signed several quitclaim deeds in blank. The deeds, when signed by Mrs. Green, were not dated, did not describe the land, and did not name a grantee. MacAdam found a buyer for one of the tracts of land owned by Mrs. Green. He filled out one of the deeds, naming Carol B. Bryson, his secretary, as grantee, and had her execute a quitclaim deed to Koskie, the purchaser. Koskie paid the purchase price to MacAdam, who appropriated the money to his own use. Mrs. Green

---

[8] *Lael* v. *Crook et al.,* 192 Ark. 1115, 97 S.W.2d 436.

[9] *Trout* v. *Taylor et al.,* 220 Cal. 652, 32 P.2d 968.

[10] *Bryant* v. *Barger,* 112 Ind. App. 17, 42 N.E.2d 429.

[11] *Calhoun* v. *Drass,* 319 Pa. 449, 178 A. 568.

brought suit to quiet title to the land, claiming that the deed to the land to Carol B. Bryson was a nullity and that Koskie acquired no title thereto. The court held the deed to be a nullity and held for Mrs. Green.

Justice pro tem Monroe said: "According to the great weight of authority, a deed executed in blank is void and passes no title. 'There must be, in every grant, a grantor, a grantee and a thing granted, and a deed wanting in either essential is absolutely void.' In the instant case each of the instruments signed by the respondent [Mrs. Green] was wanting in all three of these essentials of a valid deed. Though the decisions of other jurisdictions are not in entire harmony upon the question, it has been definitely decided in this state that under our statute of frauds the name of the grantor or the grantee or the description of the property cannot be inserted by an agent of the grantor, in the absence of the latter, unless the agent's authority be in writing. If the authority of the agent be not in writing, his insertion of the name of the grantor or grantee or description of the property does not pass title." *Green v. MacAdam et al.,* 175 Cal. App.2d 481, 346 P.2d 474 (1959).

ASSUMED AND MISSPELLED NAMES

A person may, if he wishes, use an assumed name in the transaction of business; and a deed in which an assumed name—not the true name of the grantee—is used will be valid. However, when the real estate is again conveyed, the assumed name must be used as the name of the grantor; otherwise, there will be a break in the chain of title on the record.[12]

The misspelling of the grantee's name—whether the grantee be a natural person, a partnership, or a corporation—will not invalidate the deed; however, an inconsistency in the spelling of names in a deed does create a technical defect in the record.

A PARTNERSHIP AS GRANTEE

In those states which have adopted the Uniform Partnership Act or have statutes of similar import, a deed to a partnership naming the partnership as grantee is valid. In those states in which the common-law rule applies, the names of the partners or the name of one of the partners must be used in indicating the grantee. (See Chapter 4, "Co-ownership.")

CORPORATION AS GRANTEE

Prior to the time a proposed corporation receives its charter, it has no existence, and a deed naming such a proposed corporation as grantee would be a nullity. However, in some instances when the deed was not

---

[12] *Trout* v. *Taylor et al.,* 220 Cal. 652, 32 P.2d 968.

delivered until after the corporation received its charter, the deed was held to be valid. Also, if the grantor has received the agreed consideration for the transfer, he is estopped from setting up the invalidity of the deed.[13]

If a corporation is named as grantee in a deed, the official name of the corporation as it appears in the articles of incorporation should be used. If the name in the articles of incorporation is "Beeler Bros., Inc.," that name—and not "Beeler Brothers, Incorporated"—should be used.

Three questions arise in regard to the conveying of real estate to corporate grantees:

1. What is the result if the named corporation has not been chartered at the time the deed is executed and delivered, but receives its charter at a later date?
2. What is the result if the grantee corporation is a foreign one not licensed to do business in the state?
3. What is the result if the grantee corporation has the power to "own only such land as is needed for its corporate purposes," and the land in question is not needed by the corporation for such purposes?

If a foreign corporation is not licensed to do business in a state and, under the laws of that state, has no power to own land in the state, a deed naming such a corporation as grantee is a nullity. From a legal standpoint the unlicensed corporation has no existence insofar as the state is concerned. However, if the laws of the state in which the land is located do not prohibit an unlicensed foreign corporation from owning land in the state, and the corporation has the power to own real estate, a deed naming such a corporation as grantee is valid.[14]

If land is granted to a corporation, the deed is valid; the title to the land vests in the corporation even though the corporation, under the powers granted it in its charter, does not have the power to own land in excess of the needs of the corporation and the land granted is clearly in excess of such needs. A deed by the corporation to a bona fide purchaser will vest title to the land in such buyer.

RECITAL OF CONSIDERATION

Accepted standards of conveying dictate that a deed contain a clause reciting a consideration. However, under the laws of most of the states,

---

[13] *Harwood* v. *Masquelette et al.,* 95 Ind. App. 338, 181 N.E. 380.

[14] *Spivey* v. *Spivey Building Corporation et al.,* 367 Ill. 25, 10 N.E.2d 385.

failure to recite a consideration in a deed does not affect the validity of the deed, except in the case of a deed of bargain and sale, in which event the deed is void unless a valuable consideration is given.

If a person makes a gift of his real estate, lack or failure of consideration will not render the conveyance void. If the gift deed is in the form of a warranty deed, the donee cannot enforce the covenants of warranty, since they are not supported by a consideration.

A gift deed or a deed given for a wholly inadequate consideration is valid between the parties; but if such a deed is given to defraud creditors the grantor's creditors, in an appropriate action, may have it set aside. Likewise, if a conveyance is induced by misrepresentation, fraud, duress, or undue influence, and no consideration, or an inadequate consideration, has been given, a court, in a proper action, will set the deed aside.

WORDS OF CONVEYANCE

A deed is an instrument which conveys a present interest in real estate. In order to transfer the title to the property, the deed must contain apt words of grant which manifest the grantor's intent to make a present conveyance. An expression of intention to convey at some future time is inadequate. No technical words are required; however, such words as "convey and warrant," "grant, bargain, and sell," and "convey and quitclaim" are commonly used in deeds.

Description of real estate

IMPORTANCE OF ACCURATE DESCRIPTION

One of the essentials of a valid deed is an adequate description of the thing granted. If the description in a deed of the real estate granted is to be sufficient, the real estate must be identifiable from the words in the deed, aided by evidence explaining the terms used in the deed or by references to other instruments. Such accuracy of description is of outstanding importance to a person engaged in the real estate business, for it enables him to avoid inconvenience, delay, and the expense of legal action. There is a great difference between the preciseness of a technically accurate description and a legally sufficient description of real estate. Although the courts have been exceedingly liberal in finding ambiguous descriptions of real estate to be sufficient, the cost of a court action is a high price to pay to correct an error in the record or to clarify a carelessly drafted description when care in drafting the deed would have avoided all such inconvenience and expense.

In a majority of real estate transactions the same tract of land, without alteration in its boundaries, is conveyed a number of times. In describing the land, if the description used in the caption of the abstract of title or in prior deeds is accurately copied, discrepancies in the record will be avoided.

⋁ METHODS OF DESCRIBING REAL ESTATE

The methods of describing real restate in common use are (1) governmental survey, (2) metes and bounds, (3) monuments, (4) recorded plat, and (5) informal descriptions.

⋁ GOVERNMENTAL SURVEY

After the United States gained its independence, Congress decided to raise money to pay the war debt by selling unoccupied land which the federal government had acquired. This land was a wilderness, and there were few landmarks by which it could be described. A survey of the land was ordered, and a system of rectangular surveys was adopted.

An easily identified landmark, such as the mouth of a river, was selected as the beginning point, and a base line running east and west was drawn through this point. Then a principal or prime meridian was established by drawing a line perpendicular to the base line, intersecting it at the selected point and running north and south.

Since the earth is round, it was necessary to compensate for its narrowing as the survey moved from south to north and from north to south from the base line. To accomplish this, correction lines were drawn every 24 miles. These correction lines—or *guide meridians,* as they are called—run due north and south, but run for only 24 miles until a new series of guide meridians is established. These squares are called *tracts.* Each tract is divided into townships six miles square, and each township is divided into sections one mile square.

Each township is identified by its position in relation to the intersection of the principal meridian and the base line. The position either east or west of the principal meridian is designated as the *range,* and the position either north or south of the base line is indicated by stating whether it is north or south.

Each township is divided into 36 sections, which are numbered from 1 to 36. Starting with Section 1, which is in the northeast corner of the

Divisions into townships

N

```
                          T5N
                          R1E
      First standard parallel north (correction line)
                  -6 Mi.  T4N              T4N   T4N
      24 Mi.              R1E              R4E   R5E


                                  T2N
                          meridian R2E
       meridian  T1N      meridian  T1N          meridian
W      R4W               Base line  R1E                        E
                                          T1S
                                          R3E
      Guide            Principle  T2S              Guide
                                  R1E
                                          T3S
                                          R3E
                  T4S                      T4S
                  R1W                      R4E
      First standard parallel south (correction line)
  T5S                     T5S
  R5W                     R1W
                          S
```

township, the sections are numbered west across the north side of the township to the west side, then down one tier south and back east to the east line of the township. This back-and-forth pattern of numbering is followed until all the sections are numbered.

If less than a section (640 acres) is conveyed, the land is described in relation to its position in the section, unless an uneven area is conveyed, in which event a metes-and-bounds or a monument description will be used. Such a description might read: 40 acres of land lying in the northeast one quarter of the southeast one quarter of Section 12, Township 4 north, Range 4 east of the First Principal Meridian.

Metes and bounds

A metes-and-bounds description of a tract of land is one which starts at a designated point and proceeds to bound the tract by reference to lineal units of measurement and directions.

TOWNSHIP SECTION NUMBERING

6	5	4	3	2	1
7	8	9	10	11	12
18	17	16	15	14	13
19	20	21	22	23	24
30	29	28	27	26	25
31	32	33	34	35	36

For example, suppose a tract of land is not an even fractional part of 640 acres—such as an 89-acre expanse—and does not all lie within a particular quarter of the section; such an area would be described by metes and bounds. The description might read as follows: "A portion of Section 17, T. 16 N., R. 4 E. of the 2nd P.M., Marion County, State of Indiana, beginning at a point 10½ rods west of the southeast corner of said section, thence west 89 rods, thence north 160 rods, thence east 89 rods, thence south to the place of beginning."

Portions of lots in a city are frequently described by metes and bounds.

DIVISION OF A SECTION

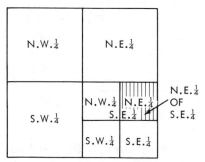

The point of beginning may be the intersection of two streets. If the point of beginning is to be the intersection of Dodds Street and Main Street, for instance, the description should read: "At the intersection of the center line of Dodds Street and Main Street or the intersection of the north side of Dodds Street with the west side of Main Street."

MONUMENTS

Monuments are visible marks or physical features, either natural or artifical, which are used to bound a property. A monument may be a stake or a stone set up as a marker of the boundary. It may be some natural object, such as a tree, a stream, or the crest of a hill. Usually, land is not described by reference to monuments alone, but by a combination of monuments, courses, and distances. For example:

Part of the N.E. ¼ of Section 17, T. 16 N., R. 4 E. of the 2nd P.M., Marion County, State of Indiana, beginning at a point in the Millerville Gravel Road, said point being 149.87 feet west of the west line of the E. ½ of the N.E. ¼ of said Section 17, thence north 51° 40′ west 216.87 feet to the center line of Fall Creek, thence south 21° 32′ west along the center line of Fall Creek 139.04 feet, thence south 35° 0′ 21′ west along the center line of fall Creek 82.71 feet, thence south 41° 22′ west along the center line of Fall Creek 181.07 feet, thence south 55° 32′ west along the center line of Fall Creek 338.13 feet, thence south 51°49′ east 412.77 feet to the center of Millerville Gravel Road, thence north 27° 52′ east along the center line of Millerville Gravel Road 731.3 feet to the place of beginning, containing 4.467 acres.

A tract of land may be described by reference to adjoining land. For example: "Bounded northerly by land now or formerly owned by Josaphat Lussier, easterly by north Broad Street, southerly by land formerly owned by Albert J. Ruel, westerly by land now owned or formerly owned by Minnie Cerute."

REFERENCE TO RECORDED PLAT OR MAP

When a tract of land is subdivided, a plat or map of the subdivision will be recorded. This plat will, as a general rule, be given a distinguishing name or a number, so that it can be identified, and it will be entered into the plat book. On this plat the size and shape of each lot will be shown, and each block and lot will be numbered. Streets, alleys, easements for utilities, and so forth, will also be indicated on the plat.

In describing a lot in a recorded plat, the lot and block number, the name or number of the plat, and the name of the city, county, and state will be given. In some descriptions, instead of the name of the city, the description by government survey of the tract subdivided will be given. A description by reference to a recorded plat might read: "Lot 2 of Block 6 in Fall Creek Place 2nd Section, an addition to the City of Indianapolis, as per plat thereof, recorded in Plat Book 27, page 62, in the office of the Recorder of Marion County, Indiana."

The same lot could be described as: "Lot 2 of Block 6 in Fall Creek Place 2nd Section, a subdivision of the W. ½ of the N.E. ¼ of Section 17, T. 16 N., R. 4 E. of the 2nd P.M., Marion County, Indiana."

✓DESCRIPTIONS TO BE AVOIDED

Although an informal description may be sufficient to convey title to real estate, such descriptions should not be used in deeds, leases, or contracts relating to interests in real estate. The courts have held descriptions by popular name—such as "my farm, Hoosier Acres"—to be adequate. The courts have also held to be sufficient such descriptions as "all my land in Monroe County, Indiana," or "all my real property in the city of Indianapolis, Indiana"; but a deed describing the property conveyed as "all my real estate" is void because of the inadequacy of the description.

Description by street number is sometimes used, especially in leases and contracts to sell improved urban property, but this practice is dangerous. Such a description gives no indication of actual boundaries, and a controversy may arise as to the amount of land included with the building at the street number.[15] Moreover, street names and street numbers may be changed.

Descriptions by areas, such as "two acres in the southeast corner of the S.E. ¼ of the S.W. ¼ of section 17, etc.," should be avoided. A description of this sort does not indicate whether the area is to be rectangular or square. In one such case the court held that the description was sufficient and that the area should be square in shape.

"The East one half of Lot 6, etc.," is sufficient to pass title but is inadequate as a description, especially if the lot is irregular in its boundaries. The courts have held that such a description would be interpreted as an intent to convey one half of the lot in area, without reference to the frontage or other considerations. A metes-and-bounds description

---

[15] *Killian* v. *Welfare Engineering Co.,* 328 Ill. App. 375, 66 N.E.2d 305.

should be used; or if the lot lines are parallel and run due east and west, and north and south, a description such as "the west 30 feet (if it is a 60-foot lot) of Lot 6, etc.," should be used. When the remaining portion of the lot is conveyed, the description used should read: "Lot 6, etc., except the west 30 feet of said lot." By such a conveyance, the entire remaining portion of Lot 6 will be conveyed. If the description reads "the east 30 feet of Lot 6" and, on resurvey, it is found that the lot is more than 60 feet wide, title to a narrow strip lying between the two portions conveyed will remain in the grantor. If the lot were found to be less than 60 feet wide, the second grantee would get less than the 30 feet he bargained for.

INCOMPLETE, ERRONEOUS, AND CONFLICTING DESCRIPTIONS

The general rule—that a description is sufficient if, by reference thereto, the real estate intended to be conveyed by the deed can be identified—is applied in determining whether or not an omission in the description in a deed invalidates the deed. Under the parol evidence rule, oral evidence is not admissible to alter or vary the terms of a written instrument; and under the provisions of the statute of frauds the deed (writing), in order to be sufficient, must contain all the material terms of the transaction. Consequently, if the omission is such that the real estate cannot be identified from the description in the deed, the conveyance will fail.

In a description of a lot by reference to a recorded plat, the omission of the block number, if the subdivision is divided into blocks and lots, will render the description inoperative, since the lot cannot be located from the description. In a description by governmental survey the omission of the prime meridian in a description, if the name of the city, county, and state are included, will not be fatal, since the real estate can be located without reference to the prime meridian.[16]

In describing real estate, errors may be made, such as indicating the "N.E. $\frac{1}{2}$" when the true description should be "S.E. $\frac{1}{4}$," or stating "thence south to place of beginning" when the description should be "thence north." When such errors, obviously clerical or typographical, are made, the court will reject the false and impossible part of the description, if the real estate can be identified from the remaining part of the description, and will hold the description to be sufficient.[17]

---

[16] *Harrington* v. *Goldsmith*, 136 Cal. 168, 68 P. 594.

[17] *Moore et al.* v. *Whitley*, 234 N.C. 150, 66 S.E.2d 785.

The courts have adopted some general rules of construction which are usually applied in interpreting descriptions in deeds when there are conflicting elements. If the description is ambiguous, parol evidence is admissible to clear up the ambiguity, but not to add to or alter the terms of the deed.

If the description is stated in general terms followed by specific terms and there is a conflict between the general and the specific terms, the specific terms will control.

If there is a conflict in a description between courses and distances and monuments, the monuments control. For example, in the description under the section "Monuments," if the last sentence had read "thence north 29° 52′ east along the center line of Millerville Gravel Road 713.3 feet to the place of beginning," and the center line of Millerville Gravel Road ran north 27° 52′ east, and the place of beginning was 731.3 feet from that point, the monument—the center line of Millerville Gravel Road—would control. Also, if, in addition to a description of land, there is a statement of area, and there is a variation between the area described and the area stated, the description of the area will control.[18]

STREETS, HIGHWAYS, AND WATERS AS BOUNDARIES

As a general rule, if a description gives a public street or highway as a boundary, the land generally runs to the center of the street or highway. This presumption may be overcome by using language in the description which will clearly indicate a contrary intent. In drafting a description of a real estate which is bounded by a tree, a highway, an alley, or a stream, controversies can be avoided by stating that the boundary is the center line of the street, highway, alley, or stream. If land is bounded by a private road or alley, the rule followed in the majority of states is the same as that applied to public streets, highways, and alleys; however, a few states hold otherwise. If land is bounded by a stream, the general rule is that the center of the stream is the boundary line.

Three deeds described the land conveyed as follows:

1. "Thirty acres in the northern part of Spanish Grant No. 2425 and West and adjoining the ten acre tract known as the Will Lemon's Tract."

2. "Forty (40) acres in the Northern part of Spanish Grant No. 2425, adjoining the ten (10) acre tract known as the Will Lemon's tract."

3. "Northwestern part of Spanish Grant No. 2425 containing twenty acres, (20) more or less, same being all the land owned by us in said Grant No.

---

[18] *Frank Towers Corporation* v. *Laviana et al.,* 140 Conn. 45, 97 A.2d 567.

2425 having previous sold (by the two other deeds) balance owned by A. N. Best."

In an action of ejectment and for rents against the Miller brothers, who claimed the title through a grant from Tom Miller, a prior owner, the Miller brothers claimed that deed No. 3 was insufficient to convey title to the land. The court held that the description of the land in the three deeds was insufficient.

Justice George Rose Smith said: "It is settled that 'part' descriptions such as these are void for indefiniteness. Although a surveyor testified that he was able to locate the tracts from the descriptions we have quoted, he must have relied upon physical evidence such as fences, for the language of the deed supplies no clue that could lead to an identification of the property. The rule is that the conveyance itself must furnish that clue." *Miller* v. *Best,* Ark., 361 S.W.2d 737 (1962).

A deed described the land conveyed as "Tract 87, Zimmerman's Map, 1904." Zimmerman's Map, 1904, was a map prepared by a surveyor employed by the county to prepare a map to be used as the basis for assessment of taxes. Although the map did not show points of beginning and was not certified to by the surveyor and was never officially made a matter of record, it did bear on its face the following endorsement: "Filed this 31st day of December, A.D. 1904, at 5 o'clock P.M. Celso Lopez, Recorder, by Deputy." From the map, directions could be determined, and aided by arroyos, natural boundaries, road crossings, and curves in arroyos shown on the map, the boundaries of the various tracts of the city could be determined. The trial court held that the description was insufficient. On appeal, this holding was reversed, and the Supreme Court held the deed valid.

Chief Justice Compton said: ". . . it is not necessary that the description of the land be contained in the body of the deed. It is sufficient if it refers for identification to some other instrument or document, but the description must be contained in the instrument or its reference, expressed or implied with such certainty that he locality of the land can be ascertained. . . . The rule has also been held to apply to maps and plats, including surveys, and to an assessor's plan. The deed is not void because the instrument referred to is incomplete, not official, unacknowledged, unrecorded or unattached or misdescribed in some particular or even invalid." *Hughes* v. *Meem,* 70 N.M. 122, 371 P.2d 235 (1962).

Estate conveyed by deed

WORDS OF INHERITANCE

At common law, if a deed did not grant the real estate to the grantee "and his heirs," a fee simple estate was not granted. Today, under the statutes generally in force throughout the United States, words of inheritance are not necessary to create a fee simple estate. The courts interpret a deed as granting a fee simple estate, unless an intent to grant a lesser estate is clearly stated or indicated in the deed.[19]

HABENDUM CLAUSE

The habendum clause in a deed usually follows the granting clause and defines the extent of the estate granted. It begins with words such as "to have and to hold." It is not an essential part of the deed and is usually not included in statutory form deeds.

At common law, if the grant was to the grantee and his heirs, a fee simple vested in the grantee, and a statement in the habendum clause that an estate less than a fee simple was granted was ineffective. If the terms of a deed were ambiguous as to the estate granted, the granting clause controlled.

However, today the courts read the deed in its entirety; and if a clear intention to grant an estate less than that indicated in the granting clause is expressed, the courts will not follow the early technical rule, but instead will give effect to the later clause in the deed.[20] In the drafting of a deed the grant should not be made to the grantee and his heirs unless the grantor intends to grant an estate in fee simple.

WARRANTIES

A warranty is not an essential element of a valid deed. A warranty deed purports to convey to the grantee title to the land described in the deed. The grantor may, in addition to transferring title, assume responsibility for stated defects in the title and obligate himself to defend against or reimburse the grantee for any loss resulting from the defects covered by the warranty. A warranty may protect only the immediate transferee, or it may be of such a nature that it "runs with the land," that is, the protection of the warranty extends to all subsequent holders who can trace their title back to the deed containing the warranty.

The warranties usually included in a warranty deed are (1) that the grantor has good title to the real estate; (2) that there are no liens and encumbrances on the real estate, except those stated in the deed; and

---

[19] *Mechtle* v. *Topp,* 78 N.D. 789, 52 N.W.2d 842.

[20] *Pachter et al.* v. *Gray et al.,* 231 Ind. 487, 109 N.E.2d 412.

(3) that the grantee and his grantees, successors, or assigns will not be evicted or disturbed by persons having title superior to that of the grantor or by a lienholder. This latter covenant "runs with the land."

At an earlier date, and today in some states, it is customary to set out in full warranties against all possible defects in title and to include covenants of seisen, covenants against encumbrances, and covenants of quiet enjoyment. Such deeds are referred to as long-form deeds. The recording of a long-form deed entails much unnecessary work. Many states have enacted statutes under which a short-form warranty deed is provided for. If the deed includes such words as "convey and warrant" or "bargain, sell, and warrant," the deed, by statutory implication, includes the usual covenants of warranty.[21]

EXCEPTIONS AND RESERVATIONS

In the event there are known defects in the grantor's title or there are known liens against the real estate conveyed and the grantor wishes to exclude these defects from his covenants of warranty, this exclusion can be accomplished by including in the covenants of warranty, if such are written into the deed, a provision expressly excepting from the covenants the known defects or liens.

If a statutory short-form deed is used, it is customary to insert therein provisions expressly excepting from the warranty the known defects or liens. For example, if there is an easement of right of way over a portion of the premises and the premises are subject to a mortgage lien, the warrant deed would contain a provision to the effect that the grantor was granting good title free from liens and encumbrances except an easement of right of way (describing it) and subject to a mortgage (giving name of mortgagee, where mortgage is recorded, original amount of mortgage debt, and unpaid balance of mortgage debt). Usually, this clause

---

[21] Form of warranty deed—Any conveyance of lands worded in substance as follows: "A B conveys and warrants to C D [here describe the premises] for the sum of [here insert the consideration]" the said conveyance being dated, and duly signed, sealed, and acknowledged by the grantor—shall be deemed and held to be a conveyance in fee simple to the grantee, his heirs and assigns, with covenant from the grantor, for himself and his heirs and personal representatives, that he is lawfully seized of the premises, has good right to convey the same, and guarantees the quiet possession thereof, and that the same is free from all encumbrances, and that he will warrant and defend the title to the same against all lawful claims (Burns' *Annotated Indiana Statues,* Vol. XI, Part 1, 56–115 I R.S. 1852, Chap. 23, § 12, 232).

will state whether or not the grantee assumes and agrees to pay the mortgage debt.

A reservation in a deed retains or withholds certain rights in the real estate. These reserved rights do not pass to the grantee but remain in the grantor. For example, the grantor might grant a fee simple title to a tract of land and in the deed include a provision reserving to the grantor an easement of right of way over a described portion of the land granted.

RESTRICTIONS

The grantor may, within reasonable limits, place restrictions on the right to use the real estate conveyed. If he wishes to place such restrictions on the property conveyed, he will include an appropriately worded restrictive covenant in the deed. Restrictive covenants will be discussed in more detail in a later chapter.

HOMESTEAD AND DOWER RIGHTS

Under the laws of some states, unless a deed contains a clause specifically waving homestead, dower, or curtesy rights, the property conveyed will be subject to such rights.

Randolph executed a deed conveying to Austin 7.51 acres of land. The granting, habendum, and warranty clauses were in the terms of a conveyance in fee simple.

After the description, but before the habendum and warranty clauses, the following provision was set forth: "And this Deed is made subject to the following conditions, reservations, and restrictions which constitute covenants running with the land and binding upon the parties hereto, their heirs and assigns, to wit: . . ." The conditions, reservations, and restrictions were then set forth in eleven separate (numbered) paragraphs. They included, among other things, restrictions that the property should be used only for residential purposes; restrictions on the size of the lots in the event of subdivision; and restrictions on the location, cost, and composition of any residence constructed thereon. Too, they included reservations of rights of way for installation of power and telephone lines.

Austin claimed that the conditions, restrictions, and reservations in the deed limited the estate granted, were in conflict with the granting clause and the habendum and warranties, and therefore were invalid. The court held that the covenants, reservations, and restrictions were valid.

Justice Bobbitt said: "In the interpretation of a deed, the intention of the grantor or grantors must be gathered from the whole instrument and every part given effect, unless it contains conflicting provisions which are irreconcilable or a provision which is contrary to public policy or runs counter to some rule of law.

"The foregoing impels us to express the view . . . that the conditions, reservations and restrictions set forth in the Randolph-Austin deed are not void *ab initio* on the ground they are repugnant to the granting habendum and warranty clauses of the deed." *Barrier* v. *Randolph,* 260 N.C. 741, 133 S.E.2d 655 (1963).

Execution of deed

✓ DATE

Although it is customary to date a deed, omission of the date does not invalidate the deed. Statutes setting out a permissive deed form may include the date of execution in the recommended form. However, these statutes are directive and not mandatory; consequently, omission of the date is not a violation of the statute and does not invalidate the deed.

✓ SIGNATURE

The signature of the grantor is essential to the validity of a deed. If there is more than one grantor named in the deed, each must sign, unless the grantors are partners—in which event, one partner, as a general rule, may sign for his copartners. Some states, by statute, require that the deed be subscribed—that is, the signature must be in writing. In such states a typed or stamped signature would not be sufficient.

A person who cannot write may sign by making his mark. In the event the deed is signed by the grantor's making his mark, it is customary for his name to be written close to the mark, together with a statement that the mark is the grantor's. Some states, by statute, require that the mark be witnessed by one or two persons, who must sign as witnesses. For example:

		John Jones
Witness	*Quinn Lloyd*	X
Witness	*Henry Hewitt*	(His Mark)

A third person may sign the grantor's name at his direction and in his presence, or with his express or implied authorization.[22]

---

[22] *Witt et al.* v. *Panek et al.,* 408 Ill. 328, 97 N.E.2d 283.

The misspelling of the grantor's name in the deed, or a variance between the spelling of the grantor's name in the deed and in his signature, does not invalidate the deed; but it does result in a technical defect in the record, and this defect may be ground for objection on the part of an attorney who examines the abstract of title.

√ SIGNATURE BY AGENT

A deed may be signed by the duly authorized agent of the grantor. At common law a deed is an instrument under seal, and the common-law rule is that the authority to sign in the name of the principal must be in writing and sealed. Under the recording statutes of most states the authority of an agent to sign a deed in the name of his principal must be in writing and executed with the same formality as is required for the execution of the deed. Such an authorization is known as a *power of attorney*.

The deed should be signed in the name of the principal, followed by the name of the agent; and the agent should sign in such a way as to indicate clearly that he is signing as agent. For example:

John Jones   (*Seal*)

By *Frank Drake*

His Agent (or His

Attorney in Fact)

√ SEAL

In its origin the seal was used to indicate that the person sealing the instrument intended to create a legally binding obligation. Today, since most people can read and write, the signature of the obligor has been accepted as the authentication of a written instrument, and the seal is not used as extensively as it was in an earlier era.

In some states, especially in the East, a deed must be sealed to be valid. In some states, deeds executed by natural persons need not be sealed, but deeds executed by persons other than natural persons (corporations and so forth) must be sealed to be valid.

Deeds are generally signed and sealed, although the seal is not essential to the validity of the deed. The seal may be in the form of a wax wafer bearing a distinctive impression, or it may be a distinctive impression in the paper on which the deed is written. It may be merely a pen scroll, and the word *seal,* or the letters *L.S.;* or the intent to seal may be indicated in some other manner.

✓WITNESSES

In a few states, if the grantor's signature is not witnessed by one or two persons, the deed will be invalid and will not pass legal title to the real property. In a limited number of states the recording statutes of the state provide that unless the signature of the grantor is witnessed by one or two persons, the deed will not be eligible for record. However, in the majority of states, witnesses to the grantor's signature are not required. As a general rule, the grantor, the grantee, or their spouses are not qualified to act as witnesses.

Acknowledgment

✓NATURE OF ACKNOWLEDGMENT

An acknowledgment is a formal declaration before an authorized official by a person who has executed an instrument that it is his free act and deed. Although it is customary to acknowledge the execution of a deed to real estate, the acknowledgment is not essential to the validity of the deed unless the statutes of the state in which the real estate is located so provide. However, in the great majority of the states, if a deed, mortgage, or other similar instrument is not acknowledged, it is not entitled to be recorded; and in addition, it is not admissible as evidence in court.

From a practical standpoint an unacknowledged deed is not a satisfactory instrument, since, if such a deed is not eligible to be recorded, the unrecorded deed would not be a valid conveyance against a subsequent innocent purchaser or mortgagee. For the protection of the grantee, all deeds should be acknowledged and recorded.

✓CERTIFICATE OF ACKNOWLEDGMENT

The notary public or officer who takes the acknowledgment fills out a certificate of acknowledgment and attaches it to the instrument, or fills in the form customarily printed on deeds and mortgages. This certifies that the grantor or grantors (naming them) appeared before him (naming his official status) and acknowledged that he (the grantor) executed the instrument as his own act and deed. The certificate will state in the caption the name of the state and the county in which it was executed. This is known as the *venue*.[23] It will be signed and sealed by the officer taking the acknowledgment; and as a general rule, if the officer is a notary public, the date of the expiration of his commission will be given.

WHO MAY TAKE AN ACKNOWLEDGMENT

Only those persons who are authorized by statute have the power to take acknowledgments. In all states a notary public has such power, and this power is generally granted to judges of courts of record and to justices of the peace.

A person acquiring a beneficial interest under the instrument being executed is disqualified from taking an acknowledgment of the person executing the instrument. This rule has been held in some states to disqualify a stockholder, an officer, or a director of a corporation, or a member of an association, from taking the acknowledgment of the corporation's officer or the association's agent who executes the instrument. As a general rule, relationship by blood or marriage will not disqualify a person from taking an acknowledgment if he acquires no beneficial interest under the instrument.

DUTY OF OFFICER TAKING ACKNOWLEDGMENT

An officer, before taking an acknowledgment, should know or satisfy himself that the person presenting the instrument for acknowledgment is the person who executed the instrument. If he does not take reasonable precautions to satisfy himself that the person presenting the instrument is the person who executed it, he may render himself liable for damages.

FOREIGN ACKNOWLEDGMENT

A deed to real estate may be executed and acknowledged in any state or county. It does not have to be acknowledged in the state in which the land is located. However, the deed form and the form of the acknowl-

---

[23] State of Indiana ⎰
     County of Monroe ⎱ ss (Venue)

Before me, John Jones (or the undersigned), a notary public (judge, or justice of the peace, as the case may be), this _____ day of _____ 19__, personally appeared (name the grantor or grantors), who dully acknowledged the execution of the annexed deed.

                          Signed   *John Jones* (Seal)
                          _____
                          (Judge or Justice of the Peace)

     My commission expires_____
     (if notary public)

edgment must comply with the statutory requirements of the state in which the land is located.

In some states, if the acknowledgment is taken outside the state in which the land is located, it must have attached to it a certificate of the clerk of the court in the county in which the acknowledgment was taken, certifying that the officer taking the acknowledgment was authorized by law to do so. This is known as a *certificate of authenticity.*

Charles Schroeder, with the connivance of a woman accomplice, mortgaged property which was owned by Charles Schroeder and his wife Marlene Schroeder. Charles Schroeder and a woman impersonating his wife were taken before a notary public, one Alice M. Pocrask, who was an assistant secretary of the mortgagee. She took their acknowledgment, although she had never seen them before. The court held that the signature of Marlene Schroeder was a forgery and that the mortgage was not a lien on her interest in the property.

Justice Schwartz said, in discussing the duties and liabilities of the notary public who took the acknowledgment of Charles Schroeder and the imposter: ". . . We are well aware that in routine procedure, notaries make little or no effort to identify a person whose oath they take or whose signature they attest. But the acknowledgment of a grantor or spouse to a deed or document relating to the transfer of real estate is by statute made an act of more than ordinary significance. Here, any competent person dealing in such matters should understand the requirements and if he does not comply with them must expect to be held responsible. The acknowledgment involved purported to be that of a wife joining a husband in the establishment of a sizeable encumbrance on their property.

"The failure of a notary, who is the mortgagee's employee and used by it to take acknowledgment of a document, properly to identify the person whose acknowledgment is taken, is chargeable to the mortgagee. The most that can be said for Avondale [the mortgagee] is that the notary was introduced to the 'Schroeders' by one of their officers who knew Charles Schroeder slightly and Marlene not at all. Such an introduction could not satisfy her duty. A requirement of personal knowledge cannot be met by introduction just prior to the acknowledgment." *Hoffman* v. *Schroeder,* 38 Ill. App.2d 20, 186 N.E.2d 381 (1962).

Delivery of deed

NECESSITY FOR DELIVERY

The act of drafting and executing a deed, although the document is complete in every respect, is not sufficient to convey the property described in the deed to the named grantee. A deed is not legally operative until it is delivered with the intent, on the part of the grantor, that it become legally effective. The physical transfer of the document, the deed, may or may not satisfy the requirement for delivery, depending on the intent of the grantor, determined objectively from all the surrounding circumstances.[24]

√ INTENT TO DELIVER

Delivery of a deed is basically a question of the intent of the grantor—not the subjective intent (what he thinks), but the objective intent (what a reasonable man familiar with all the facts and circumstances is justified in believing the grantor intended).

A grantee may be given possession of the deed for the purpose of reading it, checking the description, and so forth. This would not constitute delivery, since the grantor has in no way indicated his intent that the deed shall become effective as a conveyance of title to the real estate described in the deed.

If the grantee obtains possession of the deed without the knowledge or consent of the grantor, there is no delivery; the deed is inoperative. For example, suppose that after a deed is fully executed, the grantee steals it or obtains it by fraudulent representations or duress. In such a case, there is no delivery, and the deed is inoperative. On the other hand, mere intent to delivery the deed and transfer title, without any act or conduct giving effect to or completing the delivery, passes no title.[25]

A deed may be delivered even though the grantor retains manual custody of it. However, in such cases, there must be clear proof of the grantor's intention to deliver the instrument.[26]

Although there are certain principles which are generally followed in determining whether or not a deed has been delivered, there are no fixed rules which can be applied in all cases. In the final analysis, each case must be determined on its particular facts.

Charlie Overman lived on his 110-acre farm with his daughter Maggie and his grandson Arnold. On March 26, 1947, Charlie Overman went to Silver City and had two deeds prepared—one to Arnold for 45 acres and the other to Maggie for 65 acres, including the home site. Arnold was present at the time Charlie signed both deeds. Both deeds had the following provisions inserted at the end of the description and preceding the habendum clause:

[24] *Bryant* v. *Barger,* 112 Ind. App. 17, 42 N.E.2d 429.

[25] *Shuck* v. *Shuck et al.,* 77 N.D. 628, 44 N.W.2d 767.

[26] *In re McKitterick's Estate,* 94 Ohio App. 373, 115 N.E.2d 163.

"I hereby reserve for myself a life estate in the above described land." Upon their return home, Charlie immediately gave Arnold the deed to the 45 acres. Maggie was at work at this time, but when she returned home, Charlie handed her the deed for the 65 acres. She and Charlie went to her bedroom and put the deed in a dresser drawer. She, her father [Charlie], and Arnold regularly used this dresser drawer for their papers. Neither of the deeds was recorded until after Charlie's death in 1957. Maggie's brothers and sisters contended that the deed to Maggie was never delivered and that the 65 acres of land was part of the father's estate. The court held that there was a valid delivery of the deed to Maggie.

Justice Moore said: "The requisites to the valid delivery of a deed are three-fold. They are: (1) an intention on the part of the grantor to give the instrument legal effect according to its purport and tenor; (2) the evidencing of such intention by some word or act disclosing that the grantor has put the instrument beyond his legal control; and (3) acquiescence by the grantee in such intention. Presumption of delivery arises from registration, even after the death of the grantor, and in the absence of other evidence is sufficient to support a finding of delivery." *Jones* v. *Saunders,* 254 N.C. 644, 119 S.E. 2d 789 (1961).

DELIVERY TO THIRD PERSON

Delivery of a deed may be made to some third person for the benefit of the grantee; but the delivery, in order to be effective, must be such that the grantor surrenders all right to control the deed; and the third person must hold the deed as trustee or agent of the grantee. If the grantor reserves the right to recall the deed or to exercise control over its disposal, there is no delivery. The third person, under such circumstances, is the agent of the grantor; and possession by the agent is equivalent to possession by the principal.[27]

If delivery is made to a third person, who is to hold the deed for the grantee and deliver it to him on the happening of some future event, there is no delivery until the occurrence of the event.

The recording of a deed at the grantor's request does not necessarily amount to delivery. It is convincing evidence of intent to deliver, but a contrary intent may be established.[28]

DELIVERY AFTER DEATH

Delivery of a deed, if it is to be effective, must be made during the lifetime of the grantor. If a grantor executes deeds to real estate, and

[27] *Hooker* v. *Tucker et al.,* 335 Mich. 429, 56 N.W.2d 246.
[28] *Blachowski et ux.* v. *Blachowski,* 135 N.J. Eq. 425, 39 A.2d 94.

retains possession and control over the deeds, placing them in his strong-box or safe-deposit box, with direction that the deeds shall be delivered after his death, such deeds are ineffectual to pass title.[29]

A delivery to a third person who is to hold the deed as trustee for the benefit of the named grantee, and who is to deliver it to the grantee on the death of the grantor, is a valid delivery. However, if there is to be a valid delivery, the grantor must intend irrevocably to vest title in the grantee and to surrender all control over the deed.[30]

John Fiore, during his lifetime, executed a deed to his wife Antoinetta conveying his interest in described lands. The deed was prepared by an attorney, and was executed and acknowledged by John Fiore on September 25, 1940. It was not recorded until November 27, 1957, long after the death of John Fiore, who died on September 3, 1942. The deed, after it was executed, was left in the possession of the attorney, who was given no instructions as to its disposition. John Fiore did not tell his wife or any other member of his family that he had executed the deed, and he retained possession and control of the land described in the deed until his death. His son claimed an interest in the land, and his wife claimed the land had been conveyed to her by the deed. The court held that the deed had never been delivered and that the land had not been conveyed to the wife.

Justice Eagen said: "In order to validate defendant's [Antoinetta Fiore] claim to ownership of the property involved there are two indispensable requisites: (1) a donative intent on the part of the grantor, i.e., an intent to make a gift to the grantee then and there, when the deed was executed; (2) a delivery of the deed to the grantee, either actual or constructive, which divested the donor of all dominion over the property and invested the donee therewith. The recording of the deed was not essential to its validity or the transition of the title. Nor was it essential that the grantee have knowledge of the transaction. By subsequent acceptance, she ratified the original delivery if such had occurred.

"However, there must have been a delivery of the instrument to the grantee and while the execution, sealing, acknowledging and recording of a deed gives rise to a presumption of delivery, this is a factual presumption and as such is rebuttable.

"For a legal delivery to be effected, it is not necessary that the deed be delivered directly to the grantee. It may be placed in the possession of a third party for delivery to the grantee upon the happening of a *specified* contingency. In such cases, the legal delivery date is that when the donor effectuated his intention. However, delivery is not accomplished by the mere handing of the executed deed to a stranger. Likewise, the mere handing of the executed deed,

---

[29] *Dillion et al.* v. *Meister et al.,* 319 Mich. 428, 29 N.W.2d 846.

[30] *Dickason et al.* v. *Dickason,* 219 Ind. 683, 40 N.E.2d 965.

without more, to a third person who is an agent of the grantor is ineffective. In order for the delivery to be effectual and to result in a culmination of the transition of the title, *there must be an express and definite instruction that the deed is to be given to, the grantee then or at some future time."* *Fiore* v. *Fiore,* 405 Pa. 303, 174 A.2d 858 (1961).

✓ Taxes on deeds

In many states there is a tax imposed on deeds either directly or indirectly. In a few states there is a direct tax on the transfer of title which is represented by the deed. In others the tax in reality is upon the gross or net receipts from the sale of the property but the deed is required to show evidence that the tax has been paid before it is eligible for recording; that is, the recordation is simply a convenient way of enforcing the collection of the tax. The federal tax which formerly applied has been allowed to lapse and there are presently no federal taxes on deeds.

Deed checklist

If a contract of sale of the real estate has .been executed, the deed should be checked to make certain that it complies in every respect with the terms of the contract. Usually, the contract will state the type of deed to be given. If a warranty deed is to be given, the contract should state the exceptions, reservations, and conditions, if any, to be included in the deed.

The following points should be carefully checked, so that errors and omissions will be avoided:

1. The name of the grantor should be checked for spelling.
   a. Be certain that the name is spelled and written exactly as it was spelled in the conveyance to the grantor.
   b. If the grantor is an organization, such as a corporation or a partnership, the deed should so state.
   c. If the grantor is a natural person, the deed should state his marital status—bachelor, spinster, widower, widow, divorced and not remarried.
   d. If a wife is cograntor with her husband, her Christian name is given—Helen Doe, not Mrs. John E. Doe.
   e. If the grantor is a woman who acquired the property as grantee under one name and then later married and is granting the

property under her married name, the deed should show both names—Helen Doe, formerly Helen Roe.

2. The residence—city or county and state—of the grantor should be given.

3. The proper words of grant should be used.

   a. If the document is a warranty deed, words of warranty should be used.

   b. If the instrument is a quitclaim deed, it should so state. Check the deed form against the contract of sale to be certain that the correct deed form has been used.

4. Check the deed to be certain that the name of the grantee or the names of the grantees are spelled correctly. It is best to write out at least one given name in full—John E. Doe or J. Edward Doe, not J. E. Doe.

5. If there are cograntees, the deed must state whether or not they take as joint tenants or as tenants in common.

   a. If they take as joint tenants, this should be clearly stated in language such as "joint tenants with right of survivorship, and not as tenants in common," or in similar wording.

   b. If the grantees are husband and wife, the deed should so state.

   c. In states in which husband and wife may hold property as tenants by the entirety, it is best to state in the deed "John E. Doe and Helen Doe, his wife, as tenants by the entirety, and that they so take," although this is not necessary in all states.

6. If the grantee is an organization, its nature should be indicated, and its official name should be used.

   a. If the grantee is a partnership, it is best to name the partners, stating that they are partners, followed by the name of the partnership, as, for instance, "John E. Doe and Amos G. Roe, copartners doing business as City China Company." This is generally necessary in states which have not adopted the Uniform Partnership Act or enacted a statute enabling a partnership to acquire and transfer real estate in the partnership name.

   b. If the grantee is a corporation, check its charter and spell its name exactly as spelled in the charter—do not write out abbreviations. If the charter name of the corporation is "Doe Bros., Inc.," use that name, not "Doe Brothers, Incorporated."

   c. If the grantee is a trustee, check the trust document and spell the trustee's name as it is spelled therein, and also identify the trust. (Deeds from and to trustees, and deeds creating trusts, involve many legal technicalities and should be handled only by competent attorneys.)

7. The residence of the grantee should be given.

8. The deed should state the consideration. In some states the true consideration must be stated; but in others a recital of consideration is sufficient, such as "consideration of one dollar and other good and sufficient consideration," or language of similar import.

9. A careful check of the description is of outstanding importance. If it is taken from a prior conveyance or from the caption of an abstract, two persons should cooperate in checking the description—one to read the former deed and the other to check the new deed.

   If the description is a new one, which is by metes and bounds or by monuments, courses, and distances, two persons should check the deed against the surveyor's notes—one to read the notes while the other checks the deed.

   Descriptions by reference to plats should be carefully checked against the plat—name or number of the plat; where recorded; and block and lot numbers, if divided into blocks and lots.

10. All exceptions, reservations, restrictions, and conditions provided for in the contract should be included in the deed.

    a. If the property is sold subject to a mortgage, the deed should so state, and the mortgage should be described—name of mortgagee, amount secured by mortgage, unpaid balance, and so forth, together with a statement of where the mortgage is recorded.

    b. If a purchase-money mortgage or trust deed is given by the grantee, the amount of the unpaid balance of the purchase price, together with the material provisions of the mortgage or trust deed, should be stated in the deed.

    c. If the property is sold subject to any other type of lien—judgment lien, mechanic's lien on real estate, and so on—it should be clearly described, and a notation as to where the lien is recorded or filed should be given.

    d. If the grantor has reserved certain rights in the real property sold (such as an easement, right of way), the right reserved should be described with the same particularity as one would use in an original description in a deed. (Some conveyancers prefer, instead of including reservations in deeds, to have the grantee execute a separate deed granting back to the grantor the reserved right.)

    e. Restrictions in deeds should be drafted only by an experienced and competent attorney (restrictions are discussed in Chapter 16).

    f. Conditions, like restrictions, in deeds should be drafted by an experienced and competent attorney. A poorly and improperly worded condition usually is the source of later expensive litigation.

11. Under the laws of some states the deed must include a clause waiving dower or homestead rights. The laws of the state in which the real estate is located control in this respect and consequently must be checked.

12. Although a date is not essential to the validity of a deed, it should be dated.

13. The grantor should write his name in signing the deed in exactly the same form as is used in the body of the deed. If the grantor's name is written John E. Doe in the deed, it should be signed John E. Doe, not J. Edward Doe.

14. The deed should be sealed, if such requirement is made by the statutes of the state in which the land is located. Deeds are usually sealed even though a seal is not required.

15. In some states the signatures of attesting witnesses are required. The statutes of the state in which the land is located should be checked; and if attesting witnesses are required, the requirements of the statute as to the form of attestation and the number of witnesses should be complied with.

16. The deed should be acknowledged. The form of acknowledgment required may be set out by the statutes of the state. However, such statutes are generally directive and not mandatory, and any complete form of acknowledgment is sufficient. Check the acknowledgment to be certain that the spelling of the grantor's name therein corresponds to the spelling in the body of the deed and in the signature. Also, check the signing and sealing, and the statement of the official capacity of the officer taking the acknowledgment.

17. If the laws of the state in which the real estate is located impose a tax, check to see if the tax has been paid and if the required evidence of payment has been obtained.

18. File the deed in the proper office for recording.

6

Acquisition of title by descent or devise

Acquisition by descent

HISTORICAL BACKGROUND

AT THE TIME the feudal system of land tenure was established in England by William the Conqueror, the title to all land was vested in the king, and the highest estate an individual could hold in land was a life estate. Since the life estate was granted by the king, the rights of the life tenant, on his death, reverted to the king, who could then, if he wished, grant a life estate in the reverted land to another of his choosing. In A.D. 1215 the nobles, under the Magna Carta, forced the king to permit their rights in the land they held to descend to their heirs and to recognize the privilege of disposing of property by will. Today, in the United States, all real estate is held as alodial land, that is, the owner owes no duties to an overlord or superior; yet some of the features of feudal ownership, such as the privilege of taking land by descent or disposing of it by will, still exist. If the owner of land dies without leaving heirs, his land escheats (reverts) to the state. Also, the right of the state and federal governments to impose inheritance and estate taxes on devolution of the deceased's property is a recognition of the concept that the taking of property by descent or will is a privilege, not an absolute right.

DISPOSITION OF DECEDENT'S PROPERTY

The owner of property may direct the disposition of his property on his death by executing a will. If a person dies leaving a will, he is said to die *testate*. If a person does not make a will, the property will descend on his death according to state statutes; his personal property will descend according to the statute of the state of his domicile, and his real estate will descend according to the statutes of the state in which the real estate is located. If a person dies without leaving a will, he is said to die *intestate*.

STATUTES OF DESCENT AND DISTRIBUTION

If a person dies intestate, the state, in effect, makes a will for him. Each state has enacted statutes which set out who will share in the property of deceased persons and the share each will take. As a supplement to the statutes of descent and distribution, each state has enacted statutes defining the rights of a surviving wife or husband in the estate of the deceased spouse, and these statutes will control in the distribution of the estate of a husband or wife who dies intestate.

RIGHTS TO REAL ESTATE OF INTESTATE

The title to the real estate of a person who dies intestate vests, by operation of law, in his heirs. For the purpose of maintaining an accurate record of real estate titles, there should be recorded a court order identifying the heirs. Who the heirs of the intestate are will be determined by reference to the statutes of descent and distribution of the state in which the real estate is located. Although these statutes are similar in their general provisions, they vary widely in detail.

Under these statutes the title to real estate owned by the intestate at the time of his death passes directly to his heirs. However, the heirs take subject to the prior rights of the creditors of the deceased. If the personal property of the deceased is insufficient when liquidated to pay all the debts of the deceased, his real estate may be sold and his unsatisfied debts paid from the proceeds of such sale.

RIGHTS OF SURVIVING SPOUSE

The surviving wife or husband and the children of the deceased are, in all states, given the best claim to the property of the deceased. The widow is generally entitled to a widow's allowance of a stated sum, such as $500 or $1,000, payable out of the personal property; but in many states, if the personal property is insufficient to pay the allowance, the allowance then becomes a charge against the real estate. In all states the widow either has dower rights in the deceased husband's real estate or is given rights in lieu of dower. About one half of the states have abolished common-law dower and instead give the widow one third or some other portion of the deceased husband's real estate in fee simple.

The widow's right in the deceased husband's real estate is generally prior to the claims of heirs and general creditors. It is subject to the right of purchase-money mortgagees and the rights of other mortgagees if the wife has joined the husband in the execution of the mortgage.

In some states, if the wife has predeceased the husband and the husband dies leaving minor children, the minor children are provided for.

A husband is generally given rights in the real estate of the wife if she dies, the husband surviving. In several states the husband takes in fee simple one third of the real estate owned by the wife at the time of her death. Generally, the husband takes subject to the prior rights of the general creditors of the deceased wife.

DETERMINATION OF HEIRS

In general, the heirs of a deceased person are his close blood relatives. Under the statutes of descent and distribution, such heirs are children, parents, brothers and sisters, uncles and aunts, and, in some states, first cousins of the deceased. They take in order of the closeness of the blood relationship and by representation or, in legal terminology, *per stirpes* (by the stock). More remote relatives each take an equal share or, in legal terminology, *per capita* (by the head).

For example, suppose John E. Doe has four sons—Henry, William, Charles, and Robert. Henry marries and has two children, Mary and Thomas. Henry dies before his father and leaves surviving him his wife and his two children. The father, John, then dies intestate. The estate of John will be divided into four equal shares. William, Charles, and Robert will each take one fourth of the estate. The remaining one fourth (Henry's share if living) will be divided equally between Henry's two children (Henry's representatives). Mary and Thomas will each take one half of one fourth of their grandfather's estate. Henry's wife will take nothing. Since she is an in-law not a descendant, she is not "of the stock."

If John had had no children, and if, at his death, his closest relatives had been third cousins, each third cousin would have taken an equal share under the laws of descent and distribution of most states. No attempt is made to trace back and determine the rights of remote relatives on the basis of representation. If the owner of real estate dies intestate and leaves no descendants, his real estate escheats (goes back) to the state in which it is located.

COMMON PLAN OF DISTRIBUTION

Although there is no uniformity in the statutes of descent and distribution of the states, they do follow a common plan. They start with the closer relationships and work through all possible combinations of a kinship to the more remote relationships, which are provided for as a class.

If there are close relatives, the remote relatives take nothing. For example, if a husband dies leaving a wife and children surviving, the wife and children, under the statutes of most states, take the entire estate. If a wife and one child survive, each usually takes one half of the estate. If a wife and two or more children survive, a common distribution is for the wife to take one third of the estate and the children to take the remaining two thirds, which will be divided equally among them, the descendants of a deceased child taking his or her share by representation. If a wife and no children or no representatives of a deceased child survive, a customary division is for the wife to take one half and the parents or brothers and sisters of the deceased to take equal shares in one half.

Provisions are made for adopted children. Usually, they take from the adopting parents, but not from the ancestors of adopting parents. Illegitimate children, as a general rule, take from the mother but not from the father, unless he has admitted parentage in writing, or unless parentage has been established by legal procedure. Provisions are also made for relatives of the half blood.

On May 26, 1956, Wilfred B. Sykes died, intestate and unmarried. His father and mother had predeceased him. He was survived by an aunt, Mary E. Connell, who was a sister of his father, on whose petition Elena L. Moore was appointed administratrix of his estate on June 5, 1956. The plaintiffs were cousins of the deceased. Some were children of a deceased brother of his mother, and others were children of a deceased sister of his mother.

On October 21, 1957, the judge of probate decreed that the balance of $14,463.97 in the hands of the administratrix on her final account be distributed to said aunt, Mary E. Connell, as the only heir-at-law of the estate. Coram *et al.,* the cousins, appealed. The order of the probate judge was affirmed.

Justice Lampron said: "It has been settled law in this jurisdiction for many years that under RSA 561:1, 6, an aunt takes to the exclusion of cousins. The decree of distribution made by the probate court is in conformity with this established principle and the denial of plaintiffs' petition by the Superior Court was proper." *Coram* v. *Connell,* 103 N.H. 26, 164 A.2d 251 (1960).

Wills

NATURE OF A WILL

In legal effect a will is a gratuitous conveyance of property, to take effect on the death of the testator. The right to so dispose of property is conferred by state statute; and if a will is to be effective, it must conform to statutory requirements as to its form and execution. It differs from a deed in that the latter conveys a present interest in property, whereas a will conveys no interest in the property until the death of the testator. A deed, if it is to be valid, must be delivered in the lifetime of the grantor. A will is not delivered but is left as part of the papers of the deceased.

CAPACITY TO MAKE A WILL

The age at which a person may make a will varies from state to state, but 18 years is the lawful age in most states. In some states a will disposing of personal property may be made at an earlier age than one disposing of real estate. And in some states a woman may make a will at an earlier age than a man. The statutes of the state in which the real estate is located control as to the disposition of real estate by will.

In all states the testator must be of sound mind at the time he executes the will. There is no arbitrary test of mental capacity to make a will. The standard generally applied takes into consideration the complexity of the testator's estate and his relation to persons who would be the natural recipients of his bounty.

In order to make a valid will, the testator, at the time he executes his will, must have sufficient mental capacity to know the natural objects of his bounty, to comprehend the kind and character of his property, to understand the nature and effect of his act, and to make a disposition of his property according to some plan formed in his mind.[1]

Mrs. Stitt, a woman about 65 years of age, entered the hospital on September 28, 1958, and executed her will on the evening of September 28, 1958. Immediately after signing the will, she underwent an operation from which she never

---

[1] *Meister et al.* v. *Finley et al.,* 208 Ore. 223, 300 P.2d 778.

recovered, and she died on October 28, 1958. By her will, she distributed her property among relatives, devising most of it to relatives of her husband who had predeceased her. Neighbors and tenants testified that during the last three years of her life she became coarse and profane; that she shrieked and screamed at all hours of the day and night; that she mistreated her brother and cursed him, although he diligently preformed his tasks around the house; and that she became utterly careless in her dress, took to wearing very little clothing, rarely combed her hair or bathed, and on occasion was indecently exposed in the presence of neighborhood children. They also testified to numerous other similar idiosyncrasies. The jury found that Mrs. Sitt was mentally incompetent to execute a will, and the judge entered a judgment for the proponents of the will, notwithstanding the verdict. On appeal, the judgment was affirmed.

Chief Justice Bernstein said: "This court has recognized two types of insanity which will vitiate a will. These are (1) insanity of such broad character as to establish mental incompetence generally, and (2) mental delusion which can be shown to have directly affected the dispository provisions of the will at the time of making.

"The rule is that even though a testator does suffer from delusions or hallucinations, unless the will itself was a creature or a product of such delusions or hallucinations it is not invalid.

"While in the instant case the contestants have put on much testimony of what they might consider delusions or hallucinations, they have not put on any testimony that the will was a creature or a product of the supposed delusions or hallucinations." *In re Stitt's Estate,* 93 Arix. 302, 380 P.2d 601 (1963).

KINDS OF WILLS

There are three kinds of wills recognized by the law: (1) formal or conventional will, (2) holographic or olographic will, and (3) nuncupative will.

The formal or conventional will is one drawn and executed in the usual manner. It is drafted and executed in strict compliance with the state statute dealing with the making of wills.

A holographic or olographic will is one written entirely in the handwriting of the testator and signed by him in his own handwriting. Such wills are not witnessed or attested. Under the statutes of several states, holographic wills are valid, provided they comply with the formal requirements of the statutes. The statute may require that the will, in order to be valid, must be dated in the handwriting of the testator and must be signed at the end thereof in his handwriting, or may make other similar requirements. As a general rule, a typewritten will is not a valid holographic will, even though the typing was done by the testator.[2]

A nuncupative will is an oral one. It exists when the testator makes to witnesses an oral declaration of his wishes in regard to the disposition of his estate. In those states which recognize the validity of nuncupative wills, the property which may be disposed of by such a will is limited to personal property, the value of which does not exceed a stated amount, usually a comparatively small sum. In addition, the witnesses must reduce the oral statements of the testator to writing within a relatively short period of time, generally not exceeding six months, after the date of the making of the declaration.

REQUIREMENTS FOR FORMAL WILL

As a general rule, a formal will, if it is to be a valid conveyance of real estate, must comply with all the statutory requirements of the state in which the real estate is located; and if the will is to be a valid conveyance of personal property, it must comply with the statutes of the state of domicile (residence) of the testator. However, the Uniform Wills Act, Foreign Execution (adopted by 13 states)[3] provides that a will executed according to the laws of either the state in which it is executed or the state of the domicile of the testator shall be valid in the state in which the property is located, even though it was not executed in accordance with the statutes of that state. Several states which have not adopted the Uniform Wills Act, Foreign Execution, have included similar provisions in their wills statutes.

The statutes of all the states require that the will be in writing and that it be signed by the testator, but differ in most other respects. Usually, witnesses are required; in some states the statutes provide that the testator must sign in the presence of the witnesses, and that the witnesses must sign in the presence of the testator and in the presence of each other.

Some states require the publication of the will; that is, the testator must declare to the witnesses that the instrument is his will. He does not have to disclose the provisions of the will.

The statutes of some states provide that the testator must sign at the end of the will; in other states the place of signing is not material.

Usually, an attestation clause will follow the signature of the testator.

[2] *In re Towle's Estate,* 14 Cal.2d 261, 93 P.2d 555.

[3] The Uniform Wills Act, Foreign Execution, has been replaced by the Model Execution of Wills Act, adopted by Tennessee (1957).

This clause states the facts concerning the publication, signing, and witnessing of the will. In most states, it is not required, and its omission does not affect the validity of the will.

Fred E. Palmer executed a will dated September 22, 1960. He died on January 4, 1961. His widow presented for probate a will dated October 14, 1960, and the contestants claimed that this will was not executed as required by statute and was invalid. One of the witnesses to the will testified that she did not see Fred E. Palmer sign the will dated October 14, 1960; that she did not see Fred E. Palmer, on the evening of October 14, 1960, while in his home; that Fred E. Palmer did not request her to sign his will as a witness; that Fred E. Palmer was not present when she signed as the witness; and that Fred E. Palmer never acknowledged his signature to her. The trial court held that the will was not witnessed as required by the wills statute and was invalid. On appeal, the judgment was affirmed.

Justice Snell said: "A will that is eligible for admission to probate must be shown to have been executed in conformity with the provisions of the statute. A testator must sign his will in the presence of the subscribing witnesses or he must acknowledge that the signature exhibited is his own.

"A will must be signed by two competent witnesses at the request of the testator. . . . A request may be implied from the acts of the testator or from the surrounding circumstances. It is not necessary that the testator declare to the subscribing witnesses that the instrument to which they have attached their name as witnesses is his will." *In re Palmer's Estate,* Iowa, 122 N.W.2d 920 (1963).

DESCRIPTION OF REAL ESTATE IN WILL

In a well-drafted will which disposes of real estate, the devisees are named, and the real estate devised is described with the same degree of precision as is used in drafting a deed to the property. However, the courts, in interpreting wills, have held the designation of the party and of the real estate devised to be sufficient if it is possible from the designation to identify the party and the real estate devised. For example, a provision in a will, "I give to my son my house in Newtown," would be held to be sufficient if the testator had only one son, and if the testator lived in or near a place called Newtown and owned a house there.

CODICIL

The alteration or amendment of an executed will by erasures, striking-out of clauses, interlineations, or other similar means is not permissible.

Any such change in a will renders it void. If the testator wishes to change any of the provisions in his will, he may add a codicil (little will) or execute a new will. If the will sets up complex trusts or disposes of an extensive estate and the testator wishes to make substantial changes, the better plan would be to have a new will drafted and executed; but if the desired change is minor, a codicil would serve the testator's purpose.

A codicil, in order to be valid, must be executed with the same formality as is required for the execution of a formal will. The codicil will be attached to and become a part of the original will of the testator. In the interpretation of the will the codicil will be treated as an integral part of the will.

REVOCATION OF WILL

The testator has complete control of his will during his lifetime and may revoke it or make any change in it whenever he so desires. A will may be revoked by the execution of a later will, the provisions of which are in conflict with those of an earlier will, or it may be revoked in part by the addition of a codicil which expressly revokes provisions of the will to which it is attached or which contains provisions in direct conflict with the provisions of the principal will. In drafting a will, a customary practice is to include a provision expressly revoking all prior wills and codicils heretofore executed by the testator.

The testator may revoke his will by destroying it, by mutilating it, by canceling his signature on it, or by any other overt act which clearly indicates his intention to revoke. The accidental destruction or mutilation of a will does not amount to a revocation, and in the event of an accidental destruction or mutilation the execution of the will and its provisions may be established by oral evidence or by producing and identifying a copy of the will or notes from which the will was drafted or by other admissible evidence offered to prove a lost or destroyed document. A declaration of intention to revoke a will unaccompanied by the performance of some overt act of revocation is ineffective.

Under the statutes of some states, if the testator is unmarried at the time he executes his will and is married thereafter, the will is revoked, whereas in other states the will is not revoked unless a child is born to the marriage.

A failure to mention a child of the testator in a will does not revoke the will, but a few courts have held that there is a presumption in such a case that the child was forgotten and therefore takes the share of the parent's estate to which he would be entitled under the statutes of descent and distribution. A parent is not obligated to make a devise to a child, and a mention of the child without making a devise to him is sufficient to prevent the operation of the presumption that he was forgotten.

LIMITATIONS ON DISPOSITION BY WILL

In all states a husband cannot dispose of all his property and leave his wife nothing. The wife is given certain statutory rights in the husband's property; the husband cannot, by leaving a will, deprive her of those rights. If the husband makes some provision for his wife in his will and it is clear that he intends these provisions to be in lieu of her statutory rights and not in addition to them, the wife has the right to elect to take either under the statute or under the will.

In some states a testator is limited as to the portion of his estate he may will to charity, particularly if he leaves children surviving him.

PROBATING THE WILL

The probating of a will is the formal proving of the will in a court having jurisdiction over such matters. In most—but not all—states, there is a separate court having jurisdiction over the administration of decedents' estates. These courts are designated by various names in the different states, such as probate court, surrogate's court, and orphans' court.

The procedure to be followed is set out by the state statutes and varies from state to state. In general, the executor or some person interested in the estate presents the will for probate. One or more of the attesting witnesses verify under oath the fact that the will was executed and that the testator was of sound mind, and other facts relative to the validity of the will. Usually, the names and addresses of persons who would inherit if the testator had died intestate are filed with the clerk of the court, and notice of the probating of the will is given to each. If the judge finds that the will has been executed in compliance with the laws of the state, he will order it admitted for probate.

CONTESTING THE WILL

Any person who has an interest in the estate of the testator may contest the will. Interested persons are heirs who would take under the statutes of descent and distribution, and all beneficiaries under the will. A will may be set aside on any of the following grounds: improper execution, minority, lack of mental capacity, duress, fraud, undue influence, or forgery. The statutes of the state will set out the procedure to be followed in contesting a will.

ADMINISTRATION OF DECEDENT'S ESTATE

The administration of a decedent's estate normally involves collection and management of the assets of the estate; proof and payment of claims; determination of the rights of heirs and next of kin, if there is no will; if there is a will, determination of the rights of legatees and devisees under the will; and final distribution of the estate. In addition, estate and inheritance taxes must be determined and paid.

If the deceased has left a will naming an executor who is willing and qualified to serve, he will be appointed by the court to administer the estate. If the deceased dies intestate, or if he does not name an executor in his will, the court will, on proper petition, appoint an administrator. Under the laws of most states a surviving spouse with capacity to act has the right to be appointed administrator.

After the executor or administrator has been duly appointed and has filed the required bond, he takes possession of the assets of the estate, inventories them, and has them appraised. The procedure to be followed and the powers of an administrator will be set out in the statutes of the state. The procedure to be followed by an executor will be set out in the statutes of the state, but his powers will generally be set out in the will. However, a will cannot confer on an executor powers the exercise of which would be a violation of state statutes.

EFFECT OF ADMINISTRATION ON TITLE TO REAL ESTATE

If a person dies intestate, title to his real estate passes to his heirs. The administration of his estate has no effect on the vesting of title. The heirs own the real estate as tenants in common, and they have all the rights in the property that the deceased ancestor had. The advantage of probation is that the title to real estate can be cleared in a shorter period of time. When the estate is probated, the rights of creditors are determined and cut off within a relatively short period of time—six months to one year; whereas if there is no probating, the statute of limitations on creditors' rights must run, and the time is much longer—usually five to seven years, depending on the statutes of the state. Moreover, unpaid taxes are a lien on the assets of the estate, and the statute of limitations on taxes is ten years.

The primary purpose for estate administration is to see that the decedent's debts, including taxes generated by the fact of his death, are paid. The residue of the estate is then distributed either to his legal heirs or to those beneficiaries designated in a valid will. It is apparent therefore, that it may be necessary in some estates to sell the decedent's real estate and other property in order to make cash with which to pay debts, taxes, and the costs of administration. It is quite possible then that the heirs or beneficiaries will not in fact obtain possession of the real estate. Clearly, the quality of title which the heirs and beneficiaries have during the period of administration of the estate is very questionable.

SALES DURING ESTATE ADMINISTRATION

In the event that it is necessary or desirable to sell real estate belonging to the decedent during the administration of his estate recourse must be had to the probate law of the state in which the real estate is located. Since, as a general rule, the heirs or beneficiaries have title subject to the possibility of sale to pay debts it is necessary to follow some degree of formality in order to be sure that the sale carries with it all of the outstanding interests in the land. The safe and sure method of accomplishing this is a formal court proceeding with proper notice to all parties. This may be quite cumbersome and time consuming and the quality of title will be no better than the decedent had at his death plus the fact that the warranties in an administrator's or executor's deed may be either very limited or nonexistent. Sales or purchases of property from a decedent's estate should therefore never be undertaken without competent legal counsel.

CONCLUSION

The probate system in the United States has been under heavy attack in recent years. Its critics insist that the process is costly and time consuming out of all proportion to its benefits. On the other hand it should be clearly understood what is actually happening: the disposition of one's property to his creditors and heirs when he is not alive to defend himself from claims that may not be valid, taxes that he might feel are unjustified and gifts to those he might not wish to benefit. To safeguard the decedent and his family the probate system has created a wealth of formality to ensure proper distribution of the estate. Many of these formalities may no longer be necessary and the thrust of the probate reform movement has been to streamline and shorten the probate process by eliminating those which have outlived their usefulness. New legislation in the form of the Uniform Probate Code has become law in several states and is under serious consideration in several other states. Whether probate law will ever become uniform throughout the United States is very questionable but some degree of general probate reform to streamline estate administration and minimize its costs seems to be inevitable.

7

Acquisition of title by adverse possession

Doctrine of adverse possession

HISTORICAL BACKGROUND

THE DOCTRINE of adverse possession is based on a presumption of a lost grant. The courts, in the application of the presumption of a lost grant, have followed the reasoning of Justice Story and Chancellor Kent, who declared that it is an ancient and settled doctrine that the presumption of a grant to land will be adopted because of the infirmity of human nature, the difficulty of preserving monuments of title, and the public policy of supporting long and uninterrupted possession. The permitting of a person to acquire title to land under the doctrine of presumption of a grant or under the statutes of limitations (adverse possession) is supported by considerations of public policy, such as, for instance, the encouragment of the use of the land, and by the desirability of preventing a claimant from delaying action until documents are lost and witnesses have died.

There is a distinction between establishing title to land under the doctrine of the presumption of a lost grant and under the statutes of limitations, but the results are substantially the same. The courts have held, however, that an adverse claimant may establish title to land against the state under the doctrine or presumption of a lost grant but not under the statutes of limitations.[1]

---

[1] *McCain* v. *Wilson,* 176 Ark. 1205, 5 S.W.2d 338.

160

STATUTES OF LIMITATIONS

A statute of limitations was first enacted by Parliament in England in A.D. 1275, and similar statutes have been enacted in all of the states in the United States. These statutes are, however, not uniform in their requirements. In general, the statutes of limitations now in force set out various time limits within which a claimant must bring his action if he is to recover the property in controversy. The time limit depends on circumstances defined in the statute. For example, the Indiana statute of limitations provides that an action for the recovery of real property sold on execution and bought by the execution debtor, his heirs, or any person claiming under him, must be brought within ten years after sale. The time limit for recovery of real property sold by executors, administrators, guardians, and so forth is five years; and that on mortgages (with designated exceptions), on deeds of trust, on judgments of courts of record, and for the possession of real estate is ten years. The statute further provides that the adverse claimant must have paid the taxes and assessments falling due on the land.

REAL ESTATE WHICH MAY BE ACQUIRED BY ADVERSE POSSESSION

In general, real estate owned by the United States or a state, or owned by a subdivision of the state or a municipality, if such real estate is used for public purposes, cannot be acquired by adverse possession.[2] Under the statutes of some states, real estate owned by a county, township, school district, municipality, park commission, or similar governmental agency, if such real estate is not used for governmental purposes, can be acquired by adverse possession. Also, in some states in which there are no specific statutory provisions regarding the acquisition of such real estate by adverse possession, the courts have held that it may be acquired by adverse possession. The statutes of a few states provide that real estate owned by a religious organization cannot be acquired by adverse possession.[3]

WHO MAY ACQUIRE TITLE BY ADVERSE POSSESSION

As a general rule, any person who has the capacity to own real estate can acquire title to real estate by adverse possession. This includes natural

---

[2] *Steele* v. *Fowler, Mayor et al.,* 111 Ind. App. 364, 41 N.E.2d 678.

[3] *Davis* v. *Union Meeting House Society,* 93 Vt. 520, 108 A. 704.

persons (whether infants or adults), corporations, religious societies, states, the United States, and other governmental units.[4]

The holdings of the courts are not in accord as to the right of an alien or of a nonresident or foreign corporation to acquire title to real estate by adverse possession. Some courts hold that they may; other courts hold that they may not.

Requirements for acquisition by adverse possession

GENERAL REQUIREMENTS

Before a person can obtain title to real estate by adverse possession, the possession must be (1) actual, (2) open and notorious, (3) exclusive, (4) continuous and uninterrupted, (5) with claim of right, and (6) for the statutory period. In addition to these requirements, the statutes of some states require the payment of taxes by the adverse possessor.

POSSESSION

Actual possession, in general, consists of the exercise of positive physical acts of dominion or ownership over the land. Actual possession is composed of both act and intention; that is, before a person can acquire actual possession, his intention to hold the land must be indicated by some act.

Casual, isolated, or occasional acts of ownership are not sufficient to establish actual possession. Although the person need not establish his residence on the land, he must occupy the land and use it for the purposes for which it is reasonably suited. Under the statutes of a few states the claimant must fence or enclose the tract which he claims; but mere fencing or enclosing, without use, is generally not sufficient to establish actual possession.

Although the making of improvements or the cultivation of the land are not necessary to establish actual possession, they are generally sufficient. The mere taking of the natural products of the land, such as cutting timber, cutting grass which grows wild, tapping sugar trees, or taking sand, gravel, or stone, is not sufficient to establish actual possession.[5]

---

[4] *Trustees of University of South Carolina* v. *City of Columbia,* 108 S.C. 244, 93 S.E. 934.

[5] *West Virginia Pulp & Paper Co.* v. *Cone,* 153 F.2d 576.

Personal occupation by the adverse claimant is not necessary. He may hold possession through his agent, servant, licensee, trustee, or tenant.[6]

Whytock and Green owned adjoining lots. The lot owned by Whytock adjoined the lot owned by Green on the west. In 1920 the predecessors in title to the Green lot had built on the west side of their lot a driveway which led to a garage. A cement curb was built on the west side of the driveway. This driveway was used by Green and his predecessors. In 1951, Whytock had his lot surveyed, and it was disclosed that the driveway and garage encroached on his lot 3 feet $9\frac{1}{2}$ inches at the south end of the lot and 2 feet 6 inches at the north end. The encroachment extended 140 feet in length. Whytock started to erect a fence on the lot line, but Green brought this action, claiming this strip of land by adverse possession. Whytock conceded that Green had acquired the land on which the garage stood but claimed that Green and his predecessors in title had not been in exclusive possession of the driveway strip. The court held that Green had acquired title to the disputed strip by adverse possession.

Justice Berry said: "The construction of this curb and its continued duration can be construed as open, notorious and exclusive exercise of dominion, claim, and ownership of the strip of land in dispute by plaintiffs [Green] as opposed and adverse to that of defendants [Whytock]. . . . The law does not attempt to list all of the acts of dominion which may constitute such possession, so that which constitutes adverse possession, like the question of what constitutes negligence, often depends upon the circumstances of the particular case, as measured by the judgment of reasonable men. It has been said that such determination in a given case must largely depend upon the situation of the parties, the size and extent of the land, and the purpose for which it is adapted." *Whytock* v. *Green,* Okla., 383 P.2d 628 (1963).

OPEN AND NOTORIOUS POSSESSION

No precise statement can be made as to the particular acts which are required to establish open and notorious possession. The question of whether there is open and notorious possession must be determined from the facts of the particular case under consideration. Usually, the acts must be of such a nature that the public in general, and the people in the neighborhood in particular, will know that the land is in the exclusive use and enjoyment of the claimant. The acts required are such as an owner of the land would ordinarily perform in the appropriation of the land and its products to his own use.

---

[6] *Howell et al.* v. *Baskins,* 213 Ark. 665, 212 S.W.2d 353.

The courts consistently hold that a person purchasing land takes subject to the rights of the person in possession of the land. As a general rule, there is nothing on the record of title to the land to put the owner, the purchaser, the mortgagee, or the public on notice that the land is claimed by an adverse possessor. Consequently, the courts have held that the claimant's acts, in order to satisfy the requirement of open and notorious possession, must be of such a nature that a person of ordinary prudence inspecting the land would be aware that the land was in the possession of someone claiming rights in it.[7]

In 1943, Rall negotiated with Martin, attorney for Christ Church, for the purchase of the land in controversy. An agreement was reached, and Rall paid the agreed purchase price, but a deed to the land was never executed by the Church and delivered to Rall. There were no buildings on the land, and it was not fenced. Rall arranged with Richterberg to work the land as a tenant on a share-crop basis; and during the period from 1943 to 1961, crops of wheat and milo were raised, trees were set out, bindweed were killed with chemicals, and the land was improved by plowing. At times, cattle were pastured on the land, and an electric fence was installed. No one lived on the farm. Rall paid all taxes assessed on the land from 1943 to 1961. Christ Church tendered the taxes for 1962. In 1961, Rall sold and deeded the farm to Richterberg, and this action was brought by Richterberg against Christ Church to obtain a decree adjudging Richterberg the owner of the land. The court held that Rall acquired title by adverse possession and that this title was conveyed to and vested in Richterberg.

District Judge Daughterty said: "To establish adverse possession of land the claimant need not actually reside upon it or have it inclosed with a fence but it is sufficient if claimant is doing such acts thereon that indicate in an open, public, visible manner that he has exclusive control over the land under a claim of right to such exclusive possession." *Richterberg* v. *Wittich Memorial Church,* 222 F. Supp. 324 (1963).

EXCLUSIVE POSSESSION

To acquire title by adverse possession, the claimant must hold possession for himself to the exclusion of all other claimants. Two or more adverse claimants cannot hold exclusive possession at the same time. A claimant who holds with the title owner or a tenant of the title owner is not in exclusive possession of the property.[8]

---

[7] *La Caze* v. *Boycher,* La. App., 80 So.2d 583.

[8] *Oliver* v. *Thomas,* 173 Neb. 36, 112 N.W.2d 525.

CONTINUOUS POSSESSION

The possession of the adverse claimant, if he is to acquire title by adverse possession, must be continuous and uninterrupted for the entire statutory period. This does not mean that the claimant must be on the land every day during the period, but it does mean that he must use the land for the purpose for which it is reasonably adapted, without interruption of such use.

If land is reasonably adapted for a seasonal use, the use of the land each season without skipping a season would be considered as continuous and uninterrupted possession. For example, if the land is reasonably adapted to pasturing and the adverse claimant uses the land each year during the grazing season for the statutory period, he will have been in continuous and uninterrupted possession of the land for the statutory period.[9]

This controversy involves a parcel of land built up as an accretion to upland in the form of a peninsula with its base on the boundary of land owned by Springer and extending past Durette's land but separated therefrom by a slough. Springer's land was managed by his agent Pearmine and was occupied by either Pearmine or a tenant. The peninsula was used as pasture by the occupants of the Springer farm from April to November for a period in excess of twenty years; and during this period, Pearmine, as agent of Springer, had cut and sold timber from the disputed tract. The land was not fenced, but the river and slough formed a natural fence. The court held that Springer had acquired title to the entire tract by adverse possession, and Durette appealed. The judgment was affirmed.

Justice O'Connell said: "The fact that the land was used for grazing only during the period from April to November does not preclude the claim on the ground of lack of continuity. As stated in 3 American Law of Property § 15.3, p. 767, 'possession may exist in a person who uses the land in the way in which an average owner of the particular type of property would use it though he does not reside on it and his use involves considerable intervals in which the land is not actually used at all.'

"We find ample support for our conclusion that by his conduct in grazing cattle on the land in question the claimant has satisfied the requirement of physical possession.

"The intent with which the occupant holds possession is normally determined by what he does upon the land. Where the land is used in the manner that an owner would use it there is a presumption that the possession is adverse.

"It is not necessary for us to decide under what circumstances a tenant's

---

[9] *Kellogg* v. *Huffman,* 137 Cal. App. 278, 30 P.2d 593.

possession is sufficient to establish title by adverse possession in the landlord, because we are of the opinion that the plaintiff proved that the Pearmines were the agents and not the tenants of the Springers. The rule is clear that the possession of the agent is the possession of the principal for the purpose of acquiring title by adverse possession." *Springer* v. *Durette*, 217 Ore. 196, 342 P.2d 132 (1959).

TACKING

An adverse claimant, as soon as he takes possession of the land, acquires property rights in it which are enforceable against all persons except the true owner. These rights may be conveyed to another in the same manner as other rights in real estate are conveyed. If an adverse claimant, before he has been in possession of the land for the statutory period, passes his rights in the land to another and that person takes immediate possession, he will be required to retain possession only for the balance of the statutory period. This is known as *tacking*.

Tacking will be permitted only if privity of estate exists—that is, if the claimant of the land acquired the rights of the prior adverse claimant by grant, devise, descent, or judicial decree. If an adverse claimant abandons the land and another adverse claimant takes possession immediately, there can be no tacking, since no privity of estate exists.

The courts have held that privity of estate exists even though the land in dispute was not included in the description in the deed, if the parties understood that the disputed tract was included in the conveyance. For example, suppose that Adam claims all of a tract of land up to a cliff, but the description in the deed conveying the land to Adam does not include part of the land claimed. Then, after Adam has been in possession of the land for less than the statutory period, he conveys it to Bell and uses the same description in the deed to Bell as was used in the deed to Adam, both Adam and Bell believing that the description included the land up to the cliff. Bell would acquire Adam's rights as adverse possessor of the land not included in the description in the deed.[10]

Eli Jacobs took possession of the land in controversy in 1900. After the death of Eli Jacobs, Bill Graham, husband of Susanna Jacobs, daughter of Eli Jacobs, took possession of the land. Susanna predeceased Bill Graham, who held possession of the land until his death, when his heirs took possession and held it until they conveyed the land to D. J. Jacobs, who took possession at the time of the conveyance and has held possession since that time. During

---

[10] *Cooper et al.* v. *Tarpley et al.,* 112 Ind. App. 1, 41 N.E.2d 640.

the time Eli Jacobs and his descendants held the land, they raised tobacco on it, erected a sawmill, cut crossties and timber, and otherwise utilized the land as any owner would. International Paper Company claimed the land by virtue of paper title. Jacobs claimed the land by adverse possession. International Paper Company contended that Jacobs had not held the land for the statutory period of 20 years. The court held that Jacobs was the owner of the land.

Justice Rodman said: "To establish possession for the requisite twenty years, it was, as the court charged, permissible to tie the possession of an ancestor to that of the heir when there was no hiatus or interruption in the possession. As said by Johnson, J., in Newkirk v. Porter '. . . the adverse possession of an ancestor may be cast by descent upon his heirs and tacked to their possession for the purpose of showing title by adverse possession.' " *International Paper Company* v. *Jacobs,* 258 N.C. 439, 128 S.E.2d 818 (1963).

CLAIM OF OWNERSHIP

Possession without claim of ownership will not give the claimant title by adverse possession. The essence of adverse possession is hostile possession—that is, the party claims that he has the absolute right to possession of the property and that he does not hold in subordination to the rights of the true owner or any other person. He holds not under, but in opposition to, the title to which his possession is alleged to be adverse.

If the claimant is in possession under a license or permission, his possession cannot ripen into title by adverse possession. The possession of the claimant must be with the intent to appropriate and use the land as his own to the exclusion of all others. The claimant need not have a deed or color of title on which to base his claim of ownership, and he need not notify the title owner of record of his intention to claim ownership of the land. All that is necessary for one to establish hostile possession is that he take possession of the land and use it in the manner in which an owner would use the land, and that he perform those acts which make it apparent that he is claiming ownership of the land.[11]

COLOR OF TITLE

An instrument constitutes color of title if it purports to be a conveyance of title and is defective or void for matters not shown on the record of title. To establish title by adverse possession, the grantee in a defective or void deed must take possession of the real estate and hold it in open

---

[11] *Guaranty Title & Trust Corporation* v. *United States,* 44 S. Ct. 252, 264 U.S. 200.

and notorious possession continuously for the statutory period. The fact that the adverse claimant took possession under color of title is strong evidence that he claims title and that his possession is hostile. Under the statutes of several states a person who takes possession under color of title and pays the taxes can acquire title in a shorter period of time than one taking without color of title. Color of title, in the absence of a contrary statute, is not an essential element of the acquisition of title by adverse possession.

STATUTORY PERIOD

At common law the statutory period within which the owner could bring an action to recover land that was being held adversely was 20 years. In the United States the period for bringing an action to recover land held adversely is controlled by the statutes of the state in which the land is located. The predominant period is 20 years; however, a number of states have set a shorter period. In some states, one period is set which applies generally, and a shorter period is set which applies if the adverse claimant entered under color of title or has paid the taxes.

PAYMENT OF TAXES

The payment of taxes is not an essential element of the acquisition of title by adverse possession, unless expressly made so by the statute. Several states have enacted statutes that make the payment of each year's taxes by the adverse claimant an essential element for acquisition of title by adverse possession. Whether or not the claimant has fulfilled the requirements of the statute is a matter of statutory construction.

The statutes of some states provide for a shorter period for the acquisition of title by adverse possession if the claimant pays the taxes. Payment of taxes by the claimant is strong evidence that his possession is hostile.

CONSTRUCTIVE ADVERSE POSSESSION

As a general rule, a claimant acquires title only to the land which he occupies adversely.[12] However, under the concept of constructive adverse possession, a claimant who enters under color of title and takes actual possession of part of the land described in his muniment of title,

---

[12] *Coslin* v. *Crossett Company,* 233 Ark. 13, 342 S.W.2d 303.

but claims ownership to the entire description, can acquire title to the entire tract described in his muniment of title.[13]

TITLE ACQUIRED BY ADVERSE CLAIMANT

When an adverse claimant has satisfied all of the requirements of the statute of limitations, he not only bars any remedy for the recovery of possession which the holder of the title of record may have, but he acquires a perfect title to the real property which the courts will not permit to be disturbed. The title acquired by the adverse claimant must correspond with that on which his adverse possession operated. If he took possession under color of title, he will, in the absence of special circumstances, acquire title to the lands described in the deed under which he claims ownership; whereas if he does not take under color of title, he acquires a fee in only that land which he has occupied.

A title acquired by adverse possession is a title in fee simple[14] as perfect as though it was acquired by a conveyance. It cannot be divested by legislative enactment after it has been established, but only by written conveyance, by tax sale, or by another adverse claimant. Whether a purchaser from an adverse claimant who has satisfied the statutory requirements for obtaining title but has not yet established his title of record would be required to accept such title as a merchantable title is questionable. If the contract of purchase provided that the title must be good title of record or title satisfactory to the buyer or his attorney, the buyer would not be bound to assume the risk of establishing title by adverse possession.

ACQUISITION AGAINST CO-OWNERS, TENANTS, ETC.

If property is owned by two or more persons as co-owners, possession of one co-owner is deemed the possession of all; and the co-owner in possession cannot acquire title to the property by adverse possession unless he clearly evidences his intention to hold exclusively, which he may do by direct communication or by his acts.

Likewise, a tenant, licensee, or other person who holds permissively cannot acquire title by adverse possession unless he denies the rights of the person under whom he first acquired permissive possession, and either communicates his intention to such person and thereafter holds possession

[13] *McBeth et al.* v. *Wetnight,* 57 Ind. App. 47, 106 N.E. 407.

[14] *Meyers* v. *Canutt et al.,* 242 Iowa 692, 46 N.W.2d 72.

under claim of ownership, or so acts that his intent to hold adversely is brought forcefully to the attention of that person.

DISABILITIES

The statutes fixing the period for adverse possession usually contain a clause providing that the statute does not run against persons under stated disabilities. The persons usually protected by such provisions are infants; insane persons; married women who, under the laws of the state, do not have capacity to bring suit; and persons in prison. Under some statutes, the running of the statute is suspended during the period of disability; under others the person under disability is given a stated period after the removal of the disability in which to bring an action to recover the land which is being held adversely.

MODERN APPLICATIONS

Today, with the relative scarcity of vacant land, the classic case of "taking" another's property by adverse possession seldom occurs. Nevertheless, the doctrine is viable and quite useful as a means for settling boundary disputes and quieting title where there has been a long-standing encroachment. Modern surveying techniques frequently bring to light troublesome encroachments by old buildings and adverse possession can frequently be used to confirm title in the owner of the building. In the absence of statute, however, the doctrine of adverse possession does not apply against a governmental unit. Therefore, encroachments upon city property (such as an alley) by a building cannot be cured by adverse possession. In such cases there is usually available legislation which can be used to obtain such property from the city or obtain a so-called license to encroach.

8

Recording and evidence of title

Recording

PURPOSE OF RECORDING

THE PURPOSE of recording real estate transactions is to provide a systematic and efficient way of transferring title to real estate. The general rule that a person can acquire no better title to property than that held by his grantor applies to real property. However, the equally well-established rule that an innocent purchaser for value takes free from outstanding equities also applies.

At common law, no public records of titles or rights in land were kept. When land was sold, the grantor delivered to the grantee all the deeds, mortgages, discharges of mortgages, and so forth, which affected the title to the real estate. A lost or destroyed instrument presented a serious problem, since its absence resulted in a break in the chain of title. Under this system, if an owner of real estate had deeded or mortgaged the property to one person and then, at a later time, deeded or mortgaged the same property to another, who took as an innocent purchaser for value, the subsequent purchaser or mortgagee acquired no greater rights than those held by the grantor or mortgagor.

The rule that a person takes subject to notice of the rights of the person in possession provides some protection to a grantee if he takes possession of the property purchased, but it provides no protection to a mortgagee or to a person who purchases land which is unoccupied.

171

All of the states have enacted recording statutes which provide for the maintaining of a permanent public record of land titles and all interests in land. An unrecorded instrument is void as to an innocent purchaser or mortgagee for value, or as to other persons who have, for value and without notice or knowledge of the outstanding interest, acquired rights in the land. The recording of an instrument, as provided by the statutes, is notice to all persons of the contents of the instrument and rights created thereby.

Recording of an instrument conveying an interest in real estate has no effect on the validity of that instrument. The sole purpose of recording such an instrument is to give public notice of the right conveyed by it. If Arthur deeds or mortgages real estate to Bert, Bert acquires, on the execution and delivery of the deed or mortgage, a title to or a lien on the real estate. Recording is not required to perfect Bert's rights in the real estate and, as between Arthur and Bert, has no effect on the interest acquired by Bert.

RECORDING STATUTES

Although the recording statutes of the states are not uniform, they are alike in their major provisions. In general, they provide for the recording of instruments which affect the title to real estate. All titles to land within a county are recorded in an office located within the county, indexes of recorded instruments are kept, prerequisites for the recording of instruments are set up, the types of instruments eligible to record are defined, and the parties whose rights are affected by recording are designated.

Under the provisions of the recording statutes, a person buying real estate, or loaning money and taking a mortgage on real estate, takes with notice of all outstanding interests affecting the title if the existence of such interests would be disclosed by a careful examination of the records. The recording of an instrument properly executed, eligible for recording, and, in most states, filed for record is notice to the public of all matters contained therein. As was stated previously, the purpose of recording is to give notice. If a person has notice or knowledge of an existing interest in real estate, he is bound thereby, and recording becomes immaterial.

M. G. Austin, on August 27, 1953, had two deeds prepared, granting certain land to his son Butler and other land to his son Oliver. Oliver was present at the time the deeds were prepared and executed, and knew their contents. On October 29, 1953, M. G. Austin had a third deed prepared which granted to Oliver part of the land granted to Butler in the deed of August 27, 1953. The deed of October 29, 1953, was recorded immediately after its execution, but the deed of August 27, 1953, was not recorded until December 28, 1953. The court held that the fact that the deed of October 29, 1953, was recorded before the deed of August 27, 1953, in no way affected Butler's rights acquired under such deed.

Justice Holt said: "It is undisputed in this case that Oliver had actual notice and knowledge of his father's deed, dated August 27, 1953, to Butler when Oliver, as grantee, took the later deed, dated October 29, 1953. Butler was unaware of the execution of the deeds on August 27 and October 29 until after they were made. Since Oliver had notice of a prior unrecorded deed to his brother at the time the October deed to him was executed and recorded, Oliver was in the same legal position as if Butler's deed were actually recorded." *Austin* v. *Austin,* Ark., 372 S.W.2d 231 (1963).

PREREQUISITES FOR RECORDING.   An instrument, in order to be eligible for recording, must be drawn and executed in conformity with the provisions of the recording statutes of the state in which the real estate is located. The prerequisites for recording are not uniform. In nearly all states the instrument must be acknowledged before a notary public or other officer with authority to take acknowledgements. Some states provide that the instrument must be attested; and some states, in addition to the acknowledgment, require that the instrument be witnessed by one or more witnesses. In some states a local transfer tax must be paid on deeds and mortgages before they are eligible for recording.

The courts are not in accord as to the effect of the recording of an instrument which does not comply with all the statutory prerequisites. The majority of the courts hold that the recording of an instrument that does not comply with the statutory requirements is notice to no one.[1]

Some states have enacted curative statutes validating defective acknowledgements; under them, the instrument is to be regarded as being properly acknowledged if third-party rights have not intervened.

INSTRUMENTS ENTITLED TO RECORDING

Instruments which are eligible for recording will be set out in the statutes of the state in which the real estate is located. In all the states the statutes provide for the recording of deeds, mortgages, assignments of mortgages, discharges of mortgages, and release of liens. Usually,

---

[1] *Haverell Distributors* v. *Haverell Mfg. Corp.,* 115 Ind. App. 501, 58 N.E.2d 372.

provision is also made for the recording of land contracts, long-term (three years or over) leases on real estate, and notice of mechanics' liens on real estate; and in some states a miscellaneous record is kept, in which are recorded unclassified instruments which affect the title to real estate. In those states which have adopted the Uniform Commercial Code, provision is made for the recording or filing of security interests in goods which are, or are to become, fixtures; and in those states in which the Uniform Conditional Sales Act or similar legislation is in force, provision is made for the recording of conditional sales of personal property which is so attached to or used with real estate that it becomes a fixture.

As a general rule, only original instruments are entitled to be recorded, not copies or abstracts of instruments; and if an instrument is recorded when it is not entitled to recordation under the statutes of the state, the recording is of no effect. It is notice to no one.[2]

Six persons owned, as tenants in common, a tract of timberland. McLeod, one of the six owners, executed a contract whereby he convenanted to convey the timber on the tract to Cameron. This contract was recorded. Later, the remaining owners deeded the timber to Chandler. Cameron contended that since his agreement with McLeod was recorded, Chandler took with notice of his (Cameron's) rights. The court held that the McLeod-Cameron instrument was not eligible to record and was notice to no one.

Justice Ervin said: "We conclude, therefore, that the registration of the agreement did not give Chandler constructive notice of the existence or terms of the purely personal contract on the part of McLeod to convey to Cameron the interest in the timber which McLeod did not originally own. This is true because the record of an instrument 'does not constitute constructive notice, if it is not of a class which is authorized or required by law to be recorded.' Our conclusion is not affected in any way by the fact that the contract to convey, and the personal contract were both embodied in the same instrument because the registration of an instrument 'operates as constructive notice only when the statute authorizes its registration; and then only to the extent of those provisions which are within the registration statute.' " *Chandler* v. *Cameron,* 229 N.C. 62, 47 S.E.2d 528 (1948).

LIENS THAT NEED NOT BE RECORDED

Real estate tax liens, inheritance tax liens, franchise tax liens, and similar liens held by a governmental unit need not be recorded and are valid liens on the real estate, although not recorded.

---

[2] *Dreifus* v. *Marx,* 40 Cal. App.2d 461, 104 P.2d 1080.

WHERE INSTRUMENT IS RECORDED

The instrument must be recorded in a designated office located in the county in which the land is located. In some states a separate county office, in charge of a county officer, is established. The officer in charge is known by a variety of titles, such as county recorder, register of deeds, recorder of deeds, and registrar of deeds. In some states the county clerk or a clerk of the court is in charge of the records, and in Alabama the probate judge keeps the records.

WHEN INSTRUMENT IS RECORDED

An instrument which is eligible to record is generally held to be recorded when it has been deposited with and accepted by the authorized officer for recordation and when the statutory recording fee has been paid.[3] Generally, it is the duty of the recording officer, when he receives the instrument, to endorse thereon the date, hour, and minute it was received in his office for filing or recording, as the case may be.

HOW INSTRUMENT IS RECORDED

The statutes usually require that the instrument be recorded at length and in *haec verba* (exact words). No particular method of recording is necessary. Any method which carries out the purpose of the statutes, that is, gives the instrument publicity and perpetuity, and meets the requirements of accuracy and durability, is sufficient.[4] The early records consisted of handwritten copies of recorded instruments. Today, in some counties, the records consist of typewritten copies of instruments. In other counties, form pages are used, and the blanks are filled in. In the more populous counties the records consist of photostatic copies of instruments.

In addition to the recording of instruments, the statutes generally require the indexing of recorded instruments. The purpose of the index is to enable a person to find any recorded instrument he may wish to examine. The statutes may define in detail what indexes must be kept, or they may merely provide that adequate indexes shall be kept.

Two types of indexes are in use: the cross index and the tract index. In the cross index of names, the type of index in general use, the names of the parties to the instrument are listed in alphabetical order. The names of grantors, mortgagors, and so forth, will be indexed in one column;

---

[3] *Bank of Marlinton* v. *McLaughlin,* 123 W. Va. 608, 17 S.E.2d 213.
[4] *People* v. *Haas,* 311 Ill. 164, 142 N.E. 549.

and the names of grantees, mortgagees, and so on, will be indexed in another column. In the tract index a page is kept for each tract of land in the county, and all instruments affecting the title to the tract are indexed under the tract heading. The book and page where the instrument is recorded are given.

Under the statutes of some states the index is made a part of the record, and the recording is not completed until the instrument is indexed.[5]

ERRORS IN RECORDED INSTRUMENT

A slight error in an instrument will not affect its validity and, if recorded, will not prevent the recording from being notice. If the error is of such a nature that a prudent person would not be put on inquiry, the recording of the instrument will be ineffective as notice. An error in the description of the real estate, if it is of such a nature as to cause improper indexing of the instrument, will prevent recording of the instrument from being notice.

For example, if a deed to land in Section 18 is erroneously drafted and it reads Section 8, such deed, when recorded, would not be notice, since one examining the records would not be expected to examine deeds, mortgages, and so forth in Section 8 when he was interested in land in Section 18. A deed, mortgage, or other instrument which is recorded and which, when read in its entirety, discloses the interest conveyed, is sufficient to give notice of its contents, even though it may be defective in some respects.[6]

The party filing the instrument for record is responsible for its accuracy and validity; the recording officer does not pass on the validity of instruments offered for recordation.

H. Saxon and wife executed a deed to certain lands, and the section number—Section 13—was omitted from the description. On March 11, 1935, the grantees named in this deed conveyed the property by warranty deed, using the same description as that used in the deed to them. Both deeds were recorded. The court held that the deeds were void and that the recording did not constitute notice to subsequent purchasers.

Justice McElroy said: ". . . Constructive notice arising from the record of

---

[5] *Tocci* v. *Nowfall,* 220 N.C. 550, 18 S.E.2d 225.

[6] *Phoenix Mutual Life Insurance Co.* v. *Kingston Bank & Trust Co.,* 172 Tenn. 335, 112 S.W.2d 381.

a muniment is imputed to purchasers and creditors from a mere presumption of law, and it imputes only such knowledge as the instrument there recorded discloses, and not what a diligent inquiry into its meaning might disclose. The registration of an instrument is constructive notice to the world of the contents of the paper there recorded or intended to be recorded, and of its particular contents only, and it will have no operation or effect unless the original instrument correctly and sufficiently describes the premises which are to be affected. The effect of the registration law is to give a purchaser notice of what the instrument recorded or intended to be recorded actually conveys, and has no operation in the way of putting him on inquiry as to what premises were intended to be conveyed, unless they be substantially described therein." *Saxon* v. *Saxon,* 242 Miss. 491, 136 So.2d 210 (1962).

ERRORS IN RECORDING THE INSTRUMENT

The majority of the courts have held that when a person has filed an instrument with the proper officer for recording, he has fulfilled his duty, and the filing is constructive notice of the content of the instrument. If the recording officer makes an error in the indexing or in the recording of the instrument, the person who purchases, leases, or takes a mortgage on the property after the recording of the instrument takes subject to the erroneously recorded instrument, even though, as a result of the error, he would not have discovered the instrument by a customary examination of the records.[7] If the officer has made an error in recording an instrument, the courts have held that he has the right to correct the error in the record.

DUTY OF PARTY OFFERING INSTRUMENT FOR RECORDING

Some courts have held that the party offering an instrument for recordation owes a duty to check the records to see that the instrument is recorded and to see that no errors have been made in its recording. In these jurisdictions the person offering the instrument for recording must bear any loss resulting from errors made in its recording.

PARTIES PROTECTED BY RECORDING

Persons who have purchased or mortgaged property for value and in good faith are protected by the recording statutes. Some statutes extend protection to judgment creditors, and a few afford protection to judgment creditors and general creditors.

---

[7] *Willie* v. *Hines-Yelton Lumber Co.,* 167 Ga. 833, 146 S.E. 901.

In determining whether or not a person is a purchaser or mortgagee for value, the courts do not inquire into the adequacy of the consideration given. However, if it is established that property has been sold for a wholly inadequate consideration and conveyed for the purpose of defeating the rights of creditors or for the purpose of defeating rights acquired in the property, such deed will be set aside in a proper action. A mortgagee is entitled to payment of the debt secured by the mortgage, and no more.

A person who acquires real estate as a gift, by descent, or as devisee in a will is not a purchaser for value.

KNOWLEDGE AND NOTICE

To qualify as a good-faith purchaser, a person must acquire the property without knowledge or notice of outstanding interests. Since recording of an instrument is constructive notice to the public, a person takes with notice of all recorded instruments. He also takes with notice of all matters set out in recorded instruments. For example, suppose a recorded deed states that certain real estate is sold subject to a mortgage, and the mortgage is described in the deed. The recording of the deed is notice of the existence of the mortgage, even though the mortgage has not been recorded; and a subsequent purchaser or mortgagee of the property would take with notice of the mortgage.

The courts follow the general rule that a purchaser or mortgagee takes with notice of the rights of persons in possession of the property.[8] The fact that the purchaser or mortgagee does not have actual knowledge that the real estate is in the possession of some third person is immaterial. The purchaser or mortgagee owes a duty to inspect the real estate and is bound by the facts that would be disclosed by a reasonable inspection. If a third person is found in possession, the purchaser or mortgagee is obligated to interview the party in possession to learn what rights he claims in the property.[9]

Although a person does not have to investigate every rumor he hears relating to title to property, he is bound by any reliable information which he obtains relating to the property.

Henderson owned a 28-acre tract of land with a house thereon in which she lived. Through fradulent representations, she was induced to execute

---

[8] *Willard* v. *Bringoff,* 103 Ind. App. 16, 5 N.E.2d 315.

[9] *Sarafin* v. *Wolff et ux.,* 5 N.J. Super, 386, 69 A.2d 347.

deed to the premises, conveying them to Lila Lloyd. The deed to Lloyd was duly recorded. Lloyd conveyed the property, by warranty deed, to Lawrence. Henderson brought this action to have the deeds canceled and title decreed to be in her. She contended that Lawrence had notice or knowledge that the execution of the deed granting the property to Lloyd was obtained by fraud. The action of the trial court dismissing the bill was reversed on appeal and trial ordered.

Justice White said: "A bona fide purchaser is one who buys for a valuable consideration without knowledge or notice of facts material to the title.

"It is well established in this State that there can be no innocent purchaser of land from a vendor who is out of possession at the date of conveyance.

"The appellant, Eurydice Henderson, was in actual possession of the property in question and this alone is sufficient notice to the purchaser to put him on inquiry as to her rights in and to the property in question." *Henderson v. Lawrence,* Tenn., 369 S.W.2d 553 (1963).

GRANTEE UNDER QUITCLAIM DEED. There is a division of authority as to whether or not a grantee under a quitclaim deed can qualify as a good-faith purchaser. Some courts have held that a quitclaim deed conveys only the title that the grantor has; and consequently, the grantee takes subject to all outstanding claims against the real estate. A majority of the courts hold that a quitclaim deed is a conveyance, not merely a release, and that the grantee can take as a good-faith purchaser. No notice of outstanding interests can be implied from the giving of a quitclaim deed.[10]

RECORDATION AND THE CHAIN OF TITLE

As a general rule, the recording of an instrument is not constructive notice unless the recorded document is in the chain of title. The examiner, in examining the records, proceeds to check all instruments in chronological order; any instrument not in this chain of title would, in the normal course of the examination, be missed.

For example, suppose that a tract of land was patented by the government to Albert on May 6, 1820. This transfer would be indexed under the name of Albert. Suppose that Albert then deeded the tract to Bates on October 25, 1825. The examiner would look for instruments executed by Bates in the indexes after that date. Suppose that Bates, on April 13, 1825, executed a mortgage on the tract to Clark and Clark recorded the mortgage on that date. This mortgage would not be in the chain

---

[10] *Williams* v. *McCann,* Okla., 385 P.2d 788.

of title, and the recording of the mortgage would not be constructive notice to good-faith purchasers for value.

Again, suppose that Albert deeded the tract to Bates and Bates did not record the deed. Then Bates deeds or mortgages the tract to Clark, and Clark records the deed or mortgage. The deed or mortgage to Clark is not in the chain of title. Since the deed to Bates is not recorded, the examiner would not look in the index under "Bates" and would not discover the deed or mortgage to Clark.

A person examining the records will check the indexes under the name of a person who, according to the records, has acquired an interest in the real estate, and he will check only from the time the interest was acquired. He will not check for instruments recorded prior to the date a person acquired his interest in the real estate.

There are two exceptions to this general rule, and these exceptions are followed by a few, but not a majority, of the courts.

1. If a person executes a warranty deed to real estate which he does not own at that time, and later acquires title to the real estate and the deed by which such title is acquired is recorded, the recording of this deed is constructive notice to all persons dealing with the real estate subsequent to the recording of the deed.

2. The other exception arises under the following circumstances: Suppose that Albert owns two or more lots in a block. He deeds one of the lots to Bates, and the deed contains a covenant imposing building restrictions mutually enforceable on the owners of all the lots. Later, Albert sells another of the lots to Clark but does not insert the restrictive covenant in the deed to Clark. However, Clark purchases with constructive notice of the restriction. Some courts hold that the restrictive covenant in the deed to Bates is constructive notice of the restriction to all subsequent purchasers of the other lots.[11]

Lone Star Gas Company sold to Sheaner a gas heater and installed it in a house owned by Funk. The heater was installed in the house without Funk's knowledge or consent and as a replacement for a gas heater which was in the house. Gas Company sold the gas heater to Sheaner on a contract mortgage, which was duly recorded as a lien on the premises. Funk sold and conveyed the house to Tomlin. At the time of the sale, Funk was in possession of the house, and Tomlin had no notice or knowledge of Gas Company's claim to a lien. Gas Company contended that its lien, since it was duly recorded,

---

[11] *Hawley* v. *McCabe*, 117 Conn. 558, 169 A. 192.

was valid against Tomlin. The court held that Gas Company's lien was not valid against Tomlin.

Chief Justice McDonald said: "It is the law of this state that the record of a deed or mortgage by a stranger to the title to real estate, although duly recorded, is not constructive notice to a subsequent purchaser of the property, because the instrument is not in the chain of title to such property." *Lone Star Gas Company* v. *Sheaner,* Tex. Civ. App., 297 S.W.2d 855 (1956).

PRIORITIES

The courts are in accord in holding that if Albert deeds or mortgages real estate to Bell and Bell does not record his deed or mortgage, and, at a later date, Albert deeds or mortgages the same real estate to Clark, who takes as a good-faith purchaser or mortgagee for value and without notice, Clark's rights in the real estate are prior (superior) to the rights of Bell.

However, the courts are not in accord as to which party has prior rights in the above situation if Bell has not recorded his deed or mortgage at the time of the sale or mortgage to Clark, but does record his deed or mortgage before Clark records his. Some courts hold that the person who first records his deed or mortgage has priority. Other courts hold that if the deed or mortgage was not recorded at the time the second deed or mortgage was executed and delivered, the second purchaser or mortgagee has priority.

Torrens system

TORRENS SYSTEM OF TITLE REGISTRATION

The Torrens system of land title registration is a relatively recent development. Under the older and established system of recording title to real estate, the grantee acquires title to real estate when a properly executed deed is delivered to the grantee—recording is not essential to the validity of the transfer. Under the Torrens system the deed or mortgage has more of the characteristics of a contract than of a conveyance, and does not directly affect the title to the real estate. The deed or mortgage constitutes authority to the registrar. The title to the real estate does not pass to the grantee or mortgagee until the completion of the registration by the registrar in accordance with the statutes.[12] In those states which have adopted the Torrens system of land title registration, the older and established recording system is still in use. The owner of real estate may record his title, or he may, if he wishes, register his title under the Torrens system; registration of land titles is not compulsory.[13]

The provisions of the Torrens system statues are not uniform. However, the procedure to be followed in registering land titles is substantially the same under all of the statutes. An application in writing for the registration of the title to the real estate is made to the county court in the county in which the real estate is located. The application sets out all material information relative to the title to the real estate. The court will then inquire into the title. All persons known to have an interest in the real estate are given personal notice if they can be located. All other persons are given notice by publication. Any interested party may appear and state his claim. If no appearance is made, proof of the title in the applicant is taken, and an order is entered for the registration of the real estate.[14]

TRANSFER OF TITLE

When real estate is registered under the Torrens system, a certificate of registration is prepared and filed in the registrar's office; and at the same time, signature cards are signed by the owners of the property. A duplicate certificate is prepared and delivered to the owners. When the property is conveyed or mortgaged, or incumbered in any way, the owner delivers the deed, mortgage, or other instrument, as the case may be, to the grantee, mortgagee, or incumbrancee, together with the owner's registration certificate. All of these documents are presented to the registrar, who owes a duty to check the signatures. If everything is in order, he then registers the transfer and issues to the party the proper duplicate certificate. For example, if the owner has conveyed the property, the registrar will issue to the grantee a duplicate owner's certificate showing all encumbrances on the property. If the property is mortgaged, a "mortgagee's duplicate certificate" will be issued to the mortgagee. If the registrar accepts forged instruments and issues a certificate to the forger, it does not create rights in the registered property. Anyone, however, who

---

[12] *People* v. *Mortenson*, 404 Ill. 107, 88 N.E.2d 35.

[13] Colorado, Massachusetts, Minnesota, New York, North Carolina, Ohio, Oregon, Virginia, and Washington have statutes adopting the Torrens system.

[14] *State* v. *Westfall*, 85 Minn. 437, 89 N.W. 175.

suffers damage as the result of a mistake on the part of the registrar will be reimbursed from the fund accumulated from registration fees.[15]

Evidence of title

ABSTRACT AND OPINION

An abstract of title is a brief statement of the recorded instruments which affect the title to the real estate involved. A description of the property, the title to which is abstracted, appears in the caption of the abstract. The abstract gives, in brief form and in chronological order, all the instruments in the chain of title which affect the title to the real property.

ABSTRACTOR'S DUTY

The abstractor's duty is to examine the indexes and discover all the entries of record which are in the chain of title, and to prepare a short statement which will enable a person examining the abstract to determine the nature of the instrument and whether or not it was properly executed.

The abstract is merely a history of the title to the real estate. It is in no respect a guarantee of the validity of the title. The abstractor does not express an opinion as to the validity of any recorded instrument or the validity of the title.

The abstractor may be engaged to check the title from the original patent granted by the U.S. government; or he may be engaged to examine the records only back to the last entry on a previously prepared abstract and to bring the abstract down to date; that is, add to the abstract all instruments recorded after the last entry on the abstract.

The abstractor will attach to the abstract a certificate which will state what records have been examined and the dates covered by the abstract.

After the abstract has been prepared and certified, it will be given to an attorney, who will examine it and render an opinion. The opinion will be based on the abstract and will point out any defects in the title which are revealed by the examination of the abstract. The opinion will state the status of the title of the grantor or mortgagor.

As a general rule, the abstract and opinion do not cover matters of

[15] *Hoffman* v. *Schroeder,* 38 Ill. App.2d 20, 186 N.E.2d 381.

survey, rights of persons in possession, short-term leases, and rights to mechanics' liens arising as the result of improvements made within 60 days (or the time for filing mechanics' liens).

LIABILITY OF ABSTRACTOR

The abstractor does not guarantee the title to the real estate and is not liable if the title is defective. He is liable for losses resulting from his negligence in the preparation of the abstract. If the abstractor negligently omits an entry and, as the result of the omission, the person who has employed him suffers a loss, the abstractor is liable for the resulting loss. If the abstractor merely brings an abstract down to date, he is liable only for omissions of entries made during the period his examination was to cover.

PERSONS TO WHOM ABSTRACTOR IS LIABLE

Some courts have held that the abstractor is liable only to the party who employs him. The better view is that the abstractor is liable to anyone who relies on the abstract. The guarantee in the certificate of some abstractors runs to all persons, both present and future, who rely on the abstract. In effect, the abstract runs with the land.

CERTIFICATE OF TITLE

In some localities and in some transactions, a certificate of title is used, and no abstract is prepared. An attorney will examine the records and will issue a certificate of title which will indicate the status of the title. The certificate will state who is title owner, and will also set out all liens and encumbrances against the title. It is an opinion as to the validity of the grantor's or mortgagor's title, and as to the existence of liens and encumbrances.

TORRENS CERTIFICATE

A Torrens certificate issued by the registrar certifies as to who is title owner of the property, and as to all liens and encumbrances which are registered. The person purchasing or taking a mortgage on the real estate takes subject to liens, and so forth, which are registered but free from all other claims except short-term leases, current taxes, rights of the public, and claims arising under the laws of the United States.

Insurance of title

INTRODUCTION

The title insurance industry is an outgrowth of the abstracting business fortified by the inherent shortcomings of the abstract and opinion method of assuring title. No matter how careful the abstractor may be or how competent the attorney may be there may still be losses which result from errors in the recording system itself or errors in judgment by the abstractor or the attorney. When a loss does occur it may be difficult or impossible to obtain financial satisfaction. As a result of these factors a demand existed for some form of insurance that would provide economic protection to the property owner. Still more important, mortgage lenders who are primarily interested in recovering the funds advanced have given great support to the title insurance industry. The abstract companies, because of their familiarity with the recording system, found the title insurance business a natural area in which to expand. Attorneys have also formed title insurance companies to provide financial protection to their clients.

HOW TITLE INSURANCE WORKS

Title insurance works much like any other form of casualty insurance in that it speads the risk of loss of title over many insured parties. Rates are established on the basis of experience in a given area. When title insurance is ordered the title insurance company searches the records in much the same way that the abstractor does, however, an abstract is not prepared. Instead, only those defects which are found are noted and this information then is reviewed by the title insurance company's attorney to determine how serious the defects may be and whether or not the title is insurable. The company then decides whether or not it will insure the title and what exceptions it may take in the policy when it is finally issued. Usually the amount of coverage will be the purchase price (in an owner's policy) or the amount of the mortgage debt (in a mortgagee's policy) although additional coverage may be purchased. The purchaser of the real estate, the insured party under the policy, does not receive an abstract or an opinion; he receives instead an insurance policy which simply describes the interest being insured, the real estate, the amount of coverage and any exceptions other than the standard exceptions discussed below. In the event that there is a defect in the title the title insurance company will be called upon to pay the loss or defend the title much the same as other casualty insurers.

LIMITATIONS ON TITLE INSURANCE COVERAGE

Title insurance is based upon an examination of the quality of the title as of a particular date and time. The policy provides insurance that as of a specified moment insurable title is vested in the name of the seller of the property and that upon conveyance to the buyer he will have an insured title. As a result title insurance does *not* protect the owner against defects which come into existence after he takes title to the property. There are also standard exceptions in the typical title insurance policy against mechanics' liens which may not have been recorded at the time the title was examined; defects that a survey would have revealed, unless a survey was performed and made available to the title insurer; rights of parties in possession under unrecorded leases or conditional sales contracts. Another important limitation on the insurance coverage is that it is limited to the named insured and subsequent purchasers may not rely upon the previous owner's policy. New title insurance must be purchased by each new owner of the property. The cost of such subsequent policies, however, will likely be at a reduced cost because the insurer needs only to update his earlier examination of the title. Nor can an owner of real estate rely upon his mortgagee's title insurance policy since it provides limited coverage to the lender only for the balance of his loan.

SUBROGATION

The complexities of the law of subrogation will not be covered here; however, it is important to note that when there has been a loss the title insurer succeeds to the rights that his insured may have against other parties including, most importantly, the seller of the property. If the seller gave a general warranty deed he can be sued on his warranties by the buyer and the title insurer succeeds to this remedy. The lesson here is that the seller who provides title insurance to his buyer remains liable for defects in his title and he does not escape liability by providing title insurance. This is particularly true where the defect is created by the seller himself.

Conclusion

Title insurance is becoming more and more widely used, particularly in older metropolitan areas. Most title insurers welcome inquiries about their business from the general public, considering it a form of public relations. In addition they frequently have informative booklets and films which are often available for the asking.

9

Real estate loan institutions and mortgages

Introduction to real estate loan institutions[1]

TYPES OF REAL ESTATE LOAN INSTITUTIONS

THERE ARE several financial institutions which make loans secured by real estate mortgages. The savings and loan associations (formerly generally titled *building and loan associations*) specialize in making loans on residential property, predominantly single-family, duplex, and four-family residences. Savings banks make the major portion of their loans on real estate, favoring loans on residential properties. Commercial banks make some real estate loans, particularly the commercial banks having savings departments; but the majority of their loans are made to commercial borrowers. Life insurance companies make loans on residential property, farms, and multiple-unit housing. They have also constructed some multiple-unit housing and have purchased some properties on leaseback agreements. Although mortgage bankers and mortgage brokers do not make substantial loans on the security of real estate, they do facilitate the making of real estate loans by aiding in the finding of such loans and in the marketing of real estate mortgages. The individual cannot be classed as

---

[1] Much of the material in the section on loan institutions is adapted from Henry H. Hoagland and Leo D. Stone, *Real Estate Finance* (rev. ed.; Homewood, Ill.: Richard D. Irwin, Inc., 1961).

a real estate financial institution. However, he cannot be ignored, since the total amount of real estate loans made by individuals is substantial.

Savings and loan associations

ORGANIZATION

In their inception, building and loan associations, as they were first termed, were either unincorporated associations, partnerships, or corporations. Today, however, substantially all of them are corporations. The name *savings and loan association* has been generally used since the Federal Home Loan Bank Board was authorized to charter federal savings and loan associations. Today a savings and loan association may be chartered by the Federal Home Loan Bank Board or by one of the states.

FEDERAL CHARTERS

The federally chartered savings and loan associations are members of the Federal Home Loan Bank system and of the Federal Savings and Loan Insurance Corporation. In order to obtain their charters, they must comply with the rules and regulations established by these organizations. The state-chartered savings and loan associations, in order to obtain their charters, must comply with the statutes of the states in which they are incorporated. The state statutes are not uniform in their requirements. A state-chartered savings and loan association may, if it elects to do so and can satisfy the requirements, become a member of the Federal Savings and Loan Insurance Corporation. Also, a state-chartered savings and loan association may, by meeting the requirements, become affiliated with the Federal Home Loan Bank system. Whether operating under a federal charter or under a state charter, the savings and loan associations are corporations; their legal status does not differ fundamentally from that of banks or other financial institutions.

REGULATION

Savings and loan associations, like banks, are regulated in the interest of the public. Federally chartered savings and loan associations are subject to regulation by the Federal Home Loan Board and the Federal Savings and Loan Insurance Corporation. State-chartered savings and loan associations are subject to regulation by the chartering state; and if they are members of the Federal Savings and Loan Insurance Corporation, they must also comply with its regulations. The regulations, either federal or state, may be changed from time to time.

Although the regulations under which state-chartered savings and loan associations must operate are not uniform and federal regulations may be changed from time to time, there are common areas of regulation. As a general rule, the maximum amount permitted to be loaned on the security of a particular piece of real property is limited to a percentage of the appraised value of the property. In addition, the basis of making the appraisal and the persons eligible as appraisers are designated, thus guarding against inflated or fraudulent appraisals. These regulations generally do not apply to insured FHA and GI loans.

Other common areas of regulation are as to the types of property on which loans may be made, the amount which may be loaned on a particular piece of property, the maximum percentage of the total assets which may be loaned to one borrower, and the maximum time permitted for the repayment of the loan. Other matters which are commonly covered by regulations are loans to officers and agents of the association, purchase of mortgages, investment of funds which the association cannot loan on mortgage security, area within which the association may make loans, and rules regarding withdrawals. Federal savings and loan associations and members of the Federal Savings and Loan Insurance Corporation are subject to federal inspection, and state-chartered savings and loan associations are subject to state inspection.

OPERATION

In their origin, savings and loan associations had two basic objectives: (1) to encourage thrift and (2) to aid in the building of homes. Although the method of operation of savings and loan associations has changed materially over the years, their aims have not changed. Persons dealing with savings and loan associations may be divided into two classes: (1) loaning members and (2) borrowing members.

At one time the loaning member was obligated to loan a designated amount at stipulated periods; if he failed to fulfill his obligation, he was subject to fine. Today a loaning member may loan any amount he wishes at any time he wishes. The relationship between the loaning member and the association in this respect is no different than that of a depositor and a bank. However, the loaning member of a building and loan association, with a few exceptions,[2] is a shareholder. He has a right to vote at shareholders' meetings, and he is paid a dividend on the basis of the amount he has loaned the association; but unlike the stockholder in an industrial corporation, he may turn his shares in to the association and withdraw the amount loaned, subject to established regulations. His shares have no market value, but they may be assigned. Under present conditions, savings and loan associations permit their shareholders to make unlimited withdrawals on demand. Under regulations generally in force the association may require from 30 to 90 days' notice before a withdrawal; and if the association does not have sufficient funds to pay all requested withdrawals, it may pay them in the order of the giving of notice as it receives funds. An association usually keeps a cash balance sufficient to meet normal requests for withdrawals.

Dividends are paid out of the profits of operation. The same rate of dividend is paid to all shareholders. Under the policies of a well-operated association a reserve will be set up and a surplus accumulated, and the balance of the earnings will be distributed as dividends. If the association has a bad year, it may pay the usual dividend, drawing the amount needed to make up the deficit from the built-up surplus.

MAKING LOANS. At one time, savings and loan associations made loans only to members. Today a few associations, by their rules and regulations, are permitted to make loans only to members, but anyone wishing to borrow money may become a member by purchasing one share at some nominal price, usually $1.00.

Under the standard practice usually followed in the making of loans, the borrower must first make application for the loan. The application will include information relating to the borrower's financial worth, employment, marital status, and so forth, in addition to a description of the property on which the loan is to be made. If the loan is a construction loan, the plans and specifications and the proposed construction contract must accompany the application. An investigation of the borrower will be made, the property will be appraised, and a report to the association will be made. The directors of the association or a loaning committee will pass on the loan. If it is approved, the abstract of the property will be brought down to date; taxes and assessments will be determined; the abstract and tax history will be examined by the association attorney; surveys will be made, if deemed necessary; and if everything is found to be satisfactory, the loan will be closed.

---

[2] Ohio and California hold that persons loaning money to the association are depositors.

Savings banks

ORGANIZATION

The present-day savings bank is a corporation organized to encourage thrift and to obtain for its depositors the investment advantages enjoyed by those having substantial sums of money to invest. Savings banks are incorporated under special state statutes. Seventeen states have statutes providing for the incorporation of savings banks.[3] There are three types of organization: the cooperative savings bank, the mutual savings bank, and the stock savings bank. Under the cooperative system the depositors are the members of the corporation; and loans, except as to surplus funds, are made only to shareholders. Since the general public is invited to become shareholders, there is little difference between a cooperative savings bank and a mutual savings bank. Cooperative banks operate only in Massachusetts. The mutual savings bank has no stockholders other than the depositors. It is managed by a board of trustees elected by the members. The term of office, powers, and duties of the trustees are defined in the statutes of the state of incorporation.

CAPITAL STOCK SAVINGS BANKS

The savings bank, under the statutes of some states, may be organized as a capital stock corporation. Such savings banks are incorporated in substantially the same manner as are commercial banks. The stockholders, through their elected board of directors, manage the bank, and the profits are distributed to the stockholders as dividends.

REGULATIONS

Since savings banks are chartered by the states, they are subject to regulation by the chartering state; consequently, the regulations imposed on savings banks are not uniform. However, the areas of regulation do not differ materially. The objective of the state regulations on savings banks is the protection of the depositors. The regulations are similar, in most respects, to those imposed on savings and loan associations. In

---

[3] Connecticut, Delaware, Indiana, Maine, Maryland, Massachusetts, Minnesota, New Hampshire, New Jersey, New York, Ohio, Oregon, Pennsylvania, Rhode Island, Vermont, Washington, and Wisconsin.

general, there are limitations as to the types of investments the bank may make; the amount, expressed either in dollars or in percentage of assets, which the bank may loan to a borrower; the margin of safety required in loans on real estate; the methods of appraisal; and, in some states, the percentage of loans which may be made on real estate as security. The regulations also provide for periodic inspection. Since the 1930s, savings banks have invested a larger proportion of their funds in corporate and municipal bonds and other "legal" investments, and a correspondingly lesser proportion of their funds in real estate mortgages.

METHOD OF OPERATION

The savings bank is managed by a board of trustees, managers, or directors which appoints the officers and agents of the bank and which is the policy-making body for the bank. In managing the bank, the board must act within the scope of the bylaws, charter, and state statutes which regulate the business of the bank. The savings bank accepts deposits from the general public in any amount depositors may wish to deposit and at such times as depositors may wish to make deposits. Depositors have the right to withdraw their deposits whenever they wish, subject, however, to the bank's right to require notice, usually from 30 to 90 days. If the bank does not have liquid funds with which to pay withdrawals, it may pay in the order in which notice was received. Savings banks, as a general policy, plan to maintain a cash balance sufficiently large to enable them to pay all requested withdrawals on demand.

MAKING LOANS. The board of managers, trustees, or directors, or an investment committee, passes on all investments. In investing the funds of the bank, the persons authorized to make the investments follow customary procedures for institutional investments. They investigate the investment to be reasonably certain that it comes within the permitted type, and to determine whether or not it will provide the desired safety and income, and will fit into the needs of the bank. The types of investments will vary from time to time as general economic conditions change. In recent years the regulations of savings banks have been liberalized in some states, authorizing savings banks to pool their funds and purchase large mortgages. In New York, savings banks may pool their funds and build or acquire multiple-unit housing projects which provide housing for veterans. As a general rule, after expenses are deducted, a reserve provided, and a surplus established, the income is distributed to depositors on a prorated basis.

Commercial banks

ORGANIZATION

Commercial banks differ from savings and loan associations and from savings banks in several material respects. The commercial bank may be either a national or a state bank; but whichever it is, it is incorporated and owned by stockholders who operate the bank as a profit-making institution. The depositors do not share in the profits of the bank. The management of the bank is vested in a board of directors elected by the stockholders. The depositors have no voice in the election of directors. Commercial banks have two classes of deposits: commercial deposits and time deposits. As a general rule, no interest is paid on commercial deposits; but interest is paid on time deposits after a designated period. The commercial bank, regardless of banking regulations, must stand ready to pay its depositors on demand. Failure to make payment on demand might result in a run on the bank. Consequently, the commercial bank must maintain a position of greater liquidity than savings and loan associations and savings banks. The business interests of the community depend on the commercial bank for many services which facilitate the transaction of business, such as short-term loans, discounting of receivables, collection, and other similar services. The performance of these services does not demand the use of all of the bank's available funds. The funds not used in these short-term transactions are available for the making of longer time loans.

REGULATIONS

The time deposits of commercial banks exceed in total amount those in all other types of banks. The amount of long-term loans which a commercial bank may safely make is related directly to the amount of time deposits it has. In recent years the commercial banks have occupied a significant place in the field of mortgage lending. Although banking regulations limit the amount commercial banks may loan on conventional mortgages and also limit the percentage of the appraised value a bank may loan, the commercial banks are free to make their own appraisal. Commercial banks have favored FHA-insured and GI-insured loans. They have also made loans of substantial amounts on multiple-unit housing and industrial expansion projects. In some instances the banks have purchased mortgages from mortgage brokers or mortgage bankers. Most mortgage loans are made directly to the mortgagors.

BANK TRUST DEPARTMENT

Those banks having trust departments may have trust funds which are available for investment in real estate mortgages. The investment of trust funds is subject to the terms of the trust instrument and to the restrictive statutes of the state. Unless the trust instrument expressly authorizes a specific type of investment, the trustee must invest trust funds in "prudent" investments, as defined by the statutes of the state. First mortgages on real estate are usually included as legitimate investments for trust funds.

Life insurance companies

ORGANIZATION

Life insurance companies are organized for the purpose of writing insurance, not for the primary purpose of loaning money; yet the nature of their business is such that they have large sums of money to invest. The life insurance company knows approximately how much money it will receive during a given period and also approximately the amount it will be required to pay out; consequently, it can estimate with a high degree of certainty the sum it will have available for investment. Normally, the insured pays premiums to the life insurance company over a relatively long time, and the life insurance company will not pay out on the policy until the end of the period. This situation enables the life insurance company to make long-term loans.

RESTRICTIONS ON LOANS

The laws of the state in which the life insurance company is chartered, and of the state in which it is licensed to do business, will place restrictions on the investments of life insurance companies. However, these restrictions are not as stringent as those on savings and loan associations and on banks. As a general rule, there are no geographical limitations on the investments of life insurance companies; and since the larger life insurance companies do business in all the states, they have followed the practice of making loans in all areas of the United States.

Types of loans

Life insurance companies have made loans and have taken mortgages on residential property as security; they have used their funds to build properties, which they have managed; and they have purchased, directly from the issuing corporations, entire bond issues. In addition, life insurance companies have invested in all types of government bonds, in corporate bonds, and, to a limited extent, in preferred and common stock. A life insurance company may make loans on mortgage security through a correspondent; it may acquire mortgages from a mortgage broker; or it may buy mortgages from a mortgage banker. It may service its mortgages directly through branch officers, or through a mortgage banker. Building operations are handled either directly or through a wholly owned subsidiary. Private placements are handled directly. In some instances, two or more financial institutions have cooperated in purchasing a bond issue. These bond issues are frequently secured by mortgages on real estate.

Mortgage bankers and brokers

Nature of operation of mortgage bankers and brokers

There is a close relationship between the business of the mortgage banker and that of the mortgage broker. The services rendered by the mortgage banker range from the lending of his own funds to the sale, at some later date, of the mortgage to the person acting as a correspondent for an insurance company. The services of a mortgage broker are confined to bringing together the lender and the borrower and, in some instances, to aiding in the closing of the loan. The mortgage banker may also act as a mortgage broker.

The mortgage banker

The mortgage banking business may be carried on by an individual, a partnership, or a corporation. The business is not regulated by the federal or state governments. The mortgage banker, in addition to his mortgage banking, may sell insurance, carry on the business of a real estate broker, act as a mortgage broker, function as correspondent for insurance companies or other financial institutions, and perform other services connected with the real estate business. The mortgage banker may loan his own money, taking a mortgage on real estate as security, and take his chances on selling the mortgage to a bank, an insurance company, an individual, or some other purchaser. He may enter into a contract with one or more insurance companies whereby they are committed to purchase mortgages which satisfy certain standards, or he may establish a market with certain insurance companies and banks without having a contract to purchase with the institution. In his dealings the mortgage banker negotiates and closes the loan. He may submit the application to a prospective purchaser of the mortgage for approval and get a commitment from him before the loan is closed.

SERVICING LOANS

In addition to negotiating and closing a loan, the mortgage banker services loans, if the purchaser wishes to avail himself of this service. The mortgage banker collects payments; periodically checks the mortgaged property; checks taxes, assessments, and so forth, to make certain that they are paid when due, or pays them if they are to be paid out of the money paid by the mortgagee; keeps the property insured or sees that it is kept insured; and performs other services which may be necessary to protect the interests of the mortgagee. The service of the mortgage banker covers all phases of the mortgage transaction from the making of the loan, using his own money to make the initial loan, to the final payment of the loan and the discharge of the mortgage.

OTHER SOURCES

Since mortgages represent a form of investment a wide variety of other sources of mortgage money exist. Real Estate Investment Trusts, for example, may represent an excellent source of funds for commercial mortgages. In fact, some trusts, called Real Estate Mortgage Trusts, are designed for the exclusive purpose of investing in mortgages. Further information on sources of such investment money is included in Chapter 19 of this book.

Introduction to mortgages

HISTORICAL BACKGROUND

The mortgage had its origin in early Saxon law. At that time, it was a pledge of land made to assure the performance of an obligation; and if the obligation was not performed, the pledged land was forfeited. The forfeiture of the land, however, did not relieve the mortgagor-obligor from his duty to perform the stipulated obligation. If the mortgage was given to secure a debt and the debt was not paid on the due date, the debtor lost his land, but he was in no way relieved from his duty to pay the debt.

The classical common-law mortgage, which is the forerunner of the present-day mortgage, was not in common use in England until about A.D. 1400. It was, in form, a deed containing a defeasance clause; and under the law at that time the mortgagor lost his land if he failed to pay his debt when due. The reason for his failure to pay or the justice of the result was wholly immaterial.

The king, during this period, would frequently grant relief from the forfeiture of the land in cases of extreme hardship, and would order the mortgagee to reconvey the land to the mortgagor on the payment of the debt. Some time after A.D. 1450 the king began to delegate for determination the hearing of "conscience cases," including mortgage forfeiture cases, to his chancellor, who was a high churchman. This part of the chancellor's work was gradually organized into a systematic procedure for disposing of all petitions for special relief from the hardships of the common law; and eventually, a separate court—the chancery court—was set up to hear and determine such cases.

The chancery court became increasingly liberal in granting relief from the forfeiture of mortgaged land; and finally, in A.D. 1625 or shortly thereafter, it reached the place where it granted relief in all cases unless the mortgagor delayed an unreasonable length of time before bringing his action asking that he be granted the right to redeem his land. As a prerequisite to his right to redeem, the mortgagor was required to pay into court the principal of the debt, interest, and costs.

The mortgagee, at this time, was at a disadvantage, since he did not know how long the mortgagor might delay after a default before bringing an action and being granted the right to redeem. In order to cure this weakness in the law, the mortgagee was gradually given the right to bring suit in which he would ask the court to foreclose the mortgagor's right to redeem. At this stage in the development of our mortgage law, the courts decreed strict foreclosure of the mortgage. That is, the court would enter an order allowing the mortgagor a specific time in which to redeem the land from forfeiture; if he did not redeem within the time allowed, his right to redeem was forever foreclosed and cut off. The time allowed was discretionary with the chancellor, and was usually from two to six months. The law of mortgages had developed to the point where the courts recognized that a mortgage was a security device and that the mortgagor was, in equity, the true owner of the mortgaged real estate, although, in law, the mortgagee held title to it.

POSSESSION OF MORTGAGED REAL ESTATE

During the early period of the development of mortgage laws, Englishmen were not permitted to charge interest on money loaned, although foreign moneylenders could do so. Also, a conveyance of real estate was not valid unless the grantee took possession of the real estate. Therefore, when real estate was mortgaged, since the mortgage was a conveyance of the real estate to the mortgagee, the mortgagee took possession of it; and since he could not charge interest, he was allowed to keep the rents and profits derived therefrom.

At a later date the chancery courts required the mortgagee in possession to account for the rents and profits derived from the mortgaged real estate and to apply them in reduction of the mortgage debt. Also, by this time, the courts were holding a mortgage to be valid without change of possession. Consequently, the mortgagor, as a general rule, was left in possession of the mortgaged real estate. However, the courts recognized the mortgagee as the title owner of the mortgaged real estate and, as such, entitled to possession at any time he wished to demand it.

MORTGAGE LAW IN THE UNITED STATES

When the United States gained its independence from England, each of the states adopted, as the basic law of the state, the laws of England insofar as they were in accord with the social and economic conditions in the state. Almost from the beginning, our courts of equity—the equivalent of the English chancery courts—treated the mortgage as a lien on real estate given to secure the payment of a debt or the performance of an obligation. Some of the states recognize what is known as the *title theory* of mortgages, whereas other states recognize the *lien theory*.

The title theory is a modification of the common-law concept of the mortgage. Under the title theory the mortgage is, in form, a conveyance of the mortgaged real estate to the mortgagee, his title to be defeated on the payment of the debt. As the law developed, however, the mortgagor became the one to be recognized as the true owner of the real estate, his ownership being subject only to the superior rights of the mortgagee. Although, technically, the mortgagee has the right of possession, the mortgagor, either by the terms of the mortgage or by statutory enactment, is, as a general rule, given the right of possession until default and foreclosure. If the mortgagee is permitted to take possession, he must account for the rents and profits derived from the mortgaged real estate.

Under the lien theory of mortgages, title to the mortgaged real estate is not vested in the mortgagee but remains in the mortgagor, and only a security interest is conveyed to the mortgagee. The standard form of mortgage used in many of the lien theory states reads "mortgages and warrants" instead of "conveys and warrants." The mortgagor retains possession of the mortgaged property until default and foreclosure. Since the mortgagee's interest in the mortgaged property is a security interest, it is dependent on the debt secured, and any discharge of this debt automatically terminates the mortgagee's interest in the mortgaged real estate.

Whether the state follows the title theory or the lien theory of mortgages, the security interest of the mortgagee is personal property, and it can be transferred only with a transfer of the debt the mortgage secures. In fact, the differences between the rights of the parties to a mortgage in a lien theory state and in a title theory state are technical rather than real.

Form of the mortgage

FORMAL REQUIREMENTS

As a general rule, the formal requirements for a valid mortgage are the same as those for a valid deed[1] and are not uniform for all of the states. Usually, the mortgage must name the mortgagor and the mortgagee; must contain words of conveyance; must set out the debt to be secured;

---

[1] The formal requirements for a valid deed are discussed in Chapter 5, "Deed Checklist."

must describe the real estate mortgaged; must state, in a title theory state, the condition on which title is to be defeated (the defeasance clause); must be signed by the mortgagor; must, in some states, be sealed; must have, in some states, attesting witnesses; must be delivered and accepted; and must, if it is to be eligible for recording, be acknowledged. Acknowledgment, however, is not essential to the validity of the mortgage between the mortgagor and the mortgagee.

DEED AS MORTGAGE

From an early date the courts have held that any conveyance of real estate made as security for a debt is a mortgage, regardless of its form, and have held that the mortgagor has the right to pay the debt and redeem the mortgaged property at any time before foreclosure or the running of the statute of limitations. Any agreement entered into at the time the loan is made whereby the debtor-mortgagor is deprived of his right to redeem the mortgaged property is against public policy and is a nullity.

Before the court will declare a deed absolute on its face or declare a similar conveyance to be a mortgage, the grantor must prove by clear and convincing evidence that the true nature of the transaction was a loan and a conveyance as security for a loan. All the facts and circumstances surrounding the transaction are admissible as evidence to establish its true nature. No single fact is conclusive of the rights of the parties. Such facts as the relation between the amount paid and the value of the property at the date of the conveyance, whether the grantor retained possession of the property or surrendered possession to the grantee,[2] who paid the taxes, the relation of the parties, and the conduct of the parties prior to and subsequent to the conveyance in their relation to the property are taken into consideration.

Transactions in which property is sold and deeded by absolute deed to the grantee, who then executes to the grantor an option which gives the grantor the right to repurchase the property for the same price, plus interest at a stated rate or plus an amount equivalent to the going rate of interest, have presented some difficult problems for the courts. If the parties intended a sale and a repurchase agreement, the courts will enforce the agreement as drafted. If the seller asks the court to declare the transactions a mortgage and permit him to redeem the property after the expira-

---

[2] *Spataro et al.* v. *Domenico et al.,* 96 Cal. App.2d 411, 216 P.2d 32.

tion of the option, he will be required to prove by clear and convincing evidence that the transaction was a loan and that the deed was given as security.[3]

RIGHTS OF INNOCENT PURCHASERS

A grantor who has conveyed his real estate by absolute deed as security for a loan will not be permitted to recover the property from a person who has purchased it from the grantee, provided such person can qualify as an innocent purchaser for value.[4] The courts have held that the fact that the grantor is left in possession of the property is not notice that he has retained rights in it.[5] However, if the grantee-mortgagee sells the property, the grantor-mortgagor is not remedyless, even though he does lose his right to redeem the property. He can recover a judgment against the grantee-mortgagee for the difference between the unpaid balance of the debt plus the accrued interest and the fair market value of the property, regardless of the price at which the property was sold.[6]

McCool was living in the Home, a sanitarium for the aged. He had entered the Home on September 26, 1956; and as of March 31, 1959, he owed it $3,136.45 from room, board, medical treatment, and other things. On April 29, 1959, McCool deeded to the Home by warranty deed 240 acres of improved land with two houses, together with the usual farm outbuildings thereon. At the same time, and contemporaneously with the execution of said deed, McCool and the Home entered into an agreement in writing, whereby the Home agreed to provide for McCool during his natural life, for which service it was to be paid $200 per month, not including any doctors' fees, medicine, or laundry required by and provided for McCool. The contract further provided that William McCool and Martha Ayres, McCool's son and daughter, would have the right to redeem the property by paying the Home the amount due it for Mc-Cool's care, provided said sum was paid together with 4 per cent interest thereon within two years after the death of McCool. If the property was not redeemed, the Home was to pay William McCool $5,000. William had built on the land a house in which he and his wife lived without paying rent.

McCool died, and William and Martha did not redeem the land within the two-year period. The Home tendered $5,000 to William, and he refused the tender. The Home claimed that it was title owner of the land. William

---

[3] *Lusher et al.* v. *First National Bank of Fort Worth et al.,* Tex., 260 S.W. 2d 621.

[4] *Hoffman et al.* v. *Graaf et al.,* 179 Wash. 431, 38 P.2d 236.

[5] *Roberts* v. *Bass,* Fla., 111 So.2d 455.

[6] *Conley* v. *Henderson et al.,* 158 Ore. 309, 75 P.2d 746.

and Martha claimed that they had the right to redeem the land by paying the Home $12,222.80, the agreed amount expended by the Home in the care of McCool.

The trial court construed the warranty deed and related contract as a conveyance of the realty in fee simple to the Home. On appeal, the court held that the deed and contract created an "equitable mortgage."

Judge Kelley said: "It is noted that the involved written agreement, in the latter part of the WHEREAS clause, provides for a fixed 'flat' monthly rate of Two Hundred Dollars ($200) for the care of decedent to start from the date of execution of the agreement, thus establishing a constant rate of indebtedness to the Home which continued on to the time of decedent's death. It is held that when a deed is given in securance of an existing indebtedness, it will be held to be a mortgage.

"A rather conclusive indication that the parties intended the deed as a mortgage and that the Home intended to hold the real estate as security for decedent's indebtedness, is the provision in the next to last paragraph of the contract that 'if' the conditions thereof are carried out and fulfilled by both parties and 'there is no redemption' within two years of decedent's death, the Home 'shall be the absolute owner, in fee simple' of the real estate. Now, if the parties had intended the deed as a present conveyance of the title to the Home, said provision, as worded, would have been wholly unnecessary and, in fact, without legal application. The stated provision definitely withheld the vesting of any fee title to the real estate in the Home until the accomplishment of the expressed precedents. In other words, under the provision referred to, if the debt was not paid within the time allowed, then, and then only, was the fee title to the real estate to vest in the Home as against the appellant, William S. McCool, and the appellee, Martha Ayres. . . . Appellees earnestly contend that the rules of law pertaining to support agreements should be here applied and that, in such cases, it is held that the grantee 'takes a fee subject to a condition subsequent.' It is difficult, of course, to lay down general rules applicable to all cases. But where the parties, by their agreement, have definitely stated in clear, definite and unambiguous language the terms and conditions they have agreed upon, no room or reason exists for a forced construction contrary to their expressed intention.

"The contract contains a specific provision for 'the right to redeem the lands' within a certain time after decedent's death. Such a provision is indicative that a mortgage was intended. *McCool* v. *Ayres,* Ind. App., 192 N.E.2d 636 (1963).

EQUITABLE MORTGAGES

An equitable mortgage arises when a loan is made, when credit is given, or when a creditor has executed an extension of credit in actual reliance upon an agreement that real estate shall be mortgaged as security for the payment of the debt and then the debtor refuses or fails to execute the mortgage, or when the instrument executed is so defective that it does not create an enforceable lien on the property.

For example, suppose that Allen loaned and paid to Bert $1,000 after Bert had agreed to secure the loan by giving Allen a real estate mortgage on a house and lot owned by Bert, and then Bert, after receiving the money, refused to execute the mortgage. A court would hold that Allen had an equitable mortgage on the house and lot as security for the loan.

An equitable mortgage creates a valid lien on the real estate in favor of the creditor, but it is not valid against an innocent purchaser for value. In the above example, suppose that Bert, after promising to give Allen a mortgage on the real estate as security for the $1,000 loaned, sold the property to Call, who knew nothing about the Allen-Bert transaction, and who paid value for the house and lot. Call would take the house free from Allen's equitable mortgage.[7]

PROPERTY WHICH MAY BE MORTGAGED

As a general rule, any interest in real estate which may be sold may be mortgaged. The basic principle of property law—that one cannot convey greater rights in the property than he has—applies to the right to mortgage with equal force.[8]

Under the common law the mortgage described the land, and it created a lien not only on the land but on all the improvements which, under the law of fixtures, became a part of the land. Under the Horizontal Property acts (Condominium Property Act in some states) a person may own, convey, and mortgage an apartment in a condominium. The apartment is described by reference to a recorded declaration and plat.[9]

A mortgage may, by its terms, include both real estate and personal property. Under the recording and filing statutes of most states, such a mortgage, to be valid against bona fide purchasers and mortgagees for

---

[7] *McKeighan et al.* v. *Citizens Commercial & Savings Bank of Flint et al.,* 302 Mich. 666, 5 N.W.2d 524.

[8] See Chap. 3, "Basic Principles."

[9] The Condominium Property Act of Illinois provides (Section 7): "Every deed, lease, mortgage or other instrument may legally describe a unit by its identifying number or symbol as shown on the plat and as set forth in the declaration. . . ."

value, would have to be recorded as a real estate mortgage and also recorded or filed as a chattel mortgage.

AFTER-ACQUIRED PROPERTY

The common-law courts held that a mortgage on property to be acquired in the future was void; however, the courts of chancery decree that such a mortgage might be valid as an equitable mortgage. Today, in the United States, a mortgage on after-acquired real estate is valid insofar as the rights acquired by the mortgagee are concerned. If a mortgagor executes a mortgage on real estate which he does not own or executes a mortgage which purports to include greater rights than the mortgagor then has, the mortgage will, as between the mortgagor and mortgagee, create a lien on any rights included in the mortgage thereafter acquired by the mortgagor.[10]

A mortgagee's rights in after-acquired property will be subject to all outstanding interests in the property existing at the time the mortgagor acquires the property. For example, if a mortgagor gives a mortgage on real estate which he does not own, and he thereafter acquires the property and executes, at the time he acquires the property, a purchase-money mortgage on it, the purchase-money mortgagee will have first claim to the property.[11] Likewise, any valid mortgage or other valid lien existing on the real estate at the time the mortgagor acquires the real estate will have priority over a mortgage executed before the mortgagor acquired the real estate.

A clause in a mortgage is valid if such clause expressly states that the real estate shall become, on acquisition, subject to the mortgage, unless such clauses are expressly prohibited by statute.[12]

MORTGAGE NOT IN CHAIN OF TITLE.   If a mortgage is given on real estate by the mortgagor before he acquires an interest in the real estate and records his deed to the real estate, such mortgage would not be in the chain of title. The effect of a recorded instrument not in the chain of title on rights of third persons is discussed in Chapter 8, "Recordation and the Chain of Title."

---

[10] *California Bank* v. *Bell et al.,* 38 Cal. App.2d 533, 101 P.2d 724.

[11] *Nelson et al.* v. *Dwiggins,* 111 Fla. 289, 149 So. 613.

[12] *Walters et ux.* v. *Merchants & Manufacturers Bank of Ellisville,* 218 Miss 777, 67 So. 2d 714.

PACKAGE MORTGAGES

The so-called *package mortgage* is one that not only includes the real estate, but also expressly includes all fixtures and appliances on the premises. The package mortgage has been used extensively in recent years in the financing of houses. Such mortgages usually expressly include, as a part of the real estate, the heating and air-conditioning equipment, kitchen range, refrigerator, dishwasher, garbage disposal unit, washer and dryer, food freezer, and other such appliances.

The rights of persons having or acquiring a security interest in personal property which is to be attached to real estate so that it becomes a fixture and the rights of a person who acquires a security interest in fixtures are defined in the Uniform Commercial Code.[13]

The Code does not define fixtures, but it does provide: "(1) The rules of this section do not apply to goods incorporated into a structure in the manner of lumber, bricks, tile, cement, glass, metal work and the like and no security interest in them exists under this Article unless the structure remains personal property."

Under this provision of the Code, if the security interest attaches to the goods before they become fixtures, and is perfected as required by the Code, it takes priority as to the goods over all persons who have an interest in the real estate. If the security interest attaches to the goods after they become fixtures, it has priority over subsequently acquired interests in the real estate but is invalid against any person with an interest in the real estate at the time the security interest attaches if such person has not in writing consented to the security interest or has disclaimed an interest in the goods as fixtures. The above-described security interest in fixtures does not take priority over subsequent purchasers, lienees, or creditors who do not have knowledge of the security interest and who acquire their interest in the real estate before the security interest in the fixture is perfected. Also, an advancement under a prior encumbrance, if such advancement is made without notice or knowledge of the security interest in the fixture and before the security interest is perfected, has priority over the imperfected security interest.

Under the provisions of the Code the party having a security interest in a fixture may, in the event of default of the debtor, remove the fixture from the real estate; "but he must reimburse any encumbrancer or owner of the real estate who is not the debtor and who has not otherwise agreed

---

[13] Uniform Commercial Code, Art. 9, Sec. 9–313.

for the cost of repair of any physical injury, but not for any diminution of the value of the real estate caused by the absence of the goods removed or by any necessity for replacing them."[14]

If an item of property is not attached to or used with the real estate so that it becomes a fixture, a mortgage on the real estate would not create a lien on such property. If the real estate mortgage is so drafted that it purports to create a lien on personal property on the mortgaged premises when such property is not a fixture, the effect of the filing of such a mortgage, as a real estate mortgage, on the described personal property will depend on the laws of the state. In general, to create a lien on personal property valid against bona fide purchasers or mortgagees for value or judgment lien creditors, the mortgage would have to be filed or recorded as a chattel mortgage; or in Code states, it would have to be perfected as required by the Code.

Intermountain Food Equipment Company (hereinafter referred to as Equipment Company) sold to Waller on a conditional sales contract certain kitchen equipment for use in the Hotel Washington. At the time of the sale and the installation of the equipment in the hotel, Connecticut Mutual Life Insurance Company had a real estate mortgage on the hotel real estate and a chattel mortgage on the equipment and personal property. Equipment Company filed its conditional sales contract as required by the statutes of the state. Default was made in the payments on the real estate and chattel mortgages, and also on Equipment Company's conditional sales contract. The real estate mortgage was foreclosed, and the mortgagee claimed that it had priority over Equipment Company's conditional sales contract. Equipment Company brought an action to recover possession of the kitchen equipment covered by its conditional sales contract. The court granted Equipment Company's request.

Justice McFadden said: "In the instant action we are dealing with specific chattels sold under a duly recorded conditional sales agreement. The cause of action here is in regard to the specific items of personal property, the validity of the conditional sales agreement, and whether or not such agreement was breached as to entitle respondent to possession of such articles of personal property. In the mortgage foreclosure action the cause of action was based on the note, and the real and chattel mortgages given to secure that note. If it was to be contended in the mortgage foreclosure action that the specific articles of personal property covered by the conditional sales contract were subject to the lien of either the real estate or chattel mortgages there involved, it was incumbent upon the plaintiff in that action to make such allegation in specific terms and fully advise respondent herein. The law is generally well settled that where the removal of a fixture will not materially injure the premises,

[14] Uniform Commercial Code, Sec. 9–313(5).

a seller retaining title to such property may assert his right against any prior mortgagee or vendor of the realty. And this is true regardless of notice to the prior mortgagee or vendor." *Intermountain Food Equipment Company* v. *Waller,* Idaho, 383 P.2d 612 (1963).

The mortgage debt

NATURE OF SECURED DEBT

The rule that the debt is the life of a mortgage and that a mortgage cannot exist unless it secures a debt is well established. However, the owner of real estate can make a gift of his real estate; and likewise, he can make a gift of a mortgage on his real estate. If the owner of real estate executes a gift mortgage on the real estate, the mortgage will be valid unless the mortgagor is insolvent and the enforcement of the mortgage would defeat the rights of creditors, or unless the mortgage is part of a scheme to defraud. The fact that the debt secured is unenforceable against the mortgagor for lack of consideration does not make the mortgage void.

A mortgage given to secure a past indebtedness is valid everywhere, even though a promise based on a past indebtedness is not enforceable for lack of consideration.[15] The courts also hold that a mortgage given to secure the indebtedness of a third person is valid.

As a general rule, a mortgage is given to secure the payment of a debt owned by the mortgagor. A mortgage may be given to secure the performance of an obligation of the mortgagor, provided the damages resulting from failure to perform the obligation can be reduced to a duty to pay money. In most mortgage transactions the personal indebtedness of the mortgagor is evidenced by a negotiable note, bond, or other writing; however, a writing or a personal indebtedness of the mortgagor is not essential to the validity of the mortgage.

The debt may be created by an oral promise, and the obligation secured by the mortgage may include an express provision that the mortgagor shall not be held personally liable on the obligation. In such a case the mortgagee's rights would be confined to his rights against mortgaged property. The fact that there exists no obligation which can be enforced against the mortgagor in a personal action brought against him does not necessarily render the mortgage void.

---

[15] *Hahn* v. *Hahn et al.,* 123 Cal. App. 97, 266 P.2d 519.

FUTURE ADVANCES

The courts in all the states have consistently held that a mortgage given to secure future advances which the mortgagee is obligated to make is valid, if properly executed and recorded, against all subsequent purchasers, mortgagees, or lien claimants, even though they acquired their interest in the real estate before the advances were actually made.[16] The courts have also held that advances made by the mortgagee to protect his security—such as payment of taxes, assessments, and insurance premiums—have priority over purchasers, mortgagees, or lien claimants who acquired their rights in the real estate subsequent to the recording of the mortgage but before payments were made.[17]

ADVANCES AT OPTION OF MORTGAGEE

A more difficult problem is presented when the making of future advances is at the option of the mortgagee, or when the mortgage is given to secure all indebtedness owing by the mortgagor to the mortgagee or to become owing at any future time. A mortgage given to secure optional future advances, or a mortgage given to secure all present and future indebtedness, is valid and enforceable against the parties to the mortgage.[18] The principal problem arises in determining the rights of subsequent purchasers, mortgagees, and lien claimants.

On May 9, 1962, Welch and his wife executed a note to Union Bank of Benton for the amount of $2,500; and at the same time, they executed a mortgage on described real estate to secure the note. The mortgage included the following: "This loan shall be used for the purpose of construction of a dwelling house on the above described property and shall cover and secure additional advances to be made by mortgagee to mortgagors in the total amount of $14,500."

On May 25, 1962, Lyman Lamb Company furnished materials for the construction of the dwelling; and on June 1, 1962, Union Bank of Benton advanced Welch $2,500, for which he executed a note. Welch defaulted in his payments, and Lyman Lamb Company filed a mechanic's lien on the premises. Union Bank of Benton claimed that its advance of June 1, 1962, had priority over

---

[16] *Taulbee et al.* v. *First National Bank of Jackson et al.,* 279 Ky. 153, 130 S.W.2d 48.

[17] *Tolson et al.* v. *Pyramid Life Insurance Co.,* 221 Ark. 492, 254 S.W.2d 53

[18] *Walters et ux.* v. *Merchants & Manufacturers Bank of Ellisville,* 218 Miss. 777, 67 So.2d 714.

Lyman Lamb Company's mechanic's lien on the ground that it would relate back to the date of the mortgage, May 11, 1962. The court held that the mechanic's lien had priority.

Justice Ward said: "It is conceded by appellants that appellee's mortgage is a first lien to the extent of $2,500. This is a concession by appellants that the previously quoted language in the mortgage constitutes a compliance with the statute and our decisions so as to make it a 'construction loan'—the mortgage having been filed before any materials were furnished. However, appellants contend, and we agree, that appellee's mortgage did not constitute a prior or first lien as to subsequent advances because the bank was not obligated to make them. This obligation was a prerequisite to appellee's lien, as was clearly announced in Planters Lumber Co. v. Jack Collier East Co. There, in construing § 51–605, we said: 'The mortgagee must be bound to advance the money for the construction . . . ,' citing Ashdown Hardware v. Hughes.

"We find no language in the mortgage here which unequivocally binds the bank to make the additional loans to Welch. Rather, the contrary is indicated by certain language in the mortgage." *Lyman Lamb Company* v. *Union Bank of Benton,* Ark., 374 S.W.2d 820 (1964).

THE OPEN-END MORTGAGE

A type of mortgage known as an *open-end mortgage* is being used with increasing frequency, especially in the field of home financing. The open-end mortgage in general use includes a package provision (discussed under the heading of "Package Mortgage," above). It further provides that the mortgage secures (1) a note executed by the mortgagor to the mortgagee and (2) any advances made by the mortgagee to the mortgagor, or his successor in title, for any purpose at any time. This provision is usually followed by a statement of a maximum amount to be secured by the mortgage, exclusive of any sums the mortgagee may pay in taxes, assessments, insurance premiums, and so forth, to protect his security.

The purpose of such a mortgage is to permit the mortgagee to make advances for the purchase of appliances, repairs, and remodeling; thus the mortgagor is enabled to cover all these indebtednesses by one mortgage, thereby saving the expense of making several loans and usually enabling him to finance his borrowing at a rate of interest lower than that charged on second-mortgage loans.

The open-end mortgage is valid and enforceable between the parties to the mortgage. However, the courts are not in accord as to the rights of subsequent purchasers, mortgagees, or lien claimants who have obtained rights in the mortgaged real estate after the execution and recording of the mortgage, but before advances are made under the terms of the mortgage.

Under the laws of those states which have adopted the Uniform Commercial Code, a security interest in goods which were to become fixtures, or a security interest in fixtures perfected before any advance is made, would have priority over the lien of the open-end mortgagee's advance. The Uniform Commercial Code does not affect the rights of subsequent real estate mortgagees and lien claimants other than those having a security interest in fixtures. In regard to such claimants, a majority of the states in which the question has been litigated have held that the optional advance has priority over intervening claims, unless the open-end mortgagee has actual notice or knowledge of the intervening claims at the time he makes the optional advance.

For example, suppose that the mortgagor has executed an open-end mortgage and thereafter borrows money from a lender other than the mortgagee, giving such lender a second mortgage on the real estate. If the first mortgagee, after the second mortgage is executed and recorded, makes advances under the open-end mortgage without actual notice or knowledge of the existence of the second mortgage, such advances will have priority over the recorded second mortgage. Under this rule the mortgagee in an open-end mortgage is not required to examine the records each time he makes an advance under the mortgage.[19]

However, if the second mortgagee or someone in his behalf gives the open-end mortgagee notice of the second mortgage, or if he has knowledge of it at the time he makes the advance, the lien of the second mortgage would have priority.

The minority view[20] holds that an intervening claim has priority over a subsequent advance. In the above example, under the minority rule the recorded second mortgage would have priority over subsequent advances made under the open-end mortgage, even though the first mortgagee had no actual notice or knowledge of the existence of the second mortgage. Under the minority rule the recording of the second mortgage or other claim is constructive notice to the first mortgagee. Under this rule the holder of an open-end mortgage, in order to protect himself, must examine the records before each advancement.[21]

---

[19] *Oaks* v. *Weingartner et al.,* 105 Cal. App.2d 598, 234 P.2d 194.

[20] Held in Illinois, Michigan, Ohio, and Pennsylvania.

[21] *Ginsberg et al.* v. *Capitol City Wrecking Co.,* 300 Mich. 712, 2 N.W.2d 892.

CONSTRUCTION MORTGAGE

A construction mortgage is one given on real estate to secure a loan made for the purpose of enabling the borrower to erect a building on the real estate or to remodel or repair an existing building. Since the amount loaned will, as a general rule, be more than the value of the mortgaged real estate, either the lender will obligate himself to advance the money as it is needed to pay labor or material bills as they mature, or he will pay the entire amount to a trustee, who will be authorized to pay it out as required under the terms of the construction contract. The relation between the lender-mortgagee, the borrower-mortgagor, and the contractor will be defined either by the terms of the mortgage or by the terms of a supplemental contract entered into by the parties.

Under the usual terms of a construction mortgage the lender-mortgagee binds himself to make future advances; the total amount of which is a sum certain. Since the lender-mortgagee is obligated to disperse the money, each payment would relate back to the date of the mortgage and would have priority over claims against or interests acquired in the mortgaged property subsequent to that date but before the money is paid out.

Frequently, the sum loaned will be paid into a special bank account in the lender-mortgagee's name as trustee, or some third person may act as trustee of the fund. The trustee will sign all checks issued in payment for the work and materials. Under this arrangement the mortgage or contract may provide that checks shall be signed by the trustee and countersigned by the borrower-mortgagor. Payments are usually made only on the production of an architect's or engineer's certificate.

If the money is held in trust, the trustee will be bound by any oral promise which he makes to laborers, materialmen, subcontractors, or contractors to pay their claims out of the fund.[22] The trustee should keep accurate records of all amounts expended and all amounts promised; otherwise, he may obligate himself to make payments in excess of the amount of the trust fund or the sum covered by the mortgage.

BLANKET MORTGAGE

A blanket mortgage is one that creates a lien on several tracts of land or properties and includes a provision obligating the mortgagee to release

---

[22] *City National Bank & Trust Co. of Salem* v. *Hassler,* 9 N.J. Super. 153, 75 A.2d 546.

individual tracts or properties from the mortgage when certain stipulated payments are made on the mortgage debt. For example, suppose that Archer has purchased a 20-acre tract of land which he plans to subdivide into lots. In order to obtain the funds necessary to develop the subdivision, he borrows money from the bank and gives the bank a mortgage on the 20-acre tract to secure the loan. Archer plans to obtain the money to pay the loan by selling lots. To facilitate the carrying-out of the plan, a provision will be included in the mortgage whereby the bank will agree to release from the mortgage the lots sold, provided stipulated payments have been made in reduction of the mortgage debt. Such a mortgage is known as a *blanket mortgage.*

Rights and duties of the parties

MORTGAGOR'S RIGHT OF POSSESSION

In both the title theory and the lien theory states, the mortgagor is recognized as the owner of the mortgaged real estate. The mortgagor, as owner, is entitled to the possession of the mortgaged real estate; he has the right to all the rents and profits arising therefrom, unless there is an agreement between the parties to the contrary.

DUTIES OF MORTGAGOR

The mortgagor, as owner of the mortgaged real estate, has all the rights of ownership. His duties in relation to the property are limited to refraining from doing any acts in relation to the property which would reduce its value to such an extent that it would no longer be reasonable security for the debt. The owner owes no duty to repair or improve the structures on the mortgaged property, but he has the right to make such repairs or improvements as he wishes. In the event of gross neglect which would cause serious loss of security, the court, in a proper action, would, as a general rule, have the power to appoint a receiver to take possession of the mortgaged real estate and to do whatever would be necessary to preserve the property and thereby protect the interest of the mortgagee.

Since the mortgagor is the owner of the property, he cannot be liable for the commission of waste. However, he would be enjoined from such

acts as the tearing-down and removal of buildings, the cutting of timber in unusual quantities, or the commission of other acts which would impair the value of the property so that it would no longer be adequate security for the debt.[23]

The mortgagor in possession owes a duty to pay all taxes and assessments which would become a lien on the land. The standard mortgage usually includes a clause making the failure to pay taxes and assessments a default, and, in such a case, permitting the mortgagee to declare the debt due and payable and to bring foreclosure proceedings. Also, the mortgagee may pay the taxes and assessments, and may add the amount disbursed to the principal of the mortgage debt.

In the absence of a provision in the mortgage or in the agreement of the parties, the mortgagor owes no duty to insure the mortgaged premises for the benefit of the mortgagee. The mortgagor and the mortgagee each have a distinct insurable interest in the property. The mortgagor may insure the property for its full value, without deduction because of the mortgage.

In a mortgage foreclosure case the court allowed, as part of the mortgage debt, $996.81 plus interest in the amount of $121.68, which represented taxes on the real estate paid by the mortgagee. The United States had a tax lien on the property. The parties admitted that the face of the mortgage plus accrued interst and costs had priority over the lien of the United States, but the United States contended that its lien had priority over the mortgagee's claim for real estate taxes paid on the mortgaged property. The court held that the taxes had priority.

Judge Teigen said: "Real estate taxes subsequently levied constitute a prior lien to the mortgage lien. Where the mortgagor fails to pay the real estate taxes, the mortgagee, for his own protection, is entitled by virtue of the statute (Section 35–01–07) to pay such taxes and to enforce payment of the amount so paid by him as a part of the claim for which his mortgage lien exists. The payment of the taxes by the mortgagee extinguishes the original tax lien and the amount paid is secured by the mortgage by force of statute and by the covenants of the mortgage. It is a charge upon the mortgaged premises in addition to the original mortgage debt and of the same grade and rank. The mortgage lien attaches to such payment. This rule is the general rule. It constitutes a single and indivisible demand and claim for taxes paid are collateral and subordinate to the mortgage and may not be separated and collected in an independent action." *Fisher* v. *Hoyer,* N.D., 121 N.W.2d 788 (1963).

---

[23] *Fountain* v. *Grant,* 210 Ga. 78, 77 S.E.2d 721.

INSURABLE INTEREST

The insurable interest of the mortgagee is his security right in the property, and he cannot collect insurance in excess of the value of his security right. If the mortgagee insures in his own right, the mortgagor has no interest in insurance money paid to the mortgagee in the event of damage to or destruction of the insured buildings; and the mortgagee does not owe a duty to apply such money in reduction of the mortgage debt.[24]

STANDARD INSURANCE CLAUSE

As a general rule, the mortgage will contain an insurance clause imposing on the mortgagor a duty to keep the mortgaged property insured for its full value, or for a value stated in the mortgage, for the benefit of the mortgagee, and further providing that on the mortgagor's failure to insure the mortgaged property, the mortgagee may insure and add the cost of the insurance to the amount of the mortgage debt. Usually, insurance policies on mortgaged property provide that the insurance is for the benefit of the mortgagor and the mortgagee as their interests may appear.

Morrissetti borrowed $100,000 from Perpetual Building Association (hereinafter referred to as Perpetual) for the purpose of constructing a building on land owned by him. The loan was secured by a trust deed (mortgage) which, among other provisions, provided that the mortgagor would insure the improvement to the satisfaction and for the benefit of the mortgagee and that the mortgagee would have the right to designate the insurer. It further provided that the mortgagor would notify the mortgagee of said insurance and that, on the mortgagor's failure to keep the improvement insured, the mortgagee had the right to insure the improvement or to declare a default.

While the improvement was under construction, Morrissetti insured it for his own benefit; the interest of Perpetual was not protected. When the improvement was completed, Morrissetti insured the improvement for his own benefit; and again, Perpetual's interest was not protected. After the lapse of about four months, however, Morrissetti had Perpetual's name added to the policy as an insured. At no time did Morrissetti notify Perpetual that he had insured the improvement. Perpetual insured the improvement for its own benefit and charged the premium to Morrissetti. Morrissetti brought this suit to recover for the amount of the premiums which Perpetual had deducted from payments

---

[24] *Le Doux et al.* v. *Dettmering et al.,* 316 Ill. App. 98, 43 N.E.2d 862.

made by him. The trial court entered judgment for Perpetual, and Morrissetti appealed. The judgment was affirmed.

Chief Judge Rover said: "After trial by the court it held that under the terms of the deed of trust appellants were obligated to secure insurance on the property and to promptly notify Perpetual of that fact; that having failed to do so the latter had the right to insure the property for its protection; that appellants, when they learned of the insurance placed by Perpetual, were under an obligation to mitigate their loss by canceling the policy they had secured, but had failed to do so; and that no evidence had been adduced by appellants to show that the premiums paid by Perpetual were either improper or illegal or that the insurance procured by the latter was not worth the premiums charged. It accordingly entered judgment for Perpetual and this appeal followed. We rule the court correct.

"The rule is enunciated in 59 C.J.S. Mortgages § 328a, 447, as follows:

> A covenant to the effect that the mortgagor will keep the buildings on the mortgaged premises insured for the benefit of the mortgagee may be inserted in the mortgage and is valid and binding, if sufficient in form. . . . Under a provision requiring the mortgagor to insure the mortgaged premises the primary duty to insure is on the mortgagor, and in procuring insurance in accordance therewith the mortgagor is not an agent of the mortgagee.
>
> Unless such a provision is waived, its breach will give the mortgagee the right to take out insurance for the protection of his security at the expense of the mortgagor. . . .

Morrissetti v. *Perpetual Building Association,* Munic. Ct. of App., D.C., 150 A.2d 262 (1959).

RIGHTS OF MORTGAGEE

The principal purpose for taking a mortgage is to reduce the risk of loss resulting from the failure of the debtor to pay the debt. Consequently, the primary right of the mortgagee is to have the secured debt paid when due; and the secondary right is, on default in the payment of the debt, to have the mortgaged real estate sold and the proceeds applied in extinction or reduction of the debt. Duties other than the payment of the secured debt may be imposed on the mortgagor by the terms of the mortgage. The mortgagee has the right to have the mortgagor fulfill all such duties.

Under some circumstances, the mortgagee may be granted possession of the mortgaged real estate; or he may, on the mortgagor's default, have a receiver appointed who will take possession of the property and manage it during a pending foreclosure or other legal action involving the property. In the event the mortgagee or a receiver takes possession of the property, he must account for the rents and profits actually received by him; and any surplus over and above costs of upkeep, taxes, and other management expenses must be applied in payment of the mortgage debt. The position of the mortgagee or receiver in possession of the mortgaged property is similar in many respects to that of the manager of rental real estate. He must use reasonable diligence to keep the property rented, must keep it in reasonable repair, and must pay taxes, assessments, and other necessary items.[25] His duty to pay such items is limited to the income derived from the property. Each year the mortgagee or receiver in possession must account for the amount received, and must credit the net over and above legitimate expenditures in reduction of the mortgage debt.

ASSIGNMENT OF RENTS

A mortgagor may, at the time the mortgage is executed, make an assignment of rents to the mortgagee, the assignment to become effective on the mortgagor's default. The rent assignment may be included in the mortgage, or it may be made as a separate agreement. In either case the rent assignment should be drafted in language that will make it clear that the parties intended to assign the rents—not merely to pledge them—as security for the loan.

There are three views as to the rights acquired by the mortgagee by an assignment of rents made at the time of the execution of the mortgage:

1. Some states[26] hold, by their statutes or by court decisions, that the rent assignment is a pledge and that the mortgagee has no right to the assigned rents until default and foreclosure. Almost the only benefit the mortgagee can derive from a rent assignment in these states is that the court will, on default on the part of the mortgagor, appoint a receiver to collect rents without requiring the mortgagee to prove that the failure to appoint a receiver would result in the impairment of his security.[27]

---

[25] *Levin* v. *Carney et al.,* 161 Ohio St. 513, 120 N.E.2d 92.

[26] Arkansas, Colorado, Florida, Georgia, Illinois, Indiana, Iowa, Kansas, Kentucky, Louisiana, Mississippi, Montana, New York, North Dakota, Ohio, Oregon, South Dakota, Texas, and Wisconsin.

[27] *Fisher* v. *Norman Apartments, Inc.,* 101 Colo. 173, 72 P.2d 1092.

2. Another group of states[28] hold, by their statutes or by court decisions, that the rent assignment is a conveyance of the title to the rents and that the mortgagee may, on default, take possession under his assignment and collect the rents without court action.[29]

3. A minority of states hold,[30] by statute or court decisions, that an assignment of rents made at the time of the execution of the mortgage is against public policy and void. An assignment of rents made for a valid consideration after default is valid.

Recording the mortgage

REQUIREMENTS FOR RECORDING

The statutes providing for the recording of conveyances of real estate apply to both deeds and mortgages. The requirements for recording, the necessity of recording, and the effect of recording were discussed in Chapter 8 ,"Recording and Evidence of Title."

EFFECT OF RECORDING

Generally, a mortgage which is otherwise valid creates a lien on the real estate which is mortgaged; it is binding as between the parties to the mortgage and all persons claiming under it, even though it is not recorded. Likewise, statutes which provide that the recording of the mortgage must be renewed or reinscribed within a specified period of time do not affect the validity of the obligation as between the parties to the mortgage or the parties claiming under it.[31]

At common law, prior to the adoption of recording statutes, a valid legal mortgage given to a good-faith mortgagee for value was superior to (cut off) all existing equitable mortgages or equitable claims of which

---

[28] Alabama, California, Connecticut, Delaware, Maine, Maryland, Massachusetts, Michigan, Missouri, Nebraska, New Hampshire, North Carolina, New Jersey, Pennsylvania, Tennessee, Virginia, and West Virginia.

[29] *Mortgage Guarantee Co. et al.* v. *Sampsell,* 51 Cal. App.2d 180, 124 P.2d 353.

[30] Minnesota, Oklahoma, South Carolina, and Washington.

[31] *Dr. Joe F. Shuffield* v. *Raney,* 226 Ark. 3, 287 S.W.2d 588.

the mortgagee had no notice or knowledge at the time of the execution of the mortgage. As between successive mortgagees, the general rule was: The first in time has the superior rights.

Under the recording statutes the recording of a mortgage executed in compliance with the recording statutes of the state in which the mortgaged real estate is located is constructive notice to the public of the existence of the mortgage. However, recording does not given a mortgagee priority over outstanding equities of which he has notice or knowledge.

PURCHASE-MONEY MORTGAGE. Purchase-money mortgages, even though they are not recorded, have priority over judgments taken against the purchaser or over mortgages executed by him before taking title to the property, and over mechanics' liens, dower, curtesy, and other rights attaching to his interest on his acquisition of title.[32]

RIGHTS OF ASSIGNEE. If a mortgagee has a valid lien as a good-faith mortgagee for value, without notice or knowledge of outstanding equities of prior unrecorded instruments, his rights will pass to an assignee, his devisees, or heirs, even though such persons had notice or knowledge of the outstanding equities or unrecorded instrument. The mortgagee owns a valid lien and can convey a valid lien.

Conveyance of mortgaged real estate

RIGHT OF MORTGAGOR TO SELL

The mortgagor has the right to sell and convey, or to mortgage the mortgaged real estate or any part thereof to third persons. Any sale or mortgage or the mortgaged real estate does not affect the mortgagee's rights in the property. Ordinarily, the sale or mortgage of the mortgaged real estate may be made without the consent of the mortgagee.[33] The grantee of the mortgagor acquires all the rights of the mortgagor—that is, he has the right to the possession and use of the property, and the right to the rents and profits; but all the rights which he acquires are in subordination to the rights of the mortgagee under the mortgage.

The purchaser of the mortgaged property is not liable for the mortgage debt unless he contracts to pay it. The sale may be (1) free and clear;

---

[32] *Melrose* v. *Industrial Associates,* 136 Conn. 518, 72 A.2d 469.

[33] *Vernon* v. *Lincoln National Life Insurance Co.,* 200 Ark. 47, 138 S.W.2d 61.

(2) subject to the mortgage; or (3) subject to the mortgage, the purchaser agreeing to pay the mortgage debt.

FREE AND CLEAR

If the mortgaged property is sold free and clear of the mortgage, the seller-mortgagor contracts to obtain from the mortgagee a discharge of the mortgage either before or at the time of the closing of the sale and the execution of the deed. A substantial portion of the sales of mortgaged real estate are sales free and clear of the mortgage.

Some mortgages contain acceleration clauses maturing the mortgage debt and making it due and payable on the sale of the mortgaged real estate by the mortgagor. In other transactions the purchaser may wish to refinance the mortgage, in which case, he will arrange to pay the existing mortgage and obtain a new loan and a new mortgage. It is not uncommon for the mortgagee to discharge the existing mortgage and take a new mortgage with the purchaser of the property as mortgagor.

In any sale of mortgaged real estate free and clear of the mortgage, the mortgagor is liable to the purchaser for any damage he may suffer as the result of the mortgagor's failure to obtain a discharge of the mortgage. As a general rule, the purchaser has the right to rescind the contract of sale if the seller-mortgagor fails to obtain a discharge of the mortgage.

SUBJECT TO THE MORTGAGE

When the grantee of the mortgagor of mortgaged real estate takes the property subject to the mortgage, the conveyance amounts to a transfer to the grantee of whatever estate the mortgagor-grantor has in the mortgaged real estate after the mortgage debt is satisfied out of the real estate.[34] If the purchase price of the mortgaged real estate is a sum equal to the value of the property less the amount of the mortgage debt, the presumption is that the grantee purchased the land subject to the mortgage.

When mortgaged real estate is sold subject to the mortgage, the mortgagee's lien continues; and as between the mortgagor, the mortgagee, and the grantee, the mortgaged real estate is the primary source of the funds for the payment of the mortgage debt. If the grantee wishes to release the mortgaged real estate from the mortgage lien, he must pay

---

[34] *Wolfert* v. *Guadagno et al.*, 130 Cal. App. 661, 20 P.2d 360.

the mortgage debt.[35] However, the grantee is not personally liable for the mortgage debt; and if the mortgage debt is not paid and the mortgage is foreclosed, the mortgagee is not entitled to a deficiency judgment against the grantee.

As between the mortgagor and the mortgagee, the mortgagor, after the sale of the mortgaged real estate subject to the mortgage, is surety for the payment of the mortgage debt up to the value of the mortgaged real estate and is individually liable to the extent the mortgage debt exceeds the value of the mortgaged real estate. Consequently, if the mortgagee, knowing that the mortgagor has conveyed the mortgaged real estate subject to the mortgage, releases the mortgage to the grantee without the knowledge or consent of the mortgagor, the mortgagor will be released from his personal liability for the mortgage debt up to the value of the mortgaged real estate.[36]

If the grantee pays the mortgage debt and the mortgage is discharged and a release given, the grantee is not entitled to reimbursement. However, if the mortgagor-grantor has conveyed the mortgaged real estate subject to the mortgage and has paid the mortgage debt, he has recourse to the mortgaged real estate for reimbursement; but he cannot hold the grantee personally liable.[37]

This action was brought to recover a refund for gross income tax paid on the sale of real estate. Shirmeyer sold Prang a house on which there was a mortgage. Prang paid $800 down and later paid $2,760. The deed recited that the property was sold subject to the unpaid balance on a mortgage to Wayne Mortgage Company, Inc. Prang paid Wayne Mortgage Company, Inc., $4,200 and satisfied the mortgage on the property. Under the tax laws of the state, if Prang was not legally obligated to pay the mortgage debt, Shirmeyer was not obligated to pay the gross income tax on the mortgage debt paid by Prang, since such payment would not be classed as income to Shirmeyer. The court held that since the property was purchased "subject to the mortgage," Prang was not legally liable for the mortgage debt.

Judge Bobbitt said: "While it may be in the interest of the purchasers in this case to pay off the mortgage to Wayne Mortgage Company, Inc., yet, when they purchased the real estate here in question subject to the existing mortgage, they [the grantee-purchasers] assumed no personal liability for the

---

[35] *Barkhausen* v. *Continental Illinois National Bank & Trust Company,* 3 Ill.2d 354, 120 N.E.2d 649.

[36] *First National Bank & Trust Co.* v. *Strong,* 112 Conn. 412, 152 A. 575.

[37] *Seaman's Bank for Savings in City of New York* v. *Samdbeck* 293 N.Y. 91, 56 N.E.2d 46.

payment of the mortgage . . . ; but took said real estate charged with the payment of the debt and such property became the primary fund out of which said mortgage must be paid.

"In securing the fund out of which said mortgage was to be paid the purchasers [Prangs] assumed only an equitable obligation to pay the debt secured by the mortgage, and the legal obligation for the payment of the debt secured by said mortgage remained that the mortgagor [Shirmeyer]." *Ralph L. Shirmeyer Inc.* v. *Indiana Revenue Board,* 229 Ind. 586, 99 N.E.2d 847 (1951).

SUBJECT TO THE MORTGAGE AND ASSUMPTION OF MORTGAGE DEBT

The grantee of mortgaged real estate may take the property subject to the mortgage, and may assume and agree to pay the mortgage debt. Whether or not the grantee has assumed and agreed to pay the mortgage debt will depend on the terms of the sales contract and on the circumstances surrounding the transaction. The courts have held that the agreement to assume the mortgage debt need not be included as a provision of the deed, but may be included in the contract to sell; or it may be in a separate agreement, either written or oral; or it may be implied from the surrounding circumstances.[38]

The best practice, however, is that of including in the deed a provision stating that the conveyance is subject to a mortgage, describing the mortgage (date of mortgage, names of mortgagor and mortgagee, amount of mortgage and unpaid balance, and book and page of recordation), and further providing that the grantee "hereby assumes and personally agrees to pay the mortgage debt as part of the consideration for this conveyance." The important words are "assumes and agrees to pay the mortgage debt." If the grantee accepts a deed containing such a provision, with knowledge that the provision is in the deed, his intent to assume the mortgage debt will be clearly established.

In some instances in which the deed has stated the conveyance was subject to the mortgage but the parties, in negotiating the transaction, have agreed upon the full value of the real estate as the purchase price and have deducted from the purchase price the unpaid balance of the mortgage debt, the courts have held that the grantee was personally liable for the payment of the mortgage debt. The courts so holding have reasoned that it would be unfair to permit the grantee to withhold the grantor's money and not be liable for the payment of the mortgage debt.[39]

---

[38] California, New York, and Pennsylvania require the agreement to assume the mortgage debt to be included in the deed or in a separate written agreement.

[39] *Dimmitt et al.* v. *Johnson et al.,* 199 Iowa 996, 203 N.W. 261.

LIABILITY OF GRANTEE.   In assuming the mortgage debt, the grantee of the mortgaged real estate makes himself personally liable to the mortgagor-grantor for the payment of the mortgage debt, and he also makes himself personally liable for the mortgage debt to the mortgagee.[40] Although the courts are in substantial accord in holding that the grantee who has assumed a mortgage debt is personally liable to the mortgagee on the mortgage debt,[41] there is considerable diversity of opinion as to the basis for holding the grantee liable.

In practice, the mortgagee will, on the mortgagor's default, bring action to foreclose the mortgage and will join in such action the mortgagor and all grantees who have assumed the mortgage debt. If, on foreclosure and sale, there is a deficiency, the mortgagee will be granted a deficiency judgment against the mortgagor and all the grantees who have assumed the mortgage debt. Since the mortgagee is entitled to only one satisfaction, he no longer has a claim against any of the parties defendant when he has collected his deficiency judgment. As between the mortgagor and the assuming grantees, the last assuming grantee is liable to all prior grantors.

For example, suppose that Alberts owns real estate which he mortgages to Bates. Thereafter, Alberts sells the property to Call, who assumes the mortgage debt. Then Call sells to Deal, who assumes the mortgage debt; and Deal sells to Evans, who assumes the mortgage debt. The mortgage debt is not paid when due; Bates brings a foreclosure action joining Alberts, Call, Deal, and Evans as parties defendant. The mortgaged property, on the foreclosure sale, does not bring enough to satisfy the mortgage debt, and a deficiency judgment is entered against all the parties defendant. If Call pays the deficiency judgment, he will have a right to collect from Deal or Evans the amount paid; and if Deal pays, he can collect from Evans. Since Evans is the last assuming grantee, he is the one who is ultimately legally liable for the deficiency.

The mortgagee may expressly or by implication agree to release the mortgagor from his liability for the mortgage debt and accept the grantee in his place. This is known as a *novation.*[42]

---

[40] *Stinert* v. *Galasso,* 363 Pa. 393, 69 A.2d 841.

[41] Apparently, Massachusetts holds that the mortgagee cannot bring an action in his own name against the grantee who has assumed the mortgage debt without the consent of the mortgagor (*Provident Institution of Savings* v. *Merrill,* 311 Mass. 168, 40 N.E.2d 280).

[42] *Lynn Five Cents Savings Bank* v. *Portnoy,* 306 Mass. 436, 28 N.E.2d 418.

Hafford and Smith entered into an agreement whereby Hafford exchanged a trailer for real estate which was owned by Smith and which was subject to two mortgages. The deed executed by Smith conveying the real estate to Hafford included a clause following the description of the real estate indicating that the deed was executed subject to a mortgage to Savings and Loan Association; and the deed further recited: ". . . subject also to a deed of trust to Dave R. Ashmore and Lillian R. Ashmore, which buyer assumes and agrees to pay." Savings and Loan Association foreclosed its mortgage. Hafford contended that the assumption-of-mortgage clause was inserted by fraud and brought this action to be relieved from liability for the Ashmore debt. The court found that Hafford had agreed to assume the mortgage debt.

The court said: "It may be generally stated that a purchaser who accepts and holds land under a deed reciting that he has assumed and agreed to pay an outstanding mortgage, subjects himself to personal liability on the mortgage. This is one way in which the contract of assumption may arise.

"Admittedly, this rule is somewhat artificial—the contract of assumption is sometimes said to be 'implied' in such cases—and if the assumption clause is inserted through fraud or mistake of the grantor or scrivener, or the deed is accepted by the grantee without knowledge of the assumption clause, then the grantee incurs no personal liability to the mortgagee. Accepting the assumption clause without more, does not bind the grantee, though the deed may yet be effective as a conveyance of the land. In other words, the principle that a party must be presumed to know the content and meaning of a written instrument which he takes as evidence of title, does not extend so far as to conclusively impose on the grantee of mortgaged land a collateral personal liability for the mortgage debt formed upon a clause inserted in the deed without his knowledge and expressing an agreement which he has not made.

"It is true, as the appellants complain, that where the deed expressly provides for the grantee's assumption of an outstanding mortgage, the application of the principle is rather narrowly limited by the parol evidence rule. It appears that if a grantee who wishes to controvert the provisions of a conveyance containing an express assumption clause, after accepting it, must resort to equity to do so, he has the burden of proving non-assumption by clear and convincing proof." *Hafford* v. *Smith,* Mo. App., 369 S.W.2d 290 (1963).

SUBSEQUENT SALES

Each subsequent purchaser who, as part of the transaction, assumes the mortgage debt thereby becomes primarily liable; and all prior purchasers who have, as part of their purchase agreements, assumed the mortgage debt will become sureties along with the mortgagor. Since the assumption of the mortgage debt creates a principal-surety relationship, the law of suretyship is applied in determining the liabilities of the parties in regard to subsequent dealings.

Under the law of suretyship, if the creditor and the principal enter into an enforceable contract which alters the terms of the original contract without the surety's knowledge or consent, and the surety does not ratify the contract or waive his rights as surety, the surety will be discharged from his obligation on the contract. Under this rule, any valid extension of time for the payment of the mortgage, or any agreement materially altering the terms of the mortgage given to the grantee who is primarily liable without the consent of the prior assuming grantees or of the mortgagor, will discharge such persons from their personal liability on the mortgage debt.[43] This rule is not followed in a majority of the states in an action against the mortgagor if the mortgage debt is evidenced by a negotiable instrument. The exception is based on the negotiable instruments rule of law that an extension of time granted to an endorsee of the instrument does not discharge the party primarily liable on the instrument.[44]

Assignment by the mortgagee

NATURE OF ASSIGNMENT OF MORTGAGE

In discussing the assignment of the mortgage by the mortgagee, it is important to keep in mind the fact that the mortgagee has two things: ownership of the debt and an interest in the real estate which secures the debt. At common law the title to the real estate was vested in the mortgagee; if he wished to transfer his interests, he was required to deed the real estate and assign the debt. This situation does not exist today. The mortgage cannot be transferred separately from the debt; and all the courts hold that since the mortgage is given for the sole purpose of securing the debt, any transfer of the debt carries with it the right to the security of the mortgage.

MORTGAGE ACCOMPANIES DEBT

Suppose that a mortgagee assigns the mortgage to Arthur and the mortgage debt to Bert. In such a case the benefits of the mortgage security

---

[43] *Lynn Five Cents Savings Bank* v. *Portnoy,* 306 Mass. 436, 28 N.E.2d 418.

[44] *Mortgage Guaranty Co.* v. *Chotiner,* 8 Cal.2d 110, 64 P.2d 138.

would go with the debt to Bert. In all but a few states the courts would hold that the attempted assignment of the mortgage to Arthur was a nullity and the Arthur would take nothing by the assignment. In a minority of states the courts would decide that Arthur holds the mortgage as trustee for the benefit of Bert. In all states the practical result is the same—that is, Bert, as assignee of the debt, gets the benefit of the security.

Nonnegotiable and negotiable debt

In determining the rights and duties of the parties involved in the assignment of a mortgage and the mortgage debt, we must first determine the nature of the mortgage debt. If it is nonnegotiable in form, the rules of general contract law relating to the assignment of contracts apply in determining the rights and duties of the parties. However, if the debt is negotiable in form—that is, if the debt is evidenced by a negotiable instrument, such as a negotiable promissory note—the law relative to the negotiation of negotiable instruments applies.

It is beyond the scope of this work to discuss in detail the law of assignment of contracts and the law of negotiable instruments; however, we shall state the general rules on which the rights of the parties are based.

Assignment if debt is nonnegotiable

The assignment of a contract is, in legal effect, the sale of intangible personal property, and the basic rules of the sale of property are applied in working out the rights of the parties. Since it is fundamental in the law of property that a person cannot transfer good title to property which he does not own, it is equally fundamental in the law of the assignment of contracts that the obligee (the creditor) cannot assign greater rights in the contract (the debt) than he has. Stated in other words, the assignee of a nonnegotiable debt takes the debt subject to all defenses which the debtor has against the creditor.

Under this rule the assignee of a mortgage securing a nonnegotiable debt will be able to enforce the mortgage only to the extent that he can enforce the debt; that is, if the mortgagor-debtor has any defense to the debt—such as fraud, duress, or lack or failure of consideration or payment—these defenses will be good against the assignee of the mortgage in an action to foreclose the mortgage.

To protect himself, the assignee of a nonnegotiable debt, or someone in his behalf, should give the mortgagor notice of the assignment, since the rights of the assignee in the debt are fixed as of the time the debtor is given notice of the assignment. It must be direct notice to the debtor, but no special form is required. Good business practice requires the giving of written notice, and it should describe with certainty the debt assigned. The recording of the assignment of the mortgage is not notice to the mortgagor of the assignment, since he owes no duty to check the records before making payment to the mortgagee. When notice of the assignment is given to the mortgagor-debtor, he owes a duty to pay the debt, when due, to the assignee; payment to the mortgagee after notice will not discharge the debt and mortgage. Also, all matters by way of setoff arising after notice of the assignment will be cut off, but defenses arising under the contract (counterclaims) will not be affected.

ESTOPPEL CERTIFICATE

Since the assignee of a nonnegotiable debt cannot know of outstanding defenses, he can protect himself, at least in part, by obtaining from the mortgagor-debtor what is commonly termed a *certificate of estoppel.* This is a statement by the mortgagor to the effect that he owes the debt, that the debt is of a certain amount, and that he has no defenses to or claims against the creditor.

If the mortgagor-debtor gives the prospective assignee such a statement before the debt is assigned, the mortgagor-debtor will not be permitted, as a means of defeating the rights of the assignee, to set up any defenses arising prior to the giving of the statement. The statement, if it is to be effective, must be obtained before the assignment is made. It will not protect the assignee against defenses arising out of a default in performance by the mortgagee-creditor after the giving of the statement.[45] For example, if Bert, in the hypothetical situation stated above, gives Clark an estoppel certificate at the time of the assignment, and thereafter Arthur defaults in the performance of the contract, Clark could not recover the full contract price. He could recover only the contract price less damages for defective performance.

An oral statement by the mortgagor-debtor is sufficient to prevent him from setting up defenses arising prior to the making of the statement. However, the prospective assignee, for full protection, should get the

---

[45] *Newtown Title & Trust Co.* v. *Admiral Farragut Academy,* 84 F. Supp. 527.

statement in writing, signed by the mortgagor-debtor. Oral statements are frequently difficult to prove in the event of a court action.

ASSIGNMENT OF NEGOTIABLE DEBT

If the debt is evidenced by a negotiable instrument, the law of negotiable instruments applies in determining the rights of the parties to the debt. In all but a small minority of states[46] the courts hold that since the mortgage follows the debt and its sole purpose is as security for the payment of the debt, the holder of the negotiable instrument evidencing the debt has the same rights in the mortgage as he has in the debt.[47]

Under the law of negotiable instruments a person to whom a negotiable instrument is property negotiated and who takes the instrument for value, before it is overdue and without notice or knowledge of defects in the title or in defenses to the instrument, takes the instrument free from defenses between the parties. If the instrument is a bearer instrument, it may be negotiated by delivery alone; but if it is an order instrument— payable to the order of a named payee—it must be endorsed and delivered to be properly negotiated.

Before a person can qualify as a holder in due course—one who takes free from personal defenses—the instrument must be complete and regular on its face. If any material provision of the instrument is omitted— such as the name of the payee, in case it is an order instrument—or if there are strike-outs or erasures on the instrument, it is not complete and regular on its face.

The taker of the instrument must give value for it. If he is a donee of the instrument or inherits it, he has not given value. He must take the instrument before it is past due, and he must take it in good faith— that is, without notice or knowledge that the party primarily liable has a good defense to the instrument.

If the holder of the instrument can qualify as a holder in due course, he takes it free from such defenses as fraud, duress, undue influence, lack or failure of consideration, and all other defenses personal to the parties to the instrument. However, he does not take free from real defenses, such as forgery, lack of capacity to contract, and other defenses which might be offered to prove that the instrument was invalid from its inception—that is, that it was never a valid instrument.

---

[46] Illinois, Minnseota, and Ohio.

[47] *Patrick* v. *Kilgore et al.*, 238 Ala. 604, 193 So. 112.

If the person taking the negotiable instrument evidencing the debt cannot qualify as a holder in due course or does not take from a holder in due course, his position is substantially the same as that of the asignee of a nonnegotiable debt, and the rules relating to the rights of the assignee of a nonnegotiable debt would apply in determining his rights.

Latney and wife executed to Dorne their negotiable promissory note secured by a deed of trust. Soldoro Corporation purchased the note, which was endorsed to it. The court held that Soldoro Corporation took the note as holder in due course. Latney refused to pay the note, and Soldoro Corporation assigned the note and deed of trust to Oshinsky for collection and foreclosure. The Latneys set up as a defense that they were induced to issue the note and execute the trust deed by fradulent representations as to the condition of the house they were purchasing, which was the mortgaged property. The trial court held that the defense was not available against the holder in due course. On appeal, the holding was affirmed.

Associate Judge Hood said: "The trial court properly ruled that the corporation was a holder in due course and that the defenses raised were not available against it." *Latney* v. *Oshinsky,* Munic. Ct. of App., D.C., 169 A.2d 687 (1961).

EFFECT OF RECORDING ASSIGNMENT OF MORTGAGE

There is considerable confusion as to the effect of the recording of an assignment of a mortgage on the rights of the parties. The recording statutes of some states require the recording of assignments of mortgages; those of other states permit, but do not require, the recording of such assignments; and those of a few states are so drafted that an assignment of a mortgage is not eligible for record.

In general, the recording of an assignment of a mortgage is not notice to the mortgagor of the assignment; and if the mortgagor, without having been given personal notice of the assignment, pays the mortgage debt to the mortgagee after the assignment and recording of the assignment, such payment will discharge the mortgage debt. Recording of the assignment of a mortgage is of little importance in regard to the rights of subsequent purchasers or mortgagees. The recorded mortgage is notice of its existence, and the subsequent purchaser or mortgagee has little or no interest in knowing who owns the mortgage debt. If the mortgage debt is evidenced by a negotiable instrument, the only way the debt can be discharged is by payment to the holder in due course of the negotiable instrument. Since the debt cannot be recorded, but can be assigned or negotiated without the assignment of the mortgage, the recording of the assignment has little effect on the rights of the owner of the debt. However, the recording of the assignment is important in one respect: It makes known the person who can discharge the mortgage of record. This will be discussed under a separate heading.

PARTIAL ASSIGNMENTS

A single mortgage may be given as security for the payment of one debt or several debts, as, for instance, a series of notes or bonds. And even though the mortgage is given to secure a single debt, more than one person may eventually have an interest in it, since the mortgagee may assign interests in the debt to different assignees. In such cases the courts are not in accord as to the relative rights of the several assignees in the mortgage security.

One view, which is both logical and equitable and apparently the majority view, is that the several assignees share the mortgage security on a pro rata basis. Another view is that the assignees share in the order in which the assignments were made. A third view, which applies only to a series of notes or bonds, is that the assignees' rights attach in the order of the maturity of the notes or bonds which they hold.

The courts have generally held that if the debt is evidenced by a series of notes and the mortgagee endorses the notes with an unqualified endorsement, or guarantees the payment of the bond or debt, the holder of the notes or bonds or the assignee of the debt will have priority over the mortgagee in the security, since he is personally liable and, as guarantor, cannot compete with the holder of the debt.

Discharge of mortgage

DISCHARGE BY PAYMENT OF DEBT

In the majority of mortgage transactions the mortgage is discharged by the payment of the mortgage debt. Since the mortgage cannot exist separate and apart from the debt it secures, a payment which will discharge the debt will, by operation of law, discharge the mortgage. A change in the form of the debt, however, such as the reducing of the debt to judgment or the giving of a renewal note for the one evidencing the debt secured by the mortgage, will not discharge the mortgage, since the debt secured by the mortgage will not have been discharged. The mortgage debt may be paid by the person primarily liable or by any person at the request of the person primarily liable or by the mortgagor, but a mere volunteer has no right to pay the mortgage debt.[48]

In order to discharge a mortgage, the mortgagor or his successor must pay the mortgage debt to the person entitled to payment, or to his agent who is authorized to accept payment. If the mortgage debt is evidenced by a writing, the person making payment should demand the surrender of the written evidence of the debt along with the mortgage. If a grantee has assumed a mortgage debt and he makes payment to one who is not the holder of the mortgage and the written evidence of the debt, the mortgage is not discharged.[49] Also, if the mortgage debt is evidenced by a negotiable instrument, the person making payment should, in order to protect himself, demand surrender of the negotiable instrument when payment is made.[50]

If payment is made to one who claims to be the agent of the owner of the mortgage and mortgage debt, the person making payment must ascertain, at his peril, whether or not the agent is authorized to accept payment. Payment should never be made to an agent who does not have possession of the mortgage and the written evidence of the debt.

The courts have held that the fact that an agent has authority to collect interest on the mortgage debt does not imply that he has authority to accept payment of the principal, particularly if payment of the principal is made before the due date.

Cole Vending Industries, Inc., issued its promissory note to Exchange National Bank of Chicago. The note was secured by a mortgage on real estate owned by Albert Cole and Frieda Cole. The Coles signed the note as sureties and executed the mortgage. Payments were made on the note; and when it became due, a renewal note for the unpaid balance, extending the time of payment, was executed by Cole Vending Industries, Inc. On default in the payment of the renewal note, an action to foreclose the mortgage was brought. Cole and wife set up as a defense that the renewal of the note without their consent discharged the mortgage. The court held that the renewal did not discharge the mortgage.

Judge Tillman Pearson said, quoting Thompson on Real Property: " 'Change in form of indebtedness or in mode or time of payment as discharging mortgage lien.—No change in the form of the evidence, or the mode or time of payment,

[48] *Bourquin* v. *Feland et al.,* 189 Okla. 489, 117 P.2d 789.

[49] *Holvick* v. *Black et al.,* 57 N.D. 270, 221 N.W. 71.

[50] *Henningsen* v. *Title & Trust Co.,* 151 Ore. 318, 49 P.2d 458.

nothing short of actual payment of the debt, or an express release, will operate to discharge the mortgage unless so intended. The mortgage remains a lien until the debt it was given to secure is satisfied, and is not affected by a change of the note, or by giving a different instrument as evidence of the debt, or by a judgment at law on the note merging the original evidence of indebtedness, or by a recognizance of record taken in lieu of the mortgage note. The mortgage secures the debt, not the evidence thereof.'

"We conclude that the debt of which the note was the evidence has not been discharged and that the subsequent renewal in this case did not release the lien of the mortgage under the rule as to the release of sureties. It follows that the decree of the chancellor must be reversed." *Exchange National Bank of Chicago* v. *Cole,* Fla., 161 So.2d 715 (1964).

PAYMENT OF PORTION OF DEBT (BLANKET MORTGAGE). If a person has purchased part of mortgaged real estate, he cannot, by paying a proportionate part of the mortgage debt, get a release of the portion purchased.[51] However, when a mortgage is given on a subdivision, the mortgage agreement frequently provides that lots in the subdivision will be released from the mortgage on payment to the mortgagee of a stipulated sum for each lot released. Such agreements are enforceable; and the purchaser of the lot, on payment of the sum stipulated for the release of a lot from the mortgage, is entitled to a release.

PAYMENT BY SURETY

Under the law of suretyship, if a surety or guarantor pays the debt of his principal, he is subrogated to all rights of the creditor. If the principal, in addition to having sureties or guarantor cosign, has secured the payment of the debt by executing a mortgage on real estate and a surety or guarantor pays the mortgage debt, the mortgage will not be discharged, but such surety or guarantor will be subrogated to the mortgagee's rights and may proceed to foreclose the mortgage.

A similar situation arises when co-owners of real estate join in mortgaging the co-owned real estate and one of the co-owners pays the mortgage debt. The mortgage will not be discharged but will be kept alive for the benefit of the person making the payment. Since he is not primarily liable for the entire mortgage debt, he will be subrogated to the rights of the mortgagee against his co-owners.[52]

TENDER OF PAYMENT. The courts are not in accord as to the effect

---

[51] *Merrimon et al.* v. *Parkey et al.,* 136 Tenn. 645, 191 S.W. 327.

[52] *Hare* v. *Reddy et al.,* 222 Wis. 508, 269 N.W. 294.

on a mortgage of a tender of payment of the mortgage debt. As a general rule, a valid tender of payment of the mortgage debt will discharge the mortgage. In order to make a valid tender, the mortgagor or person primarily liable, or his duly authorized agent, must make an unconditional offer to pay the mortgage debt in money—an offer to give a personal check is not a valid tender. The tender must be made on or after the due date. The mortgagee or owner of the mortgage debt is not obligated to accept payment before the due date. If the mortgagee or owner of the mortgage debt refuses to accept the tender and his refusal is justified, the mortgage will not be discharged. As a general rule, if the mortgagee or owner of the mortgage debt does not object to the form of the tender but unconditionally refuses to accept payment, he will have waived his right to object to the form of the tender.[53] In some states the tender, if it is to be a bar to foreclosure proceedings, must be kept good—that is, the money tendered must be paid into court or to a trustee, to be held for the mortgagee or owner of the debt.

A tender does not discharge the debt, but it does stop the accumulation of interest. And if the tender is kept good and suit is later brought by the owner of the debt, the plaintiff cannot tax the cost of the suit against the defendant who made the tender.

DISCHARGE BY RELEASE

A mortgage may be discharged by a release. The release can be given only by the owner of the mortgage and mortgage debt, or by someone authorized to act for him. No particular form is required for the release of a mortgage. It may be made in any manner which clearly manifests the intent of the mortgagee or owner of the mortgage to release it. However, a formal release of a mortgage which is eligible for record and which would release the mortgage of record must be in writing and executed in compliance with the recording statutes of the state in which the mortgaged real estate is located.

DISCHARGE BY MERGER

A mortgage may be discharged by merger, that is, by vesting the interests of the mortgagor and the mortgagee in the same person. If the mortgagor, or a person to whom the mortgagor has conveyed his interest,

[53] *Harding et al.* v. *Home Investment & Savings Co.,* 49 Idaho 64, 297 P. 1101.

conveys that interest to the mortgagee, or to the assignee of the mortgagee, the mortgage will in most instances be discharged by merger.

If the merger will result in definite injury and injustice to the person acquiring the interests of both the mortgagor and the mortgagee, the court will hold that no merger resulted. For example, suppose that there are a first mortgage and a second mortgage or other junior liens on the real estate, and the mortgagor conveys his rights in the mortgaged real estate to the first mortgagee. There will be no merger. If the first mortgage were, in such a case, held to be extinguished by merger, the second mortgage or junior liens would become first claims on the real estate; this would result in increasing the value of the subordinate liens at the expense of a senior lienholder.[54]

Statute of limitations

The running of the statute of limitations on the debt does not discharge the mortgage, since it does not discharge the debt—it merely bars any action brought to enforce the debt. Some courts have held that a bar to an action on the debt is also a bar to any action on the mortgage. In some states the statute of limitations on the debt and on the mortgage are for the same period; consequently, actions on the debt and on the mortgage would, under such statutes, be barred at the same time.

Foreclosure

Nature of foreclosure

Foreclosure is the process by which all further rights existing in the mortgagor to redeem the mortgaged real estate are cut off and lost to the mortgagor. At common law the only method of foreclosure was by an action in equity. Today, there are five recognized methods of foreclosure: (1) strict foreclosure; (2) action and sale; (3) entry and possession, or writ of entry; (4) *scire facias;* and (5) power of sale.

Foreclosure statutes

Foreclosure proceedings are usually regulated by statute; one must, in bringing foreclosure proceedings, comply with the statutes of the state in which the mortgaged real estate is located. If the statutes of the state

---

[54] *Moffet* v. *Farwell*, 222 Ill. 543, 78 N.E. 925.

provide for two or more alternative methods of foreclosure, the mortgagee or his assignee may elect the method of procedure he wishes to follow, unless there is a prior agreement as to the method to be used in bringing foreclosure proceedings.

DEFAULT

A default occurs when the mortgagor is guilty of a material breach of the terms of the mortgage. Such breach may, depending on the terms of the mortgage agreement, consist of the failure to pay the mortgage debt or an installment thereof when due, failure to pay interest, failure to pay taxes, or failure to keep the premises insured. A breach may also occur on the commission of waste or on the commission of any other act which might be detrimental to the interests of the mortgagee. The party who owns the mortgage and the mortgage debt has no right to bring foreclosure proceedings until there has been a default.

WHO HAS RIGHT TO FORECLOSE

If the mortgagee has not assigned the mortgage or the mortgage debt, he is the only person who has a right to foreclose. If there has been an assignment of the mortgage and the mortgage debt, or of the mortgage debt, the laws of the state will determine who shall bring the action to foreclose. Under the statutes of many states the real party in interest, that is, the party who is entitled to receive the money due, may bring the foreclosure action in his own name.[55]

On December 7, 1936, Mr. and Mrs. J. B. Robertson issued to C. B. Robertson their negotiable promissory note and secured it by a mortgage executed by them. C. B. Robertson negotiated the note and mortgage to Mrs. Earl Deimer as security for a loan. Hugh Robertson, brother of C. B. Robertson, paid the amount of the indebtedness to Mrs. Deimer, and she transferred the note and mortgage to him. Both assignments of the mortgage were endorsed on the margin of the record of the mortgage. C. B. Robertson attempted to pay the debt to Hugh, but Hugh was in South America, and C. B. Robertson could not reach him. The note was not paid when due, and C. B. Robertson brought an action to foreclose the mortgage. The trial court held that C. B. Robertson had no interest in the note and mortgage, and dismissed the suit; C. B. Robertson appealed. The judgment was affirmed.

[55] *Linahan et al.* v. *Linahan et al.,* 131 Conn. 307, 39 A.2d 895.

Justice McFaddin said: "Did all of the plaintiff's evidence, given its strongest probative force, make a case that would support a foreclosure decree in his favor? The Trial Court answered this question in the negative, and we agree with the Trial Court. Plaintiff, on December 7, 1936, received a note and mortgage from his parents, but the same day he assigned the note and mortgage to Mrs. Earl Deimer 'without recourse for valuable consideration.' The transfer of the note carried with it the security—i.e., the mortgage lien. Thus plaintiff divested himself of ownership of the note and mortgage; and until he reacquired ownership he had no title on which to base a suit for foreclosure of the mortgage under the facts shown in this case.

"In the early case of Purdy v. Brown, . . . when an assignor assigns a note, all the legal interest vests in the assignee, and he alone is entitled to sue, unless the assignor is again invested with the legal interest by a new assignment or otherwise.' " *Robertson* v. *Robertson, 231* Ark. 573, 331 S.W.2d 102 (1960).

TRUST MORTGAGE

As a general rule, a trust mortgage or trust deed given to secure a bond issue will confer on the trustee or his successor the power to institute foreclosure proceedings; the bondholders, as individuals, will not have that right. However, if there is in the trust mortgage or trust deed no provision designating who shall have the power to bring foreclosure proceedings, any person having an interest in the mortgage debt may bring such proceedings.[56] This is also true in those situations in which the mortgage debt is owned by several persons.

JUNIOR MORTGAGE

A junior mortgagee may foreclose his mortgage, subject to the prior lien of the senior mortgagee. All parties having in the mortgaged real estate an interest which arose subsequent to the giving of the mortgage and which can be cut off by the foreclosure, and all parties having an interest in the mortgage or mortgage debt who have not joined as plaintiffs in the bringing of the foreclosure proceedings, should be joined as parties defendant. The mortgagor, even though he has conveyed the mortgaged real estate, unless he is not personally liable on the mortgage debt, should be joined as a party defendant. Under the statutes of some states the

---

[56] *Florida National Bank of Jacksonville* v. *Jefferson Standard Life Insurance Co.,* 123 Fla. 525, 167 So. 378.

rights of the holder of an unrecorded lien or interest in the mortgaged real estate will be cut off, even though he is not joined as a party defendant.

STRICT FORECLOSURE

Under a strict foreclosure, all the rights of the mortgagor are cut off by the foreclosure proceedings, and title to the mortgaged real estate is vested in the mortgagee. There is no sale of the property. Strict foreclosure is used extensively in only three states—Connecticut, Illinois, and Vermont. In Illinois, its use is restricted to cases in which the following three requirements concur: (1) The reasonable value of the premises must be not more than the amount of the debt plus interest and costs, (2) the mortgagee must take the property in full satisfaction of the mortgage debt, and (3) the mortgagor must be insolvent. In 16 other states,[57] strict foreclosure is permitted; but its use, with few exceptions, is limited to the cutting-off of the redemption rights of a junior mortgagee or lien claimant who was inadvertently omitted as a party defendant in a foreclosure by action-and-sale proceeding.[58]

FORECLOSURE BY ACTION AND SALE

Foreclosure by action and sale is permitted in all states and is the only method of foreclosure permitted in some of the states. Since the proceedings and the sale of the mortgaged property are conducted under orders of the court, the chances of a defective foreclosure are minimized. As a general rule, however, the costs incurred in a foreclosure by action and sale are greater than in a foreclosure by power of sale or entry and possession. The steps to be followed in a foreclosure by action and sale are set out by the statutes of the state in which the mortgaged real estate is located, and they must be substantially complied with.

FORECLOSURE PROCEDURE. Although the statutes are not uniform, the steps in the procedure are as follows: Suit is brought in the court having jurisdiction. If the mortgagor or his grantee or other party in interest has a defense to the foreclosure suit, he appears in the case and

---

[57] Alabama, California, Indiana, Iowa, Maryland, Massachusetts, Minnesota, Mississippi, Nebraska, New Jersey, New York, North Carolina, Oregon, Rhode Island, South Dakota, and Utah.

[58] *Sears Roebuck & Co.* v. *Camp et al.,* 124 N.J. Eq. 403, 1 A.2d 425.

sets up his defense; the case is tried in accordance with the trial procedure of the state, and a decree is entered. If there are no appearances in the case, a default decree is entered. The court will determine the amount due on the mortgage debt, and an order authorizing the sale of the mortgaged real estate will be entered.

The sale will be conducted in compliance with the statutes of the state and will, as a general rule, be reported to the court for confirmation. Unless there is evidence of fraud or other irregularity in the conduct of the sale, or unless the price bid at the sale is wholly inadequate, the judge will confirm the sale. If the property is sold for less than the amount found due on the mortgage debt, a deficiency judgment may be entered against the parties liable on the mortgage debt. If there is a surplus, it will be paid over to junior lien claimants in the order of their priority, and any amount remaining will be paid to the mortgagor or his grantee.

In substantially all states, there are statutory redemption periods during which any party having in the mortgaged real estate an interest that will be cut off by the foreclosure may redeem the property from the foreclosure.

Arizona Coffee Shops purchased two downtown lots from Phoenix Downtown Parking Association for $350,000, paying $125,000 down and executing a mortgage on the lots to secure the unpaid balance. The mortgage provided for annual payments of $11,250 and quarterly payments of interest. It further provided for acceleration in event of default in the payment of principal or interest. Timely payments were made from June 1, 1959, to March 1, 1961, when due to the illness of the bookkeeper of Arizona Coffee Shops, the March 1, 1961, payment of interest in the amount of $2,532 was inadvertently missed. On April 4, 1961, summary foreclosure proceedings were instituted. Immediately, a tender of the past-due interest was made and was refused. A summary judgment was granted, which was reversed on appeal, and a new trial was ordered.

Chief Justice Bernstein said: "Defendant contends that in its responsive pleading, and supporting affidavit, it alleged sufficient facts which, if proved, would show unconscionable conduct on the part of the mortgagee, justifying a court of equity to grant relief from the harsh consequences of foreclosure. It is universally held in equity that unconscionable conduct of the mortgagee constitutes a valid defense to a mortgage foreclosure.

"One who seeks equity must do equity. If the defendant can prove bad faith on the part of Mr. Switzer in that he realized that Mrs. Fogel was the bookkeeper, was the person upon whom defendant depended to make sure all payments were made on time, and nevertheless remained silent about the overdue interest payment so that he could pounce upon defendant and take advantage of defendant's situation, a jury might conclude that Mr. Switzer's conduct under the circumstances was so oppressive as to warrant a court of equity the right to deny the affirmative aid sought by the plaintiff." *Arizona Coffee Shops* v. *Phoenix Downtown Parking Association,* 95 Ariz. 98, 387 P.2d 801 (1963).

FORECLOSURE SALE. In foreclosure by action and sale, the sale is by court direction and is usually regulated by the statutes of the state in which the mortgaged real estate is located. These statutes vary in their terms from state to state. Also, the court, under its equity jurisdiction, generally has the power to order and direct the sale of mortgaged real estate. As a general rule, the sale is a public one, made under the direction of the sheriff or a court officer appointed for that purpose.

Usually, the statutes require the posting of a certain number of notices of the sale, and give general directions as to where the notices shall be posted. Under the statutes of some states, notice of the sale must be advertised in a newspaper having general distribution in the county in which the mortgaged real estate is located. The notice must give the time, place, manner of conducting the sale, terms of the sale, and such other information as is required by the statutes.

If the mortgage covers two or more distinct parcels of real estate, the statute may provide that the parcels shall be offered for sale separately; and if, upon sale, one or less than all of the parcels will bring a sum sufficient to satisfy the mortgage debt, only such parcels will be sold. If there are several parcels and there are junior liens on some or all of them, the court may order the parcels sold in the order of the priority of the junior lien claimants, so as to give to each lien claimant the maximum benefit to which he is entitled.

A foreclosure sale usually requires confirmation and does not become final until it is confirmed by the court. The court may set a sale aside under some circumstances and order a new sale.[59]

The Production Credit Association of Madison, Wisconsin (hereinafter referred to as PCA), commenced foreclosure proceedings against Chickering and Jacobson. The property consisted of 1,500 acres of muck farm land. PCA held a mortgage in the unpaid amount of $38,511.05. There were other liens against the land; and including the PCA mortgage, the total of the liens,

[59] *Bank of America National Trust & Savings Association* v. *Reidy et al.,* 15 Cal.2d 243. 101 P.2d 77.

exclusive of interest, was in excess of $110,000. On the foreclosure sale, PCA bid the property in for $87,000. Gumz had bid $86,000, his bid being the next high bid. Chickering and Jacobson petitioned the court to set the sale aside; and Gumz joined in the petition, offering to bid $100,000 and pay $10,000 down. PCA paid $100 down on its $87,000 bid. The petition for resale set out the inadequacy of the advertising, confusion as to the terms of the sale, and lack of authority of the representative of PCA to bid; it was also claimed that the property had special value and that this was not emphasized in the advertising of the property. The trial court granted the petition and ordered a resale. PCA appealed. The order of resale was affirmed.

Justice Wilkie said: "The main question on this appeal is whether or not the trial court abused its discretion in refusing to confirm the sale of the mortgaged premises to the State of Wisconsin and in ordering a resale. This question has been before this court on many occasions and in a very early case of John Paul Lumber Co. v. Neumeister (1900), the following rule was established which is still the law today: 'The granting or refusing of an application to set aside such sale [foreclosure] and order a resale, as a matter of favor, rests in the sound discretion of the trial court; and its determination will not be disturbed, except for a clear abuse of discretion.'

" 'A further rule is firmly established in Wisconsin that a sale will not be set aside simply because the price obtained by the sale was inadequate. As stated in A. J. Straus Paving Agency v. Jensen, this rule is confined to cases "where there is absolutely no fact appearing, except that the price is inadequate." The Straus case quotes from Griswold v. Barden (1911).

" 'Whenever other facts appear, such as mistake, misapprehension, or inadvertence on the part of the interested parties or of intending bidders, as a result of which it seems to the court the failure to obtain a fair and adequate price for the property was due in whole or in part to such mistake, misapprehension, or inadvertence, the court will readily refuse to approve the sale. No fraud is necessary to justify the court in so withholding its approval. The question simply is, is the sale under all the circumstances one of which the court, in justice to all parties, should approve?'

"In other words, a trial court may refuse to confirm a sale if he is satisfied (1) that the price received for the property was inadequate, and (2) that there was a showing of mistake, misapprehension, or inadvertence on the part of interested parties or prospective bidders." *Gumz* v. *Chickering,* 19 Wis.2d 625, 121 N.W.2d 279 (1963).

LIABILITY OF BIDDER. The bidder at the foreclosure sale is bound by his bid when the officer in charge of the sale strikes the real estate off to him, even though the sale is not finally binding until confirmation by the court. The court is required to confirm the sale, unless there are valid grounds for refusing to do so. Although some courts hold that the purchaser takes title subject to all existing defects, the better and the majority rule is that the purchaser is entitled to a marketable title, subject only to those defects set out in the notice of sale; and if the court cannot convey to him such marketable title, he may refuse to accept the defective title. The mortgagee or his assignee owning the mortgage debt has the right to bid at a foreclosure sale.[60]

FORECLOSURE BY ENTRY AND POSSESSION OR BY WRIT OF ENTRY

Foreclosure by entry and possession is a form of self-help. If the mortgagor refuses to surrender possession peaceably, the mortgagee, after default on the part of the mortgagor, may obtain possession by writ of entry. This form of foreclosure is used in four New England states—Massachusetts, Maine, New Hampshire, and Rhode Island.

When the entry is without process of law, it must be peaceable. In addition to taking possession, the mortgagee must file or record a certificate of entry executed by the mortgagor or witnesses; or he must publish the time, manner, and purpose of the entry, and must execute and file or record an affidavit of such publication.

In the action for a writ of entry the mortgagee declares on his title to the mortgaged real estate and sets out the default on the part of the mortgagor. An accounting is made to determine the amount due, and a judgment is entered, granting the mortgagee possession of the mortgaged real state if the mortgagor does not satisfy the judgment within a relatively short period of time. If the mortgagor fails to satisfy the judgment, the mortgagee is put in possession; and if the mortgagor does not redeem the real estate within the statutory period, title to the real estate vests unconditionally in the mortgagee.

In entry by both peaceable possession and writ of entry, the mortgage debt is discharged only to the extent of the reasonable value of the real estate at the time of entry, and the mortgagee is entitled to a judgment for the portion of the mortgage debt not satisfied.[61]

---

[60] *Louisville Joint Stock Land Bank* v. *Radford,* 295 U.S. 555, 55 S. Ct. 854.

[61] In addition to foreclosure by possession and writ of entry, action and sale, and power of sale, Maine permits foreclosure by advertisement or notice. The mortgagee may give public notice of default and his intention to foreclose by advertisement, and record a certified copy of the publication; or he may serve a certified copy of such notice on the mortgagor or his grantee and record the original. The mortgagor then has one year from the time of the first publication of notice or from the time of service of notice to redeem; if he does not redeem, title vests unconditionally in the mortgagee.

FORECLOSURE BY *scire facias*[62]

Foreclosure by writ of *scire facias* is used in Pennsylvania and may be, but seldom is, used in Delaware, Illinois, and New Jersey. Foreclosure by writ of *scire facias sur mortgage* originated in Pennsylvania by colonial legislation. It provides that after default by the mortgagor, a writ of *scire facias* will issue against the mortgagor, his heirs, and personal representatives to show cause why the mortgaged real estate should not be taken in execution to satisfy the mortgage debt. After determination of the amount due, the real estate is sold at a public sale; the proceeds of the sale are applied to the payment of the mortgage debt. Any surplus is paid to the mortgagor. The purchaser gets such title as the mortgagor could convey at the time of the mortgage.

Foreclosure by writ of *scire facias* cannot be brought until one year after default by the mortgagor. However, this requirement may be waived by the mortgagor.

FORECLOSURE BY EXERCISE OF POWER OF SALE

In the United States the mortgagee does not have the right to sell the mortgaged property on the mortgagor's default unless such right is expressly granted in the mortgage. When granted, it becomes a part of the mortgage and may be exercised by the mortgagee or anyone to whom he assigns the mortgage. In some states, however, the statutes of the state require that all foreclosures be by action and sale, and in these states a power-of-sale clause in a mortgage is void.[63] Foreclosure by exercise of power of sale is in general use in only eighteen states.

The advantage of a foreclosure by exercise of a power of sale is that it enables the party owning the mortgage and mortgage debt to bring about a complete foreclosure of the mortgage without the aid of the court, thereby saving both time and money. Its major disadvantage is that it does not afford the mortgagor reasonable protection from being defrauded by an unscrupulous mortgagee. If the mortgagee, however, has taken an unconscionable advantage of the mortgagor, he (the mort-

---

[62] A writ of *scire facias sur mortgage* is a writ issued upon the default of a mortgagor to make payments or observe conditions, requiring him to show cause why the mortgage should not be foreclosed, and the mortgaged property taken and sold in execution.

[63] Arizona, Colorado, Idaho, Illinois, Indiana, Iowa, Kansas, Nebraska, Oklahoma, and Oregon.

gagor) may bring an action in equity, and the court will set the foreclosure aside.

PROCEDURE UNDER POWER OF SALE. In most of the states in which foreclosure by exercise of power of sale is permitted, the procedure to be followed in the exercise of the power is set out by statute. The statutes are not uniform in their provisions; but in general, they require the party foreclosing the mortgage to give notice of the sale. Usually, the statute requires that the sale be at public auction. Under the statutes of some states the sale may be conducted by the mortgagee, but some statutes expressly provide that the sale shall be conducted by a designated public officer.

Generally, notice of the sale is required. The statute may require that public notice must be given, either by the posting of notices, or by publication, or by both; or it may require the giving of personal notice to certain designated persons. The statutes of some states require that notice to the mortgagor be served in the same manner as is required for the service of process. Notice by publication is the form most commonly required.

Such notice must state the time and place of the sale, contain a description of the mortgaged real estate, state the facts of the default, give the date of the mortgage and when recorded, specify the amount due, and give the names of the mortgagor and the mortgagee. The statutes usually designate the period of time the sale must be advertised before the mortgaged real estate is sold.

The sale must be conducted fairly and as an auction sale should be conducted, and an effort must be made to sell the property at the highest price obtainable. If there is any irregularity in the conduct of the sale or any evidence of fraud on the part of the mortgagee or his assignee, the court will, if the mortgagor or his grantee bring proper action, enjoin the sale; or if a sale has been made, the court will set the sale aside or grant whatever relief the circumstances of the case require for the protection of the interests of the mortgagor or his grantee.

MORTGAGEE'S RIGHT TO BID. There is some diversity of opinion as to whether or not the mortgagee should be permitted to bid at the foreclosure sale. The courts have generally held that if the mortgagee is conducting the sale, he will not be permitted to bid at his own sale; but if a public officer is conducting the sale, the mortgagee will be permitted to bid.

In the absence of a statute regulating the foreclosure by exercise of power of sale, the sale must be conducted in strict compliance with the terms of the power.

RIGHTS ACQUIRED BY PURCHASER. In general, the rights acquired by the person purchasing at a sale conducted under a power of sale are substantially the same as the rights acquired by a purchaser at a judicial foreclosure sale. The position of the purchaser at the sale conducted under a power of sale is weaker than that of a person purchasing at a judicial foreclosure sale, since the foreclosure in the exercise of a power of sale is not founded on a judicial decision which is binding on the parties. Consequently, the sale is vulnerable to attack for fraud or inequities.

DISTRIBUTION OF SURPLUS.   There is no uniformity in the rules governing the distribution of any surplus realized from the sale of the mortgaged real estate. The party foreclosing the mortgage would be wise to seek court determination of the right to the surplus.

Howard owned a store building on which Cordes held a mortgage. Howard moved to an adjoining state, leaving the store building vacant. Howard was in arrears in his payments on the mortgage, and Cordes took possession of the property and sold it on a land contract to Cox. Cox expended about $5,000 in making repairs and improvements on the building.

After Cox had been in possession of the premises for 19 months, Howard brought an action against Cordes and Cox, asking for possession of the premises and for the reasonable rental value of the property during the time Cox occupied them.

The trial court held that Howard was entitled to the possession of the property and granted him a judgment for nominal rent of $1.00 a month. On appeal, Howard was granted a judgment for the reasonable rental value of the premises.

The court said: "A mortgagor does not lose his right to the possession of mortgaged real property by failing to make payments on the mortgage, or by moving out of the community. The right to possession is not lost by abandonment. Nor does the mortgagee have any right to possession of mortgaged real property without a 'foreclosure and sale according to law.'

"The defendants in this case, a mortgagee and his contract purchasers (contract price $2,500), admittedly took possession of the mortgaged property without the consent of the absentee owner; and the contract purchasers, at the time this action was commenced, had conducted their business therein (Sprague Implement Company) for 19 months.

"The plaintiff, the owner of the property, was entitled under the statute (RCW 59.–04.0501) to 'reasonable rent' for that 19-month period.

"If for reasons of their own the mortgagee and his contract purchasers do not want to take the necessary steps to acquire a right of possession to the property by foreclosure and sale, they are going to have to pay the fair market value for the use and occupancy to the owner during the time they are tenants of that owner. As we pointed out in Norlin v. Montgomery, equitable principles cannot be asserted to establish equitable relief in derogation of statutory mandates." *Howard* v. *Edgren*, 62 Wash.2d 884, 385 P.2d 41 (1963).

Redemption rights

NATURE OF RIGHT

The right of redemption is the right to have the title to the mortgaged real estate restored free and clear of the mortgage lien. The right of redemption may be exercised when the mortgage debt is due; after default, but before any action to foreclose is brought; or under some circumstances, after foreclosure sale.

WHO MAY REDEEM

Under the law in the United States today the mortgagor, his grantee, or any person having in the mortgaged real estate an interest which would be cut off by foreclosure of the mortgage has the right to redeem. This would include all junior mortgagees, junior lien claimants, a wife having a dower interest in the property, a lessee whose leasehold interest would be terminated by the foreclosure, anyone becoming an owner of a fractional portion of the mortgaged real estate subsequent to the execution of the mortgage, or owners of an undivided interest in the mortgaged real estate.[64]

PAYMENT ON REDEMPTION

As a general rule, the person wishing to redeem must pay the entire amount to which the mortgagee is entitled.[65] If the person wishing to redeem has only a fractional interest in the mortgaged real estate or is a junior lien claimant, the mortgage creditor may consent to a partial redemption. Sometimes, a mortgage on a subdivision gives purchasers the right to clear by partial redemption the tracts which they have purchased.

DISCHARGE OF MORTGAGE

If the mortgage creditor, after receiving payment of the amount due him, refuses or neglects to discharge the mortgage of record or make

---

[64] *Anderson* v. *Anderson et al.*, 110 Ind. App. 577, 39 N.E.2d 806.
[65] *Brewster* v. *Terry*, 352 Mo. 967, 180 S.W.2d 600.

the assignments to which the person redeeming is entitled, such person may bring an appropriate action, and the court will force the mortgage creditor to execute the release or assignment.

REDEMPTION STATUTES

Twenty-eight states have enacted statutes permitting redemption from foreclosure. In four of the states the period of redemption starts to run when the foreclosure proceedings are started. This delays the sale until the expiration of the redemption period. In the remaining 24 states, the period starts to run when the foreclosure sale is made. Thus the title of the purchaser at the foreclosure sale is subject to defeat by redemption at any time before the expiration of the redemption period.

The provisions of the statutes vary materially, but all the statutes set out with more or less precision who may effect a redemption. All of them specify the time within which redemption may be made, although there may be one period for one class and another period for another class. All of them specify the sum which must be paid to redeem. And all of them include some provision as to the effect of the redemption.

In all states the mortgagor and his successors in interest may redeem; and in practically all states, junior lienholders may redeem. The time allowed for redemption varies from six months to two years, but a one-year period predominates. In most of the states the party redeeming the property must pay the sale price plus a stipulated rate of interest; and in some states, other items are added.

EFFECT OF REDEMPTION

The effect of the redemption on the rights of parties having an interest in the mortgaged real estate varies markedly from state to state. One general effect of redemption by the mortgagor or his successor in interest is that it nullifies the foreclosure sale. The effect of redemption by the mortgagor on the rights of claimants such as judgment creditors and similar lien claimants is too diversified and confused to permit helpful generalization.

REDEMPTION BY JUNIOR LIENHOLDER

If a holder of a junior lien redeems, he will acquire, under the provisions of most of the statutes, the rights of the person who purchased the real property at the foreclosure sale. In some states, if a holder of a junior lien redeems, his redemption has no effect on the amount owed him by the mortgagor. In other states the amount the junior lienholder pays to redeem is added to the amount due him from the mortgagor, and the redeeming junior lienholder has to bring further proceedings to enforce his original mortgage plus the amount paid on redemption. In Iowa the junior lienholder who has redeemed files a certificate stating the amount he is willing to credit on his debt; and if he files such a certificate, only the amount stated in the certificate is credited on his debt. If he fails to file a certificate, his entire debt is discharged.

If a junior lien claimant redeems, a senior lien claimant may redeem from his redemption, provided he redeems within the permitted statutory period. The mortgagor or his successor has the superior right to redeem.

Barber, on December 4, 1953, executed a real estate mortgage to Mount Morris Savings and Loan Association (hereinafter referred to as Association). Horst held against Barber a judgment which was a lien on Barbers' equity of redemption in the mortgaged property. Barber defaulted in his payments on the mortgage, and Association foreclosed the mortgage. The Messers bid the property in at the foreclosure sale. At the time the mortgage was executed, the state statute provided that a judgment creditor might redeem from a mortgage sale after the expiration of 12 months and within 15 months after the sale. The statute was later amended and at the time of the sale provided that a judgment creditor might redeem after the expiration of nine months and within 12 months after the sale. Horst, as judgment creditor, attempted to redeem the property 14 months and 27 days after the sale. The trial court held that Horst could not redeem the property, and he appealed. The holding was affirmed on appeal.

Chief Justice House said: "We are of the opinion that this case comes within the well-established rule holding time limitations to be procedural in character.

"It is argued by petitioner that if the amendment is held to apply to mortgages executed before its effective date, it is rendered unconstitutional as an impairment of contract. A sufficient answer to this argument is that he was not a party to the mortgage.

"He also asserts that a 15-month redemption period was contemplated by all parties and the Messers should be estopped to claim that any other time period is applicable. The conduct of the other parties to this proceeding cannot be made the basis of an estoppel against the Messers, nor does the fact that the Messers made no effort to obtain a deed from the master in chancery until after 15 months lend any support to petitioner's claim, since the Messers could have waited at least five years before they sought to obtain the deed.

"We hold the amendment to section 20 to be procedural and, as such, it must be applied to all foreclosure sales occurring subsequent to its effective date. The trial court properly found the attempted redemption of the petitioner Horst to be null and void." *Mount Morris Savings and Loan Association* v. *Barber,* 17 Ill.2d 523, 162 N.E.2d 347 (1959).

Checklist for mortgage

1. Name of mortgagor. The name should be spelled the same wherever it appears in the mortgage and should be spelled the same as it is spelled in the deed conveying the mortgaged property to the mortgagor. If the mortgagor is a natural person, marital status should be given—bachelor, spinster, widower, widow, divorced and not remarried. If married, the spouse's name should be given.
2. Residence of mortgagor. City, county, and state.
3. Name of mortgagee or mortgagees. Check for correct spelling.
4. Words of conveyance. Mortgage and warrant in lien state. Words of conveyance in title state.
5. Description of real estate mortgaged. Copy the description from the deed to the mortgagor, correcting obvious errors in the description.
6. Description of debt secured.
7. Defeasance clause in title-state mortgage.
8. Date of execution.
9. Signature of mortgagor.
10. Seal (in states requiring seal).
11. Acknowledgment.
12. Attesting witnesses (required in some, but not all states).

Other provisions which should be checked for inclusion in the mortgage are:

1. Provision for payment of taxes and assessments.
2. Provision for keeping improvements on the mortgaged property insured.
3. Provision giving the mortgagee the right to declare the entire debt due and payable, and to bring foreclosure proceedings on the mortgagor's failure to pay an installment of the principal, interest, taxes, or assessments when due, or on his failure to keep improvements insured.

4. Provision waiving appraisement and valuation laws on the mortgagor's failure to pay the mortgage debt.
5. Provision giving the mortgagee the right of possession on the mortgagor's default.
6. Provision assigning all rents and profits to the mortgagee, to become effective on the mortgagor's default.
7. Provision extending the lien of the mortgage to all improvements, fixtures, and appurtenants on the premises or thereafter attached to the premises—package mortgage provision.
8. Provision for making future advances under the mortgage—open-end mortgage provision.
9. Provision regarding documents to be delivered to the mortgagee—insurance policies, receipts for taxes and assessments, abstract or title certificate, policy of title insurance, and so on.
10. Provision against commission of waste by the mortgagor.
11. Provision requiring the mortgagor to obtain the mortgagee's consent in writing to use the premises for purposes other than its present use; to make alterations in the buildings; or to purchase on conditional sale and attach to the premises any apparatus, fixture, or equipment.
12. Provision requiring the mortgagor to make periodic payments to the mortgagee, to be used by the mortgagee for the payment of taxes, assessments, insurance premiums, and so on.
13. Provision requiring the mortgagor to take out life insurance payable to the mortgagee as additional security.
14. Provision covering in detail the making of advances under an open-end provision in the mortgage.
15. Provision permitting the mortgagee to advance money to pay taxes, assessments, insurance premiums, or any other charges against the mortgaged real estate, and to add the amount to the mortgage debt.
16. Provision granting the mortgagee, in the event the mortgagor conveys the mortgaged real estate, the right to extend the time of payment, forbear to sue, or deal with the grantee in regard to the mortgaged real estate without discharging the mortgagor from his personal liability on the mortgage debt.
17. Provision imposing on the mortgagor the obligation to pay all attorneys' fees reasonably incurred in connection with any dispute as to title to the mortgaged real estate, or in any suit on or foreclosure of the mortgage. Usually, the mortgagee is permitted to add sums spent for attorneys' fees to the mortgage debt.

18. Provision permitting the mortgagee to list the property and sell in the event the mortgagor moves to another city (used in connection with mortgages on homes).

19. Provision covering the rights of the parties in the event the property, or any part thereof, is taken on condemnation.

20. Provision granting the mortgagee the power of sale in the event of default (used in states permitting foreclosure by sale under power of sale).

10

Deeds of trust and land contracts

Deed of trust

NATURE OF DEED OF TRUST

A DEED OF TRUST is a deed absolute given to secure the payment of a debt. It is, basically, a real estate mortgage and is an arrangement whereby the expense and delay incident to the foreclosure of a real estate mortgage are avoided. It is a three-party instrument. The parties are the lender, the borrower, and the trustee.[1] The borrower deeds the real estate to the trustee, who holds it for the benefit of the lender. In addition to, or as a part of, the deed, the parties enter into a trust agreement whereby the trustee, on the default of the borrower, and at the request of the lender, is empowered to sell the real estate, usually at public or private sale, and pay, out of the proceeds of the sale, the debt, the accrued interest, and the costs. Any surplus then is paid over to the borrower or to the parties who have junior claims on the real estate held in trust. The trust agreement also includes such other provisions as the parties deem expedient.

The deed of trust may be used as a means of securing a bond issue

---

[1] Under the terminology of trust law the borrower who creates the trust is known as the trustor. The lender for whom the trust is created is known as the beneficiary or the *cestui que trust*. The party to whom the property is deeded is known as the trustee.

251

of a corporation. The trust agreement portion of such a deed given to secure a corporate bond issue is usually an elaborate document which sets out in detail the powers and duties of the trustee and the rights of the bondholder in the security.

CHARACTERISTICS OF DEED OF TRUST

Those courts which have followed the early rule developed in the courts of equity—that is, the rule that any conveyance of real estate given to secure a debt is a mortgage, without regard to the form of the conveyance—hold that a deed of trust is a mortgage. In these states, deeds of trust are used little, or not at all.[2]

Some states have, either by statute or by court decision, or by both, recognized the deed of trust as a conveyance in trust which vests legal title in the trustee, and have held that the statutes of the state requiring judicial foreclosure of mortgages or setting up special requirements for the foreclosure of mortgages do not apply to deeds of trust. Deeds of trust with power of sale are used extensively in such states.[3] Most of these states have enacted statutes defining the rights and duties of the parties to a deed-of-trust transaction. Although a statute of the state may set up some requirements as to the sale of the property held by the trustee in the event of default, in none of these states is foreclosure by judicial sale required, nor is the borrower permitted a statutory period of redemption after the sale.

In the other states and territories the laws are such that deeds of trust and mortgages are used without discrimination. In several of the states, whether a deed of trust or a mortgage is used is more a matter of local usage than of the legal status of the deed of trust or mortgage.

In all states in which deeds of trust are used, the courts have not, in determining the rights and duties of the parties, followed the law of trusts through to a logical conclusion. In many, if not in most, of the deed-of-trust transactions, the courts have applied the law of mortgages in determining the rights and duties of the parties. The statutes of the states in which deeds of trust are used extensively play an important

---

[2] Connecticut, Florida, Hawaii, Kansas, Louisiana, Maine, Massachusetts, Michigan, Minnesota, Nevada, New Jersey, Ohio, Oregon, Rhode Island, Utah, Vermont, and Washington.

[3] California, Colorado (power of sale valid if public trustee is used), District of Columbia, Delaware, Mississippi, Missouri, Tennessee, Texas, Virginia, and West Virginia.

part in determining the rights and liabilities of the parties. There is no uniformity in these statutes; consequently, if a person wishes to use a deed of trust, he should consult a local attorney who is familiar with the law of the state in which the real estate involved is located.

RIGHTS UNDER DEED OF TRUST

The rights of the borrower (trustor) and the lender (beneficiary) under the deed of trust are substantially the same as are the rights of a mortgagor and mortgagee under a real estate mortgage. Any interest in real estate which may be sold or mortgaged may be the subject matter of a deed-of-trust transaction. As a general rule, the trustor-borrower is left in possession of the property until default and sale by the trustee. If a borrower executes a deed of trust to real estate to which he does not at that time have title, the deed of trust, like a mortgage, will create a valid lien on the real estate conveyed if the borrower acquires title to the real estate conveyed during the life of the trust.[4]

DEED-OF-TRUST DEBT

There is no material difference between the mortgage debt and a debt secured by a deed of trust. The debt may be evidenced by a nonnegotiable or a negotiable instrument. The form of the debt—that is, whether it is nonnegotiable or negotiable—is important in determining the rights of a purchaser of the debt from the lender.

A deed of trust may be given to secure future advances in the same manner and to the same extent as a mortgage may be given to secure future advances. In the preceding chapter, package mortgages, open-end mortgages, and construction mortgages were discussed. In each of these situations a deed of trust, in those states which recognize the deed of trust as a separate type of security instrument, could be substituted for the mortgage without changing the rights and duties of the parties in any material respect.

INSURANCE

The courts have recognized that the borrower and the lender each have an insurable interest in the real estate conveyed to the trustee. In

---

[4] *California Bank* v. *Bell et al.,* 38 Cal. App.2d 533, 101 P.2d 724.

solving problems involving the rights of the parties in interest to insure the real estate and their rights to the insurance money in the event of a loss covered by insurance, the law developed in regard to the insurable rights of the mortgagor and mortgagee has been applied without material alteration to the deed-of-trust relation.[5]

Recording

The recording laws of the state in which the real estate is located apply to deeds of trust the same as they apply to any other instrument which conveys an interest in real estate. If a deed of trust is executed in compliance with the recording statutes of the state in which the real estate is located, it is eligible for recordation. However, a deed of trust, like a conventional deed or mortgage, is valid between the parties to the instrument without being recorded, and it is also binding on parties taking the real estate with notice or knowledge of the outstanding interests created by the deed of trust.

There is one material difference between a deed of trust and a mortgage in regard to discharge on the payment of the mortgage debt. A mortgage is discharged either by an entry on the margin of the record or by the execution and recording of a certificate of discharge by the mortgagee, or his assignee if the assignment of the mortgage has been recorded. The only person who can clear the record of a deed of trust is the trustee, and this is accomplished by the trustee's reconveying the real estate to the borrower or his successor in interest on the payment of the debt secured by the deed of trust.

Conveyance of real estate held under deed of trust

The granting of real estate under a deed of trust does not deprive the borrower of all his interest in the property. His rights are, in substantially all respects, the same as are the rights of a mortgagor. He has the right to redeem the real estate by the payment of the debt, and from a practical standpoint the value of this right is the difference between the market value of the real estate and the amount of the debt. The borrower may sell this interest, or he may borrow money, using this interest as security, and give to the lender a second deed of trust or a real estate mortgage. Technically, the trustee under a deed of trust

---

[5] *Le Doux et al.* v. *Dettmering et al.,* 316 Ill. App. 98, 43 N.E.2d 862.

holds only a determinable or base fee in the real estate; and the borrower-grantee has a reversionary interest in the property, that is, the title to the property revests in the borrower-grantee on the payment of the debt, provided payment is made before default and sale of the property under the terms of the deed of trust.

If the borrower-grantee sells the real estate which is the subject matter of a deed of trust, the purchaser may buy free and clear, he may buy subject to the deed of trust, or he may buy subject to the deed of trust and assume and agree to pay the debt. In determining the rights and duties of a purchaser of real estate which is subject to a deed of trust, the law of mortgages applies.

Sipe sold the real estate in question to Baker, who executed a negotiable promissory note payable to Sipe in the amount of $4,500, which was secured by a deed of trust to Linus Harding, trustee. Baker sold the real estate to Ellen Criswell, who assumed and agreed to pay "the unpaid balance owing . . ." on the $4,500 note secured by the deed of trust to Linus Harding, trustee. Sipe negotiated the note together with the lien to Southwestern Fidelity Life Insurance Company. The deed of trust included the following provision: ". . . in the event of foreclosure under the power granted hereby, the owner in possession of said property shall thereby become a tenant at will of the purchaser at foreclosure sale. . . ."

The note was not paid when due, and the real estate was sold by the trustee to Southwestern Fidelity Life Insurance Company. Criswell refused to surrender possession of the property, and this action was brought to recover possession of the real estate and to obtain a judgment for damages. Judgment was given Southeastern Fidelity Life Insurance Company, and Criswell appealed, denying the existence of a landlord-tenant relationship. The judgment was affirmed.

Justice Coleman said: "It is well settled that one agreeing to pay a note secured by a deed of trust lien, as part of the purchase price of the land so encumbered, cannot question the validity of such note or the lien securing it.

"The rights of the payee of a note secured by a mortgage, or a deed of trust, cannot be abridged or diminished by subsequent acts of the mortgagor, or grantor in such deed of trust. Mrs. Criswell, therefore, could occupy a no more favorable position than F. E. Baker. The agreement made by Baker as contained in the note assumed by Mrs. Criswell, and the deed of trust securing the same, is binding on Mrs. Criswell.

"By her acceptance of the deed from Baker, Mrs. Criswell agreed to pay the note described therein, and, from the recitation that the note was secured by a deed of trust, had constructive notice of the provisions of the deed of trust and impliedly agreed to all of them." *Criswell* v. *Southwestern Fidelity Life Insurance Company*, Tex. Civ. App., 373 S.W.2d 893 (1963).

Assignment of rights of lender

The rights of a lender under a deed of trust do not differ in any material respects from the rights of a mortgagee. He is the beneficiary under the terms of the deed of trust and as such acquires, through the trustee, a lien on the real estate as·security for the debt. He is the owner of the debt and may transfer it, together with his rights as beneficiary. The transfer of the debt carries with it the rights under the deed of trust. The debt and the lien securing the debt cannot be transferred as separate rights.

If the debt is nonnegotiable, the law of assignment of contracts applies in determining the rights of the parties. If the debt is evidenced by a negotiable instrument, the law of negotiable instruments applies in determining the rights acquired by one to whom the instrument is negotiated or transferred.

One material difference between the assignment of mortgages and the assignment of the rights of the lender in a deed of trust is in regard to the requirements for recording. Under the recording laws of most states, assignments of mortgages may be recorded and, in some states, must be recorded. When the lender in a deed of trust assigns his rights, the assignment need not be recorded; and under the recording statutes, of some states, it is not eligible for recordation. The assignment by the lender in no way affects the title or the duties of the trustee. Who owns the debt is of no concern to third persons dealing with real estate conveyed under a deed of trust. The recording of the deed of trust gives them notice of the lien on the real estate, and only the trustee or his duly appointed successor has the power to clear the record by executing a reconveyance of the real estate.

Discharge of deed of trust

The payment of the debt secured by a deed of trust entitles the borrower to a discharge, but it does not discharge the deed of trust from the record. If the trustee has died, the borrower or his successor must have a successor appointed who can execute the required reconveyance. If the trustee arbitrarily refuses to act, the borrower or his successor must bring a court action and obtain a court order forcing the trustee to act.

There is considerable confusion as to the effect of a tender. Logically, it should discharge the deed of trust, since the deed of trust is basically a lien, and tender of performance, under the general rule, discharges a lien. However, whether or not a tender discharges the lien of the deed of trust depends on the statutes and decisions of the several states. It is fairly certain that the borrower or his successor is not entitled to a court order requiring the trustee to reconvey the real estate unless the borrower or his successor pays the debt.

Under the statutes and court decisions of some of the states the running of the statute of limitations on the debt bars any action on the mortgage. In some of the states so holding, the courts have held that the running of the statute of limitations on the debt does not deprive the trustee of his power to sell the property and apply the proceeds to the payment of the debt.[6] The courts base their decisions on the ground that the trustee under the deed of trust has title to the real estate and that the statutes of limitations relating to title to real estate apply.

On May 7, 1956, MacClain executed his promissory note secured by a deed of trust on real estate owned by him to Northwestern Loan and Investment Company (hereinafter referred to as Northwestern), subject to a prior deed of trust to Federal Savings and Loan Association (hereinafter referred to as Federal). On August 30, 1956, Alcone's, Inc., obtained a judgment against MacClain and levied on the real estate. Thereafter the United States filed a tax lien on the property for unpaid income taxes, and the state of Colorado filed a second tax lien for unpaid state income tax.

MacClain became employed by Universal Securities, Inc. As part of Mac-Clain's contract, Universal Securities, Inc., paid Northwestern the amount due on the MacClain note; Northwestern marked the note paid and returned it, together with a discharge of the deed of trust, to Universal Securities, Inc., and it delivered the note and discharge to MacClain. At the request of Chisen, MacClain's attorney, MacClain delivered the note and discharge to Chisen as security for the payment of attorney's fees owed to Chisen by MacClain. Chisen contended that his claim under the Northwestern note and deed of trust had priority over the claims of Alcone's, Inc., the United States, and the state of Colorado. The trial court held that Chisen's lien had priority; and on appeal, the judgment was reversed.

Chief Justice McWilliams said: "Jones v. Sturgis . . . holds that when a note secured by a deed of trust on real property is fully paid and satisfied the deed of trust ceases to be a lien on the property.

"In the instant case Universal prompted by reasons of its own and acting on behalf of its employee fully paid and satisfied the note; it received no purported assignment of the deed of trust but on the contrary accepted a release of the same. Under these circumstances the deed of trust ceased to be a lien and the fact that MacClain later came into possession of the note, deed of

---

[6] *Grant* v. *Burr.*, 54 Cal. 298.

trust and release of deed of trust did not revive the lien interest." *Robinson* v. *Chisen*, Colo., 388 P.2d 759 (1964).

FORECLOSURE OF DEED OF TRUST

Although a deed of trust vests title in the trustee, and the trustee, under the typical trust agreement, owes a duty to sell the property on default by the borrower and on request by the lender, the sale of the property by the trustee is not the only remedy available to the lender. In some states the courts have held or the statutes provide that the power of sale in a deed of trust is cumulative and that the lender is entitled to foreclose by court action if he wishes to do so.[7] In other states the lender may resort to court action and foreclose the deed of trust as a mortgage only if he can show cause why a sale by the trustee under the terms of the trust agreement would not be fair and just.[8]

The trustee under a deed of trust is a fiduciary and must not have an interest either in the debt or in the real estate. If he has such an interest, he is disqualified and cannot conduct the sale.[9] Also, the power of sale given to the trustee is personal to him and cannot be delegated to someone else. However, he may engage some other person to perform some of the ministerial duties pertaining to the sale. In some recent cases in which the trustee was a corporation, the courts have been more liberal in permitting delegation of the duties of the trustee.[10]

The rules discussed in the preceding chapter relating to the conduct of a sale under a power of sale in a mortgage apply generally to the conduct of a sale under a power of sale in a deed of trust. The statutes of the state in which the land is located and the provisions in the deed of trust must be complied with; and if they are not complied with, the sale, on proper action brought in a court having jurisdiction, will be set aside.

As a general rule, the trustee is not permitted to buy the real estate at such a sale. The lender, however, does have the right to bid and buy.

The Tomiyasus executed a second deed of trust to a trustee to secure the payment of $13,564 to the First National Bank. This was subject and subordi-

---

[7] *Bank of Italy* v. *Bentley*, 217 Cal. 644, 20 P.2d 940.

[8] *George* v. *Zinn*, 57 W. Va. 15, 49 S.E. 904.

[9] *Morgan v. Glendy*, 92 Va. 86, 22 S.E. 854.

[10] *Randolph et al.* v. *Citizens National Bank of Lubbock et al.*, Tex. Civ. App., 141 S.W.2d 1030.

nate to a first deed of trust in the sum of $38,968.29. The Tomiyasus were in default on both debts, and the First National Bank made the payments to the holders of the first deed of trust to prevent foreclosure. The First National Bank started foreclosure, and the sale was conducted as required by the state statutes. The sale was postponed seven times to give the Tomiyasus an opportunity to refinance, but their efforts in this respect were unsuccessful. The property was sold, subject to the first deed of trust, for $18,025.73, which was $1.00 more than the unpaid balance of the First National Bank's claim. The real estate sold was of the value of $200,000. Action was brought by the Tomiyasus to have the sale set aside on the ground of irregularities, fraud, misrepresentation, and inadequacy of the sale price. The trial court found there were no irregularities, fraud, misrepresentation, or collusion but, in spite of this finding, set the sale aside. On appeal, the holding was reversed.

Chief Justice Badt said: "The effect of this rule is that where such inadequacy stands alone, unaccompanied by an unfairness or other inequitable incident, it will not authorize the vacating of the sale. But it is universally recognized that inadequacy of price is a circumstance of greater or less weight to be considered in connection with other circumstances impeaching the fairness of the transaction as a cause of vacating it, and that, where the inadequacy is palpable and great, very slight additional evidence of unfairness or irregularity is sufficient to authorize the granting of the relief sought. . . . We think there can be no doubt under the authorities that where, *in addition to gross inadequacy of price,* the purchaser has, in the language of the United States Supreme Court, 'been guilty of any unfairness or has taken any undue advantage,' resulting in such gross inadequacy and consequent injury to the owner of the property, he will be deemed guilty of fraud warranting the interposition of a court of equity in favor of the owner who is himself without fault." *Golden* v. *Tomiyasu,* Nev. 387 P.2d. 989 (1963).

Checklist for deed of trust

The deed of trust is the same as any other conventional deed, with one exception—the grantee in the deed of trust will be designated as trustee (see "Deed Checklist," Chapter 5).

The deed of trust or a separate trust agreement will set out the security features of the deed of trust. In this part of the deed the following should be considered for inclusion:

1. A description of the debt secured.
2. How the debt is evidenced (negotiable promissory note or other evidence).

3. Terms of payment of the debt.
4. Interest to be paid and when interest is payable (semiannually, annually, and so forth).
5. Provisions for reconveyance on payment of the debt, interest, and so on, in full.
6. Who pays the cost of reconveyance or release.
7. Provision for acceleration in the event of default on the part of the owner.
8. Duty of the trustee to sell the property on the borrower's default, with or without request by the owner of the secured debt.
9. Provision for the time, place, and method of sale (must comply with the statutes of the state in which the real estate is located).
10. Right to sell as an entirety or in parcels.
11. Trustee's power to sell with general warranties.
12. Statement of the order of distribution of money received from sale of the real estate (payment of costs, interest, principal, junior liens, taxes, assessments, surplus to borrower, or whatever provision is appropriate).
13. Right of the holder of the debt to bid on the real estate at the sale.
14. Right of the holder of the debt to appoint, without court action, a successor trustee in the event the named trustee dies, is incapacitated, or refuses or fails to act.
15. Statement of the rights and powers of the successor trustee when appointed.
16. Provision for insurance for the benefit of the owner of the debt secured.
17. Duty of the borrower to keep improvements in good repair.
18. Duty of the borrower to pay all taxes and assessments.
19. Right of the owner of the debt to insure and pay premiums, to pay taxes and assessments if the borrower fails to do so, and to add the amount paid to the debt.
20. Method of establishing facts of payment of insurance premiums, taxes, assessments, and so on (affidavit of the owner of the debt).
21. Provision that the deed of trust shall be a first lien on the real estate.
22. Waiver of homestead exemptions, and so on.
23. Waiver of all exemption rights.

The deed of trust is executed with the same formality as a conventional deed or mortgage.

Land contracts

NATURE OF LAND CONTRACT

Three types of real estate transactions which are closely related but which differ in some of their technical aspects are (1) the land contract, (2) a bond for title, and (3) a long-term escrow. They are all essentially security devices. In each of these the vendor of the real estate retains the technical title to the property, and the vendee takes possession and assumes the risks of ownership.

Under the terms of the land contract the buyer agrees to pay the purchase price, and the seller agrees to execute and deliver to the buyer a deed to the property when the payment of the purchase price is made. In a bond-for-title transaction the agreement between the purchaser and the seller is substantially the same as in a land contract. However, in addition to agreeing to deliver the deed, the seller executes a bond with sureties which provides for the payment to the purchaser of damages in the event the seller refuses or fails to execute and deliver the deed to the property as provided in the contract of purchase and sale. Under the terms of a long-term escrow the seller executes and delivers the deed to the escrow holder to be delivered to the purchaser when his part of the transaction has been performed. In all of these transactions the buyer is the equitable owner of the property; and his interest in it is, in some states, treated as real property.[11]

Even though, in all of these transactions, the basic objective is the securing of the payment of a debt, the courts have not treated them as security devices and have not classed them as purchase-money mortgages but have instead applied basic rules of contract law in determining the rights and liabilities of the parties.

The land contract transaction should not be confused with the agreement to purchase real estate. The land contract is, as a general rule, a long-term contract and is essentially a security device, whereas the agreement to purchase is primarily a short-term contract entered into preliminary to the conveyance of the real estate involved.

This discussion will be based on the land contract; and any important difference between the land contract, bond for title, or long-term escrow will be noted.

---

[11] *Burns Indiana Statutes,* 1953 Replacement, Vol. III, p. 6–202.

Heinrich contracted to sell to Barlow and Beus, for the sum of $65,000, real and personal property consisting of a ranch and the farming machinery and equipment situated thereon.

Under the terms of the agreement the purchasers were to deposit with Idaho National Bank, as escrow holder, certain notes valued at $15,000, payable to the order of the purchaser, and were to pay the $50,000 balance in yearly installments of $5,000. The seller was to deposit with the escrow holder a warranty deed to the real property and title insurance policies, together with a bill of sale to the personal property and certain fire insurance policies. The contract and escrow agreement expressly provided that failure to make any payment when due or the failure of the maker of any of the notes to pay a note when due would be a default on the part of the purchaser, in which event the seller would be entitled to the possession of all the property and the escrow holder would return all instruments deposited by the seller. Default was made in the payment of certain notes, and the seller brought an action of attachment whereby he attached certain of the personal property sold under the contract of sale. Under the statutes of the state a person has no right to an attachment if his claim is secured. The trial court held that Heinrich's claim was secured and dismissed the attachment. On appeal, the disimissal of the attachment was affirmed.

Chief Justice Knudson said: "In Fraser v. Clark, the court was considering a contract which, like in this case, did not contain an express provision reserving title, but provided that sufficient deed and abstract should be deposited in escrow, for delivery upon purchasers' complete compliance, and that in case of purchasers' noncompliance, deed and abstract should be returned for cancellation and contract, at vendors' option, should become null and void and vendor entitled to possession of property. The court held that: 'Such provisions of the contract clearly provided a remedy for and security to the vendors for a breach thereof and under the provisions of R.C.M., 1947, p. 93–4301, precluded a rightful attachment and seizure of defendants' personal property in an action upon the contract upon which this suit was brought.'

"We therefore conclude that the contract here involved was an executory contract of sale under the terms of which appellants retained title as security for the payment of the purchase price. This being so, the contract was one expressly providing for security within the meaning of I.C. pp. 8–501, 8–502, and the attachment was properly discharged." *Heinrich* v. *Barlow,* Idaho, 390 P.2d 831 (1964).

FORM

There are no formal requirements for a valid land contract. Basically, it is a simple contract by the terms of which one party agrees to sell and another party agrees to buy a described piece of real estate. The buyer agrees to pay the stipulated purchase price over a certain period of time, and the seller agrees to execute and deliver to the buyer a deed to the real estate when the purchase price is paid. The rules of contract law are applied in determining whether or not the parties have entered into a valid, enforceable contract. These rules are discussed in Chapter 12, "Purchase Agreement."

A land contract, in order to be valid, does not have to be acknowledged, sealed, or witnessed. However, if the parties wish to record the land contract, it must be executed in compliance with the recording statutes of the state in which the land is located.

AFTER-ACQUIRED PROPERTY

When a person contracts to sell real estate under a land contract, such contract will, in the absence of a special provision in the contract to the contrary, be construed as implying that the seller has a merchantable title to the property which he is contracting to sell. If the seller does not have a merchantable title, the buyer may, at his election, rescind the contract and recover any sum he has paid on the agreed purchase price; and he may have any note which he has given as evidence of the unpaid balance of the purchase price canceled, provided the note, if negotiable in form, has not been negotiated to a holder in due course.[12] If the seller does not have, at the time the contract is executed, a merchantable title to the real estate, but later clears his title and can convey, at the time for the execution and delivery of the deed, a merchantable title, the buyer cannot refuse to make payment and rescind the contract on the ground that the seller's title was not merchantable at the time the contract was executed.

THE DEBT SECURED BY LAND CONTRACT

The only debt which can be secured by a land contract is the unpaid balance of the purchase price of the real estate which the seller has contracted to sell to the buyer. The land contract can be used to secure no other debt; it cannot be used as security for future advances. However, the standard land contract provides that the buyer shall pay all taxes, assessments, and insurance premiums; on his failure to do so, the seller may elect to pay such taxes, assessments, and insurance premiums, and add the amount disbursed to the unpaid balance due on the land contract.

[12] *Sutton* v. *Ford et al.*, 215 Ark. 269, 220 S.W.2d 125.

As a general rule, the purchase price which the buyer has contracted to pay for the real estate, the amount of the down payment, the amount and time of each subsequent payment, and the interest to be paid and how computed are set out in detail in the land contract. Although the debt may, in addition to the provision in the land contract, be evidenced by a separate instrument—either a negotiable or a nonnegotiable note—as a general rule, no separate instrument evidencing the debt need be executed.

RECORDING

Recording is not essential to the validity of a land contract. Whether or not a land contract is eligible for recordation will depend on the recording statutes of the state in which the real estate is located. In any event, if the land contract is to be recorded, it must be executed in compliance with the recording statutes of the state in which the real estate is located.

If the buyer takes possession of the real estate and occupies it in such a way that possession and occupation are evident to any person inspecting the property, the buyer's interests would be protected without recording the land contract, since anyone buying from the seller, who is the owner of record, would take with notice of the rights of the party in possession. If the real estate is undeveloped land and the buyer cannot occupy the land in such a manner that his occupation would be obvious to others, the buyer's interests would not be protected unless the land contract was recorded, since, without recordation, a good-faith purchaser might have no notice or knowledge of the existence of the land contract and would take free of the interests of the land contract buyer.[13]

ASSIGNMENT BY THE BUYER

The buyer under a land contract has a property interest in the real estate which is the subject matter of the contract and may transfer such interest by assigning the land contract to a third person. The assignee acquires all the rights of his assigner (the buyer) and takes subject to all the obligations the assignor owes to the seller under the land contract.

---

[13] *Jarrett* v. *Arnerich et al.*, 44 Wash.2d 55, 265 P.2d 282.

The buyer, by assigning the contract, cannot release himself from his obligations to the seller, unless the seller expressly agrees that he shall be released.[14] If the land contract includes a provision denying the buyer the right to assign the land contract without the written consent of the seller, an assignment in violation of the provision would give the seller the right to declare a forfeiture. The forfeiture, however, would not be enforced if the buyer or his assignee tendered full performance to the seller on his declaration of forfeiture.[15]

If the land contract has been recorded, each assignment of the contract should be recorded. If the land contract has been recorded and subsequent assignments are not recorded, and the seller, on final payment, deeds the property to an assignee who is not an assignee of record, the failure to record the assignments would create a defect in the record.

Goodman sold, on land contract, certain real estate to Elliott-Jared Investment Company (hereinafter referred to as Elliott). The contract provided: "No assignment or conveyance by the purchaser shall create any liability whatsoever against the seller until a duplicate thereof, duly witnessed and acknowledged, together with the residence address of such assignee, shall be delivered to and accepted by the seller, and receipt thereof indorsed thereon." Elliott mortgaged its interest in the contract to National Lumber Company without complying with the above-quoted provision of the land contract. Goodman started foreclosure proceedings on the land contract, and Elliott tendered performance of the contract. Goodman refused the tender and, on suit by Elliott asking the court to enjoin the foreclosure of the contract, set up that National Lumber Company acquired no rights in the contract, since the assignment was a breach of the nonassignment provision of the contract. The court held for Goodman and refused to issue an injunction as asked.

Justice Kavanaugh said: "A similar provision to the one present in this land contract restricting alienation has been held by this court not to be invalid because of being in restraint of alienation, since it does not bar assignment of the contract but merely is an agreement between the contracting parties as to the method in which an assignment or conveyance must be made to affect the rights of the vendor. Equally well settled is the rule that the term "conveyance" embraces a mortgage of lands.

"We conclude that this personal element, which in no way affected the assignability of the contract, prevented any equities arising that would interfere with the vendor's rights to insist upon strict compliance with the contract terms." *National Lumber Company* v. *Goodman,* 371 Mich. 54, 123 N.W.2d 147 (1963).

---

[14] *Krueger et al.* v. *Campbell et al.,* 264 Mich. 449, 250 N.W. 285.

[15] *Handzel et al.* v. *Bassi et al.,* 343 Ill. App. 281 99 N.E.2d 23.

TRANSFER OF REAL ESTATE BY SELLER

The seller is the owner of record of the real estate sold under a land contract; that is, he has legal title to the real estate. He also is the owner of the debt which the land contract secures. He may assign his interest in the land contract—that is, sell the debt—or he may sell the real estate subject to the outstanding rights of the land contract buyer.

If the land contract is not recorded and the buyer or his assignee or representative is not in possession, and the seller conveys the real estate to a good-faith purchaser for value, such purchaser will take free from the outstanding claims of the land contract buyer or his assignee. However, the seller would, in such a case, be guilty of breach of the land contract; and the buyer could hold the seller liable in damages, could rescind the contract and recover all payments made, or could require the seller to account to the buyer for the full consideration of the second sale.[16] The purchaser of real estate subject to an outstanding land contract is entitled to the payments due under the contract and owes a duty to convey the real estate to the buyer or his assignee as provided in the land contract.

RIGHTS OF SELLER ON BUYER'S DEFAULT

Since the courts have not recognized the land contract as a security transaction but have held it to be a contract to sell, the basis for the determination of the rights of the seller on the buyer's default is the provisions of the contract.

The following provisions defining the seller's rights are customarily included in a land contract: a provision declaring that time is of the essence; a provision giving the seller, on the buyer's default, the right to declare the contract void and to take immediate possession of the premises and remove the buyer, and to retain all payments and improvements made as rent and liquidated damages; a provision declaring that on the buyer's default, all subsequent payments shall become due and payable, and the seller shall have the right to compel the continued performance of the contract; a provision giving the seller the right to foreclose the contract; a provision giving the seller the right to all the remedies provided for in the contract; and a provision declaring that a waiver of any breach of the contract shall not be deemed to be a waiver of any other breach.

[16] *Niles* v. *Groover,* 98 Ga. 461, 3 S.E. 899.

As a general rule, if the buyer is guilty of a material breach of the contract, such as his failure to make payment when due, or if he repudiates the contract, the seller will be entitled to repossess the real estate, particularly when the land contract so provides.[17] However, if, after default but before the seller repossesses the property, or, having repossessed, before he changes his position in relation thereto and within a reasonable time, the buyer tenders the full amount of the unpaid balance of the purchase price, interest, and legitimate costs, the seller will be required to accept the tender and deed the real estate to the buyer as required by the terms of the land contract.[18]

If the buyer, after default, refuses to surrender the property, the seller may bring an action to recover possession. The procedure to be followed in such an action will depend on the statutes of the state in which the real estate is located.

In some states the seller, as a prerequisite to the bringing of a possessory action, must give the buyer either notice to quit or notice of forfeiture. The form of such notice, the time of the notice, how and on whom served, and so forth, will be set out in the statutes of the state in which the real estate is located. In some states the giving of notice to quit or notice of forfeiture may be waived by including an express waiver in the land contract. In other states, if the land contract includes a provision making time of the essence, no notice to quit or notice of forfeiture is required.[19]

Whether or not a demand for possession, a tender of the deed to the property, or a return of the purchase money must be made as a prerequisite to the bringing of a possessory action will depend primarily on the terms of the land contract. As a general rule, demand for possession, unless waived by the terms of the land contract, must be made as a prerequisite to the bringing of a possessory action.[20]

The standard form of land contract in common use includes a provision permitting the seller, on default by the buyer and repossession by the seller, to retain all payments made and all improvements of the property as rent and liquidated damages for breach of the contract. Unless the circumstances are such that the enforcement of such provision would amount to a penalty, it will be enforced, and the buyer will be held

---

[17] *Murphy* v. *Yeast,* 59 Ariz. 281, 126 P.2d 313.

[18] *Onekama Realty Co.* v. *Carothers,* 59 Ariz. 416, 129 P.2d 918.

[19] *Whitehurst* v. *Ratliff,* 198 Okla. 639, 181 P.2d 545.

[20] *Muirhead* v. *McCullough,* 234 Mich. 52, 207 N.W. 886.

not to be entitled to the return of any of the purchase price he has paid[21] or to payment for improvements made.[22]

If the seller wishes, he may, under the procedure statutes of some states, bring an action in the nature of a strict foreclosure if the buyer defaults. A decree of strict foreclosure, since it is an equitable remedy, will not be granted if the value of the land is substantially greater than the unpaid balance due under the land contract.[23]

If, on the buyer's failure to make the payments when due, the seller does not wish to repossess the real estate, he may resort to his remedies at law. He may bring suit and recover a judgment for past-due installments; or he may, if the contract contains a provision giving him the right, declare the entire balance of the purchase price immediately due and payable, and bring an action to recover a judgment for this amount. If the seller brings suit to recover a judgment for the last installment due under the terms of the land contract or for the unpaid balance, he must tender into the court a deed which complies with the terms of the land contract.[24] Whether or not the buyer, in the event of suit for the unpaid balance of the purchase price, will be entitled to credit for installments paid or for improvements made to the property will depend on the terms of the contract and the circumstances of the particular case.

Boyd, by written contract, agreed to buy certain real estate for $17,500, of which $8,000 was represented by Boyd's promissory note payable on or before two years from its date, and the remainder was payable at $100 per month, including interest. The $8,000 note was secured by other property belonging to Boyd. Boyd defaulted in his monthly payments, and the Davies' (the sellers) gave written notice of their election to terminate and cancel the contract and retake possession. Possession of the property was redelivered to the Davies'. They then brought this suit upon the $8,000 note, to foreclose the mortgage. The trial court gave judgment to the Davies'; and on appeal, the court reversed the judgment.

Justice Noble said: "The parties to a contract may provide for its rescission upon any terms agreeable to them, and this court has indicated that a provision for forfeiture of installment payments made prior to default, which approximate rent, will be approved, at least where reasonable notice of default is required by the contract. The sellers had the option to consider the contract still in

[21] *J. F. Cantwell Co.* v. *Harrison et al.,* 95 Ind. App. 180, 180 N.E. 482.

[22] *Continental Oil Co.* v. *Bean et al.,* 171 Okla. 66, 41 P.2d 678.

[23] *Swanson* v. *Madsen et al.,* 145 Neb. 815, 18 N.W.2d 217.

[24] *Fairlawn Heights Co., Inc.* v. *Theis,* 133 Ohio St. 387, 14 N.E.2d 1; *Bridge Land Improvement Co.* v. *Myers et al.,* 129 N.J.L. 164, 28 A.2d 601.

force, sue for breach of its terms or the enforcement thereof, or, on the other hand, to disaffirm the contract and retain the payments made by purchasers as liquidated damages. Under the doctrine of election of remedies, they could not disaffirm it and sue for any part of its performance. It seems to be the general holding of the courts that a vendor may not maintain an action to recover any part of an unpaid purchase money where he has rescinded or forfeited a contract. Where a contract for sale of real estate is accompanied by the purchaser's note or other separate obligation for a part of the purchase price, termination or cancellation of the contract or claim of forfeiture under its terms, because of default by the purchaser, is generally held to destroy the consideration for the separate obligation of the purchaser and it is no longer enforceable against him.

"The trial court found as a fact that defendants only made five monthly payments, and that after written notice plaintiffs did elect to and did rescind the contract, and took possession of the real estate. Having declared a forfeiture, and elected to rescind the contract, it follows as a matter of law that there can be no recovery on the note representing an unpaid part of the purchase price. The rescission of the contract destroyed the consideration for the note which was given, not as payment, but as evidence of a payment to be made under the terms of the contract." *Davies* v. *Boyd,* 73 N.M. 85, 385 P.2d 950 (1963).

DAMAGES FOR BREACH OF CONTRACT

As a general rule, the seller, on the buyer's default, may bring an action to recover damages for breach of contract. In such a case the general rules of the law of damages would apply in determining the amount of damages to which the seller is entitled. In general, the seller is entitled to recover judgment for the amount he can prove with reasonable certainty he has lost as the direct result of the buyer's breach of the contract.

BUYER'S REMEDIES ON SELLER'S DEFAULT

If the seller refuses or fails to execute and deliver a deed to the property in compliance with the terms of the land contract, the buyer is entitled to the remedy of specific performance on the tender or payment of the purchase price and on the performance of his other obligations under the contract.[25] The buyer, on the seller's default or inability to perform, may elect to rescind the contract and recover all payments made, less

---

[25] *Sexton* v. *Waggoner,* La. App., 66 So.2d 634.

a reasonable amount as rent for the use of the real estate.[26] When the buyer has, in good faith, made substantial improvements which enhance the value of the real estate, he may recover the value of such improvements.[27]

If the seller breaches the land contract in any material respect, or is unable or unwilling to convey title to the real estate to the buyer as required by the contract, the buyer, at his election, may bring an action to recover damages for the breach of the contract. The measure of damages usually applied in such cases is the amount of loss which the buyer can prove with reasonable certainty he has suffered as the direct result of the seller's breach of the contract.

Walter L. Talley, Inc., sold certain real estate to Council on land contract. After the execution of the contract and without the knowledge or consent of Council, Walter L. Tally, Inc., conveyed an easement of right of way across the property to De Kalb County to be used for the installation of a sewer trunk line through the property. Council gave notice of rescission of the contract and brought suit to recover the money paid. The trial court granted Council a judgment; and on appeal, the judgment was affirmed.

Judge Jordan said: "Where the vendor breaches an executory contract for the sale of land, the vendee, if not himself in default, may elect to rescind the contract and recover the amount he has paid on the purchase price.

"The defendant vendor under the terms of the contract of sale was obligated to convey said property by warranty deed to the purchaser at the time the sale was consummated, subject to any incumbrances as specified in the contract. Since there were no incumbrances specified in the contract of sale, it was the vendor's duty under said contract to convey the subject property to the plaintiff vendee free and clear of any incumbrances. This is true for the reason that a general warranty in a warranty deed includes the covenant that the land being conveyed is free from incumbrances.

"Accordingly, where as here the evidence authorized the finding that the defendant vendor had placed an incumbrance upon the subject property by conveying an easement in it to De Kalb County for the purpose of installing and maintaining a sewer line through that prorperty (which according to the testimony of the plaintiff rendered the property less valuable for the use intended) and had thus rendered the performance of its contract impossible, the plaintiff vendee who was not himself in default was entitled to rescind the contract and recover the amount he had paid on the purchase price." *Walter L. Tally, Inc.* v. *Council*, Ga. App., 135 S.E.2d 515 (1964).

---

[26] *Passent et al.* v. *Peter Vredenburgh Lumber Co., Inc., et al.*, 325 Ill. App. 260, 60 N.E.2d 39.

[27] *Huggins et al.* v. *Green Top Dairy Farms, Inc., et al.*, 75 Idaho 436, 273 P.2d 399.

Checklist for land contract

Since a land contract is a contract to sell real estate, it should include the usual provisions of a purchase agreement. For these provisions, see the checklist for a purchase agreement to sell (Chapter 12). In addition to the usual provisions in a purchase agreement to sell real estate, the following provisions should be considered for inclusion in the land contract:

1. The seller's promise to convey to the buyer on payment of the purchase price.
2. The type of deed the seller is to execute and deliver (warranty deed with general warranties, warranty deed with special warranties, quitclaim deed).
3. Exceptions, reservations, restrictions, and so on, to be in the deed.
4. The seller to furnish abstract, certificate of title, or title insurance showing merchantable title.
5. The buyer's right to possession and time when possession is to be given to the buyer.
6. Title to remain in the seller until the buyer pays the purchase price in full.
7. A statement of the down payment to be made.
8. A statement of the payments to be made; the amount of each payment, and when and where paid.
9. The rate of interest to be paid on deferred payments.
10. The rate of interest to be paid on delinquent payments, if different from the rate to be paid on deferred payments.
11. How the interest is to be computed and the payments credited:
    a. Interest to be computed annually—on stated date—subtracted from the amount paid and the balance credited to the principal.
    b. Interest computed semiannually.
    c. Interest computed when each payment is made.
12. The buyer's right to pay any sum in addition to the required payments.
13. How interest is computed, if additional payments are made.
14. Whether the buyer or the seller is to pay taxes, assessments, and so forth. (Usually, the buyer pays all taxes and assessments.)
15. If the seller pays taxes and assessments, these payments are to be made out of the payments made by the buyer to the seller.

16. The type and amount of insurance to be carried by the buyer for the benefit of the seller, to be approved by the seller.
17. Insurance policies to be deposited with the seller.
18. The buyer shall not assign or sell the land contract without the written consent of the seller.
19. The buyer shall not lease or permit others to occupy the premises without the written consent of the seller.
20. The buyer shall not alter, change, remove, or add to improvements on the premises without the written consent of the seller.
21. The buyer shall keep the premises in good repair and in good condition at all times.
22. The buyer shall not commit waste on the premises.
23. In the event of breach and reentry by the seller, the buyer shall deliver up the premises in as good condition as when he took possession—ordinary wear and tear, ordinances, and acts of God excepted.
24. The buyer shall at all times use and maintain the premises in accordance with the laws of the United States, the state, and the city.
25. The seller shall have the right to enter the premises at any reasonable time for the purpose of inspecting the same.
26. The buyer assumes all risks of accident, injury, or damage to persons or property in or about the premises.
27. The buyer is in default if he fails to pay:
    a. Taxes and assessments.
    b. Insurance premiums.
    c. Installments of the purchase price.
    d. Interest on the unpaid balance when due (may provide for grace period—for example, within 30 days after becoming delinquent), or if he fails to observe or perform any other condition or term of the contract.
28. On the buyer's default the seller will have the right to exercise the following:
    a. At his option, declare the contract void.
    b. Take immediate possession of the premises.
    c. Without court action, remove the buyer or any person in possession.
    d. Retain all payments made and all improvements added to the premises as rent and liquidated damages.
    e. At the seller's option, declare that all subsequent payments shall become due and payable, and have the right to compel performance of the contract.

     f.   At his option, foreclose the land contract.

29. The seller's rights shall be cumulative.
30. The seller's wavier of any breach of the contract shall not be deemed a waiver of any other breach.
31. On the buyer's default and repossession by the seller, the seller shall be relieved of all liability to the buyer.
32. The buyer waives all right to notice to quit, to notice of forfeiture, or to demand for possession.
33. Time is of the essence in the contract.
34. The seller's right to place or maintain a mortgage on the premises in an amount not to exceed the unpaid balance of the purchase price.
35. The seller, if he places a mortgage, shall give the buyer notice of the amount and terms of the mortgage, the name of the mortgagee, and so forth.
36. A mortgage placed by the seller shall have priority over the buyer's equity.
37. The buyer, if the seller places a mortgage, shall sign a waiver of priority if requested to do so. The buyer shall not be personally liable for the mortgage debt.
38. The buyer to have the right to pay the amount of the unpaid balance of the purchase price over and above the mortgage on the premises; and the seller to execute a deed that complies with the terms of the contract, subject to the mortgage, the buyer assuming and agreeing to pay the mortgage debt.
39. Assumption of the mortgage and the mortgage debt shall satisfy the debt to the seller.
40. All covenants and agreements in the land contract shall be extended to and be binding on heirs, executors, administrators, successors, and assigns of the parties.
41. There are no representations or warranties respecting the real estate or the sale thereof, except those set out in the land contract.
42. If the contract is to be recorded, it should be executed in compliance with the recording laws of the state in which the real estate is located.

11

Real estate brokerage relationship

Introduction

THE BROKER

ALTHOUGH the real estate business is not confined to brokerage, it is an important activity of substantially all persons engaged in such business. The real estate broker is an agent employed by a seller or buyer to negotiate the sale, purchase, or exchange of real estate on a commission contingent on success. He acts as a special agent for multiple principals. His primary function is to act as an intermediary between the buyer and the seller, and to aid in the negotiations leading up to the sale, purchase, or exchange of real estate. He may, however, perform other services connected with the completion of the transaction, such as, for example, the procuring of financing.

The services performed by the real estate broker differ in many important respects from those performed by other common types of brokers— the stockbroker and commodity broker, for instance. The real estate broker's relation to the public is such that in a majority of the states, he must, before acting as a broker, obtain a license by establishing his integrity, character, and ability to serve his customers efficiently. The brokerage business is one of long standing and is very specialized. As a result, there has evolved in connection with this business a well-developed body of law which reflects for the most part the established customs and usages of the business. Generally, the applicant, in order to obtain a real estate broker's license, must show through an examination reasonable knowledge of such laws, customs, and usages.

NATURE OF THE REAL ESTATE BROKERAGE BUSINESS

A person operating a real estate brokerage business acts as an independent businessman and also as an agent in the sale, purchase, or exchange of real estate. As an independent businessman, he determines the policies of his office. He hires and compensates his employees and directs their activities in connection with the business, and in general is responsible for the operation of the business. As an agent, he represents the persons who engage his services, and he owes a duty to them to exercise care and skill in carrying out their instructions.

His duties are generally confined to the advertising of the property and to the finding of a person ready, willing, and able to deal on the terms stipulated by the broker's principal or acceptable to him. In the accomplishing of the objective of the agency, the broker may, and in many instances will, perform many connected services. Usually, the broker does not have the authority to bind his principal to a contract to sell or to make a conveyance of the listed property; such authority may, however, be conferred on him.[1]

Mrs. Todd owned real estate which she listed with Horton, a licensed real estate broker. A standard-form listing contract was executed by Mrs. Todd. Horton signed in the name of Mrs. Todd, as her agent, a contract to sell the real property. Mrs. Todd refused to perform the contract and, when sued, set up Horton's lack of authority to execute a contract to sell as her agent. The court held that Horton had no authority to execute a contract to sell as agent for Mrs. Todd.

Justice Ozner said: "It is well settled that a real estate broker, under the ordinary contract of employment, has no implied authority to execute a contract of sale in behalf of his principal. He is generally a special agent, with limited powers, whose usual duty is simply to find a purchaser ready, able and willing to enter into a contract upon the terms and conditions fixed by the owner." *Gallant* v. *Todd,* 235 S.C. 428, 111 S.E.2d 779 (1960).

THE REAL ESTATE SALESMAN

The real estate salesman occupies a unique place in the operation of a real estate brokerage business. In a majority of the states, he must,

---

[1] *Queen City Lumber Company* v. *Fisher,* N.D., 111 N.W.2d 714.

like the real estate broker, prove his character, integrity, and ability and obtain a salesman's license. The duties he is licensed to perform are more limited than those granted the real estate broker, and the salesman generally must work out of the office of a licensed real estate broker.

The salesman may be an independent contractor, or he may be an employee of the broker. If the arrangement with the broker permits the salesman to work when and if he wishes, if he is permitted to find his own prospects and is not obligated to contact prospects referred to him by the broker, and if he is in general permitted to "work on his own," his relation to the broker will be that of an independent contractor. If the salesman works regular hours under the direct supervision and control of the broker and owes a duty to follow the reasonable instructions of the broker in regard to the work to be performed, he is an employee of the broker.

In either case the primary duty of the real estate salesman is to contact persons interested in purchasing property. It is his job to learn all he can about the prospect, either from personal interviews or from outside sources; to determine which listed properties the prospect is in a position to buy and in which he may be interested; and to induce the prospect to sign a proposition to purchase a certain property. The salesman is the contact man. He makes the representations and sales talks which induce the prospect to contract to purchase the property. Many people engaged in the real estate business operate both as brokers and as salesmen. This is usually true of persons operating small real estate brokerage businesses.

Creation of the real estate broker-owner relation

RELATION OF BROKER

The broker-owner relationship is created by the agreement of the parties, and from a legal standpoint the relationship is that of principal (the owner) and agent (the broker). Although such a relationship is created by agreement, a contract of employment is not necessary for its creation. All that is necessary is that the owner expressly or impliedly indicate his willingness to be represented in a transaction by another person, the broker, who, either expressly or impliedly, indicates his willingness to act under the direction and control of the owner.

The broker may act gratuitously, and the authority to act may be either oral or in writing. The creation of the relationship and the authority to act should not be confused with the statutory requirement of a writing as the basis of a broker's right to collect a commission earned. In the real estate brokerage business the relationship of owner and broker will, with few exceptions, be created by a contract which will authorize the broker to represent the owner in a transaction involving the owner's property.

LISTING CONTRACTS

The contract between an owner and a broker whereby the broker is authorized to find a buyer or a renter for the owner's real property is known as a *listing*. A person wishing to purchase real property having certain characteristics may engage a broker to act in his behalf. An agreement of this nature is not, as a general rule, referred to as a listing; it is a contract of agency.

Some states[2] have enacted statutes, somewhat in the nature of statutes of frauds, which provide that any contract for the payment of a commission for the procuring by one person of a purchaser for the real estate of another shall not be valid unless the same shall be in writing, signed by the owner of such real estate. The statutes of some states are so worded that only contracts to pay a commission on the sale of real estate are included, whereas others stipulate that not only sales but also rentals and other transactions involving real estate are included.[3] These statutes differ in another important respect, in that some of them make the oral agreement to pay a commission null and void, and of no effect. Under this type of statute the broker can recover nothing if the contract to pay a commission is oral.[4] Other types of statutes provide that no action shall be brought to enforce an oral contract to pay a commission. The courts of some states having this type of statute have permitted the broker to recover a commission based on the benefits conferred on the owner as the result of the services rendered.[5] The suit is not on the contract, but is in quasi contract. In those states which require listing contracts to be in writing, the writing, as a general rule, need not be a complete

---

[2] Arizona, California, Idaho, Indiana, Iowa, Kentucky, Michigan, Montana, Nebraska, Utah, Washington, and Wisconsin.

[3] *Wooley* v. *Wycoff,* 2 Utah 2d 329, 273 P.2d 181.

[4] *Krause* v. *Boraks,* 341 Mich. 149, 67 N.W.2d 202.

[5] *Clinkinbeard* v. *Poole, Ky.,* 266 S.W.2d 796.

contract but only a note or memorandum; however, such note or memorandum, if it is to be sufficient, must show the broker's authority to act.

The standard listing contract form is merely an authorization for the broker to act for the owner and is not a guarantee by the broker of the sale or rental of the listed property. The broker is, as agent of the owner, obligated to use his best efforts to accomplish the objectives of the agency.

LISTING CONTRACT FORMS

The nature of a real estate broker's business is such that it makes the use of a well-drafted listing contract form very desirable. By the use of such a form the broker minimizes the risk of loss of commissions as the result of an inadequate writing or of misunderstandings.

All of the above-discussed risks may be avoided by the use of a carefully drafted and well-rounded listing contract. Listing contract forms are prepared and made available by local real estate associations. The broker may use these forms, or he may prefer to use a listing contract drafted by his attorney. If a form contract is used, extreme care should be exercised in filling in the blanks. The broker should obtain the signature of both husband and wife, if the owner is married; and the terms of the contract should be explained to the owner before he signs.

KINDS OF LISTING CONTRACTS

Listing contracts in common use are classified under four general headings: (1) open listings, (2) exclusive agency, (3) exclusive right to sell, and (4) multiple listings.

OPEN LISTINGS.   Under the terms of an open listing contract, no restrictions are placed on the owner's right to sell, either through his own efforts or through other brokers. The owner has the right to list with as many brokers as he chooses and is liable for a commission only to the first procuring broker, that is, the first broker to procure a buyer ready, willing, and able to purchase the property on the terms of the listing or other terms acceptable to the owner.[6] When a buyer is procured by any broker with whom the property is listed or by the owners, the agencies of all other brokers are automatically terminated—that is, no notice of the sale or of procurement of a buyer or of the termination of the agency is required.[7]

---

[6] *Brinkman* v. *Peel*, 222 Ark. 345, 260 S.W.2d 448.
[7] *Roberts* v. *Gardner et al.*, Okla., 275 P.2d 245.

Unless the listing contract clearly states the restrictions placed on the owner's right to sell through his own efforts or through other brokers, the courts will hold it to be an open listing. Any restrictions on the owner's right to deal with his property as he wishes must be voluntarily assumed and clearly stated. From the standpoint of the broker an open listing is not desirable. When such a listing is used and the property is listed with several brokers, a controversy may arise as to who is entitled to the commission in a situation where one broker has discussed the sale of the property with a prospect and perhaps shown it to him and then at a later date another broker or the owner concludes a sale with the prospect.

Roberts listed property with Gardner. The listing was for a reasonable time, at a specified price, and "subject to prior sale." Gardner found a buyer; but before he could present the buyer to Roberts, another broker produced a purchaser acceptable to him. The court held that the listing was a nonexclusive (open) listing.

Justice Williams said: "Since the plaintiffs were not given an exclusive right to sell, they assumed the risk of knowing that the land might be sold by the owner or another agent before they could find a purchaser, ready, able and willing to buy on the terms specified, and that such a sale would ipso facto revoke their agency." *Roberts* v. *Gardner et al.,* Okla., 275 P.2d 245 (1954).

EXCLUSIVE AGENCY. Under the terms of an exclusive agency contract the owner appoints the broker with whom he has listed the property his exclusive agent for the procuring of a purchaser for the property during the term of the listing. Under the exclusive agency contract the owner obligates himself to pay a commission to the listing broker if the property is sold during the term of the listing by the listing broker "or by any other person." An exclusive agency listing contract does not deprive the owner of his right to sell the property to a buyer procured by his own efforts; and if the owner does sell to such a buyer, the agency is terminated, and the listing broker is not entitled to a commission. In the event the listing contract is prepared for or by the broker and the terms are ambiguous, the court will hold that it is an open listing or an exclusive agency, not an exclusive right to sell.

Bursley listed a trailer court for sale with Nicholas. The listing contract provided that Nicholas was to have "for a period of six months from this date the exclusive right to sell the property at the price and terms acceptable to me: $97,000.00. Cash down payment $35,000." The contract further provided: "3. The commissions are to be paid whether the purchaser be secured by you or any other broker." Bursley sold the trailer court to Shark, a purchaser procured solely by the efforts of Bursley. The court held that the listing created an exclusive agency and that Nicholas was not entitled to a commission.

Chief Judge Allen said: ". . . the absence of an unequivocal provision in the contract that the owner has given up his inherent right to sell his property, . . . leads us to the conclusion that the lower court must be affirmed that the amended complaint failed to show an exclusive right and authority to sell sufficient to preclude the owner from selling the property without obligation to Nicholas." *Nicholas* v. *Bursley, Fla.,* 119 So.2d 722 (1960).

EXCLUSIVE RIGHT TO SELL.   Under the terms of an exclusive right-to-sell contract, the owner obligates himself to pay the broker the agreed commission if the property is sold during the term of the listing, regardless of who procures the buyer.[8] The owner has the right to sell the property through his own efforts, but the fact that the owner has procured the buyer and made the sale does not relieve him from paying the broker his commission.

If the broker wishes to obtain the advantages of an exclusive right to sell, he must draft his contract with exceptional care. Some courts have held that a listing contract which merely states that the broker has the "exclusive right to sell" creates an exclusive agency, not an exclusive right to sell,[9] whereas other courts have held that it gives the broker an exclusive right to sell.[10] A carefully drafted listing contract will protect the broker and should prevent controversy if it states in unequivocal language that the broker has the exclusive right to sell and that the broker will be paid his full commission if the property is sold during the term of the listing, no matter who procures the buyer.

Barnes listed property for sale with West. The listing contract included the following provision: "Should I, or anyone acting for me, including my heirs, sell, lease, transfer or otherwise dispose of said property within the time herein fixed for the continuance of the agency, you shall be entitled nevertheless to your commission as herein set out." Barnes, while the listing was in force, sold the property to a buyer procured by his own efforts and refused to pay West the stipulated commission. West sued Barnes, and the court granted West a judgment.

Justice Richards said: "Assuming that the listing agreement complied in all respects with the provisions of Sec. 28, Art. 6573a, V.C.S. [statute of frauds] there being no question of fraud in its execution, appellant [West] would be

---

[8] *Bell* v. *Dimmerling et al.,* 140 Ohio St. 153, 78 N.E.2d 49.

[9] *Roberts* v. *Harrington,* 168 Wis. 217, 169 N.W. 603.

[10] *Torrey & Dean, Inc.* v. *Coyle,* 138 Ore. 509, 7 P.2d 561.

entitled to recover the compensation due him under the terms of the exclusive-listing contract which had been breached by appellee [Barnes] by the sale to Ben Newman." *West* v. *Barnes,* Tex. Civ. App., 351 S.W.2d 615 (1961).

MULTIPLE LISTING.   Multiple listing is not recognized as a distinct kind of listing contract. It is an agreement among a number of the brokers in a city or area whereby any broker who is a party thereto may sell property for which another broker, who is also a party to the agreement, has an exclusive right-to-sell contract. A multiple listing starts with an exclusive right-to-sell listing. The member brokers set up a multiple listing exchange, and all listings are registered with the exchange. The usual multiple listing agreement gives each member broker the right to sell any property registered with the exchange. When a property is sold, the selling broker and the listing broker divide the commission. The basis for the division of commission is set out in the multiple listing agreement. If the listing broker sells the property, he receives all the commission.

Since an agent cannot delegate his authority to any other person without the consent, either express or implied, of the principal, a listing contract should be so worded that the owner consents to the arrangement.

Fay listed her property for sale under a multiple listing contract. Mercner, a member of the board of realtors, procured a purchaser for the property, but Fay refused to pay the stipulated commission. Fay, when sued, set up as a defense that Mercner was not named as broker in the listing contract. The court held that Mercner was entitled to the commission.

Judge Molineux said: "The multiple listing agreement herein contained an express authorization, to wit, 'the undersigned as owner hereby gives to said active broker members of the Westfield Board of Realtors the exclusive right to sell . . . the property described on the reverse side hereof. . . .' Furthermore, the multiple listing agreement was directed to all active broker members of the Westfield Board of Realtors of which plaintiff [Mercner] was one. The recent case of Looman Realty Corporation v. Broad Street National Bank of Trenton is ample authority for the proposition that an alleged party to a contract who is indicated, although not specifically named therein, may sue on the contract after proving that he was in fact an intended party." *Mercner* v. *Fay,* 71 N.J. Super. 519, 177 A.2d 481 (1962).

Checklist for listing contract

A broker who wishes to use a listing contract form should have it carefully checked by a competent lawyer. Such an attorney would be familiar with state statutes and local ordinances which would have to be taken into consideration in the drafting of the contract. The following checklist suggests the major points which should be covered in all listing contracts. The checklist is for an exclusive right-to-sell listing.

1. Names of the owner and the broker.
2. Description of the property.
3. Duration of the listing.
4. Terms on which the property is to be sold.
5. Commission to be paid.
6. When the commission is earned.
7. Consideration—the owner to pay commission, the broker to use diligence in procuring a purchaser for the property. In the consideration clause the broker may wish to promise to advertise.
8. Special provision for exclusive right to sell—"I hereby agree to pay the broker as commission 6 per cent of the selling price herein named, whether the property is sold by me (owner) or another broker or agent, or through some other sources, and whether the property is transferred or conveyed or withdrawn from sale during the term of this listing."

   If a broker wishes to protect himself from collusive sales made after the listing has expired, a clause similar to the following may be included: "In case a sale is made within [90 days] after the termination of this listing to parties with whom this broker negotiated during the term of this listing, I hereby agree to pay the broker the commission herein provided."
9. Rights of the parties in case of forfeiture of the down payment.
10. Signatures of the broker and the owner. At the time the listing contract is signed, the broker may obtain from the owner a detailed description of the property. This information is frequently written on the reverse side of the listing contract, but it is not a part of the terms of the contract.

Liability of real estate broker

RELATION OF BROKER TO OWNER

The real estate broker is the agent of the owner and, as such, owes the duties of a fiduciary to his principal, the owner. In his fiduciary relation to the owner, the broker owes a duty of undivided loyalty. He must never put himself in a position where his personal interests conflict with the interests of the owner.[11] As a professional agent, he owes a duty to advise the owner as to the various aspects of the transaction which he is negotiating on the owner's behalf. The broker will not be permitted to buy for or sell to himself property listed unless he makes a complete disclosure of all aspects of the transaction, including an honest appraisal of the value and including also any prospective increase in value of which the broker may have knowledge.

The broker is a professional agent; and by offering his services as a broker, he represents that he possesses certain special skills. He will therefore be required to possess the skill and exercise the care usually possessed and exercised by brokers engaged in similar activities in the community. This includes a knowledge of the characteristics of the area in which he is carrying on his business. He will be expected to know real estate values in his area, and will owe a duty to advise the owner as to the value of his property and as to any other matters connected with the transaction where such matters come within the scope of the services usually rendered by brokers doing business in the community. A broker cannot escape liability by pleading ignorance.

Harper, a farmer who had had little business experience, listed his 700-acre farm with Reese. The listed price was $45,000. There was a $15,000 mortgage on the farm. Reese presented to Harper a purchase agreement in which the purchase price was stated as $30,000; encumbrances—none. Reese did not explain the terms to Harper, and he executed the agreement, expecting to get $30,000 for his equity in the farm. The agreement was canceled, but Reese sued Harper to recover a commission. The court held that Reese had failed to fulfill the duties he owed to Harper and that Reese had not earned a commission.

Justice Crockett said: ". . . , persons who trust their business to such agents [brokers] are entitled to repose some degree of confidence that they will be loyal to such trust and that they will, with reasonable diligence and in good faith, represent the interests of their clients. Unless the law demands this standard, instead of being the badge of competence and integrity it is supposed to be, the license would serve only as a foil to lure the unsuspecting public in to be duped by people more skilled and experienced in such affairs than are they, when they would be better off taking care of such business for themselves." *Reese* v. *Harper,* 8 Utah 2d 119, 329 P.2d 410 (1958).

BROKER REPRESENTING BOTH PARTIES. In an exchange of property the broker may represent both parties to the exchange. In such a situation

---

[11] *Lerk* v. *McCabe et al.,* 349 Ill. 348, 182 N.E. 388.

the broker owes a duty to make a full disclosure to all parties involved, and all the parties must consent to the dual representation.[12] A failure to make a full disclosure and obtain the consent of all interested parties is a fraud on those who do not know of, and consent to, the dual representation; and on the discovery of the fraud, they may rescind the transaction. The broker cannot collect a commission from either party, since the entire transaction is tainted with fraud. If the broker has permission to act for both parties, he must act with the utmost good faith, honesty, and impartiality. If the broker favors one party or colludes to defraud one of the parties, he will be liable to the injured party for the loss suffered.

Mathews brought an action to foreclose a mortgage, and Tabrosky asked that the transaction which gave rise to the mortgage be set aside on the ground that the broker who represented Tabrosky also represented Mathews without his (Tabrosky's) knowledge or consent. The court held the transaction was voidable at the election of Tabrosky.

Judge Shannon said: "No principle is better settled than that a man cannot be the agent of both the seller and buyer in the same transaction, without the intelligent consent of both. Loyalty to his trust is the most important duty which the agent owes to his principal. Reliance upon his integrity, fidelity, and ability is the main consideration in the selection of agents; and so careful is the law in guarding this fiduciary relation that it will not allow an agent to act for himself and his principal, nor to act for two principals on opposite sides of the same transaction. In such cases the amount of consideration, the absence of undue advantage, and other like features are wholly immaterial. Nothing will defeat the principal's right of remedy, except his own confirmation, after full knowledge of all the facts. Actual injury is not the principle upon which the law holds such transactions voidable." *Tabrosky* v. *Mathews, Fla.,* 121 So.2d 61 (1960).

BROKER PURCHASING PROPERTY. The strictness with which the interests of the owner of property are guarded from fraudulent or unethical conduct of a broker is reflected in the cases in which the broker, either directly or indirectly, purchases the listed property without making a full disclosure to the owner of his (the broker's) interest in the transaction. Any such transaction is a breach of the fiduciary duty owed by the broker to the owner. If the broker purchases the property directly, or if he sells it to a relative or confederate who will at a later date convey the property to the broker, or convey it as directed by the broker and pay the broker the resulting profit or a portion thereof, or if the broker sells the property

---

[12] *Ledirk Amusement Co., Inc., et al.* v. *Schechner et al.,* 133 N.J. Eq. 602, 33 A.2d 894.

to a partnership of which he is a member or to a corporation in which he has substantial stock ownership, the courts will hold that such transactions are voidable unless a full disclosure of all the facts is made to the owner and after such disclosure the owner voluntarily consents to the transactions.[13]

Schepers listed a 160-acre farm for sale with Marvin Lautenschlager to be sold at the best available price but not less than $150 per acre. Marvin Lautenschlager learned that Yost would pay $200 per acre for the farm but did not disclose to Schepers this information and other information he had relative to the value of the farm. Marvin Lautenschlager induced Schepers to sell the farm to William Lautenschlager, Marvin's uncle, for $150 an acre, which Marvin represented as the best price obtainable. Later, William Lautenschlager sold the farm to Yost for $200 an acre. Schepers sued Marvin and William Lautenschlager for $9,200–$8,000 profit on the farm and $1,200 commission paid Marvin. The court granted Schepers a judgment of $1,200 against Marvin and of $8,000 against William.

Justice Messmore said: "An agent is required to disclose to his principal all the information he has touching the subject-matter of the agency and his relation to his principal forbids his becoming a purchaser thereof for his own benefit, in any way without the full knowledge by the principal of this fact, and the principal's acquiesence therein, with such knowledge. . . . A commission cannot be collected by the agent for his services as such, if he has wilfully disregarded, in a material respect, an obligation which the law devolves upon him by reason of his agency." *Schepers* v. *Lautenschlager,* 173 Neb. 107, 112 N.W.2d 767 (1962).

RELATION OF BROKER TO BUYER

In general, the relation of the broker to the buyer of a listed property is no different than that of any agent to a third person with whom the agent is dealing in behalf of his principal. The broker is not a party to any contract to sell negotiated for, and in the name of, the owner. If the owner fails or refuses to perform the contract to sell, the broker is not liable to the buyer for damages for breach of contract. If a down payment has been made by the buyer and the money has been turned over to the owner by the broker and the owner defaults in his performance, thus entitling the buyer to the return of the down payment, the broker is not liable to the buyer for the down payment. If the buyer has signed a proposition the terms of which differ from those stated

[13] *Utlaut* v. *Glick Real Estate Co., Inc.,* Mo., 246 S.W.2d 760.

in the listing, and the buyer makes a payment to the broker as evidence of good faith, the broker is liable to the buyer for the amount of this payment if the owner refuses to accept the offer.

An agent is liable for his wrongful acts (torts). If a broker, in selling property, knowingly misrepresents the property for the purpose of inducing the prospect to buy and the prospect does buy, justifiably relying on the broker's misrepresentations, the broker will be liable to the buyer in a tort action for deceit. In the event of such a misrepresentation, the buyer may elect to rescind the purchase, tender the property back to the owner, and recover the purchase money or any part of it which he has paid. The guilty broker would be liable to the owner for any commissions paid, unless the owner was a party to or had knowledge of the deceit.

Jeanette Clark, a saleswoman for Lelah T. Pierson, Inc., a licensed real estate broker, in showing to Beth Merrill a house which was listed for rent, neglected to warn Merrill of the dangerous stairway to the basement. Merrill, due to the dangerous stairway, fell down the stairs and suffered serious injuries. Merrill sued Buck, the owner of the house, Lelah T. Pierson, Inc., and Clark in tort, and the court granted Merrill a judgment for $65,700 against all defendants. On appeal, the judgment was affirmed.

Justice Dooling said: ". . . We are satisfied that, having affirmatively undertaken to show the house to plaintiff [Merrill] in the regular course of their [Lelah T. Pierson, Inc., and Clark] business with the purpose of earning a commission if she decided to rent it, the defendants [Pierson, Inc., and Clark] were under a duty of care to warn her of a concealed danger in the premises of which they were aware and from which her injury might be reasonably foreseen if she did become a tenant. . . .

"These defendants [Pierson, Inc., and Clark] claim that the furthest extent of their possible duty was to take care that plaintiff [Merrill] was not injured while she was examining the house in the company of defendant Clark, but this argument overlooks the fact that the tour of inspection was for the very purpose of persuading plaintiff [Merrill] to become a tenant and that the possibility of her injury from the concealed hazard if she did become a tenant was reasonably foreseeable unless she was advised of the latent danger." *Merrill v. Buck,* 25 Cal. Rptr. 456, 375 P.2d 304 (1962).

BROKER'S LIABILITY TO HIS SALESMAN

When a broker employs a salesman, they enter into a contract of employment. The primary obligation of the broker is to fulfill the contractual promises made to the salesman. Even though it is not expressly stated in the contract, if the salesman is compensated on a commission basis, the broker is obligated to give him reasonable aid in the negotiation of a deal. The broker owes a duty not to "steal" a sale from his salesman nor to collude to deprive him of his commission.

Liability of real estate salesman

RELATION OF SALESMAN TO OWNER

In most respects, the salesman's liability to the owner who has listed his property with the broker is the same as that of the broker. The salesman owes a duty of undivided loyalty to the owner. He owes the same fiduciary duty to the owner as that owed by the listing broker. In showing the property and making his sales talk, the salesman has a duty, both to the owner and to the prospective buyer, not to make false and fraudulent representations; if he does make such representations, he will be individually liable in tort for resulting injuries. If a salesman has taken a listing in behalf of the broker and, as a means of inducing the owner to list the property, has made promises he is not authorized to make, he will be individually liable to the owner for breach of such promises.

SALESMAN'S LIABILITY TO BUYER

The salesman is not liable on the contract of sale which he has negotiated in behalf of the owner unless he is expressly made a party thereto. The salesman may by express agreement make himself a guarantor or surety on the contract. If the salesman, in negotiating a contract of sale, exceeds his authority and makes promises which do not bind the owner, the salesman will be individually liable to the buyer for breach of his implied warranty of authority. However, since a salesman's authority is usually limited to the finding of a buyer, it would be only in rare instances that this rule would apply.

SALESMAN'S LIABILITY FOR HIS WRONGFUL ACTS

The salesman is individually liable for his wrongful acts. If, in order to induce a sale, he knowingly makes false representations as to material facts to the buyer, and the buyer contracts in justifiable reliance on the false representations, the salesman is individually liable in a tort action of deceit for the resulting injury. Likewise, if a salesman, in transporting a prospective buyer to a property for the purpose of showing it, drives negligently and injures the buyer by such negligence, the salesman is individually liable for the resulting injury. The same rule would apply if the prospective buyer is injured while on the property if the injury is the result of the salesman's negligence. Failure on the part of the salesman to warn the buyer of known dangerous conditions of the premises is generally held to be negligent conduct.

SALESMAN'S LIABILITY TO BROKER

The salesman—whether an employee, agent, or independent contractor—owes a duty to perform his services in such a manner that he furthers the legitimate business objectives of the broker. If the salesman is an independent contractor, he will not be under the direct control and supervision of the broker; however, he will be liable to the broker if he is guilty of a breach of his contractual obligations.

The salesman who is an employee or agent of the broker owes the duties of a fiduciary to the broker. He owes a duty to follow the instructions of the broker, unless the broker instructs him to perform an illegal or wrongful act or to follow a course of action which is detrimental to his health. The salesman must account to the broker for all money received by him in the course of his employment. If the salesman commingles money belonging to the broker or the owner with his own money, he becomes individually liable to the broker for the full amount. Depositing money belonging to the broker in the personal checking account of the salesman is a commingling of monies. If a salesman uses money or property of the broker for his individual purposes—for example, buys groceries or makes payments on his car—he is guilty of the crime of embezzlement.

When commission is earned

TERMS OF CONTRACT

A workman is entitled to his pay when his work is done. This familiar rule applies to the broker, but it does not aid in deciding when the work is completed. In order to determine when the work is finished, one must read the listing contract, in case such a contract has been drafted and signed. If the listing contract provides that the commission is payable "on the completion of the transfer of the property," no commission is earned until the transfer has been made.[14] The courts have interpreted the provision "commission is payable from the proceeds of the sale" as making the completion of the transaction a prerequisite to the owner's duty to pay a commission. Other stages in the transaction may be designated as the point at which the commission is earned. The listing contract may stipulate that the commission will be paid out of cash actually paid to the owner and will be payable only as the cash is received. In any such case the broker is entitled to his commission if the owner arbitrarily and without reasonable cause or in bad faith refuses to complete the sale.

Clark, a broker, and Hovey, an owner, executed a listing contract which included the following provision: ". . . Clark agrees to accept $500 in full payment of commissions. . . . It is further agreed by both parties that this $500 shall not be paid from the first $5,000 paid Hovey . . . but shall be paid by Hovey to Clark from the first $500 received by Hovey from Green after the $5,000 has been paid." Hovey could not give good title, and the contract of sale was never carried out. Clark sued Hovey to recover a judgment for $500 commission. The court held that Clark was not entitled to a commission.

Chief Justice Rugg said: "The rights of the parties depend upon the terms of their agreement, which is in writing and not ambiguous. It fixes the price which the plaintiff [Clark] is to receive. It stipulates in unequivocal words that the compensation shall not be paid by the defendant [Hovey] until after he has received $5,000 on account of the sale. The written agreement between the parties supersedes the ordinary rule that a broker has earned his commission when he has procured the execution of a valid agreement for sale." *Clark v. Hovey,* 217 Mass. 485, 105 N.E. 222 (1914).

IF THERE IS NO SPECIFIC AGREEMENT

If there is no specific agreement, either written or oral, as to when the commission is payable, the generally accepted rule is that the commission is earned and payable when the broker has produced a buyer ready, willing, and able to buy on the terms stated in the listing or agreed upon at the time the broker was engaged. *Ready and willing* means that the buyer will, at the present time, sign a contract to purchase the property on the terms set by the owner when the property was listed with the

---

[14] *Fowler* v. *Davidson et al.,* 44 Minn. 46, 46 N.W. 308.

broker. *Able* means that the buyer either has or can obtain the funds necessary to make the payments stipulated in the listing.[15]

Whether or not, in addition to procuring a buyer ready, willing, and able to purchase, the broker owes a duty to aid in closing the sale will depend upon local custom, in the absence of a listing contract stating the broker's duties. If the broker does follow through and aid in the closing of the sale, the courts are unanimous in holding that he has earned the commission.

MUST NEGOTIATE A BINDING CONTRACT

In order that the broker may be entitled to his commission, the buyer procured by him must be ready and willing to enter into a binding, enforceable contract to buy. If the buyer is ready and willing to make an oral promise to buy but will not sign a written contract, the broker has not earned his commission. An oral contract to purchase land is not enforceable. If the buyer reserves the right to cancel the contract on the happening of a contingency, such as his not being able to borrow money to make the down payment, the commission is not earned until the contingency has occurred and the buyer has become absolutely liable on the contract.[16] Also, if the broker induces the owner to give the buyer an option on the listed property, the broker has not earned his commission unless and until the buyer exercises the option.[17]

Gresser listed property for sale with Martineau. Martineau procured a buyer, Lotton, who signed a purchase contract which provided that Martineau would, within 30 days, arrange financing. Also, special provisions were written into the purchase contract form. Financing was not arranged within the 30-day period; and thereafter, Gresser listed the property with another broker, who sold it to Lotton. Martineau sued Gresser to recover his commission, and the court held (1) that failure to fulfill the condition for the obtaining of financing rendered the contract unenforceable and (2) that the adding of the provisions to the purchase contract amounted to the illegal practice of law and that the contract was an illegal contract.

Judge Swaim said: "A broker in pursuance of his employment, may have the parties execute a contract, after he has procured a purchaser, ready, and

---

[15] *Reynor* v. *Mackrill,* 181 Iowa 210, 164 N.W. 335.

[16] *Cooper* v. *Liberty National Bank,* 332 Ill. App. 459, 75 N.E.2d 769.

[17] *MacNeill Real Estate* v. *Rines,* 144 Me. 27, 64 A.2d 179.

willing to enter into written contract on the employer's or seller's terms, and when the written contract is entered into, there can be no issue, as to whether the person procured was 'ready and willing and able to perform.' However, it is the broker's duty, in such a case to see that the parties enter into an 'enforceable contract' and a binding contract of sale and purchase.' Here, a contract of purchase and sale was signed. Was it enforcible? Was it binding?" (NOTE: The court answered both of these questions in the negative.) *Martineau v. Gresser,* 190 Ohio Op.2d 374, 182 N.E.2d 46 (1962).

WHEN SALE IS CLOSED BY PERSON OTHER THAN BROKER

Controversy frequently arises as to who is entitled to the commission when a broker has contacted or interested a prospect but actual sale has been made by another broker or by the owner, or when the closing of the deal has been delayed until the term of the listing has expired. The general rule is that the procuring broker is entitled to the commission. Who the procuring broker is depends on the facts of the particular case.

IF LISTING IS AN OPEN LISTING

Under an open listing the broker who first finds the prospect who purchases the property has earned the commission. If several brokers have prospects for property listed on an open listing, the broker whose prospect first signs a contract to purchase the property is entitled to the commission. When a buyer has signed a contract to purchase property listed on an open listing, the agency of all other brokers is automatically canceled without the giving of notice. The courts have held that the broker is the procuring cause and is entitled to the commission in the following situations: (1) if the broker has contacted a prospect who later contracts to buy the property; (2) if a prospect, in answer to a broker's advertisement, contacts the owner and contracts to buy the property; and (3) if a broker contacts a prospect and this prospect brings the property to the attention of some third person who contracts to buy the property.

Strodtbeck listed his ranch with Wood on an open listing. Wood contacted Fulton, who agreed to purchase the ranch but did not have money to make a down payment. Arrangements were made with Strodtbeck's attorney to make the down payment on November 26 and sign a purchase contract, but Fulton did not obtain money for the down payment. On December 1, Strodtbeck sold the ranch to a purchaser obtained by another broker and paid that broker his commission. On December 2, Wood and Fulton called at the office of Strodtbeck's attorney ready to make the down payment and execute a contract for the purchase of the ranch and were told that the ranch had been sold. Wood sued Strodtbeck to recover a judgment for claimed commission. The court held that Wood was not entitled to a commission.

Chief Justice James T. Harrison said: "Under a non-exclusive listing contract defendants, [Strodtbecks] must be permitted to choose, when two buyers are under consideration, with which one to deal. The listing contract in question here provided authority to the broker to execute a preliminary contract in accordance with its terms. Plaintiff [Wood] did not see fit to do so. Too, Fulton could always have refused to go through with his proposed purchase, . . ." *Wood* v. *Strodtbeck*, Mont. 382 P.2d 170 (1963).

IF LISTING IS EXCLUSIVE AGENCY LISTING

Under an exclusive agency listing the broker is entitled to his commission if the property is sold to a buyer obtained by the listing broker or any other broker; but if the owner finds a buyer through his own efforts, the listing broker is not entitled to a commission. If the listing is either an open listing or an exclusive agency listing, the broker should give the owner notice as soon as he procures a buyer ready, willing, and able to buy. If a broker does not give notice and the owner, before he has knowledge of the broker's having procured a buyer, contracts to sell to a buyer procured by the owner's own efforts, the broker will not be entitled to a commission.

Kabel listed all the lots in a new subdivision with McKinney. The listing contract appointed McKinney Kabel's "exclusive selling agent." Kabel canceled the contract with McKinney, and McKinney sued Kabel to recover a commission on all the lots in the subdivision. McKinney was paid his commission on all lots sold by him prior to the termination of the listing. The court held that McKinney was not entitled to a commission on the unsold lots.

Judge Samuel said: "A real estate broker who has only an exclusive agency to sell is not entitled to a commission on sales made by the owner himself. Such a contract does not give the broker the exclusive right to sell the property; it simply precludes the owner from appointing any other agent during the life of the contract. The jurisprudence clearly distinguishes the appointment as an *exclusive agent* from the contract of employment conferring upon a real estate broker the *exclusive right to sell*, which latter entitles the broker to commissions on all sales during the life of the contract including those made by the owner." *McKinney Realty Company* v. *Kabel*, La. App., 131 So.2d 567 (1961).

IF LISTING IS AN EXCLUSIVE-RIGHT-TO-SELL LISTING

Under an exclusive-right-to-sell listing, the broker is entitled to his commission if the property is sold before the listing expires. Frequently, a controversy arises when the listing is for a specified time and the property is sold to a buyer who was contacted by the broker during the term of the listing, but who did not enter into the contract of sale until after the term expired. If negotiations are in progress at the time the listing expires, the courts have held that the term of the listing is, by implication, extended until the transaction is closed. In such a case the broker is entitled to his commission. If, after the listing has expired, negotiations are renewed with a prospect contacted by the broker and such negotiations culminate in a sale, the broker is not entitled to a commission unless he can prove that the owner and the buyer delayed negotiations for the purpose of depriving him of his commission, in which event the courts have allowed the broker to recover his commission. If the listing contract provides that a commission will be paid to the broker if the property is sold within a stipulated time after the listing expires to a prospect contacted by the broker during the term of the listing, the courts have enforced the provision and allowed the broker to recover his commission. Some—but not all—courts have held that if the owner and buyer have delayed closing the transaction until after the expiration of the extended period, the broker would not be entitled to a commission, even though he could show that the delay was for the purpose of depriving him of his commission.[18]

BROKER'S RIGHT TO COMMISSION IF SELLER DEFAULTS

Under the general rule that a broker has earned his commission when he has produced a buyer ready, willing, and able to purchase the property on the stipulated terms or on terms acceptable to the owner, the courts have held that default on the part of the owner to consummate the sale will not relieve him from paying the broker his commission. If the broker knows, or under the circumstances should know, that the owner's title is defective, the court will, as a general rule, hold that the broker impliedly contracts to produce a buyer who will take the property subject to the defective title or that it is the duty of the broker to work out a deal

---

[18] See *West* v. *Barnes,* Tex. Civ. App., 351 S.W.2d 615 (1961).

whereby provision is made for the removal of the defect.[19] If an owner, after he has executed a purchase-and-sale agreement, refuses, without good cause, to complete the transaction, the broker is entitled to his commission.[20]

Gaither listed his property with Williams. Williams found a buyer ready, willing, and able to purchase the property on terms acceptable to Gaither, but the transaction was never consummated. Gaither never submitted a title in accordance with the purchase agreement and refused to pay Williams a commission. Gaither, when sued, set up as a defense that the sale was never consummated. The court granted a judgment to Williams.

Presiding Justice Peek said: "Under the uncontradicted facts, since the defendants [Gaithers] accepted the offer made by persons procured by plaintiff [Williams] who were ready, willing and able to purchase the property, plaintiff [Williams] had then performed all acts incumbent upon him and he was entitled to the agreed commission. . . .

"Whether the sale was prevented by the failure of perfect title or by mere will of the vendor makes no difference. In either case the compensation had been earned by the agent." *Williams* v. *Gaither,* 20 Cal. Rptr. 779 (1962).

Termination of relation

How terminated

The relation of principal and agent may be terminated by either party at any time, with the exception of an agency coupled with an interest. The broker-owner relation is not an agency coupled with an interest. However, if the contract of employment is breached by the termination of the relation, the injured party is entitled to recover damages for breach of contract. If the owner notifies the broker that he terminates the relation and withdraws the property before the expiration of the term, the damages recoverable by the broker will depend on the circumstances of the case. If the broker is negotiating with a prospect and can prove that the prospect would have contracted to purchase the property, or if the broker can prove that the owner terminated the listing arbitrarily and without reason or in bad faith, the broker will, as a general rule, be awarded a judgment for the full amount of his commission.[21]

Under other circumstances, the judgment may be for a lesser sum.

---

[19] *Pasley* v. *Barber, Alaska,* 368 P.2d 548.

[20] *Blunt* v. *Wentland,* 250 Iowa 607, 93 N.W.2d 735.

[21] *Bartlett* v. *Keith,* 325 Mass. 265, 90 N.E.2d 308.

If no time for expiration of the listing is stated in the listing contract, the courts have generally held that the listing is for a reasonable time. Reasonable time is always determined on the basis of the facts and circumstances of each case.[22]

Licensing laws

STATE STATUTES

A majority of the states have enacted statutes making it unlawful for a person to act as a real estate broker or a real estate salesman without first obtaining a license. The purpose of these statutes is to protect the public from being defrauded by dishonest and unethical real estate brokers or salesmen. The statutes are not uniform in their provisions; yet they have many provisions which are similar as to the basic requirements. All the statutes require both brokers and salesmen to establish their honesty, truthfulness, and good reputation. The methods of establishing good character vary widely. Most statutes require the applicant for a license to establish his competence to act as a broker or salesman by taking an examination, and most states require a written examination. The license fee for a broker is more than the fee for a salesman. The license must be renewed periodically. Although the penalties for transacting business as a real estate broker or real estate salesman without a license vary widely, in no state can an unlicensed broker or salesman recover a judgment for the agreed commission in a court action, since the contract to pay the commission is an unlawful one. The effect of the licensing statute is to make illegal the contract to pay a commission.[23] The fact that the broker or salesman negotiating a contract to sell land is unlicensed does not in any way affect the legality of the contract negotiated. The only contract affected by the licensing statute is the contract of employment— the contract to pay a commission.

SCOPE OF LICENSING STATUTES

The scope of the licensing statutes varies. Some are broad and include all contracts affecting an interest in real estate, such as the negotiation

---

[22] *Harris* v. *McPherson,* 97 Conn. 164, 115 A. 723.

[23] *Firpo* v. *Murphy et al.,* 71 Cal. App. 249, 236 P. 968.

of leases and real estate mortgages.[24] Other statutes are narrower in their scope and include only contracts to sell land.

Illegal Practice of law by brokers

QUESTIONABLE ACTIVITIES OF BROKERS

In the selling or managing of real estate, a wide variety of documents must be prepared for execution by the parties involved in the transaction. In this connection, questions may arise from time to time as to the legal rights of the parties or as to the legal significance of some phase of the matter. For example, to what extent may a broker go, without engaging in the practice of law, in preparing the documents to be executed in connection with a transaction he is handling? Also, is a broker engaging in the practice of law when he advises the parties to a transaction as to the legal phases of the transaction?

These questions have not been litigated in all of the states; and even in those states in which they have been the subject of lawsuits, there is some difference of opinion. However, the courts in such states are in accord in holding that if the broker accepts a fee for preparing documents or gives advice as to the legal rights of the parties to a sale which he is handling as broker for the parties, he is engaging in the unauthorized practice of law.

LIMITS OF ACTIVITY

The extent to which a broker may go in preparing documents used in connection with a transaction he is negotiating presents a question which is difficult to answer. One view is that the broker is employed to find a buyer for the property, and that when he has found a buyer, he has fulfilled the duty he owes to his employer. Under this view the broker would be permitted to prepare only those instruments which are "preliminary" in nature—that is, instruments such as a memorandum of the transaction or deposit receipts. A licensed attorney should be employed to draft the documents necessary for the closing of the sale—as, for instance, the deed, the mortgage, the deed of trust, assignments of leases, or releases of mortgages.[25] If the broker, in addition to collecting

---

[24] *Cohen* v. *Scola,* 13 N.J. Super. 472, 80 A.2d 643.

[25] *Keyes Co.* v. *Dade County Bar Association et al.,* Fla., 46 So.2d 605.

his commission, makes an extra charge for preparing the documents exe-cut:d in connection with the closing of the sale, he has been held to be practicing law illegally.[26]

COURT DECISIONS

The more liberal view, held in the majority of the states in which the question has been litigated, is that a broker is not engaged in the un-authorized practice of law when he fills in the blanks in standardized forms which have been approved by a licensed attorney, provided that such instruments are prepared and used as an incident to a transaction the broker is handling, and provided further that no extra charge is made for such service.[27] Wisconsin has set up a commission which is authorized to approve standardized forms which a broker is permitted to use in the negotiating and closing of a sale of real estate.[28]

The holdings in other states place varying degrees of restrictions on the extent to which a broker may prepare the various documents used in the course of the negotiation and in the closing of a sale of real estate.[29] Giving advice as to the legal significance of the documents pre-pared in connection with the closing of a transaction, and advising persons as to their legal rights and duties or as to the course of action which they should follow in a real estate transaction, have been held to be engaging in the practice of law.[30] In some states the courts have held that the selection of the forms to be used and the filling-in of the blanks amount to the giving of legal advice, and that a broker who performs such services for his employer is engaged in the unauthorized practice of law.

The examination of an abstract of title and the giving of an opinion as to the state of the title to the real estate covered by the abstract are

---

[26] *Commonwealth* v. *Jones & Robbins, Inc., et al.,* 186 Va. 30, 41 S.E.2d 720.

[27] *Conway-Bogue Realty Investment Company et al.* v. *Denver Bar Association et al.,* 135 Colo. 398, 312 P.2d 998. Apparently, this view is held in Colorado, Idaho, Illinois, Massachusetts, Michigan, Minnesota, Missouri, Nebraska, New York, North Dakota, Ohio, and Pennsylvania.

[28] *Reynolds* v. *Dinger,*14 Wis. 2d 193, 109 N.W.2d 685.

[29] *Creekmire* v. *Izard, Ark.,* 367 S.W.2d 419; *Indiana State Bar Association* v. *Indiana Real Estate Association,* Ind., 191 N.E.2d 711; *State Bar of Arizona* v. *Arizona Land Title and Trust Company,* 91 Ariz. 293, 371 P.2d 1020; *Arkansas Bar Association* v. *Block,* 230 Ark. 430, 323 S.W.2d 912.

[30] *People* v. *Sipper,* 61 Cal. App.2d 844, 142 P.2d 960; *People ex rel. Illinois State Bar Association et al.* v. *Schaefer,* 404 Ill. 45, 87 N.E.2d 773.

clearly outside the province of the broker. A broker or property manager may serve notice of default in payment of rent or of default in the payment of installments on a land contract or mortgage; but he cannot bring a court action in behalf of his employer to recover a judgment for rents, or for installment payments, or for the recovery of the possession of the real estate.[31]

---

[31] *Ingham County Bar Association et al.* v. *Walter Neller Co. et al.,* 342 Mich. 214, 69 N.W.2d 713; *In re Wenger,* 61 N.Y.S.2d 686.

12

Purchase agreement

Introduction

FUNCTION OF PURCHASE AGREEMENT

A PURCHASE AGREEMENT in writing is not a prerequisite for a valid sale of real estate; it is, however, good insurance against misunderstandings and controversies which could lead to expensive legal action. If the parties reach what they believe to be a mutual understanding but do not draft and sign a purchase agreement, either party could withdraw from the deal at will without incurring legal liability. The purchase agreement should be in writing; should set out in clear, concise language the terms of the agreement, and the rights and liabilities of the parties; and should satisfy the essential requirements for a valid, enforceable contract.

THE BROKER

The broker who has negotiated the sale or purchase of real estate will not, in the normal real estate transaction, be a party to the purchase agreement and, under the laws of several of the states, will not be permitted to draft and have executed the purchase agreement. The drafting or the giving of advice to the parties to a purchase agreement has been held to be the practice of law.

A broker could become a party to such a contract by signing it as a guarantor of the performance of either the buyer or the seller. If a broker should sign such a contract as guarantor, he would be assuming an obligation which is entirely outside the normal scope of services performed by real estate brokers.

BROKER AS THIRD-PARTY BENEFICIARY

A broker might be named in the contract of sale as a third-party beneficiary; but this would not make him a party to the contract; nor would it make him liable for the performance of the contract. It would only give him certain rights under the contract. Suppose, for example, that the contract of purchase and sale expressly provides that one of the parties to the contract will pay to the broker (naming him) a stipulated sum as compensation for services rendered in the negotiation of the sale. In such a case the broker could, if he is not paid, bring a suit on the contract and recover a judgment for the amount of the promised compensation.[1]

Essentials of valid contract

ENFORCEABILITY OF PURCHASE AGREEMENT

To be enforceable by court action, the purchase agreement must fulfill certain technical requirements. The parties to the agreement must have capacity to contract, and they must reach a mutual agreement; that is, one party must make an offer which is accepted by the other party. The agreement must be entered into voluntarily and must be supported by consideration; and the objective of the agreement must be legal; that is, the performance of the agreement must not require the performance of a crime, a tort, or an act which would be a violation of public morals or detrimental to the public welfare.

CAPACITY OF PARTIES

In general, infants (minors); insane persons, or drunken persons have limited capacity to contract. Their contracts are voidable, not void. At common law married women had no legal capacity to contract; but under the married women's statutes of the states, this incapacity has been partially or totally removed. The powers of a corporation will be set out in its articles of incorporation, and it will have only such capacity to

---

[1] *Hartmann* v. *Windsor Hotel Co. et al.,* 132 W. Va. 307, 52 S.E.2d 48.

be a party to a contract involving rights in real estate as is granted to it by the state. With some exceptions, aliens have full capacity to contract.

INFANT'S (MINOR'S) CAPACITY TO CONTRACT

If an infant enters into a contract with an adult, the infant has the right to disaffirm the contract. The adult, however, has no such right. At common law the age of infancy was 21 years, but several of the states have enacted statutes changing this age. An infant may disaffirm his general contract during infancy or within a reasonable time after he reaches his majority. The courts have held, however, that an infant cannot disaffirm a conveyance of his real estate until he comes of age. Under this rule an infant would have the right to disaffirm a listing contract or a purchase agreement at any time up to a reasonable time after he reaches his majority.

An infant's right to disaffirm a contract is absolute. The infant does, however, owe a duty, if he disaffirms a contract, to return to the other party to the contract any consideration which he has received and which he still has, or any proceeds from the disposition of such consideration which he still has at the time he disaffirms, and he has the right to recover all of the consideration which he gave.[2] (There are some exceptions to this latter rule.)

The courts have held infants liable for the *reasonable value* of necessaries *furnished* to them. Necessaries are those things personal to the infant, such as, for instance, food, clothing, shelter, medical care, elemental education, training for a trade, and the tools of a trade, suitable to the infant's station in life. A house has been held to be a necessary for the married infant who is not furnished housing by his parents or guardian.[3] An infant cannot be held liable for damages for breach of a lease, but he can be held liable for the reasonable rental value of the premises during the time he occupied them, provided they would be classed as a necessary and would have been suitable to his station in life.

INSANE AND DRUNKEN PERSONS

If a person is insane or drunk at the time he enters into a contract, the contract is voidable, provided the insanity or drunkenness was such

[2] *Fletcher* v. *A. W. Koch Co.,* Tex. Civ. App. 189 S.W. 501.
[3] *Johnson* v. *Newberry,* Tex., 267 S.W. 476.

that he lacked the mental capacity to comprehend the nature of the transaction. If and when such a person regains his sanity or becomes sober, he may disaffirm the contract and recover the consideration given, but he must put the other party in *status quo.*[4]

If a person is officially adjudged insane and a guardian or conservator of his estate is appointed, any contract entered into by such insane person during the period of guardianship is void.

MARRIED WOMEN

At common law a married woman had no legal capacity, and her contracts were null and void. Every state has enacted statutes conferring some legal capacity on married women, but these statutes are not uniform in their scope. The statutes of some states give married women full capacity to contract, whereas others are so drafted that married women have no capacity to enter into certain classes of contracts.

Under the laws of some states the contracts of a married woman, if they affect an interest in her real estate, are void unless her husband joins her in the execution of the contract. The laws of the state which has jurisdiction over the contract control and should be checked to determine the capacity of a married woman to contract.

UNINCORPORATED ASSOCIATIONS

As a general rule, an unincorporated association cannot contract in the name of the association. However, a contract entered into in the name of an unincorporated association will bind the members who authorized the contract or ratified it after it was negotiated.

THE PROPOSITION

As a general rule, a broker is not authorized by the owner to execute a contract to sell the listed property. The broker's duty is to find a buyer ready, willing, and able to purchase the property on the terms of the listing or on terms acceptable to the buyer. The standard practice is for the broker to induce the prospective buyer to sign a proposition, also called an *offer to purchase.* Usually, the broker will use a printed form which has been drafted by his attorney or is furnished by the real estate association of which he is a member. A well-drafted proposition will

---

[4] *Brooklyn Trust Co.* v. *Podvin et al.,* 14 N.J. Super. 470, 82 A.2d 485.

comply with the technical requirements for a valid offer. It will state
(1) what the offeror (buyer) is willing to do and (2) what he demands
from the offeree (seller) in return.

In order to be a valid offer, the terms of the proposition must be
reasonably certain and complete. If any material term is left to be determined by the future agreement of the parties, the proposition is not a
valid offer and cannot be the basis for a binding contract.[5] Likewise,
if the terms of the proposition are stated in vague general language,
such as, "what is fair" or "an amount which I deem reasonable," the
proposition is not an offer, since the terms are uncertain. The courts
generally follow the rule that the terms of the contract must be sufficiently
definite to enable the court to determine the meaning of the contract
and to fix the rights and liabilities of the parties.[6] The courts will not
make a contract for the parties. If a printed form is used, care should
be exercised in filling in the blanks and also striking out any provisions
which do not apply. If the transaction involves much detail, one should
have an attorney draft a purchase agreement which would include terms
suitable to the particular transaction.

ACCEPTANCE

To accept the buyer's proposition, all the seller need do is indicate
his willingness to be bound by its terms. If he adds to or changes any
of the terms stated in the proposition, he will have rejected the buyer's
offer, thereby terminating it; and in turn, he will then become the offeror,
offering to sell the property on the terms stated in the buyer's proposition
as added to or changed by the seller. The buyer can then either reject
or assent to the seller's proposition.

After a proposition has been accepted, a contract results; thereafter,
neither party has the right to alter the terms of the contract in any respect
unless such alteration is made by mutual agreement.

CUSTOM AND USAGE. An offer may contain terms which are not expressly stated by the offeror but are written into the offer by custom
and usage or by operation of law. For example, suppose that Albert
offers to sell a house and lot to Bert, and the offer is silent as to whether
or not the electric light fixtures go with the house and also as to whether
Albert will convey to Bert a merchantable title to the property. Bert
accepts the offer, and in his acceptance states that the lighting fixtures

---

[5] *Bonk* v. *Boyajian,* 128 Cal. App. 2d 153, 274 P.2d 948.

[6] *Corthell* v. *Summit Thread Co.,* 132 Me. 94, 167 A. 79.

go with the house and that Albert will convey a merchantable title to the house. If it is an established custom in that community for lighting fixtures to go with the house, such a provision will be implied in the offer, and Bert's acceptance will not have added a term. Also, the general rule is that an offer of sale includes, by operation of law, a promise to convey to the buyer a merchantable title.[7]

Hudson and Buehring entered into a written contract whereby Hudson agreed to sell and convey, and Buehring agreed to purchase, Hudson's home. The contract was complete in every detail except that it stated no time for the closing of the transaction. Hudson sold the property to other parties, and Buehring sued to recover damages for breach of the contract. Hudson set up that since no time was specified for the performance of the contract, it was void for uncertainty of terms. The court held for Hudson, and Buehring appealed. The judgment was reversed, and judgment entered for Buehring.

Justice Cody said: "The fact that the contract of sale fixed no time for its performance did not evidence that the minds of the parties had not met with respect to an essential element of the contract. 'When a contract of sale fixes no time for performance, the law allows a reasonable time. In other words, if the parties do not agree upon the time, an agreement for performance within a reasonable time will be implied.' Since appellants made out a prima facie case of a contract of sale, and proved that appellees had placed it beyond their power to perform by conveying the property to a third party in April, 1946, the burden of proof, or at least of going forward with the evidence, was shifted to appellees to show either that the contract was not valid, or that it had expired or had been rescinded before the sale to the third party; or to show some ground that would excuse performance of the contract." *Buehring* v. *Hudson,* Tex. Civ. App., 219 S.W.2d 810 (1949).

Routzahn owned a tract of land consisting of 30 acres. Routzahn and his wife signed an offer to sell the property to Lucille Binus. The real estate broker who had induced the Routzahns to sign the offer returned on the day following the signing with an acceptance of the offer signed by Anna Cromer. Routzahn refused to sell, and Cromer brought suit for a decree of specific performance of the contract. The court granted the decree, and Routzahn appealed. The decree was reversed.

Judge Prescott said: "On the above statement of facts, the appellants raise several questions, but, in the view that we take of the case, it will be necessary to consider but one. It is apparent, when the Routzahns, after adding new terms and conditions thereto, signed the paper writing that had been previously signed by Lucille Binus, that this constituted a counter offer to Lucille Binus

---

[7] *Curtis Land and Loan Co.* v. *Interior Land Co.,* 137 Wis. 341, 118 N.W. 853.

by the Routzahns. It is also clear that one of the necessary terms of any proposed contract is the person with whom the contract is to be made; consequently, an offer made to one person cannot be accepted by another. And, as a party has a right to contract with whom he pleases, and another cannot be thrust upon him without his consent, it makes no difference whether it was important for the offeror to contract with one person rather than another. Therefore, when the signature of Lucille Binus was stricken from the instrument and Anna Cromer's substituted therefor, no contract between the Routzahns and Anna Cromer resulted; this instrument, after such substitution merely constituted a new offer by Anna Cromer to the Routzahns to create a contract, which, in order to ripen and culminate into one had to be accepted by the Routzahns." *Routzahn* v. *Cromer*, 220 Md. 65, 150 A.2d 912 (1959).

EFFECT OF MISREPRESENTATION, FRAUD, ETC.

If one of the parties to a contract is induced to enter into the contract by misrepresentation of a material fact or by fraud, duress, or undue influence, he is not bound by the contract and may, at his election, disaffirm the contract, tender back whatever he has received, and recover a judgment for any consideration which he has given. If a seller, in negotiating a sale of real estate, misrepresents the condition of the property, the rental received from the property, or any other material fact concerning the property, and the buyer purchases the property in justifiable reliance on the seller's misrepresentations, the buyer, on discovering the misrepresentations, may rescind the contract and recover any payments he has made. If the buyer wishes to rescind, he must act within a reasonable time after he discovers the misrepresentations.[8]

Schlemeyer owned an apartment house which he sold to Obde. At the time of the sale the apartment house was infested with termites, and this condition was known to Schlemeyer. Schlemyer had had some repairs made to the apartment house and had engaged a specialist in termite control to treat the building, but the specialist had informed Schlemeyer that the treatment was not a complete remedy of the condition. Schlemeyer did not disclose the presence of termites to Obde. Schlemeyer contended that since Obde did not raise the question of the presence of termites in the apartment house, he (Schlemeyer) owed no duty to disclose such condition to Obde. Obde brought suit in tort to recover damages for the fraudulent representation of the condition of the apartment house. Judgment for Obde, and Schlemeyer appealed. The judgment was affirmed.

Judge Finley said: "The Schlemeyers urge that, in any event, as sellers,

[8] *Halla* v. *Chicago Title & Trust Co. et al.*, 412 Ill. 39, 104 N.E.2d 790.

they had no duty to inform the Obdes of the termite condition. They emphasize that it is undisputed that the purchasers asked no questions respecting the possibility of termites.

"Without doubt, the parties in the instant case were dealing at arms length. Nevertheless, we are convinced that the defendants had a duty to inform the plaintiffs of the termite condition. In Perkins v. Marsh, a case involving parties dealing at arms length as landlord and tenant, we held that,

" 'Where there are concealed defects in demised premises, dangerous to the property, health, or life of the tenant, which defects are known to the landlord when the lease is made, but unknown to the tenant, and which a careful examination on his part would not disclose, it is the landlord's duty to disclose them to the tenant before leasing, and his failure to do so amounts to a fraud.'

"We deem this rule to be equally applicable to the vendor-purchaser relationship." *Obde* v. *Schlemeyer,* 52 Wash.2d 449, 353 P.2d 672 (1960).

CONSIDERATION

Consideration is the surrender of some right or privilege bargained for and given in exchange for a promise. It is an essential element of a valid contract. If Albert promises to deed real estate to Bert as a birthday present and then refuses to fulfill the promise, Bert cannot recover a judgment in an action against Albert for breach of promise. Albert's promise is not supported by consideration and is therefore not enforceable. Bert has given up no right or privilege (has made no payment or promise) in exchange for Albert's promise.

ILLEGALITY

Any agreement is illegal and void if the performance of such agreement would require the violation of a statute or the commission of a criminal or immoral act, or an act which would be detrimental to the general public welfare.

WRITING

The statutes of most of the states provide, in effect, that no action shall be brought on any contract for the sale of land, tenements, or hereditaments, or interest in or concerning them, unless the contract is evidenced by a note or memorandum in writing signed by the party to be bound thereby or his duly authorized agent. Such a provision makes an oral agreement to sell real estate unenforceable, not void or voidable. The statutes of several states, however, provide that an oral contract for sale of land or an interest therein is void.[9]

The note or memorandum, to be sufficient to satisfy the requirements of the statute, must contain all of the material provisions of the agreement such as the names of the parties, a description of the real estate involved which is exact enough to enable the court to identify it, credit terms, restrictions, exemptions, and so forth.

The note or memorandum may be made at the time or after the parties have reached their agreement, but it must have been made before suit was brought. It need not be contained in one document but may consist of a series of letters, a series of telegrams, or a series of letters and telegrams, provided such letters, telegrams, or letters and telegrams show on their face that they refer to the same transaction.[10]

Under the laws of a majority of the states the note or memorandum need not be signed by both parties to the contract. If it is signed by the party being sued (the defendant), it is sufficient. However, in at least two states—Kentucky and New York—the contract is not enforceable against the buyer unless the seller and the buyer have both signed the note or memorandum. The contract is enforceable against the seller if he has signed the note or memorandum, even though the buyer has not signed it.

If the parties have entered into an oral contract for the sale of real estate and the contract has been fully performed, the transaction cannot be set aside by court action. Also, if suit is brought to enforce an oral contract to sell real estate and the defendant does not set up as a defense the lack of a note or memorandum in writing signed by him or his duly authorized agent, the courts will enforce the contract. Failure to have a note or memorandum in writing signed by the party to be bound does not render the contract void or voidable; it makes the contract unenforceable, and the party for whose benefit the note or memorandum is required may waive the benefit of the protection provided.

Lowery advertised a farm for sale at auction and orally authorized Hicks, an auctioneer, to do the selling. The advertised terms of the sale were cash; but at the auction, Hicks orally stated that the terms for the sale of the farm were 10 per cent cash down payment. Couture was highest bidder, and the farm was struck off to him. The sale was held on Saturday, and the banks

[9] *Garbarino* v. *Union Savings and Loan Association,* 107 Colo. 140, 109 P.2d 638, 132 A.L.R. 1480.

[10] *Grant* v. *Auvil et ux.,* 39 Wash.2d 722, 238 P.2d 393.

were closed. Hicks told Couture that he could make the down payment on the following Monday. On Monday, Lowery refused to accept the down payment and refused to convey the farm to Couture. Couture brought suit, asking specific performance of the contract, and Lowery set up the statute of frauds as a defense. The court held that the contract to sell was oral and unenforceable under the statute of frauds.

Justice Shangraw said: "The provisions of the Statute of Frauds applicable to contracts affecting interests in land were adopted for the purpose of preventing existing estates in land from being upset by parol evidence, and their general effect is to require all contracts concerning real estate to be in writing. Its purpose is to serve as a shield against possible fraud. . . . One may admit the sale of land by a verbal contract, and yet defend the action for specific performance by pleading the statute.

"In order to hold the defendants to specific performance of the agreement to convey, they must either have personally signed a written agreement to sell the farm, or have duly authorized in writing an agent to sign for them. No such writing appears." *Couture* v. *Lowery,* 122 Vt. 239, 168 A.2d 295 (1961).

PAROL EVIDENCE RULE

If the parties to a contract have reduced the contract to writing, the writing is the best evidence of the terms of their agreement; and neither party, in the event of a suit, will be permitted to offer parol (oral) evidence to alter or vary the terms of the writing. If it is obvious that the writing is incomplete, parol evidence would be admissible to prove the omitted terms. However, if the contract is a contract to sell real estate and it is incomplete, it would not be enforced if the lack of a sufficient note or memorandum were set up as a defense.

Parol evidence is admissible to prove that a contract is illegal; or that it was induced by misrepresentation, fraud, duress, or undue influence; or that, at the time the writing was signed, the parties agreed that it was not to become binding until the occurrence of some future event and that the event had not happened. Parol evidence is also admissible to prove that the parties, subsequent to the signing of the writing, entered into a mutual agreement whereby they changed some of the terms of the existing contract.

OPTION

An option is a combination of an offer and a binding contract to hold the offer open for a stated period of time. To be valid, the option must fulfill the technical requirements for a valid offer and for an enforceable contract. The offer part of the option must state with reasonable certainty the terms of the offer, and the promise to hold the offer open must state the time limit of the offer and must be supported by consideration. If the person to whom the offer is given wishes to exercise the option (accept the offer), he must do so before the expiration date of the offer. For example, suppose that Albert offers to sell a piece of real estate to Bert, the offer setting out a description of the real estate, the price, and all of the other terms of the proposed sale, and, in consideration of $10 paid to him by Bert, Albert promises to hold the offer open for 30 days. Albert has given Bert an option on the real estate and cannot revoke his offer during the 30-day period. Bert can convert the option into a valid contract of purchase and sale of the real estate at any time during the 30 days by giving Albert notice that he elects to exercise the option and by complying with the terms of the offer.

If, after the expiration of the 30-day period, Bert attempts to exercise the option, he will, in legal effect, have made an offer to Albert which Albert may accept, thus, contracting to sell the real estate to Bert on the terms of the offer; or he may refuse to sell, thus rejecting Bert's offer. The courts have generally held the payment of $1 to be sufficient consideration to make an option binding.

The Carmodys (husband and wife) and Miller, on October 10, 1959, entered into an option agreement which provided that for a consideration of $5,000 the Carmodys "do hereby grant unto Miller the option to purchase [from the Carmodys] on or before October 10, 1960," certain described land in Jefferson County, the property being approximately 235 acres. The agreement went on to provide that "if, on or before September 10, 1960, the said purchaser [Miller] shall notify sellers [Carmodys] in writing of his intention to exercise said option, and shall on or before October 10, 1960, make a further payment of a sum equal to 20 per cent of the total purchase price, sellers do hereby agree to execute a warranty deed to said land."

Prior to September 10, 1960, Miller had the tract surveyed and a part thereof platted, and a plat thereof prepared and presented to the Carmodys. A dispute arose as to some of the terms of the option.

Miller gave notice of his election to exercise the option; but at no time before October 10, 1960, did he tender to the Carmodys 20 per cent of the purchase price of the land. The Carmodys refused to convey the land to Miller, and Miller brought action for specific performance of the contract. On the trial, he alleged that at all times he had been ready, willing, and financially able to comply with the terms of the option. He did not, however, allege that he had at any time tendered 20 per cent of the contract price of the land. The court refused to grant to Miller a decree of specific performance.

Justice McWilliams said: "After extended arguments the trial court granted Carmodys' motion for summary judgment, concluding that Miller did not comply with the provisions of the option contract which required him to make payment of a sum equal to the total purchase price on or before October 10, 1960, and further that from the affidavits it was quite evident that Miller was in no wise prevented from making such payment by any act of the Carmodys. In so holding we conclude that the trial court was correct and its action in this regard should be upheld.

" 'The general rule as stated in 91 C.J.S. Vendor and Purchaser §10 pp. 856–857 is that payment or tender is not essential to acceptance unless the option instrument makes it a condition precedent to, or a part of the option . . .' but that 'where an option contract provides for payment of all or a portion of the purchase price in order to exercise the option, to entitle the optionee to a conveyance he must, as a rule, not only accept the offer but pay or tender the agreed amount within the prescribed time.' " *Miller* v. *Carmody*, Colo., 384 P.2d 77 (1963).

Drafting the purchase agreement

PLANNING THE DRAFT

The drafting of a purchase agreement, if the transaction involved is relatively complex, should be referred to a competent attorney. The broker, however, should be familiar with the matters which will be included in a well-drafted agreement, since he will have directed the negotiations leading up to the sale. If matters which should be included in the agreement are not discussed and settled prior to the actual drafting of the agreement, disagreements may arise which could result in the loss of the sale. A competent attorney will draft a document which states in clear, well-chosen language the terms of the agreement, so that it will be free from ambiguities and can be readily understood.

It is important that the drafted purchase agreement be complete and that it cover all phases of the transaction. If the writing is incomplete, it will not serve as a note or memorandum, and the agreement will be unenforceable under the statute of frauds. If the writing is complete on its face but omits items which should have been included, neither party, in the event of a lawsuit, will be permitted, over the objection of the other party, to offer oral evidence to establish the omitted terms. If the parties so agree, omitted terms may be inserted; and in a proper action the court has the power to re-form the writing and order such terms inserted, provided the party bringing the action can prove by clear and unequivocal evidence that the omitted terms were left out by mistake or oversight. The attorney drafting the agreement has to depend, for the most part, on the broker to furnish him with the information necessary to enable him to draft a complete agreement.

MATTERS TO BE CONSIDERED

No two transactions are alike. Each transaction should be carefully checked and every possible point considered, so that the writing will be complete. The following are the principal items which should be considered and, if pertinent, included. This is not an exhaustive list of points which could arise in real estate transactions.

1. NAME OF SELLER. The seller must be named in the agreement and should be designated as *seller* or *vendor*. If the property is owned by co-owners and all are joining in the sale, all the co-owners must be named as sellers. If the seller is a partnership or corporation, the contract should so indicate. Also, if the seller or sellers are natural persons, the contract should state the marital status of each.

2. NAME OF SPOUSE. The spouse should be named in the agreement as seller and should join in the execution of the agreement if the real estate is located in a state whose laws require that a spouse must join in the execution of the deed in order to convey clear title to the real estate.

3. NAME OF BUYER. The buyer must be named in the agreement and designated as *buyer, purchaser,* or *vendee*. If there are two or more buyers, they should be named; and the agreement should state whether they are buying as tenants in common or as joint tenants, or, if husband and wife, as tenants by the entirety. If the buyer is a corporation or partnership, the agreement should so state. Also, if the buyer is purchasing the property in his capacity as trustee, the agreement should so state. In all instances the buyer's name should be spelled in the agreement as it is to be spelled in the deed of conveyance.

4. SALE PRICE. The agreement must state the sale price; otherwise, it will be incomplete.

5. EXTENSION OF CREDIT. If there is no provision in the agreement for the extension of credit to the buyers, it will be held that the terms of payment are cash. If credit is to be extended, the agreement should state the terms in detail. The amount and time of payment of the down payment, the amount of subsequent payments, when each payment is to

be made, where payable, rate of interest to be paid, whether the unpaid balance is to be evidenced by a negotiable promissory note or a series of promissory notes, and how the unpaid balance is to be secured should all be stated.

6. SECURITY TO BE GIVEN. If credit is extended, the nature of the security to be given should be stated in detail. If the unpaid balance is to be secured by a purchase-money mortgage, trust deed, installment sales contract, pledge of securities, or guarantee of payment by third persons, the terms of the security agreement should be set out in detail.

7. DESCRIPTION OF REAL ESTATE. The description of the real estate sold must be such that it can be identified from the description. However, in the drafting of the agreement the description should be as complete as the circumstances permit.

8. TYPE OF DEED. The agreement should state the type of deed which is to be executed by the seller—that is, whether general warranty, special warranty, bargain and sale, or quitclaim. If the type of deed is not stated, the court will, in the event of a lawsuit, presume that the type of deed customarily used in the community was intended.

9. TITLE TO BE CONVEYED. The agreement should state the title to be conveyed. If no statement is made regarding title, the seller will, as a general rule, be obligated to convey a marketable title. The contract may provide that the seller will convey an insurable title, a title satisfactory to the attorney of the buyer, or a title free from all defects and encumbrances.

a. *Marketable title.* A marketable title is one which is free of defects, such as mortgages, tax liens, and other liens and encumbrances. It is a title under which the buyer may have quiet and peaceful enjoyment of the property, and one which could be sold to a reasonable and prudent purchaser familiar with all the facts relative to the title to the property.[11] If the buyer wishes to refuse to close the deal on the ground that the title is not marketable, he must discover the defects in the title and point them out before he pays his money and accepts the deed.[12] After he has accepted the deed, he cannot rescind the transaction and recover his money. However, if the seller has given a warranty deed, the buyer could recover damages if the defect was a breach of the warranty.

·A provision in the agreement to the effect that the seller would convey a marketable title would justify the buyer in refusing to accept title subject

---

[11] *Myrick* v. *Austin,* 141 Kan. 778, 44 P.2d 266.

[12] *Stack* v. *Commercial Towel & Uniform Service,* 120 Ind. App. 473, 91 N.E.2d 790.

to an easement, unless the easement was visible and beneficial, such as the easements of the utility companies which service the property.[13]

As a general rule restrictions on the property, if not provided for in the agreement, are deemed to be defects in the title, which would justify the buyer in rejecting it; but restrictions imposed by zoning ordinances or state statutes on the use of the property are not defects in the title to real estate. If the buyer wishes to make a particular use of the property, he should include in the agreement a provision which would give him the right to refuse the property if it could not be used for a stated purpose.[14]

b. Title insurance. The buyer may wish to protect himself by either insuring the title or providing that the seller shall deliver with the deed a policy of title insurance insuring the title against all defects except those specifically listed in the agreement. A policy of title insurance does not guarantee a title free from defects, but it does obligate the insurance company which writes the insurance to pay for any loss suffered as the result of covered defects. The buyer may wish to provide that the seller will convey a title which will be insured by an insurance company named by the buyer.

c. Attorney's approval of title. The buyer may wish to stipulate in the agreement that the title shall be satisfactory to an attorney to be selected by the buyer. If the agreement includes such a provision, the buyer will not have to accept title until it is approved by the attorney selected. However, the attorney must act honestly. If the attorney acts collusively or capriciously in refusing to approve the title, or if he refuses to act or delays for an unreasonable length of time, the buyer will not be permitted to refuse to accept title, if title is proved to be marketable, on the ground of the attorney's failure to approve the title.

d. Title free from all defects and encumbrances. If the agreement provides that the seller will convey a title free from all defects and encumbrances, the purchaser will have the right to reject the title if it is subject to any type of defect or encumbrance. The buyer could not reject the title if it was free from all except technical defects which could be corrected by affidavits or quitclaim deeds.

10. SURVEYS. If the boundaries of the real estate are not clearly marked, the buyer may wish to have a survey made, in order to determine and correct boundaries. In such a case the agreement should stipulate who is to pay for the survey and should set out the obligations of the parties in the event the survey reveals that the true boundaries differ

---

[13] *Wheeler* v. *Beem,* 111 Kan. 700, 208 P. 626.

[14] *Campbell* v. *Heller,* 36 N.J. Super. 361, 115 A.2d 644.

from those represented to be the boundaries at the time the property was examined. As a general rule, minor differences would not justify rejection of the title, unless there was an express stipulation in the agreement to that effect.

11. ENCROACHMĒNTS.   As a general rule, if there are encroachments on the property being purchased, or if the structures on the property being purchased encroach on adjoining property or streets or alleys, such encroachments create in the title to the property a defect which would justify the buyer in rejecting the title. Some courts have held that if the encroachment is minor in nature—for example, not more than one or two inches— it is not material and will not justify rejection of the title. If there are, on the real estate sold or on the adjoining property, structures which are set close to the boundary line, there should be inserted in the agreement a clause which defines the rights of the parties in the event the structures encroach either on the property sold or on the adjoining property.

12. TIME OF EXISTENCE OF STIPULATED TITLE.   A person may agree to sell property and not be guilty of a breach of the agreement even though he does not have title to the property at the time he negotiates the sale. The seller will not need to have title to the property until the time for the delivery of the deed. If the agreement sets a time for the closing of the deal—that is, for the delivery of the deed and the payment or the securing of the purchase price—and at that time the seller cannot convey to the buyer the title provided for in the agreement, the courts will, as a general rule, give the seller some additional time in which to free the title of defect. However, if the circumstances are such that the buyer would suffer substantial injury if the time of performance were delayed, he may, if he so elects, rescind the sale if the seller does not tender performance on time. If the agreement expressly stipulates that "time is of the essence," the buyer has the right to rescind the contract if the seller does not tender performance within the stipulated time.

13. ABSTRACT OF TITLE OR TORRENS CERTIFICATE.   The agreement should provide for the furnishing of an abstract of title or, if the property is registered under the Torrens system of land titles, for the furnishing of a Torrens certificate of title. As a general rule, the seller will have an abstract of title. The abstract should be brought down to date and certified as of that date. The agreement may also stipulate that at the time the deal is closed and the deed is recorded, the abstract be again brought down to that time and certified as of that date. This will show whether any liens were acquired against the property during the time between the first certification of the abstract and the closing of the deal.

If a Torrens certificate is to be furnished, the time of certification should be stated. Title insurance may be specified.

It should be made clear in the agreement which of the parties is to pay the costs of obtaining the abstract or of bringing it down to date, or of obtaining the Torrens certificate, or issuance of title.

The time allowed the seller to obtain the abstract or have it brought down to date should be stated. Likewise, the time allowed the buyer to have the abstract examined and defects pointed out should be indicated.

Provision should be made for the removal of discovered defects and a time set within which the seller would be permitted to remove existing defects.

14. EARNEST MONEY. In many real estate transactions the buyer will make a deposit as a guarantee of his performance of the agreement. The agreement will provide that if the seller cannot perform or fails to perform, the payment made by the buyer will be returned. The agreement will usually provide that if the buyer refuses or fails to perform, he will forfeit his deposit as liquidated damages. Such a provision is enforced by the courts, unless the amount of the deposit is greatly in excess of any possible loss suffered by the seller as the result of the buyer's breach.

The amount of the deposit is a matter to be determined by the parties. The seller, for his protection, should request a deposit large enough to cover any expenses he might incur in having the abstract brought down to date; costs of surveys, if any; brokers' commissions; and any other foreseeable expenses.

15. KNOWN DEFECTS IN TITLE. As a general rule, the agreement will provide that the purchaser will accept title subject to known defects, such as easements for utilities, or restrictions. For the buyer's protection, this clause should set out specifically the defects which are excluded from the seller's obligation to convey a marketable title or are to be excluded from the coverage of a policy of title insurance. If the excluded defects are stated in broad, general language, the buyer may find that he is, in effect, contracting to accept title "as is" and will have to take whatever title the seller has, without regard to existing defects in it.

16. MORTGAGE ON PROPERTY. If there is a mortgage on the real estate sold, the seller may convey the property free and clear; the purchaser may buy subject to the mortgage, or he may buy subject to the mortgage and assume and agree to pay the mortgage debt.

a. Discharge of mortgage. If the real estate is sold "free and clear," the seller is obligated to obtain a discharge of the mortgage. Allowing the buyer to withhold from the purchase price the amount of the unpaid balance of the mortgage debt plus accrued interest is not sufficient. A mortgagee is under no obligation to accept payment of a mortgage debt until the due date and may demand a premium if he accepts earlier payment. If the seller has sold "free and clear," he must negotiate for and obtain the discharge, paying all premiums, costs, and so forth, incident to obtaining and recording the discharge.

b. Sale subject to mortgage. If the sale is subject to the mortgage but the buyer is not assuming the mortgage debt, care must be exercised in drafting the agreement. The courts have held that if the agreement states an agreed purchase price and provides that the purchaser will pay the stated price less the unpaid balance of the mortgage debt and buys "subject to the mortgage," the buyer will hold the amount of the mortgage debt as agent or trustee for the mortgagor and will be obligated to pay the mortgage debt when it falls due.[15]

If the buyer does not assume the mortgage debt, the agreement should not state a purchase price other than the amount the buyer is to pay the seller for his equity in the property. For example, suppose that the agreed value of the property sold is $15,000, and the unpaid balance of the mortgage debt and accrued interest is $8,000. The contract should state that the buyer agrees to pay $7,000 for the property "subject to the mortgage," and should describe the mortgage in detail, together with the book and page where it is recorded.

c. Sale subject to mortgage, buyer to pay mortgage debt. If the purchaser buys subject to the mortgage, and assumes and agrees to pay the mortgage debt, the agreement should set out the terms of the mortgage in detail, specify the amount of the unpaid balance of the mortgage debt and accrued interest, and state clearly that the buyer takes "subject to said mortgage, and assumes and agrees to pay the mortgage debt and accrued interest according to the terms of the mortgage and note secured thereby."

17. Conditions.   The buyer may be willing to agree to purchase the real estate but may be unable to meet the seller's terms unless he can borrow money to make the down payment or can sell property he already owns or can obtain certain employment. The seller may be willing to agree to sell subject to the buyer's negotiating the loan, selling the property, or obtaining the position.

In such a situation an agreement of purchase and sale containing all of the terms of the sale will be drafted, and a clause will be inserted providing that the buyer will not be bound to perform the agreement

---

[15] *Flynn et al.* v. *Kenrick et al.,* 285 Mass. 446, 189 N.E. 207.

unless or until the stipulated event occurs. Such a provision must be carefully worded and must describe with clarity the event which must happen before the buyer is bound. If the event is the obtaining of a loan or the selling of property, the time within which the loan must be obtained or the property sold should be stated.

In addition, the seller may wish to stipulate that he will have the right to negotiate a loan on the buyer's behalf, stating the terms of the loan or the right to find a buyer for the property to be sold. In such situations the buyer owes a duty to act honestly and use his best efforts to bring about the event; if he refuses to act, or if he follows a course which will delay or prevent the occurrence of the event, the court may hold that he is guilty of breach of the agreement.[16]

18. POSSESSION. The agreement should state the time at which the seller is to surrender possession to the buyer. If the property is in the possession of someone other than the seller, the agreement should specifically provide that the seller will take whatever action is necessary to obtain possession of the property and will surrender possession to the buyer on or before a stipulated date.

19. ASSIGNMENT OF LEASES AND ADJUSTMENT OF RENTS. If the property is rental property and is sold subject to outstanding leases, the agreement should provide for the examination of the leases by the buyer or his attorney, for the assignment of the leases to the buyer, and for the adjustment of rents. If leases are assigned, notice of the assignment should be given to the tenants; and they should be instructed to pay all rents due and payable after a stated date, to be agreed upon by the seller and buyer, to the buyer or to his order.

20. TAXES AND ASSESSMENTS. The agreement should provide for the payment of taxes and assessments which are unpaid at the time of the sale. In most communities, there is an established custom regarding the payment of taxes and assessments which will apply if no provision is included in the agreement of sale covering this point. However, misunderstanding can be avoided by including in the agreement a provision setting out specifically the arrangement regarding the payment of taxes and assessments.

21. DESTRUCTION OF BUILDINGS. The courts are not in accord as to which of the contracting parties must stand the loss if the buildings on the real estate are damaged by fire, flood, or wind after the agreement to sell is executed but before the sale is closed and the deed delivered to the buyer. The agreement should cover this contingency.

---

[16] *Lach* v. *Cahill et al.,* 138 Conn. 418, 85 A.2d 481.

The agreement may provide that in the event the buildings are materially damaged by fire, flood, or wind, the buyer will be discharged from his obligation to buy and will have refunded to him any down payment which he has made. Or it may provide that the buyer will assume the risks of the destruction of buildings by fire, flood, or wind and will, in all events, perform the agreement and pay the full purchase price. Such a clause will specifically define the risk, and the party who assumes such risk will be in a position to insure it.

22. INSURANCE.   The agreement should provide for the adjustment of the policies of insurance on the improvements on the real estate and should provide for insurance after the execution of the agreement but before the conveyance.

A policy of insurance does not go with the property insured. Insurable interest in property is determined at the time of loss. A policy of property insurance is not assignable without the consent of the insurer. If property is conveyed to the buyer and the seller no longer has any interest in the property, the buyer has no right to collect on insurance obtained by the seller, unless the seller has assigned the policies to the buyer with the consent of the insurer. In a sale of improved real estate the agreement should provide either for the assignment of existing policies and the adjustment of the premium or for the cancelation of the policies, leaving the purchaser to obtain such insurance as he wishes.

If property insured by the seller is destroyed or damaged after the execution of the agreement but before conveyance, and the seller collects the insurance, the majority of courts hold that the seller is entitled to the insurance money if the buyer has the right to rescind the agreement or if the seller must stand the loss. However, if the buyer is obligated to accept a conveyance of the property and pay the full purchase price, he is entitled to the insurance money.[17] A safe course to follow would be for both the seller and the buyer to insure their respective interests in the property, or for the buyer to insure and include a provision in the policy covering the seller's interest as it may appear.

23. SALE OF LAND AND CONTRACT TO CONSTRUCT BUILDING.   If a person agrees to sell a tract of land and to build a house or other structure on the land, the resulting contract is a combination of a contract to sell real estate and a contract to build, and should contain all the provisions essential to both types. Building contracts are discussed in Chapter 13. As a general rule, the courts will grant specific performance of a contract to sell real estate—that is, they will force the seller to convey the real estate—but will not grant specific performance of a building contract.

---

[17] *Vogel* v. *Northern Assurance Company,* 219 F.2d 409.

Some courts have granted specific performance of a combined sale of land and building contract,[18] whereas other courts have refused to do so.

24. VIOLATION OF ORDINANCES. For the buyer's protection the agreement should provide that in the event any structure on the premises is so constructed that it violates a city ordinance—lacks fire escapes, proper sanitary facilities, and so forth—the seller will correct any defect, unless the buyer is purchasing subject to the defects, in which case the agreement should so state. If the seller is to correct the defects, the closing of the deal can be expedited by getting an estimate of the cost and having the seller leave in the hands of the buyer or in escrow sufficient funds to cover the cost of the work to be done.

25. UTILITY BILLS, ETC. If the real estate is being serviced by utilities, some provision should be made for the prorating of utility bills or for having meters read and the account transferred to the new occupant at the time he takes possession.

26. FIXTURES AND CROPS. The agreement should clearly state which of the articles that are in the nature of fixtures are to go with the real estate. If the seller wishes to remove any plantings from the premises, the agreement should clearly state what plantings are to be removed and within what time they are to be removed.

If the real estate sold is farm land, the agreement should state which crops are to go with the land and which are to remain the property of the seller. It should also define the seller's right to remove reserved crops.

27. MISCELLANEOUS. During the negotiation of the sale of real estate, the parties may raise special questions regarding the property and the rights in the property which are to be retained or transferred. Careful note should be made of all such matters, and a clause setting out the agreement of the parties relative to such special items should be included.

Execution of purchase agreement

SIGNING THE PURCHASE AGREEMENT

The purchase agreement should be signed by both the buyer and the seller; and if either or both are married, the spouse or spouses also should sign. However, in those states in which either the husband or the wife may deal with his or her individual real estate without the spouse's joining, only the signature of the title owner of the real estate is necessary.

---

[18] *Edison Realty Co. et al.* v. *Bauernschaub et al.,* 191 Md. 451, 62 A.2d 354.

If the real estate is owned or is being purchased by two or more persons holding or purchasing as co-owners, all interested persons and their spouses (with the exception noted above) should sign.

If the real estate is owned or is being purchased by a corporation, the purchase agreement will be signed in the name of the corporation by an officer or agent thereof. A careful check should be made to ascertain (1) if the purchase or sale of the real estate has been duly authorized by action of the board of directors of the corporation and (2) if the officer or agent signing the agreement on behalf of the corporation is authorized to do so.

As a general rule, a partner has authority to bind the partnership, provided the purchase or sale of the real estate involved is within the scope of the partnership business.

SIGNATURE BY AGENT

The agreement may be signed by a duly authorized agent on behalf of either the buyer or the seller, or both. Oral authorization to sign is sufficient to bind the principal. However, it is customary to employ a written authorization; and if the agreement is to be recorded, the recording laws of most states require a written authorization. The written authorization must be executed with the same formality as is required for the execution of the agreement and must be recorded along with the agreement.

Good business practice requires a written authorization. A person dealing with an agent must determine the scope of the agent's authority. If the agent exceeds his authority, the principal is not bound. The agent should be required to produce his written authority, and the person dealing with the agent should read it carefully to determine the extent of the agent's authority. Authority of an agent to "sell' does not give him the authority to execute a contract to sell or a deed. Authority of an agent to execute a contract or deed does not, as a general rule, give him the authority to sell on credit.

A person may act as the agent of his undisclosed principal, in which event the agent will contract in his own name and will be bound by the contract. On the discovery of the existence of the agency, the person dealing with the agent can elect to hold either the agent or the undisclosed principal on the contract.[19] (In Pennsylvania, both are liable.)

[19] *Hollywood Holding & Development Corporation* v. *Oswald,* 119 Cal. App. 21, 5 P.2d 963.

If an owner has refused to sell to a particular individual and that particular individual employs an agent to purchase the property for him, the agent to conceal the identity of his principal, the seller may, on discovering the true principal of the agent, refuse to perform the contract.[20]

SEALED, ACKNOWLEDGED, WITNESSED, AND DELIVERED

A purchase agreement is, in legal effect, a contract; and a contract to sell real estate does not have to be sealed to be valid. Likewise, an acknowledgment is not essential to the validity of the agreement. However, under the recording statutes of most states, such an agreement would have to be acknowledged if it is to be eligible to record. As a general rule, purchase agreements are not recorded and are therefore not acknowledged.

The same rule applies to the witnessing of the purchase agreement. Witnesses are not essential to the validity of the agreement, and there is no reason for having the agreement witnessed unless the parties wish to record it and the statutes of the state require that a contract must be witnessed if it is to be eligible to record.

An agreement to sell real estate is not effective until it is delivered. The same rules of law apply to the delivery of a contract as to the delivery of a deed (see Chapter 5, "Delivery of a Deed").

It is recommended that the agreement be prepared in duplicate, and that both the buyer and the seller sign it at the same time, each signing both copies and each keeping a copy.

If the buyer submits a prepared agreement as an offer to buy, he should submit two copies; and he should include a clause in the agreement (offer) to the effect that if the seller wishes to accept the offer, he must sign and return to the buyer a copy of the agreement within a stated period of time—for example, five days. If the seller does not act within the stipulated time, the offer will terminate.

RECORDING

As a general rule, agreements to sell real estate—except the installment land contract, which is discussed in detail in Chapter 10—are short-term contracts and are not recorded. Under the recording statutes of some states, such agreements are not eligible to be recorded. There is some risk involved in not recording the agreement to sell. For instance, if

[20] *Wloczewski* v. *Kozlowski,* 395 Ill. 402, 70 N.E.2d 560.

the seller, after executing an agreement to sell, conveys the real estate to an innocent purchaser for value who has no notice or knowledge of the agreement to sell at the time the property is conveyed to him, the innocent purchaser acquires a title which is good against the contract buyer. The contract buyer's only remedy is a suit against the seller for damages for breach of contract.

Effect of purchase agreement

RIGHTS ACQUIRED BY BUYER

When an agreement to sell real estate is fully executed, the buyer acquires property rights in the real estate, although he does not acquire title until a deed to the property is executed and delivered to him. The buyer's rights in the property are called the *equitable title* to the property. This, in effect, indicates that in a proper action the court will force the seller to deed the property to the buyer if the buyer has performed or tendered performance of his obligations under the agreement.

BUYER'S RIGHT TO ASSIGN

Unless the contract of sale contains a clause prohibiting the transfer of the buyer's interest in the real estate, the buyer can sell his property right—transfer his equitable title. This is known as an *assignment* of the agreement. The assignee—buyer of the equitable title—acquires all the rights of the buyer and, on the performance of the buyer's obligations, is entitled to a deed from the seller. The buyer continues to be liable to the seller for the performance of his obligations under the agreement; he cannot relieve himself of his obligations by assigning the agreement. The buyer of the equitable title (the assignee) is not liable to the seller unless, as a part of the assignment, he assumes and agrees to perform the obligations of the buyer. The seller, the buyer, and the assignee may enter into an agreement whereby the assignee promises the seller that he (the assignee) will perform the obligations of the buyer, and the seller accepts the assignee's promise of performance in the place of the obligations of the buyer and agrees to release the buyer from his obligations. This is known as a *novation*.

BUYER'S REMEDIES

If the seller is unable to fulfill his obligations under the agreement or refuses to do so, the buyer has an election of remedies. He may (1) rescind the agreement, (2) bring an action to recover damages, or (3) bring an action asking specific performance of the agreement.

If the buyer rescinds the agreement, he thereby puts an end to it. He will be entitled to the return of any payments made or anything given in part performance and will be required to return anything which he has received from the seller in part performance. In a court action in which the remedy granted is rescission of the agreement, the court endeavors to put the parties as nearly as possible in the same positions they would have held if they had never entered into the contract.

In a suit for damages the buyer is entitled to be compensated for any financial loss which he can prove he has suffered as the direct result of the seller's breach of the agreement. The usual elements of damages would be the down payment made by the buyer or the value of any property conveyed to the seller as part payment, any actual out-of-pocket expenses paid by the buyer, and loss of profits on the transaction. To recover for loss of profits, the purchaser will have to prove beyond a reasonable doubt that the market price of the property at the time the seller was to convey it to him was greater than the agreed price. The buyer must prove the amount of this difference with reasonable certainty. When the court grants the remedy of specific performance, it forces the seller, on receiving payment of the purchase price, to give the buyer a deed to the real estate.

Whether or not a court will grant the remedy of specific performance rests in the sound discretion of the courts. If the buyer has induced the seller to enter into an unfair and inequitable agreement to sell, and its specific enforcement would impose an unjust hardship on the seller, the court may refuse to grant the remedy of specific performance.[21] As a general rule, the court will decree specific performance of an agreement to sell real estate.

DEFECTIVE TITLE

If the seller's title is defective, the buyer may, if he wishes, ask for specific performance of the agreement. If the defect in the seller's title is of such a nature that it can be compensated for by a reduction of

---

[21] *Saunders* v. *Davis et ux.,* 31 Tenn. App. 674, 220 S.W.2d 883.

the purchase price, and the buyer did not know of the defect at the time the agreement was executed, the court, as a part of its decree of specific performance, will abate part of the purchase price. For example, if the seller is only a part owner of the property, or if the land area is less than the area called for in the agreement, the court may grant a proportional reduction in the purchase price; or if there is a mortgage, mechanic's lien, or judgment lien on the property, the court will reduce the purchase price by the amount of the mortgage or lien. However, if the buyer knew of the mortgage or lien at the time he entered into the agreement, he would not be entitled to a reduction in the purchase price.

If there is a provision in the agreement that it shall be void in the event the seller's title proves defective, the buyer would not be entitled to a remedy if the seller's title is defective, but he would be entitled to the return of his down payment.

MISREPRESENTATION, ETC.

If the buyer is induced to enter into the agreement by misrepresentation or undue influence, he may rescind it. If he is induced to enter into the agreement by fraudulent representations or duress, he may rescind the agreement, or he may retain the property and bring suit in tort and recover tort damages. In a fraud case, tort damages are, as a general rule, the difference between the value of the real estate conveyed and its value if it had been as represented.

REMEDIES OF THE SELLER

The remedies of the seller correspond in most respects to the remedies of the buyer. The seller may (1) rescind the agreement, (2) declare a forfeiture, (3) recover damages, (4) tender a deed and recover a judgment for the purchase price, or (5) ask for specific performance.

If the seller rescinds the agreement, he returns what he has received and recovers possession of the real estate. If the buyer has been in possession, the seller is entitled to reasonable rent for the time the buyer was in possession.

The seller is not entitled to declare a forfeiture unless this right is expressly reserved in the agreement. When the seller declares a forfeiture, he retains all payments made by the buyer and recovers possession of the real estate.

In a suit for damages the seller must prove the amount of the financial loss he has suffered as a direct result of the buyer's breach.

In some states the seller may tender a deed and recover a judgment for the purchase price of the property. This remedy is practically the same as the remedy of specific performance. If the remedy of specific performance is granted, the court will decree the performance of the agreement on the part of the buyer. The seller, in turn, must perform his obligations under the agreement.

Seller's lien

Even though the agreement does not provide that the seller shall have a lien on the property sold for the unpaid balance of the purchase price, he will have a lien on the property; this lien may be foreclosed in the same manner as a mortgage.

Buyer's lien

If the buyer has paid part of the agreed purchase price of the real estate and the seller is unable or unwilling to convey good title to the property, the buyer will have a lien on the property for the payment he has made. This lien can be foreclosed in the same manner as a mortgage.

Checklist

An agreement to sell real estate, if it is to be enforceable, must be in writing and must comply with the following as a minimum:

1. Name of the seller.
2. Name of the buyer.
3. Reasonably accurate description of the property.
4. Statement of the sale price.
5. Signature of the party to be bound thereby. (In some states, it must be signed by both the seller and the buyer.)
6. Contract must be delivered.

In order to satisfy the statute of frauds, a formal written contract need not be executed, but there must be a written note or memorandum which sets out all the material provisions of the contract. In addition, the following should be checked and included if they apply:

1. Name of the seller's spouse.
2. Credit terms.
3. Security to be given.
4. Type of deed to be given.
5. Title to be conveyed.
6. Warranties to be made.
7. Survey to be made.
8. Encroachments.
9. Abstract of title or Torrens certificate.
10. Earnest money or down payment.
11. Exception of known defects.
12. Disposition of mortgage.
13. Conditions.
14. Assignment of leases.
15. Adjustment of rents.
16. Taxes and assessments.
17. Damage to or destruction of buildings.
18. Insurance.
19. Construction of building on the land sold.
20. Violation of ordinances.
21. Adjustment of utility bills, etc.
22. Fixtures, shrubs, and crops.
23. Miscellaneous.

If the contract is eligible for record and is to be recorded, its execution must satisfy the requirements of the recording statutes, which may require:

1. A seal.
2. Acknowledgment.
3. Witnesses.

Closing the sale

PRECAUTIONS BUYER SHOULD TAKE

Before a buyer enters into an agreement to buy real estate, he should examine the property and satisfy himself that the property is what he wants. If it is residential property, he should check the community in which it is located, the schools, churches, transportation facilities, sanitary facilities, zoning ordinances, restrictions, whether or not it is in a flood area, and anything else which might affect the value of the property.

If the property is commercial property, he should check zoning ordinances, character of surrounding property, transportation facilities, traffic flow, and similar matters. After the buyer has entered into an agreement to buy, it is too late to rescind the transaction. The seller should check the buyer's credit and satisfy himself that the buyer is able to fulfill his part of the contract.

Before the buyer accepts a deed to the property and pays or secures the purchase price, he should check each point of the agreement and be certain that the property satisfies every condition in it. When the purchaser accepts the deed and pays his money, the agreement is merged in the deed; it is then too late to object to the performance rendered by the seller. The only provisions of the agreement which are not merged into the deed are those that clearly state or unquestionably imply that they are to be performed after the transaction is closed.

One of the principal reasons for the buyer and seller of real estate to enter into an agreement to buy and sell, preliminary to the closing of the transaction, is to afford the buyer an opportunity to have the title to the property investigated. If the evidence of title is based on an abstract of title, the buyer should check to be certain that the abstract has been prepared by a competent, reliable abstractor. He should have the abstract examined by an experienced real estate attorney.

The certificate of the abstractor should be checked to ascertain what records have been examined and abstracted. Any records—such as notices of mechanics' liens, federal tax liens, old-age assistance liens, probate court records, *lis pendes* records, recognizance or bail bonds, circuit court records, superior court records, criminal court records, transcipt of judgment records of all federal courts in the state, and tax records—should be carefully checked, if the certificate of the abstractor does not include them.

If the evidence of title is to be a certificate of title, the buyer should demand or obtain a certificate of title prepared by a competent attorney experienced in making title examinations. If the property is registered under the Torrens system, the register should be checked to ascertain if there are liens and encumbrances against the property which are not mentioned in the agreement. If the title is to be an insured title, the buyer should have a commitment from the insurer who is to write the policy of insurance.

ADJUSTMENT IF TITLE IS DEFECTIVE

If the seller is unable to convey a marketable title or a title that satisfies the requirements set out in the agreement, the buyer is not obligated to accept the title and may rescind the agreement. If no specific time is set for the closing of the sale, or if a specific time is set but time is not made of the essence, the seller will have a reasonable time to cure the defects in his title. However, if the defects are such that they cannot be cured within a relatively short period of time, and especially if they are such that a bill to quiet title would be required to cure them, the seller would be in default, and the buyer would have the right to elect to rescind the agreement or to grant the seller time in which to cure the defects in his title. If an extension of time is to be granted, an agreement as to the adjustment of interest, rents, and so forth, should be drafted and signed by the parties.

MATTERS TO BE CHECKED BY BUYER

After the agreement has been executed, and before the sale is closed, the buyer should investigate the following:

1. Check the boundaries of the property. Have a survey made, if needed.
2. If a survey is made, have the surveyor indicate whether or not there are encroachments.
3. Ascertain the terms of any mortgage on the property, and obtain from the mortgagee a statement of the unpaid balance of the mortgage debt plus interest and any other charges up to date for the closing. Does the mortgage contain a clause providing that on the sale of the property the mortgage debt becomes due and payable?
4. If payments made by the mortgagee include expenditures for taxes, insurance premiums, and so on, obtain from the mortgagee a statement of the accruals in such accounts as of the closing date.
5. Check with persons in possession, and ascertain the rights which they claim in the property. Also, check with the parties in possession as to what items attached to the premises they claim as their property.
6. If the property is rental property under lease, obtain the leases, and have them examined by an attorney. Have the attorney prepare a schedule showing the principal provisions of the leases, such as options either to renew the lease or to purchase the property, unexpired term of the lease, rent received, services to be rendered by the landlord, and all other related matters.
7. Have the attorney prepare assignments of the leases, notices to the tenants of the sale of the property, and notices to make future pay-

ments of rent to the buyer; have these assignments and notices signed by the seller on the closing date.

8. If the property is an apartment house or office building or similar building which is supervised by a manager, or if the landlord-seller employs the staff which services the building, notice should be given to the manager and other building employees terminating their service. If the buyer wishes to continue their service, new contracts of employment must be negotiated. A contract for personal services is not assignable.

9. Rent adjustments should be computed as of the closing date.

10. Taxes and assessments should be investigated, and any adjustment of taxes and assessments should be computed as of the closing date.

11. All insurance policies should be checked; and if they are to be assigned, the consent of the insurer should be obtained. The adjustment of the premiums should be computed.

12. The building should be inspected to ascertain whether or not any zoning or other ordinances are being violated.

13. The premises should be checked to ascertain if any restrictions on the property are being violated.

14. Arrangements should be made to have all utility meters read (if the seller has furnished the utilities) and the account transferred to the name of the buyer. If utilities are on a tax basis and charged against the property, the meters should be read on the closing date and the utility bills adjusted.

15. The premises should be inspected immediately prior to closing the sale to make certain that no fixtures, shrubs, or chattels which are to go with the property have been removed.

16. If the seller is a corporation, the corporate records should be investigated to ascertain whether or not proper corporation action has been taken to authorize the sale, and to determine which officer or officers are authorized to execute the deed in the name of the corporation.

THE DEED FROM SELLER TO BUYER

The deed should be prepared prior to the closing date, and the attorneys of both the buyer and the seller should examine the deed and check the following:

1. The names of the grantor and grantees. Are they spelled corerctly? Is the grantor's name spelled the same in the prepared deed as it was in the deed granting the property to him?

2. The description of the property should be checked against the description in the deed granting the property to the seller. This description should not be copied slavishly; if there are errors, they should be corrected.

3. If either the grantor or the grantee is a corporation, the corporate name must be exactly as written in the charter; the state of incorporation and the location of its principal place of business should be shown.

4. The corporate deed should show the authority under which the conveyance is made.

5. Restrictive covenants. Are they properly drafted?

6. Exceptions and reservations. Do the provisions in the deed correspond to the provisions in the contract?

7. Mortgage. If the property is mortgaged or a purchase-money mortgage is to be given, is the mortgage correctly described? Does the buyer take subject to the mortgage, or does he take subject to the mortgage and assume and agree to pay the mortgage debt?

8. Liens and encumbrances. Are there any liens or encumbrances excepted in the deed which are not provided for in the contract to sell?

9. Homestead and dower rights. Are the necessary waivers in the deed?

10. Obligations which are to be fulfilled after closing should be stated in the deed.

11. Type of deed. Is the prepared deed the type of deed stipulated in the contract of sale?

MORTGAGE OR DEED OF TRUST AND NOTE

If the seller is taking a purchase-money mortgage or a deed of trust and a note to secure the unpaid balance of the purchase price of the real estate, these instruments should be prepared in advance; and the names of the parties, description of the real estate, terms of payment, rate of interest, provisions for insurance, and so forth, should be checked to be certain that they are correct and that they comply with the provisions of the contract to sell.

The buyer may borrow money and secure the loan by giving a mortgage or deed of trust on the real estate, and thus obtain the money to pay the seller in full. In such a situation the mortgage or deed of trust will be executed, as a general rule, as a part of the closing of the sale. The loan and the terms of the mortgage or deed of trust will have been negotiated as a separate transaction; but both the sale and the loan will be closed at the same time, since the lender will not wish to pay out his money until the mortgage or deed of trust and deed are executed, and the seller will not wish to deliver a deed until he is paid the agreed purchase price.

In regard to the loan, if the money is borrowed from an institution, the institution will have a standard form of mortgage or deed of trust which it will use. In Federal Housing Administration loans, government forms are used. The Veterans Administration furnishes forms to be used in its loans, but the employment of these forms is not compulsory. The loaning institution may use its own forms if they comply with Veterans Administration regulations.

Mortgages and deeds of trust are discussed in Chapters 9 and 10, respectively.

DOCUMENTS TO BE DELIVERED TO BUYER

The documents to be delivered to the buyer on the closing of a transaction will depend on the type of property which has been sold and the terms of the sale. The following is a list of the documents commonly delivered to the buyer at the closing:

1. The deed to the real estate.
2. If the sale is a sale of a part of a large tract owned by the seller and a survey has been made, the surveyor's plat is either delivered with the deed or attached to the abstract.
3. Abstract, certificate of title, or title insurance policy. If the buyer has borrowed money and given a mortgage or deed of trust on the property as security, these documents will, as a general rule, be delivered to the loaning insitution.
4. Receipt for purchase money.
5. If an existing mortgage has been paid and discharged, a discharge of the mortgage together with the mortgage and cancelled notes.
6. If an existing mortgage is assumed, a statement of the amount of the unpaid balance of the mortgage debt and accrued interest.
7. Leases and assignment of leases on the property or any portion thereof.
8. Securities deposited by tenants as security for payment of rent.
9. Letters to tenants notifying them of the sale and advising them to pay future rent to the buyer.

10. Service contracts which are not terminated at the time of the sale, such as exterminator contracts.
11. Last receipts for taxes, special assessments, water tax, and other charges.
12. In some localities the seller gives the buyer an affidavit of title covering all possible liens which would not be shown by the abstract or may have been obtained after the certification of the abstract but before the buyer has had an opportunity to record his deed.
13. A copy of the closing statement.

DOCUMENTS TO BE DELIVERED TO SELLER

If the buyer is paying the seller cash for the property, as a general rule, all that will be given to the seller is a check—usually certified—for the amount due him, together with a copy of the closing statement.

If the seller is taking a purchase-money mortgage or a deed of trust and a note for the unpaid balance, the following will be delivered to the seller on the closing of the sale:

1. Check or cash for the down payment.
2. Mortgage or deed of trust.
3. Note or series of notes for the unpaid balance. As a general rule, a simple note providing for amortized payments of principal and interest in monthly installments will be used.
4. Abstract of title, certificate of title, or policy of title insurance.
5. Insurance policies.

Closing statements

CONTENT OF STATEMENT

A closing statement which summarizes the transaction should be prepared and signed by both the buyer and the seller. Such a statement should show:

1. Date.
2. Names and addresses of the seller and buyer.
3. Address of the real estate sold, or short description, if farm land.

Following this should be an itemized statement of credits due the seller and credits due the buyer. These items should be listed in separate columns.

The items credited to the seller would usually include the following:

1. Purchase price.
2. Unearned insurance premiums.
3. Escrow deposits, taxes, and insurance.

The items credited to the buyer would usually include the following:

1. Earnest money deposit.
2. Additional down payment (if any).
3. Balance on mortgage (held by _____).
4. Interest on mortgage.
5. If there is a second mortgage on the property, the balance on the second mortgage and interest should be placed in this column. (If payments made on the mortgage include prepayment of taxes, insurance premiums, and so forth, the amount of the prepayment on these items would be placed in the seller's column.)
6. Real estate taxes.
7. Prorated rents.

Any additional items for which the buyer is entitled to credit should be itemized. Add the figures in each column, and subtract the total in the buyer's column from the total in the seller's column; this gives the total payment due the seller from the buyer.

The statement should also include an itemization of the seller's expenses if a broker has represented the seller in the negotiation of the sale. This enumeration would include all sums paid out by the broker and the commission due the broker in one column, and all payments made to the broker in another column. The difference between the totals in these two columns would be the amount to be paid to the seller or the broker, as the case may be. The following would usually appear in such an itemization: In one column would be a record of cash received by the broker; in the other column would be a listing of all cash disbursements made by the broker, such as expenditures for continuation of abstract and the broker's commission.

A short summary of the agreement of the parties relative to the transaction is recommended. Such a summary would include:

1. Date possession is to be given to the buyer.
2. Name of the person to whom the abstract was delivered.
3. Receipt for keys delivered to the buyer.
4. Receipt for copies of the survey delivered to the buyer.

5. Notation as to the assignment of insurance policies.
6. Name of the person to whom the assignment of the escrow deposit was sent.
7. Time at which the next payment on the mortgage is due, and the amount of the payment.
8. Time at which the next payments on taxes and assessments are due.
9. Time at which the notices to tenants were sent.
10. Time at which the rents are due, and amount of the rents.

Other items may be added; those to be included will depend on the nature of the particular transaction.

CHECKING STATEMENT

The statement should be carefully checked with the buyer and the seller, in the presence of each other, and should be signed by both as an indication of its correctness. A copy of the statement should be delivered to both the buyer and the seller.

IMPORTANCE OF STATEMENT

Such a statement is important in two respects: (1) Any questions or misunderstandings will be cleared up at the time the transaction is closed, thus minimizing the possibility of future disputes; (2) the parties will be bound by the statement in the event of a dispute. The statement can be set aside if one of the parties has been induced to sign by misrepresentation, fraud, or duress. Also, if a mistake has been made in computing the amounts due each person and the party benefiting from the mistake refuses voluntarily to correct the mistake, the court, in a proper action, will grant a decree ordering correction.

13

Real estate development, building, management, and appraisal

Introduction

SCOPE OF UNDERTAKING

MANY real estate brokers, in addition to acting as agents for owners in the procuring of buyers for real estate, engage in real estate development, building, management, and appraisal activities. Consequently, all such undertakings will be treated as coming within the scope of the real estate business.

LEGAL PHASES

The legal phases of real estate development, building, management, and appraisal are not well developed; and as a result, there is no unified body of law which applies specifically to these activities. However, each presents legal problems which are characteristic of the undertaking, and the rules of law which are applied to the solution of these problems are of particular importance to those operating in that area.

Real estate development

SUBDIVIDING

The first step in land development is the subdividing of the raw land into smaller tracts preparatory to further development. The subdividing

335

may consist of measuring the lots and placing stakes to indicate the boundaries of the lots; or it may involve the improvement of the tract by laying water and sewer mains, bringing in utilities, paving streets, and building sidewalks. The acquisition of the land involves no special legal problems. The conveying and financing of the purchase of land are discussed in other chapters. There are certain legal requirements and safeguards which the subdivider should consider before he undertakes his project.

GOVERNMENTAL REGULATIONS

If the tract to be subdivided lies within the boundaries of an incorporated city, or if the township or county has adopted a regional plan, the subdivider should carefully check the zoning ordinances of the city, or the regional plan of the township or county, in order to be certain that his proposed use of the land and his planned layout of streets and alleys in no way conflict with established regulations. If he cannot carry out his plan under existing regulations, he may attempt to have the zoning ordinance or regional plan amended, or try to get a waiver of the particular restriction which conflicts with his plan, or alter his plan so that there is no conflict. Usually, a planning board is given the power to waive designated restrictions included in a zoning ordinance or in an adopted land plan.

RESTRICTIVE COVENANTS

If the subdivision is located in an unrestricted area, the subdivider may wish to place restrictions on the use of the land; or if the land is in a restricted area, the subdivider may wish to place restrictions on the use of the land in excess of the restrictions under the zoning ordinance or land plan. This can be accomplished by placing appropriate restrictive provisions in the recorded plat and in the deeds of the lots. Zoning ordinances and restrictive covenants are discussed in Chapter 16.

PLATS AND DEDICATION

In establishing a subdivision, a plat is prepared and recorded. This plat should show the boundaries of each tract or lot; the roads, streets, and alleys therein; and the easements for utilities and public parks or any other rights in the land dedicated to the public. In addition, all restrictions on the use of the land should be clearly stated on this recorded plat. Since this plat will be the basis for future conveyances, the subdivision should be carefully surveyed, and all measurements and notations made by the surveyor should be accurately entered thereon.

In laying out the subdivision, it is a wise plan to establish monuments and make all measurements from these monuments. In the event of controversy as to boundaries, fixed monuments control over measurements.[1] Stone or concrete markers may be used to designate the corners of lots or tracts; and if used, such markers would control over measurements stated on the plat. The use of such markers gives a builder greater assurance that a structure erected on the lot does not encroach on the adjoining lot. When a plat has been recorded and accepted as required by law, the streets, alleys, and other portions of the land which are shown on the plat as being set aside are thereby dedicated to the public and become public property. Under the statutes of some states, such dedicated land is owned by city or other governmental unit in fee simple. Under the statutes or laws of other states the city or governmental unit acquires an easement or a determinable fee. A common-law dedication confers only an easement on the governmental unit. If land is once dedicated to a public use, the public right over such land continues until the plat is vacated or the dedicated property is abandoned. Generally, the statutes of the state set out the procedure which must be followed to effect the vacation of property dedicated to public use. Abandonment occurs when the use for which the property is dedicated becomes impossible of execution or when the objective of the use wholly fails.[2] The public right in dedicated lands is not lost by mere nonuse, and rights in land dedicated to public use cannot be acquired by adverse possession or prescription.[3]

The owners of a tract of land platted it and recorded the plat, which showed a street, Ocean View Drive, abutting the waters of New River Sound. Burkart, who purchased a block of lots abutting Ocean View Drive, claimed that since the plat showed the boundary of his lots to be the center of New River Sound, he had exclusive riparian rights to all lands between Ocean View Drive and the center of New River Sound. The city of Fort Lauderdale claimed the riparian rights for the public. The court held that the city acquired, by virtue of the dedication, an easement in the riparian rights and that Burkart had only the rights of a member of the public.

The court said: "A deed which describes property by reference to a plat makes the plat as much a part of the deed as if it were actually copied in the deed.

[1] *Village of Davidson* v. *Cartwright,* 236 Mich. 249, 210 N.W. 226.

[2] *Adams et al.* v. *Rowles,* 149 Tex. 52, 228 S.W.2d 849.

[3] *City of Billings* v. *Pierce Packing Co. et al.,* 117 Mont. 225, 161 P.2d 636.

"A dedication of lands for public street purposes, absent a clear intent to the contrary, does not divest owner of title, but only subjects the land and title to easement, and if easement is lawfully terminated, title of land remains in dedicator or his successors in interest, free and clear of easement.

"Where a street was laid out so that it was bounded on one side by navigable waters, dedication of street to public operated to relinquish to public, and to merge in the public right, dedicator's individual right of access to open navigable waters in front of dedicator's uplands, and owners of upland were not vested with riparian rights to exclusion of riparian rights accruing to the easement for the dedicated street even though they owned the underlying fee in street." *Burkart* v. *City of Fort Lauderdale,* Fla., 156 So.2d 752 (1963).

Building

PERMITS

If the area in which a builder plans to operate is regulated, the builder will be required, as a general rule, to obtain a building permit from some designated official or board. The procedure for obtaining a permit will be set out in the state statutes or municipal ordinances. There is no uniformity as to the procedure to be followed in obtaining a permit or in the standards established for the granting of a permit. As a general rule, the builder must submit the plans for the proposed building or improvement to the designated officials, who check the plans; and if the proposed building or improvement complies with established zoning ordinances and safety regulations, the permit will be granted. In many localities a building inspector checks the work as it progresses. If any phase of the construction does not comply with established building standards, the building inspector has the power to halt the work and order the defective work corrected or defective materials replaced.

If a builder is operating in an unregulated and unrestricted area, he is free to build as he wishes, being restrained only by the common-law requirement that a person will not be permitted to use his land in such a manner as to create a nuisance.

SURVEYS

Before a builder starts construction, a survey should be made of the tract on which the building is to be erected. An encroachment on adjoining land or the violation of a restriction may result in serious trouble and expense for the builder. A builder is obligated to keep the structure wholly within the boundaries of his own land. If any portion of the building—such as, for example, a bay window, the eaves, or gutters—extends over the boundaries, the builder is guilty of encroaching on the adjoining land and the owner of the adjoining land may remove the overhanging portion of the building or, by court action, force the builder to remove it. If a part of the building is on the adjoining land, the owner of that land has the right to force the removal, unless the cost would be excessive in relation to the injury caused by the encroachment, in which case the person guilty of the encroachment will, in effect, be forced to purchase the land or an easement of right to build on the land on which the encroachment stands. All doubts as to the value of the land are resolved in favor of the innocent party.

VIOLATION OF RESTRICTIONS

If the building violates existing restrictions, such as extending over the setback line or over the side yard line, any interested person may, upon discovering the violation, obtain an injunction which will enjoin the builder from continuing the work and may obtain a court order which will require the builder to alter the structure so that it will comply with the restrictions.

LATERAL SUPPORT

An adjoining landowner is entitled to have his land supported in its natural condition, but a person excavating on his land is not obligated to provide support for a structure erected on adjoining land.[4] If one is excavating on his land and the excavation is such that it will cause no damage to adjoining land in its natural state, but there are structures on the adjoining land the weight of which causes the land to sink, the injured property owner cannot recover damages for injury to his land and buildings resulting from the excavation, unless he can prove that the excavating was done negligently and that if it had been done with reasonable care, his property would not have been damaged.

One contemplating an excavation which he has reasonable ground to believe will cause damage to the land and buildings on the adjoining property owes a duty to give the adjoining property owner notice of the intent to excavate and the general nature of the proposed excavation in time to afford him an opportunity to protect his property.[5] Some state

---

[4] *Prete* v. *Cray,* 49 R.I. 209, 141 A. 609, 59 A.L.R. 1241.

[5] *S. H. Kress & Co., Inc.,* v. *Reaves,* 85 F.2d 915.

statutes and municipal ordinances have been enacted which define the duty of a person excavating on his land to protect the land and buildings of adjoining landowners.

Michelsen owned a lot 22 feet wide and 132 feet long on which there was a building 22 feet wide and 50 feet long. On the rear of the lot was a cesspool. A sewer line ran through the cesspool out to the city main. Upton, who owned the adjoining lot, excavated on his lot to a depth of eight feet below the base of the foundation of Michelsen's building. The excavation was two feet from the Michelsen lot line. Upton did not give Michelsen formal notice of his excavation activities, but Michelsen was present every day and had full knowledge of what was being done. As the result of rain, the cesspool overflowed and caused the soil under Michelsen's building to crumble and the building to collapse. Michelsen sued Upton to recover a judgment for the damage to his building. The court held that Upton was not liable.

Justice Messmore said: "Knowledge or reason to know, of the danger arising from an excavation is necessary to contributory negligence. . . . But when he knows or has reason to know of the danger he is guilty of contributory negligence if he fails to take such precautions as an ordinarily prudent man would take under like circumstances to guard his premises against harm.

"The rule in regard to contributory negligence of the adjoining owner appears to be that where such negligence is the proximate cause of the injury, or where it has materially contributed to the injury, there can be no recovery." *Michelsen* v. *Upton,* 175 Neb. 743, 123 N.W.2d 850 (1963).

TYPES OF BUILDING CONTRACTS

Although building contracts do not differ basically from other types of contracts, they may be classified as to the risks assumed by the parties. The builder may enter into a *general* contract. Under such a contract the contractor obligates himself to construct a building according to certain plans and specifications. He assumes all the risks incident to the fulfillment of the contract. He personally contracts for all labor and materials, and furnishes all tools and equipment necessary for the completion of the work. He is not an agent of the builder. Under a *unit type of operation* the builder acts as his own general contractor and contracts for certain units of the work. He is responsible for the coordination of the work but is not liable as principal for the debts incurred by his contractors for labor and materials.

In some instances the builder may do the work himself or hire the necessary labor. He may purchase the materials and supervise the work, either directly or through an employee, thereby assuming all the risks of the venture.[6]

Management

RELATION OF OWNER AND MANAGER

The real estate manager is the agent of the owner. His legal position is similar to that of the manager of a branch office or branch store. He is a general agent—that is, an agent vested with general power involving the exercise of judgment and discretion. He is usually empowered to transact all business connected with the property entrusted to him. The property manager is generally authorized to negotiate leases, collect rents, make ordinary repairs, keep the premises in a rentable condition, pay taxes, and perform many other additional services. He is a fiduciary and must use his best efforts to further the legitimate interests of his principal. The principal is liable for the acts of his manager done within the scope of the venture.[6]

AUTHORITY AND DUTIES OF MANAGER

The manager may be authorized to keep the property insured and take care of tax matters, such as attending hearings on tax assessments. However, in all his activities, he must comply with the instructions of the owner. The manager cannot lawfully substitute his judgment for the judgment of the principal (owner).[8]

The manager owes a duty to keep accurate accounts and to make an accounting to the owner at such periods as have been agreed upon, and also at any time the principal requests one. The manager owes a duty not to commingle the money of the owner with his own money. He should keep a separate account for money handled for each owner. If he does not keep separate accounts, he makes himself personally liable to the owner for all money of the owner coming into his hands.[9]

---

[6] If labor and material bills are not paid, the laborer or materialman may be entitled to a mechanic's lien on the building. Mechanics' liens on real estate are discussed in Chapter 3. The more detailed aspects of contracts to build are discussed in this chapter.

[7] *Medley* v. *Trenton Investment Co.*, 205 Wis. 30, 236 N.W. 713.

[8] *Granite State Fire Insurance Co.* v. *Mitton et al.*, 98 F. Supp. 706.

[9] *Wangsness* v. *Berdahl*, 69 S.D. 586, 13 N.W.2d 293.

Development Company engaged a rental agent to manage an apartment building. The agent had exclusive management and supervision of the building. The rents were collected by the agent, whose duty it was to pay all bills, render a monthly accounting, and remit any remainder to Development Company. The president of Development Company made periodic inspections of the premises.

The rental agent purchased coal for the heating of the building from Fadeley. The coal was billed to Development Company. The president of Development Company had purchased coal for the building on a few occasions. Development Company refused to pay for the coal, claiming that it was the obligation of the rental agent and that he had no authority to pledge the credit of Development Company. The court held Development Company liable.

Associate Justice Quinn said: "Appellee's [Fadeley's] evidence indicated that they apparently intended to contract with appellant [Development Company] through its agent, and they did offer testimony that Mr. Hamburger [Development Company's president] himself placed several orders. The fact that Mr. Hamburger ordered coal on a few occasions and also made inspections of the premises tends to show that he retained some measure of control over the rental agent's activities, the usual test in determining whether one is an agent or an independent contractor." *National City Development Company v. Fadeley*, Munic. Ct. of App., D.C., 148 A.2d 306 (1959).

Appraisal

NATURE OF APPRAISAL

An appraisal is a valuation or an estimation of the value of property. There are many situations in which an appraisal of property is required by law; but as a general rule, no standards of experience, education, or ability have been set up for the person or persons who make the appraisal. Some such qualification as "freeholder of lawful age" may be required, but little else. Almost all that is asked for is that the person appointed as appraiser act honestly and give his unbiased opinion of the value of the property he is appointed to appraise.

RECENT DEVELOPMENTS

Since about 1930, in the business world, and especially in connection with the appraising of real estate, an effort has been made to develop standards for appraisals and to train persons for the work. As a result, the appraising of real estate has come to be recognized as professional in character; and although it has not as yet reached the status of a profession, there has been much progress in that direction.

LEGAL LIABILITY OF APPRAISER

There is no developed body of law which defines the legal liability of appraisers who hold themselves out as skilled in the art of appraising and who demand a fee for the performance of their services. Such persons would, by analogy, be classed as persons performing professional services, and their liabilities would be analogous to the liabilities of such persons. Since there is a dearth of cases in which the liability of appraisers has been litigated,[10] we shall base our discussion on cases which involve the liability of certified public accountants and others performing similar services.

The person who holds himself out as possessing special skills and who contracts to perform duties requiring the exercise of such skills must possess and exercise that degree of proficiency which is usually possessed and exercised by persons in the community performing such services. Applying this rule to the appraiser, if A, who holds himself out to be an expert appraiser, is employed to make an appraisal, he must possess and exercise the same degree of care and skill in making the appraisal as is possessed and exercised by other appraisers practicing in that locality. If he fails to come up to this standard and, as a result of his lack of care and skill, his appraisal is materially in error and the person employing him acts on the appraisal to his injury, the appraiser will be liable for the resulting injury.[11]

RULES WHICH MAY APPLY

As a general rule, an agent owes the duty of care and skill, and can be held liable for breach of such duty only by his principal. However, if the agent is engaged to perform professional services, if he knows that third persons will deal with his principal in reliance on opinions rendered by him, and if he intentionally renders a false opinion, planning thereby to mislead the third person to his injury, the injured third person can recover a judgment against the agent in an action of deceit for the

[10] *Baxter* v. *Gapp & Co.,* 159 Times Reports N.S. 586.

[11] *City of East Grand Forks* v. *Steele et al.,* 121 Minn. 296, 141 N.W. 181.

damage he has suffered. The courts have extended the liability of the professional agent to third persons who have relied on the agent's report to the principal in situations where the agent has been guilty of gross negligence, in that he has failed to follow even the most elemental rules of his profession in the performance of his duties. The courts have held the agent liable to the injured third person on a theory of constructive fraud.[12]

An FHA appraiser reported that property which Neustadt was contemplating buying was eligible for a mortgage at the appraised value of $22,750; and in reliance on this appraisal, Neustadt purchased the property. The appraisal had been negligently made. The house was not properly constructed, and it cost Neustadt $8,000 to remedy the defects. Neustadt sued the United States to recover a judgment for damages suffered as the result of the negligent appraisal made by its agent. The court of appeals granted Neustadt a judgment.

Circuit Judge Soper said: "It is abundantly clear that the government owed a specific duty to the plaintiff [Neustadt] in this case even though there was no contractual relationship between them. The situation is similar to that considered by Judge Cardozo in Glanzer v. Sheppard, where it was held that a public weigher, who was employed by the seller of goods and who overstated the weight of the merchandise, was liable in damages to the buyer who bought them on the faith of the weigher's certificate. It was pointed out in the opinion that the defendant was not held merely for careless words but for careless performance of the act of weighing.

"So in the pending case, the wrongful conduct complained of does not consist merely or chiefly in the communication to plaintiffs [Neustadt] whereby they were notified that the Housing Commission had appraised the property for mortgage purposes at $22,750, but primarily in the negligent appraisal itself whereby they were led to pay more for the property than it was worth.

(NOTE: The judgment in this case was reversed. The Supreme Court, Mr. Justice Whittaker, held that the claim of the home purchaser [Neustadt] arose out of the misrepresentation and hence was not actionable against the United States under the Federal Tort Claims Act).[13] *United States* v. *Neustadt*, 281 F.2d 596 (1960).

The contract to build

A contract to build does not differ in its basic requirements from any other type of contract. That is, the parties to such a contract, if it is

---

[12] *Ultramares Corporation* v. *Touche*, 225 N.Y. 170, 174 N.E. 441.

[13] *United States* v. *Neustadt*, 366 U.S. 696, 81 S. Ct. 1294.

to be valid, must reach a mutual agreement which is supported by consideration; they must have capacity to contract; and the objective of the contract must be legal. However, the nature of the relationship created and the scope of the rights and duties of the parties to a contract to build give rise to many special legal problems, a knowledge of which is important to anyone who engages in such activity.

A person who wishes to erect a building need not necessarily enter into a contract to build. He may proceed in several different ways. He may, for instance, prepare his plans and buy the materials needed and do the work himself, or he may engage the services of laborers and direct their work; in either case, no contract to build will be involved. Ordinarily, however, the person who wishes to build will contract with a builder to construct a building according to plans which have been agreed upon by the owner and the builder. Usually, in such a situation a simple contract to build is drafted and executed by the parties. In major building operations, however, an architect will, as a general rule, be employed to draft plans and specifications; and the person who wishes to build will contract with a builder to erect such a structure according to the prepared plans and specifications. The contract will, in most instances, define and set out in some detail all the items connected with such work. A person who wishes to build may use other procedures; but such procedures will, as a matter of course, be combinations of those mentioned above.

SCOPE OF DISCUSSION

The scope of this work does not permit a detailed study of all combinations of building contracts. Consequently, we shall use as a basis for our discussion of contracts to build the situation in which an architect is employed to prepare the plans and specifications and to supervise the work, and in which the contract to build is let to a contractor, who furnishes a performance bond protecting the owner, laborers, and materialmen. During the discussion, brief reference will be made to some of the more important variations from this procedure.

The Architect

NATURE OF SERVICES RENDERED BY ARCHITECT

The first step to be taken in a major building project is the preparation of the plans and specifications by an architect. Usually, he will make preliminary sketches, followed later on by a draft of more detailed plans. He will be expected to determine the types and strength of materials to be used in the building and to answer the many technical questions which arise during the course of the planning of the building. Generally, the architect, or a fellow architect working under his supervision, will supervise the actual construction of the building. As a matter of fact, the architect performs the professional services connected with the building operation.[14]

The practice of architecture is regulated in all except a few states. In general, the regulatory statutes of the several states have as their objective the protection of the life, health, and safety of the public. In states having such statutes, a person wishing to engage in the practice of architecture must have had certain formal training, usually must have graduated from an architectural school, must have had some experience, and must pass an examination. Such a person, on qualifying, is granted a license to practice architecture in the state issuing the license.

A license to practice architecture in one state does not give a person the right to practice in any other state. Such a license is personal and cannot be granted to a corporation. And if a partnership wishes to practice architecture, all the members of the firm must be licensed.

CONTRACT OF EMPLOYMENT

The contract of employment of an architect differs in no material respect from any other contract of employment. The contract need not be in writing and signed by the parties, unless, by its terms, the employment is to continue for more than one year.[15] However, a contract in writing, defining the duties of the architect and the compensation he is to receive, should be drafted and signed by the parties. Failure of the architect and the owner to discuss the employment, to reach an agreement, and to make a written record of the agreement, signed by both parties, may result in later misunderstanding, dispute, and expensive litigation.

AUTHORITY OF ARCHITECT

An architect acts primarily as an employee or as an agent of the owner. He may, however, be called upon in some instances to decide a dispute,

---

[14] *Payne* v. *De Vaughn,* 77 Cal. App. 399, 246 P. 1069.
[15] *Lamoreaux et al.* v. *Wiseman et al.,* 136 Minn. 207, 161 N.W. 504.

in which event he will act as an impartial judge. Since the architect is to act as employee and agent of the owner, the duties, authority, and power of the architect should be carefully defined in the contract of employment. The capacity in which the architect acts will depend on the services he is to perform. If he is employed only to prepare preliminary sketches or plans and specifications, the relationship between him and the owner will be that of employee and employer, and he will owe a duty to follow the general instructions of the owner. He would not, however, be obligated to follow instructions which would result in the planning of a building which would be unsafe or in violation of regulatory statutes.

The architect may be employed to superintend the construction of the building and, in some instances, to serve as clerk of the work. In performing such services, he will be acting as agent of the owner. It will be his duty, as superintendent, to check the work as it progresses and make certain that the contractor is complying with the terms of the contract and erecting a building in accordance with the plans and specifications. If he is acting as clerk of the work, he will be on the job at all times during the construction of the building. He will inspect all materials that go into the building and keep a constant check on the work as it progresses.

As agent of the owner, the architect does not have general authority to bind his principal, but he does have authority to do whatever is reasonably necessary to carry the work to completion.[16] Unless the contract of employment confers on the architect such authority, the architect does not have the authority to change or alter the plans or specifications in any material respect.[17] He does have the authority to order minor changes which may be necessary because of minor errors in the plans or specifications.

When the architect is employed to superintend the work, he has implied authority to inspect the materials brought onto the premises by the contractor for incorporation into the building and to reject unfit materials.[18] He also has implied authority to direct the work, and to order the contractor to correct work which is not performed in a proper manner and in accordance with the plans and specifications.

---

[16] *Davis* v. *Bush & Lane Piano Co.,* 124 Ore. 585, 265 P. 417.

[17] *Nick Warisse Baking Co.* v. *National Concrete Construction Co.,* 218 Ky. 422, 291 S.W. 356.

[18] *Stimson Mill Co.* v. *Feigenson Engineering Co. et al.,* 100 Wash. 172, 170 P. 573.

348   Law of the real estate business

As a general rule, the architect is given authority to decide disputes arising during the course of the work. If the architect is employed to superintend the construction, authority to settle controversies would be implied, even though such authority is not expressly conferred on him by the contract of employment. The architect, in settling disputes, must act as an impartial judge, favoring neither the owner nor the contractor.

ASSIGNMENT OF CONTRACT AND DELEGATION OF AUTHORITY

The architect performs a personal service. He is employed because of his artistic abilities, his skill in his profession, and his reputation for honesty and fair dealing. Since the contract of employment with the architect is a contract for personal service, it is not assignable by either party to the contract without the consent of the other party.[19]

Likewise, since the services to be performed involve the exercise of personal taste and skill, and since the architect is employed because of his reputation for honesty and fair dealing, he cannot delegate any of his authority except that which is clerical in nature and does not involve the exercise of personal judgment or skill.[20]

If a firm of architects is employed, any member of the organization is authorized to perform the required services, unless the contract expressly provides that a particular member shall do so. Assistants may be employed to aid in drawing the plans and preparing the specifications, but such assistants must work under the supervision of the architect.

An architect would not have implied authority to employ another architect to superintend the work, nor would he have implied authority to employ a clerk of the work.

Huggins, as general contractor, had contracted to build a school building. He let the subcontract for the laying of the tile on the kitchen floor to Atlanta Tile and Marble Co. (hereinafter referred to as Atlanta). The subcontract provided that the tile work done by Atlanta would be subject to the approval or disapproval of "the architect." The contract named A. Thomas Bradbury as architect. Ralph Slay, an architect in the employ of Bradbury, inspected the tile work done by Atlanta and disapproved it. Huggins then had the tile floor torn out and relaid by another contractor. Huggins sued Atlanta to recover the cost of tearing out and relaying the tile floor. Atlanta set up as a defense

---

[19] *Menenberg* v. *Carl R. Sams Realty Co., Inc., et al.,* 337 Mich. 143, 59 N.W.2d 125.

[20] *Smith et al.* v. *Board of Education of City of Liberal,* 115 Kan. 155, 222 P. 101.

that the named architect, Bradbury, did not inspect and disapprove its work. Judgment for Atlanta, and Huggins appealed. The judgment was affirmed. Chief Judge Felton said: "An architect is selected and agreed upon to exercise his personal skill, discretion and judgment and his duty to exercise such skill, judgment and discretion cannot be delegated. 'The person agreed upon by the parties to pass upon the work has no right to delegate his authority to another, and if he attempts to do so, the decision of such other person is not conclusive on the parties, unless they agree to such substitution.' Under the contract the defendant had the right to have its work passed on by A. Thomas Bradbury personally and Mr. Bradbury could not delegate his duties as architect to another so as to bind the defendant without his consent such as would amount to a novation of the contract." *Huggins* v. *Atlanta Tile and Marble Co.,* 98 Ga. App. 597, 106 S.E.2d 191 (1958).

OWNERSHIP OF PLANS AND SPECIFICATIONS

In the absence of any provision in the employment contract to the contrary, the courts have held that the plans and specifications are the property of the owner, and that he—not the architect—is entitled to them.[21] If the architect refuses to deliver the plans and specifications to the owner, the architect is not entitled to his fee. The contractor has the right to possession and use of the plans and specifications during the execution of the work, but he acquires no ownership rights in them.

ARCHITECT'S DUTIES AND LIABILITIES

Although the architect is employed by the owner and in many respects acts as agent of the owner, he also, in some situations, acts as an independent judge. Since the architect is employed to perform professional services, he is obligated to bring to the work the degree of care and skill possessed by architects who practice the profession in that locality. He must possess and exercise a degree of skill which is equal to the average skill possessed and exercised by those engaged in the profession. He owes a duty to apply his skill, ability, judgment, and taste reasonably and without delay or neglect. If the architect is negligent, either in the preparation of plans and specifications or in the supervision of the work, and the owner or contractor is injured as the direct result of the architect's negligence, he will be held liable for the resulting harm.[22]

---

[21] *Hutton* v. *School City of Hammond,* 194 Ind. 212, 142 N.E. 427.

[22] *Palmer et al.* v. *Brown,* 127 Cal. App.2d 44, 273 P.2d 306.

An architect who is supervising the work owes the owner a duty of good faith and loyalty. As the agent of the owner, he must not put himself in a position in which his personal interests in any way conflict with the duties he owes to his principal, the owner. The architect should have no pecuniary interest in the building contract, nor should he act as agent for both the owner and the contractor unless he makes a full disclosure of his interest or dual employment and all parties having an interest in the work consent to the arrangement.

In the preparation of the plans and specifications the architect acts as an employee of the owner. As such, he owes a duty to follow the general instructions of the owner and to perform the work in a "good and workmanlike manner." He owes a duty to complete the work within the time stipulated or to complete it within a reasonable time if no time is set. He will be liable to the owner if, through his negligence and neglect, the work is delayed unnecessarily and, as the result of such delay, the owner suffers a loss.[23] In the preparation of the plans and specifications the owner owes a duty to cooperate with the architect, giving him such information as he needs and such other assistance as he requires to enable him to proceed with the work. If the owner refuses or neglects to cooperate in a reasonable manner with the architect and as a result the completion of the work is delayed, the architect cannot be held liable for such delay.

If the architect fails to perform his work up to the standards of the profession and as the result of his directions the owner suffers a loss, the architect will be liable to the owner for the loss suffered. He is not an insurer of his own work; he does not guarantee that the plans and specifications which he prepares will be perfect; nor does he, if he supervises the work, assure the owner that he will detect every defect in the construction of the building.[24] He does, however, obligate himself to fulfill his duty of loyalty and good faith, and to exercise care and skill in the preparation of the plans and specifications and in the supervision of the work.

Smith, wishing to build a house, employed Goff, a licensed architect, to furnish "complete architectural services, including preliminary plans, working drawings and specifications, and periodic supervision." Goff prepared the plans and specifications, but the lowest bid for the erection of the house was $16,000, which Smith felt was more than he could afford. After considerable negotiation and revision of the plans and specifications, the contractor agreed to furnish

[12] *Giffels & Vallet, Inc.* v. *Edw. C. Levy Co.*, 337 Mich. 177, 58 N.W.2d 899.

[24] *Surf Realty Corp.* v. *Standing et al.*, 195 Va. 431, 78 S.E.2d 901.

all materials and perform all work for $10,500. The contract provided that the work was to be performed in a good and workmanlike manner.

When the house was completed, the Smiths moved in, but they soon began to discover defects in the work and brought this suit against Goff, as architect, and the contractor to recover damages. The jury found for Goff, and judgment was rendered accordingly. Smith appealed, and the court of appeals affirmed the judgment.

The court said: "The issue so far as the architects are concerned was whether they used that degree of professional care required of them in the origination of the plans and specifications and in the supervision of the construction. The court instructed the jury on this issue. The use of various materials in the building which were not the same as those in the original specifications presented the question of the architects' professional judgment as to the suitability of the material for the purpose. The same is true concerning the methods employed 'to maintain the initial effect of the building.' So also, concerning the architects' supervision of construction. Architects are only required to exercise ordinary professional skill and diligence and to conform to accepted architectural standards; their contracts do not guarantee perfect plans or satisfactory results. Architects are only liable for failure to exercise reasonable care and professional skill in the preparation and execution of their plans according to their contract. Here the contract did not call for the use of any certain materials in the preparation of the plans by the architects. They were required to use their professional judgment. This issue was properly submitted to the jury by the court's instruction which stated that the law required that the architects perform their contractual duties with 'ordinary care and diligence.' This was the only issue made by the evidence as to them, for it was undisputed that architects furnish 'complete architectural services including preliminary plans, working drawings and specifications . . .' as well as '. . . revisions in his plans made necessary by excessive costs. . . .' The jury verdict is conclusive on the controverted issue." *Smith* v. *Goff*, Okla., 325 P.2d 1061 (1958).

COMPENSATION

As a general rule, the contract of employment will stipulate the method of compensating the architect, and the amount and time of payment. He may be employed on a per diem basis or on an hourly basis. A payment of a percentage of the cost of the work is the most widely used method of compensating architects. The percentage paid will usually depend on the nature of the work and on the amount of time the architect is required to devote to its supervision.

A variation of this method of payment is the fee-plus-cost method, under which the architect is reimbursed for all his costs and expenses, and is paid a fixed fee or a percentage of the cost of the work for his services.

Under the statutes of those states which, as a means of protecting the public, require a person to obtain a license to practice the profession of architecture, a person who is not licensed cannot collect fees for services rendered as an architect.[25]

If an architect guarantees that the construction of a building for which he prepares the plans and specifications will not cost more than a stated sum, and the planned building cannot be constructed for the guaranteed sum, he is not entitled to compensation for the preparation of the plans and specifications.

If the architect fails to perform his obligations under the contract of employment and, as the result of such failure, the owner is not benefited by the services rendered, the architect will not be entitled to compensation. However, if the owner accepts part performance on the part of the architect and is benefited thereby, the owner will be required to compensate the architect on the basis of the amount the owner has been benefited by the services performed by the architect.

Lien

Under the statutes of some of the states the architect is entitled to a mechanic's lien on the real estate for money due him for services rendered in the iprovement of the real estate. Mechanics' liens on real estate are discussed in Chapter 3.

Checklist for owner-architect contract

The relation of architect and owner is one of trust and confidence. To accomplish the best results for all persons concerned—owner, architect, and contractor—the owner and architect should discuss all the phases of their relationship openly and frankly, and be certain that each understands the service to be performed by the architect and the compensation to be paid him. The agreement for the employment of the architect should be in writing and signed by both parties, in order to avoid misunderstanding.

The following points should be considered and, if pertinent, should be provided for in the contract of employment:

---

[25] *F. F. Bollinger Co.* v. *Widmann Brewing Corp.*, 339 Pa. 289, 14 A.2d 81.

1. Date of the agreement.
2. Names and business addresses and residence addresses of the architect and the owner.
3. Description and location of the building to be erected.
4. The services to be performed by the architect—for example, preliminary sketches, working drawings, specifications, special drawings, large-scale drawings, detail drawings, aid in letting contract, issuance of architect's certificate, supervision of the work, and other special services to be performed by the architect—should be carefully stated in the contract.
5. Provision for employment of supervising architect, clerk of the work, engineer, or other skilled persons to aid the architect. By whom they are to be selected and by whom paid.
6. Provisions as to who is to furnish the survey of the building site; information concerning grades and lines of streets and adjoining buildings; information as to building restrictions, zoning ordinances, easements, and so forth; and information as to sewer, water, gas, electricity, and other utilities. Who is to have tests made, such as test borings, and chemical and mechanical tests of materials; and who is to pay the costs of making the surveys, of obtaining the required information, and of making the tests.
7. The making of preliminary estimates.
8. Reimbursement of the architect for expenses incurred by him and his assistants. The contract should set out in detail the expenses of the architect—for example, cost of transportation, cost of reproduction of drawings, cost of service of engineers employed on the work, payments made to special consultants, and so forth—which are to be charged to and paid by the owner.
9. Compensation of the architect. The method of compensating the architect should be clearly stated in the contract. It should also be definitely stated at what time or at what stages of the work the architect is to be paid and the amount or percentage of his fee which he is to receive at each payment date. If the architect is to be paid a percentage of the cost of the work, or if he is to be paid on the basis of a fee plus a percentage of the cost of the work, the method of determining the cost of the work should be stated in the contract.
10. Payment for extra work or special services. The contract should provide for payment of the architect for special or extra work or for services caused by changes made in the plans or specifications,

or by partial destruction of the building which would necessitate the drafting and preparing of additional plans and specifications.

11. Provision as to who would own the plans and specifications.
12. Assignment of the contract of employment.
13. Arbitration clause. If the contract of employment is to be performed in a state which has adequate arbitration statutes, a provision for the submission of all disputes arising under the employment contract is recommended. The clause should provide that the arbitration shall be carried on in accordance with the procedure recommended either by the American Arbitration Association or by the American Institute of Architects.

The contractor

LETTING THE CONTRACT TO BUILD

If a person wishes to let a contract to build, he will need to select a contractor. He may contact one he knows or one who has been recommended to him and negotiate the contract with him, or he may contact several contractors and request each to submit a bid for the job. If a governmental unit wishes to build, it will advertise for bids and let the contract to the "lowest and best" bidder. A similar practice is frequently followed by private owners—corporations, partnerships, or individuals—if the work to be done involves a subtantial outlay of money. Large developers may employe, on a full-time basis, architects, engineers, managers, and the necessary skilled and semiskilled workers whom they need for their construction, and purchase in wholesale quantities the materials needed and proceed to erect the buildings (usually homes) and sell the finished product. This type of operation is not based on a building contract.

If the job is to be let on bids, such bids will, as a general rule, be based on the plans and specifications prepared by the architect. The owner may also include with the plans and specifications a copy of the contract which the successful bidder will be required to sign, or he may state in the invitation that some standard form of contract will be used. Unless the owner advertises or states that the contract will be let to the low bidder without reservation, the bid is an offer; there is no contract until the owner notifies the bidder that his bid is accepted. If the owner, in attempting to accept a bid, alters in any material respect the terms of the bid, the bid is thereby rejected, and no contract ensues.[26] However, if the bidder consents to the change, a contract will result.

LEGALITY OF CONTRACT

A building contract is void if its execution requires the performance of an illegal act. For example, a contract to build a structure which would be in violation of a valid regulatory statute or city ordinance would be illegal and void.[27] However, a contract to construct a building which would not be in violation of any statute or ordinance, but which the owner intends to use in the operation of an illegal business, would not be illegal.[28] If the contract is illegal, the contractor, as a general rule, can recover nothing.

MISTAKE

When the contractor submits a bid and it is accepted, a contract results, and the contractor is obligated to perform. He should therefore use great care in preparing his bid, as he cannot, as a general rule, escape liability on the ground that he made a mistake in his computation. Under some circumstances, a bidder may be granted relief from a unilateral mistake.

If the mistake is not the result of negligence but is clerical and the bidder did not have a reasonable opportunity to check the figures, due to the circumstance under which the bid was made, relief will generally be granted,[29] unless rights of third parties have intervened and the parties cannot be restored to their original positions. In granting such relief, the bidder who has made the mistake may be required to stand any costs incident thereto.[30] Furthermore, an owner will not be permitted to take advantage of a mistake which he knows, or should know, has been made. For instance, if several bids are submitted and one of them is materially less than the others, the courts have held that the inadequacy of the bid is sufficient to put the owner on notice that an error has been made in preparing the bid.

[26] *R. J. Daum Construction Co.* v. *Child et al.,* 122 Utah 194, 247 P.2d 817.

[27] *Eastern Expanded Metal Co.* v. *Webb Granite & Construction Co.,* 195 Mass. 356, 81 N.E. 251.

[28] *Thomas* v. *Owens et al.,* 206 Okla. 50, 241 P.2d 1114.

[29] *Graham et al.,* v. *Clyde, Fla.,* 61 So.2d 656.

[30] *School District of Scottsbluff* v. *Olson Construction Co. et al.,* 153 Neb. 451, 45 N.W.2d 164.

Mistakes made by an architect or engineer in computing the amount due the contractor at the various stages of the work will be corrected.

The city of Portland advertised for bids on a sewage disposal project. Rushlite Auto Sprinkler Co. (hereinafter referred to as Rushlite) submitted a bid of $429,444.20 accompanied by its certified check for $21,472.21, which was to be retained by the city if Rushlite failed or refused to enter into a contract for the work. When the bids were opened, it was discovered that the next high bid was $671,600, or $242,155.80 more than Rushlite's bid. Rushlite immediately notified the city that it had omitted an item for steel of $99,225.68. Rushlite requested that its bid be withdrawn and its certified check be returned. The city refused the request and cashed the check. Rushlite brought suit to recover the amount of the check. Rushlite's bid was compiled by an adequate staff of estimators. The trial court granted Rushlite a judgment, and the city appealed. The judgment was affirmed.

Judge Rossman said: "We believe that it is manifest from the evidence that the difference between the plaintiff's bid and the next high was so large that all of those concerned with the undertaking were rendered uneasy. The plaintiff's officers at once returned to their work sheets, fearing that they must have committed a mistake. The City Engineer, according to his own words, found the variation so great that it 'scared us to death.' . . . The bid aroused suspicion in all minds. We think that the difference appraised the City that a mistake had probably been made.

"We believe that in this State an offer and acceptance are deemed to effect a meeting of the minds, even though the offeror made a material mistake in computing his offer, provided the acceptor was not aware of the mistake and had no reason to suspect it. But if the offeree knew of the mistake, and if it was basic, or if the circumstances were such that he, as a reasonable man, should have inferred that a basic mistake was made, a meeting of the minds does not occur. . . .

"It is unnecessary to state once more that the proof in cases of this kind must possess a high degree of cogency. The bidder must prove, not only that he made a material mistake, but also that the offeree was aware of it. In this case, the facts which we have mentioned are unchallenged.

"It is our belief that although the plaintiff alone made the mistake, the City was aware of it. Where it accepted the plaintiff's bid, with knowledge of the mistake, it sought to take an unconscionable advantage of an inadvertent error. Equity is always prepared to grant relief from such situations." *Rushlite Auto Sprinkler Co.* v. *City of Portland,* 189, Ore. 194, 219 P.2d 732 (1952).

INTERPRETATION OF CONTRACT

The contract to build should be prepared with care. Both parties are bound by the contract as drafted. Although the terms of the contract may be modified or canceled by the mutual agreement of the parties, neither party, in the event of a dispute and lawsuit, will be permitted to offer parol (oral) evidence to show that the terms of the contract were intended to be different than those expressed in the writing; nor will either party be permitted to offer parol evidence to add terms to the contract, unless it is clear from a reading of the contract that it is incomplete.

It is the duty of the judge to interpret a written instrument. And the judge, in interpreting a contract, will read the contract in its entirety and give the language its ordinary meaning. Technical words will be given their technical meaning, unless it is clear that such was not intended.

In the building trade, certain words have acquired a special meaning; when such words are used in a contract to build, they will be interpreted according to their accepted meaning in the trade.

As a general rule, when the contract to build refers to the plans and specifications, the court will hold that they become a part of the contract. A well-drafted contract to build will state expressly that the plans and specifications are incorporated into and become a part of the contract.

STIPULATIONS FOR ALTERATIONS AND EXTRAS

The terms of a contract will be enforced by the courts unless they have been induced by misrepresentation or fraud, or unless they are illegal. If the owner and contractor include in the building contract a provision stipulating that the owner will not be held liable for any additional costs resulting from alterations or extra work ordered unless the alteration or extra work is authorized by a written order signed by the owner, such provision will be held to be valid and will be enforced by the courts.[31]

As a general rule, such a provision in a building contract cannot be canceled or waived by the acts of the supervising architect or engineer, or by the clerk of the work.[32] The parties to the contract may, however, by mutual agreement change or cancel any of the terms of the contract, including stipulations regarding alterations or extra work. A party to a contract may, expressly or by his conduct, waive rights granted him by the contract. If an owner orally orders alterations or extra work and permits the contractor to carry out the order and then refuses to pay

---

[31] *Brandolini* v. *Grand Lodge of Pennsylvania Order of Sons of Italy in America,* 358 Pa. 303, 56 A.2d 662.

[32] *Van Buskirk et al.* v. *Board of Education of Passaic Twp., Morris County,* 78 N.J.L. 650, 75 A. 909.

for the extra costs, the courts will hold that the owner has waived his right to set up the lack of an order in writing and will hold him liable for the reasonable value of the alteration or extras in case there is no agreement as to the amount to be paid.[33]

Broderick entered into a contract with Moorehead under which Moorehead agreed to erect a warehouse for Broderick. During the course of the construction the plans were changed, and the structure actually erected was an automobile paint shop. The contract provided that any extras must be authorized in writing. Many changes were made in the plans and many extras added without written authorization.

Broderick failed to pay for the extras, and this suit was brought to impose a mechanic's lien on the property. Broderick set up as a defense that the extras were not authorized in writing. The court held that the requirement for written authority had been waived, and Broderick appealed. The judgment was affirmed.

Judge Kanner said: "The contract we are here considering specified that any extras must have been authorized in writing by the owners. This we recognize as valid. We also recognize, however, that such a provision may be waived; and a waiver of the provision may be established by the subsequent course of dealing between the parties. Ordinarily, a written agreement cannot be abrogated nor modified by executory or parol agreement; but if the parol agreement has been accepted and acted upon by the parties, this rule does not apply. 'Extras,' by statutory definition, consist of labor or services performed or materials furnished for the improvement of real property authorized by the owner in addition to labor, services, or materials covered by a previous contract between the same parties. In the case here considered, the testimony, supported in part by the exhibits, amply establishes that during construction of the building there were many changes in the plans authorized by the owners for extras incorporated in the construction, although these authorizations were not made in writing by the owners." *Broderick* v. *Overhead Door Company of Fort Lauderdale, Inc.,* Fla., 117 So.2d 240 (1959).

LIABILITY OF PARTIES

If either party to a building contract fails to perform his obligations under the contract, he will be liable to the injured party for any loss which is suffered as the direct result of the breach. Also, if the architect fails to perform his obligations, or is negligent or dishonest in the performance of his duties, with the result that either the owner or the contractor suffers a loss, the architect will be liable to the aggrieved party.

---

[33] *Frank T. Hickey, Inc.* v. *Los Angeles Jewish Community Council,* 128 Cal. App.2d 676, 276 P.2d 52.

If a principal contractor subcontracts units of the work, he owes a duty to coordinate the different units so that the subcontractor will not be caused unnecessary delay in the performance of his work. If the principal contractor fails to make such a coordination or fails to perform his part of the work, and the subcontractor is delayed in his work and thereby suffers a loss, the general contractor may be held liable to such subcontractor for the loss suffered.[34]

If the owner acts as his own general contractor and lets units of the work to different contractors, he can protect himself from the liability for failure to coordinate the work of the unit contractors by including in each unit contract a provision to the effect that each unit contractor shall be responsible to the other unit contractors for damage to work or persons, or for loss caused by neglect or by failure to finish the work at the proper time. Such a provision is a third-party beneficiary provision, and an injured unit contractor would have a right to bring suit against the unit contractor whose conduct or failure to perform was the direct cause of the loss.

The contractor is not liable for damage to or destruction of the building by fire, flood, and so forth, after the building is completed. Nor is he liable for damage to the building if such damage results from some weakness in the structure, from fault in the soil, or from similar causes.[35] The contractor is not a judge of the sufficiency of the specifications and is not liable if the completed structure is defective because of inadequacies in the plans and specifications.

The contractor does owe a duty to inspect materials delivered on the job and to reject faulty materials, but he is not liable if the defects are such that they would not be discovered by an ordinary inspection. Unless the contractor expressly warrants the work or specifically undertakes to produce a building of specified quality, he is not liable if he performs the job in a workmanlike manner in accordance with good usage and accepted practices in the community, and if he follows the plans and specifications.[36] The contractor is liable if he fails to follow plans and specifications and the deviation results in defective work, or if he is negligent in the performance of the work.

The owner is liable for his failure to make payments for the work

[34] *Guerini Stone Company* v. *P. J. Carlin Construction Company,* 248 U.S. 334, 39 S. Ct. 102.

[35] *Puget Sound National Bank of Tacoma* v. *C. B. Lauch Const. Co.,* 73 Idaho 68, 245 P.2d 800.

[36] *Mann* v. *Clowser et al.,* 190 Va. 887, 59 S.E. 2d 78.

when due, and unreasonable delay in making payments will justify the contractor in abandoning the work. The owner does not guarantee the sufficiency of the plans and specifications. If the owner is to furnish materials, he is not liable for defects in the materials furnished.

If the work is let to several contractors and a provision is inserted in each contract to the effect that each contractor shall be responsible to the others for damage to work or persons, or for loss caused by neglect or by failure to finish the work at the proper time, the owner will not be liable for damages resulting from the negligence of the several contractors.

As a general rule, the architect is not a party to the contract to build; ordinarily, he is not liable if either the contractor or the owner breaches the contract. However, if the architect is superintendent of the work and is given the authority to decide certain matters arising during the course of the work or to issue architect's certificates authorizing payment for work done, he will be held liable if, through collusion or fraud, he favors one party over the other or issues a certificate when it should not be issued. The architect is not liable for honest errors in judgment.

PERFORMANCE OF CONTRACT TO BUILD

If there are no specific provisions in the contract to build setting-up standards of performance, the contractor must perform the work up to the general standards for such work in the community.

The contract may provide that the work shall be done to the satisfaction of the owner. If the contract does so provide and the work is such that it involves fancy, taste, or judgment—as, for example, the painting of murals—the owner will not have to accept the work if he is honestly dissatisfied. If the work is such that it involves only operative fitness or mechanical utility, the owner will have to accept the work if it would be satisfactory to a reasonable person.[37]

Contracts to build provide frequently that payment of the installments due on the contract shall be made only on the production of an architect's or engineer's certificate which would state the amount due, and that the work performed was satisfactory. The contract may also contain a provision requiring, before the final payment is made, the production of a certificate by the architect or engineer which would certify that the work has been completed according to plans and specifications. If the contract

---

[37] *Erikson* v. *Ward,* 266 Ill. 259, 107 N.E. 593.

to build contains such a provision, the contractor must obtain the required certificate before he is entitled to payment. If the contract sets out the form or content of the certificate, the certificate presented must fulfill these requirements.

The certificate of the architect or engineer is conclusive as to the rights of the parties, if the contract so provides, unless the architect or engineer has exceeded his authority in issuing the certificate.

In all cases in which payment is to be made on the production of an architect's or engineer's certificate, the architect or engineer must act honestly and must exercise his honest judgment concerning the matters to which he certifies. If the owner prevents the issuing of the certificate, or if the certificate is collusively, fraudulently, arbitrarily, or capriciously withheld, the contractor will be allowed to recover without the production of such a certificate.[38] Likewise, if a certificate is collusively or fradulently issued when the contractor is not entitled to a certificate, the owner is not required to make payment on the production of the certificate.

James I. Barnes Construction Company (hereinafter referred to as Barnes) contracted to build a school building for Washington Township of Stark County (hereinafter referred to as School) for the contract price of $143,878, payment to be made on the production of an engineer's certificate issued by Zechiel. When the work was completed, the county commissioners inspected it; at that time, they discussed defects in the building and said that they would not accept the floors because they were composed of poured concrete and were very uneven. Work was done on the floors to improve them; and subsequently, Zechiel issued to Barnes a final engineer's certificate. During the course of the work, Zechiel had failed to make required tests; the walls had cracks about every 20 lineal feet, the roof leaked, the glazed tile wall was improperly finished, and the work had not been done in a workmanlike manner. School refused to make the final payment, and Barnes sued. On the trial, Barnes introduced the contract and the engineer's certificate as proof that he was entitled to the final payment. The trial court held that Barnes was not entitled to the final payment, and he appealed. The judgment was affirmed.

Judge Myers said: "It is a rule of law in Indiana that when a contract provides that work shall be done to the satisfaction, approval or acceptance of an architect or engineer, he is thereby constituted a sole arbitrator by the parties, who are bound by his decision in the absence of fraud or such gross mistakes as to imply bad faith or a failure to exercise honest judgment. His decision is not conclusive to the extent that it cannot be reviewed by a court. It is only *prima facie* correct, and the burden is upon the other parties to show fraud or mistake.

---

[38] *Haugen et al.* v. *Raupach et al.*, 43 Wash.2d 147, 260 P.2d 340.

"In our opinion there was sufficient evidence, together with all reasonable inferences deducible therefrom for the jury to have found that the engineer's certificate was not issued after the exercise of honest judgment by the engineer, or was issued as the result of gross mistake of fact on the part of the engineer." *James I. Barnes Construction Company* v. *Washington Township,* Ind. App., 184 N.E.2d 763 (1962).

STAGES OF PERFORMANCE

The courts recognize three stages of performance of a contract:

1. SATISFACTORY PERFORMANCE.   A contract to build according to plans and specifications can hardly be performed without some slight deviation from the plans and specifications. If the contractor has performed the work up to the accepted standards for that type of building in that community, he has rendered satisfactory performance and is entitled to recover the contract price.

2. SUBSTANTIAL PERFORMANCE.   If the contractor has made an honest effort to perform the work according to the terms of the contract but the result is not up to accepted standards, yet the defects are such that they do not weaken the structure, and the building will serve, in a reasonable manner, the needs of the owner, the owner will be required to accept the building. However, he will be entitled to a reduction in the contract price to compensate for the defective performance.[39]

If the faults can be corrected without unreasonable cost, the measure of damages will be the cost of remedying the defects. If the building would have to be reconstructed, or substantially reconstructed, the measure of damages would be the difference between the value of the building as constructed and its value had it been constructed according to the terms of the contract.

3. PARTIAL PERFORMANCE.   If the contractor abandons the work before completion, or if he completes the work but his performance is materially defective, he will have partially performed the contract. The nature of a contract to build is such that the owner, as a general rule, will derive some benefit from partial performance. The work cannot be returned to the contractor. If the contractor has only partially performed the contract, he cannot recover in a suit on the contract. However, he will be entitled to some payment for the benefits conferred on the owner by his partial performance. As a general rule, the amount to which the contractor is entitled is the contract price less the cost of completing the work in compliance with the terms of the contract.

---

[39] *Nees et al.* v. *Weaver,* 222 Wis. 492, 269 N.W. 266.

DEATH OR INCAPACITATING ILLNESS OF CONTRACTOR

If the contractor is prevented by sickness or death from completing the performance, recovery may be had, as a general rule, for the value of the services rendered. Likewise, if the contract calls for the remodeling or repair of a building and, during the course of the work, the building is destroyed without the fault of either party, the contractor can recover for the value of the work done and for materials furnished up to the time of the destruction of the building.[40]

OWNER'S PREVENTION OF PERFORMANCE

If the owner, without justification, prevents the contractor from completing the contract, the contractor may recover the contract price less the cost to the contractor of completing the building according to the provisions of the contract.

Reid and Kelly entered into a contract whereby Reid contracted to make designated repairs on Kelly's dwelling house and to erect a stairway adjoining it. When the work was completed, Kelly claimed that certain items were not properly done, and he refused to pay Reid the balance due. Reid offered to correct any defects in his work and set a day when he would be present to do so; but before the day arrived, Kelly notified Reid "not to come back or do anything more on the job." On the trial of the case the jury found that the defects in the work were not material and that Kelly prevented Reid from completing the work. The court entered judgment for Reid, and Kelly appealed. The judgment was affirmed.

Judge Cave said: "Thus the pleadings and the evidence clearly established that Kelly would not permit Reid to correct any deficiencies in the work, if there were any.

"The law is well established that, 'where a party to the contract forbids its performance by the other, or interferes with its performance by the other to an extent which amounts to a refusal of performance, the party thus interfered with may recover as if he had performed his contract.' There are many cases announcing this doctrine." *Reid* v. *Kelly,* Mo. App., 300 S.W.2d 542 (1957).

DELAYS IN PERFORMANCE

If there is a provision in the contract stating that the building must be completed within a certain time, failure to complete the building within that time will not justify rejection of the building, since time is not

---

[40] *Matthews Construction Company* v. *Brady,* 104 N.J.L 438, 140 A. 433.

of the essence of a contract to build. However, the contractor will be liable for damages for late performance. If there is no stipulation in the contract as to the time for the completion of the building, the contractor will owe a duty to pursue the work with reasonable diligence. Many contracts to build provide that the building shall be completed within a specified time, and that the contractor, on his failure to complete the building within the time specified, will pay a designated sum as liquidated damages for each day he is late.

Delays are excused if the contractor is prevented from completing the building by the acts of the owner. Delays resulting from strikes, inclement weather, or inability to obtain necessary materials are not excused, unless the contract to build so provides.

WAIVER

A waiver is a voluntary relinquishment of a known right, or such conduct as warrants an inference of the relinquishment of such right. The owner may accept defective performance of a contract to build and waive his right to demand strict performance. A waiver may be expressed either orally or in writing, or the waiver may be implied from the conduct of the parties.[41] If the conduct of the owner clearly indicates his intent to accept the work without making a claim for imperfections, he will have waived the defects. Acceptance of the work implies a waiver of known defects; but it does not imply a waiver of unknown latent defects— that is, defects which could not be discovered by reasonable inspection.[42]

The mere occupancy and use of the building do not constitute a waiver of defects. However, if the owner takes possession of and uses the building without in any way indicating his intent to hold the contractor responsible for deficiencies, such action is strong evidence of his intent to waive defects. This is particularly true if the defects are minor in nature.

Payment of the contract price with the knowledge of defective performance does not, as a matter of law, constitute a waiver; but such payment is strong evidence of an intent to waive known imperfections and will be held to be a waiver unless there are other facts to negate such intent. Payment is not a waiver of unknown or latent defects.

---

[41] *Standard Construction Co., Inc.* v. *National Tea Co. et al.,* 240 Minn. 422, 62 N.W.2d 201.

[42] *Michel* v. *Efferson et al.,* 223 La. 136, 65 So.2d 115.

DAMAGE TO OR DESTRUCTION OF BUILDING

When a person contracts to produce a result, he assumes the risks incident to the production of the promised result. A promisor may, by inserting appropriate provisions in his contract, relieve himself from defined risks. Also, incapacitating illness or death, intervening illegality, or destruction of the subject matter essential to the performance of the contract will, under the rule of impossibility, relieve the promisor from his duty of performance. This rule is of major importance in determining whether the owner or the contractor will bear a loss resulting from damage to or destruction of a building being erected, remodeled, or repaired.

If the contractor has contracted absolutely and unconditionally to erect a new building for a stipulated amount, he must bear any loss or damage to the building before its completion.[43] This would be true even though the building was being paid for in installments. However, if payments are to be made at various stages of the work, the courts have generally held that the owner will bear the loss resulting from damage to or destruction of the work completed and paid for, but the contractor will bear the loss of that stage of the work under construction but not completed.

The courts have usually held also that if payments are made periodically for the work completed during a stated period—for example, if payment is to be made on the tenth of each month for all materials delivered on the job and all labor done on the building up to the first of each month—the owner will bear the loss for materials paid for, and the contractor will bear the loss for that part of the period for which payment is not due.[44]

When the contract is for the remodeling or repair of or an addition to an existing building, and the building is damaged or destroyed and it is impossible to complete the work, the owner must bear the loss as to the work completed at the time of the damage to or destruction of the building, and the contractor will bear the loss resulting from his having made preparation—such as, for instance, having bought materials—for the performance of the job.

If various units of the work are let to separate contractors, the destruction of the building without the fault of either party will discharge the

[43] *Goin* v. *Board of Education of the City of Frankfort,* 289 Ky. 645, 183 S.W.2d 819.

[44] *Keel* v. *Eastern Carolina Stone & Construction Company,* 143 N. C. 429, 55 S.E. 826.

contractor from his obligation, and he will be entitled to payment for the part of the work which he has completed. If the contract is entire and indivisible, the general contractor will bear the loss; otherwise, the loss falls on the owner.[45]

This was an action by the Board of Education, Township of Woodbridge, against Kane Acoustical Company to recover for damage by fire to a partially completed school building, claimed to have been caused by the negligence of Kane Acoustical Company. As a part of the case, the judge had to determine the liability of the parties to a building contract when the building was damaged during the course of the construction.

Judge Gaulkin said: "In the absence of contractual arrangements to the contrary, the risk of loss by fire to a new building in course of construction is presumed to fall upon the builder. If it burns, it must be rebuilt by the builder, without additional compensation. Since we do not have the Woodbridge-Lyons contract, we have no means of telling whether that was the situation here.

"If these policies were builder's risk policies, in the form commonly used in New Jersey today, and if the owner had not yet paid anything for the building when the fire happened, and had no pecuniary interest therein covered by the policy, the builder ordinarily would be entitled to all of the insurance money and the owner to none. The same would be true if the builder rebuilt after the fire, before the insurance monies were paid over by the insurance companies. On the other hand, other circumstances (or the policies or contracts) may give the owner the right to some or even all of the proceeds. Again, without the data mentioned above, we cannot tell what the rights of the parties are." *Board of Education, Township of Woodbridge* v. *Kane Acoustical Company,* 51 N.J. Super. 319, 143 A.2d 853 (1958).

AGREEMENT TO MODIFY CONTRACT

The parties to a contract have the right, by mutual agreement, to cancel or alter the terms of the contract. However, any promise by an owner to pay the contractor additional compensation if he will complete the work according to the terms of the contract, or any promise by the owner to permit the contractor to substitute different or cheaper material in the performance of the contract is, as a general rule, unenforceable for lack of consideration.[46]

The courts have held that if unforeseen and unforeseeable difficulties are encountered in the course of the work and the owner promises to

---

[45] *American Surety Co. of New York et al.* v. *San Antonio Loan & Trust Co.,* Tex. Civ. App., 98 S.W. 387.

[46] *Dahl* v. *Edwin Moss and Son, Inc.,* 136 Conn. 147, 69 A.2d 562.

pay the additional cost resulting from such difficulty, the promise will be enforced.[47]

RIGHT TO RESCIND CONTRACT

Rescission of a contract is the repudiation or the unmaking of the contract and the placing of the parties in the same position that they held before entering into the contract. The parties may enter into a mutual agreement to rescind the contract; or if one of the parties is guilty of a material breach, the injured party may have the right, and may elect, to rescind the contract. If a person wishes to rescind on the ground of material breach, he must act within a reasonable time after the breach. Permitting the other party to proceed with the performance of the contract is a bar to the remedy of rescission.

A contract may be rescinded for failure of the owner to make payment when due, provided the contractor is not in default in the performance of the work. Unreasonable delay in the execution of the work is ground for rescession. The inability of either party to perform his duties under the contract is ground for rescission. If one party repudiates the contract, the other party has the right to rescind the contract.

On the rescission of the contract, no recovery can be had for damages.[48] After rescission, the parties may enter into a new contract for the work, or they may agree to changes in the terms of the contract and proceed with the work. If the parties cannot agree and the case reaches the court, the judge will decree an equitable adjustment of the matter, placing the parties as nearly as possible in the same position as that which they occupied before entering into the contract.

Checklist

No two contracts to build would, as a general rule, contain the same provisions. However, in drafting a contract to build, there are certain matters which should be considered and covered by the contract if they are applicable to the particular undertaking. The following should be considered in drafting most contracts to build. The list is not intended to be an exhaustive one.

---

[47] *Linz* v. *Shuck,* 106 Md. 220, 67 A. 286.

[48] *Miller-Piehl Equipment Co. et al.* v. *Gibson Commission Co. et al.,* 244 Iowa 103, 56 N.W.2d 25.

1. Date of the contract.
2. Name of the contractor and his address.
3. Name of the owner and his address. It is customary to name the contractor and designate him as *contractor,* and thereafter refer to him in the contract as *contractor.* Likewise, it is customary to name the owner and designate him as *owner,* and thereafter refer to him in the contract as *owner.*
4. Description, in general terms, of the building to be constructed.
5. A statement of the duties to be assumed by the contractor, such as the duty to furnish all materials and labor, and to do all other things necessary to the construction of the building.
6. A statement that the building is to be constructed according to plans and specifications prepared by the architect, naming the architect and identifying the plans and specifications by the architect's identification numbers or symbols.
7. A statement that the plans and specifications are a part of the contract.
8. A statement of the time for the completion of the work. This provision should not only state a time for the completion of the work, but should include provisions for adjustment of the time of completion in the event of changes in the work, or in the event of strikes, fire, flood, or other causes of delay which are beyond the control of the contractor.
9. A statement as to the payment of the contractor. This provision will set out the method of payment of the contractor—whether a lump sum, a unit price, the cost of the work plus a percentage of the cost, the cost of the work plus a fee, or some combination of these.

   As a general rule, payments will be made as the work progresses. The contract should define specifically when such progress payments are to be made—whether they are to be made as units of the work are completed or at stated periods; and if at stated periods, whether they are to be a portion of the total sum to be paid or are to be computed on the basis of the labor performed and materials delivered on the job.

   If the work is let on cost plus a percentage of the cost, or cost plus fee, the method of determining the cost and the reimbursement of the contractor should be stated in detail. Also, the method of determining the fee and the time of paying it should be stated.
10. A statement as to acceptance of the work and as to final payment.

The contract should provide for the final inspection and acceptance of the work and the making of the final payment. A provision should be included to the effect that the acceptance of the building and the making of the final payment will not constitute a waiver by the owner of his right to claim damages for latent defects in the work.

11. A statement as to the issuing of an architect's certificate for payment of the work. The contract should provide for payment only on the presentation of an architect's certificate stating the amount due. The general form of the certificate should be set out, and a provision should be included to the effect that the certificate does not bar the owner from making claim for defective work discovered at a later date.

12. A statement of the powers and duties of the architect. The contract should set out the general powers of the architect to supervise the work, and the contractor's obligation to follow the instructions of the architect. It should also set out the detail drawings to be prepared by the architect and the rights of the contractor if the architect delays unreasonably in preparing necessary detail drawings.

    The duty of the architect to instruct the contractor in the performance of the work should be defined, together with a statement as to the person to whom instructions are to be given—contractor, contractor's superintendent, foreman, or subcontractor—and the method of giving instructions (orally or in writing).

    The preparation of shop drawings and their approval should be covered.

13. A statement as to who shall be the owner of the drawings, plans, specifications, models, and so forth, prepared by the architect.

14. A statement as to materials, appliances, employees, etc. The contract should set out in detail which of the parties is to pay utility and material bills, pay for appliances used in the course of the work, and pay and discipline employees, and so on.

15. A statement as to the making of surveys, obtaining of permits, and so forth. It should be stated in the contract which of the parties is to provide surveys, make tests, obtain permits and easements, and so on.

16. A statement of the contractor's liability for failure to protect the work, the adjoining property, the public, and the employees of the owner, subcontractors, and contractor.

17. A statement as to the supervision of the work. The duty of the

contractor to have the work properly supervised at all times should be defined in the contract.

18. A statement as to changes in the work, extras, etc. The contract should set out in detail the owner's right to order changes in the work and to order extras. Orders for changes or extras should be in writing. Cost of such changes and extras should be determined before the work is done; all changes and extras, and the cost thereof, should be approved in writing by the architect.

19. Provision for correction of defective work, or deductions therefor.

20. A statement as to delays and extensions of time. The rights of the parties in the event of delays or extensions of time should be carefully defined.

21. A statement as to the right to rescind. The circumstances under which the owner may rescind the contract and complete the work, and the contractor's liability, should be carefully set out. Also, the circumstances under which the contractor may rescind the contract, and his rights on rescission, should be set out with equal care.

22. A statement as to insurance and bonds. The contract should state the insurance coverage each party should obtain—contractor's liability insurance; owner's liability insurance; fire, wind, and flood insurance; and so forth—together with a statement as to which party is to be protected by such insurance. Also, if bonds are to be furnished, the nature of the bonds and the beneficiary of the bonds should be set out in detail.

23. A statement as to assignment of the contract. It is customary to include a provision denying the contractor the right to assign the contract.

24. Arbitration. A clause providing for the arbitration of all disputes of every kind and nature which the parties and the architect cannot settle by mutual agreement is recommended. Such clause should set out the procedure to be followed in the arbitration.

Bonds

PURPOSE OF BOND

Whenever a person contracts to do public works, he is usually required to execute a bond with sufficient sureties to protect the governmental unit against liability and loss resulting from his defaults. The nature of the bond, the amount of the penalty, the persons protected, and all other material features of the bond will, as a general rule, be set out in the statutes or ordinances of the governmental unit having jurisdiction over the work. We shall not attempt to discuss the features of such bonds.

In private building the contractor may give a bond to protect the owner from liability and to protect him also against loss resulting from the contractor's failure to perform the contract. Sometimes the owner gives a bond to protect the contractor and others against liability or loss.

NATURE AND SCOPE OF SURETY'S LIABILITY

The extent of the liability of a surety on a contractor's bond or on an owner's bond will not exceed the liability of the contractor or the owner. If the contract is invalid, no action can be maintained against the surety.[49] The scope of the liability of the surety is determined by the provisions of the bond.

Under the common-law rule the provisions of a bond were strictly construed; all ambiguities and doubts were resolved in favor of the surety. Some courts follow this rule if sureties are individuals who are acting without compensation. However, most contractors' bonds are surety bonds, and the majority of courts construe such bonds most strongly against the compensated surety and in favor of the beneficiary under the bond.[50] As a general rule, the provisions of the contract between the owner and the contractor will be taken into consideration in construing the bond.

PERSON ENTITLED TO BENEFITS OF BOND

A carefully drafted bond will state specifically the persons who are the beneficiaries of the bond. The courts have generally held that persons furnishing materials or labor may recover on a building contractor's bond to the owner, when the bond is intended for the owner's protection against the claims of materialmen and laborers, even though they are not named as beneficiares in the bond.[51]

The intention of the parties is of outstanding importance in determining who is entitled to the benefits of the bond. The intent of the parties to the bond will be determined by reading the bond and the contract

---

[49] *Smith Engineering Co.* v. *Rice,* 102 F.2d 492.

[50] *Maryland Casualty Co.* v. *Cunningham,* 234 Ala. 80, 173 So. 506.

[51] *Knight & Jillson Co.* v. *Castle et al.,* 172 Ind. 97, 87 N.E. 976.

between the contractor and owner, and taking into consideration the conduct of the parties and all other surrounding facts and circumstances. In all cases, if the conditions of the bond are clearly stated and are unequivocal, such conditions will prevail. For example, if the bond is clearly conditioned to indemmify the owner for any pecuniary loss resulting from the breach of any of the terms of the contract between the contractor and the owner, materialmen and laborers would have no right of action on the bond.

Phoenix Indemnity Company (hereinafter referred to as Phoenix executed a performance bond as surety in connection with a contractor's public construction contract, by the terms of which Phoenix guaranteed the payment by the contractor for materials, supplies, or labor used directly or indirectly by the contractor or subcontractors and, in addition, provided for the payment of all bills for "*services* furnished to the principal in connection with the contract." The contractor failed to pay the premiums on liability insurance which, under the terms of the contract, he was obligated to carry. Suit was brought against the contractor and Phoenix to recover a judgment for the amount of the premiums. Phoenix contended that its bond did not guarantee payment of such items as insurance premiums. The trial court entered a judgment against Phoenix, and it appealed. The judgment was affirmed.

Judge Sturgis said: "While this a case of first impression in Florida, it is the general rule that whether a surety for compensation will be held liable for unpaid insurance premiums depends strictly upon the terms of the bond as construed in the light of applicable statutes.

"Contracts of suretyship for compensation are to be construed most strongly against the surety and in favor of the indemnity which the obligee has reasonable grounds to expect. They are regarded in the nature of an insurance contract and are governed by rules applicable to such contracts. The maxim that 'sureties are favored in the law' has no application to contracts of suretyship by one engaged in the business for hire. The provisions of the bond should be considered as a whole and given that effect which was logically intended by the parties as shown by the entire instrument. Applying those principles to the admitted facts in this case, it is apparent that the contractor and surety knew that no work could be done under the contract until the insurance was provided, that premiums would be charged therefor, that the insurer would become obligated to perform services on behalf of the contractor, and that such services would be consumed in the course of the work in the same sense that other materials were consumed, such as electricity, steam, transportation, and the like, which are not physical and visible materials.

"We recognize the word 'services' as having a connotation distinct from 'labor, material and supplies,' although the latter may to some extent be connected with the former. By the Mechanics' Lien Law the lien is imposed for the services of certain persons who usually are employed by the owner rather than the contractor, namely, architects, landscape architects, and engineers. The Mechanics' Lien Law also recognizes 'services' of persons other than materialmen and laborers. Thus persons who enter into contracts with the contractor for performance of part of the contractor's work are defined as subcontractors and are provided with a lien for their 'services.' Under its terms, the contract in suit could not have been fulfilled without the 'services' rendered by the appellee or some other insurer rendering a like service." *Phoenix Indemnity Company v. Board of Public Instruction of Alachua County,* Fla., App., 114 So.2d 478 (1959).

DISCHARGE OF SURETY

Usually, any alteration in the contract to build, any extension of time for performance, or any other change in the contract, if such change would affect the risk of the surety, will discharge the surety, unless he consents thereto.[52]

Any breach of a duty imposed on the owner will discharge the surety, if such breach will result in an increase of the risks of the surety. For example, if the contract requires the owner to keep the work insured against damage by fire and the owner fails to insure, thus resulting in a loss which injures the surety, the surety will be discharged.

As a general rule, a contract to build will include a provision permitting alterations as the work progresses. Although there is some diversity in the cases, the courts have usually held that if alterations are permitted by the contract, the making of alterations without the consent of the surety will not discharge the surety.[53] In all cases, if the bond expressly provides that alterations may be made, the making of alterations will not discharge the surety.

Usually, a contract to build will provide that all alterations must be authorized in writing by the architect and that the cost thereof shall be agreed upon by the parties before the alterations are made. The courts are not in accord as to the effect of making alterations without complying with the formalities set out in the contract. In some jurisdictions the courts have held that failure to observe such formalities will discharge the surety; in others the courts have decided that such formalities are for the benefit of the owner and the contractor, and that they can be waived by them without affecting the liability of the surety.

---

[52] *Woodruff* v. *Schultz et al.,* 155 Mich. 11, 118 N.W. 579.

[53] *Massachusetts Bonding & Inc. Co.* v. *John R. Thompson Co.,* 88 F.2d 825.

There are three views as to the effect on the liability of the surety when the owner makes premature payments to the contractor. (1) A few courts hold that premature payments have no effect on the liability of the surety; (2) some courts have held that a prepayment reduces the liability of the surety by the amount of the prepayment; and (3) the majority of the courts hold that premature payment discharges the surety.[54]

MATERIALMEN AND LABORERS

If a bond expressly makes materialmen and laborers the beneficiaries, a breach of the contract to build will not defeat the rights of the materialmen or laborers to recover in an action against the surety on the bond.[55]

If the surety, with knowledge of facts operating to discharge him from liability, either expressly or impliedly indicates his intention to continue to be bound as surety, he will thereby waive his right to claim he is discharged.[56]

NOTE: The following standard forms may be obtained from the American Institute of Architects, 1741 New York Avenue, N.W., Washington, D.C.:

1. Agreements between architect and owner.
2. Agreements between owner and contractor.
3. Subcontracts.
4. Performance bonds.

These forms have been carefully prepared and have been tested by use. As with all forms, the blanks must be filled in with care; the printed provisions should be carefully reviewed, and those that are not applicable to the particular work to be done should be stricken out. If there are points material to the particular work to be done which are not covered in the form, provisions covering these items should be added.

---

[54] *Anthony P. Miller, Inc.* v. *Needham*, 35 F. Supp. 332.

[55] *Hochevar* v. *Maryland Casualty Co.*, 114 F.2d 948.

[56] *Spring Garden Building & Loan Assn.* v. *Rhodes*, 126 Pa. Super. 102, 190 A. 530.

14

Escrow

Nature of escrow

THE OBJECTIVE OF AN ESCROW

AN ESCROW has been created when a deed or other instrument, the terms of which import a legal obligation, is delivered to a third person, other than the grantee in the deed or the obligee in another instrument, and such third person is to deliver the deed or instrument to the grantee or obligee on the performance of some designated act by the grantee or obligee or on the occurrence of a certain event. The third person to whom the deed or instrument is delivered is known as the *depositary* or *escrow holder*.[1]

The principal objective of an escrow is to minimize the risks incident to the sale of real estate. Where the transaction involves property of substantial value, there will be, as a general rule, several matters which must be coordinated before the deal is completed. This will necessarily cause a time lapse between the execution of the purchase agreement and the final payment and delivery of the deed. If the escrow is used and there is encountered during this time any difficulty which would prevent the concluding of the sale, each party can have returned to him that which

---

[1] *Home-Stake Royalty Corporation et al.* v. *McClish et al.,* 187 Okla. 352, 103 P.2d. 72.

he has deposited with the escrow holder and can be put in the position he occupied before he entered into the transaction.

EXAMPLE OF ESCROW TRANSACTION

The following situation will serve to illustrate the use of an escrow.

Allen has contracted to sell a house to Ball. Under the contract of sale, Allen is obligated to execute and deliver a warranty deed and an abstract of title certified to a stated date; to deliver receipted water, real estate, and personal property tax bills; and to execute an affidavit that no work has been performed on the house during the last 60 days for which a mechanic's lien could be filed. At the time Ball signed the proposition to buy, he paid $1,000 as evidence of good faith. He has contracted to pay $4,000 on the examination of the abstract, provided the abstract shows merchantable title in Allen, and to execute a purchase-money mortgage on the house securing a negotiable promissory note for $20,000 drawing 5 percent interest and payable $200 the first of each and every month, including interest computed monthly, until the note is paid in full. In this transaction, Allen and Ball enter into an escrow agreement, and First Bank is selected as depositary (escrow holder) and agrees to act as such. Instructions to First Bank will be drafted and signed by Allen and Ball.

In working out the transaction, the following steps will usually be taken: The $1,000 paid by Ball will be turned over to First Bank. Allen will execute a warranty deed and deliver it to First Bank, and will also have the abstract brought down to the stated date and certified by the abstractor. He will file the receipted water, real estate, and property tax bills, and will execute the affidavit; all of these will be delivered to First Bank and made available to Ball or his attorney for examination.

Ball will execute the mortgage and note, and deliver them to First Bank, where they will be made available to Allen or his attorney for examination. If Ball, on examination of the abstract and documents delivered to First Bank by Allen, finds them free from defects, he will pay $4,000 to First Bank.

Allen or his attorney will examine the mortgage and note; if he finds them satisfactory, he will so indicate to First Bank. When Allen and Ball have certified to First Bank that all is in order, and when all required documents have been delivered and all required payments have been made to First Bank, the documents and money in its possession will be delivered and paid to whichever of the parties is entitled thereto, thus completing the transaction.

REQUIREMENT FOR A VALID ESCROW

An escrow is a contract. Therefore, in order to have an instrument operate as an escrow, there must be sufficient parties having capacity to contract, a proper subject matter, and a consideration; and the parties must have actually and validly contracted in respect to the subject matter. The essentials of the escrow used in a real estate transaction are as follows:

1. There must be a valid, enforceable contract of purchase and sale of real estate. An oral contract to sell real estate cannot be the basis of an escrow, since such a contract is unenforceable under the statute of frauds.[2]
2. The deposit of the deed or other instruments with the depositary must be absolute and beyond the control of the grantor or obligor.[3]
3. The escrow agreement must contain a condition. By the very nature of an escrow, the delivery of the deed or instrument held by the depositary must be conditioned on the performance of some act or on the happening of some event.[4]
4. The depositary must be some disinterested person. The grantee or his agent cannot act as depositary.[5]
5. The deed or instrument delivered in escrow must be duly and validly executed.[6]

Young and Bishop negotiated for the purchase and sale of described real estate. Young as buyer and Bishop as seller negotiated an escrow agreement which set out in detail the terms of the sale. The following clause was typed on the face of the escrow agreement: "NOTE: The Escrow is subject to and conditioned upon Supplemental Trust Escrow Instructions which are to be submitted to Escrow Agent, which supplemental instructions will be made part of this Escrow." The parties did not succeed in reaching an agreement on the terms of the supplemental instructions. Young brought suit asking specific performance, and Bishop defended on the ground that no enforceable contract of sale was entered into, since no separate contract in writing for the sale of the real estate was executed, and that no supplemental instructions to the escrow were agreed upon. The trial court granted judgment on the pleadings to Bishop, and Young appealed. The judgment was reversed, and a trial was ordered.

[2] *Jozefowicz et ux.* v. *Leickem,* 174 Wis. 475, 182 N.W. 729.

[3] *Lindsey et al.* v. *Hornady,* 215 Ark. 797, 223 S.W.2d 768.

[4] *Lechner* v. *Halling et al.,* 35 Wash.2d 903, 216 P.2d 179.

[5] *Wells* v. *Wells,* 249 Ala. 649, 32 So.2d 697.

[6] *Collins* v. *Kares,* 52 S.D. 143, 216, N.W. 880.

Justice Johnson said: "Briefly stated, a contract of sale of real estate and an escrow arrangement are not interchangeable entities. A binding contract of sale must exist with respect to the subject-matter of the escrow instrument to support an enforceable escrow. A good definition of the generic term 'escrow' is this: an escrow is a written instrument which by its terms imports a legal obligation, and which is deposited with a third party, to be kept by the depository until the performance of the prescribed condition or the happening of a certain event, and then to be delivered over to the grantee, promisee or obligee. In short, an escrow is a conveyancing device designed to carry out the terms of a binding contract of sale previously entered into by the parties.

"It is the general rule that the conditions upon which the instrument is to be deposited in escrow may rest in, and be proved by, parol, and an instrument placed in escrow may be enforced although the escrow agreement is not in writing. This rule, however, does not permit enforcement of a contract for the sale of real estate unless there is a binding obligation for such sale under the statute of frauds.

". . . Suffice to say, the pleadings before us present material fact issues which preclude the granting of a judgment on the pleadings." *Young* v. *Bishop*, 88 Ariz. 140, 353 P.2d 1017 (1960).

WHO MAY ACT AS DEPOSITARY

In determining who may act as depositary of an escrow, the courts have applied basic legal principles. An escrow holder (depositary) represents both the buyer and the seller; and as such, he acts in a fiduciary capacity. He must not, therefore, put himself in a position where his personal interests conflict with the performance of his fiduciary duties. Furthermore, since he acts for both parties to the transaction, he must act with absolute impartiality. Consequently, a person who is the agent or attorney of one of the parties, and thereby owes a duty to further his principal's or client's interests, is disqualified and will not be permitted to act as depositary unless it is clear that his acting as such is not hostile to his principal's interests.[7]

Another basic legal principle which is applied in determining who may act as a depositary is that the delivery of a deed to the grantee, if the deed contains no conditional clause passes title to the grantee on delivery. And the courts have held that even though an agreement has been entered into between the grantor and grantee whereby the grantee would hold the deed in escrow until the fulfillment of a condition or the happening of some event, such an agreement would not prevent the passing of the title

---

[7] *Levin* v. *Nedelman*, 141 N.J. Eq. 23, 55 A.2d 826.

of the real estate involved to the grantee.[8] Consequently, the grantee cannot not act as the depositary, since the objective of the escrow is to prevent the vesting of the title in the grantee until the terms of the escrow are fulfilled. There are some recent decisions, however, which have not followed this rule rigidly.[9]

The mere entrusting of a deed or other instrument to the grantee or obligee is not a delivery of the instrument; and if a deed or instrument is entrusted to a grantee or obligee to be transported and given to the depositary, title will not pass at the time of the entrustment. However, if the grantee or obligee, in breach of duty, retains possession of the instrument, title will pass, and oral evidence is inadmissible to prove that the delivery was conditioned.[10]

The leaving of the deed in the possession of the grantor defeats the objective of escrow.

THE ESCROW AGREEMENT

The parties to the escrow agreement are the grantor, the grantee, and the depositary. Although the escrow agreement need not be in writing in order to be enforceable, it should be in writing for the protection of the parties. The agreement will set out the delivery of the deed or instrument to the depositary, and will state that the depositary is to hold the deed or instrument and is to deliver it to the grantee or obligee on the fulfillment of stated conditions or on the happening of certain events. As a general rule, instructions to the depositary, stating the conditions on which the deed or instrument is to be delivered to the grantee or obligee and the disposition of the deed or instrument on default, and so forth, will be set out in detail.

INSTRUCTIONS TO DEPOSITARY

The instructions to the depositary may be oral; but for the protection of all interested parties the instructions should be in writing, carefully drafted, and specific in their provisions. As a general rule, the instructions will include the following:

1. Name of the depositary.
2. Names of the buyer and seller.
3. Statement of documents to be deposited by the seller—such as deed, abstract of title or certificate of title showing marketable title in

---

[8] *Logue et al.* v. *Von Almen et al.,* 379 Ill. 208, 40 N.E.2d 73.

[9] *Chillemi* v. *Chillemi,* 197 Md. 257, 78 A.2d 750.

[10] *Carlisle et al.* v. *MacDonald et al.,* Tex. Civ. App., 200 S.W. 2d 436.

seller or policy of title insurance, insurance policies and assignments of insurance policies, leases properly assigned, notices to tenants to pay future rent to the grantee, tax receipts, receipts for payment of assessments, canceled mortgage notes, discharge of mortgage, and so forth. The documents to be deposited by the seller will depend on the nature of the property sold and the terms of the contract of purchase and sale.

4. The conditions to be performed by the buyer or the event on which delivery is to be made to the buyer—usually, payment of the purchase price, or part payment and execution of note and mortgage securing the note.

5. Disposition of the money paid to the depositary by the buyer—taxes, liens, and charges to be paid out of such money, and conditions under which the balance is to be paid over to the seller.

6. Direction for delivery of the deed, leases, assignments of leases, insurance policies and assignments of policies, and so on, when conditions are satisfied.

7. Directions for recording the deed, whether it is to be recorded immediately or on fulfillment of conditions or merely delivered to buyer without being recorded. For the protection of the buyer the deed should be recorded immediately, and the buyer should execute a quitclaim deed to the seller to be recorded in the event the seller cannot convey clear title to the buyer.

8. Time within which the seller must cure defects in his title, if any are discovered.

9. Disposition of money and documents deposited if the seller cannot convey title as provided in the contract of purchase and sale.

10. Payment of charges of the depositary, recording fees, broker's commission, attorneys' fees, and any other fees connected with the transaction.

The instructions should be signed by the buyer and the seller, and should have endorsed on them a statement to the effect that the depositary has read, understood, and approved the instructions; this statement should be signed by the depositary.

RELATION OF DEPOSITARY TO THE PARTIES

The depositary is frequently referred to as the *agent* of both parties; but he is not an agent, since he is not subject to the control of either party. He is also referred to in some instances as a *trustee;* but he is not a trustee, since he has title to none of the deeds or instruments in his possession. He is merely a conduit used in the transaction for convenience and safety. He is a third party to whom the grantor and the grantee have entrusted certain authority by the escrow agreement. When the depositary knows the terms of the agreement, he acts by virtue of his own powers and is responsible for his actions. He does not act as agent of anybody.[11]

In the event the parties to the escrow are in discord as to their rights to the instruments or to the funds held in escrow, the depositary should refuse to accede to the requests of either party. He is a mere stakeholder and should, by following the proper course of action, force the dispute into the court where his responsibility could be determined.

Foreman contracted to purchase a farm owned by Todd and Fisher. Bonner Ferry Bank acted as escrow holder, and it complied with the terms of the escrow. The title to the farm was defective, and Foreman brought suit against Todd and Fisher and Bonner Ferry Bank, contending that Bonner Ferry Bank acted as the agent of Todd and Fisher. The trial court dismissed the action against Bonner Ferry Bank, and Foreman appealed. The holding of the trial court was affirmed.

Justice McQuade said: "The authorities are divided as to whether an escrow holder is the agent of both parties to the transaction, or is a third party to whom the principals have entrusted certain duties. This is succinctly set out in Nickell v. Reser:

" '. . . the deposit of an instrument in escrow cannot be made with one who is the agent of either of the parties to the instrument . . . for if the depositary is the agent of the grantor, the instrument is retained by him; if the agent of the grantee, there is a delivery of the instrument. To the extent the term agent is applicable, it is a limited agency, with duties and powers limited to the terms of the escrow agreement.'

"Duties of an escrow holder are those set out in the escrow agreement. The holder acts as a depositary, and is not concerned with nor responsible for defects in the title to the property. Plaintiffs [Foremans] must look to their grantors, not to the despositary, nor its officer, for title." *Forman* v. *Todd*, 83 Idaho 482, 364 P.2d 365 (1961).

DUTIES AND LIABILITIES OF DEPOSITARY

The depositary is bound by the terms and conditions of the escrow agreement, and he owes a duty to follow the instructions in the escrow contract without deviating in any respect. He is obligated to withhold

---

[11] *Nickell et ux.* v. *Reser et al.*, 143 Kan. 831, 57 P.2d 101.

delivery until the conditions upon which delivery is conditioned have been fulfilled or until the event upon which delivery is conditioned has happened. He owes an equal duty to make delivery when the conditions are fulfilled or when the event has occurred.

The delivery by the depositary to the party entitled to possession of the instrument on the fulfillment of the condition or on the happening of the event is known as the *second delivery*.

If the terms and conditions of the escrow agreement are not fulfilled, the depositary owes a duty to redeliver the deed, instrument, money, or whatever has been deposited with him to the parties who deposited it.

If the depositary fails to fulfill the duties imposed on him by the escrow agreement, he will be liable in damages to the injured party for any loss resulting directly from the depositary's breach of duty. For example, suppose that the depositary, under the terms of the escrow agreement, owes a duty to hold a deed and not to deliver it until the purchase price is paid in full. And then, in breach of his duty, he delivers the deed to the grantee without being paid the purchase price. The depositary would be liable to the grantor for the full purchase price.[12]

If the seller is unable to convey a title which complies with the provisions of the contract of purchase and sale, the depositary owes a duty to return to the grantee the earnest money the depositary holds; and if the depositary fails to make such payment, he will be liable to the grantee for the full amount of the earnest money.

If written instructions are given to the depositary and at the same time, or at some later time, oral instructions are given, the depositary will not be liable if he follows the written instructions and fails to carry out the oral instructions.[13]

The courts have consistently held that if the depositary delivers the deed to the grantee without the conditions for delivery having been fulfilled or without the event on which delivery was conditioned having happened, the delivery of the deed is unauthorized, and no title passes to the grantee. However, if, after the wrongful delivery, the grantor ratifies the acts of the depositary, title will vest in the grantee.[14]

Amen entered into a contract for the purchase of a tavern. The purchase price was $74,300, payable $10,000 in cash, $54,300 by a note and deed of trust, and $10,000 by the buyer's (Amen's) assumption of certain debts.

---

[12] *Keith* v. *First National Bank of New England, North Dakota,* 36 N.D. 315, 162 N.W. 691; *Kirby* v. *Woolbert,* 48 Wash.2d 141, 291 P.2d 666.

[13] *Colorado Title and Trust Co.* v. *Roberts,* 80 Colo. 258, 250 P. 641.

[14] *Bradshaw* v. *Superior Oil Co.,* 164 F.2d 165.

Title Company acted as escrow holder. The escrow agreement was in writing and was signed by the parties and by Title Company as escrow. The agreement provided: "Any debts over $10,000 will be paid by Merced County Title Company out of the proceeds of the sale." Title Company and the sellers were given notice of a tax claim in the amount of $4,749.84, but Amen was not given notice of the claim, either by the state or by Title Company. Title Company paid $10,000 of debts exclusive of the tax claim and paid the proceeds of the sale to the seller. As a result, Amen was forced to pay the $4,749.84 tax claim. Amen sued Title Company for breach of contract and in tort for negligence. The court held Title Company was liable.

Justice Traynor said: "An escrow holder must comply strictly with the instructions of the parties. Upon the escrow holder's breach of an instruction that it has contracted to perform or an implied promise arising out of the agreement with the buyer or seller, the injured party acquires a cause of action for breach of contract. Similarly if the escrow holder acts negligently, 'it would ordinarily be liable for any loss occasioned by its breach of duty.'" *Amen* v. *Merced County Title Company*, 25 Cal. Rptr. 65, 375 P.2d 33 (1962).

EMBEZZLEMENT OF FUNDS

Frequently, the receipt of money is involved in the duties of a depositary. If the escrow agreement so provides, the depositary may deposit the money received in his own bank account; but if he does deposit it in his own account, he must keep a balance in the account equal to the amount of escrow money deposited. Failure to do so is an embezzlement of the escrow funds.

If the depositary uses for his own purposes money deposited in escrow, he is guilty of embezzlement. The deposit of money with the depositary does not create a debtor-creditor relation between the depositary and the party depositing the money.

If the depositary embezzles the money deposited with him before the fulfillment of the condition or the happening of the event, the loss falls on the party who deposited the money. The courts have held that the depositary holds such money as agent of the party who deposited it. However, if the embezzlement occurs after the fulfillment of the condition or the occurrence of the event, the party entitled to the money must bear the loss.[15]

Cradock purchased certain land from Cooper. The Internal Revenue Service had a claim against Cooper which Cradock's attorney, one Boland, claimed was a lien against the land. Cradock and Cooper agreed to allow Boland to hold $15,000 of the purchase money, out of which he was to discharge the

---

[15] *Angell* v. *Ingram et ux.*, 35 Wash.2d 582, 213 P.2d 944.

claim of the Internal Revenue Service. The parties entered into a written escrow agreement, by the terms of which the $15,000 held by Boland, as escrow holder, would be paid to Cooper if the claim was settled; and if the claim was not settled, Boland was to pay the claim out of the $15,000 and give any balance to Cooper.

The agreement was signed by Boland, attorney at law, escrow agent, Cradock, and Cooper, and the $15,000 was paid to Boland "to be held for and on behalf of W. R. Cooper, subject to the following conditions." The terms and conditions were as set out above.

Boland used $4,100 of the money to settle the claims and misappropriated the balance, $10,900. Cooper claimed that Cradock must stand the loss, since Boland was his attorney. The trial court held that each party should stand one half of the loss. Cradock appealed. The judgment was reversed, and the court held that Cooper must stand the loss.

Associate Judge Vassar B. Carlton said: "According to the law as set forth in 30 C. J. S. Escrows, paragraph 7 d, p. 1202; and in 19 Am. Jur., Escrow, Section 15, p. 432, the attorney of the grantor of the subject matter of the escrow agreement may act as escrow agent so long as his duties do not involve a conflict of interest with, or a violation of, duty to his client as principal, and so long as the condition of the escrow is not made dependent upon the client's volition.

"The primary purpose of the escrow was to remove a cloud from the title of the property. This is consistent with the interest of the defendant. The defendant retained absolutely no control of the money deposited. It was placed beyond his reach for all purposes and all times.

"Under the normal escrow situation where the escrow agent defaults prior to performance of the escrow condition, the loss falls upon the depositor, for he is deemed to have retained legal title to the subject matter of the escrow, and is deemed to be entitled to the return of such subject matter, should the other parties fail to perform.

"There is a clear exception to this rule where under the circumstances of the escrow agreement the depositor would not be entitled to the return of the subject matter under any circumstances, irrespective of performance of the terms of the agreement.

"In the instant case, the escrow money was held by Charles E. Boland under the terms of the agreement, to be paid either to satisfy a United States tax lien or to the sellers, as the remaining portion of the purchase price. It is clear that the purchaser, Cradock, retained no legal title to these funds, for he was not entitled to their return under any circumstances.

"We, therefore, conclude that as a matter of law Charles E. Boland became the agent of the sellers, the plaintiffs herein; and, accordingly, the unfortunate loss must fall upon the plaintiffs under the legal principles enunciated above." *Cradock* v. *Cooper,* Fla., 123 So.2d 256 (1960).

WHEN TITLE PASSES

The modern view, and the one most widely held today, is that the deed held in escrow becomes the deed of the grantee on the fulfillment of the conditions or on the happening of the event set out in the escrow agreement. The passing of the title to the grantee does not depend on the second delivery by the depositary.[16]

Although a deed deposited in escrow does not convey title until the conditions set out in the escrow agreement have been fulfilled or the event has happened, the courts have held that the deed will be treated as relating back to and taking effect at the time it was originally delivered to the depositary. This doctrine has been adopted by the courts to effectuate the intentions of the parties to the escrow. If, after the deed to the real estate is delivered to the depositary, but before the fulfillment of the condition or the happening of the event and the passing of title to the grantee, the grantor should die, become insane, marry, or change his legal status in any other manner, his change in status would in no way affect the validity of the deed deposited in escrow. Under the doctrine of relating back, the validity of the deed and the rights of the parties are determined as of the date of the first delivery of the deed to the depositary.[17]

The doctrine of relating back will not be applied if, by its application, the title taken by the grantee will be limited or defeated. For example, suppose that the grantor, at the time he executes the deed to the real estate and deposits it with the depositary, does not have title to the property or has defective title, but before the second delivery—the delivery by the depositary to the grantee—he acquires title or clears his title of the defects. The grantee would acquire the title which the grantor has the power to convey at the time of the second delivery—a good title free from defects.

RIGHT TO RENTS AND PROFITS

The courts have held that in the absence of a provision in the contract of purchase and sale defining the rights to the rents and profits from the real estate, the grantee is entitled to the rents and profits from the date the deed to the real estate is deposited with the depositary.[18]

---

[16] *Osborn* v. *Osborn,* 42 Cal.2d 358, 267, P.2d 333.

[17] *Cowden* v. *Broderick & Calvert, Inc., et al.,* 131 Tex. 434, 114 S.W.2d 1166.

[18] *Scott* v. *Sloan et al.,* 72 Kan. 545, 84 P. 117.

INTERVENING RIGHTS OF THIRD PERSONS

Between the time of the first delivery of the deed and the second delivery by the depositary to the grantee, third persons may acquire rights in the real estate. If, at the time the deed is delivered to the depositary, it is recorded and there is nothing in the deed or on the records to show that the deed is held in escrow, the grantee would be the owner of record. If the grantee should sell or mortgage the property and thereafter fail to fulfill the conditions set out in the escrow agreement, no title would vest in the grantee, and the purchaser or mortgagee would take nothing. However, if, in addition to permitting the recording of the deed, the grantor permitted the grantee to take possession of the property, and the purchaser or mortgagee of the property made the purchase or loan in good faith, for value, and without notice or knowledge of the existence of the escrow, such purchaser or mortgagee would be protected. The grantor would be estopped from setting up his title to defeat the rights of the purchaser or mortgagee.[19]

RECORDING OF DEED

If the deed delivered in escrow is not recorded and the grantee is not in possession of the real estate, any person, as a general rule, to whom the grantor conveys, mortgages, or leases the real estate, if such person takes in good faith, for value, and without notice or knowledge of the escrow, will acquire rights in the property.[20] However, some courts have applied the doctrine of relating back to this situation and have held that if the grantee fulfills the conditions set out in the escrow agreement, his title relates back to the first delivery, and he takes free of claims of third persons arising as the result of acts of the grantor subsequent to the delivery of the deed to the depositary.

EFFECTS OF ESCROW ON INSURANCE

Since title to the real estate does not pass to the grantee until the fulfillment of the condition or the happening of the event set out in the escrow agreement, the grantor has an insurable interest in the property, and any damage to the property before the fulfillment of the condition falls on the grantor.[21]

---

[19] *Quick* v. *Milligan,* 108 Ind. 419, 9 N.E. 392.

[20] *Meade et al.* v. *Robinson et al.,* 234 Mich. 322, 208 N.W. 41.

[21] *Dow* v. *Fireman's Ins. Co. of Newark, N.J.,* 115 Kan. 190, 221 P. 1112.

15

Landlord and tenant

Introduction

WHEN THE OWNER of real estate grants to another the right to possession of such real estate and retains a reversion in it, the transaction is called a lease; and the relation of the parties is referred to as lessor and lessee, or as landlord and tenant. Usually, the terms *lessor* and *lessee,* and *landlord* and *tenant,* are used interchangeably. In some instances, however, the courts have recognized a technical distinction and have held that the relation of lessor and lessee arises when the parties have executed the lease agreement, whereas the relation of landlord and tenant does not come into existence until the lessee has taken possession of the leased property.

LEASES, EASEMENTS, AND LICENSES

Leases, easements, and licenses have common characteristics; and in some transactions, elements of each may be present. For example, if a fence or side of a building is leased for the purpose of placing signs thereon, the elements of an easement or license predominate. On the other hand, if land is leased for the purpose of erecting billboards thereon, the characteristics of a lease predominate. Other transactions which present similar problems are, for instance, "leases" of a department in a department store, crop leases, and lodging arrangements. In such mixed transactions the courts, in determining the rights of the parties, usually give the terms of the agreement major weight but, at the same time, give some consideration to the fairness and justice of the result of applying the rules of law of leases, easements, or licenses.[1]

CREATION AND ESSENTIAL ELEMENTS OF LEASE

The relation of landlord and tenant is created by contract.[2] The lease contract is, in fact, a combination of a conveyance and contractual provisions. In the early period of the development of the law of landlord and tenant (before 1540), social and economic conditions in England were such that there was a distinct advantage in treating a lease as a contract and in holding that the property rights acquired by the tenant were personal property.[3] However, in the United States today, there is little or no justification for treating a lessee's interest as personal property or the lease as a contract; but for historical reasons, it is still generally so treated. The courts have recognized that the rights of the lessee have many of the characteristics of real estate.

ESSENTIAL ELEMENTS OF RELATION

Although the relation of landlord and tenant arises from contract, the reservation of rent is not essential to the creation of the relation.[4] However, it is essential to the relation that the occupany by the tenant be by permission of the landlord and, in addition, be in subordination to the rights of the landlord. That is, the landlord must retain such an interest in the leased property that the tenant's rights will revert to the landlord on the termination of the tenant's right of occupancy. For example, if a tenant assigns all his interest in the lease to another, the relation is that of assignor and assignee, since the tenant (assignor) has retained no rights in the leased property. But if a tenant contracts with another to permit that person to occupy a portion of the leased property or to occupy the leased property for a period of time less than the term

---

[1] *Thiokoi Chemical Corporation* v. *Morris County Board of Taxation,* 41 N.J. 405, 197 A.2d 176.

[2] *Miller* v. *Berk,* 328 Mass. 393, 104 N.E.2d 163.

[3] Hiram H. Lesar, *Landlord and Tenant,* pp. 175–77.

[4] *Peerless Sugar Co., Inc.* v. *35 Steuben St. Realty Corp.,* 66 N.Y.S.2d 839.

of the tenant's lease, the relation of landlord and tenant will arise, since the person to whom the right of occupancy is granted holds in subordination to the original tenant, and on the termination of the occupancy the rights granted revert to the original tenant.[5]

IMPORTANCE OF LEASES

The law of landlord and tenant is complex and, in many areas, archaic. Nevertheless, the lease transaction is extremely important in the real estate business because it permits one party to have the use of property that belongs to another. The interest in real estate which the tenant acquires under the lease can be substantial, approaching complete ownership, and can be used as security for financing in some cases. The fact that the law in this area is cumbersome and outdated is a matter of great concern in many quarters. While change has been slow to come in the past and may be slow to come in the future the matter is receiving attention. The reader's attention is directed to the "Model Residential Landlord-Tenant Code" prepared by the American Bar Foundation with financial support for the project from the Office of Economic Opportunity. This work represents an effort to codify the law surrounding the landlord-tenant relationshp and to clarify the rights and duties of the parties. Some form of codification appears likely in many states within the relatively near future.

Leasehold estates

TYPES OF LEASEHOLD ESTATES

There are four types of leasehold estates: (1) estates for years, (2) estates from year to year (or period to period), (3) estates at will, and (4) estates at sufferance.

ESTATES FOR YEARS

An estate for years includes all leaseholds which are to continue for a definite or ascertained period of time. The estate for years may be a

---

[5] *Fairmont Park Raceway, Inc.* v. *Commissioner of International Revenue,* 327 F.2d 780, 784.

leasehold for one year, for less than one year, or for more than one year. A lease for six months is a lease for years; likewise, a 99-year lease is a lease for years. A lease for years gives the lessee the right to possess and use the leased property to the exclusion of all other persons, including the landlord, and on the termination of such a lease the lessee owes a duty to vacate the premises. The rights of the lessor (landlord) and lessee (tenant) may, however, be altered by covenants in the lease.

ESTATES FROM YEAR TO YEAR

An estate from year to year—or from period to period, as it is sometimes termed—may be created by agreement or by operation of law. The distinguishing characteristic of this estate is that it continues for successive periods until one of the parties ends it by giving notice of termination. The landlord and tenant may enter into an agreement whereby real estate is let by the month or by the year, the relationship to continue for an indefinite number of months or years.

The estate is also created when a tenant for years holds over and the landlord acquiesces in the holding-over. Usually, the acceptance of rent is conclusive proof of the landlord's acquiescence. Other acts on the part of the landlord may be sufficient proof of his acquiescence.

If a tenant goes into possession under an oral lease, unenforceable under the statute of frauds, some courts have held that an estate from year to year results; other courts have held that an estate at sufferance ensues.

If the estate from year to year is created by the tenant's holding over, the courts have held that the successive periods of the lease will be for the term of the original lease, provided the period is less than one year; but in no event will the successive periods be more than one year. For example, if the original tenancy was for one year, six months, one month, or one week, the successive periods of the estate from year to year would be one year, six months, one month, or one week, respectively; but if the original lease was for five years, the resulting estate from year to year would be for successive periods of one year.

In order to terminate an estate from year to year, either the landlord or the tenant must give proper notice. The time at which notice must be given is generally set out in the statutes of the state; in some states the form of notice and the service of the notice are stipulated in the same statutes. As a general rule, in order to terminate an estate from week to week, one week's notice is required; in order to terminate an estate from month to month, one month's notice is necessary. There is little uniformity in the statutory time for giving notice to terminate an estate from year to year. The time ranges from six months to three months.

On June 15, Flynn entered into a written agreement with Dworkin to rent described premises and took possession on the same date. Flynn continued in possession of the premises and paid the required rental therefor until September 14, 1961, at which time he vacated the property after having advised the landlord by letter of his intention so to do.

The agreement, Section 5, reads as follows: "5. The within premises are hereby rented for a period of 12 months, commencing June 15, 1959, and this agreement shall automatically renew itself thereafter, meaning continuously for like periods, unless tenant shall give to landlord not less than thirty days' written notice, prior to the expiration of the term then running, of tenant's intention to terminate said tenancy at the expiration of the then existing time. . . ."

The agreement was not executed as provided by the statutes of the state, and the court held that the lease was void. Suit was brought to recover rent for the unexpired portion of the twelve-month period (September 14, 1961 to June 14, 1962). The trial court held for Flynn; but on appeal, the judgment was reversed, and judgment was entered for rent as claimed.

Presiding Judge Kovachy said: "However, it is also the law that while a lease in excess of three years that is not attested and acknowledged is void, the lessee in possession thereunder is, nevertheless, a tenant from year to year at the will of the lessor and subject to all the provisions of the lease excepting duration.

"The defendant tenant here started a 'third period of 12 months' on June 15, 1961, when he continued in possession of the premises without giving the landlords written notice thirty days prior to the expiration of the term, then running, of an intention to terminate his tenancy at the expiration of the then existing term as provided in the lease and by reason thereof made himself liable for the payment of rental until the end of the 'period of 12 months' namely: June 14, 1962.

"The Supreme Court in Baltimore & Ohio Railroad Co. v. West, stated the law in the syllabus as follows:

" '1.   An entry under a lease for a term of years at an annual rent, void for any cause, and payment of rent under it, creates a tenancy from year to year upon the terms of the lease, except as to its duration.

" '2.   Where, after the expiration of the term, the tenant holds over and pays rent for a part of another year, without any new agreement with the landlord, he becomes a tenant for that year at the same rent, and cannot terminate the tenancy before the end of the year without the landlord's consent.

" '3. The obligation of the tenant to pay the rent for the year, in such case, is not within the statute of frauds; the holding over being equivalent to a new entry." *Frank* v. *Flynn,* Ohio App., 197 N.E.2d 657 (1964).

TENANCY AT WILL

A tenancy at will is an estate which gives the tenant the right to possession with the consent of the landlord. It may be created by express agreement or by implication of law,[6] and during its existence the tenant has all the rights incident to the relation of landlord and tenant. The term of the estate at will is indefinite, and either party may terminate it by the giving of proper notice. At common law an estate at will was terminable without notice; but today, notice is generally required, frequently because of statutory requirements. The statutes of some states set out the time for the giving of notice, and some statutes provide the form of notice that shall be used and the method of service of notice. In those states which require notice but have no statutory requirements, reasonable notice must be given. The estate at will is terminated by the death of either the landlord or the tenant.

TENANCY AT SUFFERANCE

A tenancy at sufferance arises when the tenant comes into possession of the real property lawfully and then, after his rights have expired, holds possession of the premises without the consent of the person entitled to possession. Two common examples of an estate at sufferance are (1) a case in which a tenant for years fails to surrender possession on the expiration of his term; and (2) a case in which a mortgagor, without the consent of the purchaser, continues in possession after foreclosure, sale, and expiration of the redemption period.

An estate at sufferance may be converted into an estate at will or an estate from year to year by the acquiescence of the owner of the real estate. If a mortgagor holds over after default, foreclosure, sale, and expiration of the redemption period, and the other interested person consents, either expressly or impliedly, to the holding-over, an estate at will generally results; but if a tenant for years holds over with the consent of the landlord, an estate from year to year generally results. No notice is required to terminate an estate at sufferance. The tenant is in possession without any right of possession and is therefore not entitled to notice.

---

[6] *In re Wilson's Estate,* 349 Pa. 646, 37 A.2d 709.

The lease

ESSENTIALS OF A VALID LEASE

In determining whether or not an agreement results in a valid lease the courts have applied contract law. The parties must reach a mutual agreement (offer and acceptance), their promises must be supported by consideration,[7] the parties must have the capacity to contract, and the objective of the lease must be legal. No particular words are necessary to create the relation of landlord and tenant. The lease may be written, oral, or implied, depending on the circumstances,[8] and the provisions of any applicable statute of the state in which the leased real estate is located will become a part of the lease.

An agreement for a lease is not a lease and is not binding on the parties unless it is certain as to the terms of the future lease. If the agreement for a lease shows on its face that provisions of the proposed lease are left to future negotiation and determination, the agreement is void for uncertainty of terms.

If the tenant takes possession under an agreement for a lease, the courts will presume that the parties intended to effect a present lease and will resolve all doubts in favor of finding that a lease exists, unless the agreement is clearly insufficient to create a lease, in which case the courts will hold that the party in possession is a tenant at will. However, if the person in possession is permitted to retain possession and the owner accepts the payment of rent, some courts have held that a tenancy from year to year is created.

A lease will be declared to be void for illegality if it is made with the knowledge and intention of the landlord that the leased premises are to be used for immoral or illegal purposes.[9] There is some diversity of opinion as to what facts would be sufficient to establish "knowledge and intention" on the part of the landlord. Some courts have held that mere knowledge of the illegal use without collusion or participation in the illegal act on the part of the landlord is not sufficient to invalidate the lease. However, the courts have held the lease to be invalid if the landlord, after discovery of the illegal use, sanctions such illegal use.

[7] *In re Wilson's Estate*, 349 Pa. 646, 37 A.2d 709.

[8] *Cooperative Building Materials, Inc.* v. *Robbins & Larkey et al.*, 80 Cal. App.2d 832, 183 P.2d 81.

[9] *Weizman et al.* v. *Chapin*, 51 Ohio Abs. 26, 79 N.E.2d 668.

Requirement of writing

The provisions of the statute of frauds generally apply to leases; therefore a lease which will not be performed within one year from the making thereof must be evidenced by a note or memorandum in writing signed by the party to be bound or his duly authorized agent. However, in a few states an oral lease for a period in excess of one year is valid. For example, in Indiana an oral lease for a period not to exceed three years is valid.[10]

If the provisions of the statute of frauds are not complied with, the lease is unenforceable. The courts are not in agreement as to the character of the tenancy arising when a person enters into the occupancy of the real estate under an unenforceable lease. Some courts hold that the tenancy is a tenancy at will.[11] Other courts have held that the term of the tenancy is for the same period of time as that provided for the payment of rent in the unenforceable lease. For example, if rent is payable in monthly installments, the tenancy will be a tenancy from month to month; whereas if the rent is payable in yearly installments, the tenancy will be a tenancy from year to year. A few states have held that the tenancy will be for the period of time which can be lawfully created by a parol (oral) agreement.[12]

Minnie Newsom had a life estate in premises known as the Cox survey. Her stepson, C. W. Newsom, had inherited a one-half interest in the land. He was in possession of the land, and Mrs. Newsom brought suit to recover possession and to obtain $1,400 rent. She based her claim to rent on an oral four-year lease. The court granted Mrs. Newsom possession of the land but denied her a judgment for the rent on the ground that the oral four-year lease was unenforceable. On appeal, the denial of the judgment for rent was affirmed.

Chief Justice Grissom said: "Mrs. Minnie Newsom contends the judgment should be reversed insofar as it denies her recovery of rent on the Cox survey. The court found that Mrs. Newsom orally leased the Cox survey to C. W. Newsom for a term longer than one year. We agree with the court's holding that this parol agreement was unenforceable under the statute of frauds. The court correctly denied Mrs. Newsom a judgment for rent on the Cox survey." *C. W. Newsom* v. *Mrs. Minnie L. Newsom,* Tex. Civ. App., 371 S.W.2d 894 (1963).

[10] *Burns Indiana Statues (Annotated),* 1949 Replacement, Title 33, Sec. 101.

[11] *Greenway Wood Heel Co., Inc.* v. *John Shea Co.,* 313 Mass. 177, 46 N.E.2d 746.

[12] *Lyle* v. *Munson,* 213 Mich. 250, 181 N.W. 1002.

EXECUTION OF THE LEASE

As a general rule, the lease must be signed by the landlord. Since it is, in effect, a conveyance of an interest in real estate, the signature of the landlord is necessary to give effect to the lease. Although the signature of the landlord's spouse is not essential to the validity of a lease, the spouse should sign if it is a long-term lease, thereby conveying or releasing any claim to a dower interest in the leased real estate which would be adverse to the rights of the tenant.

If the tenant enters into possession under the lease, his signature is generally not essential to the validity of the lease; however, the absence of the tenant's signature may, under some circumstances, render the lease invalid. Good business practice requires the signing of the lease by both the landlord and the tenant.

Unless the statutes of the state in which the leased real estate is located require a seal, the lease is valid although not under seal.

Whether a lease will be valid without attestation or acknowledgment will depend on the statutes of the state in which the real estate is located. As a general rule, neither attestation nor acknowledgment is essential to the validity of the lease. However, if the lease is to be recorded, it must be executed in compliance with the recording statutes of the state in which the real estate is located. The statutes of some states expressly provide for the recording of leases for a term of five years or longer.

As is true of written instruments generally, the lease, in order to be operative, must be delivered and accepted.

PARTIES TO A LEASE

The correct names and addresses of the parties to a lease should be set out with the same degree of care as is exercised in naming the parties to a deed. If the landlord is married, the spouse should be joined, so that any interest which the spouse may have in the property will be bound by the lease. However, if a spouse joins in the execution of the lease for the sole purpose of binding his or her inchoate interest in the leased real estate, such as the dower interest of the wife, a provision should be included in the lease negating the liability of such spouse on the covenants in the lease. If the leased real estate is owned by joint tenants or tenants by the entirety, all the tenants should join in the execution of the lease. If the landlord or tenant is a corporation, its authority to execute the lease should be checked. Likewise, if the landlord or tenant is a fiduciary, the power of such fiduciary to execute the lease should be carefully investigated.

If a lease is signed by an agent of the landlord, it should be signed in the name of the landlord, with the name of the agent added, together with appropriate words designating that the agent is signing in a representative capacity. If the lease is a long-term lease which should be recorded, the agent's authority should be in writing and executed with such formality as will make the lease eligible for recordation.

DESCRIPTION OF PREMISES

The premises leased should be so described that their extent is clearly stated. A description by street number should never be used, since such a description does not identify the land intended to be included in the lease. If a lease of an entire building describes the premises by street number, the courts usually hold, in the absence of facts showing a contrary intent, that the lease includes the land generally used in connection with the building.

If the lease is for a part of a building—such as a floor of a building, office space, or an apartment—the extent of the premises should be carefully set out. If the tenant is to have the privilege of using storage space in the basement or other part of the building, such fact should be stated in the lease, since the terms of a written lease cannot be added to or altered by parol evidence.[13] In describing the leased premises, it is wise to follow the practice used in a description of real estate being conveyed by a deed and, in addition, to include a statement of the tenant's right to light and air, and use of driveways, alleys, stairways, elevators, halls, and so forth, especially if the entire premises are not leased to a single tenant.[14] If the lease is for a part of a building, the attachment of blueprints of the leased premises will make more certain the area leased.

EXAMINATION OF TITLE

As a general rule, the tenant does not demand that the landlord furnish an abstract certified to date for examination. Such a practice would be wholly unwarranted if the lease were for a relatively short term. However,

[13] *Harmony Cafeteria* v. *International Supply Co.*, 249 Ill. App. 532.

[14] *Richard Paul, Inc.* v. *Union Improvement Co.*, 33 Del. Ch. 113, 91 A.2d 49.

if the lease is for a long term, such as 50 or 99 years, and the tenant is to construct a building on the leased real estate, he should exercise the same precautions as he would if he were purchasing the property.

STATEMENT OF TERM

The term of a lease is the time the lease will run and should be set forth with precise dates. Good business practice requires that the date of the beginning of the term and the date of its ending be stated, together with a statement of the total period of the lease. The following would be an acceptable statement for the term of a lease: "for a term of 10 years beginning July 1, 1965, and ending June 30, 1975." If a lease states that the term is for "10 years from July 1, 1965," there is a diversity in the decisions as to whether the term commences on July 1 or on July 2. If the statement of the term is ambiguous and the court cannot determine with reasonable certainty the period for which the lease is to run, it will hold that the lease creates a tenancy at will.[15]

The courts have held that a lease is valid if it may be renewed at the option of the tenant as often as the tenant may elect to do so. However, the courts do not favor such terms in a lease, and will hold that a perpetual lease has not been created unless the language of the lease and the surroundings clearly indicate that such was the intention of the parties.

In some states, there is a statutory limitation on the terms of agricultural leases; and in some states, leases for 100 years or more are prohibited by statute.[16]

On October 3, 1958, Kalicki's predecessor in title, as landlord, entered into an "advertising lease" with Bell as tenant. The lease was "for a term of one or more years at a yearly rental of $15 payable in equal annual installments, and the Landlord grants the Tenant an option to renew this lease for like period or periods at the same rental." The lease provided that it "shall enure to the benefit of and be binding upon the personal representatives, heirs, successors and assigns of the parties hereto." Kalicki gave Bell notice of termination of the lease as of October 3, 1962. Bell refused to recognize the legality of the termination notice, and Kalicki brought an action for unlawful detainer. Judgment for Kalicki, and Bell appealed. Judgment was affirmed.

J. A. D. Sullivan said: "The ruling by the trial court was correct. The

---

[15] *Farris* v. *Hershfield,* 325 Mass. 176, 89 N.E.2d 636.

[16] California, Iowa, Michigan, Montana, and Nevada have statutes limiting the term of certain types of agricultural leases. Alabama, California, and Nevada have statutes prohibiting leases for a term in excess of 99 years.

law does not favor perpetual leases or covenants for continued renewals of a lease which tend to create a perpetuity. An option for renewal of a lease will not be construed as granting to the tenant the right of perpetual renewals unless the intention to create such right is clearly and unequivocally expressed in the instrument.

" '. . . It is the rule that a provision in a lease in general terms for a renewal or continuance of the lease will be construed as providing for only one renewal. This rule is based on the principle that the courts do not favor perpetuities, and unless the lease expressly or by clear implication provides that the second lease shall contain a covenant for future or perpetual renewals, it will be construed as providing for only a single renewal. . . .' 32 Am. Jur., Landlord and Tenant, p. 968, p. 813 (1941).

"Thus, it has been held that a provision in a lease (with privilege of renewals for similar periods) did not entitle the tenant to more than one renewal." *Kalicki* v. *Bell,* 83 N.J. Super. 139, 199 A.2d 158 (1964).

POSSESSION OF LEASED PREMISES

In many, but not all, states the landlord is bound to give the tenant actual possession of the leased premises. If the premises are occupied by a holdover tenant or adverse claimant at the date for the beginning of the term, the landlord would owe a duty to bring whatever action was necessary to recover possession and would have to bear the expense of putting the tenant in possession.[17] In some states the landlord is bound to give the tenant only the right of possession; in case the premises are occupied, the tenant himself must bring action to recover possession.[18] The tenant, for his own protection, should insist that the lease provide that the landlord would put the tenant in actual possession of the leased premises at the beginning of the term.

RENT

Rent is the consideration paid for the use and occupation of property. Parliament, by statute in 1738, gave a landlord the right to recover, as rent, the reasonable value of the use and occupation of land, even though there was no provision in the lease whereby the tenant expressly promised to pay rent. Many states have enacted similar statutes, and in other states the landlord has been allowed to recover reasonable rent on the theory that such right is a part of the common law. The payment of rent is

---

[17] *Adrian* v. *Rabinowitz,* 116 N.J.L. 586, 186 A. 29.

[18] *Ward et al.* v. *Hudson et al.,* 199 Miss. 171, 24 So.2d 329.

not essential, however, for the creation of the landlord-tenant relation, and such relation can be created by express agreement without a duty to pay for the use and occupation of the property.[19]

Rent is usually payable in money but may be paid in service or in property other than money. It may also be paid by the surrendering of some right or by the assumption of some burden on the part of the tenant, which right or burden he is not legally bound to surrender or assume. The lease should clearly define the rent to be paid and the medium to be used; and if no rent is to be paid, the lease should so state.

If there is in the lease no provision which stipulates when, where, and how the reserved rent is to be paid, and if, at the same time, there is no statute or established custom which controls, the rent will be payable at the end of the term of the lease, at the location of the leased premises, and in one payment. It is therefore customary to include in the lease an express provision defining when, where, and how the rent shall be paid.

For example, if the term of the lease is five years, the yearly rental $2,400, and the place of payment the office of the manager of the real estate, the following provisions would define the payment of rent adequately: "The lessee agrees to pay the lessor as rent for said premises, at the rate of $2,400 per annum, from January 1, 1965, to December 31, 1969, payable in equal monthly payments, in advance, on the first day of every month at the office of Bryan Realty Co., 163 Main Street, Odon, Indiana, or at such other place as the lessor may designate."

After a lease is in force, a promise by the landlord to reduce the rent or a promise by the tenant to pay additional rent is of doubtful validity. The courts have, in most instances, considered a lease to be a contract and have held a promise to reduce or to increase the rent to be void for lack of consideration. Some states have, however, enacted statutes which provide that a promise by a landlord to reduce rent is valid, even though not supported by consideration, if such promise is in writing.

A carefully drafted lease should clearly define rent concessions, such as, for instance, free rent for a period as a bonus for prompt payment of rent, or credit on rent for repairs made or for services rendered by the tenant, if any such concessions are to be made; and in the event the lease grants the tenant renewal rights, it should clearly state whether or not the rent concessions are to apply to the renewal or holdover term of the lease.

---

[1] *Enslein* v. *Enslein,* 84 Ohio App. 532, 82 N.E.2d 555.

The lease, especially a long-term lease, may, in addition to the payment of stipulated installments of rent, provide that the tenant will pay all real estate taxes and special assessments, will pay all water and sewer taxes, will keep the buildings insured and pay the premiums on such insurance, and will pay all other similar expenses. If such a provision is included in the lease, arrangement should be made for adjustment if the tax period or insurance period and the lease period do not coincide.

If the tenant is to pay water, sewer, and like charges, a provision should be made for the separate metering of such services, and they should be clearly defined. A provision in a lease that the tenant is to pay charges for water will not impose on him an obligation to pay charges for sewer service.[20]

If the lease provides that as part of the rent the tenant is to assume the burden of keeping the premises insured and is to pay the premium, the lease should set out in detail the risks to be covered by the insurance. In addition, the lease should provide that the property be insured with insurance companies which are reasonably satisfactory to the landlord and that the insurance policies, together with evidence of the payment of the premiums, be delivered to the landlord. Failure of the tenant to obtain the required insurance within a reasonable time after notice by the landlord is a default on the part of the tenant, and the landlord should be granted the right to obtain the required insurance and charge the premiums to the tenant.

The courts have held that failure to pay extra rent in the form of taxes, special assessments, insurance, electricity, water, and so forth, where the lease expressly provides that the tenant shall make such payments, is a default which gives the landlord the right to bring dispossession proceedings for nonpayment of rent.[21]

STABILIZING RENT RETURN

The purchasing power of the dollar fluctuates from time to time; and over long periods, it has consistently decreased. In drafting long-term leases, therefore, it is desirable to provide for increases or decreases in rent to compensate for this fluctuation. So-called escalator clauses similar to those included in labor contracts have been used, which are based on the consumer price index or on some similar index for determining price fluctuations. In some instances the value of the leased property is

[20] *Black* v. *General Wiper Supply Co.,* 305 N.Y. 386, 113 N.E.2d 528.
[21] *Chicago Housing Authority* v. *Bild,* 346 Ill. App. 272, 104 N.E.2d 666.

used as the basis for determining rent, and provision is made in the lease for periodical reappraisal of the leased property. The most common basis used in commercial leases is the amount of the business transacted on the premises by the tenant. Such leases are termed *percentage leases.*

PERCENTAGE LEASES

Percentage leases are used in the mercantile business. The rent to be paid is based, at least in part, on a percentage of the business transacted on the premises by the tenant. The lease may provide for the payment of a minimum monthly rental plus a percentage of gross sales over and above a stated amount; it may provide for the payment of a monthly rental plus a percentage of gross sales; or it may provide for the payment of a monthly rental plus a percentage of gross sales, with a maximum rental. In some instances the percentage may be based on net income or gross profits; but such provisions are not recommended, because of the difficulty of determining net income or gross profits.

A percentage lease should carefully define the basis on which the rent is to be computed. It should state the period for determining sales—that is, monthly, annually, or some other period—and whether there is to be a "carry-over" from one period to another. It should also carefully define gross sales and should state definitely whether merchandise returns, unpaid charge accounts, discounts allowed for prompt payment or payment of cash, and so forth, are included.

The type of report to be submitted by the tenant and the landlord's right to inspect the books of the tenant should be definitely set out in the lease. Generally, if the lease provides for the payment of a maximum rent and the tenant pays the maximum, the lease should provide that the landlord is not entitled to an accounting or the right to inspect the tenant's books.

The lease should provide that the tenant shall conduct the business continually throughout the year; or if the business is seasonal and is not operated during a part of the year, the lease should include a clause providing for the adjustment of rent and defining the basis for the adjustment. There are cases which hold that the court will not imply in a percentage lease a covenant which requires the tenant to continue the business for which the premises are leased.[22]

Stern leased premises at 108 North Front Street to Richard Stark. The lease provided that it could be assigned, the assignee assuming all the obligations

---

[22] *Dickey* v. *Philadelphia Minit-Man Corp.,* 377 Pa. 549, 105 A.2d 580.

under the lease, and that the premises were to be used for the purpose of operating a retail store for the sale of general wearing apparel and for no other purpose without the written consent of the leasor. The term was for five years, from August 15, 1956, to August 14, 1961. The rent received was 5½ per cent of the annual gross sales, "provided that in no event shall the annual rental agreed to be paid by the lessee during said period be less than $4,800." The $4,800 fixed minimum was payable $400 on the fifteenth of each and every month, beginning August 15, 1958. Stark leased the adjoining building, 110 North Front Street, and requested permission to break through the wall and connect the two buildings, but Stern refused to give such permission.

During the last two years of the lease period, Stark made no sales from 108 North Front Street but used it for office space and display purposes and paid the minimum rent each month. Stern sued to recover a judgment based on 5½ per cent of the gross sales made from 110 North Front Street. The court denied Stern a judgment; and on appeal, the decision was affirmed.

Judge Gabel said: "Where a lease provides for rental based on a percentage of sales with a *fixed substantial adequate minimum,* and there is no express covenant or agreement to occupy and use the premises, no implied covenant or agreement will be inferred that the lessee is bound to occupy and use the premises for the purpose expressed in the lease. Under such a lease, lessee has no obligation to occupy and use the premises for any stated definite period of time and his obligation under such a lease is limited to the payment of the basic minimum rental to the end of the term when he no longer occupies and uses the premises for the purpose expressed in the lease.

"It is therefore the judgment of the Court that first, the defendants cannot be charged with any fraud, deceit, scheme or plan to divert business from the leased premises. Second, the express conditions of said lease have not been breached by the defendants. Third, there is no express or implied covenant in said lease requiring defendants to occupy and use the premises for the sale of general wearing apparel. Fourth, the lessee in paying the minimum rental of $4,800.00 per annum paid a substantial adequate rental and the plaintiffs are not entitled to any percentage of sales made in the adjoining premises." *Kretch v. Stark,* 92 Ohio Abs. 47, 193 N.E.2d 307 (1962).

SECURITY FOR PAYMENT OF RENT

The landlord may secure the payment of the rent provided in the lease (1) by contracting for a lien on the tenant's property, (2) by requiring the tenant to pay a portion of the rent in advance, (3) by requiring the tenant to post security, or (4) by requiring the tenant to have some third person guarantee the payment of the rent. In some states the landlord is given a statutory lien on the crops and on the tenant's personal property which is on the leased premises.

The nature of the lien acquired by the landlord by inserting in the lease a clause giving him a lien on the property of the tenant as security will depend on the language of the lease. A lease clause giving a landlord a lien on the tenant's property as security for the payment of rent has been held in different cases to be a chattel mortgage, an equitable lien, and/or a declaration of trust. Such a lien has generally been held to be valid, but it will not attach to the property of a third person which has been brought onto the premises by the tenant.

As a general rule, the landlord's lien is enforceable against the tenant and all persons claiming through him with notice of the lien, but it is not enforceable against good-faith purchasers for value without notice. Whether or not the landlord can protect his interests by recording or filing the lease or a notice of the lien will depend on the statutes of the state in which the real estate is located.

The landlord may require the tenant to pay a substantial portion of the rent in advance. If the provision in the lease is properly worded and the payment is held to be a payment of rent in advance, the landlord may, on default by the tenant, retain the rent paid. However, if the provision in the lease is not carefully worded, the court may hold the advance payment to be a deposit of money as security, and require the landlord, on breach of the lease by the tenant, to refund to the tenant any amount of the deposit over and above proved damages.[23]

The tenant may post security for the payment of rent. The security posted is usually in the form of cash or securities, such as stocks and bonds, or it may be both cash and securities. If cash is deposited with the landlord as security, some courts have held that a debtor-creditor relation is created and that the landlord may use such money as he wishes. Other courts have decided that the landlord holds the deposit as pledgee and that his use of the deposit in his business is not authorized.[24]

If securities are deposited, the landlord will hold such securities as pledgee. In the absence of a provision in the lease to the contrary, the tenant will be entitled to the income from the securities so long as he is not in default. Generally, the provision for the deposits of securities will permit the tenant to substitute securities, provided the market value of the securities deposited does not fall below a stated amount.

Instead of depositing money or securities with the landlord, the tenant

---

[23] *Brooks et al.* v. *Coppedge,* 71 Idaho 166, 228 P.2d 248, 27 A.L.R.2d 645.

[24] *Colantuoni* v. *Balene,* 95 N.J. Eq. 748, 123 A. 541.

may have some person, either as guarantor or as surety, guarantee the payment of the rent. A guarantee must be in writing and signed by the guarantor or surety.

The person acting as guarantor or surety may sign, with the tenant, the lease in which the guarantee provision is included; or he may sign a separate guarantee agreement. In the event payment of rent is guaranteed by a guarantor or surety, the landlord should not enter into any agreement with the tenant which alters in any way the material provisions of the lease, unless the guarantor or surety consents to the alteration. Any alteration of the terms of the lease without the consent of the guarantor or surety will release the guarantor or surety from his liability on the lease, unless he later ratifies the alteration.

Several states have enacted statutes giving the landlord a lien on the tenant's crops and personal property on the leased premises for unpaid rent. Such statutes are not uniform in their provisions, and the statutes of the state in which the real estate is located apply.

In October, 1952, Gordon Motors, Inc., leased certain premises from Martin for a term of five years. In February, 1954, Gordon Motors, Inc., was placed in receivership, and the lease was abandoned. Martin then released the premises at the same rental but for a five-year period from May 1, 1954. At the time Gordon Motors, Inc., executed the lease, it paid five months' rent in advance The rent provision in the lease relative to the advance payment was as follows:

> The Tenant further covenants and agrees at the time of the signing of this lease to pay the Landlord the sum of Three Thousand One Hundred and Eighty-Seven Dollars and Fifty Cents ($3,187.50), representing rental for the months of June, July, August, September and October, 1957, less the sum of Seven Hundred Seventeen Dollars and Twenty Cents ($717.20), representing interest at 4½% for the term of five (5) years, or a net sum of Two Thousand and Four Hundred Seventy Dollars and Thirty Cents ($2,470.30). This payment is for the rent of such months exclusively and does not relieve the Tenant from his obligation to pay the sum of $637.50 on the first day of each and every month during the continuance except the months of June, July, August, September and October, 1957.

After the expiration of the term, Lochner, receiver for Gordon Motors, Inc., demanded that Martin refund the advance payment made by Gordon Motors, Inc. The new lessee had paid the rent in full. Martin refused, and Lochner brought suit to recover a judgment for the advance rent. The trial court held that Martin was entitled to retain the advance rent, and Lochner appealed. The judgment was affirmed.

Judge Prescot said: "The chancellor thought that the recent case of Tatelbaum v. Chertkof was controlling, and we agree. In cases of this nature, where a lease requires payment of rent in advance as distinguished from a security deposit, it is well-established law that the lessor may retain the payment upon default of the lessee in paying rent for a previous period, constituting a breach of the lease, in the absence of a provision for its refund, for the right and title thereto passes upon the execution of the lease or the payment required, and prevention of its application to the part of the term for which it was paid arises from the lessee's own misconduct.

"The reasons for the above principle are apparent. Rent does not accrue from day to day, but accrues on the day it is payable. Accordingly, the rent herein involved, although paid for a portion of the term four and one-half years in the future, was accrued, and became the property of the landlord, on the day it was paid.

"Ordinarily in determining whether money paid as in the case at bar be a payment of rent or a deposit for security, we must arrive at the intention of the parties as manifested in the terms of the lease construed in the light of surrounding circumstances. It is, of course, significant that the parties in the lease specifically termed the payment as 'rent.'

"We hold that as the money was received by the appellees for the payment of rent in advance, title thereto passed unto the appellees at the time of payment; and, under the circumstances of this case, they are not unjustly enriched by its retention." *Lochner* v. *Martin,* 218 Md. 519, 147 A.2d 749 (1959).

USE OF LEASED REAL ESTATE

In determining the tenant's right to use the leased real estate, the courts treat his interest as property and apply the rules of law relative to the alienation of property. The tenant's right to the use and occupation of the property gives him complete control; and anyone, including the landlord, who comes onto the property, without the tenant's consent, express or implied, is liable to him in an action of trespass. The tenant may use the leased real estate for any lawful purpose unless the purpose for which it may be used is expressly set out in the lease.[25] He may not commit waste; that is, he may not do anything which would damage the reversion, such as, for instance, tear down buildings or cut ornamental trees.

The tenant's use of the leased real estate may be limited by provisions in the lease which specify that the property shall be used only for certain purposes or which prohibit certain designated uses. Any provision in a lease limiting the use of the premises will be strictly construed; and if the provision is ambiguous, it will be construed most strongly against

---

[25] *Bovin* v. *Galitzka,* 250 N.Y. 228, 165 N.E. 273.

the landlord and in favor of the tenant; consequently, restrictive covenants in a lease should be drafted with great care.

A provision limiting the use of the premises to stated purposes *only* will be upheld; but if the stated purpose becomes illegal or is prohibited by governmental regulations, the lease may be terminated on the ground of commercial frustration. If the use provision is so drafted, however, that the restriction is general rather than specific and the circumstances are such that the tenant's use of the property is not totally or almost totally defeated by the regulation, the courts have generally held that the lease is not terminated.[26]

The tenant may wish to have a provision included in the lease whereby the landlord promises not to lease other parts of the building for competing uses. If such a provision does not expressly provide that the landlord himself shall not operate a competing business in the building, he will not be prohibited from doing so. Such restrictive provisions are valid; they are not contracts in restraint of trade. If restrictive provisions are not carefully worded, they may become the source of considerable ligitation.[27]

If a tenant leases an entire building for business purposes, he will have, in the absence of a restrictive provision in the lease, the right to maintain signs on the outer walls and to erect signs on the roof.[28] As· a general rule, signs cannot be maintained on residential property; consequently, if anyone, such as a doctor or dentist, leases residential property and wishes to put up a sign on the property, he should see that the lease defines his right to maintain a sign.

If the tenant leases only a part of a building, he may maintain signs on the part of the premises which he leases, provided there is no clause in the lease restricting his right. If he wishes to erect a protruding sign, a license may be required, in which case the tenant would have to acquire the license. In all leases, provisions defining the tenant's right to maintain signs should be included.

On October 6, 1958, Weiss leased a storeroom to Speedi. The purpose clause of the lease read as follows:

"7.   Lessee covenants that during the term of this lease or any renewal

---

[26] *Lloyd et al.* v. *Murphy,* 25 Cal.2d 48, 153 P.2d 47.

[27] *Peoples Trust Co.* v. *Schultz Novelty & Sporting Goods Co., Inc.,* 244 N.Y. 14, 154 N.E. 649.

[28] *400 North Rush, Inc.* v. *D. J. Bielzoff Products Co.,* 347 Ill. App. 123, 106 N.E.2d 208.

thereof: (*a*) It will use the leased premises for the conduct of a self-service laundry and the sale and display of such items as are normally sold by self-service laundries."

On October 14, 1958, Weiss leased to Bevy the adjoining storeroom to be used to "conduct and carry on a general laundry business in all its branches; to conduct and carry on the business of cleaning, pressing. . . ." The lease further provided that during the term of the lease the lessors "will not suffer occupancy of any storeroom building owned by them . . . by another dry cleaning or shirt laundry or combination of the two within a radius of three miles from the premises herein described excepting a coin-operated automatic laundry situated in the adjacent storeroom."

On November 19, 1962, Speedi started installation of two coin-operated dry cleaning machines, and Bevy brought an action asking that Speedi be enjoined "from installing and/or operating any dry cleaning equipment in the premises. . . ." The trial court refused to grant the injunction; and on appeal, the injunction was granted.

Presiding Judge Kovachy said: "Accordingly, we hold that the purpose clause of the Speedi lease was couched in plain, ordinary and unambiguous language; that in the light of the surrounding circumstances and the situation of the parties, the unmistakable import of the expression 'for the conduct of self-service laundry' was that the lessee be permitted to conduct a business for the washing of clothes with coin-operated washing machines; that the parties clearly understood and intended that only such business be conducted on the premises; that the use of coin-operated dry cleaning machines did not come within the purview of the purpose clause incorporated in the Speedi lease and that as a consequence the judgment of the Court of Common Pleas was contrary to law.

"It follows, therefore, that Speedi, by installing the two coin-operated dry cleaning machines, was competing with the dry cleaning business of Bevy's in direct violation of the lease granted it by lessors to the irreparable injury of Bevy's. Furthermore, Bevy's had a binding written promise from the lessors to protect it from competition in its business insofar as the rental of property owned by the lessors was concerned and since the lessors had failed to take steps to protect Bevy's in the matter, Bevy's had the right to invoke a court of equity to enjoin Speedi from installing and continuing the use of coin-operated dry cleaning machines in competition with it in its dry cleaning business." *Bevy's Dry Cleaning and Shirt Laundry, Inc.* v. *Streble,* Ohio App., 194 N.E.2d 595 (1963).

Davis leased certain premises to Wickline. The lease included the following paragraph:

"Fourth: It is covenanted and agreed between the contracting parties that during the term of this lease the premises hereby leased shall be used for the purpose of a drug store and for no other purpose—and that during the term of this lease or any renewal thereof the lessee shall operate the premises as a drug store.

Wickline ceased to operate the drugstore and did not use the premises for any other purpose but continued to pay the reserved rent. Davis contends that Wickline is obligated to operate a drugstore on the premises during the entire term of the lease. The trial court held that Wickline was not obligated to operate a drugstore on the premises; and on appeal, the judgment was affirmed.

Justice Wittle said: "In addition to what has been said two well defined rules of construction mitigate against the position urged by Davis in this case: (1) a contract of lease is to be construed favorably to the lessee and against the lessor; and (2) breach of covenant to sustain forfeiture is construed strictly against forfeiture. The instrument must give the right of forfeiture in terms so clear and explicit as to leave no room for any other construction.

"Keeping these principles in mind an examination of paragraph 'Fourth' of the lease is in order. The pertinent clauses are: '. . . the premises hereby leased shall be used for the purpose of a drugstore and for no other purpose.'

"This clause is clearly restrictive in nature, simply requiring the building to be used for no other purpose than a drug store. The remaining clause: 'and that during the term of this lease or any renewal thereof the Lessee shall operate said premises as a drug store.'

"This latter clause simply makes the restriction of the first clause applicable to the option to renew for a ten year term which was granted to Wickline under the lease.

"If it had been intended by Davis that Wickline operate, at all costs, a drug store for ten years, such a burdensome obligation should have been spelled out in clear and explicit terms and should have included some standard of measurement by which the conduct of Wickline could have been measured.

"We have been cited to no authority, nor have we found any, supporting Davis' contention in this case." *Davis* v. *Wickline,* Va., 135 S.E.2d 812 (1964).

REPAIRS

At common law the tenant had an implied duty to make those minor repairs which were necessary to preserve the property in substantially the same condition as that at the commencement of the term, ordinary wear excepted. Conditions have changed radically, especially as applied to domestic tenancies, and such tenants seldom make or are expected to make even minor repairs. Several states have enacted statutes either expressly imposing on the lessor a duty to keep the leased premises in reasonable repair or making his failure to repair punishable by fine or imprisonment.

In multiple-unit residential property and in office buildings the landlord usually contracts to provide such services as heat, air conditioning, hot water, elevators, and janitor. The landlord, as a general rule, retains control over the common elements—for instance, stairways, halls, lobbies, and entrances; and he therefore owes a duty to keep them in reasonable repair, and if he fails to do so, and, as a result of his breach of duty, a tenant, a guest of a tenant, or an invitee is injured, the landlord may be held liable in tort.

The lease may set out the duties of the landlord and tenant to make repairs. Repair provisions in a lease should state clearly the scope of the duties of the party who has agreed to make repairs. For example, a provision granting the landlord the right to enter the premises and make repairs imposes on the landlord no duty to make repairs.[29]

The extent of the obligation of the party who has agreed to make repairs will depend primarily on the language of the provision in the lease. A general provision to make repairs will not impose on the promisor an obligation to make structural changes in the building or to make improvements. An agreement to repair will not, as a general rule, require the promisor to restore the building to a sound or good state and to maintain it in a condition suitable for the purposes for which it is leased. In general, if a tenant agrees to keep the leased premises in repair, he is obligated to place and keep the buildings in reasonable repair.[30] An agreement to keep the leased premises in repair does not impose an obligation to rebuild a structure destroyed without the fault of the promisor.

A promise to repair made by a tenant of only part of a building imposes on him no obligation to repair parts of the building which he does not occupy. Likewise, a promise by the landlord to make specific repairs imposes on him no obligation to make repairs not specified.

A provision for repairs should clearly state whether or not the party assuming the obligation to make repairs is to repair the inside or the outside of the building, or both, and whether or not repairs to the roof are included.

If the landlord is to make repairs, he has implied assent to enter and make repairs. As a general rule, if the landlord is obligated to make repairs, he is not in default unless he has actual or constructive notice of the need for repairs, or has actual knowledge that repairs are needed and has had a reasonable opportunity to make them.[31]

---

[29] *Stone* v. *Sullivan,* 360 Mass. 450, 15 N.E2d. 476.

[30] *Ingalls et al.* v. *Roger Smith Hotels Corporation,* 143 Conn. 1, 118 A.2d 463.

[31] *Harris* v. *Edge et al.,* 92 Ga. App. 827, 90 S.E.2d 47.

In November, 1954, National Biscuit Company (NBC) leased three warehouses from Baehr. The lease provided that the lessor would keep the building painted, make all outside repairs and all repairs of a permanent nature, and all alterations and additions required by Fire underwriters, public utility companies, or municipal or state authority. Paragraph 10 of the lease provided as follows:

> 10. The Lessee covenants and agrees during the continuance of this lease to maintain landscape planting and to make all ordinary interior repairs and it is hereby agreed that any single repair job, the reasonable cost of which is $100.00 or over and which is not clearly an ordinary interior repair as distinguished from a structural repair or a repair of a permanent character, shall be considered a repair of a permanent character under the terms of this lease. Lessee agrees to make all repairs whatsoever on the demised premises made necessary by the negligence, carelessness, misconduct, or fault of the Lessee or its agents, licensees or invitees.

Incinerators in the warehouses needed extensive repairs and the parties agreed that new ones should be installed. The cost of the new incinerators installed was $1,188 each, or a total of $3,564. NBC installed the three incinerators and sued Baehr for the recovery of the cost of making the three installations. The court granted NBC a judgment; and on appeal, the judgment was affirmed.

Judge Ervin said: "It is a hornbook law that where the terms of a lease are not ambiguous, interpretation and construction of the contract are questions for the court. The court's function is to determine the intention of the parties from the language used.

"We agree with the interpretation placed upon these leases by the court below. We think it is clear that the repair here involved was one of a permanent character and that if there was any doubt about this question, the $100.00 provision of paragraph 10 requires that it be treated as a repair of a permanent character, the responsibility for which rested upon the lessor." *National Biscuit Company* v. *Baehr Brothers,* Pa. Super., 199 A.2d 494 (1964).

LANDLORD'S RIGHT TO ENTER AND INSPECT

The landlord has no right to enter the leased premises or those parts of the leased premises which are in the exclusive occupation of the tenant, unless such privilege is provided for by the terms of the lease. Generally, a lease will grant to the landlord the right to inspect the premises during the term of the lease. Such a provision should clearly define the landlord's right to inspect, stating the frequency of his inspections and the time of day when he is to make his inspections.

If the landlord is to be permitted to show the premises to prospective purchasers or lessees, his rights in this respect should be defined with a reasonable degree of certainty.

Tenant's tort liability

The tenant has the exclusive right to the occupation and control of the premises during the term of the lease; consequently, he is primarily liable for the conditions and use of the premises. If the tenant creates a nuisance on the premises, he will be answerable to those suffering therefrom. He will also be liable in tort for damages to persons who are injured while on the premises, provided such injury results from a breach of duty owed to the injured person by the tenant. The fact that the use of the premises by the tenant is not a violation of the provisions of the lease does not relieve him from liability to third persons.

Any use of property which results in an unreasonable interference with another's use and enjoyment of his property is a nuisance. No one has absolute freedom in the use of his property, since he must be restrained in his use by the existence of equal rights in his neighbor to the use of the neighbor's property. Such a rule does not prohibit all use which annoys or disturbs his neighbor in the enjoyment of his property, but' rather prohibits the use which constitutes injury to a legal right of the neighbor.

Whether the particular use constitutes a private nuisance generally turns on whether the use is reasonable under the circumstances. The test to be applied is the effect of the condition on ordinary persons with reasonable dispositions and ordinary health, and possessing average and normal sensibilities.[32] As a general rule, when a lawful business is properly operated and the location is proper, the operation of the business will not be enjoined as a nuisance, even though the operation of the business may interfere to some extent with the enjoyment of property in the vicinity.[33]

A tenant's tort liability to persons coming onto the premises or to those using the highway adjacent to the premises will be determined by the application of the law of negligence. If the tenant is in sole and exclusive occupation of the premises, he will be responsible to third persons for the condition of such premises. He will also owe a duty to persons using the highway upon which the leased real estate abuts to keep the premises free from conditions dangerous to such persons. For example, the courts have held that such a tenant would be liable to persons

---

[32] *Beckman et al.* v. *Marshall et ux.,* Fla., 85 So.2d 552.

[33] *Antonik et al.* v. *Chamberlain et al.,* 81 Ohio App. 465, 78 N.E.2d 752.

injured as the result of the tenant's having left unguarded an excavation adjacent to the highway, or of his having neglected to repair a loose sign, a defective fire escape, or a weakened structure which it was foreseeable might fall and injure a person using the highway.[34]

The tenant's liability to a person coming onto the leased real estate will depend on the relation of the tenant to the person and the surrounding circumstances. If the person is a trespasser, the tenant owes him no affirmative duty—that is, the trespasser takes the premises as he finds them. The tenant does, however, owe a duty not to injure such person willfully; and if he knows that a trespasser is on the premises, he owes a duty to use reasonable care not to cause him injury.

A licensee is a person who is on the premises with the express or implied consent of the tenant. For example, a person is a licensee if he is on the premises with the consent of the tenant for the purpose of hunting or fishing, or if he is a guest, or if he has come onto the premises to transact business with an employee of the tenant.[35] The tenant owes a duty to warn a licensee of known dangerous conditions on the premises and to refrain from conduct which it is foreseeable might injure him.

An invitee is a person who is on the premises, with the express or implied consent of the tenant, for the purpose of conducting business with the tenant. The tenant owes a duty to an invitee to keep the premises in a reasonably safe condition. The customers of a tenant who operates a retail store on the premises are invitees, and the tenant owes a duty to such persons to keep those parts of the premises in which they would ordinarily be present in a reasonably safe condition and to warn them of any condition which it is foreseeable might cause injury.

LANDLORD'S TORT LIABILITY

In general, a landlord is not liable in tort to third persons who are injured while on the leased premises, since he has no control over such premises. He does not impliedly warrant the condition of the premises, nor does he warrant that they are suitable for the tenant's purposes. He owes a duty, however, to warn the tenant of known latent dangerous conditions of the premises; and if the tenant is injured as the result of the landlord's failure to warn him, the landlord will be liable.

If the landlord has promised to keep the premises in repair, he will

---

[34] *Smith et al.* v. *Claude Neon Lights,* 110 N.J.L 326, 164 A. 423.

[35] *Gotch* v. *K. & B. Packing & Provision Co.,* 93 Colo. 276, 25 P.2d 719.

not be liable in tort for his failure to perform his contract, but he may be held liable in tort if he makes the repairs in a negligent manner and, as a result of his negligence, the tenant is injured. The courts have, under some circumstances, held that the landlord's failure to make repairs when he has notice or knowledge of the defective condition of the premises is negligence and have imposed tort liability on him.

The landlord's tort liability to third persons will depend on the relation between the landlord and such third persons, and on the circumstances of the particular case. The landlord will be liable to persons using the highways on which the leased premises abut and to neighboring landholders, if such persons are injured as the result of the landlord's having negligently permitted dangerous conditions to develop on the leased real estate. This liability will continue for such period of time after the tenant takes possession as will give him a reasonable opportunity to correct the condition.

The courts have generally held the landlord liable to third persons who are injured as the result of the dangerous or defective condition of real estate leased to a tenant if the leased real estate is to be used for public purposes. Such real estate as entertainment halls, amusement parks, athletic arenas, wharves, and so forth, would fall in this class. However, the landlord's liability does not extend to all real estate leased for purposes which require that the premises be open to the public. Such real estate as retail stores, restaurants, offices, and so on, would be included in this class.[36]

PROPERTY LEASED TO SEVERAL TENANTS.   Although the courts are not in complete accord as to the extent of the landlord's liability when the real estate is leased to several tenants and the landlord retains control of those portions of the premises used in common by the tenants, they uniformly hold that if, as the result of the landlord's negligence, such portions of the premises are permitted to become unsafe, the landlord will be liable to persons who are injured as the result of his negligence.[37] The landlord is liable not only to such injured tenants but also to third persons, such as guests of tenants or persons making business calls on tenants, if such third persons are injured while lawfully using the passageways, elevators, or other commonly used portions of the premises.

Some states have enacted statutes expressly imposing on landlords the responsibility for keeping multiple-unit dwellings in repair and holding

---

[36] *Warner* v. *Fry,* 360 Mo. 496, 228 S.W.2d 729.

[37] *Durkin* v. *Lewitz,* 3 Ill. App.2d 481, N.E.2d 151.

the landlord liable to persons who are injured as the result of the landlord's failure to fulfill his duty.

Strickland leased a residence to Zuroski and agreed to take care of the premises. The guttering and downspout near the back door of the house became defective and allowed water to fall from the roof and collect on the concrete walk immediately outside the rear door of the house. Zuroski notified Strickland that the downspout was defective and needed repair, but no repairs were made. On February 11, 1961, water from melting snow and ice on the roof of the house had collected on this walk, and ice had formed. Zuroski was injured when she slipped and fell on this ice. Zuroski sued Strickland in tort to recover damages for her injuries. The trial court granted Zuroski a judgment; and on appeal, the judgment was affirmed, Justice Bower dissenting.

Justice Boslaugh said: "As was pointed out in the Van Avery case, the American Law Institute adopted the view that the landlord is liable. Restatement Torts, s. 357, p. 967, provides as follows:

" 'A lessor of land is subject to liability for bodily harm caused to his lessee and others upon the land with the consent of the lessee or his sublessee by a condition of disrepair existing before or arising after the lessee has taken possession, if (*a*) the lessor, as such, has agreed by a covenant in the lease or otherwise, to keep the land in repair, and (*b*) the disrepair creates an unreasonable risk to persons upon the land which the performance of the lessor's agreement would have prevented.' The rule as stated is qualified under the heading of 'Comment: . . . Nature of lessor's duty': in part as follows: 'Since the duty arises out of the existence of the contract to repair, the contract defines the extent of the duty. Unless the contract stipulates that the lessor shall inspect the premises to ascertain the need of repairs, a contract to keep the interior in safe condition subjects the lessor to liability if, but only if, reasonable care is not exercised after the lessee has given him notice of the need of repairs.'

"It is our opinion that the rule as stated in the Restatement is the better view and it is the rule which we adopt as the law of this state. The reasoning which supported the decision in the Fried case supports the decision which we have reached in this case." *Zuroski* v. *Strickland's Estate,* 176 Neb. 633, 126 N.W.2d 888 (1964).

Asher Coal Mining Company (hereinafter referred to as Asher) leased some land to be mined for coal, and the lessee adopted the method of strip mining. Asher was fully aware of the nature of the mining operation thus conducted. The mining operation resulted in the displacement of topsoil, rock, shale, and other types of strata. After the cessation of the strip-mining operation, Asher did not restore the land to prevent soil erosion or excessive drainage along natural watercourses. As a result of the condition created, following a heavy rainfall, vast quantities of loose rock, dirt, and coal were washed down the mountainside, obstructing natural watercourses, causing the flooding of Green's premises, and depositing debris thereon, thereby injuring his land.

Green sued Asher in tort to recover a judgment for the damage to his land. The trial court dismissed the complaint, and Green appealed. The judgment was reversed.

Commissioner Clay said: "The authorities heretofore discussed recognize that the owner of land may be held liable for the acts of his lessee under the following conditions: the particular use or exploitation of the land must be such that harm to others is likely to ensue unless precautions are taken; the owner must consent to, authorize or be cognizant of this use; and the injury must be such as can reasonably be anticipated from such use.

"In a sense the leasing of land for exploitation is a method of use of it by the owner. He may not utilize it so as to cause injury to others. Therefore, if the expected operations under the lease result in such injury as may be reasonably anticipated, the owner has been a party to the wrong and cannot disclaim liability because he did not personally create the condition or commit the wrongful act. The significant considerations are the cognizable potentialities of danger and the reasonable predictability of injury.

"Applying the law to the facts stated in the complaint, we find a sustainable legal theory of liability. Asher was in the mining business. The leasing of this land was for the purpose of carrying out mining operations through a third party. Strip mining by the lessee was authorized. The topography of the land involved was such that debris from this operation would likely be cast or eroded into mountain streams, as a result of which damage to lower riparian owners could be reasonably anticipated." *Green* v. *Asher Coal Mining Company,* Ky., 377 S.W.2d 68 (1964).

LANDLORD'S EXCULPATORY CLAUSE

A lease may contain a provision expressly limiting the landlord's tort liability to the tenant. Such provisions are enforced in some states;[38] but in other states, they have been held to be against public policy.

ALTERATIONS

A tenant has no implied authority to make alterations or improvements to the leased premises.[39] If the lease is a long-term lease, it should, in order to protect the tenant, make provision for the improvement, altera-

[38] *Jackson* v. *First National Bank of Lake Forest et al.,* 415 Ill. 453, 114 N.E.2d 721.

[39] *Kavanaugh et al.* v. *Donovan,* 185 Va. 85, 41 S.E.2d 489.

tion, or removal and replacement of existing improvements. If the lease does not contain an express provision providing that improvements made by the tenant shall remain his property and that he shall have the right to remove the improvements at the termination of the lease, any permanent improvement made by the tenant immediately becomes the property of the landlord.[40]

If the lease contains a provision for alterations or improvements or for the erection of a building on leased real estate, blueprints and specifications for the work should be approved by the parties and attached to the lease. If this is not practical, then the parties to the lease should set out in detail the nature of the work to be done. Unless the work to be done is set out with reasonable certainty, the agreement may be held to be void for uncertainty of terms.[41]

If the work is to be done by the tenant, provision should be made protecting the landlord's interest against the filing of the mechanics' liens against the property. Under the mechanic's lien laws of most states a provision in the lease against mechanics' liens will not deprive mechanics and laborers of their right to liens. In order to protect the landlord, the lease should require the tenant to obtain waivers of liens or to post security; or it should require the tenant to pay to the landlord, his agent, or appointee the cost of the improvement, out of which payment the landlord would then pay for the improvement.

If personal property is to be attached to the leased real estate, the lease should state whether the tenant is to be permitted to remove such property on the termination of the lease or whether it is to become the property of the landlord. Such a provision should include a clause protecting the landlord from chattel mortgages on or conditional sales of such property.

DAMAGE TO OR DESTRUCTION OF IMPROVEMENTS

At common law, when leases of real estate were predominantly leases of agricultural land, the courts held that damage to or destruction of the improvements did not relieve the tenant from his obligation of pay the rent to the end of the term.[42] The major benefit accruing to the

[40] *County of Prince William, Virginia* v. *Thomason Park, Inc.,* 197 Va. 861, 91 S.E.2d 441.

[41] *Brooks* v. *Smith, Ky.* 269 S.W.2d 259.

[42] *Lewis et al.* v. *Real Estate Corporation,* 6 Ill. App.2d 240, 127 N.E.2d 272.

tenant in such leases was the use of the land. In commercial and residential leases of today, however, the principal value accruing to the tenant is the use of the improvement; consequently, the application of the common-law rule to such leases results in injustice to the tenant. Some states, by statute, have relieved the tenant from the payment of rent if the improvements on the leased premises are destroyed or are damaged to such an extent that they become unfit for occupancy.

The lease should make provision for the adjustment of the rent, for the repair or rebuilding of damaged or destroyed structures, for the time allowed for the restoration of the premises, and for the right of the tenant to terminate the lease if the improvements are destroyed or damaged extensively. If insurance has been provided, the lease should make provision for the application of insurance collected. The provision in a lease covering the destruction of or damage to the leased premises are difficult to draft. If not carefully drafted, they may be the source of expensive litigation.[43]

CONDEMNATION

If the leased real estate is taken by condemnation, the lease is terminated, and the tenant is entitled to compensation for the value of the unexpired period of his term. The value of a lease is determined by computing the difference between the rental value of the premises at the time they were condemned and the rent reserved for the unexpired term.

The tenant's claim to the award is paramount to the claim of the landlord; under some circumstances, the tenant's claim could exhaust the award and thus leave nothing for the landlord. In order to avoid this result, the parties may include in the lease a provision terminating the lease in the event of condemnation or private sale. If the lease provides that title to the tenant's fixtures or title to improvements made by the tenant shall vest in the landlord on the termination of the lease, provision should be made whereby the tenant is compensated if the lease is terminated by condemnation.

Two situations may arise which present some problems difficult to solve: (1) The condemnation may be only partial; and (2) the condemnation may be of only a part of the term—for example, two years of a ten-year term may be condemned.[44] In order to protect both the landlord and

---

[43] *Siegel* v. *Goldstein,* 148 N.Y.S.2d 266.

[44] *United States of America* v. *Petty Motor Co.,* 327 U.S. 372.

the tenant against these disadvantages, the lease should include a provision terminating the lease in the event of such a condemnation.

If only a part of the premises is condemned, the rent, as a general rule, is not abated; but the tenant has a claim against the award for the present value of the excess rent he is required to pay over and above the value of the use of the part of the premises not condemned.[45]

The rights of the parties in the event of a partial condemnation should be set out in the lease. Since it would be exceedingly difficult to work out, before condemnation, a satisfactory formula for the division of the award, the lease should provide for the right of the tenant, under defined circumstances, to terminate the lease. If the parties do not wish to provide for termination of the lease, they should provide either for the determination of the rights of the landlord and tenant by appraisal or for the arbitration of their rights.

RIGHT OF TENANT TO ASSIGN, SUBLET, OR MORTGAGE

A lease vests in the tenant a property interest in the leased real estate, and the courts have held this interest to be personal property. They have therefore applied basic principles of property law in determining the tenant's right to assign, sublet, or mortgage his interest in the leased property. Since free alienation is a basic property right, the tenant may, in the absence of statutory limitations or contractual restrictions in the lease, dispose of or encumber his interest as he wishes.[46]

When a tenant assigns his lease, such an assignment conveys his entire interest in the leased real estate. He does not, however, relieve himself from his obligation to pay rent or from his liability for damages if the lease is breached. The assignor of a lease is surety for the performance of the lease by the assignee.

As a general rule, the courts have held that a change in membership or a partnership or in the participation of a corporation in a corporate merger is not an assignment of a lease held by the partnership or the corporation. However, if a partnership or corporation enters into a lease which contains a clause restricting the assignment of the lease, express provision should be included which would define the rights of the parties in the event of a change in membership of the partnership or a merger of the corporate tenant.

When a tenant sublets all or any part of the leased premises, he then

---

[45] *City of Pasadena* v. *Porter,* 201 Cal. 381, 257 P. 526.

[46] *Hyman* v. *230 So. Franklin Corporation,* 7 Ill. App.2d 15, 128 N.E.2d 629.

becomes a landlord in relation to the sublessee, but he remains a tenant to the owner and is primarily liable to him.

When a tenant mortgages his leasehold rights, he encumbers whatever property rights the lease vests in him; and on default and foreclosure, his rights may be sold. In no event can he grant greater rights in the leased real estate than he has under the lease.

An absolute restriction on the tenant's right to assign, sublet, or mortgage would be against public policy and void, but reasonable restrictions are enforced. A restriction frequently included in a lease denies the tenant the right to assign the lease or sublet the premises or any part thereof without the written consent of the landlord. If the lease contains such a provision, it should also provide that the landlord cannot withhold his consent unless he has a valid reason for doing so. In some cases the courts have held that the landlord must act in good faith in withholding his consent.

If the landlord grants the tenant the right to assign the lease, this will not be restricted, unless the landlord, in granting such right, expressly provides that it shall be restricted.[47]

CONVEYANCE OF LEASED REAL ESTATE AND ASSIGNMENT OF LEASE BY LANDLORD

If the landlord conveys the leased real estate, his grantee will take the property subject to the rights of the tenant. The landlord will remain liable on all the covenants in the lease, unless the lease includes a provision relieving the landlord from all liability on the lease in the event of the conveyance of the leased real estate.

The landlord may assign his rights in the lease without conveying the leased real estate. Such an assignment is substantially equivalent to the assignment of a contract. The assignee acquires all the rights of the landlord under the lease, but the landlord is not released from his liability on the lease.

LANDLORD'S RIGHT TO TERMINATE LEASE FOR TENANT'S DEFAULT

The lease usually gives the landlord the right to take possession of the leased premises on the default of the tenant. In some states the landlord's right to re-enter on the default of the tenant is defined by statute. If the lease contains a clause granting the landlord the right to re-enter

---

[47] *Bauer et al.* v. *White et al.,* 225 Mo. App. 270, 29 S.W.2d 176.

on the default of the tenant, it should also contain a clause, for the protection of the tenant, requiring the landlord to give notice of default to the tenant and giving the tenant a reasonable time to cure the default.

For the protection of the landlord the lease should provide that in the event of default on the part of the tenant and re-entry by the landlord, the lease will not be terminated, and the tenant shall remain liable for all damages resulting from his default. The lease should also provide that if the landlord takes possession of the leased real estate, he does so as agent of the tenant and has the right to relet the leased real estate as agent of the tenant and hold the tenant for the rent reserved, crediting the rent received from the reletting of the premises to the amount owed by the tenant.

EVICTION OF TENANT

An eviction is the depriving of the tenant of the beneficial use or enjoyment of the leased real estate, or a material part thereof, by some intentional and permanent act on the part of the landlord or at his instigation. The essentials of an eviction are that it be effected by some affirmative act or default of the landlord, or through his procurement, or by paramount title. An eviction is not necessarily limited to a situation in which the landlord actually dispossesses the tenant. If the landlord deprives the tenant of the beneficial use of the premises, such act amounts to an eviction.[48]

The landlord's failure to perform the covenants in the lease may amount to a constructive eviction. For example, if the landlord has covenanted to keep the premises in repair or to provide certain services, his failure to perform may amount to an eviction, provided his default is material. Failure to repair the premises, allowing the premises to become untenantable, failure to supply heat or elevator service, or permitting the premises to become overrun by insects and vermin have been held to amount to a constructive eviction.

The landlord is not responsible for the acts of third persons or of cotenants, unless such acts are done with the authority or consent of the landlord. Also, acts of public authorities which deprive the tenant of the use and enjoyment of part or all of the leased real estate are not an eviction.[49]

---

[48] *Lindenberg* v. *MacDonald et al.,* 34 Cal.2d 678, 214 P.2d 5.

[49] *McNally et al.* v. *Moser et al.,* 210 Md. 127, 122 A.2d 555.

NOTICE TO TERMINATE LEASE

If a lease is for a definite term, no notice to quit is required; but if the lease is from period to period, such notice is required. The time for giving notice is set by statute in most states. At common law, if the period was from year to year, the time for giving notice was six months. In many states the time for giving notice to terminate a year-to-year lease has been shortened by statutory enactment. If the period is for less than a year—for example, from month to month—the time for giving notice is the period of the lease. A month's notice is usually required to terminate a month-to-month lease, and a week's notice is required to terminate a week-to-week lease.

There are some differences in the rules followed in the several states in the computing of time. In some states the first day of the period is counted, and the last day is not; in other states the first day is not counted, but the last day is. In a few states both the first and the last days are excluded in counting time. Sundays and holidays are counted, unless the last day falls on a Sunday or a holiday, in which case it is not counted.

If the notice given for termination of a lease is in excess of the minimum time required by the statute or by the provision in the lease, the notice is effective;[50] but if it is given for a shorter period, it is ineffective. For example, if the statute requires that 30 days' notice must be given to terminate a lease, a notice of 31 or more days would be effective, but a notice of 29 days would be ineffective. Whether or not the 29 days' notice would serve to terminate the tenancy at the end of the succeeding period would depend on the wording of the notice.

The notice should be specific and unequivocal, and in writing. Oral notice may be sufficient in the absence of a statute requiring the notice to be in writing. The notice may be given by the landlord or his duly authorized agent, and should be given to the tenant or his duly authorized agent. In giving notice to an agent of the tenant, the landlord should make certain that the agent of the tenant has authority to act in the matter.

RENEWAL PRIVILEGES

A clause in the lease may give the tenant the right to renew the lease. Such a clause may give the tenant the right to renew on the giving of

---

[50] *Hastings* v. *Nash,* 215 Ark. 38, 219 S.W.2d 225.

notice at a designated time before the expiration of the term, or it may provide for automatic renewal, unless the tenant or the landlord gives notice at a designated time before expiration of the term that he does not elect to renew the lease.

PROVISION FOR ADJUSTMENT OF RENTS

A provision in the lease for adjustment of the rent must be reasonably specific if it is to be valid.[51] A statement of the rent to be paid or a provision for the determination of the rent by an appraisal has been held to be sufficient. As a rule, a provision for renewal implies the renewal shall be on the same terms as the existing lease. However, the renewal clause should state whether the renewal lease shall include a renewal clause. It should also define the rights of the tenant to fixtures attached the improvements made to the leased real estate.

HOLDING OVER

A situation involving a holding-over arises only if the lease is for a specified term. Under such a lease the tenant owes a duty to surrender possession of the leased real estate at the expiration of the term; and if he fails to do so, he will be holding possession wrongfully and will then become a tenant at sufferance. When a tenant holds over, the landlord may elect to bring an action of ejectment and have the tenant evicted, or he may waive the wrong and treat such holding over as a renewal of the lease.[52] The tenant, since he is the wrongdoer, has no election in the matter; he cannot force himself on the landlord as a tenant. If the landlord consents to the holding-over, or the landlord and tenant enter into an agreement whereby the tenant will be given a period beyond the termination date of the lease, then he will not be held to be a tenant holding over.

There is some diversity in cases as to the nature of the tenancy created by the tenant's holding over and the landlord's acceptance of him as a tenant. Some courts have held that a tenancy at will is created. However, it is generally held that if the original term is for a year or more, the lease created by the holding-over and acceptance by the landlord will be for a year. If the term is for less than a year, the holdover term will be for the same period as the original term.[53] A few courts have

[51] *Slayter* v. *Pasley,* 199 Ore. 616, 264 P.2d 444.

[52] *Sinclair Refining Company* v. *Shakespear et al.,* 115 Colo. 520, 175 P.2d 389.

[53] *Mahoney* v. *Lester et al.,* 118 Mont. 551, 168 P.2d 339.

held the rent period to be the basis for the term of the lease after the holding-over. For example, these courts have held that if the rent reserved is payable quarterly, the term will be for a quarter; and if the rent is payable monthly, the term will be for one month.

As a general rule, failure by the tenant to surrender the premises at the expiration of the term is a holding-over, and the reasons for the tenant's failure to surrender the premises are immaterial. Some courts have held that if the tenant is prevented from surrendering the premises at the expiration of the term because of his sickness or by an act of God, his failure to surrender will be excused, and no new term will be created. If the tenant is prevented from surrendering the leased real estate because he is suffering from a contagious disease and is quarantined, there is no holding-over which will entitle the landlord to hold the tenant for another term.

There is some diversity in decisions of cases in regard to the effect of a notice given to the tenant before the expiration of the term that if the tenant holds over, the rental will be at a higher rate. Some courts have held that if the tenant holds over, he is liable for the increased rental.[54] Other courts have held that if the tenant objects to the increased rent, he will not be bound to pay the increase.

Several states have enacted statutes defining the rights of the landlord and the tenant in the event the tenant holds over.[55] Under the provisions of some such statutes the landlord may recover double or triple damages. In the absence of a statute the landlord may recover, as damages for holding over, only the reasonable rental value of the leased real estate for the period of time the tenant has held over, unless the landlord can prove that he has suffered special damages.

There may be included in the lease a provision defining the rights of the parties in the event the tenant holds over. Such provisions are enforced by the courts, unless they are of such a nature that the court would declare them void as against public policy.

Selk sold a 320-acre tract of land with a shack thereon to David Properties, Inc. (hereinafter referred to as David), and took a purchase-money mortgage on the real estate to secure an unpaid balance of $45,000. Selk was permitted to live in the shack rent-free until October 20, 1959, when the parties executed a written lease in which David leased "the house and premises heretofore

---

[54] *State ex rel. Needham* v. *Justice Court in and for Township and County of Silver Bow et al.,* 119 Mont. 89, 171 P.2d 351.

[55] *Corthouts* v. *Connecticut Fire Safety Service Corporation,* 2 Conn. Civ. 34, 193 A.2d 909.

occupied by him" to Selk for a term ending at midnight, December 31, 1959. Selk did not surrender possession; and on February 17, 1960, David wrote Selk, demanding possession of the premises and stating: "You are hereby instructed to vacate these premises immediately. Your continual occupation shall be at your own risk, and I shall charge rent for the use of these premises at the rate of $300 per month." Selk did not vacate the premises, and he paid no rent.

On February 16, 1961, David wrote Selk a second letter in which he demanded possession of the property and the payment of $3,600 rent for twelve months, and again stated that the rent would be $300 per month. David did not pay the $9,000 installment on the mortgage when due, and Selk filed suit to foreclose the mortgage. David filed a counterclaim for $7,200 past-due rent. The trial court dismissed the counterclaim, and David appealed. The dismissal of the counterclaim was reversed.

Associate Judge Roger J. Waybright said: "In answer to the contention that Selk did not occupy the entire 230 acres but only the shack, a tenant who without the consent of his landlord retains possession of part of the premises must be considered as holding over as to all. As to the counterlciam, in this case, the defendant, as the landlord, had at least several courses of action available when the plaintiff, as the tenant, continued to live on the leased property after expiration of the term of the lease. The defendant could probably have chosen to demand the 'double the monthly rent' provided for by the statute; it elected not to do so, and the plaintiff could not force the defendant to do so. The defendant undoubtedly could have treated the plaintiff as a trespasser, and sued or counterclaimed against the plaintiff for damages for depriving it of reasonable rental value and any special damages; it elected not to do so, and neither the plaintiff nor the chancellor could force it to do so. The defendant also could waive the wrong occasioned by the holding over and treat the plaintiff as a tenant, demanding an increased rent of the plaintiff if the plaintiff chose to remain on the property; this the defendant elected to do, and neither the plaintiff nor the chancellor could force it to claim damages instead of rent.

"When a landlord demands a different rent for continued possession of property it owns, and a tenant receives the demand and thereafter continues on in possession without protest, the tenant impliedly agrees to pay the rent demanded. Those were the facts shown by the evidence in the case, and that rule must be applied to the facts." *David Properties, Inc.* v. *Selk*, Fla., 151 So.2d 334 (1963).

OPTION TO PURCHASE

The lease may include a provision giving the tenant an option to purchase the property either during or at the expiration of the term. If the lease is a long-term lease and the included option is to run for a long time, there are many things which must be considered. Some definite formula for determining the price should be set up. The valuation of the real estate may be left to appraisers, provided a formula for determining the price is set up by the parties. If the price is to be agreed upon by the parties, the option is void for uncertainty of terms. If the price is specified in the lease, it may become a bargain price before the expiration of the option.

Provision for the mortgaging of the property during the term should be made. If the tenant is to erect buildings or make improvements to the property, the option—if the price is to be fixed by an appraisal— should state whether or not the value of the buildings erected or the improvements made by the tenant should be included or excluded in making the appraisal.

When the option is exercised, it immediately becomes a contract of sale. Consequently, the option should set out all the material provisions of a contract to sell—such as price, terms of payment, time and place of closing, type of deed to be given, nature of title to be conveyed, adjustments to be made, who is to furnish abstract, and so forth.[56] A contract of sale may be prepared and attached to the lease, and included in the option by reference to the contract.

The provision should also state whether or not the option is assignable. The courts have generally held that if the lease is assignable and is assigned, the option is assigned as part of the lease; and if the lease is not assignable, the option is not assignable.

The lease may provide for the termination of the option on the default of the tenant. If the landlord re-enters on the default of the tenant, the option generally terminates; but if the default on the part of the tenant is not material and the landlord does not re-enter, the option is not terminated, unless it is expressly provided that the tenant cannot exercise the option until he has fully and punctually performed all of the covenants in the lease.[57]

As a general rule, the tenant is required to give notice of his election to purchase under the option. If his notice of election to purchase changes or adds to the terms stated in the option, it is not an acceptance of the option but is, in legal effect, a rejection of the option and a counteroffer.

---

[56] *Rich* v. *Rosenthal*, 223 Ark. 791, 268 S.W.2d 884.
[57] *Cook* v. *Young*, Tex. Civ. App., 269 S.W.2d 457.

Instead of giving the tenant an option, the lease may give the tenant the first right to buy. Such a provision requires the landlord, in the event he decides to sell the property, to give the tenant the right to purchase the property at the price and on the terms of a good faith offer which the landlord is willing to accept.

Kahn leased a store building to Schoonover for the term beginning on November 1, 1956, and ending on October 31, 1959. The lease included the following provision: The lessee "shall have the option to purchase the premises leased herein for the sum of $15,000 at any time during the term of this lease by giving written notice of the same to lessor 30 days in advance of the exercise of this option." Kahn sold the premises to Dloogoff before the expiration of the term of the lease. Schoonover had made extensive improvements to the building during the term of the lease. Kahn contended that Schoonovers' only remedy was an action against Dloogoff for specific performance. The trial court granted Schoonover a judgment against Kahn for damages; and on appeal, the judgment was affirmed.

Commissioner Maughmer said: "Appellants assert that Schoonover never tried to exercise the option by giving the prescribed 30 days' notice and say he could have enforced the option against the purchasers, the Dloogoffs. Defendants by their sale of the property had made it impossible for them to perform under the option. They had breached the covenant conferring an option to purchase. As stated in 51 C.J.S. Landlord and Tenant 88, p. 648: 'In case of a breach of a covenant conferring on the lessee on option to purchase, the lessee is entitled to recover damages sustained by him.' See Barling v. Horn et al., where, under a different situation, specific performance was decreed. It is possible that plaintiff might produce evidence under which he might secure specific performance from the Dloogoffs but we shall not pursue or speculate upon this possibility. Defendants by their act in conveying the property made it impossible for them to honor the option. Plaintiff is not required to seek recompense for defendants' breach of the option covenant from the Dloogoffs. He may seek damages from the defendants directly." *Schoonover* v. *Kahn,* Mo. App., 377 S.W.2d 535 (1964).

SHARE-CROP LEASES

The relation created by an agreement to raise crops on shares will depend on the intention of the parties, as evidenced by the terms of the agreement, the conduct of the parties, and all the surrounding circumstances. The relationship may be that of employer and employee (cropper), or landlord and tenant, or the parties may be partners or joint adventurers. Although the relationship cannot be conclusively determined from any one thing, if the owner of the land retains possession, furnishes the seed, tools, and so forth, for planting and harvesting the crop, and the person who plants, cultivates, and harvests the crop is to receive a share of the crop for his work, the relationship, as a general rule, is that of employer and employee.[58]

If the exclusive possession of the land is given to the person who cultivates it, and particularly if such person furnishes the tools, part of the seed, and so forth, necessary for the raising and harvesting of the crop, the relation which arises is, as a general rule, that of landlord and tenant.[59] An agreement to raise a crop on shares does not usually constitute the parties partners or joint adventurers, unless the agreement clearly manifests an intention to create such a relationship.[60]

In some states the relation and rights of the parties to a sharecrop agreement are determined to some extent by statutes. In the absence of a statute the rights of the parties will be determined by the terms of the share-crop agreement. If the relation of the parties is that of employer and employee, the employer is the owner of the crop until it is divided. If the relation is that of landlord and tenant, the tenant is the owner of the crop until it is divided. In some states the owner of the land and the person raising the crop own the crop as tenants in common or joint tenants.

RESIDENTIAL LEASES

Residential leases, especially leases of apartments, are frequently prepared in advance by the landlord or his property manager, and the tenant accepts the lease as drawn if he wishes to rent the apartment. Also, in smaller communities, residential property is frequently rented on a month-to-month basis without the parties having any clear agreement as to their rights and duties. In such a situation, there is usually a fairly well-defined usage which will determine the rights of the parties in the event of a dispute.

If a tenant has a television set or contemplates the acquisition of one, he should be certain that his lease gives him the right to erect and maintain an outside television aerial.

---

[58] *Hampton* v. *Struve,* 160 Neb. 305, 70 N.W.2d 74.

[59] *California Employment Commission* v. *Kovacevich,* 27 Cal. 2d 546, 165 P.2d 917.

[60] *Koch* v. *Murphy et al.,* 151 Kan. 988, 101 P.2d 878.

Checklist for lease

Although it is impossible to prepare a checklist which will cover adequately all the possible combinations which may arise in leasing real estate, the following will suggest to the person negotiating a lease some of the more common points which should be discussed in arriving at an agreement and which should be considered for inclusion in the lease:

1. Date of the lease.
2. Correct names and addresses of the lessor and lessee.
3. Statement of marital status of the lessor and lessee or the nature of the entity if not a natural person—whether a corporation or partnership.
4. If the lessor or lessee is married, the name of the spouse.
5. If the landlord's wife signs for the purpose of releasing dower, a negation of her liability on the lease.
6. If the property is owned jointly, by the entirety, or in common, all the co-owners should be named.
7. If the real property is leased to more than one lessee, all the lessees should be named, and the lease should state that their liability is joint and several.
8. The premises leased should be clearly identified.
   a. If an entire building and the land on which it stands are leased, especially if the lease is a long-term lease, the legal description should be used. The same care should be exercised in describing the premises in a lease as is used in describing the premises in a deed.
   b. If an apartment is being leased, the apartment number and the street number of the apartment building are usually sufficient.
   c. If a part of a building—less than an entire floor—is leased, the part should be described by measurements, followed by the phrase, "more or less," since there may be some variance in measurements. A blueprint of the area leased should be attached to the lease.
   d. If an entire floor is leased, the lease should provide for the upkeep and use of common halls, stairways, driveways, and so forth.
   e. If parts of more than one floor are leased, each part should be carefully described.

f. If parts of a building over which a municipality has control are included, such as vaults under a street, there should be included in the lease a provision that the revocation by the municipality of the right to use such parts of the building will not terminate the lease or reduce the rent.

g. If the lease is of a store in a hotel or office building, it should include a provision giving the lessee the right to have a door leading to the lobby or rotunda and the right to keep the door open.

h. If personal property is included, an inventory of the personal property, setting out the condition of the property, should be prepared and attached to the lease.

9. The term of the lease should be made clear. This can be done by stating the year, month, and day the lease begins and ends.

10. Provide that the lessor shall give the lessee actual possession of the leased premises.

11. Provide for postponing the beginning of the term in case the lessor is unable to give possession on the date stated in the lease.

12. State clearly the amount of rent to be paid, the time of payment, and whether payable in advance.

13. Carefully define rent concessions to be made, if any.

14. Provide for payment of taxes, assessments, water, sewer, insurance premiums, and so forth, if paid by the tenant as additional rent.

15. Provide for the lessor's rights in the event the lessee fails to pay additional rent or fails to pay fixed rent.

16. State the types of insurance to be carried; amount of insurance; rights of the lessor and lessee in the proceeds if there is a loss; who the insurer shall be, or how determined, if the lessee is to provide insurance or pay premiums.

17. If the lease provides for the payment of percentage rent, the lease should:

a. Carefully define the basis upon which rent is to be computed— usually gross sales.

b. Fix minimum and maximum rent to be paid.

c. Set out what statements are to be furnished by the lessee, time of furnishing statements, and time of payment of percentage rent.

d. Fix rules relating to the conduct of the business—hours open for business, closing during slack season, closing for repairs, and so forth.

    e. Expressly provide that the lessor is not a partner.

18. Include a provision that the lessee will not violate any laws in the maintenance or use of the building and will not operate an illegal business on the premises.

19. State whether the lessor or lessee is to keep the buildings in repair.

20. Carefully set out the rights of the lessor and lessee in the event the buildings are destroyed or damaged by fire, flood, wind, or other cause.

21. State the lessor's right to enter premises for inspection, repairs, and so on.

22. State the lessee's right to assign, sublease, or mortgage his interest.

23. If the lessee is a partnership, set out the right of the lessee partnership to take additional partners or make changes in the membership of the partnership.

24. If the lessee is a corporation, set out the rights of the lessee corporation in the event of merger, consolidation, or reorganization.

25. Provide that if the lessee sublets, he shall assign the rent received to the lessor.

26. Provide that if the lessee mortgages the leasehold and defaults, the mortgagee shall give notice of the lessee's default to the lessor; also, provide that the lessor has the right to cure default.

27. Define the lessor's rights in the event the lessee defaults—give the lessor possessory as well as contractual remedy.

28. Provide that the lessor shall give the lessee notice of default and reasonable opportunity to cure this default.

29. Provide that the lessor shall have the right to damages for breach, even though the lessor has re-entered the premises.

30. If the lessee has the right or is obligated to make alterations to the building, the lease should:

    a. Set out in detail the nature of the alterations.

    b. Include a waiver of mechanics' liens, chattel mortgages, conditional sales, and other liens on the improvement.

    c. State whether or not the lessee is to post bond to protect the lessor.

    d. State whether the improvements are to remain the property of the lessee, with the right to remove, or are to become the property of the lessor.

    e. Contain a provision for adjustment of taxes, and so forth, resulting from alterations.

31. Carefully set out which articles attached to the real estate shall re-

main the property of the lessee, with the right of removal, and which shall become the property of the lessor on the termination of the lease.

32. If there is a renewal provision in the lease, the rights of the parties to fixtures, in the event of renewal, should be clearly stated.

33. The lease should provide that personal property of the lessee not removed on termination of the lease shall become abandoned property.

34. The lessor should be given the right to collect from the lessee the cost of removal of the abandoned property.

35. The lease should state clearly the lessee's duty to remove his personal property from the premises on the termination of the lease.

36. Define the lessor's right to show the property to a prospective purchaser, put "for sale" signs on property, and so forth.

37. Define the lessor's right to mortgage the property, including a provision that the lessee's interest shall be subordinate to the mortgage.

38. Provide that in the event the leased real estate is mortgaged, the lessee shall be given notice of the mortgagor's default and also be given an opportunity to cure the default.

39. Define the rights of the lessor and lessee if the building is damaged or destroyed.

40. Provide for abatement of rent or termination of the lease if the buildings are destroyed or damaged to such an extent that they are useless.

41. The lease should define the rights of the lessor and lessee in the event the leased real estate, or part of it, is taken by condemnation. The lease should provide:

    a. That in the event of complete condemnation, the lease is terminated.

    b. That if condemnation is partial, the rights of the lessor and lessee should be carefully defined.

    c. That if the right to occupy and use the leased real estate or a major portion is taken by condemnation, the lessee should be given the right to terminate the lease.

42. The lease should include a provision limiting the lessor's liability in tort arising due to the condition of the leased premises.

43. The lease should require the lessee to give the lessor notice of objectionable conditions of the premises and an opportunity to remedy the condition before the lessee has the right to claim that he has been constructively evicted.

44. Provision for security for the payment of rent should be made. Security may be provided by:

    a. Payment of rent in advance.

    b. Posting of security in the form of personal property, stocks, bonds, and so forth.

    c. Having a third person guarantee the payment of rent.

45. The lease should contain a provision for quiet enjoyment.

46. The lease should contain a provision for cancellation before the expiration of the term on payment of a premium.

47. The lease should set out the duty of the lessor to furnish services such as heat, hot water, elevator, and janitor.

48. If the lease has a provision giving the lessee the right to renew, such a provision:

    a. Should define the right to renew.

    b. Should state when notice of election to renew should be given.

    c. Should set out the terms of the renewal lease specifically and in detail.

    d. May provide that renewal will be automatic if notice to terminate is not given.

    e. Should set out the lessee's right to fixtures attached by the lessee during the term.

49. The lease should provide for terminating the liability of the lessor on lease if he sells the leased premises.

50. The purposes for which the lessee may use the premises should be carefully defined.

51. The lessee's right to erect and maintain signs on the premises, the listing of the lessee's name on a directory, and so forth, should be carefully defined.

52. The lease should provide that the lessee will surrender the premises in as good repair as when he received them, normal wear and tear and destruction by the elements excepted.

53. The lease should contain a provision requiring the lessee to comply with all reasonable rules adopted by the landlord and a definition of the limitation of the landlord's rule-making rights.

54. The lease should provide that covenants in the lease will bind the lessee's heirs, successors, and assigns.

55. The lease should include a provision that it contains entire agreement of the parties.

56. The lease may include an option giving the lessee the right to purchase the leased real estate. Such a provision should be drafted

with care and must include all the provisions necessary for a valid option.

57. The lease must be signed by the lessor and lessee.
58. In some states the lease must be sealed, especially by a corporate lessor or lessee.
59. In some states the lease must be acknowledge if it is to be recorded.
60. The lease must be delivered and accepted.

16

Restrictions and zoning

Restrictions

INTRODUCTION

THE OWNER of real estate has the right to sell and convey such real estate and the right to use it, but neither is an absolute right. The courts have distinguished between restrictions on the owner's right to sell and his right to use. In general, a provision in a deed which grants a fee simple estate to the grantee and which provides that the grantee will not sell, mortgage, or convey in any other manner the estate or an interest therein is, under the law in the United States, void; it is a direct restraint on the free alienation of the property, and as such is against public policy.[1] The Kentucky Supreme Court has held that a restraint on alienation of real estate is valid, provided the restraint is for a reasonable period.[2] Reasonable restraints on the use of real estate are generally upheld.

CREATION OF RESTRICTIONS

A restriction may be created by a reservation or condition in a deed, by a covenant included in or annexed to a deed, by a declaration in a trust imposing a restriction on the sale or use of the real estate held

---

[1] *Braun et ux.* v. *Klug et ux.,* 335 Mich. 691, 57 N.W.2d 299.

[2] *Hutchinson* v. *Loomis,* Ky., 244 S.W.2d 751.

in trust, or by a zoning ordinance. We shall confine our discussion primarily to restrictions on the use of land created by covenants either in a deed or annexed thereto, and to restrictions under zoning laws.

NATURE OF COVENANTS AND CONDITIONS

A covenant is a promise in writing, and, as we shall use the term, is a clause in a deed whereby the grantee, his heirs, and assigns are bound by the promise stated in the clause. A condition is a clause in a deed which provides that if a stated event or events happen, or if the vendee, his heirs, and assigns make a stated use of the granted real estate or fail to live up to the requirements of the condition, title to the real estate will revest in the grantor or his heirs. A deed containing a condition conveys a determinable or base fee.

There is some conflict in the decisions of the court as to whether a provision in a deed will be interpreted as a covenant or a condition where such provision is framed in the terms of a condition but does not include a clause stating that on the breach of the condition the title to the real estate will revert to the grantor and his heirs. The courts do not favor conditions; and in case of doubt, many courts have interpreted such clauses as covenants. The intention of the parties, however, governs; and if it is clear from all of the circumstances that the parties intended the provision as a condition, it will be so held. If the restraint provision expressly provides that on breach of the condition, title will revert to the grantor, his heirs, or assigns, such provision will be upheld.[3]

VALIDITY OF RESTRAINT ON USE

The validity and enforceability of a restraint on the use of real estate will depend on its scope, nature, and purpose. If it is so broad in its terms that it prevents the free alienation of the property, or if it is repugnant to the estate granted, it will not be enforced.[4] However, if the restraint is reasonable and its purpose is not against public policy, the courts will generally uphold such restriction. For example, covenants which, in order to assure the maintenance of an area as a high-class residential district, restrict the size of the lots, the location of the buildings on the lot, their design, character, and cost, and restrict businesses, especially types of businesses which are offensive, are generally upheld.

---

[3] *Superior Oil Company* v. *Johnson et al.,* 161 Kan. 710, 171 P.2d 658.

[4] *Grossman et ux.* v. *Hill et al.,* 384 Pa. 590, 122 A.2d 69.

Prior to 1948, the courts usually upheld covenants restricting the occupancy of real estate to a defined class of persons or precluding the occupancy of real estate by a defined class of persons when the classification was based on race.[5] However, in 1948, the U.S. Supreme Court held that a racial restrictive covenant was unenforceable by court action.[6] The Supreme Court held that the covenants standing alone do not violate any provision of the 14th Amendment to the Constitution and are not void, but that the enforcement of such a covenant by the courts would be a denial of the equal protection of the laws and therefore contrary to the 14th Amendment.

EFFECT OF INVALIDITY OF RESTRICTIVE COVENANT OR CONDITION

A restrictive covenant or condition which is void, inoperative, or illegal does not affect the validity of the grant or divest the grantee of the estate granted. In general, the void, inoperative, or illegal covenant or condition is, in legal effect, canceled; and the grant stands free from the covenant or condition.[7]

The Buckworths acquired lot No. 8 in block B in Sullivan Heights and shortly thereafter began to build a house thereon. Carrol County Development Corporation owned lots in Sullivan Heights and brought suit to enjoin the Buckworths from continuing to build on the ground of breach of restriction. The recorded plat of Sullivan Heights contained sixteen provisions restricting the use of the lats in that plot. Restriction No. 5 required that "before any building, or any addition or alteration thereto, shall be commenced, plans and specifications therefor, showing height, and location of building with respect to topography and ground elevation, shall first be submitted to and approved in writing by the Blooms, 'their heirs and assigns.' " The Buckworths did not comply with this requirement; and on the trial, they contended that this restriction was void.

Chief Judge Brune said: "We are unable to agree with the Chancellor's view that restriction No. 5 is void. Restrictions in similar terms requiring submission and approval of plans have been upheld in Peabody Heights Co. v. Willson. The latter cases show that approval or disapproval must be reasonable and that the power must be exercised in good faith." (Note: The court held that the development company acquired no right to enforce the restriction.) *Carrol County Development Corporation* v. *Buckworth,* Md., 200 A.2d 145 (1964).

---

[5] *Swain et al.* v. *Maxwell et al.,* 335 Mo. 448, 196 S.W.2d 780.

[6] *Shelly et ux.* v. *Kramer et ux.,* 334 U.S. 1, 68 S. Ct. 836; *Hurd et ux.* v. *Hodge et al.,* 334 U.S. 24, 68 S. Ct. 847.

[7] *Andrews* v. *Hall et al.,* 158 Neb. 817, 58 N.W.2d 201.

INTERPRETATION OF RESTRICTIONS

In no area of the law is there found a greater divergence of opinion among the courts of the several states than in the interpretation and construction of covenants restricting the use of real estate. There are basic principles of law which are generally followed, but there is little uniformity in the results. The courts recognize that since restrictions on the use of real estate are in derogation of its free and unhampered use, they are to be strictly construed and all doubts resolved against them, yet the intention of the parties governs. The intent of the parties in respect to a restrictive covenant is to be gathered from the entire context of the instrument.

In the event the language used is not clear in its meaning, it will be construed most strongly against the grantor, and the restriction will not be extended beyond the clear meaning of the language used.[8] Also, if there is any uncertainty as to whether the provision is intended as a covenant or a condition, the courts will hold that it is a covenant.[9]

RESTRICTIONS ON SUBDIVISIONS

When the plat of a new subdivision is prepared and recorded, the plat will, as a general rule, state the restrictions placed on the use of the land. Each deed will refer to the plat and the restrictions placed thereon. In this manner the restrictive covenants will be included in the deed by reference and will be binding on all grantees. If the property conveyed is not a part of a recorded plat, the restrictive covenants will be included in each deed.

A wide variety of restrictive covenants is included in recorded plats and deeds. Unless such covenants are drafted with the utmost skill and care, the desired result will not be attained. In interpreting restrictive covenants, the court will read the entire instrument and give the language used its accepted meaning. However, since restrictive covenants limit the grantee's right to use the real estate for all lawful purposes, the courts will not extend the scope of the restriction by implication.[10]

Cleveland Realty Company developed a tract of land known as the Cleveland Springs Estate. The Realty Company developed a part of the property for

---

[8] *Link* v. *Texas Pharmacal Company,* Tex. Civ. App., 276 S.W.2d 903.

[9] *Gallagher* v. *Lederer et al.,* 60 Ohio Abs. 323, 102 N.E.2d 272.

[10] *Premium Point Park Association, Inc., et al.* v. *Polar Bar, Inc., et al.,* 306 N.Y. 507, 119 N.E.2d 360.

residential and recreational purposes, and located thereon a nine-hole golf course. On May 25, 1926, it caused to be recorded a plat of the development, showing lots, streets, and the golf course. Certain provisions and restrictions were included in the plot. The provisions pertinent to the case were as follows: "Developers 'do hereby dedicate the streets and alleys as indicated on the plat to the public use forever. . . .' "

"We further dedicate the golf links and playgrounds, and the land occupied by the same indicated on the map, for such use and pleasure of the owners of the lots. . . .

"We restrict the use of all lots shown on this plat . . . in the following manner, to wit:

"1. The lots shown on this plat are to be used as the location of residences, with only one residence to the lot. . . ."

Lots in the development were sold, and homes were erected thereon. A right of way 22 feet wide across the golf course between the No. 7 green and the No. 8 tee connecting with Fairway Drive was granted to Hobbs, who began construction of the road. Residents of the development brought suit, asking that the construction of the road be enjoined and that the grant of the easement of the right of way be declared void. The trial court entered a judgment adverse to the plaintiffs; and on appeal, the holding was reversed.

Justice Moore said: "Where lots are sold and conveyed by reference to a map or plat which represents a division of a tract of land into streets, lots, parks and playgrounds, a purchaser of a lot or lots acquires the right to have the streets, parks and playgrounds kept open for his reasonable use, and this right is not subject to revocation except by agreement. It is said that such streets, parks and playgrounds are *dedicated* to the use of lot owners in the development. In a strict sense it is not a dedication, for a dedication must be made to the public and not to a part of the public. It is a right in the nature of an easement appurtenant. Whether it be called an easement or a dedication, the right of the lot owners to the use of the streets, parks and playgrounds may not be extinguished, altered or diminished except by agreement or estoppel. This is true because the existence of the right was an inducement to and a part of the consideration for the purchase of the lots. Thus, a street, park or playground may not be reduced in size or put to any use which conflicts with the purpose for which it was dedicated." *Cleveland Realty Company* v. *Hobbs,* N.C., 135 S.E.2d 30 (1964).

INTERPRETATION OF SPECIAL TERMS

In drafting restrictive covenants to be included in a deed or plat, one should avoid negative terms, since it is difficult, if not impossible, to set out specifically all of the uses which the grantor might wish to prohibit. Instead, a statement of the permitted uses should be made, and this statement should be followed by a provision prohibiting all other uses. In stating the permitted uses, broad general language and abstract terms should be avoided.

For example, such terms as "for residence purposes," "for dwelling purposes," or "not to be used for commercial purposes" are so broad in their connotation that they invite litigation. The courts have generally held that a restriction "for residential purposes only" is violated by the erection of a church, school, parking lot, filling station, or rest home, or by the operation of a retail store or a similar business in a portion of a house in which the family lives; but at the same time, the courts have held that such a restriction is not violated by the erection of apartment buildings.

The courts of the several states are not in accord in their interpretation of a covenant which restricts the use of the real estate to "dwelling purposes." One line of decisions holds that the erection of an apartment building does not violate the covenant—that apartment buildings are dwellings. The other line of decisions holds that an apartment building is not a dwelling and that the erection of an apartment building on the real estate is a violation of the covenant.

A restrictive covenant should make clear that the restriction is meant to apply to both the land and the buildings erected on the land. However, the courts have generally interpreted a restrictive covenant as applying to the use of both the land and the buildings thereon, unless the wording of the restriction is such that it is clear that the intent is that it apply only to the use of the buildings.[11]

Hunsinger owned a 35-acre tract of land. He conveyed 25 acres of the tract to Chester Villa Development Company by deed which permitted subdivision of the land into building lots. The land was subdivided, and eighty-nine separate one-family residences were constructed on the lots.

Hunsinger conveyed the remaining 10 acres by a deed which contained the following restriction: "The property shall be used for residential purposes only and the houses to be erected thereon shall contain at least 950 square feet of floor space and shall be at least seventy per cent (70%) brick or stone construction."

The grantee of the 10-acre tract planned to construct a multifamily building thereon which contained more than 950 square feet of floor space and was more than 70 per cent of brick or stone construction. The residents of the 25-acre tract brought suit asking that the construction of the multifamily build-

---

[11] *Hoover* v. *Waggoman*, 52 N.M. 371, 199 P.2d 991.

ing be enjoined. The injunction was denied; and on appeal, the order denying the injunction was affirmed.

Commissioner Davis said: "The weight of authority is said to hold that a restriction to 'residence' or 'residential purposes,' of itself, does not prohibit multiple dwellings. See 14 A.L.R.2d 1403, p. 9. In the same annotation, 14 A.L.R.2d 1376 et seq., the diversity of decisions in various jurisdictions is recorded. It is observed that the courts are in substantial agreement that a restriction to 'residence' purposes, standing alone, does not prohibit multiple dwellings, but this unanimity disappears when the modifying term 'a,' 'one' or 'a single' is prefixed to the word 'residence.'

"We must seek the intention of the grantor from the language used, considered in light of such factors as the general scheme of the subdivision. We may not substitute what the grantor may have intended to say for the plain import of what he said. We believe it is proper to assume that dratfsmen of restrictive covenants—including the covenant now before us—acquaint themselves with decisions of the court relating to their effect. Certainly, such draftsmen should be familiar with legal precedents touching upon the subject matter with which they deal; they should be entitled to place some reliance in past constructions by the courts. The McMurtry decision is old and well known; it was in full effect in 1955 when the instant restriction was drawn. We observed in McMurtry and in many other decisions that draftsmen of such covenants may readily use language expressly prohibiting the use of property. The failure to use such specific language warrants the view that it was a deliberate and intended omission.

"As noted, there is no general scheme applicable to the ten acre tract. We hold that the residents of the 25-acre tract cannot be considered beneficiaries of the subsequently written restriction of the ten acre tract. The scheme of the 25-acre tract subdivision affords no dispositive basis for construction of the restriction under consideration. Thus, we are left with language substantially identical with that used in McMurtry. We perceive no reason for departing from the rationale of McMurtry, as it applies to the facts of the case at bar." *McMahan* v. *Hunsinger,* Ky., 375 S.W.2d 820 (1964).

WHO MAY ENFORCE A CONDITION OR A RESTRICTION

If the restriction is in the form of a condition in a deed and includes a reversion clause, the grantor or his heirs, on breach of the condition, have the right of re-entry; however, a stranger to the conveyance or a creditor of the party having the right of re-entry cannot avail himself of the right.[12] At common law, such right of re-entry could not be assigned

---

[12] *Federal Land Bank of Louisville* v. *Luckenbill et al.,* 213 Ind. 616, 13 N.E. 2d 531.

or transferred; and in some states, either by statutory enactment or by court action, the common-law rule has been established. In some states, however, the right of re-entry for a condition broken is assignable or transferable after the condition is broken but not before; and in a few states, by statutory enactment, the right of re-entry has been made assignable generally.[13]

A restrictive covenant may be enforced by the parties to the agreement, and it may also be enforced by persons who are not parties to the agreement if the restriction is imposed for their benefit. If a restrictive covenant is personal to, and for the sole benefit of, the grantor, it is enforceable only by the grantor.[14]

Whether or not a restriction on the use of real estate is imposed for the benefit of others will depend on the intent of the parties to the agreement. In general, restrictions imposed pursuant to a general plan of development are imposed for the benefit of all owners of the real estate which is included in the general plan and may be enforced by any owner against any other owner who purchased with notice of the restriction.[15]

A general building scheme is one under which a tract of land is divided into building lots, the deeds to such lots to contain uniform restrictions. All the deeds, or substantially all of them, must contain restrictive covenants which are uniform or reciprocal.

A general building scheme may also be set up by recording a plat or map of the subdivided tract which contains the restrictions. Under this latter plan the deeds should include a clause which incorporates the restrictions in the recorded plat by reference—for example, "as per plat thereof, recorded in Plat Book 27, page 62, in the office of the Recorder of Marion County, Indiana." The mere conveyance of individual lots to various grantees by deeds containing building restrictions is not of itself sufficient to create a general building scheme.

Whether or not a restrictive covenant is for the benefit of common grantees or only for the benefit of the grantor will be determined from the language of the restriction, interpreted in the light of the surrounding circumstances.[16]

---

[13] *Fitch et al.* v. *State,* 139 Conn. 456, 95 A.2d 255.

[14] *Levy et al.* v. *Dundalk Co.,* 177 Md. 636, 11 A.2d 476.

[15] *Condos et ux.* v. *Home Development Company, Inc., et al.,* 77 Ariz. 129, 267 P.2d 1069.

[16] *Copelin* v. *Morris et al.,* Ohio Com. Pl., 101 N.E.2d 18.

A grantee is not bound by a restrictive covenant unless he has either actual or constructive notice of the restriction. A grantee has constructive notice of a restriction if such restriction is contained in a recorded instrument, such as a plat or map, and is referred to in his deed.[17] Also, a grantee is charged with notice of a building restriction if such restriction is contained in the recorded deed to his grantor or in a recorded deed in the grantee's chain of title.

The owner of real estate adjoining a restricted plat cannot enforce the restrictions, even though he would benefit by such enforcement, since it was not imposed on the tract for his benefit.[18]

Beeler Development Company (hereinafter referred to as Beeler) brought this action to enjoin the enforcement of a restrictive covenant providing: "No residential lot shall be re-subdivided." Dickens and other lot owners in their cross petition asked that Beeler and those holding under it be enjoined from present and future violations. Beeler contended that Dickens and the other lot owners had no right to enforce the restrictive covenant. The trial court enjoined Beeler and those holding under it from violating the restriction, and Beeler appealed. The appellate court affirmed the injunction.

Justice Thornton said: "If the language of the restriction is given its plain and ordinary meaning, it means that a lot may not be subdivided. This restriction, along with others, was used as an inducement to purchasers. When a purchaser buys and builds in reliance on the restrictions, he acquires some rights and his land is also burdened. These restrictions run with the land for the period of their existence. Every owner in the addition has a dominant estate over that of his neighbors, and the neighbors are dominant over his. Each owner has the right to enforce the covenant as written. This is true so long as the circumstances remain the same. It is also true without regard to the action of the other owners; they may waive their own rights but not those of others." *Beeler Development Company v. Dickens*, 254 Iowa 1029, N.W.2d 414 (1963).

RESTRICTIONS BY MUTUAL AGREEMENT

Restrictions may be imposed on the use of real estate by the mutual agreement of the owners of neighboring or adjoining land. For example, if the owners of all the lots in a described block mutually agree that the buildings shall be a certain distance from the street and that only one single-family dwelling shall be erected on each lot, such an agreement

---

[17] *McDonald et al.* v. *Welborn et al.*, 220 S.C. 10, 66 S.E. 2d 327.

[18] *Townsend et al.* v. *Allen et al.*, 114 Cal. App. 2d 291, 250 P.2d 292.

is enforceable by and against the parties to the agreement and their assigns having notice of the restriction.

WAIVER OR ABANDONMENT OF RESTRICTIONS

A restriction on real estate may be waived or abandoned by the party or parties for whose benefit the restriction was imposed. Whether or not a restriction has been waived or abandoned must be determined from the facts of each individual case.

Mere acquiescence in a violation of a restriction is not a waiver of the right to enforce the same restriction against another violation of the restriction, nor is it an abandonment of the restriction.[19] As a general rule, if a grantee has violated a restriction, he will not be permitted to hold another lot owner for a similar violation of the restriction. However, if his violation is minor in nature, he will be permitted to enforce the restriction against a more extensive violation by others.[20]

If the violations of the restrictions have been numerous and of such a nature that they destroy the general building scheme originally intended to be established, the restrictions will have been abandoned.

If an owner knows that a restriction is being violated, but makes no objection, and permits the violator to spend substantial sums on the property, he will not be permitted to complain of the violation. However, if the owner does not know of the violation and, in the ordinary course of events, would not learn of the violation, he has the right to bring an action against the violator when he learns of it.

Restrictions may be modified or terminated by the consent of all who are affected by it. A restriction placed on real estate by the grantor for the benefit of grantees of lots cannot be modified or terminated by the consent of the grantor alone.

Bartlett subdivided a tract of land into 107 lots of varied sizes, most of which were 165 feet in width and from 250 to more than 1,100 feet in length. The deeds to the original lots contained numerous restrictions, none of which prohibited the subdividing of the lots, but they prohibited the construction of more than one house or dwelling place on a lot as originally platted. A number of lots, at the time of this suit, had been subdivided and two houses built on the lots as originally platted.

Fritz owned lot 74, which he subdivided, the south part thereof being 275 feet in length. Fritz contracted to sell this south 275 feet of the lot to Berry,

---

[19] *Hogue et al.* v. *Dresszen et al.,* 161 Neb. 268, 73 N.W.2d 159.

[20] *Moore et ux.* v. *Adams et al.,* 200 Ark. 810, 141 S.W.2d 46.

who planned to build a dwelling thereon. Watts, who owned lot 24 in the subdivision, brought an action asking that Fritz be enjoined from subdividing his lot and from building two dwellings on lot 74. The trial court granted the injunction, and the injunction was dissolved on appeal.

Justice Hershey said: "Defendants make the further contention that while it is their position that there are no restrictions in the deed which prohibit subdividing the lots and placing more than one dwelling on a lot as originally platted, yet even if there were such a restriction, plaintiff has waived any right to enforce it by previous acquiescence in prior violations. The parties do not agree as to the facts concerning this matter. However, the evidence showed that there had been several subdividings of lots in the subdivision with the building of more than one dwelling on a lot as originally platted. Plaintiff, himself, acknowledged that one such subdividing and building took place across the street from him after he purchased his property. The developer's man in charge of his salesmen himself subdivided at least three lots and these subdivided lots had homes built on them. There is no showing that plaintiff took any action to prevent the subdividing of the lot across the street from him or the building of a dwelling on it other than to talk to the developer and possibly an attorney. No positive preventative action was taken.

"Minor violations of a restriction will not prohibit the subsequent enforcement of it. However, where there has been acquiescence of prior violations of the very substance of a general plan or particular restriction, the plaintiff will be held to have waived any right he may have had to enforce it. Thus, in Wallace v. Hoffman, the court said: 'The law is well settled that even where a general plan is shown the restrictions under the plan will not be enforced where violations have been acquiesced in.' It appears to us that even if the restrictions here were construed to prohibit the subdividing and the building thereon, yet plaintiff has so acquiesced in prior violations as to be unable to enforce any such restriction." *Watts* v. *Fritz,* 29 Ill.2d. 517, 194 N.E.2d 276 (1963).

TERMINATION OF RESTRICTION

A building restriction may be terminated by a lapse of time stated in the restrictive covenant, by merger, by material change in the neighborhood, or by the mutual agreement of the parties in interest. In some instances the restrictions are imposed on the real estate for a definite time, as, for instance, 30 years. Such a restriction is terminated by the expiration of the time limit. If a person acquires an entire plat after it has been filed along with its restrictive covenants, the restrictions on the plat are terminated, and such purchaser is not bound by them.

The courts have refused to enforce restrictions when they no longer serve their desired purpose due to material changes in the neighborhood, and instead tend to depreciate the value of the restricted property.[21] Such a situation arises when the business and industrial area of a city, due to growth, gradually encroaches on the residential area until such area is no longer suitable for residential purposes.

If all of the owners of the property in a general building scheme or all common grantees mutually agree to terminate or alter existing restrictions on their property, such agreement will be enforced unless its provisions are against public policy.

The subdivision involved was platted, and the restrictions were placed on record on May 16, 1957. Baker purchased lots 1 through 4 on February 9, 1960. At that time the tract adjacent to these lots was reserved for commerical use. Across the street was a shopping center which was constructed in 1960, and in an adjoining block was the State Tuberculosis Hospital. After Baker bought his lots, the only structure erected in the subdivision which tended to change the character of the neighborhood was a Baptist church. Baker brought this action seeking the removal of the restrictions on his lot, basing his request on the ground of changes in the neighborhood. The relief requested was denied; and on appeal, the decision was affirmed.

Acting Chief Judge Allen said: "Equity is permitted to relieve against restrictions where there has been a radical change in the character of a new neighborhood, or an entire change in the circumstances. Generally, in such controversies, the facts of each case must be considered and the case must stand or fall on these facts.

"In the present case before the Court, it does not appear that in the approximately two years and seven months, since the purchase by Plaintiffs, the neighborhood has changed so radically in character, in a manner which could not be anticipated by Plaintiffs, so as to require action by the Court. The Court finds that the only change, which has taken place, of which the Plaintiffs might not have been aware at the time of their purchase, is the construction of a Baptist Church, in another block of the subdivision. The Court finds that this, in itself, it not enough to sustain the Plaintiffs' Complaint, and under all of the circumstances, the same should be dismissed." *Baker* v. *Field,* Fla., 163 So.2d 42 (1964).

Zoning

NATURE AND PURPOSE OF ZONING

Zoning is the division of a city or other governmental unit, such as a township or county, by legislative regulation into districts, and the pre-

---

[21] *Wolff* v. *Fallon et al.,* 44 Cal.2d 695, 284 P.2d 802.

scription and application in each district of regulations having to do with structural and architecture designs of buildings and of regulations prescribing the use to which the buildings and land within the designated districts may be put. Zoning regulations are, in effect, restrictions placed on real estate by governmental action. The objective of zoning is the promotion of the health, safety, morals, and general welfare of the public. Through zoning, the character of the buildings erected, the use of the buildings, and the use of the land within the zoned district are regulated for the purpose of assuring the residents of the zoned area a suitable location in which to live, or in which to carry on their businesses or manufacturing.

Zoning differs from municipal planning in that the principal objective of municipal planning is to bring about a systematic development of the municipality or area, with particular reference to the location of streets, alleys, squares, parks, and playgrounds;[22] whereas the objective of zoning is to regulate the use to which the buildings and land within a district might be put. A municipal plan may be implemented through the enactment of zoning legislation.

SOURCE OF POWER TO ZONE

Each nation has sovereign power necessary to accomplish the legitimate ends and purposes of its government. In the United States, both the federal and the state governments have the right to restrict the individual use of real estate, provided such restriction is for the purpose of protecting the health, safety, morals, and public welfare of the people.[23] This power is generally referred to as the police power of the state. It is not an unlimited and unrestricted power; its exercise is subject to the limitations imposed on it by the federal and state constitutions. The power to enact zoning regulations is usually delegated to the municipality, and its power is subject to the limitations placed on it by the state legislature.[24] In some states the townships and counties have been given the power to enact zoning regulations.[25]

Anderson owned 3.4 acres of land which had been placed in a single residence A district (a residential district in which the minimum lot area for permitted use was 22,500 square feet). Much of Anderson's tract was swampy, as was more than 25 per cent of the town. It would have cost Anderson

---

[22] *Seligman et al.* v. *Belknap et al.,* 228 Ky. 133, 155 S.W.2d 735.

[23] *Kessler et al.* v. *Smith et al.,* 104 Ohio App. 213, 142 N.E.2d 231.

[24] *Attorney General* v. *Inhabitats of the Town of Dover et al.,* 327 Mass. 601, 100 N.E.2d 1.

[25] *Shick et al.* v. *Ghent Road Inn, Inc.,* Ohio App., 132 N.E.2d 479.

approximately $102,500 to render the land suitable for residential development, so he brought suit asking that the zoning law be declared to be void. The court held that the zoning law was valid, and the decision was affirmed on appeal.

Justice Spiegel said: "The standard by which the validity of a zoning by-law is to be determined has been stated frequently in the opinions of this court. 'Every presumption is to be afforded in favor of the validity of an ordinance and if its reasonableness is fairly debatable the judgment of the local authorities who gave it its being will prevail. . . . It will be sustained unless there exists no substantial relation between it and the expressed purposes of the statute. Conversely, it will be held invalid if it be arbitrary or unreasonable, or substantially unrelated to the public health, safety, convenience, morals or welfare.'

"There is nothing in the record to indicate that if the petitioners' land were developed for home sites, a market for this land or for the homes that could be built thereon would be lacking, nor is there any reason for us to conclude that the land is substantially better suited for nonresidential uses. The zoning by-law before us does not appear to have been adopted only because of aesthetic considerations; on the contrary, the judge of the Land Court stated that the 1955 zoning ordinance, as applied to the petitioners' land, 'has a substantial and reasonable relation to the public welfare of the town.' Finally, the judge in substance asserted that, in view of the prevalence of marshland in Wilmington, to invalidate the zoning by-law as applied to the petitioners' tract would be to 'deny the town an opportunity to adopt any zoning.' It may well be that the zoning by-law does not permit the petitioners to realize maximum profits from the use of their land, but this is not sufficient cause to invalidate it." *Anderson* v. *Town of Wilmington,* Mass., 197 N.E.2d 682 (1964).

EXERCISE AND LIMITS OF POWER

A zoning ordinance must not violate the 14th Amendment of the Federal Constitution nor the provisions of the constitution of the state in which the real estate is located, or it will not be valid. Zoning legislation is void where the means used to regulate the use of property are destructive, confiscatory, or so unreasonable that they are arbitrary.[26] The tests generally applied in determining the validity of zoning legislation are:

1. Is the zoning made by districts?
2. Is the zoning for the general welfare of the people?
3. Does the zoning promote the public health, safety, or morals?
4. Are the provisions of the zoning ordinance clear and specific?
5. Is the zoning free from discrimination?

---

[26] *Dooley* v. *Town Plan and Zoning Commission of the Town of Fairfield,* Conn., 197 A.2d 770.

6. Has the power to enact zoning ordinances been exercised in a reasonable manner?

As a general rule, the zoning, in order to be valid, must be made by districts and not by individual pieces of property. Although the establishment of the boundary lines of a district must be more or less arbitrary since the property on one side of the line will not differ greatly from the property on the other side of the line, there must nevertheless be some rational basis for the establishment of the boundary line of the district.[27]

A municipality, in establishing zoning districts, must set up classifications as the basis for their establishment. The municipality has broad discretionary powers in establishing zoning classifications; but the classifications must be reasonable, uniform, and nondiscriminatory.[28]

The answers to questions 2 through 6 will depend on the circumstances of each case. The courts have developed general standards which serve as a guide, but they are not conclusive. Building heights, setback lines, side yards, type of building materials, and similar regulations, when applied to a residential zone, have been upheld on the ground that they protect the public health and safety through the assurance of fresh air and the reduction of fire hazards. Similarly, the courts have generally upheld the regulation of lot sizes, minimum floor areas of residences, and the minimum cubic contents of buildings on lots, on the ground that the control of population density in an area reduces the amount of traffic, reduces the fire hazard, prevents overcrowding with an accompanying lowering of moral standards, and in general provides a healthier, safer area and a better moral environment in which to live and rear children.

Those opposing such ordinances argue that since there is no limit placed on the number of occupants of a house, such ordinances cannot be upheld on the basis of health. They admit that the ordinances may be justified on the ground of aesthetic considerations but contend that aesthetic considerations alone are not sufficient to support the ordinances. The final outcome of the controversy is in doubt. However, the trend is toward the upholding of such ordinances.[29]

---

[27] *Mundelein States, Inc., et al.* v. *Village of Mundelein,* 409 Ill. 291, 99 N.E.2d 144.

[28] *Katobimar Realty Company et al.* v. *Webster,* 20 N.J. 114, 118 A.2d 824.

[29] *Hitchman et al.* v. *Oakland Township et al.,* 329 Mich. 331, 45 N.W.2d 306.

In the earlier decisions the courts held that a zoning regulation could not be supported on the basis of aesthetic considerations alone. They are now, however, in accord in holding that zoning regulations may extend beyond strict considerations of health, safety, and morals, and that aesthetics should not be ignored.

The validity of a zoning ordinance prohibiting outdoor advertising signs other than those related to a business conducted on the premises was involved in an action brought by United Advertising Corporation, which wished to erect in the business and industrial area of the city outdoor billboards not related to the business conducted on the premises. The court held that the regulation was valid.

The Court said: "Much is said about zoning for aesthetics. If what is meant thereby is zoning for aesthetics as an end in itself, the issue may be said to be unexplored in our State, but if the question is whether aesthetics may play a part in a zoning judgment, the subject is hardly new. There are areas in which aesthetics and economics coalesce, areas in which a discordant sight is as hard an economic fact as an annoying odor or sound. We refer not to some sensitive or exquisite perference but to concepts of congruity held so widely that they are inseparable from the enjoyment and hence the value of property. Even the basic separation of industrial and commercial from residential, although obviously related to so much of the quoted statute as speaks of health and hazard, rests also on the aesthetic impact of uses upon the value of properties. Surely no one would say today that an industrial structure must be permitted in a residential district upon a showing that the operation to be conducted therein involves no significant congestion in the streets, or danger of fire or panic, or impediment of light and air, or over-crowding of land, or undue concentration of population. So also the recognition of different residential districts, with varying lot sizes, setbacks, and the like, rests upon the proposition that aesthetics should not be ignored when one seeks to promote 'the general welfare' as the statute says, 'with a view of conserving the value of property and encouraging the most appropriate use of land throughout such municipality.' Our cases deem aesthetics to be relevant when they bear in a substantial way upon land utilization." *United Advertising Corporation* v. *Metuchen,* 42 N.J. 1, 198 A.2d 447 (1964).

BASIS FOR ZONING

When a municipality or area is zoned, the basis for zoning is the nature of the use of the land and buildings permitted within the area. The municipality or area will first be zoned for such general uses as residential, commercial, and industrial. These areas will then be further zoned for more special purposes which fall within the scope of the general use. For example, an area zoned as residential may be further zoned for single-family, duplex, four-family, or multiunit residences. An area zoned for commercial use may be further zoned on the basis of the type of businesses carried on within the area—as, for example, retail outlets, garages and filling stations, cleaning and laundering establishments, or wholesale outlets. Likewise, an area zoned as industrial may be further zoned for specialty manufacturing, light manufacturing, or heavy manufacturing.

Also, the courts have upheld reasonable zoning regulations which restrict the use of land, apart from the use of the buildings or other structures thereon. An ordinance restricting a zone as residential may exclude such uses of the land as the excavation of clay beds, the removal of loam, the drilling of wells, or the use of the land as a private or public dump.[30]

REGULATIONS MUST BE REASONABLE

Since to be valid a zoning regulation must be reasonable, uniform, and nondiscriminatory, no dogmatic statement in regard to the basis for zoning will be accurate. However, the courts have generally upheld zoning ordinances based on certain general classifications. For example, they have usually supported ordinances restricting the use of real estate as to the architectural and structural design of the buildings, the setback line, the height of buildings, and the area of lot covered by the buildings.[31] Such restrictions can be justified on the basis of safety, health, and general welfare. For example, reduction of fire hazards and control of traffic contribute to safety; assurance of fresh air and sunlight contributes to the health; and maintenance of a desirable residential area contributes to the general welfare.

MODIFICATION OR AMENDMENT AND REPEAL OF ZONING ORDINANCE

A zoning ordinance may be modified or amended, provided the action taken is within the powers conferred on the legislative body by the state. A modification or amendment of a zoning ordinance, in order to be valid, must be justified on the ground that due to changing conditions, justice requires the modification or amendment enacted.[32]

---

[30] *Garrou* v. *Teaneck Tryon Company et al.,* 11 N.J. 294, 94 A.2d 332.

[31] *Davis et al.* v. *City of Omaha et al.,* 153 Neb. 460, 45 N.W.2d 172.

[32] *Moerder* v. *City of Moscow et al.,* 74 Idaho 410, 263 P.2d 993.

Amendments to zoning ordinances should be made with caution and only when changing conditions require a modification of the regulation. A zoning ordinance can be changed only when the change is not arbitrary and not unreasonable.

An amendment of a zoning ordinance which involves only one piece of property or a small area may be declared invalid, since such zoning would be considered spot zoning. Such an amendment should be made only when changing conditions or new or additional facts have intervened, and when a refusal to make the change would result in grave injustice to the owners of the property. Any change must be justified on the ground that it is beneficial to the health, safety, morals, or general welfare of the public.[33]

NONCONFORMING USE

When an area is zoned for a particular use, there may be property within the area which, at the time of the enactment of the zoning ordinance, is being used for purposes other than those permitted under the ordinance. Such property is known as *nonconforming property*. For example, if, at the time an area is zoned for single-family dwellings, there are in the area an apartment building and a retail store, these would be classed as nonconforming property.

As a general rule, the zoning ordinance will provide that a then existing nonconforming use may be continued;[34] to do otherwise could be, in many instances, unjust and inequitable, and it might be illegal on the ground of taking property without due compensation. To what extent a change in the nonconforming use of a building will be permitted will depend on the provisions of the zoning ordinance and the nature and scope of the change in the use of the property. As a general rule, a change to another nonconforming use of the same general character but less restrictive in its nature is allowed, but a change to a more restrictive use is prohibited.[35]

An increase in the amount or intensity of the use of nonconforming property is permitted, provided there is no material change in the character of the use made of the property. However, unless it is permitted by

---

[33] *Partain et al.* v. *City of Brooklyn et al.,* 101 Ohio App. 279, 133 N.E.2d 616.

[34] *Application of O'Neal,* 243 N.C. 714, 92 S.E.2d 189.

[35] *Steudel et al.* v. *Troberg et al.,* 76 Ohio App. 136, 63 N.E.2d 241.

the zoning ordinance, an extension of the nonconforming use to areas of the property not so used at the time the ordinance was enacted is not allowed.[36]

A building devoted to a nonconforming use at the time of the adoption of a zoning ordinance may be repaired from time to time. It may not, however, be enlarged by alteration or addition; nor will the owner be permitted to make alterations or additions which will extend the noncon- forming use or prolong the life of the building, unless provisions in the ordinance give him such right.[37]

Whether or not a building devoted to a nonconforming use may be repaired or reconstructed if it has been damaged, destroyed, or demolished will depend on the provisions of the zoning ordinance. Under the provi- sions of some zoning ordinances the repair or reconstruction of a noncon- forming building is prohibited if the damage to the building exceeds a stated part of the building or a stated percentage of the financial value of the building.

If a nonconforming use of a building which existed at the time of the adoption of the zoning ordinance is discontinued or abandoned, the right to reestablish the nonconforming use is lost. Whether or not a nonconforming use has been discontinued or abandoned is a matter of fact to be determined in each case.

A temporary or seasonal cessation of the nonconforming use is not a discontinuance or abandonment of it. Also, permitting a building to stand vacant because of inability to lease the building, because of financial inability to continue the business, or for other similar reasons is not, as a general rule, a discontinuance of the nonconforming use.[38]

The nonconforming uses of property may be (1) nonconforming build- ings, (2) nonconforming use of buildings, (3) nonconforming use of land, and (4) nonconforming lot sizes. In several states, various plans to eliminate nonconforming uses have been adopted. The nature of the nonconforming use to be eliminated has played an important part in the working-out of the plans. One plan adopted to eliminate nonconform- ing buildings and nonconforming use of both buildings and land is the compulsory amortization of the nonconforming property. This is accom- plished by compelling the discontinuance of the nonconforming use within a stated time. However, the time allowed for the discontinuance of such

[36] *De Felice et al.* v. *Zoning Board of Appeals of Town of East Haven et al.,* 130 Conn. 156, 32 A.2d 635.

[37] *Selligman et al.* v. *Von Allmen Bros., Inc.,* 297 Ky. 121, 179 S.W.2d 207.

[38] *Appeal of Langol,* 175 Pa. Super. 320, 104 A.2d 343.

use must be reasonable.[39] The constitutionality of a zoning ordinance prohibiting the continuance of a nonconforming use of property within a restricted area, provided the prohibition is reasonable and not arbitrary, has been upheld.[40] In a few instances, nonconforming property has been condemned under the power of eminent domain.

If the area is undeveloped and the lots do not conform in size, no serious problem is presented, since permits to build on the nonconforming lots could be denied, thereby forcing the owner into making the lots conform.

McKinney brought suit to enjoin Riley from operating an automobile junk yard and to compel enforcement of a zoning ordinance. McKinney's land abutted the Riley property, and the junk yard was 1,000 feet from his dwelling house. The zoning ordinance provided: "No junk yard may continue as a nonconforming use for more than one year after the effective date of this ordinance without special permit from the Board of Adjustment. The Board of Adjustment shall prescribe the conditions under which special permit shall be granted." The zoning ordinance became effective in March, 1956. Riley had started his junk yard in a small way in 1955, operating it as a part-time occupation; but by 1960, he was devoting full time to the junk business. He was burning cars on an average of three times a week. The injunction was granted, and Riley was ordered to discontinue the operation of the junk yard within forty-five days. On appeal, the holding of the trial court was affirmed.

Justice Wheeler said: "Zoning by its very nature is restrictive and regulatory as to the use of land and buildings and provisions which permit expansion and extension of existing uses are generally strictly construed. The finding that the business had been greatly extended and that its conduct was harmful and improper to a segment of the public was warranted. 'Pre-existing nonconforming uses may be "allowed to continue but not to multiply when they are harmful or improper." '

"We next consider whether enforcement of the ordinance by requiring termination of use of the land for a junk yard was a proper exercise of the police power. The validity of provisions requiring the termination of nonconforming uses within a specified period of time has been upheld as a proper exercise of the police power, provided at least that on balance, the public benefit outweighs the private injury, and the time allowed is reasonable.

"While the authorities upholding such amortization ordinances are by no means unanimous, we think that prima facie they are not unconstitutional. The defendant here had ample warning in 1957, when his application was denied, that his conduct of the business was considered a violation of the

---

[39] *City of Los Angeles* v. *Gage et al.,* 129 Cal. App. 558, 274 P.2d 34.

[40] *Hadacheck* v. *City of Los Angeles,* 239 U.S. 394.

ordinance. Yet he continued to conduct a greatly expanded nonconforming use until the operations were held to be a public and private nuisance.

"In view of the finding that the defendant's use was a public and private nuisance, the order allowing a year in which to terminate the use was a reasonable and valid application of the ordinance and within the police power." *McKinney* v. *Riley,* N.H., 197 A.2d 218 (1963).

ADMINISTRATION OF ZONING REGULATIONS

As a general rule, zoning regulations are administered by a named official, by a board, or by a commission. The powers of an official, board, or commission are only such as are conferred on them, expressly or by implication, by statute or ordinance. Such administrative officers, boards, or commissions may not abuse the discretion vested in them.

The procedure to be followed will be set out in the zoning ordinance, and it must be substantially complied with. Usually, provision is made to take an appeal from the original decision to a board of appeals. The decision of this board is subject to judicial review.

In substantially all jurisdictions a board of appeals or a similar body is given the power, within prescribed limits, to grant to property owners variances or exceptions allowing nonconforming uses of property. Variances and exceptions are granted only when the denial of the variance and exception would result in unnecessary hardship or practical difficulties.[41]

ENFORCEMENT OF ZONING RESTRICTIONS

The penalties which may be imposed for violation of the zoning ordinances depend primarily on the enabling statutes granting powers to the municipality or zoning area. Under the provisions of some ordinances, violation of the ordinance is made a criminal act; and the penalty for violation of the ordinance may be a fine or imprisonment, or both.

In addition to its power to impose a criminal penalty for violation of a zoning ordinance, the municipality may also seek the civil remedy of injunction enjoining further violation of the ordinance. And even though municipal officials have permitted the zoning ordinance to be violated for a number of years, such fact will not prevent the city from bringing an action and obtaining an injunction enjoining further violation

[41] *Ernest* v. *Board of Appeals on Zoning of City of New Rochelle,* 79 N.Y.S.2d 798; affirmed 298 N.Y. 831, 84 N.E.2d 144.

of the zoning ordinance.[42] If the violation of the zoning ordinance is of such a nature that it creates a nuisance, the city, under some circumstances, may order a building demolished.

EFFECT OF ZONING ORDINANCES ON RESTRICTIVE COVENANTS

As a general rule, a zoning ordinance will not be held to abrogate the restrictive covenants in a deed or plat;[43] but if the ordinance imposes more stringent restrictions on the use of the land or buildings in the district than those imposed by the restrictive covenants in the deeds or plats, the zoning ordinance will control. A state, under its police power, may enact legislation or confer on a municipality or other governmental unit the power to adopt ordinances which will abrogate existing covenants in deeds or plats, or which will render void certain classes of restrictions. Also, in some cases the courts have held that a zoning ordinance which classifies the land and buildings in a less restrictive category than that imposed by the restrictive covenants in the deeds or plats is evidence of a change in the neighborhood, which change justifies the court in refusing to enforce the restrictive covenants.

Building permits

NATURE OF BUILDING PERMIT

As a general rule, if a municipality or other governmental unit has adopted zoning ordinances, it will also adopt ordinances requiring any person who wishes to build, alter, or repair a building within the jurisdiction of the municipality or unit first to obtain a building permit. Such ordinances are constitutional and valid, provided the regulations are reasonable.

APPLICATION FOR PERMIT

In order to obtain a building permit, it is necessary, as a general rule, to file an application which complies with the provisions of the ordinance.

---

[42] *Leigh et al.* v. *City of Wichita et al.,* 148 Kan. 607, 83 P.2d 644.

[43] *Finn et al.* v. *Emmaus Evangelical Luthern Church et al.,* 329 Ill. App. 343, 68 N.E.2d 541.

Under the provisions of some ordinances, plans and specifications for the proposed building must accompany the application.[44]

CHECKING APPLICATION

After the application is filed, it will be checked by a designated official. If it is in proper form and the proposed building, alteration, or repair is in conformity with the zoning and building regulations, a permit will be issued. If a permit is denied, the applicant will be notified and will be given an opportunity for a hearing on the permit; and if the permit, on the hearing, is still denied, he may then resort to the courts.

RIGHTS CONFERRED BY PERMIT

A building permit is not a contract with the municipality or governmental unit; it is merely evidence of the applicant's compliance with regulations. The municipality may limit the time of starting construction under the permit; but if the permit fixes no time for starting construction, it must be started within a reasonable period.[45] The rights conferred by a building permit are not assignable, but they do pass with the land as an incident of the conveyance thereof.

---

[44] *Opinion of the Justices of the Senate,* 333 Mass. 783, 128 N.E.2d 563.

[45] *Village of Sand Point* v. *Sand Point County Day School,* 148 N.Y.S.2d 312.

17

Eminent domain

Introduction

NATURE AND SCOPE OF POWER

EMINENT DOMAIN has been defined as the right of the nation or state, or those to whom the power has been lawfully delegated, to condemn private property for public use, and to appropriate the ownership or possession of such property for such use, upon paying the owner just compensation, to be ascertained according to law.[1] This right extends to every kind of property. The power of eminent domain is an attribute of sovereignty. It is an inherent power of the state, not derived from, but limited by, the fundamental principles of the constitution.[2]

The right of the federal government to exercise the power of eminent domain is limited by the Fifth Amendment to the Constitution of the United States, which provides that (1) no person shall be deprived of life, liberty, or property without due process of law; and (2) private property shall not be taken for public use without just compensation. Like limitations are imposed on the states by the 14th Amendment, which provides, among other things, that no state shall deprive any person of

---

[1] *Leonard* v. *Autocar Sales & Service Company*, 392 Ill. 182, 64 N.E.2d 477.

[2] *Public Utility District No. 1 of Pend Oreille County* v. *Inland Power & Light Company*, Wash.2d, 390 P.2d 690.

life, liberty, or property without due process of law. Consequently, under the constitutional limitations imposed on the exercise of the power of eminent domain, private property can be lawfully taken only for public use, and it cannot be taken without just compensation.

EMINENT DOMAIN DISTINGUISHED FROM OTHER POWERS

A government has, in addition to its power of eminent domain, police power and the power to tax. In relation to individual ownership of real estate, these powers have certain common characteristics. Under each, the power of the sovereign is superior to that of the individual, and it is exercised for the general welfare of the people.

Eminent domain differs from police power in the following respects:

1. Under the power of eminent domain, compensation is required, whereas under police power the restrictions may be imposed without compensation.
2. Under the power of eminent domain the condemned right in the property is taken from the owner and transferred to the public agency to be enjoyed by it; whereas under the police power, there is no transfer of the ownership of the property effected.
3. Under the power of eminent domain the property is taken for public use, whereas under the police power the use of the property is restricted for the protection of the health, safety, or general welfare of the public.

The exercise of police power and that of eminent domain have much in common, and there is no clear line of distinction between them. If an attempted restriction under the police power deprives the owner of all the profitable use of his property and leaves him with only the burden of paying taxes and other such charges, the courts have held that such restriction is in fact a taking of property without just compensation, and they will hold the restriction to be void.[3]

There is a clear distinction between the right of eminent domain and the power to tax.[4] The tax paid by a citizen is the payment of his just share of the support of the government. If a property owner fails to

---

[3] *Granger* v. *Board of Adjustment of City of Des Moines,* 241 Iowa 1356, 44 N.W.2d 399.

[4] *State of Texas ex rel. Pan American Production Co. et al.* v. *Texas City,* 157 Tex. 450, 303 S.W.2d 780.

pay a justly assessed tax, his property may be sold at a tax sale. Property sold at a tax sale is not taken for a public use.

Under the power of eminent domain, only the property of the individual is affected, and it can be taken only for public use on payment of just compensation; whereas a tax is laid on the whole community or a class of persons in the community, and the tax constitutes the property owner's contribution to the expense of the government. A special assessment is a special tax imposed on property for the purpose of raising money to pay for an improvement which is beneficial to the property on which the tax is imposed.

In 1951, Eller owned approximately thirteen acres of land, on which were located a house, a barn, a chicken house, and a double mushroom house. In 1952 the township enacted a zoning ordinance which classified the entire township "District A," a residential and farming district. Permitted use included a "mushroom house provided it is located at least 500 feet from the nearest official roadside line and 1,000 feet from all lot boundaries." Eller's mushroom house was 400 feet from the nearest roadside line and 180 feet from the nearest property line. His mushroom house was therefore a nonconforming use. In 1956, he was granted permission to expand his nonconforming use 100 per cent. In 1959, he was denied a permit for further expansion. Eller brought an action to obtain permission for the requested expansion. The trial court held that the zoning ordinance was unconstitutional; and on appeal, the order was affirmed.

Justice Roberts said: "In the words of the court below: 'Mathematical calculation of the effect of the limitations of Sec. 24 (*e*) of the Ordinance demonstrates the absurd effect of their application upon a permitted use in an area which is part of the acknowledged mushroom growing center of the world. A set-back of 500 feet from any roadside line and a distance of 1,000 feet from any property boundary (without considering the dimensions of the mushroom house itself) requires that a property be 1,500 feet deep from the roadside line to the rear boundary and 2,000 feet in width, containing an area of 3,000,000 square feet, or 68.86 acres. Under those requirements no property containing less than about 69 acres may have even a single mushroom house. When the dimensions of a single mushroom house are necessarily calculated in addition thereto the absurdity is more apparent, and when it is considered that not less than three double mushroom houses, each 40×60 feet in dimensions, will support a growing operation without economic loss the confiscatory nature of the regulation is clear, amounting to a taking of property without compensation and a violation of due process of law.'

"Appellant urges that the constitutional issue was decided in a vacuum, that the real issue is whether it is unreasonable to prohibit the location of appellee's new mushroom house 100 feet from one property line and 200 feet from another. However, the authority on which the board necessarily based its decision is the ordinance itself. Therefore, its constitutionality was a proper issue for determination." *Eller* v. *Board of Adjustment of London Britain Township,* 414 Pa. 1, 198 A.2d 863 (1964).

WHO MAY EXERCISE POWER

Since the power of eminent domain is an attribute of sovereignty, it can be exercised by the federal government or by a state government. The federal government may condemn property within a state, a territory, or the District of Columbia. The power of a territory to condemn property will depend on the provisions of the act of Congress under which the territory is organized. As a general rule, such power will be conferred upon a territory.

A state has the right to exercise its power of eminent domain only within its borders, and such right is subject to the limitations placed on it by its constitution.

The power of eminent domain may be delegated either by Congress or by a state legislature, and such power is subject only to the limitations imposed by the federal or state constitution. It must be delegated by statute, either expressly or by implication.[5]

The right to exercise the power of eminent domain may be delegated to public corporations, agencies or boards, drainage districts, road districts, park districts, school districts or other public institutions, officers, or boards. It may also be delegated to private corporations, partnerships, or individuals. The validity of the delegation of the right to exercise the power of eminent domain does not depend on the status of the party to whom the power is delegated.[6] But the power must be limited to the taking of property for a public use, and just compensation must be paid.

If the state delegates the right to exercise the power of eminent domain, such delegated rights cannot be assigned. If a corporation transfers its property and franchises to another corporation, such transfer will not vest in the transferee the transferor's right to exercise the power of eminent domain. Although the courts are not in complete accord in their decisions, they have generally held that if a corporation leases its property,

[5] *Heppe et al.* v. *State of Nebraska,* 162 Neb. 403, 76 N.W.2d 255.

[6] *Central Louisiana Electric Company, Inc.* v. *Pugh et al.,* La. App. 96 So.2d 523.

it is not deprived of its right to exercise the power of eminent domain delegated to it by the legislature.[7] As a general rule, a consolidated corporation, after it has been consolidated, may exercise the right of eminent domain delegated to it before consolidation, provided the consolidation has been effected under a valid statute.

Whether or not the right to exercise the power of eminent domain may be delegated to a foreign corporation will depend on the provisions of the constitution and statutes of the state.

A statute delegating the right to take private property from one person and transfer it to another, the property to be used for private purposes, is void. However, property may be taken from a private owner under the power of eminent domain and then leased to private operators, provided the taking is for a public use, even though the private operators may make a profit from the operation of the leased property.[8]

Exeter & Hampton Electric Co. (hereinafter referred to as Electric Co.) condemned a right of way for a high-tension line across Harding's land. The line was intended to serve Sylvania Electric Co., but Electric Co. planned to extend the line in 1967 to serve the easterly part of Exeter and Stratham. The right to condemn the property was granted to Electric Co. by the Public Utility Commission, and its power was granted by a statute which provided: "Whenever it is necessary, in order to meet the reasonable requirements of service to the public, that any public utility should construct a line . . . across the land of another . . . such public utility may petition the public utility commission for such rights and easements and for permission to take such lands or rights, as may be needed for said purpose." Harding questioned the right of Electric Co. to condemn and contended the taking was for wholly private use. The court upheld the decision of the Commission; and on appeal, its holding was affirmed.

Justice Wheeler said: "It is elemental law that the property of an individual can not be taken for a wholly private use. The question to be determined is whether the proposed taking is for a public use, even though it will presently serve but a single customer. It will however fit into a proposed master plan to loop the town of Exeter with high voltage transmission lines and more adequately serve anticipated demands in the future. No claim is made here that such proposed service will not be open to the public generally and of service to more than one customer. The law is clear that property may be taken not only for present demands but for uses which may be fairly anticipated

---

[7] *Reuter et al.* v. *Milan Water Company, Inc.,* 209 Ind. 240, 198 N.E. 422.

[8] *Court Street Parking Company* v. *City of Boston et al.,* 336 Mass. 224, 143 N.E.2d 683.

in the future. The evidence did not require a finding that the proposed line will benefit merely a single customer or that the condemnation is for private use for that reason." *Exeter & Hampton Electric Co.* v. *Harding*, N.H., 199 A.2d 298 (1964).

PUBLIC USE

Under the provisions of the Constitution of the United States and the constitutions of the several states, the right to take property by the exercise of the power of eminent domain is either expressly or impliedly limited to a taking for a public use. Whether or not a particular use is a public one is a question to be determined ultimately by the courts.[9] However, if the legislature, by statute, has declared a particular use to be a public use, the courts will uphold the declaration, unless the declared use is clearly and manifestly of a private character.

If the property is condemned for a public use, the necessity and expediency of taking the property for such public use is a legislative—not a judicial—question; and as long as private property is taken only for public use, and damage caused is compensated, the legislature has power to determine, either directly or through agencies chosen by it, when convenience or necessity requires that the property be taken and what particular property shall be taken.[10] The decision of an agency chosen by the legislature that the taking of private property is necessary will not be set aside by a court except for fraud, capriciousness, or illegality.

From an early date the courts have recognized that the taking of private property for the establishment of public transportation systems is a taking for public use. The taking of land for highways is not limited only to land necessary for actual travel. It may include land for widening a highway or street for ornamental purposes, or land for parking space, or land for other similar purposes where common convenience and necessity justify the taking. The taking by eminent domain of land to be used for offstreet parking has been held to be a taking for a public use.[11]

The fact that property which has been taken for a public use is leased to an individual or a corporation for the purpose of operation or that a concession to operate is granted to an individual or corporation does not prevent the condemnation of such property if it is operated for the

---

[9] *McAuliffe & Burke Co.* v. *Boston Housing Authority*, 334 Mass. 28, 133 N.E.2d 493.

[10] *Slentz et al.* v. *City of Fort Wayne et al.*, 233 Ind. 226, 118 N.E.2d 484.

[11] *Poole et al.* v. *City of Kankakee*, 406 Ill. 521, 94 N.E.2d 416.

public benefit. Turnpikes, toll roads, and toll bridges, open to public travel, whether operated by a governmental unit or by a private concern, have been recognized as public uses for which private property may be taken under the power of eminent domain. Likewise, railroads; street railways; railroad, bus, and truck terminals; and similar transportation facilities which are used by public carriers to fulfill their obligation to serve the public are devoted to a public use and are granted the power of eminent domain. However, private property cannot be taken under the power of eminent domain by a common carrier if the property taken is not essential to the construction, maintenance, or operation of its transportation facility. For example, a railroad cannot condemn land to be used as building sites for houses for its employees, or for factories for manufacturing cars or locomotives, or for warehouses not used in connection with its freight service, or for the purpose of parks or flower gardens at a station or terminal.[12]

The furnishing of water to a community is a public use for which private property may be taken under the power of eminent domain. Also, the courts have held that irrigation, the erecting of dams, and the flowage of land for the creation of water power, the building of canals, the widening or deepening of streams for the improvement of navigation, the building of piers and docks, and so forth, are public uses for which private property may be taken under the power of eminent domain.

The taking of private property for public buildings, public schools, public institutions of higher learning, and parks and recreation, and for the preservation of places of historical interest, has been upheld by the courts as the taking of property for a public use.[13]

The right to take private property under the power of eminent domain in the furtherance of a slum clearance project has been held to be a taking for a public use. The taking is justified on the ground that conditions of slum areas in large cities are matters of state concern, since they affect the health, safety, and general welfare of the city.[14] However, the courts have held that private property cannot be taken under the power of eminent domain for the purpose of selling lots to working people at low cost.[15]

---

[12] *Potter* v. *Board of Public Utility Commissioners et al.,* 89 N.J.L. 157, 98 A. 30.

[13] *Craddock* v. *University of Louisiville et al.,* Ky., 303 S.W.2d 548.

[14] *Berman et al.* v. *Perker et al.,* 348 U.S. 26, 75 S. Ct. 98.

[15] *In re Opinion of the Justices,* 211 Mass. 624, 98 N.E. 611.

The City of Johnson City condemned 10.63 acres of land adjacent to a city park, the land to be used as an extension of an existing golf course. The land was being condemned for "public park purposes." Cloninger brought an action asking that the condemnation proceedings be dismissed on the ground that the use of the land for a golf course was not a "public use." The trial court dismissed the original condemnation; and on appeal, the judgment was reversed.

Justice White said: "The word 'park' is certainly broad enough, in the every day sense of the word, to include a golf course as well as a swimming pool, croquet court, baseball diamond, band shell, zoo, and a host of other recreational facilities to which the public normally turn for relaxation and recreation. It is stated that as long as the use is by the public through its officers or agents, or by its enjoyment of greater safety, health and comfort, eminent domain may unquestionably be employed and that this is true even though the public is to be rigorously excluded from the land taken.

"Where the question of 'public use' is a close one, the tendency of the courts is to be more liberal in favor of permitting a taking where the condemnor is the government or one of its subdivisions or agencies.

"In the instant case the public is not to be excluded; in fact, since it is a public park and municipal golf course every citizen will have the right to play on this golf course if he so chooses. It is true that there are those in the community who do not choose to play golf or are physically unable to do so, but this is true of almost any activity that is carried on in a park. To cite a few: swimming, tennis, and nature walks." *Johnson City* v. *Cloninger,* Tenn., 372 S.W.2d 281 (1963).

NECESSITY

In addition to the requirement that private property taken under the power of eminent domain must be taken for a public use, the property taken must be necessary for that public use. This does not mean that the property taken must be absolutely necessary and that the objective could not be attained without the taking of the property. It means only that the taking is reasonably necessary for the accomplishment of the objective in view under the particular circumstances.[16]

PROPERTY SUBJECT TO CONDEMNATION

Property of every kind and nature may be taken under the power of eminent domain. Although the taking of property under the power of eminent domain is not limited, the right to take property in a particular

---

[16] *Latchis et al.* v. *State Highway Board,* 120 Vt. 120, 134 A.2d 191.

situation will depend on the provisions of the authorizing statute, and only such property may be taken as is expressly or impliedly authorized by the statute conferring the power.[17] The authority to condemn real estate may include not only the surface soil but everything attached thereto, and all rights and interests therein, including buildings, timber, gravel, stone, oil, gas, and minerals.

The right of the government or a governmental unit to take property already devoted to a public use presents some special problems. The courts have generally held that property devoted to a public use cannot be taken under a general authorization to take property under the power of eminent domain. However, since the legislature has the power to determine necessity, it may under some circumstances authorize the taking of property already devoted to a public use and provide that such property shall be appropriated to another public use.

Also, as a general rule, the federal government or a state may, under its sovereign power, take property which is held by an individual or private corporation, even though such property is already devoted to a public use.

Property held by the United States and by it devoted to a particular purpose cannot be taken by a state under its power of eminent domain. The authorities are not in accord as to the right of a state to condemn public lands under its power of eminent domain.

Property held by a state or municipality and devoted to a public use cannot be taken under a general authorization to condemn property; but it may be taken if the authority to take is conferred, expressly or by necessary implication, by the legislature. As a general rule, property owned by a state or municipality and not devoted to a public use may be condemned in the same manner and to the same extent as privately owned property. Property owned by one state and situated in another state occupies the position of private property.

The United States filed a complaint in condemnation against the Internal Improvement Fund of the State of Florida to acquire tidal lands held in trust for the citizens of Florida. Linning and others, as citizens and taxpayers of Florida, intervened and objected on the ground that the property was held for a public use and the United States had no power to condemn it. The district court held that the United States had the right to take the property; and on appeal, the holding was affirmed.

The court said: "Ownership by or in trust for the public does not create an ownership interest in individual citizens and taxpayers such as requires or

---

[17] *Ellis* v. *Ohio Turnpike Commission,* 162 Ohio St. 86, 120 N.E.2d 719.

permits them to be parties to a condemnation action by the United States. It is well settled that the United States may acquire for its use lands held by a State even though the land be already dedicated to a public use." *Linning* v. *United States,* 328 F.2d 603 (1964).

EXTENT OF INTEREST ACQUIRED

The extent of the interest acquired by a taking under the power of eminent domain will depend on the authority granted by the legislature, the purpose for which the property is taken, and the interests requested in the pleadings of the party condemning the property. The state has the right to take, or to delegate the right to take, under the power of eminent domain, the fee in real estate, free from all liens and encumbrances; or it may take any lesser interest, such as a determinable fee, an easement, or a leasehold interest. If the state or an agency of the state wishes to take the fee free from all liens and encumbrances, it must join as defendant in the condemnation proceedings all parties having an interest in the condemned property.

As a general rule, under the statute authorizing condemnation, the party condemning can take no greater interest than is reasonably necessary for the public use for which the property is condemned. In no event can a greater interest be taken than that authorized by the legislature; however, if the condemnor wishes, he may take a lesser interest than he is authorized to take.

In the event the estate or interest to be taken is not definitely set out, no greater estate or interest may be taken than is reasonably necessary to accomplish the purpose of the public use for which the property is to be taken.[18]

When less than the fee of the property condemned is taken, the landowner may, as a general rule, enter upon and use the property for any purpose which is not inconsistent with the purpose for which the interest in the property was taken or which does not interfere with the accomplishment of that purpose. For example, when a railroad acquires a right of way by condemnation, it acquires only an easement; and to the extent the right of way is not presently needed for railroad purposes, it may be used by the original owner.[19]

---

[18] *City of Waukegan* v. *Stanczak et al.,* 6 Ill.2d 594, 129 N.E.2d 751.

[19] *Carolina & Northwestern Ry. Co.* v. *Piedmont Wagon & Manufacturing Co.,* 229 N.C. 695, 51 S.E.2d 301.

If property has been condemned for a public use and the fee is acquired on condemnation, the property may be transferred without regard to the use to which the transferee intends to put the property. However, if the fee is acquired subject to a trust to use the property for a particular purpose, it cannot be transferred, unless the transfer is authorized by the legislature. If less than the fee is condemned for a particular public use, the transferee, in the absence of special statutory authorization, can acquire only a right to use the property for that particular use or for a use which is incidental to the main purpose.[20]

COMPENSATION AND DAMAGES

The Constitution of the United States and the constitutions of the several states expressly provide that private property shall not be taken without just compensation. The constitutions of some states, in addition, provide for the payment of damages. Although it is impossible to say precisely what is meant by just compensation, the term, as it is used in law, means full indemnity or remuneration for the loss sustained as the direct result of the taking of property. Generally, no distinction is made between *compensation* and *damages,* although it has been held that *compensation* is the sum paid for the property taken and *damages* signifies the allowance made for injury to the residue of the owner's property which is not taken.[21]

The statute authorizing the taking of private property for public use is invalid if it does not make some provision for reasonable and certain compensation to the owner of the property taken and for the payment of damages to the owner of property injured, if payment of damages is required by the constitution.[22] Unless a person has an interest in the property taken, he is not entitled to compensation, even though the value of his adjoining property may be affected by the taking.[23]

DETERMINATION OF JUST COMPENSATION

The constitutional provision for the payment of just compensation for condemned property does not set up standards for its determination. That task is left to the courts, as well as the task of determining damages,

---

[20] *Rose et al.* v. *Bryant et al.,* Ky., 251 S.W.2d 860.

[21] *American Louisiana Pipe Line Company* v. *Kennerk,* 103 Ohio App. 133, 144 N.E.2d 660.

[22] *In re Opinion of the Justices,* 300 Mass. 607, 14 N.E.2d 468.

[23] *McBride et ux.* v. *Arkansas County et al.,* Tex Civ. App., 304 S.W.2d 450.

if the condemnee is entitled to such.[24] All of the elements which contribute to the value of a property must be considered, weighed, and determined; and the sum total is the amount to be awarded. Such elements as loss of access to the highway, loss of business, loss of profits, the effect of restrictions on the use of the real estate, the effect of the possibility of rezoning on the value of the real estate, and loss of the value of personal property on the condemned real estate have all been considered in determining the amount of compensation or damages to be awarded a condemnee. Each case must be considered in light of its own fact situation; no rigid rules can be laid down whereby the compensation and damages to be paid for condemned property may be determined.

The courts, however, have developed standards which aid in determining compensation and damges, and help give a degree of uniformity to the results. The standard generally applied is the market value of the real estae at the time it is taken. Although the term *market value* defies specific definition, it has attained a reasonably definite meaning in the business world and is frequently defined as "the price which would be agreed upon at a voluntary sale between an owner willing to sell and a buyer willing to buy."[25] The courts have held that testimony as to the price at which similar property located in the community had been recently sold is admissible evidence of market price.[26] If the property is of such a nature that it has no market value, such as a church or a cemetery, the true or intrinsic value must be sought by a consideration of other factors and circumstances.

If an entire tract is taken, the ordinary measure of compensation is the market value of the property at the time it is taken. In determining the market value, all the elements on the land—such as deposits of gravel, stone, and coal—which would affect its value must be taken into consideration.[27] Also, the possible uses which might be made of the property in the near future should be considered. For example, the fact that land taken is suitable for real estate development purposes, although the land has not been developed, should be considered in determining its value.[28]

[24] *Chick Springs Water Co., Inc.* v. *State Highway Department,* 159 S.C. 481, 157 S.E. 842.

[25] *Housing Authority of New Orleans* v. *Waters et al.,* 233 La. 259, 96 So.2d 560.

[26] *State* v. *Powell,* Tex. Civ. App., 376 S.W.2d 929.

[27] *United States of America* v. *69.67 Acres of Land in the Town of Oyster Bay,* 152 F. Supp. 441.

[28] *Latchis et al.* v. *State Highway Board,* 120 Vt. 120, 134 A.2d 191.

In general, the best use which may be made of the property condemned is considered in determining just compensation.

The courts are not in complete accord as to the standard to be applied in determining the compensation to be paid when only a part of the condemnee's property is taken. This problem arises when a strip of land through or along the side of a farm is taken for a highway right of way. Under the provisions of the constitutions of some states, damages resulting from the taking of property by condemnation must be included in computing the compensation to which the condemnee is entitled. If only part of his property is taken and the taking results in the dimunition of the value of the remainder, such dimunition in value of the remainder would be damages resulting from the taking. If, as the result of the taking, the remainder is enhanced in value, the question then arises as to whether this benefit should be set off against any damages suffered.

The courts have distinguished between special benefits and general benefits. Special benefits are those resulting from public works which enhance the value of property not taken when its enhanced value is the result of its advantageous relation to the improvement of the property condemned. General benefits are those that adjoining property owners share with the public generally.[29]

The various views as to the right to damages or to set off benefits in computing conpensation to be paid are as follows:

1. Neither damages nor benefits are considered.
2. Special benefits may be set off against damages to the remainder, but not against the value of the part taken.
3. Benefits, whether special or general, may be set off against damages to the remainder, but not against the part taken.
4. Special benefits may be set off against damages to the remainder and against the value of the part taken.
5. Both special and general benefits may be set off against damages to the remainder and against the value of the part taken.

If less than a fee simple interest in property is condemned, the compensation paid will be the fair market value of the interest taken. In determining the compensation to be paid for an easement, the standard generally applied is the difference between the fair market value of the whole

---

[29] *Board of Commissioners of Dona Ana County* v. *Gardner,* 57 N.M. 478, 260 P.2d 682.

premises before the taking of the easement and its fair market value immediately afterward.[30] This formula takes into consideration any element of damage resulting to the remaining property.

Where an existing easement is taken, the value of the easement is generally based on the diminished value of the servient tenement. If a leasehold estate is condemned, the value of the leasehold taken is the market value of the use and occupany of the premises for the remainder of the tenant's term, less the agreed rent which the tenant is required to pay for such use and occupancy under the terms of the lease.[31]

Union Electric Company sought to condemn 127.24 acres of land constituting a part of 134 acres owned by Saale. The county was zoned, and the land in question was zoned "agricultural." It was located six miles from the city of West Alton and 15 miles from the city of St. Charles. On the trial of the case, evidence of the value of the land as "industrial" was admitted. No proof of an intent to rezone the land as industrial was offered, nor was there proof of an application for such rezoning by Saale. A new trial was granted on the ground of the inadmissibility of this evidence. On appeal, the order of a new trial was affirmed.

Commissioner Stockard said: " 'Just compensation' for the taking by condemnation of a part of a tract of land, generally speaking, is the fair market value of the land actually taken, and the consequential damages, if any, to the remainder of the land caused by the taking. The fair market value of the land taken is what a reasonable buyer would give who was willing but did not have to purchase, and what a seller would take who was willing but did not have to sell. In the determination of what constitutes the fair market value the jury may consider uses of the land for which it is reasonably adapted or suited and for which it is *available,* having regard to the existing business wants of the community, or such as may be reasonably expected in the future. When the land is *not available* for a certain use by reason of a zoning restriction, its suitability or adaptability for such use may be shown as affecting its value as of the time of the taking if, but only if, the evidence indicates a reasonable probability of a change in the zoning restriction in the reasonably near future. The rule is well stated in Orgel on Valuation Under Eminent Domain (2d Ed.), p. 34, p. 167, as follows: 'It is generally held that although an ordinance may prohibit the use of the property for certain purposes at the time of condemnation, yet if there is a reasonable probability that the ordinance may be changed or an exception made, the value for that purpose *as affected by the existing ordinance* may be considered.' Whether such probability of a change exists is a question of fact, and whether there exists an exception as to some use

[30] *Northeastern Gas Transmission Company* v. *Tersana Acres, Inc.,* 144 Conn. 509, 134 A.2d 253.

[31] *City of Columbus, Ohio* v. *Huntington National Bank,* Ohio App., 143 N.E.2d 874.

either by the terms of the zoning ordinance or by statute is a question of law. However, if there is a showing of a reasonable probability of a change or the creation of an exception, 'an important *caveat* to remember in applying the rule is that the property must not be evaluated as though the rezoning were already an accomplished fact. It must be evaluated under the restrictions of the existing zoning and consideration given to the impact upon market value of the likelihood of a change in zoning.' " *Union Electric Company* v. *Saale,* Mo., 377 S.W.2d 427 (1964).

COMPENSATION FOR TRADE OR BUSINESS

As a general rule, injury to a trade or business is not an element to be considered in determining just compensation for property taken under the power of eminent domain. The profits from a trade or business are generally considered as arising from the investment of capital by the owner and from the industry of the owner of the trade or business, and not from the property.[32] However, the owner of a trade or business is entitled to compensation if the trade or business is condemned along with the property on which it is located.

Generally, the owner of condemned property has been held not to be entitled to compensation for loss of business caused by temporary obstruction of highway or lands not belonging to the claimant, although, in some cases, compensation has been allowed. Likewise, compensation has been denied for loss of business as the result of the diversion of traffic caused by improvement of streets or highways.[33]

Christian claimed damages resulting from loss of trade to his business due to the construction of a new highway. The new highway was built some 400 feet north of U.S. Highway 90 and behind the truck stop and residence building of Christian. After the new highway was opened to traffic, Highway 90 was still open, and the access therefrom to the remaining southern portion of Christian's property had not been impaired, but traffic preferred to travel on the new highway. As a result of the loss of traffic on the old highway, Christian's business suffered. The court denied Christian compensation for loss of business, and he appealed. The judgment was affirmed.

Chief Justice Hightower said: "Essentially, appellees are in the position of seeking to recover damages for loss of trade to their business occasioned by the limited and inconvenient ingress and egress to their place of business due to the construction of the new highway. An individual whose property abuts

---

[32] *State of New Jersey by State Highway Commissioner* v. *Hudson Circle Service Center,* 46 N.J. Super. 125, 134 A.2d 113.

[33] *Rudolph Ramelli, Inc.* v. *City of New Orleans et al.,* 233 La. 291, 96 So.2d 572.

a public way does not have a vested interest in the travel thereon. The testimony of Breazeale and particularly Davis informed the jury that appellees had suffered damages of $23,150.00 by reason of loss of business due to the construction of the new highway. There is no question but what appellees' business suffered severely by reason of said construction and the public's preference to use the same, but such was *damnum absque injuria*. In legal contemplation there was actually no evidence to support the damage award." *State* v. *Christian,* Tex. Civ. App., 376 S.W.2d 803 (1964).

PAYMENT OF COMPENSATION

The person, corporation, or political subdivision taking private property under the power of eminent domain is primarily liable for the compensation payable to the owner. Whether or not the compensation must be paid or secured before or at the time the property is taken will depend on the constitution and statutes of the state in which the land is located. Generally, if private property is taken under the power of eminent domain, by a private corporation or an individual, the compensation must be paid or secured before or at the time the property is taken.

The compensation must be paid to the person who owns the property or who has some interest in the property at the time it was taken or damaged, or to one who has taken a voluntary assignment of the rights from the owner. As a general rule, the amount of compensation to be paid for the condemned property is based on the market value of the property as a whole, and the amount awarded is then apportioned among the several owners according to their respective interests.

If the several claimants to the award cannot agree on the basis for apportionment of the award, the money may be paid into court, and the court can then determine the respective rights of the claimants. The procedure followed in determining the rights of claimants, in the event there are conflicting claims and the parties resort to court action, will depend on the statutes of the state in which the action is brought.

PROCEEDINGS TO CONDEMN PROPERTY AND ASSESS COMPENSATION

Condemnation proceedings are statutory and are distinct in character from other types of procedure. There is no uniformity in the procedure followed in the several states. Since the proceedings are statutory, and since there is no uniformity in the proceedings, any adequate consideration of this subject would entail a study of the condemnation proceedings statutes of each state; such a discussion is beyond the scope of this book.

18

Taxation of real estate

Introduction

A WIDE VARIETY of taxes apply to real estate transactions whether they be purchases of the fee simple, leases, or management arrangements. Most states include in their tax structure some form of taxation upon the mere ownership of real estate. Since these vary from state to state it is not possible here to consider them in detail, however, their existence and the manner in which they operate must be taken into account by all real estate owners. In addition, state income taxes must be considered. In some states income taxes are levied upon gross receipts rather than upon net profits from operation. Obviously, such taxes must be given careful consideration in determining the profitability of real estate operations. In most cases the impact of federal taxes will be the most important factor in determining profitability and it is usually the more difficult tax to predict or determine. Its determination will depend upon consideration of many factors because it is a tax upon *net* profits. Therefore, establishing the net profit is the basic step which must be completed. What is deductible as an expense and what must be treated as income are the two questions which may be difficult to answer. Other real estate "transactions" which may generate taxes, both federal and local, include the inheritance of real estate, the taking of real estate through eminent domain and even mortgage foreclosures, unanticipated terminations of leases and breached contracts of sale. In short, it seems safe to say that every significant event in the real estate business either will or may generate tax consequences. It is impossible to survive in the real estate business without having a working knowledge of taxation and access to competent advice on a more or less constant basis.

It is not practical here to provide a definitive analysis of the law of taxation. Constant change is the rule rather than the exception. The need of government to provide services to the general public appears to be an irresistible force which continues to impose new taxes and increase existing ones. At the same time inventive taxpayers, accountants, and attorneys are just as constantly finding new ways to avoid taxes. The result has been an extremely complex federal tax structure that almost defies understanding. Nevertheless the subject is far too important to neglect for it is inherent in every real estate transaction. Even the sale of one's own residence creates income tax consequences, either a taxable profit or a nondeductible loss. Again, it cannot be overemphasized that the material presented herein is limited to basic fundamentals and that competence in this area must be acquired by additional study of the law of taxation. Except to the extent that they have an impact under the federal income tax law, state taxation is ignored in the discussion which follows.

Operation of real estate

Operation of real estate, whether by the owner, a tenant, or a manager, when it is profitable, will result in taxation on the profit earned. The profit which is earned by any operator of real estate is taxed at ordinary income tax rates. That is, it is taxed in the same way that wages, interest, dividends, and so on, are taxed. Since by definition the tax is imposed upon the profits it is essential that we determine what is profit and therefore taxable income under the income tax law. To arrive at that portion of gross income which will be taxed we must take into account two basic factors: what is included in the term "income" and what is meant by the term "deductible expense." That is, we must establish what is *net taxable income* under the tax laws. This may or may not be the same as "net income" under sound accounting rules and practices. One must resist the temptation to apply the rules of logic in the area of federal income taxes.

The initial fact to be determined is the gross income attributable to the operation of real estate. Clearly, all rents received are income. Not so clearly, rents paid in advance are also income *when received*. Even less clearly, amounts paid by a tenant for the cancellation of a lease also constitute income. In the normal operation of real estate, the renting of it to tenants, the rentals paid represent income when received. It is true of course that their receipt may be reported either on an accrual (when earned) or cash (when received) basis. Nevertheless, the payment of rent by the tenant to the owner results in taxable income to the owner. This amount is the starting point in the establishment of net income for tax purposes. Once the income is established we turn to the matter of deductions which are generally the expenses incurred in the production of that income. Certain expenses are obviously associated with the production of income from real estate: salaries of employees, maintenance, insurance, local real estate taxes, and so forth. All of these are deductible from the income received as the legitimate expenses incurred in producing that income. Other expenses which may be deducted are perhaps not so clearly attributable but are nonetheless real and are deductible; depreciation of improvements (*not* the land itself) and interest expense on a mortgage on the real estate. None of these are mysterious on the surface, however, their application under the income tax laws can become complex. For example, the depreciation allowance which will be permitted under the tax laws must be within published guidelines or it may become subject to negotiation between the taxpayer and the Internal Revenue Service. The useful life over which the improvements may be depreciated must be clearly established in order to determine the validity of the deduction claimed. At the same time certain options are available to the taxpayer which permit him to use an accelerated form of depreciation for tax purposes regardless of whether or not it is realistic under sound accounting principles. Salaries paid are also subject to examination by the IRS and may be found to be partly or completely nondeductible. Such examinations are usually limited to the salary paid to the owner for his services or to close family members. Perhaps the most troublesome deduction for the operator of real estate is the establishment of maintenance expenses. It is frequently difficult to classify an expenditure either as a normal repair or as a capital improvement. The difference is quite important from a tax standpoint since normal repairs and maintenance are fully deductible against current income in determining taxable income, whereas capital improvements must be depreciated over their useful life and only the current portion may be deducted. Further complicating this question is the economic fact that very often normal maintenance must be deferred in times when income is insufficient to pay for it. As a result, when income does become available and the deferred maintenance is accomplished, there is a distortion which makes what is actually maintenance look suspiciously like a capital improvement. The determination of which it is for income tax purposes can be quite important from a cash flow standpoint. If the "repairs" must be paid for in cash at the time they are made but are determined to be capital improvements for tax purposes, the cash outlay must come from current profits without the benefit of a tax deduction. This is doubly distressing to the taxpayer because lenders are loath to entertain requests for long-term financing of what is obviously, from a sound accounting standpoint, current expense. Lenders generally look askance at businesses which must borrow on a long-term basis to pay current maintenance expense. This dilemma occurs more frequently than might be expected.

The interest cost of borrowed money utilized to purchase the asset, build it or operate it is clearly an expense of production of income. To this very limited extent the cost of the land can be utilized to generate income tax deductions. As noted above, land itself does not depreciate for tax purposes. When interest rates are not exorbitant and the income stream to service the debt is assured (such as exists in some shopping centers enjoying occupany under long-term leases from national companies) a relatively high ratio of debt to asset value can be quite advantageous to the owner as a means of freeing capital for other ventures. This is true because the actual cost of borrowing is reduced by the deductibility of the interest cost. For example a 50 percent taxpayer paying 8 percent interest on a secured loan and deducting all interest from current income taxes is actually paying, on an after-tax basis, only 4 percent for the use of the money. To the extent that his secured loan approaches 100 percent of the cost of his investment (not as uncommon as one might imagine) he can be free to utilize his own capital on other ventures where secured borrowing rates are not available. A truism has grown up in the real estate industry to this effect: never use your own money to invest in real estate when commercial financing is available. To a great extent the income tax laws support this approach and make it work.

Salaries to employees needed to operate real estate are a necessary expense in the production of income. Normally, the deductibility of this expense for income tax purposes is not a problem; however, it can become a problem if the employee is a close relative. This is particularly true if that relative does not have proven capability which applies to the management or operation of the real estate and if he does not devote a substantial part of his time to the conduct of the business. Paying one's son $20,000 per year for working part time as a leasing agent is certain to bring serious trouble if the return is audited by the IRS, particularly if the son's chosen field of endeavor is dentistry. There is, of course, no reason why a businessman may not hire his relatives to work in his business; however, when he does so he must be prepared to justify his claim that their salaries are a legitimate cost of the production of his income and therefore deductible for tax purposes.

Local real estate taxes which are imposed upon the ownership of real estate are a necessary cost of being in the business of owning and operating real estate. Since these taxes are frequently based upon the value of the improvements, the business which is conducted upon the property and so forth, it is not uncommon for this burden to be shifted from the owner to his tenant. That is, the tenant may be obligated to pay all or part of these taxes as part of his rent. When this occurs the owner's deduction for the payment of these taxes is offset by the fact that payment of his debt by someone else is income to him. The same result is reached in the area of insurance on the property.

Local income taxes are also a factor to be reckoned with. Again, they represent an expense incurred in the production of income and are deductible in determining for federal income tax purposes the net taxable income. If such local income taxes are based upon net income they are still a factor in determining profitability. If, however, as is true in some states, they are a tax upon gross receipts without regard to profitability they may be quite onerous.

Clearly, in determining the profitability on an after-tax basis of the operation of real estate, a wide variety of factors must be taken into consideration. The gross rent which must be earned from a property is significantly affected by the income tax treatment of the expenses of producing that rent. In its simplest terms taxation is another expense which must be given careful consideration in projecting profitability and it must be controlled to achieve that profitability. How does one forecast, manage, or control taxes? To a great extent, of course, it is not controllable by the individual property owner; however, there are certain aspects which are subject to control and serious consideration must be given to them. Consider, for example, the construction and rental operation of a new apartment building which has been built largely with borrowed funds. Some of the considerations which ought to be explored are the following:

1. Depreciation. Because it represents new residential construction an apartment building can qualify for accelerated depreciation, which permits high deductions during the early years of its life with rapidly diminishing deductions during the later years of its useful life.

2. On an amortized mortgage during the early years a greater percentage of the payments made will be deductible as interest and this will decline in later years. During the first year or two as much as 95 percent of the payments made will be deductible interest.
3. New apartments traditionally command higher rentals while they are new or relatively new than they do as they age and decline.
4. Real estate taxes, based on some function of market value, should be higher when the building is new and should, hopefully, be subject to reduction as the market value of the property declines in later years.
5. Maintenance, on the other hand, should be rather low when the building is new and should increase as the building ages.

The first two factors alone represent clear opportunities for deductions while the fourth is somewhat questionable. The other two factors (higher rents and lower maintenance) suggest that profitability from operations should be at its highest during the earlier years of the building's useful life. It would appear that from a tax planning standpoint it would be advantageous to take as much depreciation as the law allows in order to offset this income; however, maybe the interest expense and the usual straight-line depreciation will be sufficient to hold the taxable income at a reasonable level. In either event a thorough analysis based on realistic projections into the future is in order. Is it more advantageous to maximize after-tax profits in the early years on the theory that the operation will necessarily become less profitable in later years? The need for sound tax accounting advice should be obvious.

Another important consideration to the operator of real estate is the likelihood that the real estate will be sold at some time in the relatively near future; that is, before it wears out. By "relatively near future" a time from five to ten years hence is meant. Certain problems present themselves under the so-called recapture rules of the Internal Revenue Code. That is, the tax laws are based on the premise that accelerated depreciation is an advantage that is offered to taxpayers to encourage them to invest in new facilities needed in our economy. They are not meant to provide them with windfall profits for a few years followed by a sale at cost or even a profit. When such a sale occurs the deductions which have been taken in excess of "straight-line" depreciation are "recaptured" by being classified as ordinary income. That is, to the extent that the taxpayer has had the advantage of "excess depreciation" deductions these amounts become taxable to him as ordinary income in the year of sale at a price which exceeds his cost basis (cost less depreciation deductions). This "bunching" of ordinary income into a given year can have a very serious impact on his tax liability due to the graduated rate structure applied to ordinary income. This rule comes into play in accordance with schedules published in the tax code which specify the length of time one must hold the property in order to avoid this unhappy consequence. For example, residential rental property must be held for 200 months before a complete escape from the recapture rules will occur. On commercial property there is no limit, and the recapture rules will apply at any time there is a sale. It should be stressed that the recapture applies only to the deductions taken in excess of straight-line depreciation.

Sales of real estate

As suggested above in connection with the recapture provisions of the federal income tax laws, a different set of tax problems are encountered upon the sale of real estate. When real estate is sold there will be either a profit (or "gain") or a loss. To the extent that there is a profit or gain there will be imposed an income tax called a "capital gains" tax. As with the determination of what is net taxable income, considered above, the beginning point in the determination of gain is cost. We must first allocate to the property sold all provable cost for its acquisition and improvement. As might be expected, those costs which have been deducted against ordinary income (interest, real estate taxes, insurance, salaries and maintenance) may not be deducted again. Only costs related to acquisition and capital improvement may be considered. In addition, to the extent that costs have been claimed against ordinary income as depreciation deductions they must be deducted from the cost for tax purposes. By this method we arrive at the tax cost "basis." An example is set out below:

Purchase of property, 6–1–70 at		$25,000.00
Depreciation deductions, 1970	$ 500.00	
Depreciation deductions, 1971	1,000.00	
Depreciation deductions, 1972	1,000.00	
Depreciation deductions, 1973	1,000.00	
Total		3,500.00
Adjusted basis at end of 1973		21,500.00
A sale on January 1, 1974 at		24,000.00
Adjusted basis		21,500.00
Taxable capital gain		$ 2,500.00

The next step in calculating profit or gain from the sale is of course to establish the true selling price. In arriving at this figure certain expenses are taken out of the sales price, those which are incident to or caused by the sale itself. Brokerage fees, expenses of a survey, abstract continuation, title insurance fees and the like are deducted from the sales price to arrive at the true proceeds of sale. Of course, the payoff of an existing mortgage would be deducted. With the true selling price and the tax cost basis it is then a simple matter to establish what the gain has been on the sale. At this point, however, we must take into account still another factor: the classifications of the gain for income tax purposes; that is, is it a capital gain or is it ordinary income? The difference is critically important to the taxpayer because capital gains are taxed at a much lower rate (basically, one-half of the taxpayer's income tax rate) and the net after-taxes is dramatically different. If it is a capital gain, is it a long-term or short-term capital gain? Again, the answer has a significant impact on after-tax profit because short-term gains are taxed at the same rates as ordinary income. Obviously, the taxpayer much prefers that his taxable gain be classified as a "long-term capital gain" because of the favorable tax treatment of his profit (losses are considered below, but they present the same classification problem in reverse). He gets to keep more of it if it is a long-term capital gain. Two hurdles he must clear in achieving this goal are set out below:

1. The "holding period" during which the taxpayer held title to the property being sold is crucial in determining whether he has experienced a long- or short-term gain. He must hold title for a minimum of six months in order to receive long-term capital gains treatment on the profit. It appears on the surface that this mechanical test is easy to deal with. One has either owned the property for six months or he has not, and in most cases the problem is just that simple. In other cases the problem is not so simple, as where the "owner" simply had an option to purchase the property, exercised it and then immediately sold the property. Does the holder of an option to purchase have the equivalent for tax purposes of absolute ownership? The tax laws say no. (A somewhat different answer would result if he sold his option after holding it for six months.) Clearly, the transaction should be so structured that the holding period can be easily established.
2. The second question presented: is it a capital gain at all? A troublesome feature of the tax laws as they relate to capital gains treatment

of profit on the sale of an asset is that the asset sold must be a "capital" asset as opposed to one which is held primarily for sale in a trade or business. The ownership of development real estate may be clearly a capital asset when held by one who is an investor, a doctor, for example. Clearly, the ownership of vacant ground is not related to his occupation, nor is the sale of real estate a normal part of his professional activity. On the other hand, suppose that the owner of development real estate is a real estate broker. It is not quite so clear that the sale of such real estate is not a part of the broker's normal business, that it is not "stock in trade" held for sale to customers as part of his normal business. The real point here is that it is up to the taxpayer who claims capital gains treatment to establish the fact that he is not in the business of marketing real estate. What difference does it make if he is unable to establish this fact? If he cannot support this position the profit is not a capital gain taxed at perhaps half his income tax rate; it is instead ordinary income fully taxed at his top income tax bracket. The difference in his net after-tax profit from the sale is significant.

Even if the seller of real estate is able to establish that he is not in the trade or business of selling his own real estate he must be aware of what is his tax cost basis, as discussed above. That is, to the extent he has claimed depreciation deductions in prior years his basis is reduced below his actual cost. The extent of his gain is consequently increased to the extent that he has already had an income tax deduction advantage in prior years. In addition, he may suffer additional penalties to the extent that he has taken depreciation in excess of straight-line depreciation under the recapture rules. Oversimplified, these rules simply say that, to the extent that the depreciation taken is in excess of normal (straight-line) depreciation the excess is recaptured as ordinary income in the year of sale. There are schedules adopted by the tax laws which show how long the property must be held in order to avoid recapture and they are adjusted from time to time to support government policy in encouraging or discouraging certain classes of new construction. It is worth noting in this connection that the rules may be imposed even if the sale is *involuntary* such as a mortgage foreclosure or condemnation. The sole criterion is whether or not the taxpayer has received a tax advantage in earlier years against ordinary income which, policywise, must be repaid at the time of sale. Prior to the 1969 Reform Act most real estate operations permitted accelerated depreciation to be taken with relatively easy recapture provisions. It was then possible to "expend" that portion of depreciation which exceeded straight line during the first seven years of the life of the improvements which, coupled with the high proportion of interest included in the debt service, provided massive deductions against net operating income which was usually at its highest during the early years. At that point a unique feature of the income tax law provided another advantage which included a windfall for the property owner. He sold it with little or no recapture. The new buyer was permitted to start over again on a new accelerated depreciation schedule and, probably, a new mortgage loan with interest comprising most of his payments. As a result, resale values were relatively high. The 1969 Reform Act severely limited these advantages by restricting rapid acceleration to *new* improvements used for residential purposes; stretched out the time for recapture so that it extended the time during which depreciation in excess of straight line will be recaptured; and, most importantly, provided that accelerated depreciation could not be applied to used improvements. In effect this forced the original owner to find a market for his property on the merits of its profitability rather than its tax advantages and placed a premium on skillful management of the property so as to be able to prove its profitability when a sale is sought. In addition, of course, the Reform Act limited some of the advantages inherent in the depreciation deduction (as well as other "preference" items) for high bracket taxpayers. It has by no means, however, eliminated these advantages, and investments in real estate by high bracket taxpayers still provide attractive "shelter."

Establishing the true profit at the time of sale involves, of course, the treatment of several items other than just gross sales price versus adjusted cost. The expense incurred in achieving the sale may be deducted from the gross sales price in arriving at the true net proceeds of sale. This will include the brokerage commission paid, legal fees, and the expense of proving merchantable title. On the other hand there are certain adjustments typically made at the real estate closing which may increase the purchase price without specifically being identified. Typical of these is the handling of real estate taxes which in many states are assessed one year (and become a lien in that year) but are not payable until the following calendar year. The buyer will usually prefer to pay these taxes himself when they become due rather than to rely upon the seller who will, of course, have little interest in attending to their prompt payment since he will have sold the property long before the taxes become due. To the extent that the buyer agrees to pay real estate taxes in excess of his pro rata share, however, the buyer will be paying a premium for the property in excess of the stated purchase price; at the same time the seller will be receiving more than the stated price. How are the parties affected income taxwise? Their treatment is inconsistent:

Seller: Receives a little more for the property so he must increase his net proceeds of sale and pay a higher capital gains tax; but, since these taxes are usually his personal liability he is entitled to a deduction against ordinary income when they are paid *regardless of who pays them*. Therefore he has traded a capital gain for an ordinary income deduction which may be quite beneficial to him.

Buyer: Pays a little more for the property but does not have to pay it until the taxes are payable a year or more later, *but* he may not deduct those taxes from his ordinary income because they are not his taxes. He may only add those taxes to his cost of the property so that he will increase his tax cost basis in the event of a later sale. Presumptively, he is paying less for the property and some of his cost is deferred as to payment and to obtain these advantages he sacrifices a deduction from ordinary income—which he could not have claimed anyway.

Something for everyone without the risk of violating the income tax rules? Today, yes, but future treatment of the private agreement which shifts the burden of local real estate taxes may change. It is frequently misunderstood by the parties and in many cases neither one of them takes full advantage of the rules. Nevertheless, the informed broker or property owner may increase the profitability of a sale for his client or himself with knowledge of the income tax laws as they apply to real estate sales.

SALES OF RESIDENCES

Sales of residences are singled out for special treatment under the federal income tax laws. Even if there is a gain on the sale of property used by the taxpayer as his residence that gain will not be recognized for tax purposes to the extent that the proceeds from the sale of the old residence are invested in a new residence. To the extent that these proceeds are not used for the purchase of a new residence the gain must be recognized and the capital gains tax paid. Basically, this nonrecognition of gain feature is available only if the taxpayer buys an existing home either one year before or one year after the sale of his old residence; in the alternative, if he builds a new house, it must be commenced during the above two-year period and used as a residence within another six months. There is a gain *realized* but it is not *recognized* for tax purposes if the above conditions are met. The gain is not, however, completely ignored because the taxpayer must reduce the cost of his new residence by the amount of gain not recognized at the time of sale of the old residence. At a later time when he sells the new residence, his basis for determining gain (or loss) is the cost of the new residence *reduced by* the gain not recognized when the old residence was sold. To illustrate:

5–1–54 Taxpayer buys residence for	$10,000.00	
5–1–64 Taxpayer sells residence for	13,000.00	
Taxable gain *realized*	3,000.00	
7–1–64 Taxpayer buys new residence at		$18,000.00
His basis is reduced by the unrecognized gain from first sale		3,000.00
Cost basis		$15,000.00
7–1–65 Taxpayer sells new residence		20,000.00
Cost basis (from above		15,000.00
Taxable gain		$ 5,000.00

If the cycle is repeated (i.e., every time he sells, he immediately buys a more expensive house) the taxation of all this accumulated gain can be deferred until such time as he finally sells without reinvesting. At that point *all* accumulated gain is taxable. (*One important exception:* the taxpayer is entitled to a one-time, limited exclusion of this gain if the ultimate sale of residential property occurs after age 65. It is, therefore, possible to partly avoid this accumulated capital gain.) An important point is that the sale must take place after the taxpayer achieves age 65. It is quite common for a person approaching age 65 to attempt a sale of his residence so as to be able to travel or move to some other locale in retirement. Frequently the tax saving is lost and the tax payable at a time when his income has been substantially reduced by virtue of retirement. This results from the fact that the tax payable for the year in which he becomes age 65 comes due the following calendar year. In the example used above, assume that the taxpayer becomes age 65 on July 10, 1965. Under normal employment practices his retirement (and reduction in income) would come in that same month. The capital gains tax would not become payable until April 15, 1966. Sales of personal residential property at a loss do not result in a deduction, however, because it is nonbusiness property.

FORCED SALES

"Forced" sales of real estate have traditionally been thought of as "loss" sales; however, for income tax purposes the enforced seller may find to his sorrow that there has been a taxable gain even if the liquidation was not his choice. Condemnation proceedings under the doctrine of eminent domain frequently result in taxable gain since the condemning authority must normally pay the "fair market value" for that which is taken. Such sales are, for tax purposes, no different than the usual sales of property and have the same tax results including the recapture of excess depreciation. Less clearly, the cash loss which results from a sale upon foreclosure of a mortgage may be only the tip of the iceberg. If the property has been depreciated below the actual proceeds of sale there is nevertheless a "sale" for tax purposes and there may be a taxable gain over the adjusted basis which has resulted from accelerated depreciation. Still worse, if this occurs during the time that the recapture rules still apply the result may be a recapture at ordinary income tax rates which spells disaster for the taxpayer. Does this ever happen? Unfortunately it does when high bracket taxpayers purchase property solely for the tax shelter it provides without determining whether the project is operated on a sound business basis, has competent management, and whether projections are realistic or not. Should the broker or developer be concerned? He may face a fraud charge if he has sold participations in a project without full disclosure of the risk involved. The reader is invited to obtain and read a prospectus on any legitimate offering of participation in any current apartment project. The disclaimers made are such that one wonders why anyone ever invests in them.

INSTALLMENT SALES

Once the decision to sell real estate at a profit is reached and even assuming that capital gains treatment will be available the amount of tax generated may still be so high as to make a sale undesirable. At the same time no matter how attractive the property may be there will be a limit to the price at which it can be sold. That is, the buyer will not be willing to pay a premium for the property simply because the seller has an income tax problem on his profit. Capital gains taxes, since they are levied at a reduced tax rate that applies only to the profit, seldom generate much sympathy for the taxpayer on the part of his purchaser. Nevertheless there is a way in which the capital gain can be spread over a period of years if the transaction qualifies as an installment sale. Usually what happens is that the sale is structured on a conditional sales contract with the seller receiving part of the payment each year for several years. He reports only that proportionate amount of gain he receives in the year it is actually received. To qualify for such treatment the seller is limited as to the percentage of the purchase price he may receive in the first year to not more than 30 percent with 29 percent usually used by practitioners to be conservative. Caution must be exercised in this area and competent tax counseling should be sought before entering into an agreement intended to achieve installment sales treatment. The rules for the timing of receipts and the definition of what constitutes a payment and when it is reported are complex and strictly applied. Of critical importance is just what will be counted as a receipt in the year of sale and great care must be exercised to meet this requirement because if it is not met the entire gain will be taxable in the year of sale even though the total payment is not received in that year. Care must be taken by the seller to "insulate" himself from constructive receipt of later payments by the buyer.

Since there is a delay in ultimate payment it is normal to expect that the buyer will pay interest on the unpaid balance. For tax purposes, it is not just customary; it is mandatory. Even if the parties agree that no interest is to be paid the tax authorities will impute interest at a realistic rate and to this extent a part of the receipts will be taxable to the seller as ordinary income just as any other interest income would be taxed, at ordinary income tax rates rather than capital gains rates. While the 30 percent limitation in the year of sale applies to the principal payment only and not interest paid on the balance, conservative practitioners usually structure such sales in such a way that interest is not paid until the following year in order to avoid any possible claim that the 30 percent rule has been exceeded. Even winning the argument with IRS on this point can be expensive in terms of accountant's and attorney's fees. As a result, the approach to such a sale should be very conservative.

Some practical problems must also be faced. Assuming that the property is of sufficient value and the capital gain is great enough to justify the use of the installment sale approach the seller must satisfy himself that the purchaser is a good credit risk so that the sale will ultimately be completed. He will want assurance that the total price will ultimately be paid. The purchaser, on the other hand, will usually require title to the property himself or that the title be protected so that he will be assured of receiving value for his money when the contract price has been paid. It is not uncommon for the property to be of great value only if it can be developed immediately which usually means that the purchaser must have title so as to be able to mortgage the property to obtain development funds. A true dilemma results which is capable of solution only by an experienced real estate and tax lawyer. An illustration of a possible solution is set out below:

The GBG Co. desires to purchase 150 acres of vacant land from farmer Smith who inherited the property many years ago and has a cost basis of $100 per acre or $15,000 total cost basis. The GBG Co. intends to develop the ground for an apartment complex which will take about four years to complete. The parties agree that the purchase price should be $2,500 per acre or a total of $375,000. Smith's tax advisor shows him that he can save substantial taxes on his gain of $360,000 if he spreads it over four tax years and Smith suggests to GBG a conditional sales contract. GBG is agreeable because this will permit them to postpone the layout of cash for several years even though their cost is increased by the amount of interest they will pay on the unpaid balance. GBG, however, cannot wait for four years to start their apartment complex. They must start at once in order to effectively employ their capital. They intend to borrow substantial sums to begin Phase I of their development and must therefore have title to 30 acres so that it can be mortgaged to secure their borrowing. In addition they want to take title to the other 120 acres at the rate of 40 acres per year for the next three years and they need assurance that Smith's title will continue to be clear for that period of time. The impasse is removed when GBG's attorney suggests that at the time of the closing Smith receive 25 percent of the total price and immediately convey 30 acres to GBG and convey the remaining 120 acres to Smith's bank as trustee under a trust agreement which is subject to the conditional sales contract and of which Smith is the beneficiary. GBG is satisfied that the bank as trustee will protect its title while Smith has the assurance that the property will not be conveyed until it is paid for and that, under the terms of the trust and the conditional sales contract, he will not become entitled to receive any further money which will be taxable to him and disqualify him from receiving installment sale treatment. The bank, in return for assuming these responsibilities and duties, will extract a trustee's fee for its services.

The above arrangement must be carefully structured in order to assure the intended tax benefits and protection of both parties. This should only be done by a highly qualified attorney. Other devices have been used to accomplish the same result; however, there is substantial risk involved in any such device which is intended to permit the seller to have his cake and eat it too.

TRANSFER AT DEATH

Admittedly, the consequences of the death of the owner of real estate are not within the province of the average real estate broker or salesman. Nevertheless, the fact remains that any asset an individual is likely to own during his liftime he is also likely to own at the time of his death. As a result, sales of real estate out of decedents' estates represent an important market for one engaged in the real estate business. The death tax consequences upon the real estate owned by the decedent represent a highly sophisticated body of tax law completely apart from the income tax law. No pretense is made here that the treatment of this subject which follows is exhaustive. Quite the contrary; it is intended to simply introduce the reader to the subject so that he will not be unaware of its significance.

Real estate, in common with any other assets, owned at the time of death, must be valued at its "fair market value" for estate and inheritance tax purposes. State death taxes, because of the wide variations from state to state, are not considered here, but should not be ignored in practice. From a federal estate tax standpoint, since it is universal in its application and frequently dramatic in its consequences, the subject of death taxes is considered below in some detail. It is not correct to imply that there is a "sale" at the date of death for death tax purposes, however, the requirement that property owned by the decedent, including his real estate, be valued at its "fair market value" requires some analysis of that term. The term "fair market value" is defined as "the price at which a sale would be consummated between a willing buyer and a willing seller, neither one of whom is under any compulsion to deal." Such a valuation, while it may be closely approached by an experienced and qualified appraiser, is not binding upon the federal government and the ultimate value for federal estate tax purposes remains subject to negotiation in the event the estate tax return is audited. The sometimes harsh reality of the situation is the fact that estate taxes are imposed on this value without regard to the deceased owner's actual cost. Assume, for example, that even after all deductions have been taken it is determined that a parcel of land is valued at $100,000 in the deceased owner's estate. Whether he paid $20,000 for it or $80,000 is irrelevant. The essential fact is that he died owning an asset valued at $100,000 and the estate tax is imposed on this amount. If this represents an appreciation in value over his cost then, to this extent, the estate tax is similar to the capital gains tax in that it imposes the estate tax as though the property had been sold at the date of death at the agreed upon value for estate tax purposes. If, on the other hand, he had paid $200,000 for the same property valued at $100,000 in his estate there is no benefit in the form of deduction in his estate tax return for this loss in value. What is the impact of this tax? The answer requires consideration of several factors. There are several facets to consider:

1. Owners rarely sell on the date of death. Therefore, the true significance of the estate tax is its impact upon the heirs. The fact that the estate tax is levied upon the date of death market value means, in effect, that for tax purposes there has been a sale. That is, in the hands of the heirs the tax cost basis is the value established for estate tax purposes. There is, in tax parlance, a "stepped-up" basis, an increase from the deceased owner's basis to the value at death.

    In the example cited above, the tax cost basis in the hands of the heirs is $100,000 regardless of what the deceased owner paid for it. Should they sell it for $100,000 there is neither gain nor loss. If they sell it for a price of, say, $120,000 this gain is 20,000, long-term or short-term depending upon their holding period. A sale at less than $100,000 will result in a loss for income tax purposes.

2. The difference between the rates of estate and income taxation, age and physical condition of the owner, the marketability of the property at the price desired, and so forth, all enter into the decision to sell before death or hold and let the estate or heirs sell after death, or make a gift of the property during lifetime. The estate tax is graduated based upon the "adjusted" gross value of the estate; the capital gains tax is based upon the owner's income tax rate which is also graduated. The decision to sell during lifetime is made more difficult by the fact that the capital gains tax may be incurred shortly before death, before the owner has an opportunity to give the proceeds to his heirs, and the net proceeds may be taxed again at his death at estate tax rates. There may therefore be double taxation on the gain which can have a serious impact on the net value of the estate which the owner may leave to his heirs. It takes careful investigation of the alternatives to determine the more favorable approach.

No matter how carefully the calculations and planning are accomplished the fact is that natural deaths are not capable of being planned on a precise timetable. The risk of an untimely death must be considered in arriving at the decision to sell or hold. Another fact that complicates the decision is that markets are fleeting things. The decision to pass up an opportunity to sell property in favor of holding it for a "stepped-up basis" after the death of the present owner may look pretty foolish if the demand for the property has slackened or even vanished in the interim. While there has been a general rise in real estate values for many years the best price attainable for a given piece of property may only exist for a relatively short period of time, for properties frequently "compete" with each other for a particular application. Shopping center developments are good examples of this phenomenon. Prior to the building of a significant shopping center in one quadrant of a metropolitan area there may be several tracts of ground which are suitable for this purpose and speculation may be feverish in these properties. Once one of them is selected and development has actually begun, however, the value of the properties not selected may spiral downward just as rapidly as it rose. Withholding a property from the market under such circumstances solely to avoid taxes may be self-defeating. If there is no profitable sale the tax questions become academic.

The imposition of death taxes, particularly the federal estate tax, poses another difficult problem for the estate of the deceased owner: liquidity, for the taxes must be paid with cash, not with the property itself. Under existing rules the tax generated (based upon its "fair market value" as earlier defined) must be paid within nine months after the death of the owner with certain exceptions in hardship cases. For a tract of ground of significant value this will usually be too short a time to develop a market for the property at a realistic price. Planning the estate of one who is heavily invested in real estate is a challenging and difficult problem. The creation of liquidity from some source other than a sale of the real estate itself requires ingenuity, careful planning, and expense. Ignoring the problem, however, may wipe out the anticipated profit from the investment.

A wide variety of tax problems must be confronted in the real estate business. Their range is quite broad and there is no logic which can be relied upon to lead one to them. Some of them are considered below in random fashion.

1. *Sales of timber.* Trees are not really legal fixtures, however, for purposes of establishing property rights in them we treat them as though they were fixtures. That is, when they are growing and are firmly attached to the real estate they are a part of the real estate

for property law purposes at least. When they are severed and become logs they become personal property for property law purposes. Their treatment for tax purposes, however, is unusual and whether a sale of timber will be taxed as a capital gain or an ordinary income is a thorny problem.

2. *The hobbiest operator.* A farmer whose expenses exceed his income has an ordinary loss that will be deductible against income he may have from other sources (such as wages from some secondary occupation) on a direct basis. The same result may not apply to a loss suffered by the so-called gentleman farmer, one whose *primary* source of income is his trade or profession while any income he might obtain from operation of his farm is secondary and upon which he is not dependent. In such a case the losses incurred from farming may be characterized by the federal government as costs of indulging in a "hobby" rather than a trader business. In such a case expenses incurred to the extent they exceed income may not be deductible against income from the owner's primary occupation.

OWN OR LEASE REAL ESTATE?

For the user of real estate, either for business or personal purposes, important decisions must be made on the basis of the federal income tax laws. The treatment of the business user of real estate and improvements differs substantially, however, from the treatment afforded the use of them for personal purposes. Each is considered separately below.

BUSINESS USER OF REAL ESTATE AND IMPROVEMENTS

For the business which must have real estate and buildings the basic question which must be answered is whether it is more desirable to own or lease the necessary property. Charging the cost of the land and buildings to the business itself is the primary consideration. Already discussed above is the depreciation question. If property is held as a capital asset it can be depreciated, *but* only the improvements may be depreciated not the land and the cost of the land may be a very significant cost factor. It is therefore apparent that the ability to pay for this investment by charging it to current business operations as it is used (or "used up") is limited. On the other hand, if the business leases the land and improvements its rental payments are totally deductible as a current expense of operations and are deductible from gross income in determining net taxable income. Clearly, the use of the real estate by the business permits it to, in fact, deduct the cost of the use of the real estate, an advantage denied to it if it owns the real estate. A possible disadvantage to this arrangement is the fact that the rental expense is one which must be met every year with "hard" or actual cash dollars and it may be a severe burden to the business in years in which its gross income is unusually low. Still another option is available and that is the leasing of the ground alone (which is still a deductible expense) plus the construction by the tenant-business of improvèments tailored to its needs. In this case the tenant is not compelled to depreciate the buildings but instead may *amortize* them over the life of his lease. He must spread the cost over the term of his lease in equal annual installments without any option similar to accelerated depreciation. An obvious disadvantage to this arrangement is the fact that at the termination of the lease the improvements are the property of the landlord not the tenant. Clearly the basic business decision to be made here is not a simple one, but at least there is some degree of flexibility and knowledge of this fact will be important to the planning of the conduct of the business. It will be important to the owner of the real estate as well to be aware of the fact that these options are available to him. That is, it may be more advantageous to him to have ordinary income for a relatively long period of time rather than to receive a large capital gain without a better investment to make with the net proceeds after taxes. For example, assume that a $100,000 piece of real estate which can be leased for a period of 30 years at $8,500 per year. The rate of return is obviously 8.5 percent. Assume further that in the event of a sale at $100,000 the capital gains tax is $20,000. The net proceeds of $80,000 must be put to work at 10.6 percent in order to yield $8,500 per year. Such a rate of return may not be attainable without incurring unnecessary risk. Further, the owner of the real estate may be quite willing to build improvements to suit a reliable, financially strong tenant so as to go into the business of managing real estate, much as the owner of an apartment building does. All of the above considerations make it clear that knowledge of the tax treatment which will be accorded to both the owner and the user of real estate is important to anyone active in the real estate business.

PERSONAL USER OF REAL ESTATE

A note of caution must be interjected at this point. The tax benefits which may be available to the owner or user of business property are not available to the individual who uses land and improvements as his personal residence. Since the renting of residential space is a personal rather than a business expense incurred for the production of income it is nondeductible. There are, however, certain deductions which are available to the homeowner even though his use of his home is for purely personal purposes. Two major benefits of home purchase and ownership are the deductibility of interest payments on borrowed money used to purchase the home and the deductibility of local real estate taxes. Aside from these, however, the deductions available to the owner of business property (such as insurance, maintenance, and depreciation) are not available to the homeowner. The individual who rents residential space is of course contributing to the payment of interest and taxes but only indirectly and since they are not his legal obligation to pay they are not deductible for him. This combination of tax rules has lent impetus to the condominium movement in the United States because the user of residential condominium space is considered the legal owner even for tax purposes. He purchases the space and is therefore entitled to the same tax treatment afforded to the owner of a single-family residence. These factors have led to a wide variety of claims made in the advertising for residential real estate for sale to the effect that there are great and significant income tax advantages which flow from home (or condominium) ownership as opposed to leasing an apartment. These claims may very well be true as far as income taxes are concerned. There is, however, another side to the coin and that is that purchase as opposed to a lease of residential space obligates the purchaser (usually) to a substantial long-term debt and exposes him to the risk of market loss in the event of a subsequent sale. These are burdens not assumed by the apartment dweller who retains his maneuverability without severely limiting his ability to obtain credit for other purchases or investments. That is, the impact on the individual's personal balance sheet or net worth of home ownership may be an important factor. Perhaps this fact illustrates an important lesson: as important as taxation is in making the most fundamental decisions (such as whether to own or rent residential space) it is not the *only* consideration. While taxation cannot be ignored in making either business or personal decisions with respect to real estate a proper perspective must be maintained in order to avoid the achievement of favorable tax treatment at the expense of a loss in terms of real dollars.

19

Real estate investment vehicles

Introduction

A GREAT DEAL of notoriety has been given to the great fortunes which have been amassed by investing or speculating in real estate. Additional impetus to the desire to invest in real estate has resulted from the tax shelter which real estate investments can provide. Unfortunately, the unit cost for a parcel of real estate is astronomical when compared with the cost of a share of common stock or a share in a mutual fund. As a result the small investor was for a long time frozen out of the real estate investment world so far as major projects were concerned. Another inhibiting factor has been the lack of availability of adequate, reasonably priced financing. In spite of these obstacles the desire to invest in real estate ventures was a compelling force that would not be denied. For every small individual investor there was a promoter who desired the use of that investor's money as badly as the investor (or pigeon in some cases) wanted access to the action. This combination of forces has resulted in some relatively effective solutions which permit the individual investor today to share in major real estate ventures, both in the profits and the losses. The sophisticated, knowledgeable investor with capital or access to it has found that he can share his ventures (thus minimizing his personal exposure to loss) and obtain not only a return on his investment but compensation for his expertise—a double profit opportunity which has motivated him to find ways in which to structure the real estate venture in such a manner that there is advantage to both groups. The profit motive is a compelling force in shaping business organization and in imaginative use of existing vehicles. Even though innovations are the order of the day the basic fundamental laws of property rights remain their essential framework and a reemphasis of them is important to understanding their limitations. In the materials which follow a variety of investment vehicles is considered ranging from the simple forms of co-ownership discussed in Chapter 4 to the real estate investment trust. Each has its desirable features and drawbacks, and each also has its applications.

Simple co-ownership as an investment vehicle

Frequently a real estate investment requires no more than a very few investors either because of its relatively low cost or because of the financial capacity of the investors themselves. When this is true the investment vehicle can be kept relatively simple. For example, the "Real Estate Syndicate" which conjures up visions of a very complex arrangement is very often nothing more or less than a tenancy in common. Obviously, there must be something more than this simple tenancy to delineate the aims and goals of the investors and to provide some element of control of the venture. This is true because, without some overriding agreement, each tenant owns an undivided interest in the real estate with which he can deal as he pleases without consulting with his co-owners. To permit this situation to exist is to permit potential chaos in the event of disagreement between the cotenants. Granted this fact, consider the confusion and loss of control which would result upon the death of one of the cotenants or his financial death through insolvency or bankruptcy. It is apparent that the utilization of the tenancy in common as an investment vehicle requires considerable care in the selection of the cotenants and that there should also be a written, enforceable contract between the cotenants so that basic investment decisions can be made, such as: selling or continuing to hold; the sales price to be sought and/or accepted; conditions under which the cotenancy will be continued; options and option prices at which one cotenant can be removed; restrictions upon the right of one cotenant to sell or otherwise dispose of his interest with or without the consent of his cotenants. All of these are matters which must be considered in the agreement between the investors. It should be recalled at this point that in the tenancy in common there is no requirement that the interests of the tenants be equal and frequently the agreement will reflect a greater degree of control in the investors who contribute the greater proportion of the investment. There is then at least some degree of flexibility which is possible through the use of the simple tenancy in common. There are, of course, mechanical problems in dealing with the title to the property which multiply with the number of investors or tenants. For example, in those states which still recognize some form of dower or other interest in an owner's spouse, the wives of all the tenants may be necessary parties to any sale, mortgage, lease, or other formal dealings with the property. As a result of these factors the tenancy in common has inherent limitations when more than a few investors are involved. Nevertheless, it should not be overlooked as a possibility because of the advantages of its simplicity and one more very important tax advantage: each investor or tenant preserves his independence as a separate tax paying entity. That is, the tax consequences of dealing with the investment for each investor are unaffected by the tax consequences which may befall his cotenant. It is conceivable, for example, that one investor in the venture may qualify for capital gains treatment on a profit from subsequent sale of the investment even if his cotenant is classified as a dealer and taxable on his profit at ordinary income tax rates. Clearly the use of the tenancy in common even with a well-drafted agreement between the parties should not be undertaken without the benefit of qualified legal and tax counseling. Even more obvious, it should never be undertaken without an agreement between the parties, however, it sometimes is and the results can be disastrous and costly when close business associates disagree on policy or even tactics.

The joint tenancy of real eastate suffers from all the shortcomings of the tenancy in common with the additional complication of survivorship itself. It would require unique circumstances indeed for an investor to desire that his interest in the venture be transferred at death to his fellow investors rather than to his estate or to his heirs. This is not to say that the joint tenancy is never useful as an investment vehicle. In certain situations, such as an investment by co-investors who are close family members, it may have desirable results such as assurance of control of the title by the surviving investor and the avoidance of the delays and expenses attendant upon probate proceedings in the deceased co-owner's estate. On the other hand, it may have serious adverse economic consequences in the deceased tenant's estate not the least of which may be the lack of liquidity for payment of death taxes coupled with complete loss of control of a valuable asset which might be mortgaged to raise the necessary cash because it is not owned by the surviving tenant. There are serious problems to be faced in the use of the joint tenancy as an investment vehicle and it should be done only under unusual circumstances. The need for competent legal and tax advice is obvious. Other forms of co-ownership which include the feature of survivorship, such as the tenancy by the entireties or the community which are unique to the marital relationship have the obvious advantages of continuity of control and the dispensation with formal probate proceedings to transfer title to the surviving spouse and on the surface appear quite advantageous in what is the classic example of a "close family relationship." Nevertheless, the estate tax consequences may be quite undesirable and the selection of another available form of co-ownership may have distinct advantages. In this area the qualified estate planner should be consulted and the need for his advice becomes more important with the advancing age of the parties.

The partnership

The partnership is far from a new device. It has been a recognized vehicle for the conduct of a wide variety of businesses for many years. Under the common-law partnership a great degree of flexibility in the conduct of business was possible. At the same time there were several drawbacks, not the least of which was the fact each partner was exposed to unlimited liability for the acts of his partner. That is, not just the assets of the partners which were devoted to the business were subject to the losses of the business but the personal assets of each partner could be reached as well. This unlimited exposure to liability was, and still is, an inhibiting factor in the use of the partnership as an investment vehicle.

The advent of the Uniform Partnership Act and its widespread adoption throughout the United States has eliminated many of the technical difficulties which previously existed at common law. For example, under the Uniform Partnership Act the partnership itself can hold title to real estate rather than requiring the partners themselves to hold title as individuals. The impact of the UPA has, however, been one of merely streamlining the mechanics of doing business rather than working any basic changes in the underlying concepts of partnership law. This is particularly true of the feature of unlimited personal liability of each partner for the acts of his copartners which remains as a deterrent to the use of the partnership even under the Uniform Partnership Act. Even with its limitations, however, the partnership remains as a viable and useful device and as an attractive vehicle for investment in real estate ventures. The element of ease of control remains and this is supplemented by attractive income tax treatment of the partnership as opposed to corporations other than Subchapter S corporations, discussed later in this chapter. That is, the income earned by the partnership is "passed off" to the partners and is taxed directly to them rather than being taxed once to the business entity and then again to the participants as is true with the typical corporation. These factors continue to make the partnership attractive as an investment vehicle. Even so, the most important element in the use of the partnership is, just as with the syndicate, a well-drafted partnership agreement. The same considerations discussed above in connection with the tenancy in common need to be considered in structuring the partnership: control, division of profits, buyout of a dissenting partner, settlement of accounts at death, and so on. All of these matters demand the services of an attorney in the preparation of the agreement as well as continuing advice in the management of the enterprise.

The corporation

The corporation as a vehicle for real estate investment has the classic advantage of the corporation for other business ventures: limited liability for the shareholder. He is exposed to loss only up to the amount he has paid for his stock in the absence of unusual circumstances. By the same token the individual shareholder has a limited voice in the management of the corporation depending upon his percentage of ownership which determines his power to elect directors who appoint the officers of the corporation who conduct its business. Since the goal of the corporation investing in real estate is profit the income tax treatment of the corporation is an important consideration. While it is true that recognition of income can be sheltered to some extent by the corporation by retention for reserves, and so forth, the income which will be paid out to the shareholders is exposed to liability for income taxes twice rather than once. That is, the corporation itself is a tax paying entity which must pay its own income taxes on net income it has earned. From the residue, after taxes, is paid to the shareholders their distribution of earned income: the dividend. In the individual shareholder's hands the dividend is taxable as ordinary income. Clearly, the earned income from the enterprise is taxed twice before the investor can measure his net, spendable return on his investment. This appears to be a severe penalty to pay in return for limited liability, however, this depends upon the character of the investment. For example, for the investment in raw ground with a goal of subsequent sale at a profit the penalty appears too severe because the exposure to liability is slight. Investment in an apartment complex, on the other hand, may expose the investor to substantial liability for personal injuries on the premises and a variety of other sources. Another consideration which favors the selection of the corporation is the need for large amounts of money. That is, when vast sums are required because of the cost of the investment, its development and marketing, the corporation may be an attractive vehicle simply because the unit cost of investment may be kept very low and the funds obtained from many investors.

Subchapter S corporations

For many investors the low unit cost of investment and freedom from personal liability are enough to make the corporation an attractive vehicle in spite of the limited amount of control exercizable by each shareholder. With the additional feature of double taxation upon the income, however, the corporation as a vehicle for real estate investments is far less attractive. One possible alternative exists: the so-called Subchapter S Corporation which is a creation of the federal income tax laws. A detailed discussion of the Subchapter S Corporation and all of its ramifications is beyond the scope of this book, however, certain fundamental points should be noted for further investigation. Essentially, the Subchapter S Corporation is a corporation in the true sense of the legal term, however, it may elect to be treated as though it were a partnership for purposes of federal income taxes and, in some states, for state income tax purposes. In order to qualify for this treatment, which eliminates the tax on the corporation and taxes all net income directly to the shareholders, certain rigid requirements must be met. Perhaps the most significant are these two: the number of shareholders is limited to ten in number; and *all* of the earned income, with few exceptions, must be actually charged to the shareholders for tax purposes. The obvious advantages are: that the net income is taxed directly to the shareholders only, and not to the corporation and then the shareholders; limited liability. The disadvantages include: (1) the limitation upon the number of shareholders which inhibits the accumulation of large sums; (2) the fact that substantially all of the net income must be charged to shareholders when earned even though this may fluctuate widely from year to year thereby "bunching" income in some years which sends individual tax rates soaring in a given year; and (3) the degree of control exercisable by an individual shareholder is limited by the percentage of his ownership and his limited right to elect directors to control the business. There are other, highly technical aspects to the use of the Subchapter S Corporation which need to be considered with competent legal and accounting advice such as: the impact on the corporate structure of the death of one of the shareholders; the fact that certain entities, such as trusts, cannot qualify as shareholders under the tax laws; and the requirements of the Internal Revenue Code must be met on a continuing basis in order to avoid disqualification from Subchapter S status. In those situations which justify its use the Subchapter S corporation can be invaluable; however, it is surrounded with many technical rules of income tax law and should be the result of only a carefully considered decision.

Simple trusts

The use of the trust in the real estate field is hardly a novel or new idea. It goes back to before the time this country was organized. The development of the trust for use as a real estate investment vehicle has, however, in recent years been the subject of a great deal of sophisticated development both from a legal standpoint and a tax standpoint. In an oversimplified way the trust results in a split of the rights of ownership between the holder of the legal title, the "trustee," and the holder of the equitable title, the "beneficiary." Under basic trust rules the trustee, even though he has the legal title, is obligated to deal with the trust property for the profit of the beneficiaries only and not for the trustee himself. The creator of this arrangement is called the "settlor" or "grantor" of the trust estate. Almost universally the trust must be created in writing either to comply with the statute of frauds or applicable state trust law. The settlor of the trust may become the beneficiary of the trust when it is established and there is no limit on either the number of settlors or beneficiaries. Neither is there any limit on the number of trustees, however, due to the general rule that trustees must act unanimously in making certain decisions it is seldom that more than one trustee is appointed. While the creation of the trust can be relatively simple the relationship is governed by many complex rules and its operation is governed by applicable state laws. A thorough discussion of these matters is beyond the scope of this book; however, the trust is such a useful device that a limited discussion of its working is in order.

In its simplest terms the real estate trust is an arrangement under which the settlor transfers title to real estate to the trustee subject to the terms of the trust agreement which spell out in detail the duties, powers, obligations, and liabilities of the trustee, as well as specifying his compensation. The trust agreement will charge the trustee with the responsibility of managing or dealing with the property solely for the benefit of the named beneficiaries who may also be given the right to direct the trustee in his conduct with respect to the trust property. In a real estate trust the realty will be conveyed to the trustee *as trustee* and not outright. This will be a formal legal conveyance of the title to the realty but subject to the obligations and limitations spelled out in the trust agreement. The trust has several significant advantages over many forms of co-ownership. Among these are the ease with which the transfer of title can be accomplished; no matter how many beneficiaries there may be a deed from the trustee will pass the legal title since the trustee is the sole legal titleholder. This eliminates the need for a conveyance from many individuals who may be beneficiaries of the trust and, as such, the true parties in interest. The fact of participation in the benefits from the trust can remain a private matter in most cases; that is, the names of the beneficiaries, the true owners of the property, are not a matter of public record. (In some states today their identities can be forced to be revealed by the trustee under certain circumstance such as the violation of certain health and fire regulations.) A certain amount of notoriety has resulted from this secrecy aspect because it has been used at times to conceal the identity of the true owners of real estate which has been involved in public scandals; however, the device is nevertheless very valuable and useful for the smooth accomplishment of many perfectly legitimate business transactions.

A trust is a separate tax paying entity just as is a corporation; however, for tax purposes it can be structured in such a way that it is treated as is a partnership. That is, if all the earnings are paid out to the beneficiaries of the trust the trust files an information return only, disclosing the amounts and the distributees and the tax liability is passed off to the beneficiaries.

Because of the nature of the relationship between the trustee and the beneficiaries and the fact that the trustee has the legal title to the trust property and could easily convert it for his own use and benefit, the law surrounds the relationship with substantial safeguards. It is characterized as a "fiduciary" relationship requiring a much higher standard of good faith on the part of the trustee than is required of either party in any normal business transaction. The penalties for breach of this relationship are harsh and will usually not be limited to the actual monetary loss suffered by the wronged beneficiary. As a result, trustees generally do not serve without compensation which is related to the degree of risk assumed. On the other hand, the care and selection of the trustee is a serious decision which must be based upon matters such as his integrity and financial responsibility. Performing this function has become an important business of banks acting through their trust departments. There is, however, no reason why an individual may not act as a trustee. Generally, corporations other than banks are prohibited from the trust business by applicable state law.

The real estate investment trust

The real estate investment trust (REIT) is a creature of the income tax laws. It was authorized by the Real Estate Investment Trust Act by Congress in 1960.[1] The effect of this legislation is to permit the organization of an unincorporated trust or association for the purpose of investing in real estate, real estate mortgages, and other interests in real estate. Such trusts and associations are relieved from the payment of corporate income taxes provided they are organized and operated in compliance with the act. The more important provisions which must be met are: (1) there must be 100 or more certificateholders (or beneficiaries) during each year and five or fewer of those holders must not own more than 50 percent of the certificates outstanding; (2) the purchase and sale of real estate may not be a substantial part of the trusts' business; and (3) the major portion of its income must be derived from dividends, interest, rents from real property, or gains from the sale of real property. In addition, in order to avoid being taxed as a corporation it must pay out at least 90 percent of its earned taxable income each year. Failure to meet all of the requirements of the act during any given year will result in the taxation of the trust as though it were a corporation. Such failure to qualify would, of course, seriously limit the advantages of the REIT to its certificateholders. It should be noted that there are other rules which

---

[1] Public Laws 86–779, Sec. 856, United States Code, Annotated, Title 26, §§ 856, 857.

must be met in order to qualify under the act and that the above information is greatly oversimplified.

The REIT has become tremendously popular as an investment vehicle because certificates of beneficial ownership can be issued in small denominations and prices just as can stock in a corporation. Markets for these certificates have been organized so that they can be traded in much the same way corporate stock is traded. Rates of return on investment have been attractive to many investors and many REITs have been quite successful. There have, however, been many failures of such trusts with disastrous consequences for the certificate holders. As with any other business the ability and integrity of its management are key ingredients to success. The development of capable management (both real estate and financial) has not occurred as quickly as the explosive growth in popularity of the REIT itself. Great care must be taken by the investor to assure himself of the quality of management of the REIT. On the other hand, qualified management of such trusts commands a premium for its services and this field therefore represents an attractive career field for knowledgeable real estate people.

The limited partnership

The limited partnership represents an attempt to combine the flexibility and the tax treatment of the partnership with the insulation from liability of the investors which is available in the corporation. In the limited partnership one or more general partners exercise control of the enterprise and assume a geater degree of risk. The limited partners contribute money to the enterprise and share in the profits proportionately. Up to this time the attraction of the limited partnership has been its ability to pass off to the limited partners all or substantially all of the income tax deductions generated by the enterprise, such as depreciation, interest, and local taxes. Frequently the motive for investment is almost solely the acquisition of those deductions which the limited partner may apply against ordinary income from other sources (such as salaries for highly paid executive and fees for successful professionals) and the attractiveness of the investment is directly related to the investor's income tax bracket. The term "tax shelter" is particularly appropriate in this context because the deductions generated by the limited partnership's activity can be used to "shelter" income from other sources. The marketing of limited partnership interests has been aimed therefore at the sophisticated investor and the number of limited partners has generally been rather small (although some limited partnerships are quite large because of the size of the venture itself and the need for large amounts of capital). In addition to the normal risks of any real estate enterprise (such as the construction and management of an apartment complex) there are very real risks from an income tax standpoint. That is, in addition to the possible loss of the investment itself if the project fails there is risk of exposure to serious income tax "recapture" penalties. For this reason the investment opportunities in the limited partnership area have so far been restricted to the truly sophisticated investor who can demonstrate that fact plus the fact that he can afford the investment. The reader is invited to obtain a copy of the prospectus or proposal on such a limited partnership venture and to study the qualifications imposed upon the investor himself as well as the disclaimers of responsibility on behalf of the general partner and the promoter.

Conclusions

There will undoubtedly be additional investment vehicles designed in order to attract the small as well as the large investor into the real estate field. In addition there are frequently combinations of the existing vehicles already in use. A few observations about the real estate investment are in order. First, it must be borne in mind that the promoter or salesman is no longer selling real estate; he has entered into the securities business which has its own legal framework and its own system of regulation. The regulations imposed will be both state and federal and they are designed to protect the investor from fraud. The penalties for failing to comply with these regulations can be quite severe. Anyone intending to pursue this field as a career should therefore seek additional education and training in the securities business. This is true even with the relatively simple vehicles such as the private trust or even the tenancy in common. Many states, for example, restrict the number of investors who may be *solicited* for such an investment even if the number of actual investors still stays below the statutory number of participants. This is the difference between a private offering which can be quite simple and a public offering which may require registration and control by a state agency.

Second, it should be unnecessary to point out that the basic reason for a higher rate of return on investment almost universally carries with it a higher degree of risk. Even in those investments in which the income tax advantages increase the net return there is always the risk of change in the income tax law which can seriously impair marketability and result in partial loss of the investment. This is in addition to the normal risks encountered in any real estate investment. An important factor to consider is the fact that real estate investment properties are high-unit value investments and their marketability is therefore impaired. Quick reactions to changes in economic conditions are not always possible. The liquidation of a real estate investment may be quite costly in terms of economic loss and may be a disaster from an income tax standpoint. It is not intended to imply that losses are not possible in the stock and bond markets, however, the character of the real estate investment itself is unique and this must be kept in mind by the investor as well as his counselor.

20

Governmental regulation of the real estate business

Introduction

THE REGULATIONS which affect the real estate business cover a broad spectrum of state and federal laws. It would be literally impossible to give consideration here to all laws which have some impact on the industry. Indeed many laws which affect the real estate business were not intended to restrict the activities of the real estate broker or salesman but do so indirectly. In this chapter are considered some of the more important areas of governmental regulation with which the active real estate person should have some acquaintance. Real estate licensing statutes, which represent direct regulation of the conduct of the activities of real estate brokers and salesmen, are covered in Chapter 11 and are not repeated here.

Civil rights legislation

Civil rights legislation so far as real estate is concerned, is intended to provide assurance that all citizens will have an equal opportunity to acquire the ownership or use of suitable housing facilities and that they are not subjected to discrimination in obtaining housing. Controls over the real estate industry are exerted by both federal and state legislation in this area much of which is overlapping. Such legislation universally provides a means for its enforcement in the courts; however, in most cases it also provides for enforcement through a public commission which is designed to speed enforcement without the delays attendant upon litigation and to achieve the goals of the civil rights program through administrative persuasion rather than requiring formal legal action. As a result of the fact that legislation in this area is of rather recent vintage the definitions which are used are still being shaped and changed by court decisions and administrative rulings. Many practices which have been traditional in the real estate brokerage business have been found to result in *de facto* discrimination whether this was their intent or not. Certain forms of advertising, for example, may be discriminatory because they inhibit a member of a minority group from seeking housing through the advertiser where such advertising makes it appear that he will be an unwelcome customer. "Panic selling" which frequently results when the basic character of a neighborhood's racial makeup begins to change has been specifically singled out in some states as a form of discriminatory practice. The mere fact of placing "For Sale" signs on listed properties in such a neighborhood has been held to be discriminatory. Clearly, a refusal to sell or rent to all comers is discriminatory as is a refusal to process a legitimate offer to purchase. The active real estate broker or saleman cannot avoid responsibility for discrimination by taking the position that his principal is the one who is practicing discrimination and thereby insulate himself from the sanctions imposed by the applicable legislation. These sanctions can be quite severe, including, in many states, the loss of the broker's or salesman's license. It is therefore quite obvious that anyone becoming active in the real estate business should carefully investigate the laws and regulations in his own state in order to avoid an unintended violation which can be quite costly. More than this, this area of regulation should be carefully investigated before going into the real estate business to determine the rules and guidelines regarding record-keeping, for example, which will provide positive evidence of compliance. It is frequently impossible to accurately reconstruct such records after the fact. It should be noted also that this is an area in which new interpretations may be put on commonly accepted practices from time to time and, therefore, anyone active in the business should make it a point to keep current with new developments. A further point that should be kept in mind: the civil rights acts, so far as they relate to the real estate business, are not limited in their application to real estate broker and salesmen; they are all inclusive and the owner-operator or owner-seller of real estate needs also to be informed so that his compliance will be assured.

Truth in Lending (*Federal Consumer Credit Protection Act*)

Truth in Lending legislation, as its name implies, was originally designed to control the practices of those in the business of granting credit. From the very outset its application was expanded to include the real estate sales industry. While the primary impact of Truth in Lending on the real estate business has been in the area of advertising to the extent that credit terms are included, it is important that all persons in the real estate sales industry be aware of the fine line that divides the real estate business from the finance business. This requires some knowledge of the fundamental purposes and provisions of the law which are discussed below.

Contrary to popular opinion Truth in Lending legislation does not purport to *control* interest rates. A lender could charge 200 percent on a credit obligation without violating the Truth in Lending law (although he might very well be violating some form of usury statute) because Truth in Lending does not control his interest charge. What Truth in Lending laws do require is that the cost of credit be disclosed to the borrower. The logic of the law is simple: not all borrowers are entitled to be treated equally so far as the cost of credit is concerned; this will depend upon the individual borrower's ability to repay and his reputation for willingness to repay any extensions of credit to him. The purpose of Truth in Lending is to permit the borrower to "shop" for credit, to compare between lenders the expense of borrowing. Many transactions are not covered because they involve loans of such size or such type that the borrower is presumed to be sophisticated enough to be able to discern the cost of credit for himself. For the typical residential sale, however, the legislation is clearly applicable and this is one reason that brokers and salesman need to be knowledgeable about it.

The second important reason for considering Truth in Lending is that there is an important definition to understand: who is a "creditor" under the act? Clearly, those in the normal business of lending money are governed by the act. Usually, the real estate salesman or broker is not in this category, however, the act also applies to those who *arrange for* credit which is extended by others. It is not at all unusual for a real estate salesman or broker to assist a buyer in finding credit with which to consumate the sale. Indeed, this ability and service frequently represents the difference between completing the sale (and earning a commission) and losing it. In normal real estate brokerage operation Truth in Lending will not apply unless two tests are met: the broker has knowledge of the terms of credit *and* he participates in the preparation of the loan documents. Then he is engaged in the business of granting credit and is responsible to see that there is a full disclosure of the terms and that evidence of the borrower's understanding is obtained. Short of this degree of participation the broker (or salesman) need not concern himself with compliance during the lending process.

Perhaps the most important feature of Truth in Lending as far as the real estate sales industry is concerned is the regulation of advertising of real estate for sale. Simply stated, the law requires a full disclosure of the credit terms being offered. While some relaxation in the rules relating to advertising has occurred since the inception of this legislation it is still quite important that credit terms, when advertised in connection with the sale of residential property, be clearly stated in compliance with the act. Advice of an attorney should be sought in determining the form and content of the advertising program to be pursued. The penalties for violation of Truth in Lending can be severe and under certain circumstances can even include imprisonment. It is therefore important to be aware of its impact on the real estate business.

Interstate Land Sales Full Disclosure Act

The classic basis for federal control of business which appears to be wholly confined within state borders has traditionally been the fact that some of that business is conducted across state lines making such business a matter of federal concern and federal jurisdiction. Until recent years it was thought that real estate sales being local in nature, were immune from significant federal control. This notion is now dispelled largely through the use of advertising media such as radio and television which easily reach large segments of the population, frequently reaching, inadvertently, a market not sought by the advertiser. This has resulted in federal legislation intended to control interstate land sales but which in fact imposes a new layer of regulation on sales which are primarily *intrastate*. The Interstate Land Sales Full Disclosure Act has a purpose similar to Truth in Lending: full disclosure of material facts and the prohibition of misrepresentation of those facts.

The act requires the filing of a statement of facts relating to the property and the representations which are made to prospective borrowers with an office of the federal government. Unfortunately, there is no requirement that this office (the OILSR of HUD at present) formally approve the documentation. The penalties can be severe if there is a material misrepresentation or a failure to state material facts and the report must be furnished to prospective buyers, even if they are residents of the state in which the property is located. The normal mechanics for enforcement (such as the power of subpoena and the power to enter binding orders) are present. Sanctions for willful violations may include either fines or imprisonment or both. The terms of the act are complex and it is dangerous to generalize, however, it appears that when more than 50 lots are involved, in a common plan of sale, interstate sales are likely or advertising is likely to go beyond state lines, the only safe course to follow is to comply with the terms of the act. This is a highly technical matter and the advice of an attorney should be sought in connection with any program which conceivably might be covered. It is possible to obtain an exemption, however, this approach may be more difficult than compliance.

Regulation of the credit industry itself

A wide variety of regulations directly affect the financial industry which have an impact upon the real estate business. They range from the restrictions upon the investments which are permissible to the terms upon which such investments may be made. Even further afield are such laws as the Fair Credit Reporting Act which has had the effect of substantially reducing the flow of accurate credit information from financial institutions to those not directly engaged in the granting of credit. Banking and insurance industry regulations have an impact upon the real estate business simply because they regulate the flow of money into the industry to finance the purchase of real estate assets. The wide range of such regulations prohibits a detailed discussion of them here. Nevertheless, it is important to recognize that regulation of other industries may have a significant impact upon the real estate business.

Environmental controls

While most of the forms of environmental legislation are not aimed directly at control of the real estate business it is clear that they have a significant impact on the uses to which private property may be put and that they must therefore be given consideration in making real estate decisions. Great emphasis has been placed upon environmental control during the past ten years and the cause of antipollution is receiving wide support from many sources. The problem is not new and neither is legislative control a new idea. As far back as 1899 the United States had on its books water pollution control legislation (Refuse Act of 1899) which included provisions for fines and prison sentences, however, its enforcement left a great deal to be desired. Today we have on the books a wide variety of air, noise, water, and pesticide pollution statutes, and it is clearly beyond the scope of this book to consider them all even in limited fashion. Nevertheless, the reader should bear in mind that any of them might have a substantial impact on a particular real estate project.

At the same time there is a more direct body of controls that cannot be ignored: regulation against the misuse of land. Today it is not at all unusual for the developer of real estate to find himself burdened by many restrictions which only a few short years ago would have been considered necessary only for aesthetic purposes. That is, the requirements of dedication of a portion of a subdivision for common use by all residents, the preservation of open space between structures, and so forth, are frequently imposed today as conditions for the granting of approval to proceed with development. The basic tool for controlling the development of real estate is the police power manifested by the exercise of zoning controls. In addition to this of course the power of eminent domain may be utilized to take property for environmental purposes. It is also important to recognize that private legal action in the form of lawsuits against nuisance and trespass is becoming a more and more widely accepted method of forcing environmental control.

The basis for the present-day impetus behind environmental control is the National Environmental Policy Act of 1969 (Public Law 91–190) of January 1, 1970, which clearly established a national policy to "encourage productive and enjoyable harmony between man and his environment" and, among other things, "to establish a Council on Environmental Quality." This was followed shortly by the Environmental Quality Improvement Act of 1970 (Public Law 91–274) of April 3, 1970, which established the Office of Environmental Quality. A series of Executive Orders followed these two pieces of legislation which were designed to implement the policy established by the congressional action. The thrust of federal action in this area has been to impose the requirement that *all* federal agencies control activities under their jurisdictions in such a way that they will "protect and enhance the quality of the environment."

At the same time there has been a corresponding movement by the courts to recognize that the protection of the environment is a legitimate basis upon which individuals should be entitled to bring suits (usually for injunctive relief) whether or not they can demonstrate clearly that the action complained of will result in substantial economic loss. That is, the courts have recognized what Congress has recognized: that protection of man's environment is a fundamental right which is entitled to be protected by legal action. Also, the courts appear to have relaxed their traditional reluctance to grant injunctive relief which has always been considered an extraordinary remedy. In large part this shift stems from the fact that an injunction which halts a development is the only effective way to prevent irreparable harm which may not even be measurable in terms of money damages.

State legislation in the area of environmental protection and control exists in many states as well as the federal action noted above. Real estate business people need to be familiar with these requirements because of their impact on the purely business aspects of real estate. More importantly it must be noted that this body of law and regulation is still developing and is in an almost constant state of change. At the same time it must be recognized that certain other national policies may be in conflict with the cause of environmental control and improvement either in a specific area or at a specific time. It cannot be expected that there will be an orderly, logical development. It appears clear, for example, that the developing "energy crisis" will create serious conflicts in governmental policy and that these conflicts will have a significant impact upon the development of the law of environmental control.

Conclusion

No pretense is made that the regulations discussed above are all of those which have a direct bearing upon the real estate business. Those discussed above are important, but the significance of their treatment here is that the range of regulation which they represent should suggest that others will also have an impact upon the conduct of any phase of the real estate business.

Index

513

This book has been set in 11 and 10 point Garamond, leaded 2 points. Chapter numbers and titles are in 30 and 18 point Scotch Roman italic. The size of the type page is 27 by 45 picas.